W9-BKG-919

ADULT DEVELOPMENT & AGING

BIOPSYCHOSOCIAL PERSPECTIVES

ADULT DEVELOPMENT & AGING

BIOPSYCHOSOCIAL PERSPECTIVES

Fifth Edition

Susan Krauss Whitbourne, Ph.D.
University of Massachusetts Amherst

Stacey B. Whitbourne, Ph.D.
VA Boston Healthcare System

WILEY

VICE PRESIDENT & EXECUTIVE PUBLISHER	George Hoffman
EXECUTIVE EDITOR	Christopher Johnson
EDITORIAL ASSISTANT	Kristen Mucci
MARKETING MANAGER	Margaret Barrett
PHOTO EDITOR	Elizabeth Blomster
ASSOCIATE PRODUCTION MANAGER	Joyce Poh
PRODUCTION EDITOR	Yee Lyn Song
COVER DESIGNER	Kenji Ngieng
COVER PHOTO	JHLloyd/iStockphoto

This book was set in 9.5/11.5 BerkeleyStd-Book by Laserwords Private Limited, and printed and bound by Courier Kendallville. The cover was printed by Courier Kendallville.

This book is printed on acid free paper.

Founded in 1807, John Wiley & Sons, Inc. has been a valued source of knowledge and understanding for more than 200 years, helping people around the world meet their needs and fulfill their aspirations. Our company is built on a foundation of principles that include responsibility to the communities we serve and where we live and work. In 2008, we launched a Corporate Citizenship Initiative, a global effort to address the environmental, social, economic, and ethical challenges we face in our business. Among the issues we are addressing are carbon impact, paper specifications and procurement, ethical conduct within our business and among our vendors, and community and charitable support. For more information, please visit our website: www.wiley.com/go/citizenship.

Copyright © 2014, 2011, 2008, 2005 John Wiley & Sons, Inc. All rights reserved. No part of this publication may be reproduced, stored in a retrieval system or transmitted in any form or by any means, electronic, mechanical, photocopying, recording, scanning or otherwise, except as permitted under Sections 107 or 108 of the 1976 United States Copyright Act, without either the prior written permission of the Publisher, or authorization through payment of the appropriate per-copy fee to the Copyright Clearance Center, Inc. 222 Rosewood Drive, Danvers, MA 01923, website www.copyright.com. Requests to the Publisher for permission should be addressed to the Permissions Department, John Wiley & Sons, Inc., 111 River Street, Hoboken, NJ 07030-5774, (201)748-6011, fax (201)748-6008, website http://www.wiley.com/go/permissions.

Evaluation copies are provided to qualified academics and professionals for review purposes only, for use in their courses during the next academic year. These copies are licensed and may not be sold or transferred to a third party. Upon completion of the review period, please return the evaluation copy to Wiley. Return instructions and a free of charge return shipping label are available at www.wiley.com/go/returnlabel. Outside of the United States, please contact your local representative.

Library of Congress Cataloging-in-Publication Data

Whitbourne, Susan Krauss.
  Adult development and aging : biopsychosocial perspectives / Susan Krauss Whitbourne, Stacey B. Whitbourne. – Fifth edition.
    pages cm
  Includes bibliographical references and index.
ISBN 978-1-118-42519-0 (pbk.)
1. Gerontology. 2. Older people–Psychology. 3. Older people–Health and hygiene.
4. Older people–Social conditions. I. Whitbourne, Stacey B. II. Title.
  HQ1061.W48 2014
  362.6--dc23   2013039716

Printed in the United States of America

10 9 8 7 6 5 4

PREFACE

Everyone ages. This very fact should be enough to draw you into the subject matter of this course, whether you are the student or the instructor. Yet, for many people, it is difficult to imagine the future in 50, 40, or even 10 years from now. The goal of our book is to help you imagine your future and the future of your family, your friends, and your society. We have brought together the latest scientific findings about aging with a more personal approach to encourage you to take this imaginative journey into your future.

The fifth edition of *Adult Development and Aging: Biopsychosocial Perspectives* incorporates material that we believe is vital to your understanding of this rapidly developing and fascinating field of study. Much of what you will read comes directly from Susan's classroom teaching of the Psychology of Aging course at the University of Massachusetts Amherst. She continues to incorporate her day-to-day teaching of the course into the text, which keeps the material current, fresh, and engaging. At the same time, her active involvement in research on the psychology of adult development and aging gives her the ability to sift through the available findings and pull out those that are central to an understanding of individuals as they change from the years of early adulthood through late life.

Stacey was inspired to pursue the field of aging after taking her mother's course in 1999. She continued her graduate work in social and developmental psychology, focusing on cognitive functioning in later adulthood. Stacey is the program director for a major national initiative that is building a health and genomic database for future studies of military veterans. Having also taught adult development and aging at Brandeis University and the University of Massachusetts Boston, she is also attuned to student needs and interests.

We are proud to say that the addition of Stacey as a coauthor brings a third generation into the field in a tradition begun by Theodore C. Krauss, M.D., Susan's father, an innovator in geriatric medicine. Susan became interested in the scholarly field of aging as an undergraduate when she decided to write a paper on personality and adaptation in a developmental psychology course. At the same time, her father's professional activities had a profound influence and made the choice of gerontology (the scientific study of aging) a natural one.

It is our hope and belief that you will find yourself as engrossed in the psychology of adult development and aging as we are. Not only is everyone around you aging, but also the issues that researchers in field examine range all the way from the philosophical to the practical. Why do living things age? Is there a way to slow down the aging process? How will society deal with the aging of the Baby Boomers? How will job markets be affected by an aging society? Will the young adults of today age differently than did their parents and grandparents? Bringing it to a personal level, as you take the course, you'll start to ask questions about your own life. What challenges await you as you begin your career? What will it be like to start a family? How will you manage the transition into your early adulthood as you leave college behind to pursue your own life? All of these, and more, are questions that you will find yourself asking as you explore the many complexities of the process that causes people to change and grow throughout life. You will learn not only how people grow older but also how to grow older in a way that is healthy and satisfying.

THEMES OF THE BOOK

The biopsychosocial model emphasized in our text is intended to encourage you to think about the multiple interactions among the domains of biology, psychology, and sociology. According to this model, changes in one area of life have effects on changes in other areas. The centerpiece of this model is identity, your self-definition. You interpret the experiences you have through the framework provided by your identity. In turn, your experiences stimulate you to change your self-definition.

This is an exciting time to be studying adult development and aging. The topic is gaining increasing media attention and tremendous momentum as an academic discipline within life span development. The biopsychosocial model fits within the framework of contemporary approaches taking hold in the sciences in general that emphasize the impact of social context on individuals throughout all periods of life. Entirely new concepts, sets of data, and practical applications of these models are resulting in a realization of the dreams of many of the classic developmental psychologists whose work shaped the field in the early 20th century.

Adult development and aging are areas that have no national boundaries. Aging is now being recognized as a priority for researchers and policy makers around the world, not only in the United States and Canada. We can all benefit from this international perspective both for our own countries and for those of citizens around the world.

ORGANIZATION

If you read the chapters of this book in order from start to finish, you will progress from the basics in the first three chapters to more complex issues, starting in Chapter 4, that place relatively more emphasis on the "bio," the "psycho", and the "social." However, not all instructors choose to proceed in this fashion, and we have designed the book with this flexibility as an option. We emphasize the biopsychosocial model throughout, in that many of the topics, regardless of where they appear in the book, span areas as diverse, for example, as driving and diabetes.

We do recommend, though, that the last chapter you read is not the one on death and dying, as is often the case in other books in the field. Our last chapter covers successful aging. Many students and instructors have shared with us their appreciation of our ending on a "high note." Even though death is obviously the final period of life, we each have the potential to live on after our own ending through the works we create, the legacies we leave behind, and the people whose lives we have touched. These are the themes that we would like you to take with you from this book in the years and decades ahead.

FEATURES

Up-to-Date Research

The topics and features in this text are intended to involve you in the field of aging from a scholarly and personal perspective. You will find that the most current research is presented throughout the text, with careful and detailed explanations of the studies that highlight the most important scholarly advances. We have given particular attention to new topics and approaches, including neuroscience and genetics, as well as continuing to bring to students the latest advances in cognition, personality, relationships, and vocational development as well as highlighting sociocultural influences on development, including race, ethnicity, and social class.

Aging Today

Susan writes a highly popular *Psychology Today* blog entitled *Fulfillment at Any Age*. Each chapter opens with a condensed version of one of the blog entries relevant to that chapter's content. These informal chapter openings will stimulate students to think about the academic material they will read in the subsequent pages, and in some cases, include practical self-help tips so popular with readers.

Engaging Figures and Tables

Each chapter is illustrated with photographs, figures, and tables intended to bring a strong visual element into the text. Many of these figures clearly summarize important research findings and theoretical models. Our selection of these materials connects to the PowerPoint slides that instructors can download from the Wiley website.

Contemporary Approach

With coauthors literally one generation apart, it's been our goal to find the balance between the "professor" and the "student" perspectives. As a result, you will find many current examples relevant to people in your age group, whether you're a returning student or a student of traditional college age. Instructors, too, will find material that they can relate to their own experiences, whether they are relative newcomers or more seasoned academics.

STUDENT LEARNING AIDS

Glossary Terms

We have made a concerted effort in this edition to provide a large number of glossary terms, indicated in bold in each chapter, and listed at the end of the book. Although it may seem like you will have a great many terms to memorize, the fact of the matter is that you will need to learn them anyway, and by having them provided in your glossary, you'll find it easier to spot them when it comes time to review for your exams. Susan finds that her students like to study from flashcards that they make up, and if you find this a useful study tool, the glossary terms will make that process much more straightforward. The majority of these terms relate specifically to adult development and aging, but where we felt it was helpful for you to review a term that you may not have encountered for a while, we also included several terms of a more general nature.

Numbered Summaries

You will find a numbered summary for each chapter that will supplement your studying and help you narrow down your reviewing to the chapter's main points. Together with the glossary terms, these will give you a comprehensive overview, though they will help you the most if you actually read the chapters themselves.

CHANGES IN THE FIFTH EDITION

The first edition of *Adult Development and Aging: Biopsychosocial Perspectives* was intended to provide a fresh and engaging approach to the field of the psychology of adult development and aging by focusing on three themes: a multidisciplinary approach, positive images of aging, and the newest and most relevant research. We continue this tradition in the fifth edition because we want you, our readers, to feel as connected to the material as possible. Our thinking is that students will be more motivated to complete their reading if they like the text and feel that they can relate to it. At the same time, instructors will find their job that much easier because students sitting in their classrooms will come to class ready to discuss what they've read.

Instructors who have developed their course based on earlier editions will not need to change the basic structure of their lectures and assignments. However, to reflect this ever-changing field, we shifted material within the chapters, in some cases deleting topics that by now are no longer considered relevant in order to make room to cover the newer approaches that have come into prominence within the past three years.

Although many of the classics remain, we have included nearly 500 references from the past 3 years, up through early 2013. In virtually all cases where we reference population data, we rely on sources from 2012 or 2013. We also give expanded coverage to global population and health data in keeping with our stated goal of providing an international perspective.

We have added a number of specific topics that expand the potential for this course to reach students interested in neuroscience, clinical psychology, social psychology, health, and applied psychology. In taking on these new topics, we are sensitive to the need to keep the overall length of the book the same, so we have dropped other areas that are now past their prime.

In the area of statistics, within the research methods chapter, we now include a section on multivariate analyses that explains the use of structural equation modeling and path analysis. These are topics that are now becoming part of the standard literature in many areas of the psychology of aging, if not psychology in general. We also expand our treatment of research methods to include epidemiology and meta-analysis, both of which are critical to understanding, again, many of the findings we present throughout the book. Because we draw heavily from several large-scale studies such as MIDUS and Whitehall II, we also explain them in the early chapters of the book.

Within the section on the nervous system, we cover brain scanning methods as well as expanded treatment of plasticity models. We include new research on sleep and memory and the brain's default network. The chapter on health now reviews measurement of functional activity (ADLs and IADLs), and we renamed the section on dementia "Neurocognitive Disorders," reflecting the changing terminology in DSM-5.

Our chapters on cognition underwent significant revision, though we have kept the basic structure the same. Specifically, we now include new sections on videogames and aging, have expanded the treatment of driving and aging, cover executive functioning and neuropsychological assessment, and include the latest research on using virtual reality training to help older adults compensate for memory loss. We have added new theories of intelligence and include a detailed discussion of the WAIS-IV, which was a radical departure from previous versions of the WAIS. New research on reading and aging, bilingualism, and cognitive plasticity also make these chapters timely and relevant.

Our coverage of personality and aging has been revised to discuss minority identity issues, the emerging field of narrative research, and changes in the approach to studying attachment in adulthood and later life. We have, of course, included the most up-to-date coverage of the personality and health relationships.

In the relationships and family chapter, which is among the favorites of students who take this class, we have expanded our treatment of cohabitation, same-sex families, and the intergenerational solidary and ambivalence models. We have added new studies on "helicopter parents" as well as several that focus on adult children who return home to live with their parents. Widowhood was previously broken up between the relationship and bereavement chapters; we now present the topic in its entirety within the context of family. Adding to our coverage of long-term relationships, we also discuss the enduring dynamics model of intimacy.

Within the vocational development chapter, we focus on the latest findings on work–family relations, revising the previous edition to examine the differing models with the most recent research as well as touching on the topic of family-friendly workplaces. We address the issue of employment among military veterans, and cover several areas of work stress, including workplace bullying and emotional labor. The fascinating topic of vocations as "callings" also allows us to provide a new perspective on vocational satisfaction. Within the section on leisure, we also present studies that examine the travel patterns of retired adults. Our coverage of the financing of pensions and Social Security now includes sections on the changes occurring in Europe and how they affect the global economy.

The entire chapter on mental health follows the 2013 publication of psychiatry's newest diagnosic manual, the DSM-5. In addition, we present data from the most recent models on aging and psychopathology. We include the use of telepsychology in the treatment of older adults, a field that is rapidly gaining momentum in clinical psychology in general. In the area of elder abuse, we present new data gathered since the last edition that clarifies the types and prevalence of this tragic situation.

In the long-term care chapter, we have reorganized the sections to make the distinctions among types of settings more clear, and also include a section on "aging in place." We look once again at the abuses within nursing homes and also present the positive side of new models of care. An important topic in this chapter is health care (in the U.S.) and the future of Medicare, which we present in a way that will help students realize why this is of such vital concern to them, regardless of their age. We also culled through the many statistical compilations of data on nursing homes, which is surprisingly difficult to find, and summarize the numbers in a way that drives home their importance.

The chapter on death and dying contains many of the same topics as previous editions, but is slightly reorganized to make the organization of topics clearer to the reader. We also provide an update on the international data on mortality as these reflect on global health issues. The chapter also includes an expanded treatment of advance directives and the topic of living wills. The bereavement section updates the theoretical perspectives on attachment theory, reflecting the latest research in this area.

Finally, in the chapter on creativity, we completely reorganized our coverage to give expanded treatment to successful aging and slightly less attention to the specifics of the creativity and aging model. The new successful aging sections expand on the traditional definitions of this term and include greater emphasis on social context. We found the World Health Organization's model of successful aging to provide a particularly useful framework, and present this in detail. In our last section, on creativity and aging, we now discuss the concept of "lastingness" as the enduring quality of the work of late life creative individuals. Once again, we highlight the fact that anyone can leave a legacy, whether eminently creative or not. We leave our readers with what we hope are inspirational messages that will guide them through their own future development.

Supplements

Wiley is pleased to offer an online resource containing a wealth of teaching and learning materials at http://www.wiley.com/college/whitbourne.

Website Links

References in this edition show the websites that students and instructors can consult to gather updated information on changes in the field.

INSTRUCTOR RESOURCES

Instructor's Manual

The content in the Instructor's Manual reflects the 40 years of experience that Susan has in teaching this course. You will find chapter outlines, key terms, learning objectives, and lecture suggestions. We have updated our suggestions for videos and also provide instructors with resources for films, music, and literature.

PowerPoint Slides

Prepared for use in lectures, we provide you with a complete set of PowerPoint slides tested in Susan's class and designed specifically for this book. Instructors can easily adapt them for their own specific needs.

Test Bank

Instructors have access to a complete downloadable test bank that includes 50 questions in each chapter that follow the order in which concepts are presented in the text. Each multiple-choice question is labeled according to the concept it tests, along with its difficulty level (based on class testing). We include short answer and essay questions that correspond with each section of the chapter. Because they are in convenient Microsoft Word format, instructors can adapt them to their own particular needs.

ACKNOWLEDGMENTS

Our first set of acknowledgments goes to our families. Husbands Richard O'Brien and Erik Gleason have graciously provided important support that allowed us to spend the many hours we needed over the period of a year to revise the book. Jennifer O'Brien, daughter and sister, is a wonderful sounding board for our ideas; as she continues her career in clinical psychology, we look forward to continued "collaboration" with her. We would also like to thank the newest members of our family—namely Theodore James Gleason, age 2 at the time of this writing, and Scarlett Beth Gleason, who is now just a few months old. Susan is thrilled to be a grandmother, experiencing the joys of this special status on a first-hand basis.

Throughout the writing of this book, students in the Psychology of Aging class at the University of Massachusetts Amherst provided valuable insights and observations. As we were revising the book and preparing the lectures, student continued to provide us with fresh perspectives. Their good humor, patience, and willingness to experiment with some new ideas have made it possible to add the all-important student viewpoint to the finished product. We also appreciate the contributions of Susan's graduate teaching assistants, who serve as sounding boards in her preparation and review of lecture content.

We feel extremely fortunate to have had the guidance of editor Chris Johnson at John Wiley & Sons. He helped us prepare this and previous editions as well. His insights, support, and friendly advice have been central to our ability to maintain the book's strength while widening its appeal. We would also like to give special thanks to our associate editor, Kristen Mucci. She maintains the tradition of Wiley's efficiency and helpful attention that we have had the good fortune to receive throughout the revision process. Photo editor, Billy Ray, helped us tremendously in meeting our requests for great illustrative material. We feel particularly grateful to our production editor Yee Lyn Song, who once again in this edition provided helpful, friendly, and thoughtful feedback. The marketing team and sales representatives are in contact with us on a regular basis to ensure that you and your colleagues receive the best

service, and that your students are given the best options to meet the instructor's course requirements. Finally, the work of designer Kenji Ngieng guaranteed that the book's design is attractive and pedagogically presented. These individuals on the Wiley team provide behind-the-scenes help that every author knows is invaluable to the creation of an excellent text.

Our final thanks go to the reviewers who provided helpful comments and suggestions throughout the revision process. Their insightful observations and thoughtful proposals for changes helped us tighten and focus the manuscript and enhance the discussion of several key areas of interest in the field. Thank you to Alex Bishop (Oklahoma State University), Sue Burdett-Robinson (Hardin-Simmons University), Alvin House (Illinois State University), Gary Montgomery (The University of Texas-Pan American), and Nancy Partika (Triton College). We have also benefited from informal reviews provided by our colleagues who use the book in their teaching. We greatly appreciate their helpful suggestions.

In conclusion, we hope that we have given you something to look forward to as you venture into the fascinating field of adult development and aging and that the subsequent pages of this book will fulfill these expectations. We aim to present a comprehensive but clear picture of the area and hope that you will be able to apply this knowledge to improving your own life and the lives of the older adults with whom you may be preparing to work. We hope you will come away from the course with a positive feeling about what you can do to "age better" and with a positive feeling about the potentialities of later life. And maybe, just maybe, as has happened on many past occasions with people who read this book and take our courses, you will decide to pursue this field and we can welcome you as colleagues in the coming years.

Finally, we would like to comment on the process of working together as a mother–daughter team. The first author was pregnant with the second author when she embarked on her first textbook in the field, the precursor to the present volume. Little did she know that the child she was about to have would become a psychologist, much less a specialist in aging. We greatly enjoy writing this book, and are proud and happy to be able to share our perspectives with you, the reader.

Susan Krauss Whitbourne, Ph.D.
Stacey B. Whitbourne, Ph.D.
November 2013

ABOUT THE AUTHORS

Susan Krauss Whitbourne, Ph.D., professor of psychology at the University of Massachusetts Amherst, received her Ph.D. in developmental psychology from Columbia University in 1974 and completed a postdoctoral training program in clinical psychology at the University of Massachusetts at Amherst, having joined the faculty there in 1984. Her previous positions were as associate professor of education and psychology at the University of Rochester (1975–1984) and assistant professor of psychology at SUNY College at Geneseo. Formerly the Psychology Departmental honors coordinator at the University of Massachusetts Amherst, she is director of the Office of National Scholarship Advisement where she advises students who apply for the Rhodes, Marshall, Fulbright, Truman, and Goldwater Scholarships, among others. In addition, she is faculty advisor to the University of Massachusetts Chapter of Psi Chi, a position for which she was recognized as the Eastern Regional Outstanding Advisor for the year 2001 and as the Florence Denmark National Faculty Advisor in 2002. She served as eastern region vice president of Psi Chi in 2006–07 and as chair of the program committee for the National Leadership Conference in 2009. Her teaching has been recognized with the College Outstanding Teacher Award in 1995 and the University Distinguished Teaching Award in 2001. Her work as an advisor was recognized with the Outstanding Academic Advisor Award in 2006. In 2003, she received the American Psychological Association (APA) Division 20 (Adult Development and Aging) Master Mentor Award and the Gerontological Society of America (GSA) Behavioral and Social Sciences Distinguished Mentorship Award.

Over the past 20 years, Dr. Whitbourne has held a variety of elected and appointed positions in APA Division 20 including president (1995–96), treasurer (1986–89), secretary (1981–84), program chair (1997–98), education committee chair (1979–80), Student Awards Committee chair (1993–94), Continuing Education Committee chair (1981–82), and Elections Committee chair (1992–93). She has chaired the Fellowship Committee and serves as the Division 20 representative to the APA Council (2000–2006 and 2009–present). She is a fellow of Divisions 1 (General Psychology), 2 (Teaching of Psychology), 9 (Society for the Study of Social Issues), 12 (Clinical Psychology), 20, and 35 (Society for the Psychology of Women). She served on the APA Committee on Structure and Function of Council, chaired the Policy and Planning Board in 2007, served on the APA Membership Board, chairs Women's Caucus and Coalition of Scientists and Applied Researchers in Psychology, and is now on the Board of Educational Affairs. In 2011, her contributions were recognized with an APA Presidential Citation.

Dr. Whitbourne is also a fellow of the American Psychological Society and the Eastern Psychological Association, for which she served on the Executive Board. She is a fellow of the Gerontological Society of America, and chairs the Behavioral and Social Sciences Fellows Committee. She is past president of the Council of Professional Geropsychology Training Programs. A founding member of the Society for the Study of Human Development, she was its president from 2005 to 2007. She is also a founding member of the Society for the Study of Emerging Adulthood. She also serves on the Board of Directors of the National Association of Fellowship Advisors. In her home of Amherst, Massachusetts, she has served on the Council on Aging (2004–07) and was the president of the Friends of the Amherst Senior Center (2007–09).

Her publications include 15 published books, many in multiple editions, and more than 140 journal articles and chapters, including articles in *Psychology and Aging, Psychotherapy, Developmental Psychology, Journal of Gerontology, Journal of Personality and Social Psychology*, and *Teaching of Psychology*, and chapters in the *Handbook of the Psychology of Aging, Clinical Geropsychology, Comprehensive Clinical Psychology (Geropsychology)*, the *Encyclopedia of Psychology*, and the *International Encyclopedia of the Social and Behavioral Sciences*. She has been a consulting editor for *Psychology and Aging*, serves on the editorial board of the *Journal of Gerontology* and was a consulting editor for *Developmental Psychology*. She is editor-in-chief of the Wiley-Blackwell *Encyclopedia of Aging*. Her presentations at professional conferences number over 250 and include several invited addresses, among them the APA G. Stanley Hall Lecture in 1995, the EPA Psi Chi Distinguished Lecture in 2001, and the SEPA Invited Lecture in 2002. In addition to her professional writing, she writes a blog

for *Psychology Today* called "Fulfillment at Any Age," and posts to the Huffington Post "Post 50" website.

Stacey B. Whitbourne, Ph.D., received her Ph.D. in social and developmental psychology from Brandeis University in 2005 where she was funded by a National Institute on Aging training fellowship. She completed her post-doctoral fellowship at the Boston University School of Public Health, Department of Epidemiology, funded by a National Institute on Aging Grant and a Department of Veterans Affairs Rehabilitation Research and Development Service Grant. Currently, she is a research health scientist at the Massachusetts Veterans Epidemiology and Research Information Center (MAVERIC), an independent research center housed within the VA Boston Healthcare System. She also serves as program director for the Million Veteran Program, a longitudinal health and genomic cohort funded by the Department of Veteran's Affairs Office of Research and Development. In addition, she is an instructor of medicine at Harvard Medical School and an associate epidemiologist at the Division of Aging at Brigham and Women's Hospital. The author of several published articles, she is also a coauthor on a chapter for the Sage Series on Aging in America. She is a member of the American Psychological Association Division 20 and the Gerontological Society of America. A member of the Membership Committee of Division 20, she has also given more than 30 presentations at national conferences. As an undergraduate, she received the Psi Chi National Student Research Award. In graduate school, she was awarded the Verna Regan Teaching Award and an APA Student Travel Award. She has taught courses on adult development and aging at Brandeis University and the University of Massachusetts Boston.

CONTENTS

CHAPTER 4

Physical Changes   63

CHAPTER 5

Health and Prevention   93

1

Themes and Issues in Adult Development and Aging

What's Your Real Age?

TOPICS

Themes and issues

Models of development

Methods

Physical changes

Health

Memory and attention

Higher-order cognition

Personality

Relationships

Work and retirement

Mental health

Long-term care

Death and dying

Successful aging

If you want to know your true age, don't look at the calendar. The calendar tells you what your chronological age is, but this number may be far from accurate in defining who you are. All you know from your chronological age is how many times you've sat on the earth while it orbits around the sun. As an index of aging, chronological age is deeply flawed.

Perhaps the biggest reason for this is that industrialized societies such as our own measure productivity in terms of time. Agrarian societies kept track of time by referring to markers in the seasonal variations of the sun, moon, and planets. As society became industrialized, people increasingly relied on clocks to set the pace of work. Age then became part of that industrialized system. Atomic clocks that measure the tiniest fraction of a second give us no respite from time's arrow.

Just as age and time become woven into our society's fabric, so too is the way that society defines each of us in terms of this magic number. Did you ever notice that the first piece of information in a news article or even a wedding announcement, right after the subject's name, is his or her age? If you'd rather your neighbors didn't know your exact age, you'd better be sure not to get involved in a jaywalking accident or fender bender. Your age will follow your name, and there's no way around that.

Yet, age may not always tell us very much about a person. Think of the older-than-her-years, hypermature 15-year-old who could easily pass for 22. How about the older adult who lives down the street from you, whose sprightly step would rival that of someone 40 years her junior? In thinking about yourself, as Satchel Paige once said, "How old would you be if you didn't know how old you was?"

Perhaps the best way to test your functional age is to ask yourself this very simple question: How old do you feel? Forget what the calendar says, and even forget what your functional age is. The age you feel may very well be the most important factor in determining your health, happiness, and longevity. Research consistently demonstrates that the people who are happiest and best adjusted in their middle and later years are those who don't focus on their limitations, worry about their memories, or become preoccupied with whether others view them as old. Being able to subtract a few years from this subjective age, or age that you feel, may actually buy you a few more objective years of healthy and productive life.

Posted by Susan Whitbourne and Stacey Whitbourne

Aging affects everyone. Your aging process began the moment you were born. If you are of traditional college age, you're undergoing a time of transition that lasts from adolescence to adulthood. The concept of being an adult may be new to you, and the idea of being an older adult may seem far off. Our purpose in writing this book is to help you think about your own aging as well as the aging process more generally. You may have decided to take this course to help you understand your aging family members or trends in society; however, before long, we hope that you think about what will happen to you as you yourself get older.

Let's start by asking you what comes to mind when you think of your current age. Is it an important part of who you are or do you not think about your actual age? Next, ask yourself whether you consider yourself to be an "adult." What does the word adult mean to you? Is it a term you would use to describe others who are older than you are now? Finally, what are your thoughts about the aging process? When you think of older adults, do you immediately regard them as unable to care for themselves? What is the "typical" older adult like, in your eyes?

Just by thinking about these questions, you've already started to focus on what age means in terms of your overall sense of self. These are the types of questions that we'll explore throughout the book. Even as we discuss in-depth the effects of the aging process throughout adulthood, we will often come back and question how much we really know about a person based on age alone. We'll also show you that some age distinctions are almost arbitrary. Someone decided that a certain age means you're in a certain stage of life; from that point forward, people attribute a great deal of meaning to that particular number. In reality, however, the aging process isn't completely linked to the passage of time alone.

Our goal is to encourage you to take personal explorations as you gain factual information about the aging process. Not only will the material help you in your career (regardless of what field you go into), but it will also help you understand yourself and how you change over time. You'll also learn, perhaps surprisingly, that you don't have to sit back and let the aging process passively affect you. There are active steps you can take to make sure that you keep functioning as well as possible for as long as possible throughout your entire life. With a few simple precautions, you can avoid the illnesses that limit people's ability to enjoy themselves into their later decades.

If you're a traditional college-age student heading into your twenties, we hope to help you appreciate that it is never too early to start incorporating these changes into your lifestyle. And for our readers of nontraditional college age, we hope to help you see that it's never too late to initiate behaviors that can maintain, if not enhance, your everyday

functioning. A key goal in writing this book is to involve you in the progression of your aging process and show you ways to be an active part of your own development.

THE BIOPSYCHOSOCIAL PERSPECTIVE

We organize the book around the **biopsychosocial perspective**, a view of development as a complex interaction of biological, psychological, and social processes. Aging is not a simple, straightforward progression through time. Your body undergoes biological changes largely influenced by your genetics or physiology. At the same time, you change psychologically in ways that reflect what's happening to your body that, in turn, affect your body's changes. All of this takes place in a social context. Holding biology and psychology constant, people age differently depending on where and when they live, whom they interact with, and what resources they have available to them.

Figure 1.1 captures this complex biopsychosocial interaction. Biological processes refer to how the body's functions and structures change throughout the aging process. We cover these changes in the chapters on normal aging and health. Psychological processes include the individual's thoughts, feelings, and behaviors related to growing older. We examine these changes in the chapters on cognition, personality, and emotions. The social processes of aging reflect the cultural, historical, and interpersonal influences on the individual. We cover these in chapters about relationships, family, work, and institutionalization. In Chapter 2, we will explore how life-span development theories grapple with explaining how these complex processes all interrelate. You'll find that there's a great deal more to aging than you probably imagined when you first started reading this chapter.

FIGURE 1.1

The Biopsychosocial Model

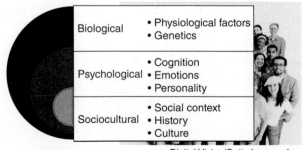

Digital Vision/Getty Images, Inc.

As you can see from the biopsychosocial model, we intend to go beyond "psychology" in teaching you about the processes involved in adult development and aging. In fact, **gerontology**, the scientific study of the aging process, is an interdisciplinary field. People who devote their professional lives to the study of gerontology come from many different fields—biology, medicine, nursing, sociology, history, and even the arts and literature. To be a gerontologist, applying this integrative view to your work is crucial. Knowledge, theories, and perspectives from all disciplines contribute importantly to the study of the individual over time.

To help put it all together for you as you develop throughout adulthood, we will pay special attention to the concept of **identity**. Identity is defined as a composite of how people view themselves in the biological, psychological, and social domains of life. The interaction of these domains forms an overall view of the "self."

FOUR PRINCIPLES OF ADULT DEVELOPMENT AND AGING

We begin our study of adult development and aging by sharing a set of four principles that form the foundation of our biopsychosocial approach (see Table 1.1). As you read the book, you'll find that we return frequently to these principles, which we highlight when they appear in the chapter. If you begin to understand them now, you will find the course material much easier to master.

1. Changes Are Continuous Over the Life Span

First and foremost, changes over the life span happen in a continuous fashion. According to the **continuity principle**, the changes that people experience in later adulthood build on the experiences they had in their earlier years. This means we can never isolate the later years of life without considering the years preceding them. Since time moves in a forward direction, the changes throughout life build upon themselves in a cumulative fashion. If you were hard

TABLE 1.1

The Four Principles of Adult Development and Aging

Principle	Meaning
1. Changes are continuous over the lifespan	*Individuals remain the "same" even though they change*
2. Only the survivors grow old	*Aging individuals are increasingly self-selected*
3. Individuality matters	*People vary within and between age groups*
4. Normal aging is different from disease	*Intrinsic aging processes are different from those associated with illness*

on your body as a young adult, chances are the changes you'll undergo when you're older will be more negative than if you took good care of yourself.

The continuity principle also applies to the way that people think about their own identities. You know that you're the same person you always were, despite getting older. Birthdays don't transform you into a different person. You don't look the same to others, but you feel essentially the "same" on the inside.

When others look at you, however, they don't necessarily share this perspective. People don't meet you for the first time and think about what you were like when you were younger—they see you as you are now. Unless they are close relatives or friends, they have no way of knowing what you were like when you were in your childhood or teenage years. Anyone meeting you now judges you on the basis of your current appearance because he or she has no other data from which to draw.

Similarly, when you look at a middle-aged or older adult, it's unlikely that you judge that person on the basis of how he or she may have been in the past. You see an older woman, perhaps walking with a little difficulty, and don't stop to think that this person used to be more vigorous and healthy. However, that very same older woman knows that she is the "same" person she's always been. She may seem surprised, in fact, to realize that she's seen as an "old

Robert L. Zentmaier/Photo Researchers, Inc.

Robert L. Zentmaier/Photo Researchers, Inc.

Robert L. Zentmaier/Photo Researchers, Inc.

Over the progression of time, as shown in these photos of the same man from ages 3 through 82, people may feel the same inside even though their outer appearance changes.

woman" instead of as the Jane, Barbara, or Mary she knows herself to be.

Therefore, when working with older adults, it is important to remember that they would prefer to be treated as the people they always were, rather than as "old people." As we'll see later, older adults are often stereotyped as weak and infirm, when in reality, they want to be viewed as individuals who've lived a long time. They don't want to be stereotyped on the basis of the way they look to you right now. Some nursing home administrators, eager to remind their employees of this fact, display pictures of the residents from their younger years. The residents know they're the same people they have always been, and it's helpful if those who work with them are reminded of this fact as well.

2. Only the Survivors Grow Old

The **survivor principle** states that the people who live to old age are the ones who managed to outlive the many threats that could have caused their deaths at earlier ages. Perhaps this is obvious because clearly, to grow old, you have to not die. However, the survivor principle is a bit more complex than that. Contrary to the Billy Joel song "Only the Good Die Young," it's not the good who die young, but the ones who fall victim to the forces that cause people to lose their lives. Some of these are random, to be sure, such as being killed by someone else in an accident, by an act of war, or in a natural disaster. However, many other factors that lead some to survive into old age are nonrandom.

Thus, survivors not only manage to avoid random causes of their own fatalities, but also are more likely to take care of their health and not engage in risky behaviors (such as driving too fast or getting involved in crime) or use drugs and alcohol excessively. The very fact that survivors avoid death until late in life suggests they may have inherited good genes or at least managed to maintain their physical abilities (biological factors), are emotionally healthy (psychological factors), or have surrounded themselves with a good support system (social factors). These, or a combination of the three, plus a dose of good luck, allow them to be with us today.

Table 1.2 shows the five most common behaviors that prevent people from living a longer life (Kamimoto, Easton, Maurice, Husten, & Macera, 1999). We somewhat ironically call these "Five Ways to Shorten Your Life." Most people would prefer not to shorten their lives, and certainly not to develop poor health in their later years, but many do not think about the ramifications of engaging in risky behaviors. Survivors most likely do not engage in these behaviors. Therefore, not only are they different because they may have been born healthier, but they also likely took

---

TABLE 1.2
Five Ways to Shorten Your Life

1. Being overweight
2. Drinking and driving
3. Eating inadequate fruits and vegetables
4. Being physically inactive
5. Smoking

Source: Adapted from Kamimoto, L. A., Easton, A. N., Maurice, E., Husten, C. G., & Macera, C. A. (1999). Surveillance for five health risks among older adults—United States, 1993–1997. *Morbidity and Mortality Weekly Reports, 48(SSO8)*, 89–130.

---

care to maintain their health and preserve their longevity. When you consider what it takes to become an older adult, it is hard not to appreciate that the people who survive to later adulthood have some incredibly special characteristics.

The survivor principle has important theoretical implications. Clearly, all older adults who participate in research are survivors of the conditions that others did not endure. As time goes by, more and more of the older population will die. When they reach their 90s or 100s, they most likely represent a different population than their now-deceased age mates. The older they get, the more select they become in such key characteristics as physical functioning, health, intelligence, and even personality (Baird, Lucas, & Donnellan, 2010).

Consequently, when we examine differences between younger and older people, we must keep in mind that older people alive today were a special group when they were young. The younger adults have not yet been subjected to the same conditions that could threaten their lives. Some of them will die before they reach old age. Knowing who will be the survivors is almost impossible to predict meaning we may be comparing highly select older adults with a wider range of younger adults. Therefore, we cannot conclude that age "caused" the older adults to have the characteristics they have now because they might always have been a special subset of their own age group.

To help illustrate this principle, consider data on the psychological characteristic of cautiousness. One of the tried and true findings in the psychology of adult development and aging contends that older people are less likely to take risks than are younger people. Similarly, older adults are less likely to engage in criminal behavior. It's possible that as people age they are better able to avoid behaving in ways that could bring them harm or get them arrested. Alternatively, it's possible that they did not change at all and are the only ones left standing from their generation.

The people more likely to make risky decisions early on in life died at younger ages or were imprisoned. Certainly, those who made poor health decisions would be less likely to have survived into old age.

As a result of the survivor principle, you need to remind yourself continually throughout this book that the older adults we study may have become less risky, more honest, or better able to take care of their health. On the other hand, they may not have changed at all—only survived long enough for us to study them.

3. Individuality Matters

A long-held myth regarding development is that as people age, they all become alike. This view is refuted by the principle of **individuality**, which asserts that as people age, they become more different from each other. This divergence occurs in people's physical functioning, psychological performance, relationships, interest in work, economic security, and personality.

In one often-cited study, still considered a classic, researchers examined a large number of studies of aging to compare how differently older versus younger adults responded to the same measures (Nelson & Dannefer, 1992). Rather than their scores converging, they grew farther apart. Research continues to underscore the notion that individuals continue to become less alike with age. Such findings suggest that diversity becomes an increasingly prominent theme during the adult years, a point we will continue to focus on throughout this book.

The idea of increasing divergence among older adult populations does not mean that everyone starts out at exactly the same point when they're young. There are always going to be differences within any sample of people in almost any characteristic you can name. The issue is that as people get older, these differences become magnified. The top-performing person in a sample of young adults

may be 10 points higher than the next highest performer. By the time this person reaches his or her 70s or 80s, these differences may grow by a factor of two, three, or more. In part, this is a statistical fluke. As you'll learn in Chapter 3, it's difficult to find a sample of older adults who are as close in age as are the young adults researchers tend to study (who are often within 2 or 3 years of each other). If age is related to performance, then the odds are that the older group will differ simply because they differ more in age.

However, the increasing variation among older adults isn't just a statistical artifact. Even if you had a sample of older adults who were exactly the same age, it's likely that they would differ more among themselves than they would have when they were younger because they've lived through more experiences affecting everything from their health to their psychological well-being. Those experiences have cumulative effects, causing them to change at different rates and to differing degrees.

Consider what's happened to you and the people you grew up with by this point in your life. You have made the decision to go to college, while others in your age group may have enlisted in military service. You may meet your future spouse in college, while your best friend remains on the dating scene for years. Upon graduation, some may choose to pursue graduate studies as others enter the workforce. You may or may not choose to start a family, or perhaps have already begun the process. With the passage of time, your differing experiences build upon each other to help mold the person you become. The many possibilities that can stem from the choices you make help illustrate that the permutations of events in people's lives are virtually endless. Personal histories move in increasingly idiosyncratic directions with each passing day, year, and decade of life.

There are actually two types of differences that come into play when we talk about individuality. **Interindividual differences** are differences *between* people. We've shown an example of interindividual differences in Figure 1.2. In

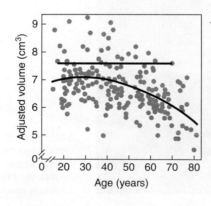

Age (years)

FIGURE 1.2

Interindividual Differences in Development

This figure shows age differences in the volume of cells in the hippocampus, a part of the brain involved in memory. The straight line shows that people in their 70s may have the same brain volumes as people in their 20s.

Source: Reprinted by permission from Macmillan Publishers Ltd: Nature Reviews Neuroscience. Hedden, T., & Gabrieli, J. D. (2004). Insights into the ageing mind: A view from cognitive neuroscience. *Nature Review Neuroscience*, 5, 87–96.

this figure, each dot represents the size of the hippocampus, a part of the brain involved in memory thought to grow smaller as people get older. As you can see, people of the same age can vary so dramatically from one another that they may more closely resemble people from different age groups. Follow the straight line showing two dots—one representing a 20-year-old and one representing data from a 70-year-old. The hippocampus of this 70-year-old actually equals that of at least one 20-year-old. Many of the 70-year-olds have hippocampal sizes that equal those of people in their 40s. These interindividual differences clearly show that not all 70-year-olds are alike.

As this example shows, some older adults can outperform younger adults on tasks typically shown to decline with age. This sort of occurrence happens in many areas of study. Although traditionally younger adults have faster reaction times than older adults, exceptions to the norm are common. While you may think of average-age college students as being able to run faster, lift heavier weights, or solve crossword puzzles in a shorter time than people three times their age, consider the differences between a sedentary 21-year-old and a 72-year-old triathlete. Chances are, the triathlete will outperform the sedentary adult in all categories. We will continue to explore the notion that functioning does not necessarily need to "go downhill" as people get older.

Intra-individual differences refer to the variations in performance within the same individual. In other words, not all systems develop at the same rate within the person. Some functions may increase over time, others decrease, and others stay the same. Even within a construct such as intelligence, an individual may show gains in one area,

losses in another, and stability in yet another domain. Intra-individual differences illustrate the fact that development can proceed in multiple directions within the same person (Baltes & Graf, 1996), a concept known as **multidirectionality**.

4. "Normal" Aging Is Different From Disease

The principle that **normal aging is different from disease** means that growing older doesn't necessarily mean growing sicker. It is important for both practical and scientific reasons to distinguish between normal aging and disease. Health care specialists who work with middle-aged and older adults need to recognize and treat the onset of a disease rather than dismiss it simply as "getting older." For example, an 80-year-old man exhibiting symptoms of depression can be successfully treated, assuming that the clinician does not write his symptoms off as a feature of normal aging. Personality development in adulthood does not inevitably lead to the depressive symptoms of lowered self-esteem, excessive guilt, changes in appetite, or lack of interest in activities. Older adults may experience some moderation in personality qualities such as becoming a bit less judgmental in relation to others. However, the development of psychological disorders for the first time in later life is not typical. Clinicians who mistakenly think that these symptoms are part of the normal aging process won't take the proper course of treatment that could alleviate the depressed person's suffering.

Gerontologists translate the principle that normal aging is different from disease into terms that distinguish these

©Ty Allison/Getty Images, Inc.

This highly fit triathlete has physical skills that would rival those of a sedentary young adult, further illustrating the principle of individual differences. He also provides an example of optimal aging.

processes. **Primary aging** (or **normal aging**) refers to the normal changes over time that occur due to universal, intrinsic, and progressive alterations in the body's systems. Changes over time leading to impairment due to disease rather than normal aging are referred to as **secondary or impaired aging**. These changes are not due to universal, intrinsic processes but are a function of an abnormal set of changes afflicting a segment rather than the entirety of the older population (Aldwin & Gilmer, 1999). Skin wrinkling is an example of primary aging; the development of skin cancer in later life is an example of secondary aging. Toward the very end of life, individuals experience a rapid loss of functions across multiple areas of functioning; this is called **tertiary** aging (Gerstorf, Ram, Lindenberger, & Smith, 2013).

Primary, secondary, and tertiary aging refer to processes that, over time, accumulate, and in the absence of accident or injury, cause the individual's death. Gerontologists believe that despite the changes in the body that lead to loss, aging can also involve gains. The term **optimal aging** refers to age-related changes that improve the individual's functioning. Changes due to optimal aging may reflect the preventative or compensatory measures that adults take to counter the toll that aging would normally take on their physical and psychological functioning. However, some individuals do not even make special efforts to alter their own aging, but for reasons not always entirely clear, seem to age at a slower rate than their peers. They may be the ones who never seem to get sick right until the very end of their lives, when a sudden illness leads to their death (i.e., tertiary aging).

Throughout life, age-related losses due to primary, secondary, and tertiary aging eventually overtake age-related gains, as we show in the left side of Figure 1.3.

FIGURE 1.3

Age-Related Losses and Gains

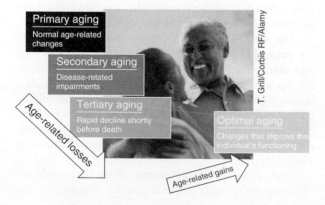

THE MEANING OF AGE

The study of aging implies that age is the major variable of interest. As we describe in more detail below, there is value in categorizing individuals in later life based on their age. At the same time, there is an arbitrariness to the numerical value attached to people based on the continuous processes that occur over time. The crossing from an age that ends in "9" to an age that ends in "0" (such as going from 39 to 40) often leads people to engage in self-scrutiny if not somewhat disturbing birthday cards from friends invoking the "over the hill" metaphor. In truth, however, the body does not change in such discrete fits and starts.

Chronological age has some value in describing a person, but like other descriptive features of a person, such as gender or eye color, it is the social meaning attached to chronological age that often outweighs any intrinsic usefulness. As we have already discussed, people of the same age can vary substantially from one another, and people of different ages can be more similar to each other than their differing age might lead you to expect. Chronological age is a number based on events in the universe that occur, and its units are not necessarily inherently tied to the aging process.

The body does keep time in a cycle that approximates a 24-hour period, but there is no evidence at the moment to suggest that this time pacemaker is related to aging. To say that chronological age (or time) "means" anything with regard to the status of the body's functioning is, based on current evidence, questionable. The popularity of such phrases as "30 being the new 20" and "60 the new 50" capture the difficulty of defining age based solely on a number.

Using Age to Define "Adult"

Now that we have you thinking about the meaning of age, we will move on to the next challenge—the meaning of the word "adult." Earlier, we asked you to decide whether you consider yourself an adult. When you think of that word, perhaps the synonym of "mature" comes to mind. This, in turn, may conjure up images of a person reaching a certain level of accomplishment or growth. Consider, for example, the term "mature" in reference to an apple. A mature apple is one that is ready to be eaten, and you can judge that by examining the apple's color, size, and texture. An apple's maturity level is relatively easy to measure compared to judging the maturity of humans because the complexity of the biopsychosocial processes are far more difficult to quantify.

You might think that the most logical definition of maturity should be based on physical development. Yet, you also know that a 13-year-old male who has essentially reached his full physical development would, in contemporary Western society, be regarded as anything but an adult. Although his physical attributes define him as an adult, the psychological and social standards would not.

Perhaps a standard based on ability is a better option. Consider 16 years, the age when most people can legally drive. Or, alternatively, consider the age 18, when U.S. society ordains the person with the right to vote. Using the age of 21 presents another possible point of entry into adulthood. Because it is the age when American adults can legally drink alcohol, for many, the turning of 21 represents a defining mark of the beginning of adulthood. However, the United States is in a small minority of nations that set the drinking age at 21. Some Canadian provinces set the drinking age at 19 (though it is 18 in most); countries such as Germany, Barbados, and Portugal set it at 16. These conflicting age demarcations for even such a seemingly concrete behavior as drinking alcohol show that deciding when a person is an adult on this basis has very limited utility.

Parenthetically, the variations in the legal drinking age shown from country to country (and even within a country) illustrate the interaction of biological and sociocultural factors in setting age-based parameters around human behavior. People in Canada who are 18 years old are, on average, not all that physiologically distinct from 18-year-olds who live in France. For that matter, they are probably not even psychologically different. It's the culture that distinguishes whether they're able to drink alcohol without getting arrested.

If you're like many students, the age of 25 may hold special importance for you. This is the age where, in the United States, you can rent a car (without having to pay a tremendous surcharge). This age has no inherent meaning, but it is used by car rental companies because the chances of having an auto accident are lower after the age of 25. It's possible that a switch is flicked on a person's 25th birthday so that the unsafe driver now has become a model of good behavior on the road. However, there are statistically higher odds that people under age 25 are more likely to engage in the risky combination of drinking and driving.

Another set of criteria related to the age of adulthood pertains to when people can marry without the consent of their parents. There again, we find huge variation. Within the United States alone, the age of consent varies from state to state (in South Carolina it is 14, while other states deem 16 or 18 the appropriate age). Moreover, the age when people actually marry reflects factors such as the health of the economy; in bad economic times, the median age of marriage goes well above the age of consent. During these times, people in their 20s (or older) may find they're forced to move back in with their parents because they aren't earning sufficient income to rent or buy their own place.

Does that mean that people become less "adult" when the economy lags?

Given these contradictory definitions of "adult," it might be wise to recommend that we set the threshold into adulthood based on the individual's having reached the chronological age associated with the expectations and privileges of a given society or subculture. For example, in the United States, individuals may be considered to have reached adulthood at the age when they are eligible to vote, drink, drive, and get married. For the majority of U.S. states, the age of 21 is therefore considered the threshold to adulthood. In other countries, these criteria may be reached at the age of 18. Regardless of the varying definitions, up to as many as the first 10 or 11 years of adulthood represent the period of **emerging adulthood**, or the transition prior to assuming the full responsibilities associated with adulthood, normally the years 18 to 29 (Arnett, 2000). These responsibilities may occur during the years that follow college graduation or, for those individuals who do not attend college, when they face the need to find full employment or make family commitments.

Divisions by Age of the Over-65 Population

Traditionally, 65 years of age has been viewed as the entry point for "old age." There was no inherent reason for the choice of this age other than that in 1889, the German Chancellor Otto von Bismarck decided to set this as the age when people could receive social insurance payments. Now, we accept age 65 without giving it much thought.

Gerontologists recognized long ago that not only was 65 an arbitrary number for defining old age, but that it also resulted in people being placed into too broad of a category when defined as older adults. All other things being equal, a 65-year-old faces very different issues than someone who is 85 or 90. There are certainly 65-year-olds in very poor health and 95-year-olds who have no serious ailments. But because, on average, 65-year-olds are so different than those who are 20 or more years older, we use a convention to break the 65-and-older category into subgroups.

The subgroups most frequently used in gerontology are **young-old** (ages 65 to 74); **old-old** (ages 75 to 84); and **oldest-old** (ages 85 and older). We shouldn't place too much credence on numbers, as we've already said, but these are good approximations for roughly categorizing the 65-and-older population. Bernice Neugarten, one of the early pioneers in psychological gerontology, proposed these distinctions in the mid-1960s, and they have remained in use to this day.

With more and more people living to the oldest-old category, though, gerontologists are reexamining the divisions of the 65+ age group. Specifically, people over the age of 100, known as **centenarians**, are becoming more and more commonly represented in the population, as we will show later in the chapter. It will not be long before the very highest age category becomes more prominent—the **supercentenarians**, who are 110 and older. Typically, the oldest person in the world at any given time is between the ages of 114 and 116. Jeanne Louise Calment, the oldest documented living human, was 122 at the time of her death. Supercentenarian will probably retain its definition as 110 and over, though, at least for the foreseeable future.

Functional Age

Discontented with the entire concept of chronological age, a number of gerontologists are devising a new classification system that is based not on what the calendar says but on **functional age**, which is how people actually perform (see Figure 1.4). With functional instead of chronological age as the basis for a system of studying aging, we could gain a better grasp of a person's true characteristics and abilities. When we talk about research methods in Chapter 3, we'll see further advantages to using measures other than chronological age to study the aging process.

Biological age is the age of an individual's bodily systems. Using biological age instead of chronological age would tell us exactly how well people are able to perform such vital functions as pumping blood through the body and getting oxygen to the lungs. With biological age, you could also help people learn how best to improve their muscle and bone strength, for example. To accomplish this,

we would need a large repository of data showing what's to be expected for each major biological function at each age. For example, we'd need to know the population values for blood pressure readings in people with different chronological ages. Then, we would assign people a "blood pressure age" according to which chronological age of healthy people their numbers most closely match. A 50-year-old whose blood pressure was in the range of normal 25- to 30-year-olds would then have a biological age that was 20 or 25 years younger than his or her chronological age.

Popular culture has certainly caught on to the notion of biological rather than chronological age. There are a multitude of online calculators in which you answer various questions to estimate how long you will live. In addition, there are slightly more sophisticated "biological age tests" that let you calculate your "lung age," for example. Though we don't have reliable biological age measures yet, these measures are becoming more sophisticated and may eventually serve a purpose.

Psychological age refers to the performance an individual achieves on measures of such qualities as reaction time, memory, learning ability, and intelligence (all of which are known to change with age). Like biological age, a person's performance on these tasks would be compared with those of other adults, and then scaled accordingly.

Social age is calculated by evaluating where people are compared to the "typical" ages expected for people to be when they occupy certain positions in life. These positions tend to center on family and work roles. For example, a grandparent would have an older social age than would a parent, although the grandparent might easily be chronologically younger than the parent.

Social age can have some interesting twists. For example, people can be grandparents in their late 20s (with a social age of 60 or older). Conversely, women can become mothers in their late 60s. In 2010, a TV series aired an episode called "Pregnant at 70." Similarly, a retiree would have an older social age than would a person still working, although again their chronological age might be in reverse order. Athletes typically retire in their 30s or earlier, depending on their sport; politicians or religious figures may not retire until their late 80s, if at all.

As stated earlier, an advantage of using functional indices of aging is that they can be more accurate than chronological age. Of course, it's much easier to use chronological age than to use these more sophisticated calculations. Furthermore, functional ages must be constantly calibrated and re-calibrated to ensure that they continue to be accurate. For example, a biological index based in part on blood pressure may require adjustments as health practitioners change the definition of what is considered "old." Changes in both medical knowledge and population norms

FIGURE 1.4

Alternative Indices of Aging

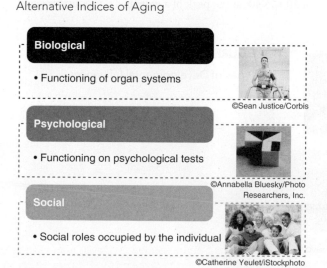

Biological

• Functioning of organ systems

©Sean Justice/Corbis

Psychological

• Functioning on psychological tests

©Annabella Bluesky/Photo Researchers, Inc.

Social

• Social roles occupied by the individual

©Catherine Yeulet/iStockphoto

for particular age groups may mean that the definition of normal blood pressure for an average 60-year-old shifts to be more typical of a person in the 70s. Psychological age and social age indices are also likely to change over time. Despite its faults, chronological age may be the most expedient index for many areas of functioning, as long as we keep in mind that it does not tell the whole story.

Personal Versus Social Aging

The aging process occurs within the individual, but as you have learned already, it is shaped by events occurring in the individual's social context. When developmental psychologists study the aging process, it is difficult to disentangle those internal changes from those that reflect a changing world, though we try to do so by applying the appropriate controls in our research.

Personal aging refers to changes that occur within the individual and reflect the influence of time's passage on the body's structures and functions. **Social aging** refers to the effects of a person's exposure to a changing environment. Over time, then, the changes we see within the individual represent the unique blend of personal and social aging as these play out in that individual's life.

Within the category of social aging, the changes that take place in an individual's life can reflect a multitude of interacting factors. At any one time, the individual's life reflects one or more of three basic categories of three social influences (see Figure 1.5). These influences, identified by psychologist Paul Baltes (1979), include normative age-graded influences, normative history-graded influences, and nonnormative influences. We'll look at each of these in turn.

Normative age-graded influences lead people to choose experiences that their culture and historical period attach to certain ages or points in the life span. The term "normative" stems from the term "norm," which is a social expectation for behavior. In Western society, age norms traditionally dictate that individuals graduate from college in their early 20s, get married and begin a family in their 20s or 30s, retire in their 60s, and become grandparents in their middle to later years, usually in the decades of the 50s, 60s, and beyond. These are influences on behavior to the extent that people believe that they should structure their lives according to these age demarcations.

Events that occur in response to normative age-graded influences occur in part because a given society has developed expectations about what is assumed for people of certain ages. The decision to retire at the age of 65 years can be seen as a response to the norm regarding when it is appropriate (and, for many, desirable) to leave the labor market. Graduation from high school generally occurs at the age of 18 years for most because in most industrialized societies, children start school at the age of 5 or 6 and the educational system is based on 12 or 13 grades.

Normative age-graded influences exert their impact because people are socialized into believing that they *should* structure their lives so that they conform to these influences. When they don't, they feel that there is something wrong with them. For example, a 40-year-old office worker may consider retiring but feel reluctant to do so because it is not what is expected for a person of that age in that field of employment. Similarly, a 35-year-old may prefer not to marry or to have children, but feel pressured into doing so by other family members, friends, or the society at large by virtue of having reached their mid-30s.

The normative age-graded influences are partly linked to the biological aging process, particularly in the area of family. Parenthood traditionally occurs between the ages of 20 and 40, at the peak of a woman's reproductive cycle.

FIGURE 1.5

Types of Developmental Influences

(First Left): B2M Productions/Getty Images, Inc.; (First Middle): digitalskillet/iStockphoto; (First Right): Huchen Lu/iStockphoto; (Middle): Compassionate Eye Foundation/Chris Ryan/OJO Images Ltd/Photodisc/Getty Images, Inc.; (Right): Mark Edward Atkinson/Getty Images, Inc.

This age range sets the normative age period for biologically becoming a parent. Once this age is set, then a lower limit is set on the age at which the adult can become a grandparent. If the child also follows a normative age-graded influence, the parent will likely become a grandparent for the first time between the ages of 55 and 65 years.

Normative history-graded influences are events that occur to everyone within a certain culture or geopolitical unit (regardless of age) and include large-scale occurrences, such as world wars, economic trends, or sociocultural changes in attitudes and values. The impact of these events on people's lives may be felt immediately. They can continue to have a lasting impact for many years on the subsequent patterns of work, family, and quality of life of the people affected by those events. For example, World War II veterans who entered the military after their families were already established were more likely upon their return to get divorced or separated, to suffer career setbacks, and experience poorer physical health after they turned 50 (Elder, Shanahan, & Clipp, 1994).

An individual does not have to experience a historical event directly to be affected by a normative history-graded influence. For example, you may have been too young to have your job affected by the 2008 recession, but because the recession affected large sectors of the economy, you may have suffered anyway. Anytime there is a significant enough event or set of events affecting a large number of people, the event's aftermath may continue to impact aspects of each person's life for years to come.

If the life course was influenced only by normative age- and history-graded influences, predicting the course of development of people of the same age living in the same culture would not be easy, but it would be a manageable problem. Plug in a person's age and the year of the person's birth, and you'd be able to figure out which combination of age-graded and history-graded influences set the course of that person's life. However, people's lives are also affected by **nonnormative influences**, which are the random idiosyncratic events that occur throughout life. They are "non-normative" because they occur with no regular predictability.

There are almost an infinite number of examples of nonnormative influences. Some are due to good luck, such as winning the lottery or making a smart investment. Nonnormative influences can also be negative, such as a car accident, fire, or the untimely death of a relative. One moment your life is routine and predictable, only to be permanently altered in the course of a single event. Other nonnormative influences may unfold over a gradual period, such as being fired from a job (due to personal, not large-scale economic reasons), developing a chronic illness not related to aging, or going through a divorce. In everyday language, you talk about someone benefiting from the "right place, right time" effect or—conversely—suffering a negative fate from being in the "wrong place at the wrong time."

As you have read about the various types of influences on life, it may have crossed your mind that the way in which they interact with each other is also important. Consider the example of divorce. Although society's norms have changed considerably regarding this life event, many would still consider this a nonnormative occurrence because the norm (and certainly the hope) of married couples is to remain married. And although a divorce is a personal occurrence, it may be seen in part as a response to larger

ASSOCIATED PRESS

The devastating effects of Hurricane Sandy in 2012 impacted residents of the New Jersey shoreline, providing an example of a normative history-graded influence.

social forces. For example, a couple who is exposed to financial hardship because one or both partners lost a job due to living in harsh economic times (normative historical influence) is now faced with severe emotional stress. If they are in their middle years, when couples are expected to have reached a degree of financial comfort (age-graded normative influence), their problems may be exacerbated. Yet some couples may feel closer to each other when exposed to such adversity, and this is where the idiosyncratic nonnormative factors come into play.

This example illustrates the dilemmas faced by researchers in human development who attempt to separate out not only personal from social aging, but also the impact of particular influences that fall into the category of social aging. Though challenging, the very complexity of the equation fascinates those of us who try to understand what makes humans "tick" and what causes that ticking to change over the decades of the human lifespan.

KEY SOCIAL FACTORS IN ADULT DEVELOPMENT AND AGING

As we've just seen, social factors play an important role in shaping the course of our lives. Here we make explicit exactly how we define and use the key social factors that we will refer to in this book.

Sex and Gender

In discussing the aging process, there are important male–female differences related to the socialization experiences of men and women. We will use the term **gender** to refer to the individual's identification as being male or female. Gender is distinct from biological **sex**, which refers to the individual's inherited predisposition to develop the physiological characteristics typically associated with maleness or femaleness. Both sex and gender are important in the study of adult development and aging. Physiological factors relevant to sex influence the timing and nature of physical aging processes, primarily through the operation of sex hormones. For example, the sex hormone estrogen is thought to play at least some role in affecting a woman's risks of heart disease, bone loss, and possibly cognitive changes.

Social and cultural factors relevant to gender are important to the extent that the individual assumes a certain role in society based on being viewed as a male or female. Opportunities in education and employment are two main areas in which gender influences the course of adult development and becomes a limiting factor for women. Although

progress has certainly occurred in both domains over the past several decades, women continue to face a more restricted range of choices and the prospects of lower earnings than do men. Furthermore these differences are important to consider when studying the current generation of older adults, as they were raised in an era with more traditional gender expectations.

Race

A person's **race** is defined in biological terms as the classification within the species based on physical and structural characteristics. However, the concept of race in common usage is broader than these biological features. Race is used in a more widespread fashion to refer to the cultural background associated with being born within a particular biologically defined segment of the population. The "race" that people use to identify themselves is more likely to be socially than biologically determined. In addition, because few people are solely of one race in the biological sense, social and cultural background factors assume even greater prominence.

The U.S. Census, a count of those living in the United States conducted every 10 years, attempts to provide an accurate depiction of the size and makeup of the country. The 2010 U.S. Census defined race on the basis of a person's self-identification. The most frequently-used racial categories in data reported from the census are White, Black or African American, American Indian or Alaska Native, Asian, and Native Hawaiian or Other Pacific Islander.

In addition to these racial categories, the census also included categories based on national origin and allowed individuals to select more than one racial category. To the extent that race is biologically determined, however, racial differences in functioning in adulthood and aging may reflect differences in genetic inheritance. People who have inherited a risk factor that has been found to be higher within a certain race are more likely to be at risk for developing that illness during their adult years.

Racial variations in risk factors may also interact with different cultural backgrounds associated with a particular race. For example, people at risk for a disease with a metabolic basis (such as inability to metabolize fats) will be more likely to develop that disease depending on whether cooking foods high in fat content are a part of their culture.

Social and cultural aspects of race may also alter an individual's development in adulthood through the structure of a society and whether there are systematic biases against people who identify with that race. As we will demonstrate throughout this book, many illnesses have a higher prevalence among the African American population than among the White population, and this has led to significant disparities in the health of the two groups. Part of the differences in health may be attributed to lack of opportunities for education and well-paying jobs, but systematic discrimination is also believed to take a toll on health by increasing the levels of stress experienced by African Americans (Green & Darity, 2010).

Ethnicity

The concept of **ethnicity** captures the cultural background of an individual, reflecting the predominant values, attitudes, and expectations in which the individual has been raised. Along with race, ethnicity is often studied in adult development and aging as an influence on a person's familial attitudes and experiences. For example, people of certain ethnic backgrounds are thought to show greater respect for older adults and feel a stronger sense of obligation to care for their aging parents. Ethnicity also may play a role in influencing the aging of various physiological functions, in part through genetic inheritance, and in part through exposure to cultural habits and traditions. Finally, discrimination against people of certain ethnic backgrounds may serve the same function as race in limiting the opportunities for educational and occupational achievements.

The term ethnicity is gradually replacing the term race as a categorical variable in social research. We will follow that tradition in this book unless there is a clear-cut reason to refer specifically to race (i.e., if we are describing research that also uses this term). However, there are occasional points of confusion in that the U.S. Census occasionally combines race (White or Black) and ethnicity (Hispanic or non-Hispanic).

Socioeconomic Status

Socioeconomic status (SES), or "social class," reflects people's position in the educational and occupational ranks of a society. Technically, SES is calculated through a weighted formula that takes into account a person's highest level of education and the prestige level of his or her occupation. There is no one set way to calculate SES, however. Various researchers have developed scales of socioeconomic status that give differing weights to these values in coming up with a total score. People with higher levels of education tend to have occupations that are higher in prestige, and so some researchers use level of education alone as the index of SES.

Income levels are not necessarily associated with socioeconomic status. High-prestige jobs (such as teachers) are often associated with mid- or even low-level salaries. However, as a proxy for or in addition to SES, some researchers use income as the basis for analyzing social class differences in health and opportunities.

Throughout the book, we will return to studies published from a landmark investigation known as **Whitehall II**, a survey of a large sample of British adults focusing on the relationships among health, social class, and occupation. The original Whitehall study was established in 1967 and involved 18,000 men working in civil service occupations in the United Kingdom. This study showed that the men in the lowest employment brackets had poorer health than their health habits would predict. In 1985, Professor Sir Michael Marmot and a team of investigators from University College London set out to determine other factors that might contribute to the poorer health of both men and women at the lower ends of the socioeconomic scale. By 2008, the study had generated a wealth of data (Council of Civil Service Unions/Cabinet Office, 2004), and Marmot's appointment to the World Health Organization Commission on Social Determinants of Health is moving the findings squarely into global public policy.

Religion

Religion, or an individual's identification with an organized belief system, has received increased attention as a factor influencing development in adulthood. Organized religions form an alternative set of social structures that are partly connected with race and ethnicity. More important, religion provides many people with a source of coping strategies, social support in times of crisis, and a systematic basis for interpreting life experiences (Klemmack et al., 2007).

Unfortunately there is relatively little research on the role of organized religion in the lives of aging adults, and even less on spirituality and its role in middle and later adulthood. There are some researchers who are now beginning to examine this area but there is much that remains to be learned.

THE BABY BOOMERS GROW UP: CHANGES IN THE MIDDLE-AGED AND OLDER POPULATIONS IN THE UNITED STATES AND THE WORLD

A quick snapshot of the U.S. population according to age and sex appears in Figure 1.6 (Vincent & Velkoff, 2010). The age–sex structure provides a useful way of looking at the population. A "young" population is shaped like a pyramid, an "old" population is depicted by an upside-down pyramid, and a population considered stable is shaped like a rectangle.

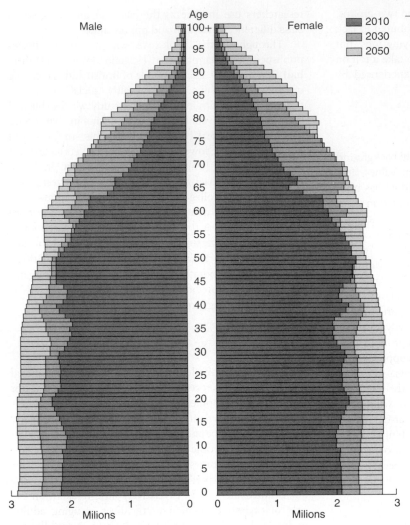

Source: Vincent, G. K., & Velkoff, V. A. (2010). The next four decades. The older population in the United States: 2010 to 2050. *Current Population Reports*. Retrieved from http://www.census.gov/prod/2010pubs/p25-1138.pdf

FIGURE 1.6

Age and Sex Structure of the Population for the United States: 2010, 2030, and 2050

You can clearly see in this figure the prominence of the **Baby Boom generation**, the term used to describe people born in the post-World War II years of 1946 to 1964. The term Baby Boom generation was coined in the U.S. to reflect the huge increase in babies born to couples after servicemen returned home from the war. The boom continued until the early 1960s during years of economic prosperity. Having labeled this generation with a term, social commentators then developed terms for other generations, including the "Silent Generation" (those in their teens in the 1950s), the "Greatest Generation" (those who fought in World War II), "Gen X" (the children of the Baby Boomers), and "Gen Y" (also called the Millennials, born around the year 2000).

Figure 1.6 clearly shows the influence of the Baby Boom generation as a "bulge" in the age range of those who are now in their 50s and 60s. As this bulge continues to move upward throughout the 21st century, the Baby Boom generation will have a continued impact on the nature of society, particularly in the way everyone views aging (as indeed it already has) (Whitbourne & Willis, 2006).

United States

In 1900, the number of Americans over the age of 65 years made up about 4% of the population (constituting 3.1 million people). By 2010, this number increased to 40.3 million. People 65 and older now represent 13% of the total U.S. population, which is a 15% increase from 2000 (Howden & Meyer, 2011). Figure 1.7 illustrates these dramatic increases as well as showing the growth

FIGURE 1.7

Population Age 65 and Over and Age 85 and Over, Selected Years 1900–2008 and Projected 2010–2050

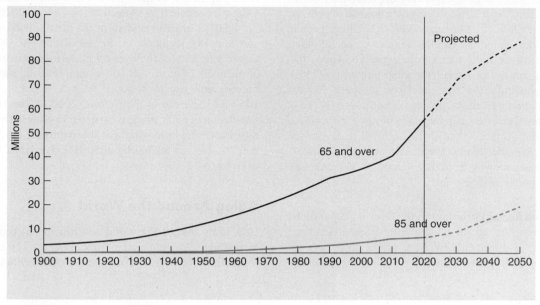

Source: Federal Interagency Forum on Age-Related Statistics. (2012). Older Americans 2010: Key indicators of well-being, from http://www.agingstats.gov/agingstatsdotnet/Main_Site/Data/2010_Documents/Docs/OA_2010.pdf

curves separately for the over-65 population as a whole and within that, those who are 85 and older (Federal Interagency Forum on Age-Related Statistics, 2013).

By 2050, the U.S. Bureau of the Census estimates that there will be 83.7 million adults 65 and older, representing 21% of the total population; the 85 and older adults alone will number 17.9 million or 5% of the population. Perhaps most impressive is the estimate in the growth in the number of centenarians. In 1990, an estimated 37,306 people over the age of 100 lived in the United States. By 2010, this number had increased to 53,364; by 2050 it will increase eight times to 442,000 (Howden & Meyer, 2011; U.S. Bureau of the Census, 2012a).

The major explanation for these large increases in the 65 and older population can be accounted for by the movement of the Baby Boomers through the years of middle and later adulthood. It is important to consider not just that these individuals were born during a period of high birth rates, but that they are expected to live into their 80s, 90s, and 100s. This will increase the number of very-old individuals that society will experience throughout the century.

Increases in the aging population reflect the vast advances that have taken place in the average length of life. **Life expectancy** is the average number of years of life remaining to the people born within a similar period of time. To calculate life expectancy, statisticians take into account death rates for a particular group within the population and use these figures to project how long it will take for that entire group to die out completely. Life expectancy is not the same as **life span**, which is the maximum age for a given species. The life span of humans has not changed, but more people are living to older ages, leading to the life expectancy increase we are currently witnessing.

Life expectancy from birth rose overall from 62.9 years in 1940 to 78.7 years in 2010. Many factors have contributed to increases in life expectancy, including reduced death rates for children and young adults. People are also living longer once they reach the age of 65, at which point the life expectancy becomes 84.1 years of age (National Center for Vital Statistics, 2013).

A related concept is **health expectancy**, which is the number of years a person could expect to live in good health and with relatively little disability if current mortality and morbidity rates persist. The ideal situation in a given society is that individuals have both long health and life expectancy, meaning that they are able to be productive and free of chronic illness until close to the time that they die. This is also called **compression of morbidity**, meaning that the illness burden to a society can be reduced if people become disabled closer to the time of their death (Vita, Terry, Hubert, & Fries, 1998).

Geographic Variations Within the United States. As you can see from Figure 1.8, the over-65 population of the United States population is very unevenly distributed geographically. As of 2010, slightly over one half of persons 65 and over lived in 11 states. With 4.3 million people 65 and older, California has the largest number of older adults, but because the state's population is so large, this age group constitutes a relatively small proportion (11%) of the population. As you may have guessed, Florida has the highest percent of people 65 and older (17.4%). The greatest increases in percentage of aging population between the years 2000 to 2010 occurred in the states of Alaska, Nevada, Idaho, Utah, Arizona, and Colorado, with increases ranging from 31% (Utah) to 50% (Alaska) (Administration on Aging, 2012).

Gender and Racial Variations in the Over-65 Population. Women over the age of 65 currently outnumber men, amounting to approximately 58% of the total over-65 population. This gender disparity is expected to diminish somewhat by the year 2050 as the last of the Baby Boomers reach advanced old age. At that time, 56% of the 65 and older population in the United States will be female and 44% will be male (U.S. Bureau of the Census, 2010d).

Changes are also evident in the distribution of White and minority segments of the population. As shown in Figure 1.9, 20% of the over-65 population was made up of members of racial and ethnic minorities in 2006. This number will rise to between 39 and 42% by the year 2050 (U.S. Bureau of the Census, 2010d). The Hispanic population of older adults is expected to grow at the fastest rate, increasing from what was approximately 6 million in 2003 to over 18 million by 2050 (He, Sangupta, Velkoff, & DeBarros, 2005).

Aging Around the World

Data from around the world confirm the picture of an increasingly older population throughout the 21st century. In 2010, there were 531 million people worldwide over

FIGURE 1.8

Persons 65+ as a Percentage of Total Population, U.S., 2011

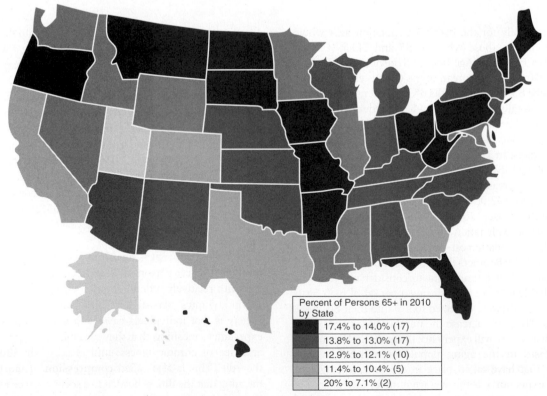

Percent of Persons 65+ in 2010 by State	
	17.4% to 14.0% (17)
	13.8% to 13.0% (17)
	12.9% to 12.1% (10)
	11.4% to 10.4% (5)
	20% to 7.1% (2)

Source: Administration on Aging. (2012). A profile of older Americans: 2011. Retrieved from http://www.aoa.gov/aoaroot/aging_statistics/Profile/2011/docs/2011profile.pdf

FIGURE 1.9

Population Age 65 and Over, by Race and Hispanic Origin, 2008 and Projected 2050

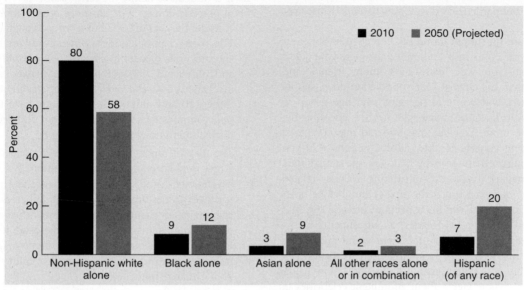

Source: Federal Interagency Forum on Age-Related Statistics. (2012). Older Americans 2010: Key indicators of well-being, from http://www.agingstats.gov/agingstatsdotnet/Main_Site/Data/2010_Documents/Docs/OA_2010.pdf

the age of 65. Predictions suggest that this number will triple to 1.53 billion by the year 2050 (U.S. Bureau of the Census, 2010a). China currently has the largest number of older adults (106 million), but Japan has the highest percentage of people 65 and older (20%) (Kinsella & He, 2009). (U.S. Bureau of the Census, 2010b).

World population statistics are often reported in terms of "developed" and "developing" countries. Developed countries include all those in Europe, North America,

Japan, Australia, and New Zealand, plus some nations formerly in the Soviet Union. All other nations of the world are classified as developing (Kinsella & He, 2009). The developing countries are those that have an agrarian-based economy, typically with lower levels of health care, education, and income.

As shown in Figure 1.10, the proportion of the population 65 years and over living in developing countries will show a precipitous rise in the next decade and will continue

FIGURE 1.10

Average Annual Percent Growth of Older Population in Developed and Developing Countries, 1950–2050

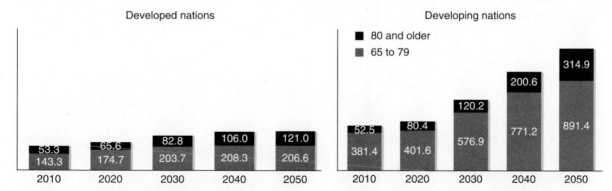

Source: U.S. Bureau of the Census. (2009). Census Bureau Reports World's Older Population Projected to Triple by 2050. Retrieved from http://www.census.gov/Press-Release/www/releases/archives/international_population/013882.html

to exceed the rate of growth in developed countries. The larger proportion of the aging population in the world will place a strain on the economies and health care systems of all nations, but particularly developing nations (Kinsella & He, 2009).

What are the implications of these figures for your future as you enter into and move through your adult years? First, you will likely have more friends and associates than the current older population does, simply because there will be more peers of your age group to socialize with. If you are male, the news is encouraging; you will be more likely to live into old age compared to the current cohorts of older adults. For those of you who are younger than the Baby Boomers, the statistics are also encouraging if you are considering a career related to the field of aging, given the higher number of older clientele. Changes in various aspects of lifestyle can also be expected in the next decades, as adjustments to the aging population in the entertainment world and media are made. Just as society is getting used to the idea of an aging Paul McCartney, many others will follow in his footsteps to change views about prominent celebrities in Western society and, indeed, around the world.

SUMMARY

1. This book uses the biopsychosocial perspective, which regards development as a complex interaction of biological, psychological, and social processes. The four principles of adult development and aging include the assumptions that changes are continuous over the life span; only the survivors grow old; individual differences are important to recognize; and "normal" aging is different from disease. Distinctions must be drawn between primary aging (changes that are intrinsic to the aging process) and secondary aging (changes due to disease).

2. It is difficult to define the term "adult" given the range of possible criteria. For purposes of this book, we will consider the ages of 18–22 to serve as a rough guideline. The over-65 population is generally divided into the subcategories of young-old (65–74), old-old (75–84), and oldest-old (85 and over). Centenarians include individuals 100 and older, and supercentenarians are those 110 and older. These divisions have important policy implications as well as highlight the need to make distinctions among individuals over 65.

3. The idea of functional age bases age on performance rather than chronological age. Additionally, biological, psychological, and social age all provide alternative perspectives to describe an individual. Whereas personal aging refers to changes within the individual over time, social aging refers to the effects of exposure to a changing environment and includes normative age-graded influences, normative history-graded influences, and nonnormative influences.

4. Social factors important to the study of adult development and aging include gender, race, ethnicity, socioeconomic status, and religion.

5. Society will experience a great impact as the Baby Boom generation begins to enter older adulthood. 40.3 million Americans are over the age of 65, constituting 13% of the total U.S. population; these numbers are expected to rise dramatically in the coming years as a result of the Baby Boomers. Gender and racial variations are also expected to change. Countries around the world will show increases in the over-65 population as well, particularly among developing countries. These changes will impact the way in which you view your own later adulthood, as well as prepare for what will happen in your later years.

2

Models of Development: Nature and Nurture in Adulthood

It's Time for a New Look at Nature and Nurture

TOPICS

Themes and issues

Models of
  development

Methods

Physical changes

Health

Memory and attention

**Higher-order
  cognition**

Personality

Relationships

Work and retirement

Mental health

Long-term care

Death and dying

Successful aging

Genetic explanations provide us with great rationales for behaviors we would rather disavow. Drive too fast? You're genetically programmed to be Type A, so of course you're always in a hurry. Uncomfortable with close relationships? Well, blame it on your family, especially Grandpa, who never could communicate with anyone. Finding it hard to keep your weight in check? Well, just look at some of your relatives who love to eat and hate to exercise.

Yet research evidence shows that all of these behaviors are highly modifiable. We can change them if we want to. Other than the truly, 100% genetically determined characteristics such as those you can see (eye color, birth marks) and those you can't (blood type), many of your traits can be altered by the choices you make.

There are also surprising ways that the environment influences even those components of our body's cells that we think are subject only to genetic influence. Parts of the cell's instructions for constructing proteins (basic elements of life) can be altered by stress. While pregnant, a mother's exposure to trauma can alter the way she builds these instructions in her growing child's cells.

There are even more surprising facts about identical twins. Did you know, for instance, that there is more than one type of monozygotic (MZ) set of twins? Only 1% are completely identical, meaning that they shared one placenta and one amniotic sac—the sources of nutrition while in utero. About three-quarters share one placenta but mature within two separate amniotic sacs. The remaining one-quarter or so do not share either a placenta or an amniotic sac. As a result, though their genes are identical, the prenatal environments of most MZ twins are not.

Think about the meaning of these findings. People love to say that they got their personality from their aunt and their interest in cars from their dad. But when we start to think about nature–nurture issues in terms of more complex relationships, we start to think about our lives differently. It's unlikely that you would agree with the claim that, for example, you got your love of 90s music from your daughter or possibly your son; however, because development is a two-way street, you are just as likely to be influenced by a child as the other way around. The people in your life, including those who are no longer alive, have become a part of "who" you are, and they alter whatever shoe-loving or high-strung genes you inherited in many complicated ways.

It's important to keep a critical eye whenever you read a new study that claims to have solved the nature–nurture puzzle. It's just as important to be on the lookout for researchers who provide valid criticisms of such studies, even though these critiques might not make the news. We can control our genetic destinies—for worse but, let's hope, also for better.

Posted by Susan Whitbourne and Stacey Whitbourne

The study of adult development and aging has evolved from the field of developmental psychology to incorporate the years beyond childhood and adolescence into a unified view of the life span. For many years, the field of developmental psychology was synonymous with the field of child development. Starting in the 1960s, several influential theorists determined that the emphasis in the field should extend through the entire life span. They argued that designating a point when people stopped developing did not make sense because people do not stop growing and changing once they reach full maturity. Although developmental psychology still retains an emphasis on the early years, the importance of the middle and later years has solidified within the field. In part based on the shifting demographics of the world, this expanded view is reflected in a higher number of programs that train future developmentalists.

KEY CONCEPTS IN THE STUDY OF THE LIFESPAN

The **life span perspective** views development as continuous from childhood through old age (see Figure 2.1). This extended outlook of the life span also includes a focus on the **contextual influences on development**, which incorporates the effects of sex, race, ethnicity, social class, religion, and culture. For decades, developmental psychologists debated whether changes in life occurred primarily due to nature or nurture. However, researchers now consider both nature *and* nurture as influences on life span change.

Reflecting these changes, the term **developmental science** is gradually replacing the term developmental psychology as the focus on life span development continues to

encompass a broader variety of domains than a sole focus on the psychology of the individual (Magnusson, 1996). The use of the term "science" rather than "psychology" conveys this shift toward an understanding of the systematic effects of multiple influences on the growing individual over time.

Developmental scientists no longer look solely at psychological domains such as cognition and personality, but instead apply their analytic methods to areas of functioning traditionally used in other fields such as biology, health, and sociology. The inclusion of social context implies that it is not sufficient to look only within the individual's immediate environment in order to understand change over time (Ford & Lerner, 1992). Particularly important to the field of developmental science is a desire to understand the dynamic interactions among and within each level of analysis of change, from the biological to the social (Lerner, 1996).

With the refocus toward developmental science, researchers now attempt to explain the underlying processes of development rather than simply use a descriptive approach to catalog the changes over time that occur as people get older. The descriptive approach to development was practiced for many decades as researchers attempted to establish the ages at which particular events occur within the individual. Examples of this approach include the work of child psychologists such as Arnold Gesell, who wrote books about "the child at two," "the child at three," and so on. Developmental scientists are attempting to discover orderly principles underlying growth through life: the "whys," not just the "whats."

Developmental science is also increasingly relying on advances in the field of neuroscience, or the study of brain-behavior relationships. Researchers in developmental neuroscience use brain scanning methods to correlate changes in the structures of the nervous system with changes in behavior from birth through later life. They may also draw from research on species other than humans in which experimental methods can be used to manipulate both genes and the environment in ways that are not possible with humans.

The growth of the lifespan approach to development was also spurred on by advances in gerontology. Distinct from **geriatrics**, which is the medical specialty in aging, gerontology is an interdisciplinary field that draws from biology, sociology, anthropology, the humanities, and other behavioral and social sciences.

In summary, the emerging role of developmental science suggests that individuals continue to grow and change over the entire course of their lives. Additionally, consideration of multiple influences is important, as well as the understanding that social context plays an integral role in examining change over time.

FIGURE 2.1

Expanded Views of Development

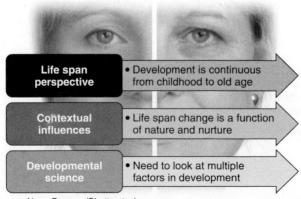

Life span perspective
• Development is continuous from childhood to old age

Contextual influences
• Life span change is a function of nature and nurture

Developmental science
• Need to look at multiple factors in development

Alena Brozova/Shutterstock

MODELS OF INDIVIDUAL–ENVIRONMENT INTERACTIONS

What causes people to change over time? We know that nature and nurture influence the individual's growth, but how much can we attribute to nature and how much to nurture? When you think about your own development, do you tend to say you must have your mother's this or your father's that? Or do you connect your current behaviors with the city or town you grew up in, what your friends were like, and where you went to school? Questions such as these fall into the category of individual–environment interactions in development. Just as you think about the causes of your own behavior, so do developmental scientists.

Early in the 20th century, developmental psychologists took a largely "nature" approach. They regarded growth in childhood as a clock-like process that reflected the unfolding of the individual's genetic makeup. This was the assumption of early 20th-century writers such as Arnold Gesell (1880–1961), who took on the task of chronicling a child's changes from birth to adolescence. According to these early developmental theorists, such changes reflected the influence of ontogenesis, or maturational processes, as they unfolded within the child. These authors gave minimal emphasis to the environment. They believed that parents needed to provide the right growing conditions, much as you would provide water and light to a plant seedling. Other than that, the child's genes would dictate the pace and outcome of development.

Challenging the nature position was the founder of American behaviorism, John B. Watson (1878–1958).

Writing some 20 years after Gesell, Watson took the extreme "nurture" position that a child's development was entirely dependent on the environment the parents provided.

The nature–nurture debate stimulated many of the classic studies in child development. Researchers from the opposing viewpoints attempted to prove their positions by contrasting, for example, differences between identical twins reared together and those reared in separate homes. The theory behind these studies was that since identical twins shared 100% of their genetic material, any differences between those reared apart would be due to the environment in which they grew up.

Perhaps the most hotly debated of these discussions was the issue of whether intelligence is inherited or acquired. The debates took on a different tone as researchers understood more and more that neither influence alone could account for individual differences in performance on intelligence tests—in children or adults. One contribution that changed the tone of the nature–nurture debate occurred when developmental psychologist Sandra Scarr introduced the concept of **niche-picking** (Scarr & McCartney, 1983), the proposal that genetic and environmental factors work together to influence the direction of a child's life. According to this concept, children quite literally pick out their "niche," or area in which they develop their talents and abilities. Once they start down that particular pathway, they experience further changes that influence the later development of those particular abilities.

Consider the example of a child whose genetic potential predisposes her to be a talented dancer. She has a great deal

Age fotostock/SUPERSTOCK

These young girls are expressing an interest in dance, which will become their "niche" as they continue to develop further their interests and abilities.

of flexibility, poise, and a good sense of rhythm—all characteristics that reflect strong "dance" genes. At the age of 4, her parents take her to a ballet performance. She sits glued to her seat, fascinated by the pirouetting and leaping that she sees on stage. This event triggers pleas to her parents to enroll her in ballet lessons, and soon they do. The child has chosen dancing as her "niche," having been exposed to the ballet performance, and once allowed to pursue her talent, she continues to thrive. Thus, her "dance genes" lead her to develop an interest in exactly the activity that will allow her talents to flourish. Similarly, had she possessed strong athletic abilities, she would have pursued a game such as soccer or field hockey that, in turn, would have given her the niche in which to develop those strengths.

There are three prominent models in developmental science, each gives differing emphasis to genetics, the environment, and the interaction of the two (Lerner, 1995). In Table 2.1, we summarize the essential elements of these models.

Armed with the basic information we've covered so far, ask yourself once again where you think you come out on the nature–nurture–interactionist debate. If you're on the side of genetics, you agree with the **organismic model** (taken from the term "organism"), which proposes that heredity drives the course of development throughout life. Changes over time occur because the individual is programmed to exhibit certain behaviors at certain ages with distinct differences between stages of life.

In contrast, the **mechanistic model** of development (taken from the word "machine") proposes that people's behavior changes gradually over time, shaped by the outside forces that cause them to adapt to their environments. People who believe in the mechanistic model propose that growth throughout life occurs through the individual's exposure to experiences that present new learning opportunities. Because this exposure is gradual, the model assumes that there are no clear-cut or identifiable stages. Instead, development is a smooth, continuous set of gradations as the individual acquires new experiences.

The **interactionist model** takes the view that not only do genetics and environment interact in complex ways to produce their effects on the individual, but that individuals actively shape their own development. This model is most similar to niche-picking because it proposes that you can shape *and* be shaped by your own environments.

With increasing evidence from studies showing that genetics and environmental influences on development do not operate completely independently from one another, the interactionist model is gaining traction. A related concept is also becoming increasingly accepted: that individuals can alter not only the nature of their interactions with the environment, but also the rate and direction of the changes associated with the aging process. According to the principle of **plasticity in development**, the course of development may be altered (is "plastic"), depending on the nature of the individual's specific interactions in the environment. The type of interactions most likely to foster plasticity involve active interventions such as mental and physical exercise. Other ways to promote plasticity involve taking steps to prevent causing harm to their bodies by avoiding, as much as possible, engaging in risky behaviors.

With this framework in mind, you will be able to place each theory of development into perspective. Theories proposing that development is the result of ontogenetic changes fall within the organismic model. Learning theory, which proposes that development proceeds according to environmental influences, is categorized into the mechanistic model. Theories that regard development as the product of joint influences fit within the interactionist model. Clearly, the biopsychosocial perspective falls within the interactionist model of development because it considers multiple influences on development and views the individual as an active contributor to change throughout life.

As we explore the processes of development in middle and later adulthood, the usefulness of the concepts of multidimensionality, multidirectionality, and plasticity will become apparent. We have already discussed the need to examine the aging process from a multidimensional

TABLE 2.1
Models of Individual–Environment Interactions

	Organismic	Mechanistic	Interactionist
Nature of change	Qualitative	Quantitative	Multidirectional Multidimensional
Contribution of organism	Active	Passive	Active
Main force in development	Biological (intrinsic)	External (environmental)	Reciprocal

Source: Adapted from Lerner, R. M. (1995). Developing individuals within changing contexts: Implications of developmental contextualism for human development, research, policy, and programs. In T. J. Kindermann & J. Valsiner (Eds.), *Development of person-context relations* (pp. 13–37). Hillsdale, NJ: Lawrence Erlbaum.

point of view, and along with this notion is the idea that development can proceed in multiple dimensions across life. The concept of plasticity fits very well with the notion of compensation and modifiability of the aging process through actions taken by the individual, a concept that we will continue to explore throughout this book. From our point of view, the interactionist model provides an excellent backdrop for the biopsychosocial perspective and a basis for viewing the processes of development in later life on a continuum with developmental processes in the early years.

Reciprocity in Development

You can see that an important assumption of the interactionist model is that adults are products of their experiences. However, adults also shape their own experiences, both through active interpretation of the events that happen to them and through the actions they take. We would like to explore this idea now, because it is so fundamental to the principles we articulate throughout the text.

The concept of **reciprocity in development** states that people both influence and are influenced by the events in their lives (Bronfenbrenner & Ceci, 1994). This means that not only are you shaped by your experiences, but that you in turn shape many of the experiences that affect you.

Consider the reciprocal process as it has affected your own life. You were influenced by earlier events to choose a particular course that has brought you to where you are right now. Perhaps you and your best friend from high school decided to apply to the same college, and as a result you are at this college and not another one. Perhaps you chose this college because you knew you wanted to major in psychology and you were impressed by the reputation of the faculty in your department. Or perhaps your choice was made randomly, and you are unsure of what exactly led to your being in this place at this time. In any case, you are where you are, having been influenced one way or another by your prior life events. That is one piece of the reciprocal process.

The second piece relates to the effect you have on your environment; this in turn will affect subsequent events in your life. For example, by virtue of your existence, you affect the people who know you, your "life footprint," as it were. It is not only very possible but very likely that their lives may have already been altered by their relationship with you. Your impact as a student at your college may have lasting effect on both you and your institution.

Everyone knows of great student athletes, scholars, or musicians who bring renown to their institutions. Even if you don't become a famous alum, your contributions to the school may alter it nevertheless. Have you ever asked a question in class that may have taken your professor by surprise? Perhaps, as a result, you may have permanently altered the way that professor approaches the problem in the future. It is not improbable to imagine that your question stimulates your professor to investigate a new research question. The investigation may ultimately produce new knowledge in the field, changing it permanently by virtue of this new knowledge.

Though you may not become the source of ground-breaking research by one of your professors, you may nevertheless influence the people around you in much smaller ways that lead to important changes. Some of these influences may be good ones, as when you express kindness to a stranger who in turn has reason to smile, and for that instant, feels a bit better about the world. Others may be less positive, as when a single wrong turn while you are behind the wheel has the unfortunate effect of causing an accident. In a split second, any person can influence others for better or worse, forever changing the course of someone's life.

The reciprocal process takes as a basic assumption the idea that that people are not passive recipients of environmental effects. Instead, choices and behaviors that each and every one of us makes leave a mark on the world. Subsequently, the changes in that environment may further alter people in significant ways, which leads to further impacts on society. Reciprocal views of development regard these continuing processes as both ongoing and, to some extent, unpredictable.

SOCIOCULTURAL MODELS OF DEVELOPMENT

The models of development we have just examined set the stage for looking in greater depth at particular theoretical approaches to adult development and aging. We begin by focusing on those approaches that give relatively more emphasis to the environment as an influence on development.

Ecological Perspective

The **ecological perspective**, proposed by developmental theorist Urie Bronfenbrenner (1994) identifies multiple levels of the environment as they affect the individuals over time (see Figure 2.2). As shown in Figure 2.2, the ecological perspective defines five levels of the environment or "systems," all of which interact in their influence on the individual. Bronfenbrenner proposed that each of these five systems influences your development in different ways. You are aware of some of these influences, but the further you go out from the center, the less likely you are to have direct experiences with those systems (Swick & Williams, 2006).

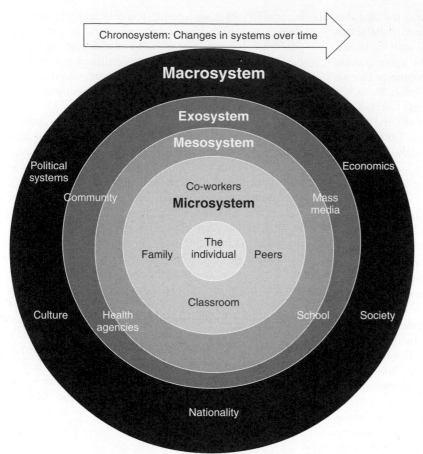

FIGURE 2.2

Bronfenbrenner's Ecological Perspective

According to Bronfenbrenner's ecological perspective, our development is affected by processes at multiple levels.

In the center of the ecological model is the **microsystem**, the setting in which people have their daily interactions and which therefore have the most direct impact on their lives. The **exosystem** includes the environments that people do not closely experience on a regular basis but that impact them nevertheless. These environments include such institutions as the workplace and community centers as well as extended family, whom you may not see very often. The **macrosystem** includes the larger social institutions ranging from a country's economy to its laws and social norms. The macrosystem influences the individual indirectly through the exosystem. The **mesosystem** is the realm of the environment in which interactions take place among two or more microsystems. For example, you may be having difficulties at home that you carry over into your relationships with co-workers.

All of these systems interact over time. The **chronosystem** refers to the changes that take place over time. The interacting systems within the ecological model are affected by historical changes. These can include events within the family, for example, as well as events in the larger society that indirectly affect the individual by affecting the macrosystem.

In thinking about this model, it is important to keep in mind the fact that development in one sphere interacts with development in other spheres. The concentric circles are not just static in that sense. Events that take place in the outer perimeter of the circle, such as changes in your country's economy or political systems or changes in the world as a whole, also have an impact on your life, even at the inner biological level. For example, when the economy suffers, as it did in the late 2000s and early 2010s, people experience deprivation in ways that affect their physical functioning and overall health, not to mention their mental health. Furthermore, in keeping with the concept of reciprocity, people can affect their own development. Like ripples from a stone hitting the water, individuals can have an impact on the exosystem, and even the macrosystem, should their influence spread far enough into society.

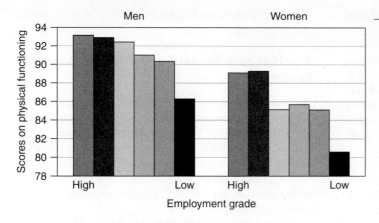

Men   Women

FIGURE 2.3

Results from the Whitehall II Study

As can be seen from this figure, scores on physical functioning were lower among men and women in Whitehall II from lower employment grades.

Source: Marmot, M., & Brunner, E. (2005). Cohort profile: The Whitehall II Study. *International Journal of Epidemiology*, *34*, 251–260 by permission of Oxford University Press.

Research from the Whitehall II study provides compelling evidence to support the importance that social factors play in determining health status (Kouvonen et al., 2011). Although you may typically think of your overall health as functioning within your inner biological level, researchers working within the Whitehall II study have consistently demonstrated the significance of relations with others and social roles on health. In Figure 2.3, we have illustrated one of the key findings that participants who reported negative characteristics of close relationships had a higher likelihood of being overweight. Additionally, research from Whitehall II provides evidence that social support from a relationship identified as the closest relates to maintained levels of physical activity, even after controlling for factors such as physical functioning and self-rated health. This particular study, then, demonstrates specifically the role of the microsystem in influencing health.

The Life Course Perspective

The ecological model's emphasis on social context provides an excellent background for understanding a concept central to social gerontology. According to the **life course perspective**, norms, roles, and attitudes about age have an impact on the shape of each person's life (Settersten, 2006). The term life "course" is not the same as life span. The life "course" refers, literally, to the course or progression of a person's life events, a course that is heavily shaped by society's views of what is appropriate and expected to occur in connection with particular ages.

Within the life course perspective, specific theories attempt to link society's structures to the adaptation, satisfaction, and well-being of the people who live in that society. Social gerontology focuses on age as the primary structure that influences an individual's quality of adaptation. Social class, family roles, and work are additional areas of study by gerontologists studying the life course.

Age norms in adulthood are linked to the **social clock**, the expectations for the ages at which a society associates with major life events (Hagestad & Neugarten, 1985). These expectations set the pace for how people think they should progress through their family and work timelines. People evaluate themselves according to these expectations, deciding whether they are "on-time" or "off-time" with regard to the social clock. Those who see themselves as off-time may become distressed, especially when they are criticized by others who expect people to follow the normative prescriptions for their age group. Nonevents, which are the failure to experience an expected life change,

For many people, the social clock provides a measure of evaluating their life's successes.

may have as much of an influence on an individual's life as actual events.

Increasingly, however, individuals are setting their own unique social clocks, as exemplified by people like former astronaut and Ohio senator John Glenn. At the age of 77, Glenn joined the space shuttle *Discovery* crew on a 9-day orbital mission in 1998. His ability to meet the arduous physical requirements of the voyage was aptly captured in his statement: "Too many people, when they get old, think that they have to live by the calendar."

Not only is age linked to the social clock, but also to people's social roles, the resources available to them, and the way they are treated by those with whom they interact. One of the guiding frameworks regarding age and role satisfaction is **activity theory**, the view that older adults are most satisfied if they are able to remain involved in their social roles (Cavan, Burgess, Havighurst, & Goldhamer, 1949). If forced to give up their roles, they will lose a major source of identity as well as their social connections. According to activity theory, older adults should be given as many opportunities as possible to be engaged in their work, families, and community.

A contrasting perspective to activity theory is **disengagement theory** (Cumming & Henry, 1961), which proposed that the normal and natural evolution of life causes older adults to purposefully loosen their social ties. This natural detachment, according to disengagement theory, is not only inevitable but desirable, and that aging is accompanied by a mutual withdrawal process of the individual and society. Within this approach, retirement and isolation from family members are sought out by older adults and results in higher levels of well-being.

When first proposed in the early 1960s, gerontologists were highly skeptical if not outraged by the propositions of disengagement theory. The idea that older adults wanted to be put "on the shelf" and could even benefit from social isolation only reinforced negative treatment of older adults by society. Rather than describing a desirable end product of a mutual withdrawal process, critics of disengagement theory regarded it as disrespectful of older adults and as a justification for what is already harsh treatment by society of its older adult members.

Yet, it makes sense that not all older adults wish to be as active and involved in their work, family, and community as they were when they were younger. **Continuity theory** (Atchley, 1989) proposes that whether disengagement or activity is beneficial to the older adult depends on the individual's personality. Some older adults prefer to withdraw from active involvement with their families and communities; others are miserable unless they are in the thick of the action. Older adults experience lower life satisfaction when they don't want to be excluded from their social roles by virtue of age. Either forced retirement or forced activity will cause poorer adjustment and self-esteem in middle-aged

and older adults than finding the amount of involvement that is "just right."

Ageism as a Social Factor in the Aging Process

The social context in which aging occurs is, unfortunately, one that is not necessarily favorable to the overall well-being of older adults. Many are affected by **ageism**, a set of beliefs, attitudes, social institutions, and acts that denigrate individuals or groups based on their chronological age. Similar to other "isms" such as racism and sexism, ageism occurs when an individual is assumed to possess a set of stereotyped traits.

Ageism does not only affect older adults. Theoretically, the term could also apply to teenagers, who are often stereotyped as lazy, impulsive, rebellious, or self-centered. However, for all practical purposes, ageism is used to refer to stereotyped views of the *older adult* population. Disengagement theory was thought of by its critics as a justification for ageism, as a way to conveniently move older people to the backdrop of society. Moreover, by implying that all older adults have the same drive to withdraw, the theory perpetuates the stereotype that all older adults have similar personalities.

The primarily negative feature of ageism is that, like other stereotypes, it is founded on overgeneralizations about individuals based on a set of characteristics that have negative social meaning. Oddly enough, that negative social meaning may have a positive spin (Kite & Wagner, 2002). Ageism applies to any view of older adults as having a set of characteristics, good or bad, that are the same for

Maggie Kuhn (1905–1995), founder of the "Gray Panthers," whose grassroots activities protested against ageism in public and governmental policies, including age discrimination, pension rights, and nursing home reform.

everyone. Calling an older adult "cute" or "with it" is as much an expression of ageism as is referring to that person as "cranky" or "senile."

One effect of ageism is to cause younger people to avoid close proximity to an older person. In fact, ageism may also take the form of not being openly hostile but of making older adults "invisible": that is, not worthy of any attention at all. Ageism is often experienced in the workplace, and although prohibited by law (a topic explored in Chapter 10), older workers are penalized for making mistakes that would not incur the same consequence if made by younger workers (Rupp, Vodanovich, & Crede, 2006). Ironically, aging is the one stereotype that, if you are fortunate enough to survive to old age, you will most likely experience. Unlike the other "isms," people who hold aging stereotypes will eventually become the target of their own negative beliefs as they grow old.

What are your stereotypes about aging? Table 2.2 shows the most common stereotypes, along with refutations by the World Health Organization with examples from around the world of older adults who defy these stereotypes.

Research on college students shows that the ones most likely to harbor ageist attitudes are those who

TABLE 2.2

Fighting Stereotypes about Aging

Stereotype	Counter-evidence	Example
Older people are "past their sell-by date"	Most individuals maintain cognitive abilities well into later life. Older adults possess experience and institutional memory. Physical declines are much less than expected.	On October 16, 2011, British national Fauja Singh became the first 100-year-old to complete a marathon by running the Waterfront Marathon in Toronto, Canada.
Older people are helpless	Older people may be vulnerable in emergencies, but in general they are not helpless.	After the 2007 Cyclone Sidr in Bangladesh, older adults served in active roles to help survivors. In 2011, after the earthquake and tsunami in Japan, older adults volunteered at disaster sites, saying they were not afraid of becoming contaminated with radiation.
Older people will eventually become "senile"	Occasional memory lapses occur at any age. Although dementia (loss of intellectual abilities) risk increases with age, its symptoms are not normal signs of aging.	Most older adults can manage their financial affairs and everyday lives and can give informed consent for treatment or medical interventions. Some types of memory stay the same or improve in later life.
Older women have less value than younger women	Women's roles as caregivers are often overlooked because society equates a woman's worth with beauty, youth, and the ability to have children. In most countries, women tend to be the family caregivers. Many, including those of advanced age, take care of more than one generation.	In sub-Saharan Africa, 20% of rural women aged 60 and older are the main carers for their grandchildren.
Older people don't deserve health care	Conditions and illnesses in older adults are often overlooked as being a "normal" part of aging but they are not. Age does not necessarily cause pain and only extreme old age is associated with limited bodily functions.	80-year-old Simeon from Moldova is a counselor for war veterans, providing social, legal, and health advice and support for them, informing them of the rules and their rights.

Source: World Health Organization. (2012) World Health Day 2012: Ageing and health. http://whqlibdoc.who.int/hq/2012/WHO_DCO_WHD_2012.1_eng.pdf

identify most strongly with their own age group (Packer & Chasteen, 2006). In other words, the more likely you are to think of yourself as a teen or twenty-something, the more likely you'll hold biased views of older adults. As a result of taking this course, however, we hope you will gain knowledge that will cause you to challenge your own stereotypes about aging and older adults.

Why does ageism exist? Of the many possible causes, perhaps the root is that we view older adults negatively because they remind us of the inevitability of our own mortality (Martens, Greenberg, Schimel, & Landau, 2004). According to **terror management theory**, people regard with panic and dread the thought of the finitude of their lives (Solomon, 1991). They engage in defensive mechanisms to protect themselves from the anxiety and threats to self-esteem that this awareness produces. Younger people therefore unconsciously wish to distance themselves as much as possible from older adults. Having acquired ageist attitudes when younger, older adults themselves may express ageist beliefs because they wish to distance themselves from what they have come to learn is a devalued social identity (Bodner, 2009).

Sociologists emphasize, in contrast, that older adults are seen negatively because they have lost their utility to society. According to the **modernization hypothesis**, the increasing urbanization and industrialization of Western society is what causes to be older adults to be devalued (Cowgill & Holmes, 1972). They can no longer produce, so they become irrelevant and even a drain on the younger population.

Some sociologists argue that the modernization hypothesis is overly simplistic (Luborsky & McMullen, 1999). For example, in the United States, even when life expectancy was lower and there were fewer older adults in the population, attitudes toward age were not consistently positive (Achenbaum, 1978). Evidence for negative attitudes toward elders is also found in current preindustrialized societies. Conversely, in some highly developed countries, older adults are treated with reverence and respect and are well provided for through health care and economic security programs. Modernization alone does not seem able, then, to account for ageism.

Whatever its cause, older adults must nevertheless cope with ageist attitudes. Many too must cope with other "isms" that affect the way they are regarded in society. The **multiple jeopardy hypothesis** (Ferraro & Farmer, 1996) states that older individuals who fit more than one discriminated-against category are affected by biases against each of these categorizations. Women are subject to ageism and sexism, and minority-status women are subject to racism, ageism, and sexism. Heterosexism and classism (biases against people of working class backgrounds) further add to multiple jeopardy. These systematic biases interact with age to produce greater risk for discrimination in attitudes and the provision of services to specific subgroups of older adults.

It's possible, however, that older adults are somehow protected from multiple jeopardy. The **age-as-leveler view** proposes that as people become older, age overrides all other "isms." Older adults, whatever their prior status in life was, all become victims of the same stereotypes. Regardless of minority status, gender, or other social characteristics, all older adults are viewed with the same harshly negative views. Consider the case of a wealthy older adult male and an older lower-income minority woman. Though the man almost certainly would have enjoyed many advantages over the woman when he was younger, they are now seen as having an equally low social ranking because they are old. Therefore, there's only a single jeopardy of ageism facing older adults rather than multiple jeopardy resulting from a combination of isms.

Older adults potentially facing multiple jeopardy may also be protected from its effects and even perhaps fare better than those with higher social standing. According to the **inoculation hypothesis**, older minorities and women have actually become immune to the effects of ageism through years of exposure to discrimination and stereotyping. These years help them to develop a tolerance, so that they are better able to withstand the negative attitudes applied to older adults than are their counterparts. The upper-income white male may actually find it more difficult to accept the stereotypes of ageism than does the low-income minority woman, who is used to being treated as a less desirable member of society after years of discrimination.

These views of ageism become important in examining the health and well-being of older adults. Interestingly, neither ageism nor multiple jeopardy appears to have deleterious effects on feelings of happiness and well-being, a topic we explore in Chapter 14. However, the effects of less access to health care and exposure to negative views of aging on those who are subjected to the "isms" may take their toll on physical health and are therefore a matter of vital concern.

PSYCHOLOGICAL MODELS OF DEVELOPMENT IN ADULTHOOD

In the broadest sense, psychological models attempt to explain the development of the "person" in the person–environment equation from the standpoint of how adaptive abilities unfold over the course of life. Psychologists approach aging by focusing on the changes that occur in the individual's self-understanding, ability to adjust to life's challenges, and perspective on the world.

Erikson's Psychosocial Theory

According to developmental psychologist Erik Erikson (1963), people pass through a series of eight stages as they progress from birth through death. A psychoanalyst by training, Erikson attempted to understand how people navigate the major life issues that they face when they encounter each of life's new challenges.

Erikson's **psychosocial theory of development** proposes that at certain points in life, a person's biological, psychological, and social changes come together to influence our personality. He defined each stage of development as a "crisis" or turning point that influences how people resolve the issues they face in a subsequent period in life. The "crisis" is not truly a crisis in the sense of being a catastrophe or disaster. Instead, each psychosocial stage is a time during which the individual may move closer to either a positive or negative resolution of a particular psychosocial issue. Figure 2.4 illustrates the eight-stage matrix.

Erikson maintained that these stages are universally experienced, although the way in which individuals negotiate them may vary. The **epigenetic principle** asserts that each stage unfolds from the previous stage according to a predestined order. These stages are set in much the same manner as the programming for the biological development of the individual throughout life. They are built, according to Erikson, into the hard-wiring of the human being.

The earliest four stages are central to the adult's ability to build a solid sense of self and engagement with others. **Basic trust vs. basic mistrust** involves the infant's establishing a sense of being able to rely on care from the environment (and caregivers). In **autonomy vs. shame and doubt**, young children learn ways to act independently from their parents without feeling afraid that they will venture too far off on their own. In the **initiative vs. guilt** stage, the child becomes able to engage in creative self-expression without fear of making a mistake. The last stage associated with childhood, **industry vs. inferiority**, involves the individual's identifying with the world of work and developing a work ethic.

The first of the eight stages directly relevant to adulthood is **identity achievement versus identity diffusion**, when individuals must decide "who" they are and what they wish to get out of life. This stage emerges in adolescence,

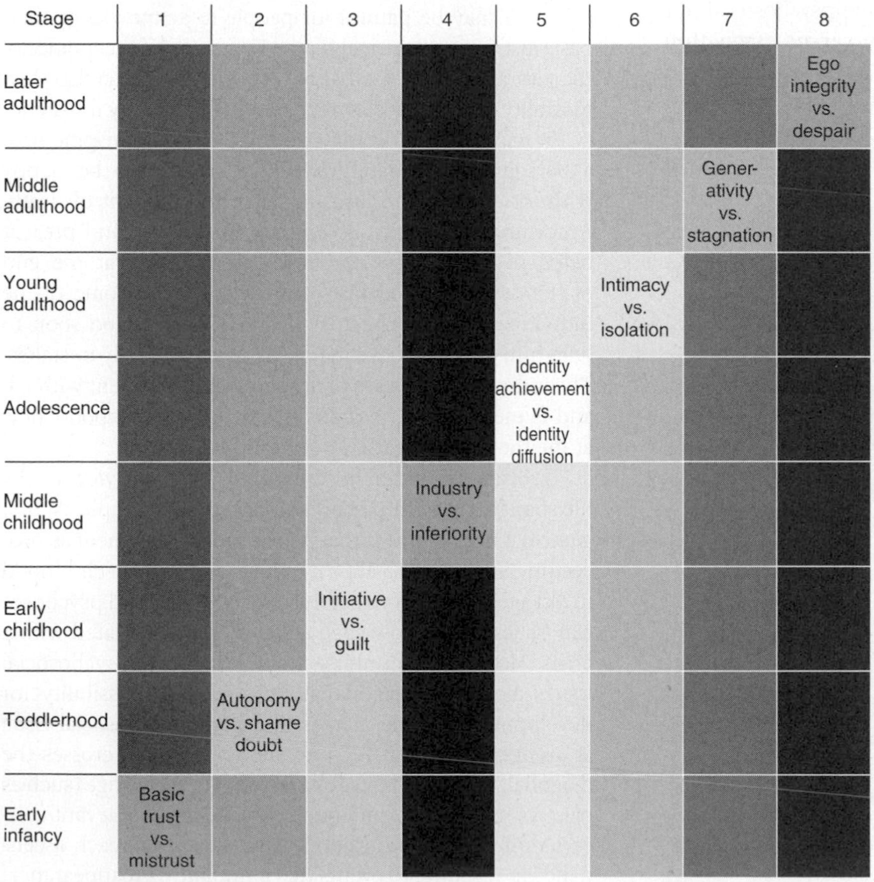

FIGURE 2.4

Stages in Erikson's Psychosocial Theory

Stage	1	2	3	4	5	6	7	8
Later adulthood								Ego integrity vs. despair
Middle adulthood							Generativity vs. stagnation	
Young adulthood						Intimacy vs. isolation		
Adolescence					Identity achievement vs. identity diffusion			
Middle childhood				Industry vs. inferiority				
Early childhood			Initiative vs. guilt					
Toddlerhood		Autonomy vs. shame doubt						
Early infancy	Basic trust vs. mistrust							

Source: Adapted from Erikson, E. H. (1963). *Childhood and society* (2nd ed). New York: Norton.

yet continues to hold importance throughout adulthood, forming a cornerstone of subsequent adult psychosocial crises (Erikson, Erikson, & Kivnick, 1986; Whitbourne & Connolly, 1999). An individual who achieves a clear identity has a coherent sense of purpose regarding the future and a sense of continuity with the past. By contrast, identity diffusion involves a lack of direction, vagueness about life's purposes, and an unclear sense of self.

In the **intimacy versus isolation** stage, individuals are faced with making commitments to close relationships. Attaining intimacy involves establishing a mutually satisfying close relationship with another person to whom a lifelong commitment is made. We can think of the perfect intimate relationship as the intersection of two identities; this is not a total overlap because each partner preserves a sense of separateness. The state of isolation represents the other end of the spectrum, in which a person never achieves true mutuality with a life partner. Theoretically, isolation is more likely to develop in individuals who lack a strong identity because establishing close relationships with others depends to some extent on how securely formed the individual's sense of self is.

The motive for caring for the next generation emerges from the resolution of the intimacy psychosocial crisis. During the stage of **generativity versus stagnation**, middle-aged adults focus on the psychosocial issues of procreation, productivity, and creativity. The most common pathway to generativity is through parenthood, an endeavor that involves direct care of the next generation.

Chabruken/Taxi/Getty Images, Inc.

Mentoring is one activity associated with generativity; as shown here, this older worker is trying to give helpful advice to his younger colleague.

However, individuals who do not have children can nevertheless develop generativity through such activities as teaching, mentoring, or supervising younger people. A career that involves producing something of value that future generations can enjoy is another form of generativity.

The main feature of generativity is a feeling of concern over what happens to the younger generation, along with a desire to make the world a better place for them. Stagnation, by contrast, occurs when the individual turns concern and energy inward or solely to others of one's own age group rather than to the next generation. A person who is high on the quality of stagnation lacks interest or may even go so far as to reject the younger generation. Of course, being a parent is no guarantee of achieving generativity; the crucial component of generativity is concern and care for the people who will follow one's own generation.

Toward the end of adulthood, individuals face psychosocial issues related to aging and facing their mortality, the key issues in the stage of **ego integrity versus despair**. Older individuals who establish a strong sense of ego integrity can look back at their experiences with acceptance. Ego integrity also involves an ability to look at and accept the positive and negative attributes of one's life and self, even if it may be painful for people to acknowledge their past mistakes or personal flaws. This sense of acceptance of the past and present self allows the individual to also view mortality with the acceptance that life inevitably must end.

It may be difficult for a young person to imagine how a person who is happy with life could also be happy with, or at least not devastated by, the thought of death. According to Erikson, acceptance of the past and present helps people attain acceptance about being at the end of their lives. In contrast, despair is the outcome of the individual's realization that death is coming too soon to help him or her achieve major life goals or rectify mistakes. The individual in a state of despair feels discontent with life and is melancholic, perhaps to the point of despondency, at the thought of death.

Erikson presented an organized, cohesive view of the life span that is both elegant and deceptively simple. At first glance, it might appear that he viewed development as proceeding in a series of steps moving steadily from childhood to old age. The diagonal in the matrix of ages and psychosocial issues shows how each age period is associated with a crisis. However, the intersection of ages and psychosocial issues along the diagonal is not the only possibility for development. People may experience a psychosocial issue at an age other than the one shown where it crosses the diagonal. Thus, the issues characterizing each stage (such as trust vs. mistrust for infancy) may coexist as relevant concerns throughout adulthood. Any stage may reach ascendancy in response to events that stimulate its reappearance.

Let's look at an example to show how these "off-diagonal" situations might occur. An 80-year-old woman walking on a city sidewalk is suddenly attacked, robbed of her purse, and left alive but emotionally shaken and in pain. This incident may traumatize her for some time and in the process, she becomes fearful of leaving her home. In Eriksonian terms, she is reliving the issues of "trust" experienced in infancy and must regain the feeling of safety in her environment. The woman may also be left feeling vulnerable that with her increasing years, declines in her physical functioning have made her a target.

Another implication of the epigenetic matrix is that a crisis may be experienced before its "time." A 35-year-old woman diagnosed with breast cancer may be faced with issues relevant to mortality, precipitating her to contemplate the psychosocial issues that normally confront much older people. The crisis stages can be considered "critical periods" during which certain issues are most likely to be prominent, but they are not meant to be discrete steps that proceed from youth to old age.

Erikson's views about development were a radical departure from the personality theories prevalent in the mid-1900s, when childhood was given sole emphasis as a time of important change. By reenvisioning the life span, Erikson provided a new but enduring perspective that recognized development as a lifelong set of processes that help to mold and shape and reshape the individual.

Piaget's Cognitive-Developmental Theory

Just as Erikson crafted a new model of personality development throughout the life span, a Swiss psychologist by the name of Jean Piaget brought an entirely new perspective to bear on the process of cognitive development. Rather than being content simply with describing children's development, as his predecessors had done, Piaget tried to explain the processes underlying their growth of cognitive abilities. After watching his own young children explore their environment while at play, Piaget hypothesized the existence of a set of underlying processes that allowed them eventually to achieve understanding and mastery of the physical world.

Piaget believed that development involves continuing growth of the individual's knowledge about the world through a set of opposing, complementary processes. These processes target what Piaget called **schemas**, the mental structures we use to understand the world. Children's schemas change and mature as they explore their environment—a process that, ideally, helps them to bring their schemas increasingly in tune with reality.

Through the process that Piaget called **assimilation**, people use their existing schemas as a way to understand the world around them. In this context, the term assimilation does not have its usual meaning, as when you say that a person has become assimilated to a new culture. Rather, in Piaget's model, assimilation has the opposite meaning: it refers to the situation in which individuals change their interpretation of reality to fit the schemas they already hold. Instead of changing themselves to fit the culture, they change their perception of the culture to fit their own way of understanding it.

As an example, let's say that you have a very limited understanding of different varieties of birds. You may call all little birds "sparrows" and all large birds "crows." You are forcing into two categories what actually may be 8 or 10 different varieties of birds in your neighborhood. According to Piaget, people engage in this assimilative process until they are able to gain experiences that allow them to refine their concepts or schemas. If you go for a walk with an avid bird watcher who points out the differences among sparrows, finches, and chickadees (all small birds), you will emerge with a refinement to your previous categorization system.

When you change your schemas in response to new information about the world you are, in Piaget's terms, using the process of **accommodation**. This process is actually more like the way we commonly speak about cultural "assimilation." In Piaget's terms, when you change yourself in order to fit the larger culture that you're now a part of, you are engaging in accommodation: you are the one who is changing.

It's unfortunate that Piaget's terms mean the opposite of their use in common speech, especially the concept of assimilation. However, it might be easier to understand assimilation and accommodation in the Piagetian sense if you remember that Piaget was describing the process of schema development. You impose your schemas onto the world, making the world fit you, in assimilation. You change your schemas about the world, changing in response to knowledge from experiences, in accommodation. (If all else fails, remember that the "s" in assimilation means "same," and the "c" in accommodation means "change.")

These processes of assimilation and accommodation occur continuously throughout development. Children are constantly exploring their worlds, changing their schemas as they accommodate them to fit the reality of their experiences. At certain points in childhood, according to Piaget, there are major shifts in children's understanding of their experiences. These correspond to the stages associated with early infancy (sensorimotor stage), preschool (preoperational period), middle childhood (concrete operations stage), and adolescence through adulthood (formal operations stage). Each stage represents a time of **equilibrium**, when assimilation and accommodation are perfectly balanced. The equilibrium achieved in formal operations is the most stable, because it is when the individual is able to use the highest level of thought to understand and learn from experience. However, throughout life, people rely on all forms of thought, ranging from sensorimotor (non-verbal) to concrete (the here and now).

Identity Process Theory

As you've learned, identity is a central issue in adulthood. How identity changes is a question that we will explore throughout this book. We will rely heavily on the framework of **identity process theory** (Whitbourne, Sneed, & Skultety, 2002), which proposes that identity continues to change in adulthood in a dynamic manner.

In identity process theory, we assume that people approach their experiences from the vantage point provided by **identity**, which is the set of schemas that the person holds about the self. Your identity is your own answer to the question "Who am I?" For most people, this includes their views about their physical self, their cognitive abilities, their personality characteristics, and their social roles. Identity also includes the individual's sense of connection to his or her cultural heritage, a process of particular importance to adolescents and emerging adults from immigrant and minority groups (Rodriguez, Schwartz, & Whitbourne, 2010; Schwartz et al., 2012). Figure 2.5 illustrates the general framework of identity process theory.

Identity Assimilation, Identity Accommodation, and Identity Balance. Just as in Piaget's theory, people use assimilation to interpret their experiences in terms of their existing schemas, the process of **identity assimilation** refers to the tendency to interpret new experiences in terms of a person's existing identity. You may see yourself as being a good student, for example. This view of yourself colors your academic experiences. If you are, in fact, a good student, you'll have plenty of instances that bolster this view. You receive

good grades, your professor seems to like you, and other people may come to you for help. Occasionally, however, you may have experiences that contradict this self-image. You do poorly on an exam, an assignment is returned with many critical comments, or you're stumped in class when you're called upon to answer a question. How do you reconcile these experiences with your positive identity as a student? If you're using identity assimilation, you won't change your identity at all. Instead, you'll still see yourself as a good student, but one who ran into some rough material, an unfair test, or an inordinately harsh professor.

When people use identity assimilation, they tend to resist changing their identities in the face of criticism or disconfirming experiences. In fact, most people prefer to see themselves in the positive light of being physically and mentally competent, liked by others, honest, and concerned about the welfare of others. The advantage of identity assimilation is that it allows people to feel reasonably happy and effective, despite being less than perfect. The downside of identity assimilation is that it can lead you to distort your interpretation of experiences when change would truly be warranted. Returning to our example of seeing yourself as a good student, by blaming the material or the professor for your bad grade, you may not realize how your own academic weaknesses contributed to the situation you're in now.

We can see, then, that although identity assimilation has the advantage of allowing you to preserve a positive view of who you are, there may be negative consequences of refusing to incorporate these experiences into your identity. If you continue to blame the professor or the test for your poor grades, you will never find yourself at fault for your failures. Eventually, these limitations need to be confronted. Whether this signifies that you are in the wrong major, are not studying hard enough, or may not be as smart as you once thought, learning to accept your imperfections is vital to your own growth.

Ideally, people eventually use **identity accommodation**, in which they make changes in their identities in response to experiences that challenge their current view

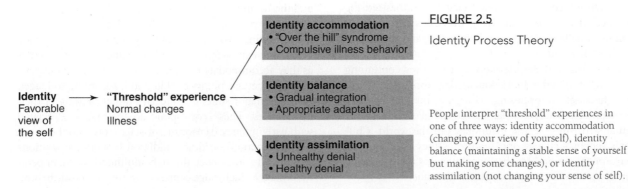

FIGURE 2.5

Identity Process Theory

People interpret "threshold" experiences in one of three ways: identity accommodation (changing your view of yourself), identity balance (maintaining a stable sense of yourself but making some changes), or identity assimilation (not changing your sense of self).

of themselves. Identity change may be difficult, particularly at first, because you must come to grips with your weaknesses. However, the result will ultimately produce a self-image that is more in sync with reality.

It's possible, also, for an individual to use identity assimilation to bolster a negative rather than a positive view of the self. As we will learn later in the book, people who suffer from chronic depression often take an unduly pessimistic view of their identities, focusing on their weaknesses rather than their strengths. In that case, identity accommodation can help them develop a more realistically positive set of schemas about their personal characteristics and strengths.

Both identity assimilation and identity accommodation are most beneficial when they operate in tandem. The process of **identity balance** refers to the dynamic equilibrium that occurs when people tend to view themselves consistently but can make changes when called for by their experiences. If you had that tendency to avoid letting your academic disappointments permeate your identity through identity assimilation, it would benefit you to use identity accommodation to acknowledge your areas of weakness, such as not being well-suited to your college major, perhaps. Although you wouldn't want to go overboard and conclude that you should give up school altogether, by using some identity accommodation, you could first admit to your problems and then set up a plan to improve your study habits.

As with identity assimilation, however, relying too heavily on identity accommodation can have destructive consequences. Individuals who define themselves entirely on the basis of their experiences, such as being viewed negatively by others, may be devastated by an event when they feel rejected. Imagine if every criticism ever leveled at you throughout your life caused you to question your personal qualities and think that you are a deeply flawed person. You would become extremely insecure, and your identity would fail to include the central compass that would ultimately allow you to have confidence in your abilities. In this case, you would benefit by ignoring those experiences that unrealistically caused you to question yourself.

Ideally, as in Piaget's theory, a balance between identity assimilation and identity accommodation can be achieved in adulthood. Piaget proposed that the natural tendency is to use assimilation when confronted with a new situation. People use what has worked in the past to help understand what is happening in the present. However, when the situation warrants changes, you should be able to make those adjustments. Though it would hardly be ideal to change your self-view completely when someone criticizes

For many people, age-related changes in appearance serve to stimulate changes in identity.

you, if the criticism is consistent enough and comes from enough different quarters, you may be well advised to look honestly at yourself and see whether you should change something.

When identity balance is operating successfully, the individual feels that he or she has a strong sense of **self-efficacy**, a term used in the social psychological literature to refer to a person's feelings of competence at a particular task (Bandura, 1977). As we will see throughout the book, older adults high in particular types of self-efficacy recognize that they have experienced age-related changes but nevertheless feel in control of their ability to succeed.

The Multiple Threshold Model. Throughout adulthood, identity processes are constantly brought to bear on the physical and cognitive changes that everyone experiences. These changes can be thought of as occurring through a sequence of phases over time, or a set of "multiple thresholds" (Whitbourne & Collins, 1998). The **multiple threshold model** of change in adulthood proposes that individuals realize that they are getting older through a stepwise process as aging-related changes occur. Each age-related change (such as wrinkling of the skin or a decreased reaction time) brings with it the potential for another threshold to be crossed. People are likely to monitor the areas of the greatest significance to their identities with great care or vigilance, while paying less attention to the thresholds that don't mean as much to them. You may be preoccupied with the fact that your hair is thinning or turning gray, but less focused on the changes in your muscles. Someone else may feel oppositely, and disregard gray hair but fixate on the loss of muscle strength.

Whatever the area of greatest relevance, at the point of crossing a threshold, people are prompted to recognize the reality of the aging process in that particular area of functioning. It is during the process of moving from identity assimilation to identity accommodation through the occurrence of these thresholds that a new state of balance is reached. Ultimately, people will only be able to adapt to age-related changes once they have examined the meaning of the change and incorporated it into their existing view of the self.

Figure 2.6 represents identity changes in terms of threshold experiences. Almost all young adults see themselves as "youthful." In Western society, this youthful image is one that many people would like to preserve and therefore they resist making changes to this image. You perhaps feel this way now. It's true that you're no longer an adolescent, but you almost certainly still regard yourself as being young. You may feel this way for years, if not decades, identifying yourself with the younger generation.

It won't be too long, however, until you encounter experiences that lead you to your first "threshold." Perhaps you feel a little stiff when you get up from a chair, or find out that your blood pressure is higher than it used to be. Many people say that the first time they felt old was when someone called them "sir" or "ma'am." At that point, you may start to challenge the view you had of yourself as a young person. Your options now are to disregard the whole experience and not change your identity to see yourself as not-so-young (identity assimilation). Or you might become completely thrown by the experience and conclude that you are heading more swiftly than you hoped to middle age (identity accommodation). It's also possible that you might note the experience, admit that you're not a teenager any more, and feel perfectly fine with the fact that people are treating you with a bit more dignity (identity balance).

FIGURE 2.6

Selective Optimization with Compensation

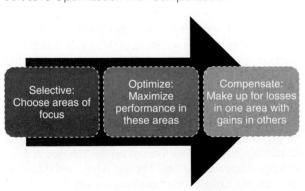

Identity assimilation can be healthy or unhealthy. The unhealthy type of identity assimilation occurs when people ignore warning signs that the changes their body is going through require attention. If your blood pressure really is too high, you should explore ways to lower it, no matter what your age. It would not be healthy to deny the condition. On the other hand, a healthy denial occurs when people avoid becoming overly preoccupied with age-related changes that are truly inconsequential to their overall health and well-being, especially if there is nothing they can do to ameliorate the process. Healthy deniers continue or begin engaging in preventive behaviors without overthinking their actions and reflecting at length about their own mortality. However, at some point, everyone needs to confront these changes, to some extent. You can't completely ignore the fact that you are getting older no matter what your age.

Let's look next at identity accommodation in which people change their identities in response to experiences. Theoretically, identity accommodation helps to keep identity assimilation in check. However, people who conclude that one small age change means they are "over-the-hill" may be just as likely to avoid taking preventative actions as those who engage in unhealthy denial. They incorrectly conclude that there's nothing they can do to slow down the aging process, so why try? Similarly, people who are told they must watch their blood pressure may go overboard and do nothing but worry about what this means for their health. They "become" their illness, which they allow to take over their identity.

Eventually, if the pendulum swings from identity accommodation back to identity assimilation, the individual can reestablish a middle ground between becoming overly preoccupied with change versus pretending that changes are not occurring. People who use identity balance accept that they are aging without adopting a defeatist attitude. They take steps to ensure that they will remain healthy, but do not become demoralized about conditions or limitations they may already have developed. Additionally, they are not deluded into thinking that they will be young forever.

The advantages of identity balance (and to an extent healthy denial) are that the older adult adopts an active "use it or lose it" approach to the aging process. By remaining active, people can delay or prevent many if not most age-related negative changes. On the other hand, there are many "bad habits," or ways in which a person's behavior can accelerate the aging process. Some of the most common negative behaviors, described in Chapter 1, include overexposure to the sun and smoking. Ideally, people adapt to the aging process by taking advantage of the use-it-or-lose-it approach and avoiding the bad habits.

Less of a strain will be placed on both identity assimilation and accommodation if people can maintain functioning designed to promote good health for as long as possible.

The Selective Compensation with Optimization Model

We see, then, that people adapt mentally to the age-related changes they experience by shifting their priorities. According to the **selective optimization with compensation model (SOC)**, adults attempt to preserve and maximize the abilities that are of central importance and put less effort into maintaining those that are not (Baltes & Baltes, 1990) (see Figure 2.6). Older people make conscious decisions regarding how to spend their time and effort in the face of losses in physical and cognitive resources.

The SOC model implies that at some point in adulthood, people deliberately begin to reduce efforts in one area in order to focus more on achieving success in another. It is likely that the areas people choose to focus on are those that are of greater importance and for which the chances of success are higher. Time and health limitations may also be a factor. If someone who has enjoyed high-impact aerobics finds the activity too exerting or hard on the knees, this person may compensate by spending more time doing yoga. Similar processes may operate in the area of intellectual functioning. The older individual may exert more effort toward solving word games and puzzles and spend less time on pastimes that involve spatial and speed skills, such as fast-moving computer games. If reading becomes too much of a chore due to fading eyesight, the individual may compensate by switching to audio books.

Concepts from the multiple threshold model would seem to fit well with the SOC model. People may make choices based on what aspects of functioning are central to their identities. Those who value the mind will compensate for changes in mental abilities by finding other intellectually demanding activities that they can still perform rather than switching their focus entirely. Those who are able to make accommodations to age-related changes without becoming overwhelmed or preoccupied will be able to reestablish a sense of well-being after what may be an initially difficult period.

Although the SOC model may seem to present a negative view of aging, in that it emphasizes the way that people adapt to loss, it can also be seen as offering a realistic perspective on the fact that there are losses in adulthood that can often outweigh the gains (Heckhausen, 1997). However, people adapt to these changes by re-adjusting their goals and, in the process, can maintain their sense of well-being (Frazier, Barreto, & Newman, 2012).

BIOLOGICAL APPROACHES TO AGING IN ADULTHOOD

Biological changes throughout later life, as is true in the years of infancy, childhood, and adolescence, are based on genetically determined events or changes in physiological functioning brought about by intrinsic changes within the organism. Inevitably, the body's biological clock continues to record the years. As we discussed at the beginning of this chapter, however, the interactionist model of development predicts that environmental factors influence the expression of biological or genetic predispositions. According to the principle of *reciprocity*, people's actions interact with their genetic inheritance. The result is that relatively large individual differences occur in the nature and timing of age-related changes in physical and cognitive functioning. Ultimately, the aging of the body sets the limit on life's length, but people can compensate through behavioral measures for many of the changes associated with the aging process to alter the timing of these events.

Acknowledging the role of biology begs the question: Why do living organisms grow old and die? If you are a fan of science fiction, you have surely read stories of a world in which aging does not occur, or occurs so slowly that people live for hundreds of years. While these fictional accounts may be engrossing and even tempting to imagine, there are some obvious problems associated with such a world. Outcomes such as overpopulation, a lack of adequate resources, and intergenerational strife are just some of the possibilities. Presumably, to keep the population in check, birthrates would be reduced to a virtual standstill.

Although it's not possible to know "why" aging occurs, the fact is that death does occur, and with it the inevitability of aging. Yet researchers who study aging continue to explore whether aging is in fact the result of a correctable defect in living organisms. A related possibility is that organisms are programmed to survive until they reach sexual maturity. Having guaranteed the survival of their species, living creatures are programmed to deteriorate or diminish once the genes programmed to keep them alive past that point are no longer of use to the species. Biologically speaking, according to this view, reproduction is the primary purpose of life, and once this criterion has been met, there are no specific guidelines to determine what happens next.

Genes and DNA

Inherited characteristics are found in the **genome**, the complete set of instructions for "building" all the cells that make up an organism (see Figure 2.7). The human genome is found in each nucleus of a person's many trillions of

FIGURE 2.7

From Genome to Protein

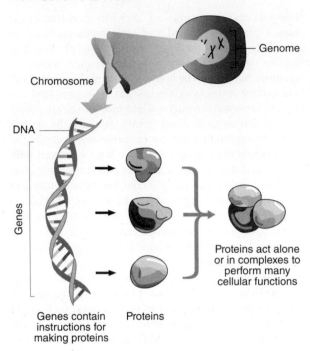

Genome

Chromosome

DNA

Genes

Proteins act alone
or in complexes to
perform many
cellular functions

Genes contain
instructions for
making proteins

Proteins

cells. The genome is contained in **deoxyribonucleic acid (DNA)**, a molecule capable of replicating itself that encodes information needed to produce proteins. There are many kinds of proteins, each with different functions. Some proteins provide structure to the cells of the body, whereas other proteins called enzymes assist biochemical reactions that take place within the cells. Antibodies are proteins that function in the immune system to identify foreign invaders that need to be removed from the body. The entire process of protein manufacture is orchestrated by the genetic code contained in DNA.

A **gene** is a functional unit of a DNA molecule carrying a particular set of instructions for producing a specific protein. Human genes vary greatly in length, but only about 10% of the genome actually contains sequences of genes used to code proteins. The rest of the genome contains sequences of bases that have no apparent coding or any other apparent function. Some of the proteins that the genes encode provide basic housekeeping duties in the cell. These genes constantly stay active in many types of cells; more typically, a cell activates just the genes needed at the moment to carry out a task and suppresses the rest. Through this process of selective activation of genes, a cell becomes a skin cell, for example, rather than a bone cell.

The genome is organized into **chromosomes**, which are distinct, physically separate units of coiled threads of DNA

and associated protein molecules. In humans, there are two sets of 23 chromosomes, one set contributed by each parent. Each set has 23 single chromosomes: 22 are called "autosomes" and contain non sex-linked information, and the 23rd is the X or Y sex chromosome. The presence of the Y chromosome determines maleness, so that a normal female has a pair of X chromosomes and a male has one X and one Y in the 23rd chromosome pair. Although each chromosome contains the same genes, there is no rhyme or reason to the distribution of genes on chromosomes. A gene that produces a protein that influences eye color may be next to a gene that is involved in cellular energy production.

When DNA reproduces itself, the process often occurs without a problem, and the DNA copy is the same as the original molecule. However, for various reasons, genes may undergo the alterations known as **mutations**. When a gene contains a mutation, the protein encoded by that gene will most likely be abnormal. Sometimes the protein can function despite the damage, but in other cases, it becomes completely disabled. If a protein vital to survival becomes severely damaged, the results of the mutation can be serious. Genetic mutations are either inherited from a parent or acquired over the course of one's life. Inherited mutations originate from the DNA of the cells involved in reproduction (sperm and egg).

When reproductive cells containing mutations are combined in one's offspring, the mutation is in all the bodily cells of that offspring. Inherited mutations are responsible for diseases such as cystic fibrosis and sickle cell anemia. They also may predispose an individual to developing cancer, major psychiatric illnesses, and other complex diseases.

Acquired mutations are changes in DNA that develop throughout a person's lifetime. Remarkably, cells possess the ability to repair many of these mutations. If these repair mechanisms fail, however, the mutation can be passed along to future copies of the altered cell. Mutations can also occur in the mitochondrial DNA, which is the DNA found in the tiny structures within the cell called mitochondria. These structures are crucial to the functioning of the cell because they are involved in producing cellular energy. Unlike DNA found elsewhere in the cell, mitochondrial DNA is inherited solely from the mother.

Geneticists have provided many fascinating and important perspectives on the aging process. The completion of the Human Genome Project in 2003 and progress by the International HapMap project (Frazer et al., 2007) paved the way for researchers to identify successful analytic techniques to map complete sets of DNA. A **genome-wide association study** is a method used in behavior genetics in which researchers search for genetic variations related to complex diseases by scanning the entire genome. Another method in behavior genetics is a **genome-wide linkage study**, in which researchers study the families of people with specific psychological traits or disorders. These methods offer a promising avenue for research on the genetics of aging. Hundreds of studies have successfully identified novel genes involved in aging-related diseases such as heart failure (Velagaleti & O'Donnell, 2010), Alzheimer's disease (Harold et al., 2009), and osteoarthritis (Richards et al., 2009).

In genome-wide association studies, researchers seek to identify causes of aging involving **single nucleotide polymorphisms (SNPs)**, which are small genetic variations that can occur in a person's DNA sequence. Four nucleotide letters—adenine, guanine, thymine, and cytosine (A, G, T, C)—specify the genetic code. An SNP variation occurs when a single nucleotide, such as an A, replaces one of the other three. For example, an SNP is the alteration of the DNA segment ATGGTTA to AAGGTTA, in which an "A" replaces the second "T" in the first snippet. Although many SNPs do not produce physical changes in people, researchers believe that other SNPs may predispose people to resistance to disease or the potential for a longer life span.

As genomic research continues to make advances in understanding the complexity of disease and genes, more and more individuals will be offered the opportunity to have their genome scanned to determine their risk for developing a disease. However, you might wonder, if this were available to you, whether you would want to find out which diseases you may potentially be at risk for developing. Would you change your lifestyle based on this information, and if so, would you want other family members tested? Questions such as these will dominate the biomedical field for years to come, raising important ethical and personal questions.

Programmed Aging Theories

Genetics are involved in all biological theories of aging, but to differing degrees (Hayflick, 1994). **Programmed aging theories** propose that aging and death are built into the hard-wiring of all organisms and therefore are part of the genetic code. Every living organism has, then, "aging genes" that count off the years past maturity, just as "development genes" lead to the point of maturity in youth.

One argument long used to support programmed aging theories is based on the fact that species have different life spans. For example, butterflies have life spans of 12 weeks, and giant tortoises have life spans of 180 years. Humans have the longest life span of any mammals at 120 years. The fact that life spans vary so systematically across species supports the role of genetics in the aging process, according to many biologists.

Variations among species in life spans are clearly illustrated when age is plotted against death rates. The **Gompertz function** plots the relationship between age and death rates for a given species. The originator, Benjamin Gompertz, was an 18th-century British mathematician who worked as an actuary, a profession where the financial impact of risk is calculated. In 1825, he applied calculus to mortality data and showed that the mortality rate increases in a geometric progression with age. When plotted as a logarithmic function, it takes the form of a straight line.

Figure 2.8 compares the plots resulting from the Gompertz function for several species of field and deer mice (Sacher, 1977). The horizontal axis of this graph shows the age of the organism in days with the longest-living species reaching about 9 years and the shortest-living about 1 and a half years. The vertical axis shows the death rate per day (transformed) and the plot points show the number that die per day with increasing age of the species. There is a different Gompertz function for each species, supporting the idea that longevity is an inherited, species-specific trait even within these six species of rodents.

Findings in support of genetic theories are particularly intriguing in view of the considerable progress being made in the field of genetics. The ability to identify and then control the "aging" gene or genes would go a long way toward changing the very nature of aging. The idea that there is one or multiple genes that control the aging process from birth to death is very appealing, but the approach has its limits. We cannot say for sure that evolution has selected for the aging process so that old generations die in order to make room for new ones. Historically, few species survived long enough to be exposed to the evolutionary selection process.

A more defensible alterative to genetic theory is that evolution has selected for species that are vigorous through the period of optimal sexual reproduction and then less important once that period has passed. According to the "good genes gone bad" theory (Hayflick, 1994), aging genes take over in the postreproductive years and lead to the ultimate destruction of the organism. Researchers continue to investigate the notion that the very genes that have a positive effect on development during early life create susceptibility to a variety of diseases in later life (Caruso et al., 2000). For example, senescent cells may act as a protective device against the continued growth of cancerous cells. The senescent cells, in turn, are eliminated by the immune system. However, the immune system does not destroy all of the senescent cells, and so they continue to remain present in the body's tissues (Hornsby, 2009).

The most compelling attempts to explain aging through genetics are based on the principle of **replicative senescence**, or the loss of the ability of cells to reproduce.

FIGURE 2.8

Gompertz Curve

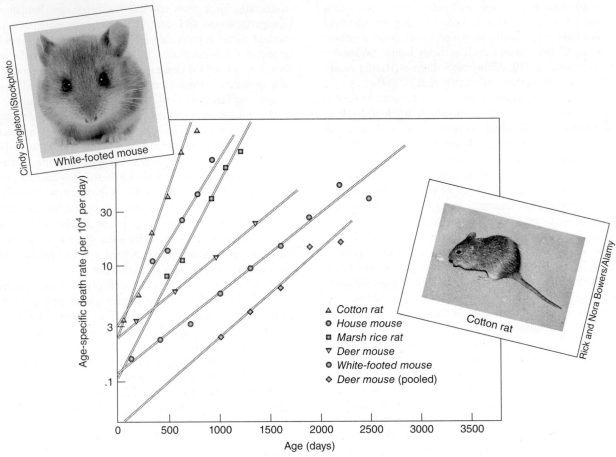

This figure shows the relationship between the age in days of six species of mice and rats and the rate of dying per day. The fact that different species have different functions supports the notion of genetic contributions to longevity.

Source: Sacher, G. A. (1977). Life table modification and life prolongation. In C. E. Finch & L. Hayflick (Eds.), *Handbook of the biology of aging* (pp. 582–638). New York: Van Nostrand Reinhold.

Scientists have long known that there are a finite number of times (about 50) that normal human cells can proliferate in culture before they become terminally incapable of further division (Hayflick, 1994). Until relatively recently, scientists did not know why cells had a limited number of divisions. It was only when the technology needed to look closely at the chromosome developed that researchers uncovered some of the mystery behind this process.

As we saw in Figure 2.2, the chromosome is made up largely of DNA. However, at either end of the chromosomes are **telomeres**, repeating sequences of proteins that contain no genetic information (see Figure 2.9). The primary function of the telomeres is to protect the chromosomes from the damage to them that accumulates over repeated cell

replications. With each cell division, more of the telomeres are lost, exposing more and more of the active part of the chromosome. Once telomeres shorten to the point of no longer being able to protect the chromosome, adjacent chromosomes fuse, the cell cycle is halted, and ultimately the cell dies (Shin, Hong, Solomon, & Lee, 2006). Evidence linking telomere length to mortality in humans suggests that the telomeres may ultimately hold the key to understanding the aging process (Cluett & Melzer, 2009).

However, biology does not completely explain the loss of telomeres over the course of life. Supporting the idea of biopsychosocial interactions in development, researchers have linked telomere length to social factors. Analyzing blood samples from more than 1,500 female twins,

FIGURE 2.9

The Telomere Theory of Aging

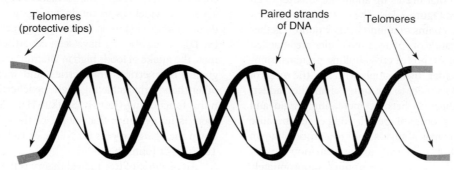

Telomeres
(protective tips)

Paired strands
of DNA

Telomeres

According to the telomere theory, aging is caused by loss of telomeres from the ends of chromosomes.

researchers in the United Kingdom determined that telomere length was shorter in women from lower socioeconomic classes (Cherkas et al., 2006). There was a difference of seven "biological years" (measured in terms of telomeres) between twins with manual jobs and their co-twins in higher-ranking occupations. The researchers attributed this difference to the stress of being in a lower-level occupation in which people have less control over their day-to-day activities. Body mass index, smoking, and lack of exercise were additional factors influencing telomere length. A subsequent study on this sample provided further research of the important role of lifestyle factors. Even after the researchers adjusted for such factors as age, socioeconomic status, smoking, and body mass index, people who engaged in higher levels of physical activity had longer telomeres than those who did not (Cherkas et al., 2008).

Although many cells in the body are thought to be affected by the shortening of the telomeres, not all experience this effect of the aging process. For example, when tumor cells are added to normal cells, they replicate indefinitely. Because of the danger posed by these multiplying tumor cells, senescence may be thought of as a form of protection against cancer. The key to extending the life span based on the telomere theory would be for scientists to find a way to keep cells replicating longer without increasing the risk of cancer cell proliferation (Ohtani, Mann, & Hara, 2009).

Another candidate for a genetic cause of aging involves the **FOXO genes**, a group of genes that may operate to influence the rate of cell death. Using SNP analysis, researchers are finding that interactions involving these genes may contribute to human longevity (Tan et al., 2013). Although nicknamed the "longevity gene," it may be premature to believe that the cause of aging will be identified as involving one gene, or even a set of genes. However, this research offers intriguing leads into what

may eventually produce important breakthroughs in the search for genetic contributions to the aging process.

Random Error Theories

Random error theories are based on the assumption that aging reflects unplanned changes in an organism over time. The **wear and tear theory** of aging is one that many people implicitly refer to when they say they feel that they are "falling apart" as they get older. According to this view, the body, like a car, acquires more and more damage as it is exposed to daily wear and tear from weather, use, accidents, and mechanical insults. Programmed aging theories, in contrast, would suggest that the car was not "built to last," but rather meant to deteriorate over time in a systematic fashion. (See Table 2.3.)

Cross-linking theory proposes that aging causes deleterious changes in cells of the body that make up much of

TABLE 2.3

Random Error Theories of Aging

	Brief Summary	*Supporting Evidence*
Cross-linking	• Collagen molecules form cross-links	• Cross-links do increase in older organisms
Free radical	• Free radicals cause destructive changes in cells	• Mixed data on anti-oxidants, caloric restriction, and resveretrol
Error catastrophe	• Mutations lead to deleterious changes	• Errors in mitochondrial DNA may be a source of harmful changes

the body's connective tissue, including the skin, tendons, muscle, and cartilage. The cross-links develop in **collagen**, the fibrous protein that makes up about one-quarter of all bodily proteins (see Figure 2.10). The collagen molecule is composed of three chains of amino acids wound together in a tight helix. Strands of collagen molecules are attached through horizontal strands of cross-linking proteins, similar to rungs on a ladder. Increasingly with age, the rungs of one ladder start to connect to the rungs of another ladder, causing the molecules to become increasingly rigid and shrink in size. The process of cross-linking occurs because exposure to certain types of sugars leads to a process known as glycation, which in turn leads to the formation of what are called advanced glycation end-products (appropriately named "AGE"). The AGEs induce cross-linking of collagen, which in turn increases, for example, stiffness of skeletal muscle and cartilage (Semba, Bandinelli, Sun, Guralnik, & Ferrucci, 2010).

An issue yet to be determined is whether the cross-linking theory adequately explains the cause of aging or whether it describes a process that occurs due to the passage of time and cumulative damage caused by a lifetime of exposure to sugar in the diet. Another theory focuses on **free radicals**, unstable oxygen molecules produced when cells create energy. The primary goal of a free radical is to seek out and bind to other molecules. When this occurs, the molecule attacked by the free radical loses functioning. According to **free radical theory** (Sohal, 2002), the cause of aging is the increased activity of these unstable oxygen molecules that bond to other molecules and compromise the cell's functioning.

Although oxidation caused by free radicals is in fact a process associated with increasing age, researchers have

FIGURE 2.10

Diagram of a Collagen Molecule

Collagen is a long fibrous protein whose strands form a triple helix. It makes up much of the connective tissue in the body (skin, cartilage, tendons, bone, lens of the eye), so when it forms cross-links, these tissues become less flexible.

questioned the utility of free radical theory to explain the aging process in general (Perez et al., 2009). **Antioxidants**, chemicals that prevent the formation of free radicals, are advertised widely as an antidote to aging. The active ingredient in antioxidants is the enzyme superoxide dimutase (SOD). No doubt you have seen advertisements that promote the intake of foods high in vitamins E and C, including grapes, blueberries, strawberries, and walnuts. However, other than perhaps having slight beneficial effects on cognitive functioning (Joseph, Shukitt-Hale, & Willis, 2009), there is no evidence that intake of these foods will slow down the aging process (Lapointe & Hekimi, 2009; Park, Tedesco, & Johnson, 2009).

An offshoot of free radical theory is the **caloric restriction hypothesis**, the view the key to prolonging life is to restrict caloric intake (Walford, Mock, Verdery, & Mac-Callum, 2002). Caloric restriction is thought to have a beneficial impact in part because it reduces the formation of free radicals. After many years of experimental research involving nonhuman species, particularly rodents, evidence is beginning to emerge to support the value of caloric restriction in humans, with or without exercise (Lefevre et al., 2009).

Promising findings regarding free radical theory suggest that resveratrol, a natural compound found in grapes and consequently wine, is a highly potent antioxidant. Levels of resveratrol are highest among varieties of red wine. Laboratory mice fed on a high-calorie diet plus resveratrol had a survival rate approximating that of mice on a normal diet, both of whom had higher survival rates (but not longevity rates) than animals on a high-calorie diet (Pearson et al., 2008). Exercise further increases the life-enhancing effect of resveratrol (Murase, Haramizu, Ota, & Hase, 2009). Although it has now become fairly well established that red wine is related to reduced effects of aging, researchers debate the cause of these positive effects. Rather than having its effects through mechanisms involving free radicals, other researchers propose that red wine's benefits are the result of procyanidins, tannins present in red wine, which have beneficial effects on the arteries.

The **autoimmune theory** of aging proposes that aging is due to faulty immune system functioning in which the immune system attacks the body's own cells. Autoimmunity is at the heart of certain diseases prevalent in older adults, such as some forms of arthritis, systemic lupus erythematosus, and cancer (Larbi, Fulop, & Pawelec, 2008).

Error theories of aging propose that mutations acquired over the organism's lifetime lead to malfunctioning of the body's cells. According to the **error catastrophe theory**, the errors that accumulate with aging are ones that are vital to life itself. Researchers are now finding that the source of the errors is in the mitochondrial DNA

(Kukat & Trifunovic, 2009). Mice with mutations in the mitochondrial DNA show accelerated signs of aging, including graying, hair loss, and loss of muscle mass and spine strength.

Biologists have made significant advancements in trying to solve the puzzle of why humans and our counterparts across the animal kingdom experience the changes associated with aging that eventually lead to death. At the present time, genetic theories are considered more likely to hold the ultimate answer, but other approaches cannot yet be ruled out. Furthermore, though it is likely that aging ultimately will be accounted for by a combination of these theories, it is also likely that some theories provide better ways to understand age-related changes in the body than others. Rather than exploring one overarching theory, many researchers take the approach of applying specific theories to specific alterations with age in particular organ systems or tissues, such as using cross-linking theory to explain changes in the body's connective tissues.

In looking at perspectives on the aging process that derive from the social sciences, it is important to keep in mind the central role of biological factors. These factors form the "nature" component to the complex "nature–nurture" interactions assumed to characterize development in the adult years. Clearly, all three models must be brought to bear in attempting to understand the complexities of nature and nurture.

SUMMARY

1. The life span perspective views development as continuous from childhood to old age and incorporates the effects of sex, race, ethnicity, social class, religion, and culture. The term "developmental science" is emerging to reflect the need to take a broad, interdisciplinary approach to the study of change over time, including the fields of biology, health, and sociology.

2. The three prominent models of developmental science offer differing emphasis on genetics, the environment, and the interaction of the two. The organismic model proposes that heredity drives the course of development throughout life and that changes occur over time because individuals are programmed to exhibit behaviors at certain ages. The mechanistic model proposes that people's behavior changes gradually over time, shaped by the outside forces that cause them to adapt to their environments. Rather than clear-cut stages, development is viewed as a smooth, continuous set of gradations as the individual acquires new experiences. The interactionist model of development emphasizes processes such as niche-picking, in which there is a reciprocal interaction between the individual and the environment. The concepts of multidimensionality and multidirectionality are central, and plasticity is considered an important element of development. The biopsychosocial perspective fits within the interactionist model.

3. Sociocultural models of development emphasize the effects of the environment on individuals, focusing on variables such as age and sex structures within the population, income, and social class. Ecological perspectives examine multiple levels of organization within the environment, such as the proximal social relational level and the sociocultural level. The life course perspective highlights age-related norms, roles, and attitudes as influences on individuals. Age norms in adulthood are tied to the social clock, the expectations for the ages at which a society associates with major life events. Theories that relate the well-being of the older individual to the level of social involvement include disengagement theory, activity theory, and continuity theory. These propose different relationships between individuals and society.

4. Ageism is a set of stereotyped views about older adults, reflected in negative as well as positive images. Some historians believe that older adults were more highly regarded in preindustrial societies, a view known as the modernization hypothesis. However, it appears that mixed views of aging have existed throughout history and across cultures. According to the multiple jeopardy hypothesis of aging, older adults who are of minority status and are female face more discrimination than White male individuals. In contrast, the age-as-leveler view proposes that as people become older, age overrides all other "isms." Older adults potentially facing multiple jeopardy may also be protected from its effects and even perhaps fare better than those with higher social standing. According to the inoculation hypothesis, older minorities and women have actually become immune to the effects of ageism through years of exposure to discrimination and stereotyping.

5. Erikson's psychosocial development theory is an important psychological model of development in adulthood. It proposes a series of eight psychosocial crisis stages that correspond roughly to age periods in life in the growth of psychological functions. The eight stages follow the epigenetic principle, which means that each stage builds on the ones that come before it. However, later stages can appear at earlier ages, and early stages can reappear later in life. According to Piaget's theory of development, individuals gain in the ability to adapt to

the environment through the processes of assimilation and accommodation. The ideal state of development is one of equilibration or balance. According to the identity process theory, identity assimilation and identity accommodation operate throughout development in adulthood as the individual interacts with experiences. The multiple threshold model was proposed as an explanation of how identity processes influence the interpretation of age-related events such as changes in physical or cognitive functioning.

6. According to the selective optimization with compensation model (SOC), adults attempt to preserve and maximize the abilities of central importance and put less effort into maintaining those that are not. Older people make conscious decisions regarding how to spend their time and effort in the face of losses in physical and cognitive resources.

7. There are two major categories of biological theories, all of which regard aging as the result of changes in the biological makeup of the organism. Programmed aging theories are based on the observation that species differ in life spans (represented by the Gompertz equation) and propose that aging is genetically determined. The telomere theory, which emerged in part from observations of replicative senescence, proposes that cells are limited in the number of times they can reproduce by the fact that each replication involves a loss of the protective ends of chromosomes known as telomeres. Random error theories view aging as an accident resulting from cellular processes that have gone awry, including the wear and tear theory, the cross-linking theory, and the free radical theory. Studies on caloric restriction provide support for the free radical theory, which also proposes that antioxidants can slow down the aging process.

3

The Study of Adult Development and Aging: Research Methods

AGING TODAY

What Your Grandmother Didn't Tell You About Her Sex Life

For many people, aging implies a complete loss of sexuality. Yet, logically, there is no reason why anyone 40, 50, 60, or older should give up his or her sex life. Why do we "de-sex" our elders? One obvious reason is that if people older than you are having sex, this could mean that your parents—or worse—your grandparents are "doing it." That's a tough image for many people to swallow. The National Social Life, Health, and Aging Project (NSHAP) was conducted on a large national sample of adults 57 to 85 years of age. The study was intended to test the hypothesis that older adults with strong sexual and intimate relationships would have more favorable health in general. They defined sexuality as reflecting a combination of physical ability, motivation, attitudes, opportunity, and actual sexual behavior (Waite, Laumann, Das, & Schumm, 2009a).

You might wonder just how to go about constructing a survey to test these potentially sensitive personal questions, particularly to people who (if the stereotypes are true) may feel uncomfortable answering them. However, the researchers believed that the best way to get the information was just to ask for it. They certainly respected their respondents, but didn't hesitate to ask them the tough questions needed to gain as complete a picture as possible of their sexual history, practices, and attitudes. The researchers clearly had to get over the mindset that they were asking their parents, or their grandparents, to provide such private information. The best way to approach this problem was to make the questions as straightforward as possible, to act professionally, and not to become embarrassed themselves by the answers they were getting.

The researchers obtained much of the information about sexuality through interviews, including the standard information about sex and marital status of the respondents. These were reasonably straightforward questions, the stuff of much survey research. The questions became more delicate, however, if respondents weren't married. People who answered something other than being married or cohabiting were asked if they had a romantic, intimate, or sexual partner. The interviewers then went on to ask the remaining questions about this sexual partner, whom they labeled the "current partner." Remember, again, that some of these respondents could have been as old as 85 years. You might think of questions about a sexual partner as more appropriate for a person 50 or more years younger than these participants. If so, you're already confronting one of the stereotypes that we have about aging. This reaction can give you insight into why scientific objectivity is so important in any kind of research, but particularly in research that touches on sensitive topics such as sexuality and aging.

Posted by Susan Whitbourne and Stacey Whitbourne

Aging is inherently linked with the passage of time. The relationship between age and time presents a dilemma that researchers in adult development and aging must confront when designing and implementing research. As difficult as it is to understand the nature of change over time, the importance of such research is crucial to the scientific understanding of the aging process. Without empirical data, there would be little basis for establishing an understanding of how the aging process affects people. In this chapter, we examine the methodologies designed by researchers to capture information that can gain an accurate view of development in adulthood and later life.

VARIABLES IN DEVELOPMENTAL RESEARCH

Let's start with a few basic definitions that are helpful for understanding how aging is measured and studied. A **variable** is a characteristic that "varies" from individual to individual. Understanding why people vary as a function of their age is at the heart of the study of development. In scientific research in general, the **dependent variable** is the outcome that researchers observe. The **independent variable** is the factor that the researcher manipulates. The researcher can set the value of the independent variable according to the study's conditions. Researchers choose these variables to test a particular hypothesis. The hypothesis, in turn, is based on the question the researcher wishes to investigate. Typically, these questions arise from a theoretical interest of the researcher.

Researchers who use an **experimental design** to study a question of interest decide on conditions that will allow them to manipulate a particular independent variable. In the typical experimental study, the researcher randomly assigns respondents to groups. These groups represent different levels of the independent variable such as exposure to a treatment (in the experimental group) vs. no exposure to treatment (in the control group). The researcher then compares the performance of the two groups on the dependent variable. Should people differ on the dependent variable, the researcher assumes that this is because they were exposed to different levels of the independent variable. Clinical trials typically compare the effectiveness of a drug on one group compared to another and as long as the proper controls were in place, the findings can suggest that the drug helps people improve. One of these controls involves ensuring that participants are randomly assigned to experimental vs. control groups; if not, the findings are compromised.

Although developmental psychologists classify age as an independent variable, age is truly not "independent" because its value cannot be controlled or manipulated. An experimenter cannot randomly assign people to a particular age group by making some people young and some people old. This means that you can never state with certainty that aging "causes" people to receive certain scores on a dependent variable of interest. What you can establish is whether different age groups varied in their responses to the experimental manipulation.

For example, consider an experiment in which the experimenter wishes to test the hypothesis that the memory performance of older adults is particularly sensitive to instructions that help them to feel more confident going into the experiment. To test this hypothesis, the researcher compares older and younger adults in two conditions. In the experimental condition, the researcher gives the confidence-boosting instructions to both age groups prior to the memory test. In the control condition, the researcher provides standard instructions to both age groups prior to the test. The independent variable is the instructions and the dependent variable is memory performance. The experimenter then compares memory scores in the two age groups and the two conditions. If people in both age groups get higher scores in the experimental group, but the older adults improve more, the researcher would have evidence to support the hypothesis.

The example of the memory experiment illustrates what happens when the findings show an interaction between variables—the manipulation affects both groups, but the effect is stronger for one group than for the other. We still can't conclude that age "caused" differences in responses to the treatment groups, but we do know that older adults seemed to benefit more when researchers help them to feel better about their cognitive skills.

Because age cannot be experimentally manipulated, we say that studies of aging represent the **quasi-experimental design** in which researchers compare groups on predetermined characteristics. The same is true of studies that examine sex, ethnicity, or social class differences. You cannot conclude that the predetermined characteristic caused the variations in the dependent variable, but you can use the results to describe the differences between groups. Consider a study in which researchers compare adults living in the community with older adults in assisted living facilities. Since the researchers could not assign the older adults randomly to these groups, they cannot conclude that living situation caused higher levels of happiness in one group over the other. Other factors may account for the differences in happiness rather than living situation. What researchers can do in this situation is attempt to rule out other alternatives, such as levels of physical functioning, which may account for differences in happiness. Once they feel that other explanations have been ruled out, and if the differences are repeatedly demonstrated, researchers can make the cautious inference that living situation had something to do with the variations in people's happiness scores.

Similarly, when comparing age groups in performance on a variable of interest, such as performance on memory for lists of numbers, you cannot conclude that age caused older adults to perform differently than the comparison age groups. As you will see later, ruling out alternative explanations is of tremendous importance not only when diverse age groups are compared, but also on other characteristics associated with age.

DESCRIPTIVE RESEARCH DESIGNS

As you just learned, studies of aging are by definition quasi-experimental and thus do not allow for cause and effect conclusions. The second problem in studies on aging is that effects we think are due to age are actually due to other variables that are associated with age but aren't intrinsically associated with the aging process. These factors relate to the social and historical period in which researchers are testing them. To be able to make legitimate claims about "age" and not the social or historical period, researchers must be able to build controls into their data designs and analyses that can rule out these social and historical factors. Fortunately, there are such tricks up the developmental researcher's sleeve. Therefore, even though age is an imperfect variable, many researchers have figured out ways around the thorniest problems it creates.

The great majority of studies on aging use what we call here a **descriptive research design**, which provides information about age differences but does not attempt to rule out social or historical factors. For example, a study may show that older adults are more likely to have a certain health problem than are younger adults. You have no way of knowing whether that health problem is a natural result of the aging process or a result of environmental conditions that were present during the individual's lifetime. Perhaps the older people were exposed to worse nutritional practices than their younger counterparts; therefore, the findings reflect disparities in their early life experiences rather than age. Further research, using adequate controls, would be needed to rule out this possibility.

In this section, we break down the descriptive research designs and show you both their strengths and limitations. Before getting to these, we need to explain the three basic concepts manipulated in these designs: age, cohort, and time of measurement.

Age, Cohort, and Time of Measurement

The three factors that jointly influence the individual's performance on a given psychological measure at any point in life are age, cohort, and time of measurement. We summarize these three factors in Table 3.1.

TABLE 3.1

Age, Cohort, and Time of Measurement

Term	Definition	Measurement of:
Age	• How many years (or months) the person has lived	• Change within the individual
Cohort	• Year (or period) of a person's birth	• Influences relative to history at time of birth
Time of measure-ment	• Year or period in which a person is tested	• Current influences on individuals being tested

Age is an objectively determined measure of how many years (and/or months or days) a person has lived up to the present moment. **Cohort** is the term we use to describe the year (or period) of a person's birth. **Time of measurement** tells us the year or period in which a person is tested.

Researchers who study development would like to be able to test hypotheses involving age, meaning that they are primarily interested in the impact of chronological time on a person's functioning. However, as we discussed above, researchers face the thorny problem of disentangling a person's age from the period of history in which the person is living. People in their 70s now were born at a time (approximately the 1930s) in which many people experienced economic hardship. We don't know, therefore, whether a 70-year-old person's performance reflects aging or the circumstances associated with growing up in the 1930s and 1940s. Descriptive research designs can never hope to provide solutions to this problem because they don't allow researchers to manipulate age and environmental influences in such a way as to pull them apart.

You may not be particularly familiar with the term "cohort," but you almost certainly know about "generational" effects. A generation is simply a period that spans about a 20- to 30-year time frame. Cohort can be any length of time, which is why researchers use it rather than generation.

Cohort effects refer to the social, historical, and culture influences that affect people during a particular period of time. In many cases, cohort effects are taken to mean the influences present during the early years of development that cause individuals to behave in a certain way at the current time. For example, the Baby Boomers were thought to have become rebellious because their parents were permissive in raising them, a fact that could be traced to the popularity of a particular parenting advice book. When the Baby Boomers reached their adolescent years, this "anything goes" attitude combined with the natural tendency of teenagers to forge their own paths to produce

TABLE 3.2
Designs in Developmental Research

Year of birth (Cohort)	Year of testing (Time of measurement)			
	1980	*1990*	*2000*	*2010*
1940	40 yrs	50 yrs	60 yrs	70 yrs
1930	50 yrs	60 yrs	70 yrs	80 yrs
1920	60 yrs	70 yrs	80 yrs	90 yrs

Longitudinal

Cross-sectional

an authority-flaunting generation. Another way to think about cohort effects is that they are normative history-graded influences present at or around the time of a person's birth.

Social, historical, and cultural influences that are presently affecting people participating in developmental research are called **time of measurement effects**. As used in developmental research designs, time of measurement effects are similar to cohort effects in that they are also normative history-graded influences that affect many people who are alive at the same time. In the 2010s, such time of measurement effects could include the rapid growth of personal technology, a slowing of the world's economy, and the impact of political and social change in the Middle East on global relations. As in Bronfenbrenner's ecological model, time of measurement effects may be far removed from the individual but still impact people indirectly by affecting the conditions that actively impinge on their lives. For example, the rising cost of gasoline can limit a family's finances, which, in turn, has an effect on the health of individual family members.

As you can see from these simple definitions, once you know the value of two of these variables (i.e., age, cohort, or time of measurement), you automatically know the third. A 40-year-old person tested in 2015 must, by definition, have been born in 1975. To test a person born in 1999 at the age of 25 means that the testing must take place in 2024. These connections among age, time of measurement, and cohort create difficulties when investigators attempt to sort out the extent to which people's scores on measures thought to be sensitive to age are actually due to age rather than the historical and social context.

Descriptive research designs are unable to offer any solutions to the inevitable confound between age and context. They fall into two categories based on whether an individual is tested on multiple occasions over time or whether two or more differing age groups are compared,

which you can see in Table 3.2, illustrating designs in developmental research.

Longitudinal Designs

In a study using a **longitudinal design**, people are followed repeatedly from one test occasion to another. By observing and studying people as they age, researchers aim to determine whether participants have changed over time as the result of the aging process.

A variant of the longitudinal design is the **prospective study**, in which researchers sample from a population of interest before they develop a particular type of illness or experience a particular type of life event. For example, researchers who wish to study widowhood may sample a population of married individuals while they are still married. Over the ensuing period of the study, they can expect that a certain percentage of these individuals will suffer the death of their spouses.

The typical longitudinal studies that psychologists carry out in their labs are very similar to those that you experience in your own life as you watch the people around you change over time. Consider your own experience from the start of kindergarten to high school graduation. Perhaps you attended school with the same set of students throughout high school, watching your friends and peers grow and develop along with you. Perhaps you marveled at how some friends remained the same over the years while others were not at all like they were when they were younger. Now that you are in college, your relationships with your childhood friends will change even more with the passage of time. You may attend their weddings or even find romance with past loves.

Fast forward to your 10-year reunion (or if you have already attended yours, reflect back), when you are reminded of the person you were during your adolescent development. Many of your former classmates will look

Joseph Sohm/Visions of America, LLC/Alamy

A longitudinal study in action. The Class of 1966 High School reunion 40th anniversary pose in front of Webster Groves High School in Webster Groves St. Louis.

and act the same, and you may remark that the years have done little to change these people. However, other classmates may be difficult or impossible to recognize. Of course, you are also changing along with them. Maybe you were too harsh to judge the cheerleader or nerd and it is only now that you can see them as the complex and multifaceted people they were all along.

Just as psychologists develop hypotheses about why the participants in their studies change over time, you also develop your own hypotheses regarding reasons for the changes in the people you know. Did the cheerleader who joined the Peace Corps change her personality because of the influence of volunteering in an impoverished nation, or did she choose to volunteer for the Peace Corps because she had a hidden side that none of her friends saw in high school? How about the math whiz? Did he blossom because his business acumen gave him access to a broader social network? Or was he really more social than you realized and simply waiting until he had more financial resources before letting his true personality shine through?

As with these two examples, researchers also face the challenge of determining whether changes observed over time in longitudinal studies result from the person's own aging or the result of the changing environment in which the person functions. The individual cannot be removed from the environment to see what would happen if he or she had lived in a different time or place. It is simply not possible to know if people are inherently changing or whether they alter due to the circumstances in which they are aging. This is the key limitation to longitudinal studies: the inability to differentiate between aging within the individual from changes in the social and historical context.

In addition to this thorny theoretical problem, practical problems also plague longitudinal research. The most significant is perhaps the most obvious. It takes years, if not decades, to see the study come to fruition, making it both expensive and technologically challenging—in other words, it takes money and a great deal of clerical effort to keep the project going. On top of this, the results are not available for many years, meaning that researchers cannot focus their entire professional energy on this one study. In many cases, the original investigator may not even live long enough to see the results come to fruition.

Further complicating the longitudinal study is the problem of attrition, as participants either die or drop out of the study for other reasons. As the number of participants diminishes, researchers find it increasingly difficult to make sense of the data because there are too few participants left to allow for statistical analyses across the multiple time points of the study.

The problem of losing participants is compounded by **selective attrition**, the fact that the people who drop out of a longitudinal study are not necessarily representative of the sample that was originally tested. They may drop out due to illness, lack of motivation, instability, death, or an inability to continue in the study because they have moved so frequently that the researcher loses track of them. Another reason that becomes an increasingly significant problem is the death of participants who perhaps were initially in poorer physical health.

One direct consequence of selective attrition is that the data from the study become increasingly skewed as the study wears on. In a process called **terminal decline**, individuals gradually lose their cognitive abilities as they draw closer to death (MacDonald, Hultsch, & Dixon, 2011). After that point, they quite obviously cannot be tested; however, while they were in the sample in their declining years, they may have pulled down the group's average. The researcher may erroneously conclude that participants in the sample "improved" when, in reality, the sicker and perhaps less motivated are simply gone from the sample, leaving the higher performers alone to contribute scores. You can compare this to a marathon run. As the race nears its conclusion, only the hardiest remain on their feet to make it to the finish line. If you measured the finishers at the beginning of the race, they would have scored higher than the dropouts on such critical factors as endurance and speed.

Figure 3.1 illustrates the problem of selective attrition with a hypothetical longitudinal study conducted over four time points. The bottom line shows the data of the subgroup who die in between Times 3 and 4. As you can see, their scores steadily declined prior to that point. The top line shows the people who remained in the study across all four times of testing. Their scores did not change at all. However, if the researcher calculates the average score for Times 1 through 3 that includes the people who will die before Time 4, that average will seem to increase when the ones who were showing terminal decline are no longer in the sample. Their presence at Time 3 brought down the overall average, and when they were gone, it might look like the survivors had increased when in fact they remained stable.

To address the problem of selective attrition, longitudinal researchers typically conduct analyses to determine whether the pattern of participant dropout was random, or whether it reflected a systematic bias that kept the healthier and more motivated participants in the sample. Such a technique is referred to as nonrandom sampling, and means that successive samples are increasingly unlike the populations they were intended to represent. Various statistical techniques are employed to determine whether nonrandom sampling has occurred, and if so, whether relationships between the variables are affected. Without such procedures, the study's results become difficult to interpret. Beyond a certain point, however, there is little that the researcher can do. The healthiest individuals will always be the last ones standing at the end of a study and therefore may never have been representative of their age group (Hofer & Sliwinski, 2006).

Practice effects are another theoretically thorny issue that complicate longitudinal studies (Hoffman, Hofer, & Sliwinski, 2011). Because they repeatedly take the same tests, participants may improve simply because they become better able to answer the questions. If the test measures intelligence, participants may purposely learn the answers in between testing occasions. Similarly, in studies examining personality, a participant may suspect or find out the meaning of a response that implies something unfavorable. On the next test occasion, the respondent may be less likely to endorse that statement.

The investigator faces a far more serious dilemma with regard to the nature of the tests themselves which, over time, may become outdated. The cutting-edge theory developed in the 1980s may have since been refuted, but the researcher is still left with measures based on that theory. One way to address this problem is to reanalyze or rescale the test scores to correspond to the newer theory, if possible. This was the strategy used in studies of personality development by researchers at the Institute for Human Development in Berkeley, who began a study of child development in the late 1920s, a project that continued far longer than initially planned. By the time participants were in their adult years, the original measures were no longer theoretically relevant. The researchers rescored the data using newer theoretical and empirical frameworks.

A variety of methods can also address the practical problems that researchers encounter when they conduct longitudinal studies. Most importantly, investigators need to monitor and maintain their databases of contact information. Administrative personnel whose job it is to retain study participants can maintain the "care and feeding" of the sample in between testing occasions. Research staff may send out greeting cards for holidays and birthdays or update participants on study progress via newsletters and

FIGURE 3.1

The Problem of Selective Attrition in Longitudinal Studies

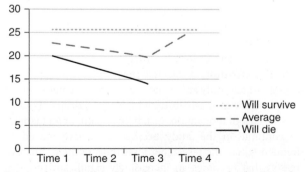

Data in a longitudinal study are distorted by those who die. Here, the average appears to increase between Times 3 and 4 even though the survivors never changed.

emails. Many longitudinal studies use websites to allow participants to engage interactively. Creating a personal touch encourages respondents to continue their involvement and also enables investigators to keep better track of moves, deaths, or email updates.

The problem of having to wait years, if not decades, for results can also be partly overcome. Investigators often publish multiple studies from the same investigation, some of which may be spinoffs addressing slightly different research questions. They can also look at analyses based on measures taken at the same testing point that are not dependent on the longitudinal analyses.

Despite their flaws, longitudinal studies have the potential to add invaluable data on psychological changes in adulthood and old age. Furthermore, as data accumulate from multiple investigations concerning related variables, a body of evidence builds up that helps to inform the larger research questions. Even though one study may have its problems, convergence across several investigations allows researchers to feel greater confidence when findings are similar from one study to the next.

Cross-Sectional Designs

In a study using a **cross-sectional design**, researchers compare groups of people with different ages at one point in time. Typically, older adults (ages 60 or 65 and higher) are compared with younger adults (often of college age). The cross-sectional design is by far the more frequently used research method in the field of developmental science in general, but particularly in research on aging.

Because research on aging is focused on age *changes*, the cross-sectional design, which looks at *age differences*, would seem to hold limited value. However, given the expense,

technical, and practical problems that plague longitudinal studies, many researchers have little choice other than to turn to the cross-sectional method. The challenge they face in cross-sectional research is to make sure they are actually studying the effects of age rather than simply documenting differences between cohorts.

A researcher needs to design a cross-sectional study, then, in a way that controls as much as possible for the effect of cohort that could potentially obscure or exaggerate the effects of age. The key to controlling for cohort differences is to select younger samples comparable in important ways to the older sample. For instance, in a study of aging and verbal memory, it would be important for researchers to ensure that the age groups being compared have similar vocabulary or verbal comprehension skills if not actually similar educational backgrounds.

The cross-sectional design reflects not only differences between cohorts, but also the effects of current social and cultural influences. In other words, everyone participating in the study at about the same time is affected by normative history-graded influences. For example, you and everyone else living now are going through the same events affecting your country, if not the world. What would make this even more problematic from the standpoint of studies on aging is if younger and older adults experienced these events differently.

One case illustrating the problem of cohort differences in cross-sectional studies is shown in Figure 3.2. The graph is from an investigation comparing the relative amounts of white matter in the brains of young, middle-aged, and older adult samples (Brickman et al., 2006). The higher the amount of white matter, the better the individual's brain functions. From the figure, it would seem that because the younger age groups have more white matter, their brains are functioning better compared to the older adult brains.

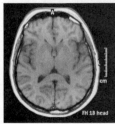

Salih Dastan/iStockphoto

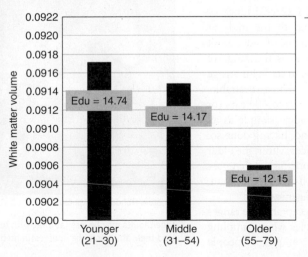

FIGURE 3.2

The Problem of Cohort Differences in Cross-Sectional Research

This cross-sectional study, showing apparent decreases in white matter volume with age (see photo), fails to take into account cohort differences in years of education.

Source: Reprinted from *Biological Psychiatry, 60(5)*, Brickman, A.M., Zimmerman, M. E., Paul, R. H., Grieve, S. M., Tate, D. F., Cohen, R. A., ... Gordon, E., Regional white matter and neuropsychological functioning across the adult lifespan, 444–453, Copyright (2006), with permission from Elsevier.

However, the story is not so simple. The age groups were not comparable in education; the older adults had the fewest years of formal schooling. The cohort difference in education makes it impossible to know whether it was age or education that most strongly influenced the white matter of these three age groups.

Selective survival, the bane of longitudinal investigators, also serves to challenge the work of researchers whose primary work involves the cross-sectional design. Study participants, by definition, are survivors of their respective age groups. Thus, they may represent a healthier or luckier group of people than those in their cohort who did not live as long. Perhaps they are the ones who are more cautious, smarter, and genetically hardier and so were able to avoid the many diseases that could have caused their death prior to old age. As a result, older adults in a cross-sectional study may look different from the younger ones because the two groups are drawn from two different populations—those who will die young (but are still represented in the young adult group) and those who survive to be old. The sampling of young adults drawn exclusively from a college population, a common technique in psychological research, may not be representative of the younger cohort either.

Unlike a longitudinal study, however, cross-sectional studies do not specifically show terminal decline. In other words, since the participants are not followed over time, deteriorations in performance as they become ill or impaired cannot be observed. It is possible that on any given occasion, a participant who will be dying in the next few months or years is in the sample of a cross-sectional study. However, this person's scores will not be tracked over time and so will not appear in the data.

Researchers conducting cross-sectional studies must make numerous decisions as they plan their sample. For example, if researchers wish to compare "young adults" with older adults, they have to decide whether to restrict themselves to the sort of typical 18- to 22-year range or instead allow the age range to expand to the mid- or even late-20s. As it turns out, the age range of older adult samples is rarely defined as narrowly as is the range of those in college. Often, researchers have to settle for an age range for the older group that is larger than is desirable. In some studies, the range is as large as 20 to 30 years (or more). Some researchers define the "older" sample as all respondents over the age of 50 or 60 and, having done so, fail to look for any possible age differences within the older sample. By the time all is said and done, age differences in the older sample may be as great, if not greater than, differences between the older and younger samples.

A related problem to determining acceptable age ranges is the question of how to divide samples when sampling the adult years. Is it better to divide samples of people in cross-sectional studies into decades and then examine age differences continuously across the adult years? Or is it better to compare people at the two extremes of the adult span? Researchers increasingly include middle-aged samples along with the younger and older adults rather than compare only those at the two extremes of the age distribution. The inclusion of three age groups creates a more justifiable basis for "connecting the dots" between their scores on measures of psychological functioning across the adult years.

Another area of concern to researchers conducting cross-sectional studies is the need to take into account the possibility that different age groups will react differently to the test materials. In studies of memory, for example, there is a risk that the older adults will find some of the measures challenging and perhaps intimidating because they are not used to having their abilities evaluated in a formal setting such as the psychology lab. Young adults are far more comfortable with test situations either because they are currently or have recently been in school, where testing is part of the fabric of everyday life. To an older adult, particularly one who is sensitive to memory loss, anxiety about the situation rather than actual performance can result in decreased scores, a topic we address further below.

Task equivalence also applies to the way different cohorts react to measures of personality and social attitudes. For example, a measure of depression may have been tested on a young adult sample but not on an older sample. Items on such a scale concerning physical changes, such as alterations in sleep patterns (a symptom of depression), may in fact reflect normal age-related differences and not differences in depression. Older adults will therefore receive a higher score on the depression scale by virtue of

Amanda Rohde/iStockphoto

Older adults may be less familiar with test-taking, a factor that may lead their abilities to be underestimated in a laboratory setting.

changing their sleep patterns alone, not because they are actually suffering from depression.

These problems aside, cross-sectional studies are relatively quick and inexpensive compared to longitudinal studies. Another advantage of cross-sectional studies is that the latest and most up-to-date technology can be brought to bear on the problem. If a new tool or technique comes out one year, it can be tested through a cross-sectional method the next year. Researchers are not tied to obsolete methods that were in use some 30 or 40 years ago.

The best cross-sectional studies, though never able to permit causal inferences about aging, employ a variety of controls to ensure that differences other than age are kept to a minimum and that the ages selected for study span across the adult years. Most researchers regard their cross-sectional findings as tentative descriptions of the effects of aging on the function of interest. They are aware of the importance of having their findings replicated and verified through studies employing a longitudinal element.

Throughout this book, we endeavor to sift through and find the best available evidence to report to you about the aging process. We will emphasize the studies that do the best job of controlling for factors extraneous to age, whether they are longitudinal or cross-sectional. The next section covers methods that are superior to descriptive designs; however, unfortunately these methods are still only rarely used. In areas where there is relatively little research, we may find that we have to turn to studies that didn't necessarily control that well for confounds other than age. However, we will aim to point these problems out to you so that you are still getting the best information possible. Even if you do not pursue a research career, you will learn to be an educated consumer of research on a topic that is so vital to many areas of your life.

SEQUENTIAL RESEARCH DESIGNS

We have probably convinced you by now that the perfect study on aging is virtually impossible to conduct. Age can never be a true independent variable because it cannot be manipulated. Furthermore, age is inherently linked with time, and so personal aging can never be separated from social aging. However, considerable progress in some areas of research has been made through the application of **sequential designs**. These designs consist of different combinations of the variables age, cohort, and time of measurement.

Simply put, a sequential design involves a "sequence" of studies, such as a cross-sectional study carried out twice (two sequences) over a span of 10 years. The sequential nature of these designs is what makes them superior to the truly descriptive designs conducted on one sample,

followed over time (longitudinal design) or on different-aged samples, tested on one occasion (cross-sectional design). Not only do sequential studies automatically provide an element of replication, but when they are carried out as intended, statistical analyses can permit remarkably strong inferences to be drawn about the effect of age as distinct from cohort or time of measurement.

The Most Efficient Design

One of the most influential articles to be published in the field of adult development and aging was the landmark work by psychologist K. Warner Schaie (1965), in which he outlined what would later be called the **Most Efficient Design**, a set of three designs manipulating the variables of age, cohort, and time of measurement. It is "most efficient" because it enables the most amount of information to be condensed into the most inclusive data framework.

The three designs that make up the Most Efficient Design and the respective factors they include are the **time-sequential design**, in which the data are organized by age and time of measurement, the **cohort-sequential design**, in which cohorts are compared at different ages, and the **cross-sequential design**, in which cohorts are examined at different times of measurement.

Referring back to Table 3.2, for example, in the time-sequential design, the researcher would compare the scores of three or four age groups at three or four times of measurement (e.g. 30- and 40-year olds in the 2000s and 2010s). The cohort-sequential design would consist of two cohorts (e.g. 1940 and 1930) compared at two ages (40 and 50). The time-sequential design would involve comparing two or more cohorts (e.g. 1940 and 1930) at two or more times of testing (2000 and 2010).

Depending on the pattern of significant effects, the researcher may be able to draw conclusions about the relative influences of age, cohort, and time of measurement. For example, if age effects are significant in the time-sequential and cohort-sequential designs and not in the cross-sequential design, then a strong argument can be made for the possibility that the effects reflect the influence of personal rather than social aging. Alternatively, if time of measurement differences are established in both the time-sequential and cross-sequential designs, these findings would suggest it was the time rather than the age of the participants that most influenced the pattern of scores. Similarly, if the cohort factor is significant in the two designs in which it is used, and significant age or time of measurement effects are not observed, then the researcher may look at early childhood environmental factors in these samples because the performance differences would have been attributable only to cohort.

CORRELATIONAL DESIGNS

An alternative approach to describing group differences using the quasi-experimental design is the **correlational design**, in which relationships are observed among variables as they exist in the world. The researcher makes no attempt to divide participants into groups or to manipulate variables.

Simple Correlational Designs

Comparisons of age groups or groups based on divisions such as year of birth or time of measurement are useful for many research questions in the field of gerontology. However, often this approach is neither the most efficient nor the most informative. By grouping people into categories, researchers lose a great deal of information that could be preserved if they used actual age in years. Age is a continuous variable, meaning that it does not have natural cutoff points, as does a categorical variable such as gender. There may be a difference between people of 42 and people of 45 years of age, but when they are all grouped in the "40-year-old" category, this distinction is obscured.

In the correlational design, age can be treated as a continuous variable and it is therefore unnecessary or even desirable to put people into arbitrarily defined groups. The relationship between age and another variable is expressed through the statistic known as the **correlation** (represented by the letter r), whose value can range from $+1.0$ to -1.0. A significant positive correlation indicates that the two variables are positively related so that when the value of one variable increases, the other one does as well. A significant negative correlation indicates that the two variables are negatively related so that when one increases in value, the other one decreases. A correlation of zero indicates no relationship between the variables.

In a correlational study, the researcher makes no assumptions about what caused what—there are no "independent" or "dependent" variables. A correlation between two variables means simply that the two variables are related, but like the proverbial chicken and egg, the researcher cannot say which came first.

Let's consider as an example the relationship between age and response speed. The correlation between these two variables is most often positive; that is, when age increases, response speed does as well (keep in mind that a higher response speed indicates slower performance). When interpreting this relationship, the researcher may be tempted to conclude that age "caused" the increase in response speed. However, this conclusion is not justified, because age was not experimentally manipulated. In a correlational study, there are no independent or dependent variables. Therefore, the possibility that variable A accounts for variable B is equal to the possibility that B accounts for A. It may be tempting to assume that response speed doesn't cause increasing age; rather, age causes increasing response times. However, because an experiment was not conducted, the possibility that increased response speed caused aging cannot be ruled out.

Figure 3.3 shows another example of a correlational study in which men with cardiovascular disease were tested on a hostility questionnaire (Brydon et al., 2010). The rise in their blood pressure was measured after they had completed a laboratory task designed to induce stress (defending themselves publicly against a fabricated shoplifting charge). As you can see in this figure, hostility was positively correlated with increases in blood pressure, meaning that the higher their levels of hostility, the more their blood pressure increased. We might be tempted to conclude that the hostility caused their blood pressure to soar, as it seems unlikely that the increase in their blood pressure would lead their hostility to spike in response to the experimental stress.

However, if you are a psychology student, you have probably incorporated the mantra "correlation does not equal causation" into your everyday language. You know, because you've heard it so many times, that correlations do not allow researchers to state that one variable was the direct cause of another. However, it's also true that two variables may appear to be correlated with each other because there is a third unmeasured variable that both are correlated with. Returning to the case of age and response speed, this third variable might be "number of functioning

FIGURE 3.3

Correlation Between Hostility and Blood Pressure

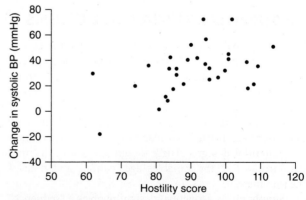

Source: Reprinted from *Journal of Psychosomatic Research, 68(2)*, Brydon, L., Strike, P. C., Bhattacharyya, M. R., Whitehead, D. L., McEwan, J., Zachary, I., … Steptoe, A.. Hostility and physiological responses to laboratory stress in acute coronary syndrome patients, 109–116, Copyright (2010), with permission from Elsevier.

brain cells." Age may be related to number of brain cells, and number of brain cells may be related to response speed. The apparent correlation between age and response speed might disappear entirely when the number of brain cells is measured and factored into the relationship.

With this in mind, thinking about hostility and blood pressure, it is possible that their apparent relationship might be accounted for entirely by an unmeasured third variable such as cigarette smoking. Perhaps people who have higher levels of hostility are more likely to smoke cigarettes, and cigarette smoking is related to higher blood pressure. As it turns out, to control for this possibility, the investigators did take smoking status into account before calculating the hostility–blood pressure correlation. However, researchers are not always able to anticipate every single factor that may affect an apparent correlation between two variables.

When examining data from a typical correlational study, then, it is important to keep in mind that causation cannot be inferred from correlation and to be on the lookout for competing hypotheses related to unmeasured variables. Because arguments that increasing age "causes" changes in other variables are so compelling, it is difficult to remember that there can be other causes lurking in the background.

Correlational studies contain a wealth of information despite their inability to determine cause and effect. The value of the correlation itself provides a useful basis for calculating the strength of the relationship. Furthermore, it is possible to manipulate a larger number of variables at one time than is generally true in studies involving group comparisons. Advanced correlational methods have become increasingly available in the past 20 years that allow researchers to navigate the difficulties involved in causality with traditional correlational methods, and we will turn to those next.

Multivariate Correlational Designs

In contrast to simple correlational designs, which involve determining the statistical relationship between two variables (called a bivariate relationship), a **multivariate correlational design** involves the analysis of relationships among more than two variables. Table 3.3 identifies some of the advantages to using a multivariate design. For example, the researcher using a multivariate design can simultaneously evaluate the effects of many potentially important factors rather than being restricted to the study of two variables, which can lead to overlooking an important third (or fourth) variable.

Multivariate correlational methods also enable researchers to test models in which a set of variables is used to "predict" scores on another variable. In **multiple regression analysis**, the predictor variables are regarded as equivalent to the independent variables, and the variable that is predicted is regarded as equivalent to a dependent variable. Although the design is still correlational in that the experimenter does not manipulate an independent variable, the statistics involved enable investigators to suggest and test inferences about cause–effect relationships.

A variant of multiple regression is **logistic regression**, in which researchers test the likelihood of an individual receiving a score on a discrete yes–no variable. For example, a group of investigators may want to test the probability that a person will receive a diagnosis of cardiovascular disease or not, depending on whether the person has one of several risk factors. Logistic regression is often used to determine whether nonrandom sampling has occurred, as discussed earlier with subject attrition in longitudinal studies. Using the yes–no variables of "survivor" and "dropout," researchers can attest to whether differences between survivors and dropouts are due to chance or to other factors.

TABLE 3.3
Advantages of Multivariate Correlational Design

- Control for confounds related to age
  - ✓ Can add in other variables

- Allow investigations of "causality"
  - ✓ Significance of paths can be tested

- Provide ways to examine change over time
  - ✓ Can model individual variations in growth

Evgeny Kuklev/iStockphoto

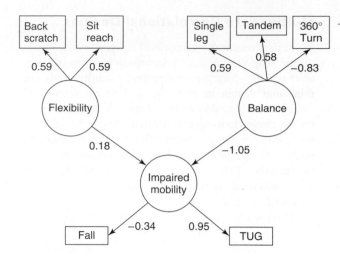

FIGURE 3.4

Example of Structural Equation Modeling Predicting Mobility from Flexibility and Balance in Older Adults

Source: Reprinted from *Archives of Gerontology and Geriatrics, 55(3),* Dai, B., Ware, W. B., & Giuliani, C. A., A structural equation model relating physical function, pain, impaired mobility (IM), and falls in older adults, 645–652, Copyright (2012), with permission from Elsevier. doi: 10.1016/j.archger.2012.06.005

Multivariate correlational designs have the potential to test complex models that reflect multiple influences, including age, on the outcome variables of interest to the researcher. For example, the researcher may believe that education positively affects life satisfaction in older adults because of a third variable, such as health status. The researcher can conduct a statistical test of **mediation**, in which the correlation between two variables is compared with and without their joint correlation to a third variable. If the correlation between education and life satisfaction is smaller when health status is included than when it is not, then the researcher can assume that health serves in this mediational role. Researchers can also test for **moderation**, when two variables are believed to have a joint influence on a third. For example, both age and education may correlate with life satisfaction.

Researchers can test for multiple types of mediation and moderation by conducting a single analysis that includes different types of proposed relationships. In **path analysis**, researchers test all possible correlations among a set of variables to see if they can be explained by a single model. In our example of education, health, age, and life satisfaction, a path analysis would allow the researcher to test whether education and age both affect life satisfaction (moderation) through their joint effect on health (mediation), which in turn affects life satisfaction.

Depending on the data available to a researcher, there may be several measures that all tap a similar construct. In this case, they can use a **latent variable**, which is a statistical composite of several variables that were actually measured. In the example we are using, the researchers may have three measures of life satisfaction rather than just one. They can construct a latent variable that then serves to capture all three measures. In **structural equation modeling (SEM)**,

researchers test models involving relationships that include latent variables. As in path analysis, they propose a set of relationships among variables; however, some are directly measured and others are constructed as latent variables.

Figure 3.4 shows an example of structural equation modeling applied in a study where researchers sought to determine which older adults were at greatest risk for limitations in their mobility (Dai, Ware, & Giuliani, 2012). In this figure, the ovals represent latent variables, meaning that they were constructed from variables that were actually measured. As you can see from the figure, the latent variable of flexibility consisted of scores on tests in which participants had to scratch their backs and reach from a seated position. The latent variable of balance consisted of scores reflecting the ability to maintain balance with one and two legs, and while turning. The latent variable of impaired mobility, which the researchers were trying to predict, was made up of an answer to the question of whether the participant had a history of falling, and the speed at which he or she was able to get up from a chair, walk around a tape marker on the floor, and return to the chair. Looking at this figure, you can see that both flexibility and balance predicted the risk of impaired mobility in older adults. The results suggested that balance was the most important predictor of fall risk. The researchers had also obtained measures of aerobic endurance and strength, but models including these variables failed to meet the statistical criterion of providing a good fit to the data.

SEM is typically used to assess the relationships among variables collected at one point in time. To take advantage of data obtained in longitudinal studies, researchers turn to a multivariate method that takes into account the patterns of people's scores over time. In **hierarchical linear modeling (HLM)** (Raudenbush & Bryk, 2002), individual patterns of change are examined over time rather than simply comparing mean scores of people at different ages. Such a technique is particularly important in longitudinal research, because not every participant exhibits the same patterns of change over time. While some individuals may increase, others may decrease, and some may not change at all. Solely looking at overall mean scores fails to capture this individual variation. In HLM, individual patterns can be explored statistically in addition to examining whether particular variables affect some individuals more than others.

TYPES OF RESEARCH METHODS

Data on adult development and aging can be captured using a variety of data collection strategies or research methods. Each method has advantages and disadvantages that are important to consider according to the particular field of study, the nature of the sample, available resources, and desired applications.

Laboratory Studies

The majority of information about physical and cognitive changes associated with the aging process comes from **laboratory studies**, in which participants are tested in a systematic fashion using standardized procedures. The laboratory method is considered the most objective way of collecting data because each participant is exposed to the same treatment, using the same equipment and the same data recording procedures. For example, in a study of memory, participants may be asked to recall a set of items presented on a computer. At a later point, they may be asked at to recall as many of those items as possible using some type of automated response system.

There are obvious advantages to the laboratory study. The objective and systematic ways in which data are recorded provides the investigator assurance that the results are due to the variables being studied rather than to extraneous factors. For instance, in the memory study, all participants would be presented with the recall items systematically, in a way that does not depend on the voice inflections of the researcher, the quality of the visual stimuli, or the amount of time used to present the items.

A limitation of the laboratory study is the inability to apply the stimuli presented to real-life experiences of most adults. It is possible that the older person feels uncomfortable when tested in an impersonal and possibly intimidating manner using unfamiliar equipment. Consequently, the findings may underestimate the individual's abilities in everyday life and may not generalize to real-world scenarios.

Qualitative Studies

There are often instances in which researchers wish to explore a phenomenon of interest in an open-ended fashion. The investigation of social influences on adult development such as, for example, personal relationships, may demand the researcher use a method that captures potentially relevant factors within a broad spectrum of possible influences (Allen & Walker, 2000). The **qualitative method** allows for the exploration of such complex relationships outside the narrow restrictions and assumptions of quantitative methods. In other cases, researchers may be working in an area in which conventional methods are neither practical nor appropriate for the problem under investigation. Qualitative methods are also used in the analysis of life history information, which is likely to be highly varied from person to person and not easily translated into numbers. The main advantage for using qualitative methods is that they provide researchers with alternative ways to test their hypotheses. The qualitative method can be adapted in a flexible manner to the nature of the problem at hand.

Archival Research

In **archival research**, investigators use existing resources that contain data relevant to a question about aging. The archives might consist of a governmental data bank, or the records kept by an institution, school, or employer. Another source of archival data is newspaper or magazine reports.

An advantage of archival research is that the information is readily accessible, especially given the growth of Web-based data sets including those of the U.S Census. Data files can be downloaded directly from the Internet, or publications can be accessed using portable document files (PDFs) that are easily read and searched. Disadvantages are that the researcher does not necessarily have control over the form of the data. For instance, a governmental agency may keep records of employment by age that do not include information on specific occupations of interest to the researcher. Another disadvantage is that the material may not be systematically collected or recorded. Newspaper or school records, for example, may have information that is biased or incomplete.

Surveys

Researchers rely on the **survey method** to gain information about a sample that can then be generalized to a larger population. Surveys are typically short and easily administered with simple rating scales to use for answers. For instance, poll voters are surveyed on for whom they will

REENA ROSE SIBAYAN/The Jersey Journal/Landov LLC

Data from the 2010 U.S. Census are collected through survey methodology; the results become archived and available for historical analyses.

cast their ballots in upcoming elections. Occasionally, more intensive surveys may be given to gain in-depth knowledge about aging and its relationship to health behaviors, health risks, and symptoms. The U.S. Census is collected through survey methodology. However, it is considered archival in that it has extensive historical records going back to the year 1750 when the first U.S. Census was conducted.

The U.S. Census Bureau is redesigning the decennial (every 10 years) census by providing social, demographic, economic, and housing data annually for local U.S. communities. The American Community Survey (ACS) is a nationwide sample survey of approximately 3 million households collected every month on about 250,000 households. Many of the statistics we present in this book about families, work, and other key social indicators come from the ACS. The ACS website has many downloadable tables, making up-to-date statistics more accessible than has ever been the case in prior years (U.S. Bureau of the Census, 2013).

Surveys have the advantage of providing data that allow the researcher to gain insight into the behavior of more people than it would be possible to study in the laboratory or other testing site. They can be administered over the telephone or, increasingly, via the Web. Interview-based surveys given by trained administrators provide knowledge that is easily coded and analyzed while still providing comprehensive information about the behavior in question. Typically, however, surveys tend to be short, with questions that are subject to bias by respondents who may attempt to provide a favorable impression to the researcher. Consequently, although the data may be generalizable to a large population, the quality of the data itself may be limited.

However, surveys also offer the opportunity to gather data on far larger samples than would be possible in the laboratory. The Midlife in the United States Survey (MIDUS) was conducted in 1995 on over 7,100 adults ages 45 and older (MIDUS I). The investigators then received further funding to conduct follow-ups and were able to reach over 4,900 of the original participants in 2004 (MIDUS II). The interdisciplinary nature of MIDUS, the fact that it had a longitudinal component, and its inclusion of the midlife years has made it an important data source for studies spanning such wide-ranging areas as genetics, personality, mental and physical health, and sociodemographic factors.

Epidemiological Studies

Governments, funding agencies, or interested researchers often need to gather data on the frequency of a particular disease in the population. **Epidemiology** is the study of the distribution and determinants of health-related states or events (including disease), and the application of this study to the control of diseases and other health problems (World Health Organization, 2013).

An epidemiological study may use a survey methodology in which questionnaires asking about a particular disease or set of diseases are sent to a representative sample of the population. Epidemiologists may also collect data through interviews and, increasingly, by obtaining biological samples for genetic and genomic analysis.

The results of epidemiological studies can provide researchers with two types of population estimates. **Prevalence statistics** provide estimates of the percentage of people who have *ever* had symptoms in a particular period.

Incidence statistics provide estimates of the percentage of people who *first* develop symptoms in a given period. For example, the lifetime prevalence of a disorder signifies what percentage of the population had the disease at any time since they were born. A one-year incidence estimate would tell you what percentage of the population develops symptoms of the disease within a one-year period.

Case Reports

When researchers want to provide an in-depth analysis of particular individuals, they use the **case report**, which summarizes the findings from multiple sources for those individuals. Data may be integrated from interviews, psychological tests, observations, archival records, or even journal and diary entries. The focus of the case report is on the characteristics of the individual and what has influenced his or her development and life experiences. Personal narratives may also be obtained with this method, in which individuals describe their lives as they have experienced them along with their ideas about why their lives have evolved in a given manner.

Although the case report has the benefit of providing insights into the lives of individuals as they change over time, it relies heavily on clinical judgments by the researcher. Therefore, for a case report to provide valuable information, a high level of expertise is required so that the findings are presented in a manner that balances the objective facts with the subjective analysis of the researcher.

Focus Groups

A less formal research method is a **focus group**, which is a meeting of respondents asked to provide feedback about a particular topic of interest. In a focus group, an investigator attempts to identify important themes in the discussion and keep the conversation oriented to these themes. The goal is to develop concrete research questions to pursue in subsequent studies. For example, attitudes toward mental health providers by older adults may be assessed by a focus group in which participants 65 and older share their concerns and experiences with counselors and therapists.

An advantage of the focus group is that issues can be identified prior to conducting a more systematic investigation. This approach, often considered a pilot study, is particularly useful when little preexisting research on the topic is available. An obvious disadvantage is that the method is not particularly systematic, and the data cannot readily be analyzed or systematically interpreted.

Daily Diaries

Researchers who wish to examine the day-to-day variations in a measure of interest use the **daily diary method** in which participants enter data on a daily basis. The data may consist of ratings on such variables as happiness, perceived stress, or interactions with friends, family, or co-workers. The participants may be asked to record their ratings at the same time every day, or they may be sent messages on a mobile device reminding them to enter their data. Typically, these studies are carried out over a period of weeks or months.

By obtaining data on a frequent basis over a period of time, researchers can track small variations in conditions that they believe may influence people's day-to-day functioning. Moreover, the statistical analyses made possible by these numerous data points provide researchers with more extensive information than they could obtain by single-point investigations.

Observational Methods

In the **observational method**, researchers draw conclusions about behavior through careful and systematic examination in particular settings. Recordings may be made using videotapes or behavioral records. In one type of observational method known as participant observation, the researcher participates in the activities of the respondents. For example, a researcher may wish to find out about the behavior of staff in a nursing home. The researcher may spend several days living with people in the nursing home. The researcher's subjective experiences would become part of the "data."

There are elaborate procedures available for creating behavioral records in which the researcher precisely defines the behavior to be observed (the number of particular acts) and specifies the times during which records will be made. This procedure may be used to determine whether an intervention is having its intended effects. If an investigator is testing a method to reduce aggressive behavior in people with Alzheimer's disease, behavioral records could be made before and after the intervention is introduced. After observing the effects of the intervention, the method's effectiveness could be determined by a return to baseline condition to assess whether the aggressive behavior increases without the intervention.

Meta-Analysis

In comparing the findings across investigations that examined similar phenomena, researchers can take advantage of **meta-analysis**, a statistical procedure that allows them to combine findings from independently conducted studies. For example, it is common for multiple researchers to test the effect of a particular psychological treatment, such as psychotherapy. The investigator who conducts the meta-analysis sets criteria for including particular studies such as the type of therapy, use of similar outcome measures, and gender distribution of the sample. Then the investigator calculates a statistic that reflects the extent of the therapy's effect, known as the "effect size." This statistic can then be used to estimate, across studies, the statistical significance of the outcomes observed in the studies included in the analysis.

Studies on aging also benefit from meta-analysis. In these cases, investigations that include estimates of age differences or age changes can then be compared using a single statistic. That statistic then provides an estimate that incorporates all the studies that the researcher includes.

Meta-analysis is far superior to the approaches previously used in which researchers would have no statistical basis for comparing one study with another. Although somewhat rare at this point in the field, with the accumulation of more research investigating similar problems, these may become more common and therefore provide a more accurate picture of how a given variable or set of variables change over the adult years.

MEASUREMENT ISSUES IN ADULT DEVELOPMENT AND AGING

Research designs, no matter how cleverly engineered, are unable to yield worthwhile results if the methods used to collect the data are flawed. Researchers in adult development and aging, like all other scientists, must concern themselves with the quality of the instruments they use to capture data. The task is made more difficult because the instruments must be usable with people who are likely to vary in ability, educational background, and sophistication with research instruments. Earlier we pointed out the problems involved in comparing older and younger adults on measures used in cross-sectional studies. Here we will look specifically at some of the ways developmental researchers can ensure that their measures are equivalent across age groups.

The first measurement issue to consider is that of **reliability**. A measure is reliable if it yields consistent results every time it is used. The importance of reliability is highlighted by considering the analogy of measurements used in cooking. If your tablespoon were unreliable (say, it was made of floppy plastic), the amount of ingredients added would vary with every use. Your cookies may be hard and crunchy one time and soft and gooey the next. A psychological test must also provide similar scores upon repeated administration. This principle is one of the first qualities psychologists look for in a measure—its ability to provide consistent scores. Reliability can be assessed by test–retest reliability, which is determined by giving the test on two occasions to assess whether respondents receive similar scores across both administrations. Another form of reliability relates to internal consistency, which indicates whether respondents answer similarly on comparable items.

The second criterion used to evaluate a test is **validity**, meaning that the test measures what it is supposed to measure. A test of intelligence should measure intelligence, not how good your vision is. Returning to the example in the kitchen, if a tablespoon were marked "teaspoon," it

Michael Newman/PhotoEdit

In a behavioral observation, researchers collect data by counting the frequency of specific behaviors.

would not be measuring what it is supposed to measure, and your baked products would be ruined. Tablespoons are fairly easy to assess for validity; however, psychological tests unfortunately present a far greater challenge. For this reason, validity is a much more difficult quality to capture than reliability.

The concept of validity varies depending on the intended use of the measure. Content validity provides an indication of whether a test designed to assess factual material accurately measures that material. Your next exam may very well include questions testing how well you have understood the topics covered in this chapter. Criterion validity indicates whether a test score accurately predicts performance on an indicator measure, as would be used in a test of vocational ability that claims to predict success on the job. Finally, construct validity is used to assess the extent to which a measure intended to assess a psychological construct is able to do so.

Construct validity is difficult to establish and requires two types of evidence: convergent and discriminant validity. Convergent validity is needed to determine that the measure relates to other measures that are of theoretical similarity. A test of intelligence should have a positive relationship to another test of intelligence that has been well validated. Discriminant validity demonstrates that the measure does not relate to other measures that have no theoretical relationship to it. A test of intelligence should not be correlated with a test of personality, unless the personality test assesses some aspect of intelligence.

Although psychologists are generally aware of the need to establish the reliability and validity of measures used in both research and practical settings, less attention is focused on psychometric properties when used in gerontological research. Measures whose reliability and validity were established on young adult samples are often used inappropriately without testing their applicability to samples of adults of varying ages. The process can become quite complicated. If Form A of a measure is found to be psychometrically sound with college students but only Form B has adequate reliability and validity for older adults, the researcher is faced with the prospect of having to use different forms of a test within the same study. Nevertheless, sensitivity to measurement issues is crucial if conclusions drawn from the research are to have value.

ETHICAL ISSUES IN RESEARCH

All scientists who engage in research with humans or other animals must take precautions to protect the rights of their participants. In extreme cases, such as in medical research, the life of an individual may be at stake if he or she is subjected to risky procedures. Research in which respondents are tested or put through stressful experimental manipulations also requires that standard protocols are followed. Recognizing the importance of these considerations, the American Psychological Association developed a comprehensive set of guidelines for psychologists that includes the appropriate treatment of human participants in research (American Psychological Association, 2003). We have summarized the main features of these guidelines in Table 3.4.

Researchers must present a potential respondent as full a disclosure as possible of the risks and benefits of becoming involved in any research project. When the individual is a minor child or an adult who is not able to make independent decisions, the researcher is obligated to inform the individual's legal guardian about the nature of the study. Having provided information about the study, the researcher must then obtain a legal signature indicating that the participant understands the risks and benefits involved in the study. At this point the researcher is able to obtain the full **informed consent** of the respondent or the respondent's legal representative. When the individual is an animal, the researcher is similarly bound to ensure that the animal is not mishandled or subjected to unnecessary harm, although different protective procedures are followed.

TABLE 3.4

Summary of APA Ethical Guidelines for Research on Human Participants

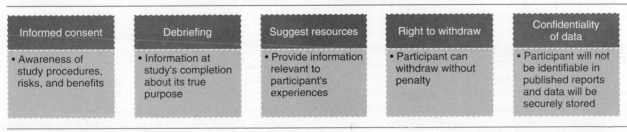

Informed consent	Debriefing	Suggest resources	Right to withdraw	Confidentiality of data
• Awareness of study procedures, risks, and benefits	• Information at study's completion about its true purpose	• Provide information relevant to participant's experiences	• Participant can withdraw without penalty	• Participant will not be identifiable in published reports and data will be securely stored

Source: Adapted from American Psychological Association. (2003). Ethical Principles of Psychologists and Code of Conduct. Retrieved from http://www .apa.org/ethics/code2002.html&8_02.

Research participants are also entitled to know what the study was about after completion in a process called **debriefing**. If you have ever participated in research, you may have been curious during the course of the study to know what was being tested. In some cases you might have been surprised to find out about the "real" purpose of the study. Perhaps you were told that you were going to be asked to fill out a series of questionnaires in a quiet laboratory room. In the middle of the questionnaire, you hear a loud noise in the hallway, followed by a man screaming. Although you may think the point of the study is to gather information about you, the goal of the research was to assess your response to the sudden commotion. After the experiment is over, the researcher is obligated to tell you the truth about the purpose of the study. You may be embarrassed if in fact you did not get up to help, but you at least had a right to know that you were being tested on this attribute. The debriefing might make you feel better because you would realize that your response of not helping reflected the experimental manipulation rather than a malevolent personality attribute you possess.

As this example illustrates, research participants may learn information about themselves that is potentially upsetting or damaging. In fact, ethical guidelines for research in psychology dictate that the researcher not only provide feedback but also must be ready to suggest support or counseling for people who become distressed while involved in the experiment. Respondents are also entitled to withdraw from a study without risk of penalty should they choose to do so. The experimenter should not coerce them into completing the study, and even if they decide to discontinue participation, they should still receive whatever reimbursement was initially promised. If they are students in a class or clients receiving services (such as hospital patients), they should not fear having their grades lowered or services withheld from them.

Finally, research participants are entitled to know what will happen to their data. In all cases, the data must be kept confidential, meaning that only the research team will have access to the information provided by the participants. The other condition usually attached to the data is that of anonymity. Participants are guaranteed that their names will not be associated with their responses. The condition of anonymity obviously cannot be kept if the study is a longitudinal one because the researchers must maintain access to names for follow-up purposes. In this case, the condition of confidentiality applies, and the researchers are obligated to ensure that all records are kept private and secure.

These ethical standards are enforced in all institutions receiving federal or local funding for research through Institutional Review Boards (IRBs), which review all proposed studies to be carried out at that institution or by anyone employed by that institution. These reviews ensure that the rights of research participants are adequately protected according to the criteria discussed above. In addition, the American Psychological Association's ethical guidelines ensure that studies conducted specifically in the field of psychology meet predetermined criteria for protection of human and animal subjects. An important development in the area of protection of human participants was the implementation in April 2003 of national standards within the United States to protect the privacy of personal health information. The Health Insurance Portability and Accountability Act, referred to as HIPAA, is the first-ever federal privacy standards to protect patients' medical records and other health information provided to health plans, doctors, hospitals and other health care providers. HIPAA protects research participants by ensuring that a researcher must meet standards to maintain the privacy of health-related information. With these guidelines in place, there is assurance that respondents in research will be appropriately treated.

SUMMARY

1. The study of aging is intimately linked with the passage of time, making research on aging difficult to design and implement. A variable is a characteristic that "varies" from individual to individual. The dependent variable is the outcome that researchers observe while the independent variable is the factor that the researcher manipulates. In experimental study designs, researchers decide on conditions that will allow them to manipulate a particular independent variable based on the question of interest using random assignment. Because aging can never be randomly assigned, studies on aging are considered quasi-experimental.

2. Descriptive research designs include longitudinal and cross-sectional. Both of these designs are quasi-experimental because they do not involve the manipulation of age as an independent variable. Each has advantages and disadvantages, but the main problem is that they do not allow for generalizations to be made beyond a single cohort or period of history.

3. The variables in developmental research are age, cohort, and time of measurement. Age represents processes going on within the individual, and cohort and time of measurement are regarded as measures of social aging. These three variables are interdependent because as soon as two are known, the third is determined. Cohort effects refer to the social, historical, and culture influences that affect people during a particular period of time.

4. Longitudinal research designs involve people being followed repeatedly from one test occasion to another in an attempt to determine whether participants have changed over time as the result of the aging process. A variant of longitudinal research is the prospective study, in which researchers sample from a population of interest before they develop a particular type of illness or experience a particular type of life event. Longitudinal designs have several limitations, including selective attrition, terminal decline, practice effects, outdated tests, and length of time to follow the results. A variety of methods can be employed to account for these limitations.

5. A cross-sectional design compares groups of people of different ages at one point in time and is the more frequently used method in research on aging. The challenge of cross-sectional designs is to ensure that the effects of age are studied rather than differences between cohorts. Researchers design cross-sectional studies to control for cohort effects as best as possible. Limitations of cross-sectional research include concerns about survival effects, unrepresentative populations, age range definitions, test material reaction, and task equivalence. Despite these drawbacks, researchers employ a variety of controls to ensure that differences other than age are kept to a minimum.

6. Sequential designs consist of different combinations of the variables age, cohort, and time of measurement, and attempt to control for the effects of social aging by allowing researchers to make estimates of the influence of factors other than age on performance. The Most Efficient Design was developed by Schaie to provide a framework for three types of sequential studies and involves a set of three designs manipulating the variables of age, cohort, and time of measurement.

7. Correlational designs involve studying the relationship between age (or another variable) and other measures of interest. A simple correlational design involves two variables, and a multivariate correlational design involves analyzing relationships among multiple variables. Structural equation modeling is a form of multivariate correlational analysis in which complex models involving age can be statistically evaluated. In hierarchical linear modeling, patterns of change over time are analyzed, taking into account individual differences in change.

8. There are several methods of research available to investigators who study aging. In the laboratory study, conditions are controlled and data are collected in an objective manner. Qualitative studies allow for exploration using an open-ended method. Archival research uses existing records, such as census data or newspaper records. Surveys involve asking people to provide answers to structured questions, with the intention of generalizing to larger populations. Epidemiologic studies gather data on the frequency of a particular disease in the population. Case reports are used to provide in-depth analyses of an individual or small group of individuals. Focus groups gather information about people's views on particular topics. Observational methods provide objective data on people in specific settings and under specific conditions. Meta-analysis allows for a statistical procedure that allows researchers to combine findings from independently conducted studies.

9. Researchers in adult development and aging must concern themselves with finding the most appropriate measurement tools available. The science of studying measurement instruments is known as psychometrics. Of particular concern is the need to establish the appropriateness of the same measurement instrument for adults of different ages. Reliability refers to the consistency of a measurement instrument, and validity assesses whether the instrument measures what it is intended to measure.

10. Ethical issues in research address the proper treatment of participants by researchers. Informed consent is the requirement that respondents be given adequate knowledge about a study's procedures before they participate. Debriefing refers to notification of participants about the study's real purpose. Respondents also have the right to withdraw at any time without penalty. Finally, respondents must be told what will happen to their data, but at all times the data must be kept confidential. All research institutions in the United States are required by federal law to guarantee the rights of human and animal subjects.

4

Physical Changes

AGING TODAY
Six Reasons to Exercise

We all know that exercise and physical activity are good for us. Unfortunately, this does not always translate into action. Embarking on a workout can fall to the bottom of our to-do list in the face of life's many stresses. In this chapter we focus on a variety of physical changes that can accompany the aging process, and highlight the role that physical activity plays in coping with these changes. Before we begin, we want to provide you with some food for thought about the benefits of physical activity.

1. Exercise builds aerobic power and improves breathing. Ordinarily, people lose about 1% of their aerobic power each year, or, if you'd like to do the math, 10% per decade. That's a lot of unnecessary huffing and puffing. Both long- and short-term exercise training studies show that you can cut this loss in half, so that you lose 15% rather than 30% in a 30-year period.

2. Exercise reduces blood pressure, the number one form of heart disease, by giving your heart a workout. The stronger your heart muscle gets, the greater its ability to pump blood through the arteries, which also helps to reduce your blood pressure.

3. Exercise lowers the risk of type 2 diabetes, an illness that is becoming a worldwide public health crisis. Even if you don't care about the health of the world, you should care about your risk of diabetes. The complications of adult-onset type 2 diabetes pose a serious risk to your physical well-being. By engaging in regular physical exercise, you improve your body's ability to metabolize glucose, the key to staving off this disease.

4. Exercise maintains the functioning of your auto-immune system, protecting you from infection and other chemical toxins. Even short-term exercise programs can reverse some of the deleterious effects of aging on this sensitive, complex, and crucial regulatory system that controls so much of your everyday health.

5. Exercise helps keep bones strong and build muscle mass. At a rate of 1% loss per year for both bone mineral strength and muscle mass, it is important to engage in resistance or strength training to offset this loss.

6. Exercise can also lower your risk of developing dementia based on cardiovascular illness by improving the flow of blood throughout your body, including your brain. Preserving the neurons in your brain can give you an added advantage should you develop dementia. It's even possible that exercise can help slow or prevent Alzheimer's disease by improving your glucose and fat metabolism; some of the brain alterations found in Alzheimer's disease may be due to abnormalities in these processes.

Posted by Susan Whitbourne and Stacey Whitbourne

In this chapter, we examine changes in the body, brain, and sensory systems throughout middle and later adulthood and demonstrate how these changes interact with an individual's identity. People's feelings about themselves strongly reflect perceptions of their physical appearance and competence. Furthermore, reflecting the interactionist model of development, physical changes affect a person's behavior, which, in turn, can modify the actions the individual takes to slow or modify those changes. As people experience mobility changes, for example, they may exercise less often, which further exacerbates these alterations in mobility.

Following the interactionist model, you will find that there are ways to prevent many age-related changes, or at least substantially slow them down. If you adopt these changes now, you can grow older more successfully, regardless of your current age. You will see that we frequently suggest physical activity. We admit we have a bias toward adopting and maintaining a physically active lifestyle: we are both avid exercisers. However, it may surprise you to see just how beneficial this lifestyle can be.

Changes that occur in the body reflect social factors such as class, race, and gender. These social factors, in turn, affect how people interpret changes in their physical functioning. For example, women in Western culture are socialized to care more about their appearance than are men. This means that women are more likely to feel differently about themselves as they age. However, women may also be more likely to take preventative steps to maintain their appearance.

Throughout this chapter, we will explore the interactions of physical changes with identity and social context and look at how people are affected by the way in which they age.

APPEARANCE

When you think about which physical changes are the most telling about the aging process, wrinkles and gray hair are generally at the top of the list. Even though these outward signs are not necessarily good indicators of what is happening inside the body, many adults regard these as the most important aspects of the changes that occur as they get older.

Skin

Skin, the largest organ in the body, is most vulnerable to a series of age-related changes that become visible as early as the 20s and continue throughout adulthood.

The first signs of aging generally appear in the 30s, when the skin starts to show small wrinkles, slight drooping or loss of resilience, and some changes in color and texture. Later, the skin also becomes more translucent, and it is easier to see the underlying bones and veins, particularly in the hands. Skin discolorations and small outgrowths accumulate, so that by the 50s, the skin (particularly in the face) shows distinctive marks of the passage of time.

What you see on the skin's surface reflects the changes that occur underneath. The outermost layer of the skin, known as the **epidermis**, consists of a thin covering that protects the underlying tissue. Over time, and not visible to the naked eye, the epidermal skin cells lose their regular patterning. The **dermis**, the middle layer of the skin, contains protein molecules of collagen and elastin, among which various nerve cells, glands, and the hair follicles reside (see Figure 4.1).

Over time, collagen undergoes the cross-linking process we described in Chapter 2, leading the skin to become less flexible. Elastin, a molecule that is supposed to provide flexibility, becomes less able to return to its original shape after it is stretched during a person's movements. With the changes in collagen and elastin, the skin eventually can no longer return to its original state of tension and begins to sag. At the same time, the sebaceous glands, which normally provide oils that lubricate the skin, become less active. Consequently, the skin surface becomes drier and more vulnerable to damage from being rubbed or chafed.

The **subcutaneous** fat layer is the bottom-most layer of skin, giving the skin its opacity and smoothing the curves of the arms, legs, and face. Starting in middle adulthood, this layer starts to thin, providing less support for the layers above it, which then exacerbates the wrinkling and sagging caused by changes in the dermis. The blood vessels beneath the skin therefore become more visible.

The skin's coloring also changes over the course of adulthood, most visibly in fair-skinned people. People develop discolored areas referred to in colloquial terms as "age spots" (officially called *lentigo senilis*). These areas of brown pigmentation that show up on the skin of fair-skinned people are more likely to occur in the sun-exposed areas of the face, hands, and arms. Also developing on the skin are pigmented outgrowths (moles) and elevations of small blood vessels on the skin surface (angiomas).

Nails are a part of the skin and are also subject to age-related changes. Toenails, in particular, grow more slowly and may become yellowed, thicker, and ridged. In addition to normal age-related changes in the nails, many older adults develop fungal infections in their toenails, causing the nails to thicken and separate from the nail bed. Older adults with limited joint movement and flexibility

FIGURE 4.1

Cross-Section of the Skin

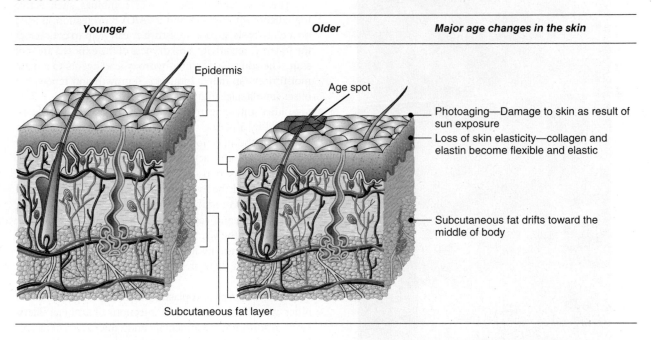

Younger	*Older*	*Major age changes in the skin*

Epidermis

Age spot

Photoaging—Damage to skin as result of sun exposure

Loss of skin elasticity—collagen and elastin become flexible and elastic

Subcutaneous fat drifts toward the middle of body

Subcutaneous fat layer

experience more difficulty caring for their own feet and lower extremities (Mitty, 2009).

The general changes that occur in the skin contribute to the aging of the face; however, the face's underlying structure also changes as a result of bone loss in the skull, particularly in the jaw. Changes in the cartilage of the nose and ears cause them to become longer, further altering the face's shape. The muscles of the face also lose their ability to contract; this means that a face that is smiling becomes more similar to a face at rest (Desai, Upadhyay, & Nanda, 2009).

Loss of enamel surface leads the teeth to become yellow: stains accumulate from a lifetime intake of coffee and tea, certain types of food, and—for smokers—tobacco. With increasing age, many people lose their teeth, a process that affects not only their appearance but aspects of their health in general. In the United States, about 26% of all adults 65 and older have lost all their natural teeth (Schoenborn & Heyman, 2009). The rates are double for people in lower income brackets and those without private medical insurance. Middle-aged adults may suffer less from problems related to tooth loss than previous generations; this is due to improvements in dental hygiene in the past several decades, particularly increased rates of flossing.

Nevertheless, some changes in the teeth are bound to occur—and if not in the teeth, then in the gums (Deng, Miao, Liu, Meng, & Wu, 2009).

Changes in the skin also affect the appearance of the eyes, which develop bags, small lines at the creases ("crows feet"), areas of dark pigmentation, and puffiness. The need for eyeglasses, which increases in middle adulthood as we discuss later in this chapter, means further changes.

Genetic background plays an important role in the rate of skin aging. Fair-skinned people tend to display more rapid effects of aging than those with darker skin. Above and beyond genetic inheritance, lifestyle habits are perhaps the next greatest influence on the aging of the skin. The most significant lifestyle habit is exposure to the sun; radiation from the sun causes age changes known as **photoaging** (Coelho et al., 2009). The sun's ultraviolet rays accelerate the process of cross-linking, causing mutations that alter protein synthesis by the cells and increasing the production of free radicals. Other harmful habits can interact with exposure to the sun, most notably cigarette smoke (Burke & Wei, 2009).

This list of changes in the skin is daunting, indeed. Many of these changes are intrinsic to the aging process, but even these vary depending on the individual's lifestyle

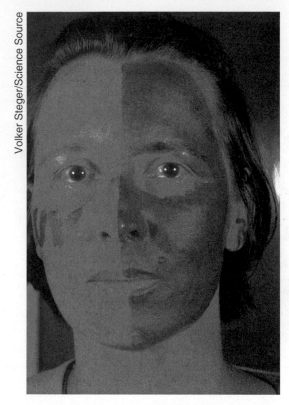

Volker Steger/Science Source

The photo demonstrates how sun damaged skin looks under UV light.

tretinoin (the active ingredient in retinol) (Tucker-Samaras et al., 2009).

The best type of moisturizer combines such active ingredients with SPF-15 and UVA/UVB protection. If used on a daily basis, a good moisturizer can help to counteract the fragility, sensitivity, and dryness of the exposed areas of skin. The addition of alpha-hydroxy acid agents to a basic moisturizer can help stimulate cell growth and renewal to offset sun damage (Yamamoto et al., 2006).

Other antiaging treatments for the face can only be provided by a plastic surgeon or dermatologist. The most popular is the injection of botulinum toxin (Botox®). In a Botox treatment, a syringe containing a small amount of a nerve poison is injected into the area of concern, such as around the eyes or in the middle of the forehead muscle. This procedure paralyzes the muscle, relaxing the skin around it and causing a temporary reduction in the appearance of the wrinkle. Although cosmetics companies have invested heavily in finding over-the-counter alternatives, at present there are no substitutes for this procedure (Beer, 2006).

Dermatologists and plastic surgeons perform a host of other antiaging interventions: injections of artificial fillers, laser resurfacing treatments, and microdermabrasion. Increasingly, products that simulate these procedures are being introduced into the market; in the coming years, people who seek to reverse or alter the facial aging process will have a wider variety of affordable and convenient options.

Hair

One of the most obvious changes to occur as the body ages is the graying of the hair. But less obvious is the fact that the hair does not, literally, turn gray. Instead, the number of pigmented (colored) hairs diminishes over time while the number of hairs that are no longer pigmented increases. Hair loses its pigment when the production of melanin, which gives hair its color, slows and eventually ceases. It is very likely that by the time a person reaches the age of 75 or 80, there are virtually no naturally colored hairs left on the scalp or other hair-covered areas of the body. There are variations in the rate at which this change takes place. You may have an older relative or friend whose hair is only slightly gray or, conversely, know people in their 20s who have a significant amount of gray hair already.

The thinning of the hair, though more visible in men, actually occurs in both sexes. In general, hair loss results from the destruction of the germination centers that

habits. The most significant is the use of sunscreen. Because it is not possible to avoid the sun's rays completely, people who want to protect themselves from photoaging should use sunscreen with a sun protection factor (SPF) of at least 15. The sunscreen should also block both UVA and UVB light.

Though most health-conscious people are aware of the importance of sunscreen, even the most knowledgeable may not completely understand how to use it properly (Wang & Dusza, 2009). Others may know, but not care. Younger adults, in particular, continue to tan excessively, either outdoors or in a tanning salon. The cosmetics industry—taking advantage of many people's desire for a youthful appearance—is flooding the marketplace with new antiaging products. Although many of the early formulations were nothing more than glorified moisturizers, newer entries use technology developed from advances in the biology of aging combined with the improved delivery systems of such ingredients as collagen and

FIGURE 4.2

Forms of Male and Female Pattern Baldness

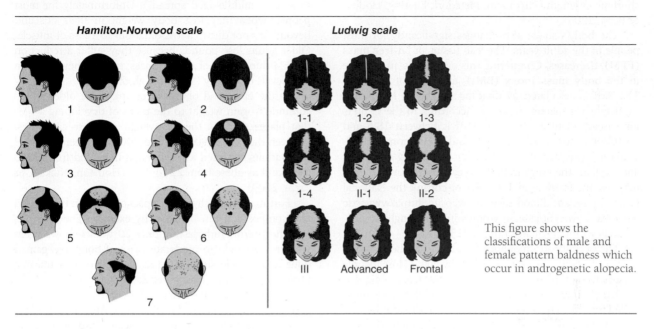

This figure shows the classifications of male and female pattern baldness which occur in androgenetic alopecia.

produce the hair in the hair follicles (see Figure 4.2). The most common form of hair loss with increased age is male and female pattern hair loss, technically known as **androgenetic alopecia**. This is a condition that affects 95% of adult men and 20% of adult women, to some degree. Androgenetic alopecia causes the hair follicles to stop producing the long, thick, pigmented hair known as terminal hair and instead produce short, fine, unpigmented and largely invisible hair known as vellus hair. Eventually, even the vellus hair is not visible, because it no longer protrudes from the follicle, which itself has shrunk. Although hair stops growing on the top of the head where it is desired, it may appear in larger amounts in places where it is not welcome, such as the chin on women, the ears, and in thicker clumps around the eyebrows in men.

Pharmaceutical companies are actively working to find a solution for baldness. The multitude of products designed to stop or mask the balding process range from chemicals applied directly to the scalp, most notably topical minoxidil (Rogaine), to herbal remedies and surgically implanted hair plugs. Available by prescription only, oral finasteride (Propecia) is another alternative. Although there is no "cure" for gray hair or baldness, improvements in products that stimulate hair growth and the

production of melanin are probably not far off in the future. Researchers are currently investigating the efficacy of a steroid used in treating a condition in which the prostate gland becomes enlarged (which we discuss later in the chapter) as a way to reverse hair loss in men (Alsantali & Shapiro, 2009).

BODY BUILD

The concept of being "grown up" implies that you are done growing and your body has reached its final, mature form. However, throughout adulthood, the body is a dynamic entity, continuously changing in size and shape. By the time people reach their 50s and 60s, their bodies may have only a passing resemblance to what they looked like when they first reached physical maturity.

The first set of changes in body build involves height. Cross-sectional and longitudinal studies convincingly show that people get shorter as they get older, a process that is more pronounced for women. So although you may think of yourself as 5 foot 9 now and for the rest of your life, the chances are good that you will lose as much as an inch of height over the coming decades. This loss of height is due to the loss of bone material in the vertebrae. With the weakening of the vertebrae, the spine collapses and shortens in length (Pfirrmann, Metzdorf, Elfering, Hodler, & Boos, 2006).

The body's shape also changes significantly for most people in the adult years. The lean tissue, or **fat-free mass (FFM)**, decreases. Countering this decrease is an increase in the **body mass index (BMI)**, an index of body fat. The BMI is calculated by dividing weight (in kilograms) by height (in meters squared). According to the Centers for Disease Control, the ideal BMI is between 18.5 and 25 (Centers for Disease Control and Prevention, 2010a). Table 4.1 presents the formula for calculating your BMI and explains the range in BMI. To calculate your BMI, you may use the formula in Table 4.1 or consult the National Heart, Lung, and Blood Institute website: http://www.cdc.gov/healthyweight/assessing/bmi/adult_bmi/english_bmi_calculator/bmi_calculator.html (2013).

The overall pattern of body weight in adulthood shows an upside-down U-shaped trend by age. Most people experience an increase in their weight from their 20s until their mid-50s, after which they tend to lose those added pounds. The weight gain during middle adulthood is mainly due to an increase in BMI (Ding, Cicuttini, Blizzard, Scott, & Jones, 2007) representing the accumulation of body fat around the waist and hips (commonly referred to as the "middle-aged spread"). Unfortunately for most people, when they lose body weight in their 60s and beyond, it's not due to a loss of fat but to a loss of muscle. Older adults lose pounds because they suffer a reduction of FFM due to loss of muscle mass, even if they maintain high levels of activity (Manini et al., 2009).

At the other end of the spectrum, some older adults continue to gain weight to the point of developing a BMI that places them in the overweight or obese categories. Between the mid-1990s and mid-2000s, the percentage of older adults classified as overweight increased from 60 to 69%, and as obese from 22 to 31% (Houston, Nicklas, & Zizza, 2009).

Fortunately, much of the impact of aging on body build and composition can be offset by exercise. For example, one short-term study lasting only 20 weeks showed that women with mild to moderate cases of bone loss gained bone and muscle strength in as a result of this training (Tolomio, Ermolao, Travain, & Zaccaria, 2008).

On the basis of extensive research on both short- and long-term exercise benefits, the American College of Sports Medicine and the American Heart Association

TABLE 4.1
Calculate and Interpret Your BMI

Measurement Units	Formula and Calculation
Kilograms and meters (or centimeters)	Formula: weight (kg) / [height (m)]^2. With the metric system, the formula for BMI is weight in kilograms divided by height in meters squared.
	Since height is commonly measured in centimeters, divide height in centimeters by 100 to obtain height in meters.
	Example: Weight = 68 kg, Height = 165 cm (1.65 m) Calculation: $68 \div (1.65)^2 = 24.98$
Pounds and inches	Formula: weight (lb) / [height (in)]^2 x 703. Calculate BMI by dividing weight in pounds (lbs) by height in inches (in) squared and multiplying by a conversion factor of 703.
	Example: Weight = 150 lb, Height = 5'5" (65")
	Calculation: $[150 \div (65)^2]$ x 703 = 24.96

BMI	Weight Status
Below 18.5	Underweight
18.5—24.9	Normal
25.0—29.9	Overweight
30.0—39.9	Obese
40 and over	Extreme Obesity

Source: Centers for Disease Control and Prevention. (2010). About BMI for adults. Retrieved from http://www.cdc.gov/healthyweight/assessing/bmi/adult_bmi/index.html#Interpreted

(ACSM/AHA) (Chodzko-Zajko et al., 2009) recommend specific amounts and forms of exercise for older adults, as shown in Table 4.2.

These guidelines are meant to be adjusted for the older adult's individual needs. The ACSM/AHA states that the intensity and duration of physical activity should be low at the outset for older adults who are functionally limited or have chronic conditions that affect their ability to perform physical tasks. It recommends that the progression of activities should be tailored to the individual and that strength and/or balance training may need to precede aerobic training until the individual has gained some strength. Even if the individual is unable to engage in the minimum amount of activity, he or she should perform some type of physical activities to avoid being sedentary. For example, older adults who have impaired balance and mobility can be given chair aerobics to perform, such as raising and lowering their arms. Individuals who have mobility problems or are frequent fallers can be given balance training that includes progressively difficult postures, dynamic movements—such as turning in circles, heel stands, toe stands—and standing with their eyes closed.

Exercise, even in small doses, can have beneficial effects not only on physiological status but also on feelings of psychological well-being. Recall our discussion at the beginning of the chapter on the interactions of aging and identity. One intriguing study provides dramatic support for this relationship. Researchers tested older adults on a measure of "social physique anxiety," the extent to which one is afraid of what other people think of one's body. Over the course of a 6-month exercise training study, older adults decreased their social physique anxiety and felt more fit. They also gained on a measure of self-efficacy, or the feeling of confidence in being able to complete physically demanding tasks (McAuley, Marquez, Jerome, Blissmer, & Katula, 2002). In subsequent studies, social physique anxiety in middle-aged obese women predicted their level of involvement in physical activity (Ekkekakis, Lind, & Vazou, 2009).

MOBILITY

You are able to move around in your environment due to the actions of the structures that support this movement, including your bones, muscles, tendons, and ligaments. In the average person, all these structures undergo age-related changes that compromise their ability to function effectively.

Beginning in the 40s (or earlier in the case of injury), each component of mobility undergoes significant age-related losses. Consequently, people walk more slowly as they get older (Shumway-Cook et al., 2007). You have probably observed these changes when you're interacting with older relatives or friends, who tend to take longer than you to reach the same destination. Unfortunately, older adults may find it hard to adapt to their slower walking speed, leading them to be more likely than the young to make mistakes when predicting how long it will take them to cross the street (Lobjois & Cavallo, 2009). Thus, there are practical implications of these changes in mobility that can have far-reaching consequences on the older adult's life and health (see Figure 4.3).

Muscles

The adult years are characterized by a progressive age-related loss of muscle tissue, a process known as **sarcopenia**. The number and size of muscle fibers decrease, especially the fast-twitch muscle fibers that you use in speed and strength. As indicated by research from cross-sectional studies, muscle strength (as measured by maximum force) peaks in the 20s and 30s, remains at a plateau until the 40s to 50s, and then declines at a faster rate of 12 to 15% per decade (Kostka, 2005), with more pronounced decreases for men (at least in a cross-sectional view).

In contrast to the declines in speed and strength, people retain their muscular endurance, as measured by isometric strength (Lavender & Nosaka, 2007). There are

TABLE 4.2
Recommendations for Exercise from the American College of Sports Medicine and American Heart Association

Type of exercise	Frequency	Intensity (0–10 scale)	Duration	Type
Endurance	3–5 times per week, more if moderate, fewer if intense	5–6 for moderate 7–8 for intense	10 minutes for moderate 20 minutes for intense	Walking, swimming, or stationary cycle
Resistance	2 days per week	5–6 for moderate 7–8 for intense	8–10 exercises for each muscle group	8–12 repetitions per muscle group
Flexibility	2 days per week	5–6		Sustained stretches

Source: Chodzko-Zajko, W. J., Proctor, D. N., Fiatarone Singh, M. A., Minson, C. T., Nigg, C. R., Salem, G. J., et al. (2009). American College of Sports Medicine position stand. Exercise and physical activity for older adults. *Medicine & Science in Sports & Exercise, 41*, 1510–1530 Wolters Kluwer Health.

FIGURE 4.3

Age-Related Changes in Muscles, Bones, and Joints

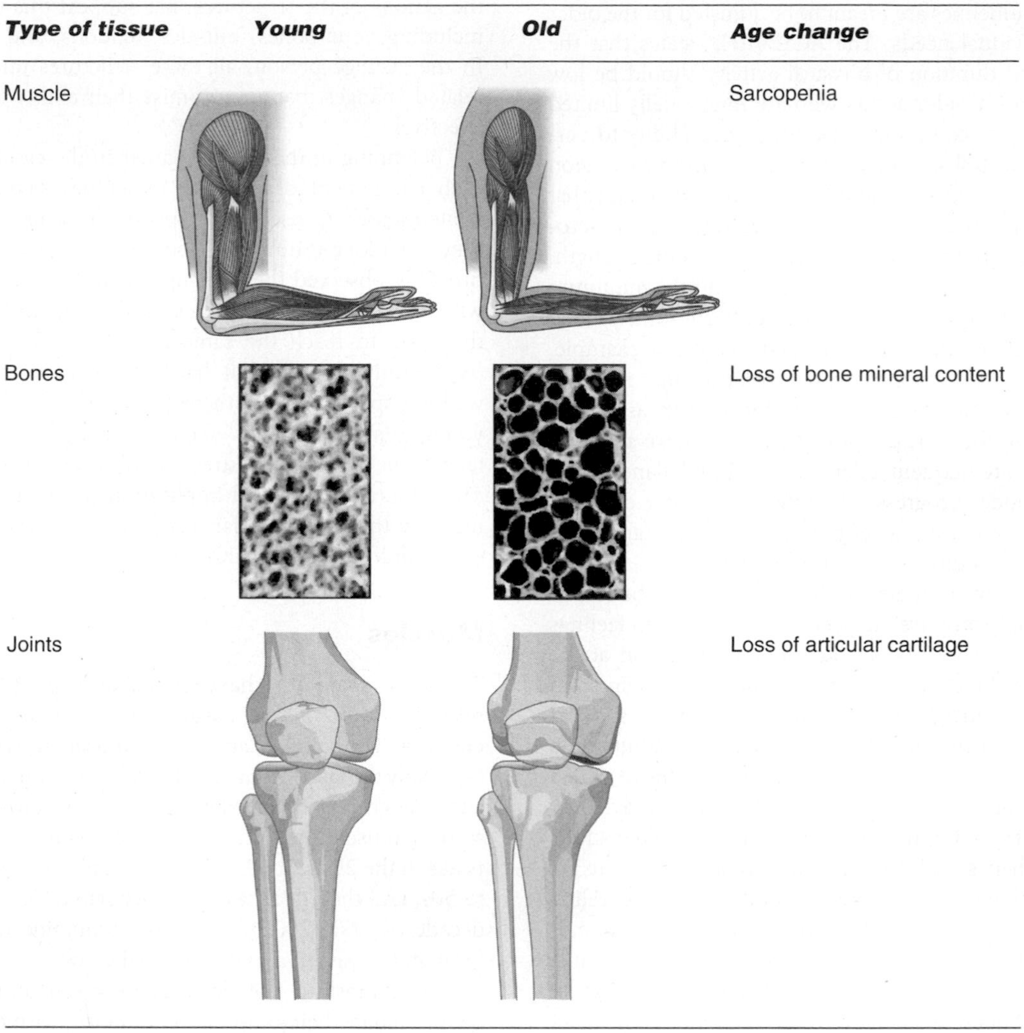

Type of tissue	Young	Old	Age change
Muscle			Sarcopenia
Bones			Loss of bone mineral content
Joints			Loss of articular cartilage

also relatively minor effects of age on eccentric strength, the action involved in such activities as lowering arm weights (such as the downward motion of a bicep curl) or going down the stairs. Eccentric strength is preserved through the 70s and 80s in men and women (Roig et al., 2010).

Changes in muscle mass strongly, but not entirely, predict age-related reductions in strength in adulthood (Raj, Bird, & Shield, 2010). One other contributor to loss of muscle strength comes from disrupted signals that the nervous system sends to the muscles telling them to contract (Klass, Baudry, & Duchateau, 2006). Third, the tendons become stiffer, which makes it more difficult to move the joint and thus exert muscular strength (Carroll et al., 2008).

The loss of muscle mass brings with it a set of negative consequences, including increased risk of falling, limitations in mobility, and reduced quality of everyday life. Unfortunately, sarcopenia can become part of a vicious cycle: the greater the loss of muscle mass, the greater the difficulty in undertaking exercise, leading to more muscle loss weakening (Lang et al., 2009). If sarcopenia occurs in the presence of gains in fat, a condition known as sarcopenic obesity may develop, in which the individual both loses muscle and gains body fat (Zamboni, Mazzali, Fantin, Rossi, & Di Francesco, 2008).

Strength training with free weights or resistance machines is the top preventative measure that can counteract the process of sarcopenia in adulthood (Jones et al., 2009). Although older adults do not achieve as high a degree of improvement as do younger adults, even a program as short as 16 weeks of resistance training can build fast-twitch muscle fiber numbers to the size of those found in the young (Kosek, Kim, Petrella, Cross, & Bamman, 2006). There seems to be no age limit on who can benefit, as adults in their 90s also show improvements in muscle strength after training (Kryger & Andersen, 2007).

Effective muscle strength training typically involves 8 to 12 weeks, three to four times per week, at 70 to 90% of the one-repetition maximum. In order for these benefits to be maintained, the individual has to keep exercising. It's not enough to exercise for a year or two and then stop. Aerobic exercise can provide additional benefits to boost the effects of muscle training (Harber et al., 2009).

One of the major benefits of muscle training is that the stronger the muscles become, the more pull they exert on the bones. As we will see next, loss of bone strength is as, if not more, significant a limitation on the health and well-being of older adults than is loss of muscle mass.

Bones

Bone is living tissue. It constantly reconstructs itself through a process of **bone remodeling**, in which old cells are destroyed and replaced by new cells. The general pattern of bone development in adulthood involves an increase in the rate of bone destruction compared to renewal and greater porosity of the calcium matrix, leading to loss of bone mineral content. The remodeling process that leads to these changes is controlled in part by a set of protein-like substances that act on the bone cells (Cao et al., 2005). These substances are, in turn, under the influence of the sex hormones estrogen for women (Maltais, Desroches, & Dionne, 2009) and testosterone for men (Travison et al., 2009). Therefore, as people experience decreases in sex hormones, they also lose bone mineral content (Sigurdsson et al., 2006).

Estimates of the decrease in bone mineral content over adulthood are about 0.5% per year for men and 1% per year for women (Emaus, Berntsen, Joakimsen, & Fonnebo, 2006). Further weakening occurs due to microcracks that develop in response to stress placed on the bones (Diab, Condon, Burr, & Vashishth, 2006). Part of the older bone's increased susceptibility to fracture can be accounted for by a loss of collagen, which reduces the bone's flexibility in response to pressure (Saito & Marumo, 2009). The problem is particularly severe for the upper part of the thigh bone right below the hip, which does not receive much mechanical pressure during walking and therefore tends to thin disproportionately (Mayhew et al., 2005).

People lose bone at varying rates as the result of a number of other causes. Genetic factors are estimated to account for as much as 70% of bone mineral content in adulthood (Ferrari & Rizzoli, 2005). Consequently, not all older adults experience loss of bone mineral; in one longitudinal study of aging and bone mineral density, a subset of older adult women showed no significant bone loss (Cauley et al., 2009).

Heavier people in general have higher bone mineral content, so that they lose less in adulthood, particularly in the weight-bearing limbs involved in mobility. However, the amount of muscle mass rather than the weight is important since greater fat mass is related to higher loss of bone mineral content (Hsu et al., 2006). Perhaps reflecting their greater mobility, people living in rural areas have higher bone density than people living in cities (Pongchaiyakul et al., 2005). Bone loss is greater in women, especially White women, who lose bone density at a higher rate than do African American women (Cauley et al., 2008). Conversely, African American men seem to lose bone mineral density at a higher rate than do White men (Sheu et al., 2009).

Fortunately, most people aren't significantly affected by bone loss until they are in their 50s or 60s. The good news is also that people can stave off this significant bone loss by modifying their lifestyle and diet. The key lifestyle factors are to exercise, not smoke, and maintain a BMI of approximately 25 (Wilsgaard et al., 2009). Resistance training with weights in particular can help slow down the rate of bone loss (Tolomio et al., 2008). Diet is a fourth key way to maintain bone health, including eating high amounts of dietary protein (Devine, Dick, Islam, Dhaliwal, & Prince, 2005), increasing calcium intake prior to menopause, and taking vitamin D (Dawson-Hughes & Bischoff-Ferrari, 2007). Additional dietary controls include taking in adequate quantities of magnesium (found in foods such as bananas, certain types of nuts, and potatoes) (Ryder et al., 2005) and carotenoids (Sahni et al., 2009).

Environmental factors also play a role in maintaining bone health. People who live in climates with sharp demarcations between the seasons appear to be more likely to suffer from earlier onset of bone loss; for example, people living in Norway have among the highest rates of bone fracture of anyone in the world (Forsmo, Langhammer, Forsen, & Schei, 2005).

Joints

Although most people do not feel that they are getting "creaky" until their 40s, the joins are already undergoing significant changes even before you reach the age of skeletal maturity. These changes continue steadily throughout the adult years and appear to affect women more than men (Ding et al., 2007). By the 20s and 30s, the articular cartilage that protects the joints has already begun to degenerate, and as it does so, the bones start to suffer as well. The fibers in the joint capsule become less pliable, reducing flexibility even further.

Unlike muscles, joints do not benefit from constant use. On the contrary, stress and repeated use cause the joints to wear out more rapidly. As they become less flexible and more painful, people find it increasingly hard to move the affected limbs, hands, and feet. In fact, over half of the adults in the United States report that they experience chronic joint pain or movement restriction (Leveille, 2004).

Exercise can ameliorate some effects of aging on the joints if you use caution (Hunter & Eckstein, 2009). The best form of exercise is strength, in which you build the muscles that support the joints while, at the same time, avoiding putting stress on impaired tendons, ligaments figments, and arterial surfaces (Boling, Bolgla, Mattacola, Uhl, & Hosey, 2006). In addition to increasing muscle strength (see below), resistance training in which people use weight machines can also increase the flexibility of the tendons, allowing joints to move more comfortably and effectively (Reeves, Narici, & Maganaris, 2006). Particularly important is flexibility training that increases the range of motion of the joint such as stretching or practicing gentle forms of yoga (Oken et al., 2006). Because the increased weight associated with obesity contributes to joint pain and stiffness and loss of cartilage volume (Teichtahl et al., 2009), an exercise program should also focus on lowering body fat.

If you take precautions early (such as setting up your computer workstation posture properly), you can reduce the likelihood that you will lose joint mobility in your middle and later years (see Table 4.3). Wearing the proper shoes is one of the most important of these precautions (Dufour et al., 2009). Second, you should protect your upper limbs by using ergonomically designed accessories such as curved and cushioned computer keyboards. You should also adjust the height of your chair and its distance from the computer screen. These precautions can help reduce the probability that you will develop the painful condition known as carpal tunnel syndrome.

Middle-aged individuals already experiencing joint damage can benefit from flexibility exercises that expand a stiff joint's range of motion. Exercise that strengthens the muscles supporting the joint also helps to improve its functioning. Both kinds of exercise have the additional benefit of stimulating circulation to the joints, thereby enhancing the blood supply that promotes repair processes in the tendons, ligaments, and surfaces of the exercising areas.

TABLE 4.3
Evaluation Checklist from the U.S. Occupational Safety and Health Administration for a Safe Workstation

WORKING POSTURES–The workstation is designed or arranged for doing computer tasks so it allows your:	Y	N
1. **Head** and **neck** to be upright, or in-line with the torso (not bent down/back). If "no" refer to Monitors, Chairs, or Work Surfaces.	☐	☐
2. **Head, neck**, and **trunk** to face forward (not twisted). If "no" refer to Monitors or Chairs.	☐	☐
3. **Trunk** to be perpendicular to floor (may lean back into backrest but not forward). If "no" refer to Chairs or Monitors.	☐	☐
4. **Shoulders** and **upper arms** to be in-line with the torso, generally about perpendicular to the floor and relaxed (not elevated or stretched forward). If "no" refer to Chairs.	☐	☐
5. **Upper arms** and **elbows** to be close to the body (not extended outward). If "no" refer to Chairs, Work Surfaces, Keyboards, or Pointers.	☐	☐
6. **Forearms, wrists**, and **hands** to be straight and in-line (forearm at about 90 degrees to the upper arm). If "no" refer to Chairs, Keyboards, or Pointers.	☐	☐
7. **Wrists** and **hands** to be straight (not bent up/down or sideways toward the little finger). If "no" refer to Keyboards or Pointers.	☐	☐
8. **Thighs** to be parallel to the floor and the **lower legs** to be perpendicular to floor (thighs may be slightly elevated above knees). If "no" refer to Chairs or Work Surfaces.	☐	☐
9. **Feet** rest flat on the floor or are supported by a stable footrest. If "no" refer to Chairs or Work Surfaces.	☐	☐

Source: U.S. Department of Labor. (2009). Good working positions: Computer workstations, from http://www.osha.gov/SLTC/etools/computerworkstations/

VITAL BODILY FUNCTIONS

The major organs of the body that keep us alive are in the cardiovascular, respiratory, urinary, and digestive systems. As a very general estimate, we can say that the age-related change across all of these vital systems is in the neighborhood of 0.5% per year (Bortz, 2005) (See Figure 4.4). This sounds like a high number, especially when you multiple it by the 40 to 50 years of adulthood. Fortunately, you can significantly reduce or offset the impact of aging on the majority of these functions by taking preventive actions. Not surprisingly, we will refer repeatedly to physical activity as one of the best strategies you can follow to accomplish this goal.

Cardiovascular System

The cardiovascular system includes the heart, the arteries that circulate blood throughout the body away from the heart, and the veins that bring the blood back to the heart. The most significant changes in the cardiovascular system involve the heart muscle itself and the arteries, leaving the veins relatively spared.

In the heart itself, the left ventricle is the chamber that pumps the oxygenated blood out to the arteries; therefore, its performance is key to the efficiency of the entire cardiovascular system. However, due to a combination of aging of the muscle and changes in the arteries themselves, the walls of the left ventricle lose their ability to contract

FIGURE 4.4

Age-Related Changes in Vital Organ Systems

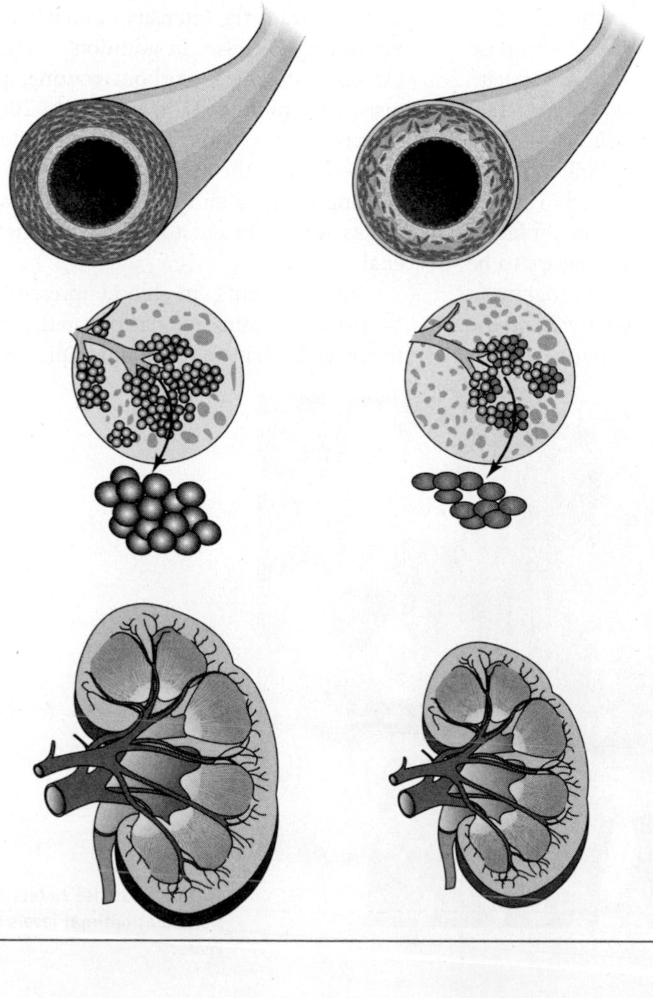

Bodily system	Young	Old	Age change
Cardiovascular			Decrease in aerobic capacity of 1% per year
Respiratory			Decrease in expiratory volume
Urinary			Slower excretion rates

enough so that they can accomplish an efficient distribution of blood through the arteries (Nikitin et al., 2006). The arteries accommodate less blood flow that, in turn, further stresses the left ventricle (Otsuki et al., 2006). The reason the arteries accommodate less blood flow is that fats circulating throughout the blood eventually form hard deposits inside the arterials walls known as **plaque**, consisting of cholesterol, cellular waste products, calcium, and fibrin (a clotting material in the blood).

Cardiovascular efficiency is indexed by **aerobic capacity**, the maximum amount of oxygen that can be delivered through the blood, and **cardiac output**, the amount of blood that the heart pumps per minute. Both indices decline consistently at a rate of about 10% per decade from age 25 and up, so that the average 65-year-old has 40% lower cardiovascular efficiency than a young adult (Betik & Hepple, 2008). The decline is more pronounced in males than females (Goldspink et al., 2009). Maximum heart rate, the heart rate achieved at the point of maximum oxygen consumption, also shows a linear decrease across the years of adulthood.

Declines in aerobic capacity occur even in highly trained athletes; however, those who continue to exercise at a high level of intensity maintain their aerobic capacity longer than nonathletes (Tanaka & Seals, 2003). One study of former football players followed into middle age showed that they had favorable body composition and reduced risks of cardiovascular disease and osteoporosis (Lynch, Ryan, Evans, Katzel, & Goldberg, 2007). The major factor determining whether an athlete remains fit appears to be the difficulty of maintaining an active training program in the late 70s. Complications other than those involving the cardiovascular system, such as joint pain, interfere with even the most motivated person's ability to participate in high-intensity exercise (Katzel, Sorkin, & Fleg, 2001).

Continued involvement in exercise throughout adulthood therefore does not appear to result in stopping the biological clock. However, exercise and avoiding bad habits (such as smoking and eating a high-fat diet) can slow down the clock by benefiting functional capacity, lifestyle, and changes in body mass (Heckman & McKelvie, 2008).

Short-term training studies further reinforce these conclusions about the value of exercise for middle-aged and older adults (Chodzko-Zajko et al., 2009). To be maximally effective, exercise must stimulate the heart rate to rise to 60 to 75% of maximum capacity, and this training must take place three to four times a week. People benefit from many forms of aerobic activities, including walking, hiking, jogging, bicycling, swimming, and jumping rope. However, even moderate or low-intensity exercise can have positive effects on previously sedentary older people.

The increasing popularity of incorporating a heart rate monitor (such as a chest strap that connects wirelessly to a watch) into an exercise program is making it relatively simple to track the intensity of how hard the heart is working during exercise. In addition to incorporating aerobic exercise into one's workout routine, people should add resistance training (Karavirta et al., 2009). Not only does exercise help maximize the heart's functioning, but it also can counteract the increased stiffness of the arteries. In one training study, a simple program of daily walking for 12 weeks was sufficient to have beneficial effects (Teichtahl et al., 2009).

Improvements in blood pressure associated with short-term training may in part reflect the favorable effect that exercise has on enhancing lipid metabolism. Exercise

Catherine Yeulet/iStockphoto

Healthy exercise habits can keep adults functioning at optimal levels throughout their later years.

increases the fraction of **high-density lipoproteins (HDLs)**, the plasma lipid transport mechanism that carries lipids from the peripheral tissues to the liver where they are excreted or synthesized into bile acids. In contrast, **low-density lipoproteins (LDLs)** transport cholesterol to the arteries. The ideal combination in terms of heart health is a low overall blood cholesterol level, in which HDLs are greater than LDLs (Cooney et al., 2009). In the same way that exercise positively effects aerobic power and muscle strength, even moderate levels of exercise can have a beneficial impact on cholesterol metabolism (Walker, Eskurza, Pierce, Gates, & Seals, 2009). Conversely, smoking has deleterious effects on cholesterol, leading to decreased HDLs and increased LDLs as well as the accumulation of other harmful forms of fat in the blood (Kuzuya, Ando, Iguchi, & Shimokata, 2006).

In summary, although there are a number of deleterious cardiovascular changes associated with aging, they are by no means uniformly negative. More important, there are many ways that you can both prevent and compensate for these changes. With regard to aerobic functioning, exercise is one of the best ways you can slow down the rate of your body's aging process.

Respiratory System

The function of the respiratory system is to bring oxygen into the body and move carbon dioxide out. The respiratory system accomplishes these goals through the mechanical process of breathing, a process that involves several structures, including the diaphragm and the muscles of the chest wall. The exchange of gases takes place within the innermost reaches of tiny airways in the lungs, in the tiny air sacs known as the **alveoli**.

Aging affects all components of the respiratory system. The respiratory muscles lose the ability to expand and contract the chest wall, and the lung tissue itself is less able to expand and contract during inspiration (Britto, Zampa, de Oliveira, Prado, & Parreira, 2009). Consequently, starting at about age 40, all measures of lung functioning in adulthood tend to show age-related losses. These losses are more severe in women (Harms, 2006) and are particularly pronounced during exercise, when people place the most stress on their respiratory systems (Zeleznik, 2003).

The normal age-related changes contribute to the measure of **lung age**, which is a mathematical function showing how old your lung is based on a combination of your age and a measure obtained from a spirometer called forced expiratory volume. By calculating lung age, individuals can determine how much they are placing themselves at risk by engaging in behaviors such as smoking that are known to compromise respiratory function.

People who want to minimize the effects of aging on the lungs have two main strategies they can follow. The first may be the most obvious—to stay away from or quit smoking cigarettes. People who smoke lose more forced expiratory volume in later adulthood than those who do not (Mitsumune, Senoh, Nishikawa, Adachi, & Kajii, 2009). Although it is better to quit smoking than continue smoking, there are unfortunately deleterious changes in the body's cells that remain for at least several decades after a person has quit smoking (Masayesva et al., 2006).

Other lifestyle changes involve diet and exercise. Researchers have determined that obesity is related to poor respiratory functioning (Harrington & Lee-Chiong, 2009). Exercise can strengthen the muscles of the chest wall, and, in the process, compensate at least in part for the lost elasticity of the lung tissue (Womack et al., 2000).

Urinary System

The urinary system is made up of the kidneys, bladder, ureters, and urethra. The kidneys are composed of **nephrons**, cells that serve as millions of tiny filters that cleanse the blood of metabolic waste. These waste products combine in the bladder with excess water from the blood to be eliminated as urine through the urethra.

At one time, researchers believed that the fate of the kidneys in late life was to decline steadily due to loss of nephrons over time. However, the jury is still out on this question. There do appear to be age differences in the kidney (Lerma, 2009), but many factors other than age can compromise the nephrons. One of these factors is cigarette smoking. This can lead to serious kidney disease in older adults with other risk factors (Stengel, Couchoud, Cenee, & Hemon, 2000), perhaps through its effect on changes within the nephron's ability to filter wastes (Elliot et al., 2006).

Studies conducted on samples in the past may have yielded exaggerated estimates of the effects of normal aging on the kidneys, reflecting instead the fact that a large percentage of the population smoked cigarettes for much of their adult lives. However, this fact doesn't account for the entire effect of age on the kidneys. Illness, extreme exertion, or extreme heat all serve as stresses that greatly compromise the kidney's ability to do its job (Fuiano et al., 2001).

Regardless of the cause of changes in the kidney with age, there are important implications to consider. Glomerular filtration rate (GFR) is the volume of fluid filtered through the kidneys and is most typically measured by creatinine clearance, which compares the level of creatinine in urine with the level in the blood. Older adults are likely to have slower excretion rates of chemicals from the body, as evidenced by lower GFR even in healthy older adults (Sun et al., 2009). Given these changes, health professionals prescribing medication must carefully monitor middle-aged and older adults to avoid inadvertent overdoses (Wyatt, Kim, & Winston, 2006).

Changes with aging may also occur in the elastic tissue of the bladder, making it no longer capable of efficiently retaining or expelling urine. Older adults also experience slight changes in the perception that they need to urinate, although the bladder itself does not shrink in size in normal aging (Pfisterer, Griffiths, Schaefer, & Resnick, 2006). Adding to intrinsic changes in the bladder that lower the rate of urinary flow in men is the fact that many men experience hypertrophy (enlargement) of the prostate, a gland located on top of the bladder. This puts pressure on the bladder and can lead men to feel frequent urges to urinate.

Approximately 30% of all adults 65 and older suffer from **urge incontinence**, a form of urinary incontinence in which the individual experiences a sudden need to urinate and may even leak urine. In **stress incontinence**, the individual is unable to retain urine while engaging in some form of physical exertion. According to one estimate (Anger, Saigal, & Litwin, 2006), the prevalence of daily incontinence ranges from 12% in women 60 to 64 years old to 21% in women 85 years old or older. Of all women reporting incontinence, 14% experience it on a daily basis and 10% on a weekly basis. Among the risk factors for urge incontinence in women are being of White race; having diabetes, which is being treated with insulin; experiencing symptoms of depression; and currently using estrogen (Jackson et al., 2004).

A condition related to urge incontinence is **overactive bladder**; in addition to incontinence, symptoms include a need to urinate more frequently than normal. Overactive bladder is estimated to affect 25% of the population 65 and over (Wagg, Wyndaele, & Sieber, 2006). Although conditions associated with bladder function can be particularly distressing, the large majority of older adults are symptom-free. Consequently, it is important to remember that urinary incontinence is not a part of normal aging.

However, older adults with overactive bladder and incontinence often experience a number of associated psychological problems, including symptoms of depression, difficulty sleeping, and various forms of sexual dysfunction (Coyne et al., 2007). These individuals are also likely to experience embarrassment and concern over having an accident. They may also be more likely to fall and suffer a fracture if their incontinence leads them to have to hurry to the bathroom.

A variety of treatments are available to counteract incontinence; however, because people often mistakenly assume that bladder dysfunction is a normal part of aging, they are less likely to seek active treatment. In one study of more than 7.2 million patients diagnosed with overactive bladder, 76% went untreated (Helfand, Evans, & McVary, 2009). Medications such as tolderodine (Detrol LA) are becoming increasingly available to help control bladder problems.

Behavioral controls used alone (Burgio, 2009), or combined with medication (Tran, Levin, & Mousa, 2009), can also help to reduce the symptoms of overactive bladder and incontinence. Pelvic muscle training (also known as "Kegel" exercises) can be particularly effective for this purpose (Felicissimo et al., 2010). In this exercise, the individual contracts and then relaxes the urinary sphincters for a short period of time to strengthen them. Individuals can also set regular schedules for bathroom use, which helps

SOMOS/SuperStock

Kegel exercises, or pelvic muscle training, can help compensate for or even prevent urinary incontinence.

prevent spillages. Eliminating excess fluid intake can also be helpful, particularly in the hours before bedtime. Such behavioral methods not only reduce incontinence but also help to alleviate the depression often associated with this condition (Tadic et al., 2007).

Digestive System

You no doubt hear a great deal in the media about middle-aged and older people requiring aids to their digestive system, such as treatments for heartburn (acid reflux), gas, bloating, and bowel irregularity. Surprisingly, the reality is that the majority of older people do not experience significant losses in their ability to digest food.

Physiological changes in the esophagus are relatively minor (Achem & Devault, 2005), as are changes (for people in good health) in the stomach and lower digestive tract (Bharucha & Camilleri, 2001). There are decreases in saliva production (Eliasson, Birkhed, Osterberg, & Carlen, 2006), fewer gastric juices are secreted, and the stomach empties more slowly in older adults (O'Donovan et al., 2005). There is also a decrease in liver volume and blood flow through the liver (Serste & Bourgeois, 2006). However, these changes vary tremendously from person to person, in part due to variations in overall health status (Drozdowski & Thomson, 2006). Smoking status and medications also affect digestive system functioning in older adults (Greenwald, 2004).

Though troubling when it occurs, fecal incontinence affects only 4% of the over-65 population (Alameel, Andrew, & Macknight, 2010). As is true with urinary incontinence, training in behavioral controls can help to manage the condition (Byrne, Solomon, Young, Rex, & Merlino, 2007). Increasing the amount of fiber in the diet can also help older adults maintain bowel regularity and prevent incontinence (Markland et al., 2009).

Physiology is not the only determinant that regulates how well a person's digestive system functions in later life. Many lifestyle factors that change in middle and later adulthood contribute to overall digestive health. For example, families typically become smaller as children move out of the home, financial resources may decrease when people retire, and age-related mobility and cognitive problems can make cooking a more difficult task for the older adult to manage. As a result, the older adult may be less motivated to eat, or to eat a healthy diet.

Unfortunately, by being exposed to constant advertising about the need for older adults to use dietary supplements, digestive aids, and laxatives, older adults may suffer changes that could otherwise be avoided. The best way for older adults to maintain their digestive health is to eat a diet that includes a balance among foods containing protein, complex carbohydrates, and fats.

BODILY CONTROL SYSTEMS

Each of the organ systems we have discussed so far plays a crucial role in a person's daily physical and mental well-being; however for these systems to work properly, their functioning must be coordinated. This is the job of the endocrine and immune systems. Together, these systems have important roles in a variety of areas related to health and quality of life.

Endocrine System

The **endocrine system** is a large and diverse set of glands that regulate the actions of the body's organ systems (referred to as "target" organs). **Hormones** are the chemical messengers produced by the endocrine systems.

Changes with age in the endocrine system can occur at many levels. Because there are so many complex regulatory pathways, changes in one can have numerous effects on others. For example, the endocrine glands themselves may release more or less of a particular hormone. The target organs may also respond differently to stimulation from the hormones. Complicating matters are findings that demonstrate that the endocrine system is highly sensitive to levels of stress and physical illness. These outside factors can further disturb whatever intrinsic changes would normally occur due to aging.

The hypothalamus and anterior (front) section of the pituitary gland, located deep within the base of the brain, are the main control centers of the endocrine system. **Hypothalamus-releasing factors (HRFs)**, hormones produced by the hypothalamus, regulate the secretion of hormones in turn produced by the anterior pituitary gland. HRFs are not the only source of stimulation for pituitary hormones, however. The pituitary hormones also respond to signals from target organs carried through the blood, indicating that more pituitary hormones are needed. The HRFs then stimulate greater hormone production by these endocrine glands. Because the hypothalamus is also a part of the nervous system and thus a neuroendocrine structure, it also may release HRFs in response to information sent from other parts of the nervous system.

Six hormones are produced by the anterior pituitary: growth hormone (GH, also called somatotropin), thyroid-stimulating hormone (TSH), adrenocorticotropic hormone (ACTH), follicle-stimulating hormone (FSH), luteinizing hormone (LH), and prolactin. Each of these hormones acts on specific target cells within the body and some (such as TSH) stimulate the production of other hormones. Below we focus on the growth and thyroid-stimulating hormones as they relate to the aging process.

Growth Hormone (GH). In youth, GH stimulates the growth of bones and muscles and regulates the growth of most internal organs. Throughout life, GH affects the metabolism of proteins, lipids, and carbohydrates. A related hormone produced by the liver, IGF-I (insulin-like growth factor-1), stimulates muscle cells to increase in size and number.

Together, GH and IGF-1 are called the somatotrophic axis (GH and IGF-1). A decline in their activity, called **somatopause of aging**, is thought to account for a number of age-related changes in body composition across adulthood, including loss of bone mineral content, increases in fat, and decrease in muscle mass as well as losses in strength, exercise tolerance, and quality of life in general (Lombardi et al., 2005). There are also age differences in the activity of GH. In young people, GH production shows regularly timed peaks during nighttime sleep; in older adults, this peak is smaller, a pattern that may contribute to changes (Espiritu, 2008), a topic we will discuss shortly. GH also rises during exercise, but in adults age 60 and older this response is attenuated (Weltman et al., 2006).

Given the importance of GH to so many basic processes affected by aging, GH replacement therapy has been increasingly viewed by some as an antidote to reverse or at least slow the effects of the aging process. Low doses, administered in conjunction with testosterone to men, have demonstrated positive effects in increasing lean body mass, reducing fat mass, and improving overall aerobic capacity (Giannoulis et al., 2006).

However, many questions remain about the practicality of GH alone or GH in combination with testosterone as a way to counter the effects of aging. In addition to being extremely expensive (US$10,000 to $30,000 per year), researchers maintain that the substantial potentially harmful side effects outweigh its possible advantages (Hersch & Merriam, 2008). GH is linked to joint pain, enlargement of the heart, enlargement of the bones, diabetes, high blood pressure, and heart failure. As a result, human growth hormones (HGH) are banned from most competitive sports, despite the fact that HGH has not been demonstrated to improve athletic performance (Liu et al., 2008).

Cortisol. We turn next to **cortisol**, the hormone produced by the adrenal gland. Given that cortisol provides energy to the muscles during times of stress, researchers regard it as the "stress hormone." Cortisol serves the function of energizing the body, making it ready to react to a stressful encounter. Unfortunately the increase in cortisol negatively affects memory and other forms of cognitive functioning in older adults (Comijs et al., 2010).

The idea that aging causes dangerous increases in cortisol levels is known as the **glucocorticoid cascade hypothesis** (Angelucci, 2000). According to this view, increased cortisol levels accelerate neuronal loss in the hippocampus. Repeated (cascading) increases in cortisol over the lifetime lead to further degeneration.

Not all studies support the glucocorticoid cascade hypothesis. Some researchers find that age changes are not demonstrated under normal conditions (Feldman et al., 2002). Most significant is that when the data are collected longitudinally rather than cross-sectionally (which is true for all of the above studies), individual variations exist in the pattern of changes over time (Lupien et al., 1996). Obesity is another factor that may relate to cortisol levels. At one time, researchers believed that obesity presented a risk for higher cortisol, but in a large-scale longitudinal study, it was weight loss rather than gain that was associated with higher cortisol levels in men (Travison, O'Donnell, Araujo, Matsumoto, & McKinlay, 2007).

Thyroid Hormones. Controlling the rate of metabolism (also known as the **basal metabolic rate (BMR)**) are hormones produced by the thyroid gland, located in the neck. The BMR begins to slow in middle age and is responsible for the weight gain that occurs even when a person's caloric intake remains stable. Changes in BMR are at least in part related to age-related decreases in thyroid hormones over adulthood (Meunier et al., 2005). Subclinical hypothyroidism can affect as many as 15 to 18% of adults over the age of 60 (Diez & Iglesias, 2004) and is associated with cognitive impairment (Hogervorst, Huppert, Matthews, & Brayne, 2008).

Melatonin. Sleep–wake cycles are controlled in part by **melatonin**, the hormone manufactured by the pineal gland, located deep within the brainstem. **Circadian rhythm**, the daily variations in various bodily functions, is therefore affected by this hormone. As we will discuss later in this chapter, some researchers believe that significant changes in circadian rhythm that occur throughout middle and later adulthood correspond to declines in melatonin production across adulthood (Mahlberg, Tilmann, Salewski, & Kunz, 2006).

A segment of the research community believes that melatonin supplements can reduce the effects of aging and age-associated diseases, especially in the brain and immune system. It is true that melatonin supplements for women can lead to improved pituitary and thyroid functions (Bellipanni, Bianchi, Pierpaoli, Bulian, & Ilyia, 2001) and reduce the incidence of sleep problems (Gubin, Gubin, Waterhouse, & Weinert, 2006). However, melatonin use can produce significant side effects, including confusion, drowsiness, headaches, and constriction of blood vessels, posing a danger to people with high blood pressure. The dosages usually sold in over-the-counter medications may be as high as 40 times the amount normally found in the body, and the effect of such large doses taken long term has not been determined (National Library of Medicine, 2010).

In addition to concerns about safety, melatonin supplements can interfere with sleep cycles if taken at the wrong time of day. Thus, between the questions about effectiveness, side effects, and dosages, older adults should most likely not be using this hormone to regulate their circadian patterns or sleep.

DHEA. The most abundant steroid in the human body, **dehydroepiandrosterone (DHEA)**, is a weak male steroid (androgen) produced by the adrenal glands. DHEA is a precursor to the sex hormones testosterone and estrogen and is believed to have a variety of functions, such as increasing the production of other sex steroids and the availability of IGF-1 as well as positively influencing some central nervous system functions.

DHEA, which is higher in males than females, shows a pronounced decrease over the adult years, decreasing by 60% between the ages of 20 and 80 (Feldman et al., 2002). This phenomenon, termed **adrenopause**, is greater in men, although men continue to have higher levels than women throughout later life because they start at a higher baseline. Extremely low levels of DHEA have been linked to cardiovascular disease, some forms of cancer, immune system dysfunction, and obesity (von Muhlen, Laughlin, Kritz-Silverstein, & Barrett-Connor, 2007).

Although there are no definitive answers about DHEA's role in aging other than the likely decline in DHEA, DHEA replacement therapy rivals GH and melatonin in the antiaging industry. However, like GH therapy, DHEA use presents notable health risks, mainly liver problems and an increase in risk of prostate cancer (Arnold et al., 2007). A natural substitute for some of the positive effects of DHEA replacement therapy is exercise, which can help to compensate for its loss in the later adult years (Igwebuike et al., 2008).

Female Hormonal Changes. Technically speaking, **menopause** is the point in a woman's life when menstruation stops permanently. As used in common speech, however, menopause has come to mean a phase in middle adulthood covering the years in which a woman's reproductive capacity diminishes. The more precise term for this gradual winding down of reproductive ability is **climacteric**, a term that applies to men as well. For women, the climacteric occurs over a 3- to 5-year span called **perimenopause**], which ends in menopause when the woman has not had her menstrual period for 1 year. The average age of menopause is 50 years, but the timing varies among individuals. Menopause occurs earlier in women who are thin or malnourished or who smoke.

Throughout perimenopause, there is a diminution in the production by the ovarian follicles of estrogen, the primary female sex hormone. Because the other female hormone, progesterone, is produced in response to ovulation, progesterone levels also decline during this time. The process of estrogen decline begins about 10 to 15 years before menopause, at some point in the mid-30s. By the mid-40s, the ovaries have begun to function less effectively and produce fewer hormones. Eventually, menstrual cycles by the early to middle 50s have ended altogether. There is still some production of estrogen, however, as the ovaries continue to produce small amounts and the adrenal glands stimulate the production of estrogen in fat tissue. Follicle-stimulating hormone (FSH) and luteinizing hormone (LH) levels rise dramatically during the perimenopausal period, as the anterior pituitary sends out signals to produce more ovarian hormones. In turn, the hypothalamus produces less gonadotropin-releasing factor (GnRH).

Although women vary considerably in their progression through the menopause (as they also do during puberty), there are certain characteristic symptoms, many of which you have probably heard discussed by middle-aged and older women. One of the most prominent symptoms is the occurrence of "hot flashes," which are sudden sensations of intense heat and sweating that can last from a few moments to half an hour. These are the result of decreases in estrogen levels, which cause the endocrine system to release higher amounts of other hormones that affect the temperature control centers in the brain. Fatigue, headaches, night sweats, and insomnia are other physiological symptoms that result from fluctuating estrogen levels. Menopausal women also report that they experience psychological symptoms such as irritability, mood swings, depression, memory loss, and difficulty concentrating; however, the evidence regarding the connection between these symptoms and the physiological changes involved in menopause is far from conclusive.

Along with hormonal changes, menopause is associated with alterations in the reproductive tract. Because of lower estrogen levels, there is a reduction in the supply of blood to the vagina and surrounding nerves and glands. The tissues become thinner, drier, and less able to produce secretions to lubricate before and during intercourse. The result is the possibility of discomfort during intercourse (da Silva Lara et al., 2009). In addition, women may become more susceptible to urinary problems, such as infections and stress incontinence.

More widespread throughout the body are other effects of menopause associated with the impact of decreasing estrogen levels on other bodily systems. Weaker bones, high blood pressure, and cardiovascular disease become more prevalent among postmenopausal women. Estrogen appears to provide protection against these diseases, but is lost at menopause. There are also deleterious changes in cholesterol levels in the blood associated with menopause, causing postmenopausal women to be at higher risk of atherosclerosis and associated conditions.

Estrogen-replacement therapy (ERT) was introduced in the 1940s to counteract the negative effects of estrogen loss on postmenopausal women. Later, estrogen was combined with the hormone progestin to reduce cancer risk. Administration of both hormones is referred to as **hormone replacement therapy (HRT)**.

Initial studies on HRT's effects on the body provided enthusiastic support, citing positive impact on skin tone and appearance, bone mineral density, immune functioning, thickness of the hair, sleep quality, prevention of accidental falls, and improvements in memory and mood. However, starting in 2002, the pros and cons of HRT became hotly debated by researchers, and the jury is still out on whether the benefits outweigh the risks (Alexandersen, Karsdal, & Christiansen, 2009). There is also evidence that the specific chemical composition of the hormone replacement may have differing effects on cancer risk (Schneider, Jick, & Meier, 2009). At the same time, there may be as yet unidentified benefits of HRT such as reduced risk of colon cancer (Weige, Allred, & Allred, 2009).

For women not willing to experiment with HRT given the conflicting data, alternatives are available. Other recommended approaches to counteract the effect of hormonal changes include exercise, quitting smoking, lowering the cholesterol in the diet, and perhaps, more enjoyably, having one alcoholic drink a day.

Male Hormonal Changes.   Although men do not experience a loss of sexual function comparable to menopause (despite what you might hear about "male menopause"), men undergo **andropause**, which refers to age-related declines in the male sex hormone testosterone. The decline in testosterone is equal to 1% per year after the age of 40, a decrease observed in longitudinal as well as cross-sectional studies (Feldman et al., 2002). The term "late-onset hypogonadism" or "age-associated hypogonadism" has begun to replace the term andropause, although all three terms are currently in use.

Abnormally low levels of testosterone levels are found in 6 to 10% of men between the ages of 40 and 70, but these rates are far higher (15–30%) in men who are diabetic or obese (Tostain & Blanc, 2008). Testosterone supplements for aging men were long considered an unnecessary and potentially dangerous proposition. However, with greater empirical support and acceptance in the medical community, testosterone supplements are in greater use, with the stipulation that treatment is accompanied by regular medical screening (Theodoraki & Bouloux, 2009). The benefits associated with testosterone supplements include maintained or improved bone density, greater muscle strength, a lowered ratio of fat to lean, and lower rates of cognitive decline (Janowsky, 2006).

In contrast to findings from early studies, there is no evidence that prostate mass increases as long as the treatment maintains a man's testosterone within a normal range. Also in contrast to previous research, higher testosterone levels are associated with lowered cardiovascular risk, including more favorable cholesterol levels (Munzer, Harman, Sorkin, & Blackman, 2009).

Erectile dysfunction (ED), a condition in which a man is unable to achieve an erection sustainable for intercourse, is estimated to increase with age in adulthood, from a rate of 31% among men age 57 to 65 to 44% of those 65 and older. Compared to younger men, however, premature climax is less common in the 65 and older population (Waite, Laumann, Das, & Schumm, 2009). However, ED is related to health problems in older men, including metabolic syndrome (Borges et al., 2009).

You are no doubt familiar with the "cure" for ED, the little blue pill known as Viagra. Phosphodiesterase type 5 inhibitors, including Viagra (the technical term is sildenafil), can be effective in treating ED, alleviating the difficulties experienced by men and their sexual partners (Morales, Mirone, Dean, & Costa, 2009). Researchers now believe that the combination of testosterone supplements with other ED medications can be particularly beneficial (Corona & Maggi, 2010). However, there are risks for men who have cardiovascular disease, and they are warned not to use these treatments.

Based on the relationship between ED and metabolic syndrome as well as hypertension, diabetes, and obesity (Chitaley, Kupelian, Subak, & Wessells, 2009), however, a safer alternative, at least as an initial approach, would be to exercise more frequently to reduce these conditions (Lamina, Okoye, & Dagogo, 2009).

Immune System

Regulating the body's ability to fight off stress, infection, and other threats to well-being and health is the immune system. In addition to protecting the body, the immune system is closely linked to the nervous system and, consequently, to behaviors, thoughts, and emotions (Lupien, McEwen, Gunnar, & Heim, 2009).

Researchers believe that there are widespread age-related declines in immune system functioning, a process known as **immune senescence** (see Figure 4.5). The two

<u>FIGURE 4.5</u>

Age-Related Changes in the Immune System

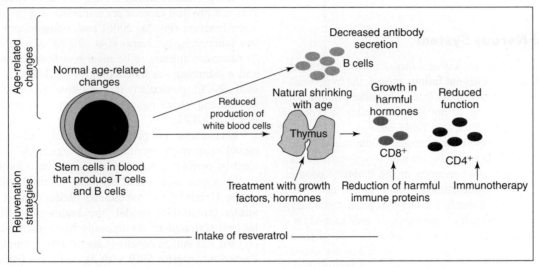

Source: Reprinted from *Current Opinion in Immunology*, *21(4)*, Dorshkind, K., & Swain, S., Age-associated declines in immune system development and function: causes, consequences, and reversal, 404–407, Copyright (2009), with permission from Elsevier.

primary types of immune lymphocytes include "T cells" and "B cells," both of which are involved in destroying bodily invaders known as antigens. In immune senescence, these cells fail to develop properly and lose their ability to perform effectively, causing older adults to be less resistant to infections (Grubeck-Loebenstein, 2010). Thus, although children are more likely to develop an influenza infection during flu season, mortality from such a disease occurs almost entirely among older adults unless the flu viruses were ones to which they were exposed as children or young adults.

Interactions between the immune system and other physical and psychological changes are important to consider as factors that affect the aging process. For example, cortisol and DHEA have opposing actions on the immune system and changes in their balance with age can alter the activity of immune system cells (Buford & Willoughby, 2008). Micronutrients, found in certain vitamins and minerals such as vitamin E and zinc, are believed to improve immune responsiveness and prevent infection (Mocchegiani et al., 2008). Protein intake is also crucial to maintaining adequate immune functioning in older adults (Aoi, 2009). Moderate exercise can play a role in enhancing immune functioning and can offset age-related declines (Senchina, 2009). Conversely, chronic stress can accelerate the rate of the immune system's aging (Gouin, Hantsoo, & Kiecolt-Glaser, 2008).

Previous research examining the effects of aging on the immune system may have failed to control (statistically) for variables measuring diet and exercise. Perhaps for this reason, studies produce differing results on how aging affects the immune system (Dorshkind, Montecino-Rodriguez, & Signer, 2009). There may also be some protective mechanisms not completely understood at present that help maintain the immune functioning of certain healthy agers. For example, studies of centenarians reveal that some of the basic cells in the immune system were as healthy in this hardy group of older adults as in young adults (Alonso-Fernandez, Puerto, Mate, Ribera, & de la Fuente, 2008).

The many conflicting studies on aging and the immune system support the principle of interindividual variability in the aging process. This variability may reflect as much the different samples who were studied as the fact that health, diet, and exercise, not to mention biological differences, all play a role in affecting the rates at which any one individual experiences immune system changes.

NERVOUS SYSTEM

It is no exaggeration to say that the nervous system controls all behavior. Without a functioning nervous system, organisms would be unable to carry out the various maintenance activities of the body or to enact voluntary, learned behavior. The central nervous system makes it possible to monitor and then prepare responses to events in the environment, conceive and enact thoughts, and maintain connections with other bodily systems. The autonomic nervous system controls involuntary behaviors, the body's response to stress, and the actions of other organ systems that sustain life.

Central Nervous System

Early research on nervous system functioning in adulthood was based on the **neuronal fallout model**, the hypothesis that individuals progressively lose brain tissue over the life span because neurons do not have the ability to replace themselves when they die (see Table 4.4).

The data to support the neuronal fallout model came primarily from autopsy studies in which neuroanatomists counted the number of neurons in the brains of people of different ages. These studies tended not to take into account the cause of death, the fact that brain tissue may be destroyed after death by the methods used to study it, and the possible diseases that the subjects suffered from while alive. All of these factors may have biased the results and caused an exaggerated picture of the extent to which brain tissue is lost in later life.

Newer findings are presenting a different view of the effect of aging on the nervous system. It now seems clear that in the absence of disease, the aging brain maintains much of its structure and function. Moreover, it is possible that neurons may actually gain in both structure and function even until late in life. The **plasticity model** proposes that the neurons which remain alive are able to take over the function of those that die (Goh & Park,

2009). For example, areas of the brain involved in complex language and word processing skills continue to develop and reach maturity in middle age (Bartzokis et al., 2001). Diet and physical exercise are important ways to maintain brain function (Pinilla, 2006) and, consequently, cognitive functioning (Dishman et al., 2006). Aerobic exercise in particular appears to be most beneficial in preserving and maximizing the functioning of the brain (Colcombe et al., 2006), particularly in areas involved in attentional control and verbal memory (Erickson & Kramer, 2009) (see Figure 4.6).

Researchers also propose that older adults can show neural plasticity by recruiting brain regions not ordinarily used to perform a function to compensate for declines in the region that would normally be used. According to the **Hemispheric Asymmetry Reduction in OLDer adults (HAROLD) model**, the brains of older adults become activated in the opposite hemisphere when the original area suffers deficits (Cabeza, 2002). Similarly, the **Posterior–Anterior Shift with Aging (PASA) model** proposes that the front (anterior) of the brain in older adults becomes more responsive to make up for the lower responsiveness found in the rear (posterior) of the brain (Davis et al., 2008).

The Hemispheric Asymmetry Reduction in OLDer adults (HAROLD) model proposes that the brains of older adults become activated in the opposite hemisphere compared to younger adults and are therefore less lateralized.

The Posterior–Anterior Shift with Aging (PASA) model proposes that the front (anterior) of the brain in older adults becomes more responsive to make up for the lower responsiveness found in the rear (posterior) of the brain (Davis, 2008).

Many of these new findings are made possible by the increasing availability of brain scanning methods now being used in many laboratories that in the past were only accessible in hospitals or major research centers. There are several types of scanning methods that can produce pictures of brain structures or activity, depending on the goal of the research.

The **electroencephalogram (EEG)** is a brain scanning method that measures electrical activity in the brain. EEG activity reflects the individual's state of consciousness and the state of the brain's arousal while the individual is asleep. The EEG pattern also shows particular patterns of brain waves when an individual engages in particular mental tasks. Clinicians use EEGs to evaluate clients for conditions such as epilepsy, sleep disorders, and brain tumors.

Computed axial tomography (CAT or CT scan) is an imaging method that clinicians and researchers use to provide an image of a cross-sectional slice of the brain from any angle or level. CT scans provide an image of the

TABLE 4.4
Models of Aging and the Nervous System

Model	Proposed effects of aging	Relevant research
Neuronal fallout	Losses occur in numbers of neurons and synapses	Decreases in prefrontal cortex, hippocampus. Increases in white matter hyperintensities.
Plasticity	Continued growth through dendritic elaboration	Diet and exercise preserve brain function and cognition.

FIGURE 4.6

Impact of Aerobic Exercise on Brain Functioning

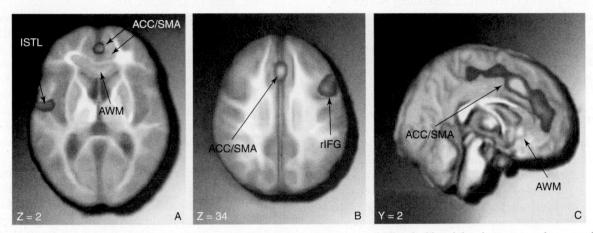

MRIs of the brains of older adults who engaged in an aerobic fitness training program compared with older adults who participated in a stretching and toning program. A and B show horizontal slices of the brain, and C shows a vertical slice. The dark areas indicate increased gray matter volume in aerobic vs. non-aerobic exercisers, and the lighter highlighted regions show increased white matter, all areas that help promote memory.

Source: Colcombe, S. J., Erickson, K. I., Scalf, P. E., Kim, J. S., Prakash, R., McAuley, E., ... Kramer, A. F. (2006). Aerobic exercise training increases brain volume in aging humans. *Journal of Gerontology Series A: Biological Sciences and Medical Sciences 61A*, 1166–1170, by permission of Oxford University Press.

fluid-filled areas of the brain, the ventricles. The method is useful when clinicians are looking for structural damage to the brain.

Magnetic resonance imaging (MRI) is a brain imaging method that uses radio waves to construct a picture of the living brain based on the water content of various tissues. The person is placed inside a device that contains a powerful electromagnet. This causes the nuclei in hydrogen atoms to transmit electromagnetic energy (hence the term *magnetic resonance*), and the activity from thousands of angles is sent to a computer, which produces a high-resolution picture of the scanned area. The picture from the MRI differentiates areas of white matter (nerve fibers) from gray matter (nerve cells) and is useful for diagnosing diseases that affect the nerve fibers that make up the white matter.

Neither the CT scan nor the MRI can show changes in the brain when the individual is involved in a task because they both provide static images. In contrast, **functional magnetic resonance imaging (fMRI)** is a type of scan that can be used to show changes in the brain over the course of a mental activity. Researchers are increasingly using fMRIs to understand the brain areas involved in the processing of information, giving an "inside look" at age differences in cognition.

Two other scans show brain activity but require injections of radioactively labeled compounds into the blood. **Positron emission tomography (PET) scan** and **single photon emission computed tomography (SPECT)** detect

these radioactive compounds as they pass through the brain. The images they provide show blood flow, oxygen or glucose metabolism, and concentrations of brain chemicals. Vibrant colors at the red end of the spectrum represent higher levels of activity, and colors at the blue-green-violet end of the spectrum represent lower levels of brain activity.

Using these scanning techniques, researchers have accumulated a rapidly-growing body of evidence about how aging affects the normal brain. Normal aging seems to have major effects on the prefrontal cortex, the area of the brain most involved in planning and the encoding of information into long-term memory, as well as in the temporal cortex, which is involved in auditory processing (Fjell et al., 2009). The **hippocampus**, the structure in the brain responsible for consolidating memories, becomes smaller with increasing age, although this decline is more pronounced in abnormal aging such as in Alzheimer's disease (Zhang et al., 2010). Nevertheless, evidence exists in support of the plasticity model within the cells of the hippocampus (Lister & Barnes, 2009).

Aging is also associated with changes in the frontal lobe in the form of abnormalities known as **white matter hyperintensities (WMH)**. These abnormalities are thought to be made up of parts of deteriorating neurons. Their presence appears to interfere with long-term memory because they disrupt the integrity of the white matter (Charlton, Barrick, Markus, & Morris, 2009). These structures seem to be associated with hypertension and therefore are not necessarily a universal phenomenon (Burgmans et al., 2010).

Many puzzles remain in understanding WMH's role in the aging of the nervous system and the impact, in turn, on memory. For example, in individuals over 60 years of age, these abnormalities account for a significant amount of the variation in cognitive functioning (Vannorsdall, Waldstein, Kraut, Pearlson, & Schretlen, 2009).

Sleep

The literature on sleep in adulthood clearly refutes a common myth about aging, namely, that as people grow older they need less sleep. Regardless of age, everyone requires 7 to 9 hours of sleep a night (Ancoli-Israel & Cooke, 2005). However, sleeping 8 hours or more a night is associated with higher mortality risks and greater incidence of stroke in women (Chen et al., 2008). Middle-aged and older adults who experience changes occur in sleep-related behavior and sleep problems can suffer adverse effects on their mental and physical well-being. Unfortunately, sleep problems seem to affect up to half of all older adults (Neikrug & Ancoli-Israel, 2009).

Sleep problems in middle and later life relate in part to lifestyle as well as physiology. You almost certainly know from your own experience that your sleep is more disrupted when you are experiencing periods of stress. For instance, middle-aged adults who live with high degrees of job-related stress suffer sleep disturbances. Other lifestyle

factors also play an important role, including obesity, physical inactivity, and alcohol use (Janson, Lindberg, Gislason, Elmasry, & Boman, 2001).

Whatever the cause, we know that older adults spend more time in bed relative to time spent asleep. They take longer to fall asleep, awaken more often during the night, lie in bed longer before rising, and have sleep that is shallower, more fragmented, and less efficient (Fetveit, 2009). Their sleep patterns on an EEG show some corresponding age alterations, including a rise in Stage 1 sleep and a large decrease in both Stage 4 and REM (rapid-eye movement) sleep (Kamel & Gammack, 2006). These changes occur even for people who are in excellent health.

At some point during middle to late adulthood, people also shift from a preference to working in the later hours of the day and night to a preference for the morning. Adults over 65 tend to classify themselves as "morning" people, while the large majority of younger adults classify themselves as "evening" people (see Figure 4.7). The biological basis for this shift in preferences presumably occurs gradually throughout adulthood, along with changes in hormonal contributors to sleep and arousal patterns (Benloucif et al., 2004).

One intriguing implication of the changes in circadian rhythm with age is the possible confound that time of day presents in studies of aging and cognitive functioning. Older adults tested at their nonoptimal hours (such as late afternoon) are more disproportionately affected than are young adults (Rowe, Hasher, & Turcotte, 2009). This can

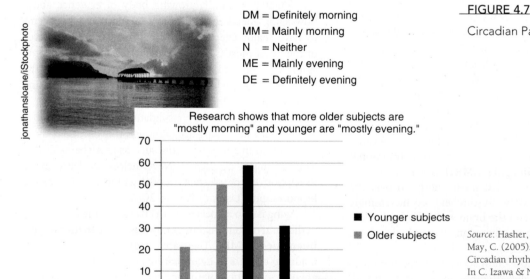

jonathansloane/iStockphoto

DM = Definitely morning
MM = Mainly morning
N   = Neither
ME = Mainly evening
DE = Definitely evening

Research shows that more older subjects are "mostly morning" and younger are "mostly evening."

■ Younger subjects
■ Older subjects

FIGURE 4.7

Circadian Patterns and Aging

Source: Hasher, L., Goldstein, F., & May, C. (2005). It's about time: Circadian rhythms, memory and aging. In C. Izawa & N. Ohta (Eds.), *Human learning and memory: Advances in theory and application* (Vol. *18*, pp. 179–186). Mahwah, NJ: Lawrence Erlbaum.

result in a systematic bias that exaggerates the extent of age differences in performance. The effect of time of day on memory performance is less pronounced among older adults who engage in regular patterns of physical activity compared with their sedentary peers (Bugg, DeLosh, & Clegg, 2006).

Changes in sleep patterns in middle and later adulthood may be prevented or corrected if the individual makes a few simple changes in sleep habits. A sedentary lifestyle is a major contributor to sleep problems. Therefore, another reason for older adults to exercise is to improve their sleep quality. A variety of psychological disorders can also interfere with the sleep of middle-aged and older adults, including depression, anxiety, and bereavement (Kim et al., 2009). Seeking psychological intervention for these disorders may ultimately benefit a person's sleep, which will in turn help to alleviate these mental health conditions.

There are a number of medical illnesses that can disrupt a person's sleep. These include arthritis, osteoporosis, cancer, chronic lung disease, congestive heart failure, and digestive disturbances (Bloom et al., 2009; Spira, Stone, Beaudreau, Ancoli-Israel, & Yaffe, 2009). People with Parkinson's disease or Alzheimer's disease also suffer serious sleep problems (Gabelle & Dauvilliers, 2010).

Finally, as we discussed earlier, people experience normal age-related changes in the bladder that lead to a more frequent urge to urinate during the night. As a result of these changes, the individual is likely to experience sleep disruptions. Menopausal symptoms can also lead to frequent awakenings during the night, although exercise seems to help minimize the impact of menopause on aging (Chedraui et al., 2010). Periodic leg movements during sleep (also called nocturnal myoclonus) are another source of nighttime awakenings (Ferri, Gschliesser, Frauscher, Poewe, & Hogl, 2009).

When these conditions interrupt sleep, they can lead to daytime sleepiness and fatigue. This creates a vicious cycle: the individual starts to establish a pattern of daytime napping, which increases the chances of sleep interruptions occurring at night (Foley et al., 2007), or is too tired to exercise. Sleep problems also can increase the risk of falling, cause difficulty concentrating, and lead to negative changes in quality of life (Ancoli-Israel & Cooke, 2005).

One physical condition that particularly interferes with sleep is **sleep apnea**, a disorder in which the individual becomes temporarily unable to breathe while asleep. People who suffer from this condition typically let out a loud snore followed by silence due to the closing of the airway. The respiratory control centers in the brain respond to the lack of oxygen, and the sleeper awakens. The periods of snoring and choking may occur as many as 100 times a night. To make up for the lack of oxygen that occurs during each

episode, the person's heart is forced to pump harder to circulate more blood. As a result, the person experiences large spikes in blood pressure during the night and elevated blood pressure during the day. Over time, the person's risk of heart attack and stroke is increased. Because so much of the night is spent awake, the individual becomes sleepy during the day and finds it difficult to complete everyday activities.

Sleep apnea is more common in older adults with cardiovascular or cerebrovascular disease (Fetveit, 2009). The condition can be treated with a continuous positive airway pressure (CPAP) device, which keeps airways open during sleep; however, users often complain that the burdensome equipment inhibits sleep patterns (Wolkove, Elkholy, Baltzan, & Palayew, 2007).

Although changes in sleep occur as a normal feature of the aging process, severe sleep disturbances do not. Exercise can help in improving disturbed circadian rhythms (Benloucif et al., 2004). Sleep specialists can offer innovative approaches such as light therapy, which "resets" an out-of-phase circadian rhythm, and encouragement of improvements in sleep habits (Klerman, Duffy, Dijk, & Czeisler, 2001).

Temperature Control

Every summer or winter, when regions of the country suffer extreme weather, older adults are among those reported to be at greatest risk of dying from hyper- or hypothermia, conditions known together as **dysthermia**. Approximately 700 people per year die from hyperthermia; 40% are 65 or older. Over a 20-year period (1979–1998), a total of 13,970 deaths were attributed to hypothermia (Centers for Disease Control and Prevention, 2006). Aging alone, however, does not seem to be the main cause of deaths due to hyperthermia, as the majority of those who die in conditions of extreme heat have heart disease (Luber & Sanchez, 2006).

There are also increasing numbers of deaths due to hypothermia in older adults (Fallico, Siciliano, & Yip, 2005). The cause of the higher death rates under conditions of hypothermia may be an impaired ability of older adults to maintain their core body temperature during extremely cold outside temperatures (Thompson-Torgerson, Holowatz, & Kenney, 2008).

In less extreme conditions, older adults are less able to adjust their internal bodily temperature. This is because their sweat output is reduced, causing their core temperatures to rise (Dufour & Candas, 2007). Adding to this is the fact that the dermal layer of the skin becomes thinner, making it more difficult to cool the skin (Petrofsky et al., 2009).

SENSATION AND PERCEPTION

A variety of changes occur in adulthood throughout the parts of the nervous system that affect sensation and perception. (see Table 4.5).

Vision

You may associate growing older with the need to wear reading glasses, and in fact, this is what occurs. Most people require some form of corrective lenses by the time they reach their 50s or 60s.

Presbyopia is the loss of the ability to focus vision on near objects, and is the primary culprit for the need for reading glasses. The cause of presbyopia is the thickening and hardening of the lens, which is the focusing mechanism of the eye (Sharma & Santhoshkumar, 2009). These changes mean that the lens cannot adapt its shape when needed to see objects up close to the face. By the age of 50, presbyopia affects the entire population.

There is no cure for the presbyopia. Bifocals had been the only correction available since the time of Benjamin Franklin (who invented them). Today, however, multifocal contact lenses are increasingly available (Woods, Woods, & Fonn, 2009).

Though you cannot cure presbyopia, you may be able to alter its onset; lifestyle habits seem to affect the rate at which the presbyopic aging process occurs. For example, smoking accelerates the aging of the lens (Kessel, Jorgensen, Glumer, & Larsen, 2006).

Older adults are also likely to experience the loss of visual acuity, or the ability to see details at a distance. The level of acuity in an 85-year-old individual is approximately 80% less than that of a person in his or her 40s. Turning up the lights is one effective strategy to compensate for loss of acuity, but at the same time, older adults are more sensitive to glare. For example, older drivers are more vulnerable to the glare caused by the lights of oncoming traffic on a dark road at night or the light of the setting sun shining directly on the windshield. As a result, making lights brighter may actually impair rather than improve an older person's visual acuity.

In addition to experiencing normal age-related changes in vision, older people become increasingly vulnerable to visual disorders. In fact, about one-half of adults over the age of 65 years report that they have experienced some form of visual impairment. The most common impairment and the main form of eye disease is a **cataract**, a clouding or opacity in the lens. This results in blurred or distorted vision because the retina cannot clearly focus the images. The term "cataract" reflects a previous view of this condition as a "waterfall" behind the eye that obscured vision.

Cataracts affect about 17% of the over-40 population (Congdon et al., 2004). Cataracts usually start as a gradual cloudiness that progressively grows more opaque and bothersome. Although they are most often white, they may also appear to be yellow or brownish in color. If the cataracts have a yellow or brown tone, colors will take on a yellow tinge similar to the effect of wearing colored sunglasses. Cataracts appear to develop as a normal part of the aging process, but other than the changes that occur in the lens fibers, their cause is not known. Factors such as heredity, prior injury, and diabetes may play a role in cataract formation. Cigarette smoking and nutritional deficits are additional risk factors (Rhone & Basu, 2008). Evidence suggests that a high intake of carbohydrates may increase the probability that a person develops cataracts (Chiu, Milton, Gensler, & Taylor, 2006). Conversely, taking vitamin C may reduce their formation (Yoshida et al., 2007).

As the cataract develops, the person's vision becomes increasingly impaired both under conditions of low light, as acuity is reduced, and under conditions of bright light, due to increased susceptibility to glare. Bright lights may seem to have a halo around them. These are significant limitations and can alter many aspects of the person's everyday life. It is more difficult to read, walk, watch television, recognize faces, and perform work, hobbies, and leisure activities. Consequently, people with cataracts may become more dependent on others because they cannot drive or go out at night on their own.

Fortunately, cataracts can be successfully treated with little inconvenience or pain. Enormous strides have been made in the treatment of cataracts due to advances in surgical procedures. Currently, people who undergo cataract surgery are through in an hour or less, under local anesthesia and with no hospital stay. They recover their vision

TABLE 4.5
Age-Related Changes in Vision and Hearing

Sense	Changes	
Vision	Presbyopia cataracts	Purestock/Getty Images, Inc.
Hearing	Presbycusis	MedicalRF.com/Alamy

within 1 to 7 days, and many people's vision is so improved that they rely only minimally on corrective lenses.

A second significant form of blindness that becomes more prevalent in later adulthood is **age-related macular degeneration (ARMD)**, a condition caused by damage to the photoreceptors located in the central region of the retina known as the macula. This area of the retina is normally used in reading, driving, and other visually demanding activities so that the selective damage to the receptors in the macula that occurs is particularly incapacitating. An estimated 15% of people 80 and older have this disease (ONeill, Jamison, McCulloch, & Smith, 2001), which is one of the leading causes of blindness in those over the age of 65 (Coleman, Chan, Ferris, & Chew, 2008).

Although there is no known treatment for ARMD, antioxidants and the avoidance of cigarette smoking (once again) can serve to reduce a person's risk (Zanon-Moreno, Garcia-Medina, Zanon-Viguer, Moreno-Nadal, & Pinazo-Duran, 2009). Exposure to light is yet another risk factor, so wearing protective lenses may serve as prevention (de Jong, 2006). If you find yourself squinting outside in the sunlight, you might think about decreasing your risk of developing ARMD in the future by putting on a pair of sunglasses. Treatments for the "wet" form of ARMD, which is related to damage to the vascular supply to the retina, so far include only medications that can slow its progression by reducing the growth of new blood cells (Brucker, 2009).

Glaucoma is the term used for a group of conditions causing blindness related to changes in pressure within the eyeball. The most common type of glaucoma develops gradually and painlessly without symptoms. Therefore, it may not be detected until the disease reaches advanced stages. Eventually, glaucoma causes a loss of peripheral vision and, over time, may cause the remaining vision to diminish altogether. More rarely, the symptoms appear suddenly: they include blurred vision, loss of side vision, perception of colored rings around lights, and experience of pain or redness in the eyes.

Glaucoma is the third most common cause of blindness in the United States, and the most common form of glaucoma is estimated to affect about 3 million Americans. It is diagnosed in 95,000 new patients each year. Blacks are at higher risk than Whites, as are people who are nearsighted, have diabetes, or have a family history of glaucoma. Arthritis (Perruccio, Badley, & Trope, 2007) and obesity (Imai et al., 2010) are additional risk factors. Some forms of glaucoma can be controlled but not cured, and others can be treated successfully through surgery.

Visual disturbances in older adults, whatever their cause, require the attention of health care professionals. Not only might they be treatable, but even if they're not, their presence can relate to psychological symptoms, including depression and isolation. Moreover, visual problems can create difficulties in other areas of functioning, such as increasing the likelihood of a person's falling or making medication errors that can have serious consequences in their own right (Pelletier, Thomas, & Shaw, 2009).

Hearing

Hearing loss is a common occurrence in later adulthood, as depicted in Table 4.5. The most common form of age-related hearing loss is **presbycusis**, in which degenerative changes occur in the cochlea or auditory nerve leading from the cochlea to the brain. Presbycusis is most often associated with loss of high-pitched sounds, because the cochlear cells that are triggered by high-frequency stimuli are located toward the front of the cochlea, the area that receives the most stimulation by noise waves in general.

Hearing loss clearly has an effect on the older adult's ability to engage in conversation (Murphy, Daneman, & Schneider, 2006). In turn, older adults may be more likely to avoid potentially noisy situations, such as eating at a restaurant.

Fortunately, although hereditary factors play a role in presbycusis, there are steps you can take to protect yourself from the environmental contributors that are almost, if not more, important. Various health problems such as diabetes, heart disease, and high blood pressure can also put a person at higher risk (Aimoni et al., 2010). However, exposure to loud noise is the most frequent cause of presbycusis (Mohammadi, Mazhari, Mehrparvar, & Attarchi, 2009). The next time you turn up the music playing in your headphones or go to a loud concert, think about the long-term effects on your hearing, particularly if you wake up the following morning with your ears still ringing (see Figure 4.8).

Another hearing disturbance that is relatively common in older people is **tinnitus**, a symptom in which the individual perceives sounds in the head or ear (such as a ringing noise) when there is no external source. The condition can be temporarily associated with the use of aspirin, antibiotics, and anti-inflammatory agents. Changes in the bones of the skull due to trauma and the buildup of wax in the ears may also contribute to tinnitus. Although treatments are available for tinnitus (generally dependent on the cause of the symptom), there is no cure.

Using hearing aids can help adults with hearing loss overcome many hearing-related problems. With increasing improvements in the quality of hearing aids as well as reductions in their size, people no longer need to rely on devices that are visible to others. These miniature devices considerably reduce the social stigma many associate with the need to wear a hearing aid. They are also more effective,

FIGURE 4.8

How Loud Is Too Loud?

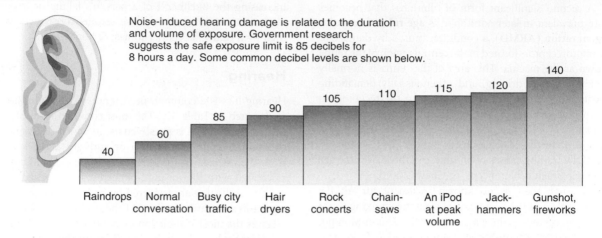

Noise-induced hearing damage is related to the duration and volume of exposure. Government research suggests the safe exposure limit is 85 decibels for 8 hours a day. Some common decibel levels are shown below.

Raindrops	Normal conversation	Busy city traffic	Hair dryers	Rock concerts	Chain-saws	An iPod at peak volume	Jack-hammers	Gunshot, fireworks
40	60	85	90	105	110	115	120	140

and particularly so because people are more likely to use them given that they are so small and easily hidden.

Even without a hearing aid, however, it's possible for older adults to improve their ability to understand speech if they take advantage of various communication strategies. The first is to look directly at the person speaking to them and to make sure that there is enough light so that they can clearly see the person's face. Older adults should also turn down background noise that could interfere with the audio stream they are trying to follow, whether it's a person, a television, or the radio. At restaurants and social gatherings, they should find a place to talk that is as far as possible from crowded or noisy areas. They can also ask the people speaking to them not to chew food or gum while talking and not to speak too quickly (Janse, 2009).

Many people talking to an older adult (with or without hearing loss) tend to over-compensate and raise their voices unnecessarily high. This has the unfortunate effect of interfering with the speech signal. It is also important for the speaker to enunciate carefully, speak in a low tone (to offset presbycusis) and look straight at the older adult. Most importantly, if you're the speaker, you should avoid talking to the person as if he or she were a child. This also includes referring to the individual in the third person or leaving the person out of the conversation altogether (based on the assumption that he or she can't hear).

Providing context is also useful because this provides additional cues to the listener about your topic of conversation. You can also gauge whether you are being understood by paying careful attention to how the other person is responding to you, both verbally and nonverbally. Finally, rather than becoming frustrated or upset with the listener, maintaining a positive and patient attitude will encourage the listener to remain more engaged in the conversation.

Balance

As important as the maintenance of visual and auditory functioning are with increasing age, the sense of balance can mean the difference between life and death. Loss of balance is one of the main factors responsible for falls in older adults (Dickin, Brown, & Doan, 2006). In 2005 alone, more than 15,800 people 65 and older were known to have died directly from injuries related to falls (Kung, Hoyert, Xu, & Murphy, 2008), 1.8 million were treated in emergency departments for fall-related nonfatal injuries, and about 460,000 of these people were hospitalized (Stevens, Ryan, & Kresnow, 2006). Older adults who become injured in a fall also have a higher risk of requiring institutionalization and a higher rate of mortality (Porell & Carter, 2012).

In addition to experiencing changes in balance, people who are more likely to fall have a history of previous falls, are weaker, have an impaired gait, and are more likely to be on medications (Tinetti & Kumar, 2010). Older individuals who have more difficulty detecting body position are more likely to lose their balance or fail to see a step or an obstacle in their path on a level surface.

It is natural that people who have had a painful and perhaps frightening experience of a fall become anxious in a subsequent situation where they feel insecure; they then become even more unsteady in their gait

Hans Neleman/Getty Images, Inc.

Practicing Tai Chi can help older adults maintain their balance and flexibility to offset age changes that can increase their risk of falling.

(Reelick, van Iersel, Kessels, & Rikkert, 2009). The **fear of falling** can create a vicious cycle in which older individuals increasingly restrict their movement. When they become less physically active, they further risk losing their strength, which in turn increases the risk of a fall. You can think of fear of falling as a form of low self-efficacy as much as an actual fear. The individual is convinced that he or she lacks the ability to avoid a fall.

The two symptoms most frequently associated with age-related vestibular dysfunction are dizziness and vertigo. **Dizziness** is an uncomfortable sensation of feeling light-headed and even floating. **Vertigo** refers to the sensation of spinning when the body is at rest.

Because the vestibular system is so intimately connected to other parts of the nervous system, people may experience symptoms of vestibular disturbance in the form of problems such as headache, muscular aches in the neck and back, and increased sensitivity to noise and bright lights. Other signs of vestibular disturbance include fatigue, inability to concentrate, unsteadiness while walking, and difficulty with speech. Increased sensitivity to motion sickness is another common symptom. Some of these changes may come about with diseases that are not part of normal aging; others may occur as the result of normative alterations in the vestibular receptors.

Exercise can help older adults learn to compensate for factors that increase their chance of falling (Kim, Yoshida, & Suzuki, 2010). The most beneficial forms of exercise include learning how to step with assistance (Hanke &

Tiberio, 2006) and strengthening the leg muscles (Takahashi, Takahashi, Nakadaira, & Yamamoto, 2006). People who are concerned about falling should also cut back on the medications they take for other conditions that can cause confusion or disorientation (Kannus, Uusi-Rasi, Palvanen, & Parkkari, 2005).

Falls can also be prevented if a person wears proper eyeglasses, uses a prosthetic aid in walking, outfits the home with balance aids such as handrails, and develops greater sensitivity to the need to take care while walking. Having an accurate eyeglass prescription is crucial, given that vision provides important cues to navigating the environment. Accordingly, older adults with uncorrected visual problems are more vulnerable to falls (Vitale, Cotch, & Sperduto, 2006). Older adults can also benefit from Tai Chi to help them improve their balance and lessen the likelihood of falling (Harmer & Li, 2008). Most recently, researchers have suggested martial arts training as an effective intervention (Groen, Smulders, de Kam, Duysens, & Weerdesteyn, 2010).

Although a person may resist using a walking stick, this is an adaptation to changes in balance that can lead to significant improvements in mobility. At home, people can also make relatively simple adaptations that prevent falls, such as getting a shower chair or bath bench in the tub and installing a handheld shower head. Learning to sit while performing ordinary grooming tasks, such as shaving, further reduces a person's risk of falling. People can also outfit their kitchens to minimize the fall risk, such as bringing in a tall (but stable) chair or stool that they use while they cook. Having multiple telephones in the home is another useful strategy so that the need to hurry to reach the phone (and possibly fall) is avoided. Even better, keeping a cell phone close by reduces this risk entirely. The person at risk of falling can also derive feelings of security, and a lower risk of falling, by having the cell phone nearby in case he or she actually does fall and needs help.

In addition to practical strategies, older individuals can learn to develop greater sensitivity to the floors that they navigate, such as when they step onto a tile floor from a carpet. They can also be trained to recognize situations that realistically should be avoided, such as bumpy sidewalks or wet floors. As they do, they gain a greater sense of personal control over the likelihood of falling, lowering their fear of it and increasing their ability to navigate around their environments within safe limits (Zijlstra et al., 2009a).

Smell and Taste

You are able to enjoy food thanks to your taste buds (responsible for the sense of gustation or the act of tasting) and smell receptors (responsible for the sense of olfaction or smell). Smell and taste belong to the chemical sensing system referred to as chemosensation. The sensory receptors in these systems are triggered when molecules released by certain substances stimulate special cells in the nose, mouth, or throat. Despite the fact that the olfactory receptors constantly replace themselves, the area of the olfactory epithelium shrinks with age, and ultimately the total number of receptors becomes reduced throughout the adult years. At birth, the olfactory epithelium covers a wide area of the upper nasal cavities, but by the 20s and 30s, its area has started to shrink noticeably.

Approximately one-third of all adults 65 and older suffer some form of olfactory impairment (Shu et al., 2009) with almost half of those 80 years and older having virtually no ability to smell at all (Lafreniere & Mann, 2009). The loss of olfactory receptors reflects intrinsic changes associated with the aging process, as well as damage caused by disease, injury, and exposure to toxins. Research suggests that these environmental toxins may play a larger role in olfactory impairment than changes due to the aging process. Chronic diseases, medications, and sinus problems may be a more significant source of impairment than age per se over the life span (Rawson, 2006).

Tobacco smoke is a major source of interference with taste and smell. Although people who quit smoking eventually experience an improvement in their sense of smell, this can take many years (equal to the number of years spent smoking). Dentures are another cause of loss of taste sensitivity: they may block the receptor cells of the taste buds. Add to this the fact that certain medications also interfere with taste disorders (Schiffman, 2009), and it is difficult to determine whether aging brings with it inherent changes in taste or not.

Cognitive changes are also believed to be associated with a loss of smell sensitivity. Older adults who have experienced the greatest impairment in cognitive functioning may be the most vulnerable to loss of odor identification abilities. In one longitudinal study, researchers followed older adults over a 3-year period and observed that people with the most rapid decline in cognitive processes had the greatest rate of decline in the ability to label various odors (Wilson, Arnold, Tang, & Bennett, 2006).

Although nothing can be done to reverse age-related losses of smell and taste once they occur, people who suffer from severe losses may benefit from medical evaluations and treatments for underlying conditions (Welge-Lussen, 2009). Apart from such interventions, older people can also take advantage of strategies to enhance the enjoyment of food, such as expanding their food choices, planning meals in pleasant environments, and finding good dining companions.

Somatosensory System

You are able to move around in the environment through the operation of the somatosensory system, which translates information about touch, temperature, and position to your nervous system. Awareness of bodily position is made possible by proprioception, which provides information about where your limbs are placed when you are standing still. Kinesthesis applies to the knowledge that receptors in your limbs provide when your body is moving. Through proprioception, you would know that you are poised at the top of a staircase, ready to take your first step downward; through kinesthesis, you would know that you are actually moving down those stairs.

Touch. A well-established body of evidence links the loss of the ability to discriminate touch with the aging process throughout adulthood. Age differences have been documented in such areas as the ability to differentiate the separation of two points of pressure on the skin and the detection of the location of a stimulus applied to the skin. One estimate places the loss at 1% per year over the years from 20 to 80. However, the rate of loss varies according to body part. The hands and feet are particularly subject to the effects of aging compared with centrally located areas such as the lip and tongue. These losses can compromise the adult's ability to grasp, maintain balance, and perform delicate handwork and can interfere with speech (Wickremaratchi & Llewelyn, 2006).

Pain. The question of whether older adults are more or less sensitive to pain is a topic of considerable concern for health practitioners. Changes in pain perception with age could make life either much harder or much easier for individuals with illnesses (such as arthritis) that cause chronic pain.

There is no evidence that older adults become somehow immune or at least protected from pain by virtue of age changes in this sensory system. Lower back pain for at least 30 days in the past year was reported among 12% of a large-scale sample of Danish elders (Leboeuf-Yde, Nielsen, Kyvik, Fejer, & Hartvigsen, 2009). Although benign back pain shows a decrease across adulthood, back pain that is more severe and disabling increases in the later years (Dionne, Dunn, & Croft, 2006).

Most older adults are able to maintain regular functioning despite the presence of chronic pain; however, as one would expect, the pain makes it more difficult for them to carry out their everyday activities (Covinsky, Lindquist, Dunlop, & Yelin, 2009).The experience of pain can also interfere with cognitive performance, in addition to being a limitation in an individual's everyday life. In one sample of more than 300 older adults, poorer performance on tests of memory and spatial abilities was observed among individuals who suffered from chronic lower back pain (Weiner, Rudy, Morrow, Slaboda, & Lieber, 2006). In a study of more than 11,000 elders in the United Kingdom, researchers found that regardless of the presence of other complicating conditions such as depression and anxiety, the experience of chronic pain had a direct relationship to an experience of cognitive symptoms (Westoby, Mallen, & Thomas, 2009). You should keep this finding in mind when you evaluate studies of cognitive performance in older adults, because it is possible that many reports of age differences reflect the fact that they are distracted by pain.

Psychological factors may also interact with the experience of pain in older adults. Symptoms of benign pain may diminish along the aging process because older adults have become habituated to the daily aches and pains associated with changes in their bones, joints, and muscles. It is also possible that cohort factors interact with intrinsic age changes to alter the likelihood that complaints about pain will be expressed. The experience of pain is associated with the personality trait of stoicism (the tendency to suffer in silence) (Yong, 2006). Older adults may simply not wish to admit to others, or even themselves, that they are feeling some of those aches and pains.

People can reduce the risk of pain in later adulthood can by controlling for the factors related to greater pain prevalence. Obesity is highly associated with chronic pain even after controlling for education and related conditions such as diabetes, hypertension, arthritis, and depression (McCarthy, Bigal, Katz, Derby, & Lipton, 2009). Thus, controlling for weight would seem to be an important and effective intervention. At the same time, rather than relying on pain medications, all of which carry the risk of abuse or at least interactions with treatments for other conditions, it is also advisable for older adults to learn to manage their pain through holistic methods (McCleane, 2007).

In summary, changes in physical functioning have important interactions with psychological and sociocultural factors, and can influence the individual's identity in the middle and later years of adulthood. Fortunately, there are many preventative and compensating steps that people can take to slow the rate of physical aging.

SUMMARY

1. Appearance is an important part of a person's identity, and throughout adulthood, the components of appearance all undergo change. Following the interactionist model of development, physical changes affect a person's behavior, which can modify the actions the individual takes to slow or modify those changes. Many age changes in the skin are the result of photoaging. The hair thins and becomes gray, and in men in particular, baldness can develop. There are significant changes in body build, including loss of height, increase of body weight into the 50s followed by a decrease, and changes in fat distribution. However, adults of all ages can benefit from exercise, which can maintain muscle and lower body fat.

2. Mobility reflects the quality of the muscles, bones, and joints. Age-related losses in mobility typically start in the 40s. The process of sarcopenia involves loss of muscle mass, and there is a corresponding decrease in muscle strength although muscular endurance is maintained. Strength training is the key to maintaining maximum muscle functioning in adulthood. Bones lose mineral content throughout adulthood, particularly among women, in large part based on genetic factors. Diet and exercise are important areas of prevention. The joints encounter many deleterious changes, and although exercise cannot prevent these, middle-aged and older adults can benefit from strength training, which builds muscles that support the joints, and flexibility training, which maintains range of motion even in damaged joints.

3. The cardiovascular system undergoes changes due to alterations in the heart muscle and arteries that lower aerobic capacity, cardiac output, and maximum heart rate. It is crucial for adults to avoid harmful fats in the diet and to engage in a regular pattern of aerobic exercise to minimize changes in the cardiovascular system. The respiratory system loses functioning due to stiffening of lung tissue starting at about age 40. Important preventive actions include avoiding (or quitting) cigarette smoking and maintaining a low BMI. Although age changes in the kidney are likely due to nephron loss, other environmental factors, such as smoking, illness, or extreme exertion appear to play a role. Changes in the urinary system make the kidney more vulnerable to stress and less able to metabolize toxins, including medications. The bladder of older adults becomes less able to retain and expel urine, but the majority of people do not become incontinent. Behavioral methods and/or medication can correct normal age-related changes in urinary control. The digestive system becomes somewhat less efficient in older adults, but there is not a significant loss of functioning. In addition to the physiological changes, lifestyle factors impact overall

digestive health. Many older people are misinformed by the media and take unnecessary corrective medications to control their gastrointestinal functioning.

4. The endocrine system is the site of many changes in the amount and functioning of the body's hormones as people age. The growth and thyroid-stimulating hormones affected by age include growth hormones, cortisol, thyroid hormones, melatonin, and DHEA. The climacteric is the period of gradual loss of reproductive abilities. After menopause, which typically occurs at the age of 50, women experience a reduction in estrogen. Decreases in testosterone levels in older men, referred to as andropause, are not consistently observed. Erectile dysfunction is observed in 44% of men age 65 and older. Changes in the immune system, referred to as immune senescence, are observed primarily in a decline in T cell and B cell functioning. Diet and exercise can counteract the loss of immune responsiveness in older adults while chronic stress can accelerate the immune system's aging.

5. Normal age-related changes in the nervous system were once thought of as neuronal fallout, but it is now recognized that there is much plasticity in the aging brain. The increasing availability of brain scanning methods for research purposes has revealed considerable variation in age-related alterations in brain structure. There is a rise in Stage 1 and a decrease in Stage 4 and REM (dream-related) sleep. Changes in circadian rhythms lead older adults to awaken earlier and prefer the morning for working. Poor sleep habits and the coexistence of psychological or physical disorders (such as sleep apnea) can interfere further with the sleep patterns of middle-aged and older adults. In many cases, dysthermia (including hyper- or hypothermia) is related to the presence of disease.

6. Visual acuity decreases across adulthood, and presbyopia leads to a loss of the ability to focus the eye on near objects. Cataracts, age-related macular degeneration, and glaucoma are medical conditions that can lead to reduced vision or blindness. Presbycusis, the most common form of age-related hearing loss, can interfere with the ability to communicate. Hearing aids can help older adults overcome many hearing-related problems. Older adults are more vulnerable to a loss of balance, particularly when they suffer from dizziness and vertigo. Balance training can compensate for these changes and help reduce the fear of falling. There is loss of the perception of the position of the feet and legs, adding to other age-related changes in balance. Smell and taste show some losses with age, but both senses are extremely vulnerable to negative effects from disease and environmental damage, in particular from tobacco smoke. A loss of the ability to discriminate touch is observed in aging, particularly in the hands and feet. Findings on changes in pain perception with aging are inconclusive.

5

Health and Prevention

The Kiss of Health

You may not believe it, but kissing may improve your health, your well-being, and your intimate relationships. Kory Floyd and colleagues investigated the possible benefits of kissing in a sample of 52 married or cohabitating adults (Floyd et al., 2009). They wanted to know whether the physical act of kissing provided tangible, measurable benefits and if it can improve one's health.

In what has to be one of the most unusual "experimental" treatments in all of social science, the researchers assigned half their sample (ages 19 to 67) to a frequent kissing condition and the other half to a control condition with no special instructions to kiss: "The point is for the two of you to kiss each other more often and for longer periods of time than you typically do right now." But this was more than a one-night stand: "We hope you will both make increased kissing a priority over the next six weeks." There were no such instructions given to the control group, who did not know the purpose of the study (though obviously, they did give informed consent).

At the end of the study, the kissing group in fact stated they felt less stressed and more satisfied in their relationship. Importantly, for their health, their cholesterol levels (the "bad" kind) decreased as well. Compared to the control group, the couples in the kissing group also reported that they exercised more, argued less, had less conflict, and understood each other better. As a result, the researchers had to rule these factors out statistically when examining the group differences in cholesterol. Even with these factors controlled, the kissing group still retained their health advantage.

These findings give new meaning to the term "healthy relationship." Kissing can improve both your intimate relationships, and beyond that, perhaps your risk of heart disease by improving your response to stress. If you're in a long-term relationship, the takeaway is clear: kiss early and kiss often. If not, expressing affection in other ways can also provide you with stress-buffering boosts.

Posted by Susan Whitbourne and Stacey Whitbourne

TABLE 5.1

Percent Within Age Groups of Chronic Conditions 2010

Age	Heart Disease	Coronary Heart Disease	Heart Attack	Stroke	Cancer, All	Arthritis	Diabetes
45–64 years	12.2	6.9	3.7	2.7	8.4	29.3	11.0
65–74 years	26.7	18.0	10.1	6.7	18.7	46.6	19.3
75–84 years	35.9	24.2	13.7	10.8	25.5	52.3	18.4
85 and over	41.2	28.6	15.3	14.0	27.1	54.7	14.1

Source: Centers for Disease Control and Prevention. (2012). Health data interactive. Retrieved from http://www.cdc.gov/nchs/hdi.htm

Chronic illnesses can significantly interfere with the quality of a person's daily life. People with chronic illnesses find it difficult to carry out many simple tasks of everyday living. They may be limited in their ability to move, experience pain and anxiety, and be unable to complete simple mental tasks. Psychologists providing services to older adults with chronic illnesses may find that these chronic illnesses make it more difficult to diagnose and treat psychological disorders. Although it is important to distinguish illness from normal aging, there are significant chronic diseases to which people become increasingly susceptible with age. You can see a summary of the prevalence of the major chronic illnesses from ages 45 and older in the United States in Table 5.1.

KEY CONCEPTS IN HEALTH AND PREVENTION

Health is more than the absence of illness or disability. According to the World Health Organization (1948), **health** is a state of complete physical, mental, and social well-being. This multidimensional definition fits well with the biopsychosocial model, as it emphasizes all realms of the individual's functioning. In addition, as we shall see throughout this chapter, people who are healthy are not just not ill, but are able to maintain a sense of well-being.

It is important to keep in mind, then, that health is not simply the absence of disability. However, disability can limit the individual's ability to adapt to the requirements of everyday life. Many health researchers and practitioners find it useful to assess an older adult's ability to perform **activities of daily living (ADL)**, which are the tasks of bathing, dressing, transferring, using the toilet, and eating. An expanded measure evaluates the **instrumental activities of daily living (IADL)**, which include the ability to use the telephone, go shopping, prepare meals, complete housekeeping tasks, do the laundry, use private or public transportation, take medications, and handle finances (Lawton & Brody, 1969). These measures provide a functional assessment of health status by indicating the degree of independence the individual can maintain whether living at home or in an institution.

The behavioral risk factors for chronic disease include a sedentary lifestyle, smoking, alcohol use, and unhealthy diets (see Figure 5.1). According to the World Health Organization (Mendis, Puska, & Norrving, 2011), of the 57 million deaths worldwide in 2008, 36 million, or 63%, were due to chronic disease; these diseases also contribute heavily to the health care costs around the world. To the extent that individuals are able to reduce their risk factors for chronic disease, they therefore improve not only their quality of life, but also the economic health of society.

DISEASES OF THE CARDIOVASCULAR SYSTEM

We begin with **cardiovascular disease**, a term that refers to a set of abnormal conditions that develop in the heart and arteries. The number one cause of death worldwide, cardiovascular disease can also cause chronic disability.

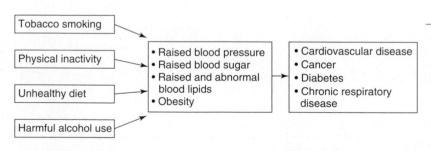

FIGURE 5.1

Behavioral Risk Factors for Chronic Diseases in Adulthood

Source: Adapted from Mendis, S., Puska, P., & Norrving, B. (2011). *Global atlas on cardiovascular disease prevention and control.* Geneva, Switzerland: World Health Organization.

Because the distribution of blood throughout the body is essential for the normal functioning of all other organ systems, cardiovascular disease can have a widespread range of effects on the individual's health and everyday life.

Cardiac and Cerebrovascular Conditions

Chronic diseases that fall into the category of cardiac and cerebrovascular conditions are linked by the fact that they involve disturbances of the cardiovascular system.

As we described in Chapter 4, fat and other substances accumulate in the walls of the arteries throughout the body as part of the normal aging process. One of the most pervasive chronic diseases is **atherosclerosis**, a term that derives from the Greek words *athero* (meaning paste) and *sclerosis* (meaning hardness). In atherosclerosis, fatty deposits collect at an abnormally high rate, substantially reducing the width of the arteries and limiting the circulation of the blood (see Figure 5.2). **Arteriosclerosis** is a general term for the thickening and hardening of arteries. Everyone experiences some degree of arteriosclerosis as part of normal aging.

It is possible to live with atherosclerosis and not encounter significant health problems. However, atherosclerosis eventually leads to a buildup in plaque in a particular artery such that blood no longer reaches its destination.

FIGURE 5.2

Development of Atherosclerosis

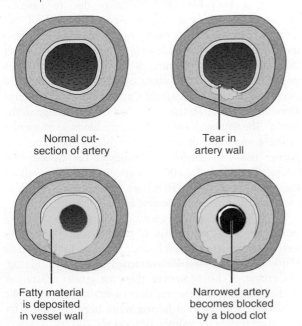

Normal cut-section of artery

Tear in artery wall

Fatty material is deposited in vessel wall

Narrowed artery becomes blocked by a blood clot

The organs or tissues that are fed by that artery then suffer serious damage due to the lack of blood supply. When this process affects arteries that feed the heart muscle, the individual is said to have **coronary (or ischemic) heart disease**. The term **myocardial infarction** refers to the acute condition in which the blood supply to part of the heart muscle (the myocardium) is severely reduced or blocked.

An individual with **hypertension** suffers from chronic abnormally elevated blood pressure. The technical definition of hypertension is based on the two measures of blood pressure. Systolic is the pressure exerted by the blood as it is pushed out of the heart during contraction, and diastolic is the pressure when the blood is relaxed between beats. Blood pressure is measured in units of "mm Hg," or millimeters of mercury, referring to the display on a blood pressure scale. A person is diagnosed with hypertension when his or her blood pressure is greater than or equal to 140 mm Hg systolic pressure or 90 mm Hg diastolic pressure.

Atherosclerosis contributes to hypertension in the following way. The accumulation of plaque forces the blood to be pushed through narrower and narrower arteries. As a result, the pressure on the blood as it is being pumped out of the heart becomes greater and greater, and the person now is at risk for hypertension.

Hypertension itself creates dangerous changes in the arteries. The more pressure that the blood exerts in its passage through the arteries, the greater the strain on the arteries' delicate walls. Over time, these walls become weakened and inflamed. As they do, they accumulate even more plaque, which tends to settle into those cracks and weak areas. Consequently, the individual's hypertension becomes even more pronounced. This problem is more severe in the larger arteries, particularly the ones leading from the heart, which take the full force of the heart's pumping action.

In addition to damaging the arteries, hypertension increases the workload of the heart. Because the arteries have narrowed, the heart must pump harder and harder to push out the blood. The heart muscle in the left ventricle (the part that pumps out the blood) becomes thickened and overgrown. This hypertrophy of the left ventricle further compromises the health of the cardiovascular system.

Congestive heart failure (or heart failure) is a condition in which the heart is unable to pump enough blood to meet the needs of the body's other organs. Blood flows out of the heart at an increasingly slower rate, causing the blood returning to the heart through the veins to back up. Eventually, the tissues become congested with fluid. This condition can result from a variety of diseases, including coronary heart disease, scar tissue from a past myocardial infarction, hypertension, disease of the heart valves, disease of the heart muscle, infection of the heart, or heart defects present at birth. People with congestive heart failure are unable to exert themselves without becoming exhausted and short of breath. Their legs may swell due to edema, a condition in which fluid builds up in their bodies. They may also experience fluid buildup in their lungs along with kidney problems.

The term "cerebrovascular disease" refers to disorders of circulation to the brain. This condition may lead to the onset of a **cerebrovascular accident**, also known as a "stroke" or "brain attack," an acute condition in which an artery leading to the brain bursts or is clogged by a blood clot or other particle. The larger the area of the brain deprived of blood, the more severe the deterioration of the physical and mental functions controlled by that area. Another condition caused by the development of clots in the cerebral arteries is a **transient ischemic attack (TIA)**, also called a ministroke. The cause of a TIA is the same as that of a stroke, but in a TIA, the blockage of the artery is temporary. The tissues that were deprived of blood soon recover, but chances are that another TIA will follow. People who have had a TIA are also at higher risk of subsequently suffering from a stroke.

Incidence

Heart disease is the number one killer in the United States, resulting in 24% of all deaths in the year 2010. Together, heart and cerebrovascular disease accounted for 33% of all deaths in the United States of people 65 and older (National Center for Vital Statistics, 2013), a figure that is comparable to the rate observed in Canada (Tu et al., 2009). Though these numbers are high, the percentage is even greater in older adults; half of all deaths of people 75 years and older in the U.S. are due to heart disease, making it the deadliest illness among the oldest segment of the population.

Worldwide, coronary heart disease and stroke were the leading causes of death in 2010, amounting to 12.9 million deaths or 25% of all deaths (Wang et al., 2012). The countries with the highest death rates from these ailments as of 2009 were Russia, Bulgaria, Hungary, and Romania; the United States ranked 13th and Canada ranked 26th in the world (Lloyd-Jones et al., 2010).

Behavioral Risk Factors

Lifestyle factors contribute significantly to all forms of heart disease. Even people who have a strong genetic predisposition to cardiovascular disease can reduce (or raise) their risks through the choices they make on a daily basis. Referring back to Figure 5.2, we will now consider each of the four risk factors in terms of cardiovascular disease.

Looking first at tobacco smoking, approximately one-fifth of all adults in the United States smoke. The rates of current smokers decrease across age groups of adults to 10% of those 65 and older (National Health Interview Survey, 2009). It is very possible that the smoking rates decrease not only because older adults are less likely to smoke but also because the nonsmokers are more likely to survive.

Although it is not known exactly why smoking increases the risk of heart disease, most researchers believe that it damages the arteries, making them more vulnerable to plaque formation and ultimately leading to the deleterious changes we outlined earlier. Though having long-lived parents is related to lower levels of cardiovascular risk factors, the benefits of heredity are offset among women who smoke (Jaunin et al., 2009).

A sedentary lifestyle is the next major risk factor for heart disease. There is a well-established relationship between leisure activity and heart disease (Yung et al., 2009), with estimates ranging from a 24% reduction in the risk of myocardial infarction among nonstrenuous exercisers to a 47% reduced risk among individuals engaging in a regular pattern of strenuous exercise (Lovasi et al., 2007). As it happens, the majority of adults at highest risk for heart disease (i.e., those 75 and older) are the least likely to exercise. Only about 36% of people 65 to 74 and 16% of those 75 and older engage in vigorous leisure activity (National Health Interview Survey, 2009).

An unhealthy diet places the individual at risk of developing a BMI in the overweight or obese range. An analysis of 57 longitudinal studies conducted in Western Europe and North America showed a causal relationship between a high BMI and mortality due to vascular disease (Whitlock et al., 2009). According to the CDC, dramatic increases in the number of overweight and obese individuals have occurred among United States adults over the past 20 years. Currently, 30.3% of the United States population is considered obese by government standards. According to the International Organization for Economic Development (2007), this is the highest percentage in the world. The intake of high-cholesterol foods in particular is the component of obesity that places individuals at greater risk for developing cardiovascular disease and stroke (Erqou et al., 2009). Conversely, high levels of the "good" cholesterol (HDL) are related to lower risk of cardiovascular disease (Cooney, et al., 2009).

Finally, some alcohol consumption appears to have a protective effect on the risk of cardiovascular disease as well as on functional health declines in general (Chen & Hardy, 2009), at least for women (Djousse, Lee, Buring, & Gaziano, 2009). Moreover, there are gender differences in the relationship between alcohol intake and metabolic syndrome, with alcohol having more negative effects for men than it does for women (Buja et al., 2009).

These risk factors combine to produce higher rates of stroke in the United States within the southeastern region of the country. The Southeast is considered the "stroke belt" of the United States, with 8 to 12 states in this region having substantially higher stroke mortality than the rest of the country. Three states comprising the "stroke buckle" include North Carolina, South Carolina, and Georgia. The high rates of stroke are attributed in part to diets in this region that are based on high consumption of sodium, monounsaturated fatty acids, polyunsaturated fatty acids and cholesterol, and the low consumption of dietary fiber (see Figure 5.3).

Although stroke rates are in general elevated for the stroke belt, they are particularly high for Blacks. In a study of more than 23,000 men and women 45 years and older, researchers found higher scores for Blacks than Whites on measures related to stroke risk, including hypertension, systolic blood pressure, diabetes, smoking, and hypertrophy of the left ventricle of the heart (Cushman et al., 2008). The stroke belt's higher risk also reflects the fact that the region has lower levels of education and less access to health care than is true for other areas within the United States. (The high costs incurred by this at-risk population for health care is a topic we will cover in more detail in Chapter 11).

The cluster of symptoms associated with these high risk factors for cardiovascular (and other) diseases is known by the term **metabolic syndrome** (see Table 5.2). The symptoms include high levels of abdominal obesity, high blood fats (known as triglycerides), abnormal levels of blood cholesterol (low "good" cholesterol or HDL and high "bad" cholesterol or LDL), hypertension, and high glucose. Even possessing three of the risk factors involved in the metabolic syndrome increases a person's risk of mortality from cardiovascular disease (Clarke et al., 2009).

Prevention of Heart Disease and Stroke

Advances in the understanding of the cause of heart disease and stroke have resulted in safer and more effective medical and dietary supplements, which have lowered

FIGURE 5.3

The "Stroke Belt" in the U.S., 2010

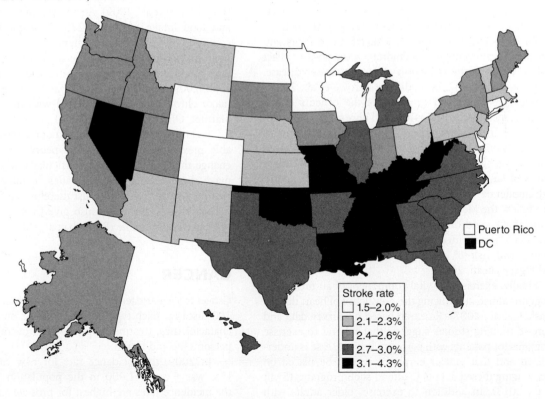

Stroke rate
- 1.5–2.0%
- 2.1–2.3%
- 2.4–2.6%
- 2.7–3.0%
- 3.1–4.3%

☐ Puerto Rico
■ DC

The "stroke belt" can be seen in this map as the Southeastern portion of the United States where stroke rates are highest.

Source: http://apps.nccd.cdc.gov/gisbrfss/map.aspx

TABLE 5.2
Criteria for the Metabolic Syndrome

Risk factor	Defining level
Abdominal obesity (waist circumference)	Men: > 40 in Women: > 35 in
Triglycerides	> = 150 mg/dL
HDL cholesterol (the good kind)	Men: < 40 mg/dL Women: <50 mg/dL
Blood pressure	Systolic BP > 130 or diastolic > 85 Hg mercury
Fasting glucose	> 100 mg/dL

Diagnosis requires three or more of the five characteristics.
dL = milligrams per deciliter.

cardiovascular death rates. The lowering of cholesterol through preventive medications is becoming the primary mode of intervention. Chief among these medications are statins, which work by lowering the levels of harmful cholesterol (LDL) in the blood. However, in addition to or instead of medication, anyone can benefit from control of diet and participation in exercise as preventive strategies; the earlier you begin to follow these strategies, the better.

As we noted in Chapter 1, a diet high in fruits and vegetables significantly lowers mortality; the positive effect is mainly due to the reduction of cardiovascular disease, particularly ischaemic heart disease (Crowe et al., 2011). Research has continued to advocate the benefits of the "Mediterranean style diet" as a way of lowering one's risk of cardiac death (Nordmann et al., 2011). This diet promotes the consumption of meals that include minimally processed fruits, vegetables, nuts, seeds, grains, olive oil as the main source of fat, low amounts of red meat and dairy foods, with moderate amounts of wine during meals. People who follow the Mediterranean diet have a diminished risk of metabolic syndrome and higher levels of high-density lipoprotein (Kastorini et al., 2011) as well as less cognitive decline and risk of dementia (Féart, Samieri, Allès, & Barberger-Gateau, 2013).

Finally, exercise is a vital component of all preventive programs aimed at reducing the prevalence of heart disease (Haskell et al., 2007). Research based on survey data and exercise training studies suggests that referral to exercise programs for patients with coronary heart disease is under-utilized and that greater emphasis should be placed on encouraging these patients to attend such programs (Swift et al., 2013). In addition to exercise, older adults with hypertension can also benefit from relaxation training; even a 12-session audio relaxation training program was shown in one study to have beneficial effects (Tang, Harms, Speck, Vezeau, & Jesurum, 2009).

There are significant national differences in risk of heart disease as well as other major illness. Eastern European countries, such as Russia, Bulgaria, Romania, and Poland, have the highest death rates from cardiovascular disease (Lloyd-Jones et al., 2009). An analysis of the dietary habits and food intake of almost 27,000 people living in the countries of Central and Eastern Europe suggested that poor dietary habits contribute significantly to the high rates of morbidity and mortality in these countries (Boylan et al., 2009). The United States has higher rates of the six major chronic diseases associated with mortality (Banks, Marmot, Oldfield, & Smith, 2006).

It is important to remember in our discussion of available preventive treatments that people are reluctant to change their lifestyle habits, particularly when they must make these changes after decades of unhealthy habits. Health care professionals must therefore not only educate high-risk individuals, but also give them encouragement that change is possible (Resnick et al., 2009).

CANCER

Cancer is a generic term that includes a group of more than 100 diseases. Each type of cancer has its own symptoms, characteristics, treatment options, and overall effect on a person's life and health.

In 2009, the incidence rate for new cancers in the U.S. was 4.6 per 1,000 in the population. In the U.S., the incidence rates are highest for prostate (in men only), breast (female), and lung; however, lung cancer is associated with twice the death rate than for either prostate or

TABLE 5.3
Risk Factors for Cancer

Risk factor	Relevant data
Exposure to sun	Increased risk in higher UV exposed cities
Cigarette smoking	80–90% of lung cancer deaths are due to smoking
Diet	Intake of red meat related to colon cancer
Environmental toxins	Work-related toxins associated with increased cancer risk

salih dastan/iStockphoto

breast cancers (Centers for Disease Control and Prevention National Center for Injury Prevention and Control, 2013a). The overall cancer rates for these sites have dropped since 1975, but since 2005, death rates for skin, liver, pancreas, and the uterus have risen (Jemal et al., 2013). The American Cancer Society (2013) estimates that in 2013, 1.66 million new cancers will be diagnosed, not including some forms of skin cancers not reported to cancer registries. Approximately 580,000 are expected to die from cancer in 2013. However, the 5-year relative survival rate for cancers diagnosed between 2002 and 2008 is 68%, which is an increase of almost 20% since 1977.

Around the world, 12 million new cases of cancer were diagnosed in 2008, according to the World Health Organization (2010b). This translates into an age-standardized rate of 1.8 per 1,000 in the population; 7.6 million died in that year alone. Among men and women, lung cancer is the most frequent cancer, followed by breast and colorectal cancers.

Risk Factors and Prevention

All cancer is genetically caused in the sense that it reflects damage to the genes that control cell replication. Some damage is associated with genetic mutations that people inherit. These inherited risks are particularly important for breast and colon cancer. About 5% of women with breast cancer have a hereditary form of this disease. Similarly, close relatives of a person with colorectal cancer are themselves at greater risk, particularly if many people within their extended family have had the disease. However, most cancer is not of the inherited variety. Instead, cancer develops when random mutations occur that cause the body's cells to malfunction. The mutations

develop either as a mistake in cell division or in response to injuries from environmental agents such as radiation or chemicals (see Table 5.3).

Most cancers become more prevalent with increasing age in adulthood because age is associated with greater cumulative exposure to harmful toxins (carcinogens) in the environment. Skin cancer, the most common form of cancer in adults, is directly linked to exposure to ultraviolet (UV) radiation from the sun. In the United States, for example, melanoma is more common in Texas than it is in Minnesota, due to the fact that levels of UV radiation from the sun are stronger in the South than the northern Midwest. Around the world, the highest rates of skin cancer are found in South Africa and Australia, which are also areas that receive substantial amounts of UV radiation. Artificial sources of UV radiation, such as sunlamps and tanning booths, can cause skin cancer despite the claims that the manufacturers make about their safety. In fact, researchers have determined that women in developed countries who use tanning beds before the age of 30 increase their risk of developing skin cancer by 75%. Even cancer of the eye is also more likely to develop in people who use artificial tanning devices (El Ghissassi et al., 2009).

Cigarette smoking is in many ways more dangerous than UV exposure because the forms of cancer related to cigarettes are generally more lethal than skin cancer. Most lung cancer is caused by cigarette smoking. People who smoke also place themselves at risk for developing cancers of the mouth, throat, esophagus, larynx, bladder, kidney, cervix, pancreas, and stomach. The risk of lung cancer begins to diminish as soon as a person quits smoking. People who had lung cancer and stopped smoking are less likely to get a second lung cancer than are people who continue to smoke. Being exposed to cigarette smoke ("secondhand smoke") can present just as great a risk, if not greater, for lung cancer.

Though you are probably aware of the risks of cigarette smoke in developed countries such as the United States, Canada, and Europe, you may not realize that carcinogens are present in substances such as betel quid, which includes the toxic substance areca nut. Approximately 600 million people in India (as many as 80% of adults) and parts of Southeast Asia, chew betel quid. Even if the betel quid contains no tobacco quid, people who engage in this habit are at greatly increased risk of liver and esophageal cancer (Secretan et al., 2009).

Being overweight is linked to a variety of cancers of the gastrointestinal system. A nationwide study of over 900,000 adults in the United States who were studied prospectively from 1982 to 1998 played in important role in identifying the risks associated with a high BMI. During this period of time, there were more than 57,000 deaths within the sample from cancer. The people with the highest BMIs had death rates from cancer that were 52% higher for men and 62% higher for women compared with men and women of normal BMI. The types of cancer associated with higher BMIs included cancer of the esophagus, colon and rectum, liver, gallbladder, pancreas, and kidney. Significant trends of increasing risk with higher BMIs were observed for death from cancers of the stomach and prostate in men and for death from cancers of the breast, uterus, cervix, and ovary in women (Calle, Rodriguez, Walker-Thurmond, & Thun, 2003). We can conclude from this research that maintaining a low BMI is a critical preventive step in lowering your risk of cancer.

In addition to BMI, eating specific foods seems to play a role in cancer risk. Stomach cancer is more common in parts of the world—such as Japan, Korea, parts of Eastern Europe, and Latin America—in which people eat foods that are preserved by drying, smoking, salting, or pickling. By contrast, fresh foods, especially fresh fruits and vegetables, may help protect against stomach cancer. Similarly, the risk of developing colon cancer is thought to be higher in people whose diet is high in fat, low in fruits and vegetables, and low in high-fiber foods such as whole-grain breads and cereals. For instance, New Zealand and the United States have the higher rates of colon cancer and also consume the largest amount of meat (National Cancer Institute, 2010).

There are several additional specific types of environmental toxins in the air, food, and water that make certain people more vulnerable to cancer. Such compounds include asbestos, arsenic, beryllium, cadmium, chromium, and nickel. Exposure to these compounds significantly increases a person's risk of cancer in various sites in the respiratory system, including the lung and nasal cavity. People exposed to arsenic are at risk for bladder cancer, and those to asbestos more likely to develop ovarian cancer. In addition, people exposed to leather, silica, and wood dust are more likely to develop respiratory cancers (Straif et al., 2009). People in certain occupations are more at risk for exposure to these carcinogenic substances, including those who work in iron and steel founding or manufacture isopropyl alcohol, paint, and rubber (Baan et al., 2009).

People make many other lifestyle choices that can further contribute to their risk of developing cancer. In the intensive efforts to find the causes of breast cancer, a variety of lifestyle factors have been suggested, such as amount of alcohol consumed and having an abortion or a miscarriage. The evidence is somewhat stronger for the effect of personal history in the case of cervical cancer, which has a higher risk among women who began having sexual intercourse before age 18 and/or have had many sexual partners. For men, efforts are under way to determine whether having had a vasectomy increases their risk for prostate cancer.

In addition to a person's lifestyle and history of disease, people's race and ethnicity may contribute to certain types of cancers. Skin cancer is more likely to develop in people with fair skin that freckles easily; Black people are less likely to develop any form of skin cancer. Uterine cancer is more prevalent among Whites, and prostate cancer is more prevalent among Blacks. Stomach cancer is twice as prevalent in men and is more common in Black people, as is colon cancer. Rectal cancer is more prevalent among Whites.

Finally, certain hormones may increase the risk of cancer, interacting in complex ways with other factors that we have already mentioned. Although the cause of prostate cancer is not known, the growth of cancer cells in the prostate, like that of normal cells, is stimulated by male hormones, especially testosterone. Estrogen in postmenopausal women is thought to increase their likelihood of developing uterine cancer. However, women may counter this risk by taking HRT that includes both progesterone and estrogen (Grosse et al., 2009).

The link between BMI and uterine cancer in women may be due to increased production of estrogen among heavier women, so that the estrogen rather than fat increases the risk of uterine cancer. Likewise, findings that diabetes and high blood pressure increase the risk of uterine cancer may be related to the fact that these conditions are more likely to occur in overweight women who have higher levels of estrogen (Wedisinghe & Perera, 2009).

Treatments

The best way to avoid cancer is to prevent it by staying away from known carcinogens. People at risk based on their age, sex, and lifestyle should also undergo screenings as recommended by health care professionals. Organizations in the United States such as the American Cancer Society and the Canadian Cancer Society in Canada publicize the need for tests, such as breast self-examination and mammograms for women, prostate examinations for men, and colon cancer screenings for both men and women.

As important as detection is, however, public health officials often revise their recommendations for the frequency and nature of cancer screening. For example, in November 2009, the U.S. Preventive Services Task Force released a controversial update to the 2002 recommendation statement for breast cancer screening. The 2002 recommendation advocated breast mammography every 1 to 2 years for women over 40. The 2009 statement, citing insufficient evidence to assess the benefits and harms of screening, recommends against routine mammography screening in women between the ages of 40 and 49. Biennial screening mammography is recommended for women between the ages of 50 and 74. For women over the age of 75, the USPSTF determined insufficient evidence to assess the additional benefits and harms of mammography. Uncertainties pertaining to the harm of screening (including misdiagnosis) were cited as a basis for the recommendations. When the report was made public, countless groups and organizations were quick to harshly criticize the recommendations, sparking debate in the medical field and media outlets (Woolf, 2010).

In order to determine the impact of the USPSTF recommendations, researchers examined self-reported mammography rates between 2006 and 2010. Although mammography rates declined slightly across all age groups over 40 (adjusted for a variety of demographic factors including race/ethnicity) in 2010, the differences were not statistically significant (Howard & Adams, 2012). A national telephone survey conducted a year after the revised recommendations suggested that less than half of women surveyed were aware of the changes in screening guidelines and that those who were younger and had higher rates of education and income were more aware of the changes (Kiviniemi & Hay, 2012).

Similar changes occur in guidelines for colon and prostate cancer screening. In each case, physicians and their patients must weigh the risks incurred by undergoing screening (and possibly receiving a false positive) against the failure to detect a treatable cancer. Your best advice as a patient is to keep up with the literature for your own gender and age group, and advise your relatives to do the same.

Depending on the stage of cancer progression at diagnosis, various treatment options are available. Surgery is the most common treatment for most types of cancer when it is probable that all of the tumor can be removed. Radiation therapy involves the use of high-energy X-rays to damage cancer cells and stop their growth. Chemotherapy uses drugs to kill cancer cells. Patients are most likely to receive chemotherapy when the cancer has metastasized to other parts of the body. Biological therapy uses substances called biological response modifiers that improve the way the body's immune system fights disease and may be used in combination with chemotherapy to treat cancer that has metastasized.

As more information is gathered through the rapidly evolving program of research on cancer and its causes, new methods of treatment and prevention can be expected to emerge over the next few decades. Furthermore, as efforts grow to target populations at risk for the development of preventable cancers (such as lung cancer), we can expect that cancer deaths will be reduced even further in the decades ahead.

DISORDERS OF THE MUSCULOSKELETAL SYSTEM

Musculoskeletal diseases include a range of conditions that develop in the bones and joints. Not fatal in and of themselves, these diseases can be crippling and may lead to injury or bodily harm that can eventually lead to the death of the afflicted individual (see Table 5.4).

Osteoarthritis

Arthritis is a general term for conditions affecting the joints and surrounding tissues that can cause pain, stiffness, and swelling in joints and other connective tissues. **Osteoarthritis**, the most common form of arthritis, affects joints in the hips, knees, neck, lower back, and small joints of the hands. These are joints vulnerable to injury that people sustain due to repeated overuse in the performance of a particular job or a favorite sport. Obesity is another risk factor for osteoarthritis because the extra weight of the obese person's body puts stress on the joints in the lower part of the body. Individuals who are obese are four times more likely to have knee osteoarthritis compared to the general population. Researchers followed patients with osteoarthritis who underwent bariatric (or weight loss) surgery to assess the effect on knee symptoms and saw significant improvement of the arthritis symptoms at 6- and 12-months postsurgery (Edwards et al., 2012).

Injury or repeated impact contributes to osteoarthritis by thinning or wearing away the cartilage that cushions the ends of the bones in the joint as they rub together. The synovial fluid that fills the joint loses its shock-absorbing properties as well, further contributing to the development of osteoarthritis. Bony spurs and joint swelling also develop as the disease progresses. These changes in the joint structures and tissues cause the individual to experience pain and loss of movement.

TABLE 5.4
Osteoarthritis and Osteoporosis Risk Factors and Treatments

Disease	Risk factors	Treatment
Osteoarthritis: *Painful, degenerative joint disease*	• Overuse • Obesity • Injury	• Pain management • Flexibility • Replacement
Osteoporosis: *Abnormal loss of bone mineral content*	• Race • Ethnicity • Hormonal changes • Lack of vitamin D	• Exercise (resistance) • Nutritional supplements • Medications

Tomaz Levstek/iStockphoto

People with osteoarthritis require pain management. Medications used to help alleviate the pain of osteoarthritis include aspirin, acetaminophen, ibuprofen, and non-steroidal anti-inflammatory drugs (NSAIDs). Although these can help alleviate the individual's pain, NSAIDs can create their own set of problems. People who take NSAIDs on a chronic basis are at risk for kidney disease as well as ulcers. Another strategy is to inject corticosteroids directly into joints to reduce swelling and inflammation. These drugs are used sparingly, however, because they can themselves destroy bones and cartilage.

Even the best pain medications only alleviate symptoms; they do not provide a cure for the disease. More active forms of treatment for osteoarthritis are increasingly becoming available. One approach is to receive an injection of a synthetic material into an arthritic joint to replace the loss of synovial fluid. A second option is to be injected with sodium hyaluronate directly into the joint. This is a version of a chemical normally present in high amounts in joints and fluids.

When these pain or injectable treatments no longer produce relief, the individual with osteoarthritis may undergo the total replacement of the affected joint. Although hip or knee replacement surgery may seem like a drastic measure, it is one that typically proves highly satisfactory. Following the surgery, many individuals are able to lead not only pain-free lives, but are also able to resume some of their former activities.

Exercise can also help to reduce the pain of osteoarthritis, particularly when the disease is in its early stages (Kujala, 2009). The best exercise for osteoarthritis helps the individual strengthen the muscles around the joint (Verweij, van Schoor, Deeg, Dekker, & Visser, 2009) and stretch the tendons. People whose osteoarthritis is made worse by their obesity can also benefit from a program of exercise that focuses on weight loss. Another benefit of exercise is that it can offset the effects on mood of the chronic pain associated with osteoarthritis.

Osteoporosis

As we saw in Chapter 4, people steadily lose bone mineral content throughout the decades of adulthood. This loss of bone mineral content occurs due to an imbalance between the rates of bone resorption vs. bone growth. **Osteoporosis** (literally, "porous bone") is said to occur when the bone mineral density reaches the point that is more than 2.5 standard deviations below the mean of young, White, non-Hispanic women.

As many as 8 million women and 2 million men in the United States suffer from osteoporosis (Sweet, Sweet, Jeremiah, & Galazka, 2009). Rates of osteoporosis-related bone fracture is equivalent to the rates of myocardial infarction (Binkley, 2009). Women (particularly postmenopausal women) are at higher risk than men because they have lower bone mass in general. However, osteoporosis is a significant health problem in men. Women vary by race and ethnicity in their risk of developing osteoporosis; White and Asian women have the highest risk, whereas Blacks and Hispanics the lowest. In addition, women who have small bone structures and are underweight have a higher risk for osteoporosis than heavier women.

Excessive use of alcohol and a history of cigarette smoking increase an individual's risk of developing osteoporosis. Conversely, people can reduce their risk by taking in adequate amounts of calcium present in dairy products, dark green leafy vegetables, tofu, salmon, and foods fortified with calcium such as orange juice, bread, and cereal (a regimen similar to that recommended to prevent heart disease). Other dietary measures include eating foods high in protein and nutrients such as magnesium, potassium, vitamin K, several B vitamins, and carotenoids (Tucker, 2009). Vitamin D, obtained through exposure to sunlight (while wearing sunblock, of course!), or as a dietary supplement, is another important preventative agent (Bischoff-Ferrari et al., 2009). Exercise and physical activity are also significant factors in reducing a person's risk of osteoporosis, particularly when that exercise involves resistance training with weights (Guadalupe-Grau, Fuentes, Guerra, & Calbet, 2009).

Once an individual develops osteoporosis, there are a variety of medications currently available to slow or stop bone loss, increase bone density, and reduce fracture risk. The bisphosphonate known as alendronate is a medication used to increase bone density. Unfortunately, it can have serious side effects, particularly bone loss in the jaw. The naturally occurring hormone calcitonin may also be given to help regulate calcium and bone metabolism. However, calcitonin may actually cause bone pain and a set of other unpleasant side effects.

A deficiency of sex hormones, in both men and women, may be a contributing cause to osteoporosis; as discussed above, the risks of hormone replacement therapy need to be weighed against the gains in preserving bone health (Pietschmann, Rauner, Sipos, & Kerschan-Schindl, 2009). Calcitrol, though linked to risks involving buildup of calcium by-products in the body, may also prove to be effective when combined with other treatments (Peppone et al., 2009). Interestingly, certain types of alcohol may be preventive for women. In a study of beer drinkers compared to women who drank no alcohol or other forms of alcohol, the women who consumed beer had the lowest rates of osteoporosis, perhaps due to the fact that beer contains a form of estrogen (Pedrera-Zamorano et al., 2009).

DIABETES

People with **diabetes** are unable to metabolize glucose, a simple sugar that is a major source of energy for the body's cells. **Adult-onset diabetes**, also known as **type 2 diabetes**, develops over time, gradually reducing the individual's ability to convert dietary glucose to a form that can be used by the body's cells.

Characteristics of Diabetes

Normally, the digestive process breaks food down into components that can be transported through the blood to the cells of the body. The presence of glucose in the blood stimulates the beta cells of the pancreas to release insulin, a hormone that acts as a key at the cell receptors within the body to "open the cell doors" to let in the glucose. Excess glucose is stored in the liver or throughout the body in muscle and fat, at which point its level in the blood returns to normal.

In type 2 diabetes, the pancreas produces some insulin, but the body's tissues fail to respond to the insulin signal, a condition known as insulin resistance. Because the insulin cannot bind to the cell's insulin receptors, the glucose cannot be transported into the body's cells to be used. Eventually the excess glucose overflows into the urine and is excreted. The body therefore loses a main source of energy, while large amounts of glucose remain in the blood.

The symptoms of diabetes include fatigue, frequent urination (especially at night), unusual thirst, weight loss, blurred vision, frequent infections, and slow healing of sores. If blood sugar levels dip too low (a condition known as hypoglycemia), the individual can become nervous, jittery, faint, and confused. The only way to correct for this condition is for the individual to eat or drink a sugary substance as quickly as possible. Alternatively, in hyperglycemia, when blood glucose levels become too high, the person can also become seriously ill. Type 2 diabetes is associated with long-term complications that affect almost every organ system, contributing to blindness, heart disease, strokes, kidney failure, the necessity for limb amputations, and damage to the nervous system.

Incidence and Risk Factors

A large fraction of the over-65 population suffers from type 2 diabetes. Diabetes is estimated to afflict 10.3 million people 60 years of age and older, which is approximately 21% of adults in this age category. The CDC estimates that having diabetes doubles the risk of death compared with others in one's own age group (Centers for Disease Control and Prevention, 2010b). In addition, more children are developing type 2 diabetes as a function of the increase in childhood obesity. Such findings will have important health implications for future generations of older adults.

According to the World Health Organization, the number of people suffering from diabetes worldwide was approximately 171 million in 2010, a number that will double by 2030. Approximately 3.2 million deaths per year are due to complications of diabetes. The United States is third following India and China in the number of people who suffer from diabetes, but the increase in number of cases is greater in the developing countries (World Health Organization, 2010a).

Diabetes can be understood in terms of the biopsychosocial perspective in that it involves physical, behavioral, and sociocultural risk factors (see Figure 5.4) noted earlier in the chapter as risk factors for heart disease.

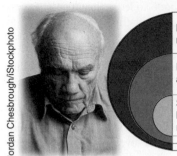

Biological = Changes in glucose metabolism, obesity

Psychological = Sedentary lifestyle; also associated with depression and stress

Sociocultural = Habitual eating patterns, lack of education, low economic resources

Jordan Chesbrough/iStockphoto

FIGURE 5.4

Biopsychosocial Model of Diabetes

Researchers in this area warn that older adults are becoming increasingly likely to experience metabolic syndrome, insulin resistance, high lipid levels, and hypertension, leading to greater risk of cardiovascular and kidney disease (Bechtold, Palmer, Valtos, Iasiello, & Sowers, 2006). Echoing the findings of other research on the benefits of moderate consumption of alcohol, research on diabetes risk also suggests that people can protect themselves against diabetes by taking 1-2 ounces per day as long as this doesn't conflict with other medications or conditions people may have (Baliunas et al., 2009).

Race and ethnicity also contribute to diabetes risk. The incidence of diabetes is about 60% higher in African Americans and 110 to 120% higher in Mexican Americans and Puerto Ricans compared with Whites. The highest rates of diabetes in the world are found among Native Americans. Half of all Pima Indians living in the United States, for example, have adult-onset diabetes.

Prevention and Treatment

Given the clear relationship between obesity and diabetes, the most important means of preventing type 2 diabetes include the control of glucose intake, blood pressure, and blood lipids.

People with diabetes require frequent testing, usually accomplished by measuring blood levels. Depending on the severity, once an individual has type 2 diabetes, diet and exercise may be sufficient to control its symptoms. If not, then the individual requires insulin injections or oral forms of diabetes medications. There are currently six classes of oral diabetes medications, each of which works in a unique way to control blood glucose levels.

RESPIRATORY DISEASES

The main form of respiratory disease affecting adults in middle and late life is **chronic obstructive pulmonary disease (COPD)**, a group of diseases that involve obstruction of the airflow into the respiratory system. Two related diseases—chronic bronchitis and chronic emphysema—often occur together in this disease (see Figure 5.5). People with COPD experience coughing, excess sputum, and difficulty breathing even when they carry out relatively easy

FIGURE 5.5

Components of COPD

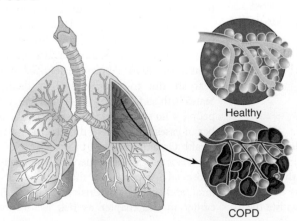

Healthy

COPD

- Chronic emphysema: Loss of elasticity in the alveoli
- Chronic bronchitis: Bronchial tubes inflamed and irritated
- Main cause is smoking

tasks, such as putting on their clothes or walking on level ground.

According to the international group Global Initiative for COPD (2009), the disease is the fourth leading cause of chronic illness and death and the fifth in the world in terms of the burden of disease. COPD's prevalence increases with age throughout adulthood. By 75 and older, an estimated 25% of the population has COPD (Iyer Parameswaran & Murphy, 2009).

Chronic bronchitis is a long-standing inflammation of the bronchi, the airways that lead into the lungs. The inflammation of the bronchi causes an increase in mucus and other changes, which in turn leads to coughing and expectoration of sputum. People with chronic emphysema are more likely to develop frequent and severe respiratory infections, narrowing and plugging of the bronchi, difficulty breathing, and disability.

Chronic emphysema is a lung disease that causes permanent destruction of the alveoli. Elastin within the terminal bronchioles is destroyed, causing the airways to lose their ability to become enlarged during inspiration and to empty completely during expiration. The result is that the exchange of carbon dioxide and oxygen becomes compromised. People with COPD experience this situation as shortness of breath, making it difficult for them to complete the tasks of daily life (Reardon, Lareau, & ZuWallack, 2006).

Although the cause of COPD is not known, most who study the disease generally agree that its main cause is cigarette smoking. Exposure to environmental toxins such as air pollution and harmful substances in the occupational setting also may play a role, but even these have much more pronounced effects in people.

The specific mechanism involved in the link between smoking and emphysema is thought to involve the release of an enzyme known as **elastase**, which breaks down the elastin found in lung tissue. Cigarette smoke stimulates the release of this enzyme and results in other changes that make the cells of the lung less resistant to elastase. Normally there is an inhibitant of elastase found in the lung, known as alpha-1 antitrypsin (AAT). However, cigarette smoke inactivates AAT and allows the elastase to destroy more lung tissue. Of course, not all smokers develop COPD, and not all people with COPD are or have been smokers. Heredity may also play a role. There is a rare genetic defect in the production of AAT in about 2 to 3% of the population that is responsible for about 5% of all cases of COPD.

Apart from quitting smoking, a necessary first step in prevention and treatment, individuals with COPD can benefit from medications and treatments. These include inhalers that open the airways to bring more oxygen into the lungs or reduce inflammation, machines that provide oxygen, or, in extreme cases, lung surgery to remove damaged tissue.

NEUROCOGNITIVE DISORDERS

People receive the diagnosis of **neurocognitive disorder** when they experience a loss of cognitive function severe enough to interfere with normal daily activities and social relationships. You may be familiar with the term **dementia**, which is also used in common speech to refer to a loss of cognitive abilities. Clinicians distinguish major neurocognitive disorder from mild neurocognitive disorder, which, like the term **mild cognitive impairment (MCI)**, refers to a form of neurocognitive disorder that signifies that the individual may be at risk for developing Alzheimer's disease.

People who suffer from **amnesia** have as their main symptom profound memory loss. Their amnesia may involve an inability to learn or remember information encountered after the damage (anterograde—into the future) or the inability to recall information learned prior to the damage (retrograde—going back into the past). Amnesia can be caused by chronic substance use, medications, exposure to environmental toxins, head trauma, loss of oxygen supply to the brain, or the sexually transmitted disease of herpes simplex.

Alzheimer's Disease

Alzheimer's disease is a form of neurocognitive disorder in which the individual suffers progressive and irreversible neuronal death. Over the years, Alzheimer's disease has been called by a variety of names, including senile dementia, presenile dementia, senile dementia of the Alzheimer's type, and organic brain disorder.

Identified as a disease in 1906, Alzheimer's disease is named after Alois Alzheimer (1864–1915), the German neurologist who was the first to link changes in brain tissue with observable symptoms. Alzheimer treated Auguste D., a woman in her 50s who suffered from progressive mental deterioration marked by increasing confusion and memory loss. Taking advantage of what was then a new staining technique, he noticed an odd disorganization of the nerve cells in her cerebral cortex. In a medical journal article published in 1907, Alzheimer speculated that these microscopic changes were responsible for Auguste D.'s dementia. The discovery of brain slides from this patient confirmed that these changes were similar to those seen in the disease (Enserink, 1998). In 1910, as a resulting number of autopsies from severely demented individuals showed the same abnormalities, a foremost psychiatrist of the era, Emil Kraepelin (1856–1926), gave the name described by his friend Alzheimer to the disease.

Prevalence. The World Health Organization estimates a prevalence of Alzheimer's disease worldwide of people over 60 as 5% of men and 6% of women (World Health Organization, 2001). The incidence rates of new cases is less than 1% a year for those aged 60 to 65 or possibly as high as 6.5% in those 85 and older (Kawas, Gray, Brookmeyer, Fozard, & Zonderman, 2000).

In contrast to the World Health Organization's estimates, U.S. sources often cite a percentage of 12%, or 5–5.5 million people. They report that among people 85 and older, the prevalence rises to about half. On the basis of these estimates, we see projections of a staggering 14 million individuals in the U.S. alone who will suffer from the disease by 2050 unless a cure is found (Alzheimer's Association, 2010).

What would account for the discrepancies between the U.S. and global statistics? Unfortunately, the answer lies in part in the politics of the disease. The estimates you read about in the U.S. news media originate from a non-peer-reviewed publication produced yearly by the privately funded Alzheimer's Association. It bases its projections in large part on a study of 856 U.S. residents living in 42 states, age 71 and older (Plassman et al., 2007). This approach of generalizing from a relatively small U.S. sample has characterized much of the Alzheimer's prevalence research and thus has led to disputes among researchers about the validity of this estimate. Some argue that the reasons are due to the funding structure behind the organizations that sponsor this type of research. The Alzheimer's Association partners with the National Institute of Aging along with several major pharmaceutical companies. There are definite financial incentives attached to erring on the high side when presenting prevalence data.

Over a decade ago, critics of the U.S. figures reported a far lower prevalence closer to that of global statistics equaling about 5–6% of the 65 and older population (Brookmeyer, Corrada, Curriero, & Kawas, 2002; Hy & Keller, 2000). They argued that the original projections were flawed because they were based on inadequate samples. Not only were those original samples small, but they were less well-educated than the over-65 population at large (Beeri et al., 2006).

In point of fact, however, the press releases intended to inform the public about the prevalence of Alzheimer's disease may not be that far off, as long as you read the fine print. They include not just the prevalence of Alzheimer's disease, but also on the prevalence of other forms of neurocognitive disorder. As you have already learned, people can have neurocognitive disorder caused by cerebrovascular disease, with estimates placing this rate perhaps as high as 20% of cases of neurocognitive disorder (Knopman, 2007). By counting forms of neurocognitive disorder

other than Alzheimer's disease in the overall prevalence estimates, this contributes to those artificially high rates.

The distinction between Alzheimer's disease and other forms of neurocognitive disorder is an important one. Other forms of neurocognitive disorder are different in their cause, prognosis, and treatment. They may even be preventable.

From a sociocultural point of view, what the public hears about the prevalence of Alzheimer's disease is important because this information shapes people's attitudes toward aging. If you believe that half of all people 85 and older have this form of neurocognitive disorder, it would seem to justify the view of old age as a time of "senility." Moreover, people who see these statistics may inaccurately conclude that they are doomed to develop the disorder and that there is nothing they can do to prevent it. If a more accurate message was communicated to the public, more people would realize that by controlling their lifestyle choices, they could in fact prevent the forms of neurocognitive disorder that are caused by cardiovascular disease.

Psychological Symptoms. The psychological symptoms of Alzheimer's disease evolve gradually over time (see Table 5.5). The earliest signs are occasional loss of memory for recent events or familiar tasks. Although changes in cognitive functioning are at the core of this disease's symptoms, changes in personality and behavior eventually become evident as well. By the time the disease has entered the final stage, the individual has lost the ability to perform even the simplest and most basic of everyday functions. The rate of progression in Alzheimer's disease varies from person to person, but there is a fairly regular pattern of loss over the stages of the disease. The survival time following the diagnosis is 7 to 10 years for people diagnosed in their 60s and 70s, and drops to 3 years for people diagnosed in their 90s (Brookmeyer, et al., 2002).

Biological Changes. One of the most pervasive set of changes to occur in the brain of a person with Alzheimer's disease is the formation of abnormal deposits of protein fragments known as **amyloid plaques**. Amyloid is a generic name for protein fragments that collect together in a specific way to form insoluble deposits (meaning that they do not dissolve). The form of amyloid most closely linked with Alzheimer's disease consists of a string of 42 amino acids and is therefore referred to as **beta-amyloid-42**.

Beta-amyloid is formed from a larger protein found in the normal brain, referred to as **amyloid precursor protein (APP)**. As APP is manufactured, it embeds itself in the neuron's membrane. A small piece of APP is lodged inside the neuron, and a larger part of it remains outside. In healthy aging, the part of APP remaining outside the

TABLE 5.5
Stages of Alzheimer's Disease

Not Alzheimer's	Early-stage	Middle-stage	Late-stage
• Forgetting things occasionally • Misplacing items, like keys, eye glasses, bills, paper work • Forgetting the names or titles of some things, like movies, books, people's names • Some reduction in ability to recall words when speaking • Being "absent-minded" or sometimes hazy on details • "Spacing things out," such as appointments	• Short-term memory loss, usually minor • Being unaware of the memory lapses • Some loss, usually minor, in ability to retain recently learned information • Forgetting things and unable to dredge them up, such as the name of a good friend or even family member • Function at home normally with minimal mental confusion, but may have problems at work or in social situations • Symptoms may not be noticeable to all but spouse or close relatives/friends	• Short-term memory loss deepens, may begin to forget conversations completely, name of street where you live, names of loved ones, or how to drive a car • Mental confusion deepens, trouble thinking logically • Some loss of self-awareness • Friends and family notice memory lapses • May become disoriented, not know where you are • Impaired ability to perform even simple arithmetic • May become more aggressive or passive • Difficulty sleeping • Depression	• Severe cognitive impairment and short-term memory loss • Speech impairment • May repeat conversations over and over • May not know names of spouse, children, or caregivers, or what day or month it is • Very poor reasoning ability and judgment • Neglect of personal hygiene • Personality changes; may become abusive, highly anxious, agitated, delusional, or even paranoid • May need extensive assistance with activities of daily living

Source: "Evaluating Prescription Drugs used to Treat: Alzheimer's Disease Consumer Reports Best Buy Drugs" Copyright 2012 by Consumers Union of U.S., Inc. Yonkers, NY 10703-1057, a nonprofit organization. Reprinted with permission from *Consumer Reports Best Buy Drugs*™ for educational purposes only. www.CRBestBuyDrugs.org.

neuron is trimmed by enzymes called **secretases** so that it is flush with the neuron's outer membrane. In Alzheimer's disease, something goes wrong with this process so that the APP is snipped at the wrong place, causing beta-amyloid 42 to form. The cutoff fragments eventually clump together into beta-amyloid plaques, the abnormal deposits that the body cannot dispose of or recycle (see Figure 5.6).

Apart from its tendency to form insoluble plaques, beta-amyloid seems to have the potential to kill neurons. **Caspase** theory proposes that beta-amyloid stimulates the production of substances called caspases, enzymes that are lethal to neurons. This destruction of neurons, referred to as **apoptosis**, ultimately leads to the loss of cognitive functioning that occurs in Alzheimer's disease (Galvan et al., 2006).

The second major change to occur in the brain is a profusion of abnormally twisted fibers within the neurons themselves, known as **neurofibrillary tangles** (literally, tangled nerve fibers). It is now known that the neurofibrillary tangles are made up of a protein called **tau** (see Figure 5.7), which seems to play a role in maintaining the stability of the microtubules that form the internal support structure of the axons. The microtubules are like train tracks that guide nutrients from the cell body down to the ends of the axon. The tau proteins are like the railroad ties or crosspieces of the microtubule train tracks. In Alzheimer's disease, the tau is changed chemically and loses its ability to separate and support the microtubules. With their support gone, the tubules begin to wind around each other and they can no longer perform their function. This collapse of the transport system within the neuron may first result in malfunctions in communication between neurons and may eventually lead to the death of the neuron.

Like the formation of plaques, the development of neurofibrillary tangles appears to occur early in the disease process and may progress quite substantially before the individual shows any behavioral symptoms. The earliest changes in the disease appear to occur in the hippocampus and the entorhinal region of the cortex, the area near the hippocampus, which is critical in memory and retention of learned information (Reitz, Honig, Vonsattel, Tang, & Mayeux, 2009).

Proposed Causes. One certainty about Alzheimer's disease is that it is associated with the formation of plaques and tangles, particularly in areas of the brain controlling

FIGURE 5.6

Steps in the Formation of a Beta-Amyloid Plaque

(a)

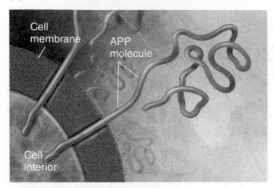

(b)

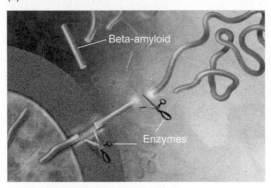

(c)

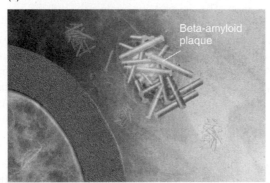

Proposed steps in the formation of beta-amyloid plaque. (a) As it is being made, APP sticks through the neuron's membrane. (b) Enzymes cleave beta-amyloid protein, releasing it into the space outside the neuron. (c) Clumps of beta-amyloid collect and begin to form a plaque.

memory and other vital cognitive functions. Uncertainty remains as to what causes these changes. It is also not clear whether the development of plaques and tangles is the cause of neuron death, or whether these changes are the result of other underlying processes that cause neurons to die and produce these abnormalities in neural tissue as a side product.

Moreover, the existence of plaques and tangles in the brain is not a sure sign that an individual will have cognitive symptoms, highlighting the fact that this is a disorder affected by environmental as well as biological factors (Styczynska et al., 2008). Although the progression of Alzheimer's tends to lead to an inevitable loss of functioning, there is variability in its physical and cognitive symptoms (Burton, Strauss, Hultsch, Moll, & Hunter, 2006).

The theory guiding most researchers is that genetic abnormalities are somehow responsible for the neuronal death that is the hallmark of Alzheimer's disease, with new "suspects" regularly being introduced into the literature (Tanzi & Bertram, 2008). The genetic theory began to emerge as an explanation after the discovery that certain families seemed more prone to a form of the disease that struck at the relatively young age of 40 to 50 years. These cases are now referred to as **early-onset familial Alzheimer's disease**. Although it is a tragic situation, scientists have been able to learn a tremendous amount from studying the DNA of afflicted individuals. The four genes discovered so far, thought to account for about half of all early-onset familial Alzheimer's disease, are linked to excess amounts of beta-amyloid protein.

Since the discovery of the early-onset form of the disease, genetic analyses have also provided evidence of another gene involved in familial Alzheimer's disease that starts at a more conventional age of 60 or 65 years. This form of the disease is called **late-onset familial Alzheimer's disease**. However, only 5% of all cases of Alzheimer's disease are familial, and the rest show no inherited pattern.

Clearly, even though genetic theories have considerable appeal, they do not tell the whole story. One of the prime genes thought to be involved in the late-onset familial pattern is the **apolipoprotein E (ApoE) gene**, located on chromosome 19. **ApoE** is a protein that carries cholesterol throughout the body, but it also binds to beta-amyloid, possibly playing a role in plaque formation.

Although the ApoE gene has received more attention, the first genetic defects found to be associated with familial Alzheimer's disease were on the **APP gene** on chromosome 21. The APP gene appears to control the production of APP, the protein that generates beta-amyloid.

Most early-onset familial Alzheimer's disease cases are associated with defects in the so-called **presenilin genes (PS1 and PS2)**. Researchers speculate that these genes somehow lead APP to increase its production of beta-amyloid, which in turn causes neurofibrillary tangles and an increase in amyloid plaques (Zhang et al., 2009). Neuroinflammation, or inflammatory pathways in the

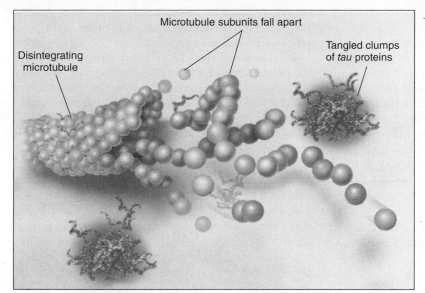

Disintegrating microtubule

Microtubule subunits fall apart

Tangled clumps of *tau* proteins

FIGURE 5.7

Formation of a Neurofibrillary Tangle in Alzheimer's Disease

brain, is another mechanism believed to be involved in the progression of Alzheimer's based on observations that administration of long-term anti-inflammatory drugs was related to lower rates of Alzheimer's (Imbimbo, Solfrizzi, & Panza, 2012).

Higher education and continued mental activity throughout life are environmental factors that can protect the individual from developing Alzheimer's. In a unique longitudinal study of aging among the Sisters of Notre Dame, nuns who agreed to donate their brains upon their death were studied while alive and their cognitive performance related to the studies of their brain upon autopsy. One of the original findings of the study was that despite the appearance of plaques and tangles in autopsy, many of the sisters did not show symptomatic deficits in cognitive performance. More recently, researchers found that higher mental activity in early adulthood seemed to protect the sisters from showing signs of cognitive decline in later life despite the presence of these changes in the brain (Iacono et al., 2009).

Extensive social networks appear more generally to be a protective factor against Alzheimer's disease, reducing the risk even among people who have high levels of brain pathology (Bennett, Schneider, Tang, Arnold, & Wilson, 2006). Physical exercise also seems to serve a protective function against the type of cognitive changes that may precede the development of Alzheimer's disease, particularly if it is performed at least at a moderate level of intensity (Geda et al., 2010).

Limited alcohol intake in earlier adult life may be protective against neurocognitive disorder later in adulthood (Peters, Peters, Warner, Beckett, & Bulpitt, 2008). Also

related to lower risk is higher thyroxine levels (de Jong et al., 2009). The extent to which the individual participates in exercise may be another lifestyle contributor to the development of or progression of Alzheimer's disease. Both physical exercise and exercise in the form of stimulation along multiple sensory channels aid in slowing cognitive decline and could potentially provide success to individuals with neurocognitive disorder (Briones, 2006). Finally, one of the most intriguing prospects in the search for causes of Alzheimer's disease relates to diet. People who follow the Mediterranean diet have a lower risk of developing the disease, even after controlling for factors such as ApoE4 genotype, BMI, age, sex, and smoking (Lopez-Miranda et al., 2009).

Diagnosis. The diagnosis of neurocognitive disorder is made when there is significant and progressive cognitive decline in one or more areas including social cognition, memory, **aphasia** (loss of language ability), **apraxia** (loss of ability to carry out coordinated movement), **agnosia** (loss of ability to recognize familiar objects), and disturbance in **executive functioning** (loss of the ability to plan and organize) (American Psychiatric Association, 2013).

The diagnosis of Alzheimer's disease through clinical methods is traditionally carried out using the process of exclusion, where other possible diagnoses are ruled out. This is because no one specific test or clinical indicator can definitively identify the disorder. Though methods of diagnosis are improving considerably, it is still the case that only an autopsy will reveal the presence of neurofibrillary tangles and beta-amyloid plaques that are the sure signs of the presence of Alzheimer's disease rather than another form of neurocognitive disorder.

In an attempt to improve diagnostic accuracy, the National Institute of Neurological and Communicative Disorders and Stroke (NINCDS) teamed up with the Alzheimer's Disease and Related Diseases Association (ADRDA) to develop a comprehensive set of criteria specific to Alzheimer's disease (McKhann et al., 1984). They based their criteria on medical and neuropsychological screening tests, behavioral ratings, and mental status measures based on observations of large numbers of cases. At the time, these recommendations significantly improved the chances of a correct diagnosis, with 85 to 90% accuracy in the disease's later stages.

Through the continued improvement of brain scanning, the ability to provide a reliable diagnosis in the early to moderate stages of the disorder is becoming ever more likely (Xiong, Yang, Gong, & Zhang, 2010). Ultimately, as treatments improve, early diagnosis would make it possible for clinicians to intervene and either slow or stop the degeneration of the patient's brain.

Medical Treatments.   As researchers continue to make advances in identifying the cause or causes of Alzheimer's disease, the hope is that medications will be found that can reverse its course. Current medications temporarily alleviate memory loss but do not slow the progression of the disease (Salloway, 2008) (see Figure 5.8).

One category of Alzheimer's medications target **acetylcholinesterase** (also called cholinesterase), the enzyme that normally destroys acetylcholine after its release into the synaptic cleft. The actions of this enzyme seem to reduce the amount of acetylcholine available to the hippocampal neurons, thus leading to memory loss. **Anticholinesterase** treatments inhibit this enzyme. The anticholinesterase

FIGURE 5.8

Medications Used to Treat Symptoms of Alzheimer's Disease

- Anticholinesterases: Decreases action of cholinesterases, allowing more acetylcholine to remain in the brain
- Memantine: Block glutamate receptors, which reduces neuronal death
- Antioxidants: Make oxygen more available to neurons

Tatiana Popova/iStockphoto

treatments approved by the U.S. Food and Drug Administration (FDA) are **tetrahydroaminoacridine (THA)**, also called tacrine and given the brand name Cognex; **donepezil hydrochloride**, called Aricept; and **rivastigmine**, with the brand name of Exelon. By inhibiting the action of acetylcholinesterase, these drugs slow the breakdown of acetylcholine, maintaining it at normal levels in the brain.

After tacrine was approved by the FDA in 1993, the initial enthusiasm about its potential to treat the disease's symptoms was followed by disappointing reports that it could produce toxic effects in the liver if taken in doses large enough to reduce a person's symptoms. Three years later, the FDA gave approval for the use of Aricept and, although it also has gastrointestinal side effects (diarrhea and nausea), these generally were not as serious as those of tacrine. However, the side effects are considerable and can include, in addition to the gastrointestinal effects, dizziness; drowsiness; fainting; frequent or painful urination; headache; joint pain, stiffness, or swelling; depression; unusual bleeding or bruising; weight loss; clumsiness or unsteadiness; confusion; changes in blood pressure; loss of bladder or bowel control; aggression; agitation; delusions; irritability; nervousness; restlessness; tremors; and respiratory difficulties. As you can tell from this long list of possible side effects, some are potentially as problematic as the disease itself, such as confusion, depression, and incontinence.

Anticholinesterase treatments give the patient at best a few months to a year of relief from the troubling cognitive symptoms that occur in the early stages of the disease (Gilstad & Finucane, 2008). Individuals and their families need to weigh whether the benefits are worth the risk of unpleasant and perhaps life-threatening side effects.

Memantine (Namenda), another type of medication for Alzheimer's disease, targets the excitatory neurotransmitter, glutamate. The theory is that glutamate essentially overexcites the neurons, causing them to die. By targeting glutamate, memantine is thought to exert a protective effect against this damage (Lipton, 2006). However, memantine's effectiveness is very limited (Clerici et al., 2009).

A diet rich in antioxidants has long been touted as a way to prevent Alzheimer's. Antioxidants such as ginkgo biloba, melatonin, polyphenols, and vitamins E and C have been proposed to help improve memory and thinking in people with Alzheimer's although few studies have yet to validate these claims. Research from a sample of Germans suggests that the serum concentration of vitamin C and beta-carotene are lower among patients with mild neurocognitive disorder compared with the control participants (von Arnim et al., 2012).

Current research is aimed at identifying medications that will interfere with the disease progression rather than at treating its symptoms (Gauthier & Scheltens, 2009). One approach targets beta-amyloids, and the second focuses on neuroprotective agents that will protect neurons from cell death. These agents would be most effective if used in the early stages of the disease, when it is possible to intervene most effectively (Salloway, 2008). Efforts to develop novel drugs for Alzheimer's have been met with limited success, although there are some promising avenues for treatment with existing drugs. Bryostatin, a drug used for chemotherapy, acts to reactivate the defective enzymes, possibly helping to restore memory (Sun, Hongpaisan, & Alkon, 2009). The compound MDA7 (an anti-inflammatory drug) produces immune responses that slow the progression of Alzheimer's in animal models (Wu et al., 2013). Another drug, Gammagard, which also targets immune functioning, was thought to have the potential to help remove amyloid. Unfortunately, its effectiveness in treating Alzheimer's symptoms is as yet unproven. Nevertheless, these novel drugs provide directions to guide researchers in developing alternative treatments to anticholinesterases.

Researchers believe that a medical cure for Alzheimer's disease will eventually be found, and may occur in your lifetime. However, it is unlikely that one "magic bullet" will serve this function. Instead, treatments will need to be targeted for specific at-risk individuals based on their genetic vulnerability, medical history, and exposure to environmental toxins (Roberson & Mucke, 2006).

Psychosocial Treatments. As intensively as research is progressing on treatments for Alzheimer's disease with the hope of someday soon finding a cure, the reality is that no cure presently exists. Meanwhile, people with this disease and their families must find ways to deal on a daily basis with the incapacitating cognitive and sometimes physical symptoms that accompany the deterioration of brain tissue. Clearly, until a cure can be found, mental health workers will be needed to provide assistance in this difficult process, so that the individual's functioning can be preserved for as long as possible.

A critical step in providing conscientious symptom management is for health care professionals to recognize that Alzheimer's disease involves families as much as it does the patients. Family members are most likely to be the ones providing care for the patient, particularly when the patient is no longer able to function independently. This responsibility most likely falls to wives and daughters.

Caregivers are those individuals, usually family, who provide support to people with chronic diseases. They have been the focus of considerable research efforts over the past 30 years. We now know that caregivers are very likely to suffer adverse effects from the constant demands placed on them. The term **caregiver burden** is used to describe the stress that caregivers experience in the daily management of

their afflicted relative. As the disease progresses, caregivers must provide physical assistance in basic life functions, such as eating, dressing, and toileting. As time goes by, the caregiver may experience health problems that make it harder and harder to provide the kind of care needed to keep the Alzheimer's patient at home.

Given the strain placed on caregivers, it should come as no surprise that health problems and rates of depression, stress, and isolation are higher among these individuals than among the population at large. For example, research suggests that daughters caring for parents with neurocognitive disorder suffer significantly more cardiovascular stress compared to wives caring for their spouse (King, Atienza, Castro, & Collins, 2002).

Fortunately, support for caregivers of people with Alzheimer's disease is widely available. Local chapters of national organizations in the United States such as the Alzheimer's Association provide a variety of community support services for families in general and caregivers in particular. Caregivers can be taught ways to promote independence and reduce distressing behaviors in the patient as well as to learn ways to handle the emotional stress associated with their role. We summarize suggestions from the National Institute of Aging (2009) for caregivers to care for themselves in Figure 5.9.

FIGURE 5.9

Suggestions for Caregivers

Caring for yourself
Taking care of yourself is one of the most important things you can do as a caregiver. This could mean asking family members and friends to help out, doing things you enjoy, using adult day care services, or getting help from a local home health care agency. Taking these actions can bring you some relief. It also may help keep you from getting ill or depressed.

How to take care of yourself
Here are some ways you can take care of yourself:

- Ask for help when you need it.
- Join a caregiver's support group.
- Take breaks each day.
- Spend time with friends.
- Keep up with your hobbies and interests.
- Eat healthy foods.
- Get exercise as often as you can.
- See your doctor on a regular basis.
- Keep your health, legal, and financial information up-to-date.

Source: National Institute of Aging. (2009). Caring for a person with Alzheimer's Disease. NIH Publication Number: 09-6173. Retrieved from http://www.nia.nih.gov/NR/rdonlyres/6A0E9F3C-E429-4F03-818ED1B60235D5F8/0/100711_LoRes2.pdf.

An important goal in managing the symptoms of Alzheimer's disease is to teach caregivers behavioral methods that will help to maximize the patient's ability to remain independent for as long as possible. The idea behind this approach is that, by maintaining the patient's independence, the caregiver's burden is somewhat reduced. For example, the patient can be given prompts, cues, and guidance in the steps involved in getting dressed and then be positively rewarded with praise and attention for having completed those steps. Modeling is another behavioral strategy, in which the caregiver performs the desired action (such as pouring a glass of water) so that the patient can see this action and imitate it. Again, positive reinforcement helps to maintain this behavior once it is learned (or more properly, relearned). The caregiver then has less work to do, and the patients are given the cognitive stimulation involved in actively performing these tasks rather than having others take over their care completely.

Second, caregivers can also use behavioral strategies to reduce or eliminate the frequency of actions such as wandering or being aggressive. In some cases, this strategy may require ignoring problematic behaviors, with the idea that by eliminating the reinforcement for those behaviors in the form of attention, the patient will be less likely to engage in them. However, it is more likely that a more active approach will be needed, especially for a behavior such as wandering. In this case the patient can be provided with positive reinforcement for not wandering. Even this may not be enough, however, and the caregiver may need to take such precautions as installing a protective device in doors and hallways.

Third, caregivers should, as much as possible, operate according to a strict daily schedule. The structure provided by a regular routine of everyday activities can give the patient additional cues to use as guides for which behaviors to carry out at which times of day.

Fourth, the caregiver should identify situations in which the patient becomes particularly disruptive, such as during bathing or riding in the car. In these cases, the caregiver can learn how to target those aspects of the situation that cause the patient to become particularly upset and then modify them accordingly. For example, if the problem occurs while bathing, it may be that a simple alteration such as providing a terry cloth robe rather than a towel helps reduce the patient's feeling of alarm at being undressed in front of others.

It is also important for caregivers to understand what to expect as the disease progresses. In a study of more than 300 nursing home patients with advanced neurocognitive disorder, fewer interventions considered burdensome, such as tube feeding, were used when those responsible for the patient's treatment were aware of the prognosis and typical course of the disease (Mitchell et al., 2009).

Creative approaches to managing the recurrent stresses involved in the caregiver's role may help to reduce the feelings of burden and frustration that are so much a part of daily life. Along with the provision of community and institutional support services, such interventions can go a long way toward helping the caregiver and ultimately the patient (Callahan et al., 2006).

Other Forms of Neurocognitive Disorder

The condition known as neurocognitive disorder is frequently caused by Alzheimer's disease in later life; however, many other conditions can affect the status of the brain and cause the individual to experience loss of memory, language, and motor functions.

People with **vascular neurocognitive disorder** progressively lose cognitive functioning due to damage to the arteries supplying the brain. The most common form of vascular neurocognitive disorder is **multi-infarct dementia or MID**, which is caused by transient ischemic attacks. In this case, a number of minor strokes ("infarcts") occur in which a clogged or burst artery interrupts blood flow to the brain. Each infarct is too small to be noticed, but over time, the progressive damage caused by the infarcts leads the individual to lose cognitive abilities.

There are important differences between MID and Alzheimer's disease. The development of MID tends to be more rapid than Alzheimer's disease. The higher the number of infarcts, the greater the decline in cognitive functioning (Saczynski et al., 2009). Smaller hippocampal volume is also related to the presence of infarcts and poorer memory functioning (Blum et al., 2012).

Vascular neurocognitive disorder seems to be related to risk factors that are similar to those for cardiovascular disease. Diabetes mellitus is associated with moderate cognitive deficits and changes in the physiology and structure of the brain, increasing the risk of neurocognitive disorder (Baquer et al., 2009). These cognitive deficits are particularly likely to develop early in the course of the disease (van den Berg et al., 2008). Metabolic syndrome also is associated with a higher risk of vascular neurocognitive disorder (Solfrizzi et al., 2009). Excess fat (adiposity) in the midsection further increases the risk of neurocognitive disorder in late life (Whitmer et al., 2008).

Neurocognitive disorder that specifically involves the frontal lobes of the brain is known as **frontotemporal neurocognitive disorder (FTD)**. The individual with FTD experiences personality changes such as apathy, lack of inhibition, obsessiveness, addictive behaviors, and loss of judgment (Caycedo, Miller, Kramer, & Rascovsky, 2009). Eventually the individual becomes neglectful of personal habits and loses the ability to communicate.

People who develop **Parkinson's disease** show a variety of motor disturbances, including tremors (shaking at rest), speech impediments, slowing of movement, muscular rigidity, shuffling gait, and postural instability or the inability to maintain balance. Neurocognitive disorder can develop during the later stages of the disease, and some people with Alzheimer's disease develop symptoms of Parkinson's disease. Patients typically survive 10 to 15 years after symptoms appear.

There is no cure for Parkinson's disease, but medications are available that can treat its symptoms. The primary drug used is Levadopa (L-dopa); however, over the years, this medication loses its effect and may even be toxic. Another, more radical, approach involves applying high-frequency deep brain stimulation of subcortical movement areas of the brain that in the past were excised surgically (Espay, Mandybur, & Revilla, 2006). Research examining the activation of brain cells with flashes of light offers promising treatment for Parkinson's disease (Gradinaru, Mogri, Thompson, Henderson, & Deisseroth, 2009). This quickly emerging field of optogenetics presents exciting avenues to better understand the mechanisms involved in Parkinson's disease to advance and improve treatment (Vazey & Aston-Jones, 2013).

Lewy bodies are tiny spherical structures consisting of deposits of protein found in dying nerve cells in damaged regions deep within the brains of people with Parkinson's disease. **Neurocognitive disorder with Lewy bodies,** first identified in 1961, is very similar to Alzheimer's disease in that it causes progressive loss of memory, language, calculation, and reasoning as well as other higher mental functions. Estimates are that this form of neurocognitive disorder accounts for 10 to 15% of all cases of neurocognitive disorder (McKeith, 2006). Neurocognitive disorder with Lewy bodies can fluctuate in severity, at least early in the disease. The disease also includes episodes of confusion and hallucinations, which are not typically found in Alzheimer's disease.

A relatively rare cause of neurocognitive disorder is **Pick's disease**, which involves severe atrophy of the frontal and temporal lobes. This disease is distinct from frontotemporal neurocognitive disorder because, in addition to deterioration of these areas, the individual's brain accumulates unusual protein deposits (called Pick bodies). The symptoms of Pick's disease include disorientation and memory loss in the early stages, but the disorder eventually progresses to include pronounced personality changes and loss of social constraints, similar to frontotemporal neurocognitive disorder. Eventually the individual becomes mute, immobile, and incontinent.

Reversible neurocognitive disorders are due to the presence of a medical condition that affects but does not destroy brain tissue. If the medical condition is left untreated, permanent damage may be done to the central nervous system, and the opportunity for intervention will be lost. Furthermore, if the condition is misdiagnosed as Alzheimer's disease, the patient will be regarded as untreatable and not be given the appropriate care at the appropriate time.

A neurological disorder known as **normal-pressure hydrocephalus**, though rare, can cause cognitive impairment, dementia, urinary incontinence, and difficulty in walking. The disorder involves an obstruction in the flow of cerebrospinal fluid, which causes the fluid to accumulate in the brain. Early treatment can divert the fluid away from the brain before significant damage has occurred.

Head injury can cause a **subdural haematoma**, which is a blood clot that creates pressure on brain tissue. Again, surgical intervention can relieve the symptoms and prevent further brain damage. The presence of a brain tumor can also cause cognitive deficits, which can be prevented from developing into a more severe condition through appropriate diagnosis and intervention.

Delirium is an acute cognitive disorder that is characterized by temporary confusion. It can be caused by diseases of the heart and lung, infection, or malnutrition. Unlike neurocognitive disorder, however, delirium has a sudden onset. Because this condition reflects a serious disturbance elsewhere in the body, such as infection, it requires immediate medical attention.

Delirium has many causes, including substance use, intake of medications, head injury, high fever, and vitamin deficiency. Most cases of delirium subside within days, but the condition may persist for as long as a month. Although relatively frequent in acute care medical settings, occurring in up to nearly 40% of hospitalized older adults (Boustani et al., 2010), the condition is uncommon within community-residing populations. Therefore, when an older person shows signs of delirium, treatment should be given right away (Andrew, Freter, & Rockwood, 2006). Unfortunately, the individual with delirium may be misdiagnosed with dementia, and an opportunity for intervention will have been lost or at least made more complicated.

Prescribed medications given in too strong a dose or in harmful combinations are included as other potentially toxic substances that can cause neurocognitive disorder-like symptoms. A condition called **polypharmacy**, in which the individual takes multiple drugs sometimes without the knowledge of the physician, can be particularly lethal. Recall that the excretion of medications is slower in older adults because of changes in the kidneys, so that older adults are more vulnerable to such toxic effects of medications.

Wernicke's disease is an acute condition caused by chronic alcohol abuse involving delirium, eye movement disturbances, difficulties maintaining balance and movement, and deterioration of the nerves to the hands and feet. Providing the individual with vitamin B1 (thiamine) can reverse this condition. Unfortunately, if it is not treated, Wernicke's disease progresses to the chronic form of alcohol-induced neurocognitive disorder known as **Korsakoff syndrome**.

Older adults who suffer from clinical depression may show cognitive changes that mimic those involved in Alzheimer's disease. The symptoms of depression in older adults may include confusion, distraction, and irritable outbursts, symptoms that may be mistaken for Alzheimer's disease. When these cognitive symptoms appear, causing impairment similar to neurocognitive disorder, the individual is said to have **pseudodementia**. Depression may also occur in conjunction with dementia, particularly in older adults who are in the early stages of a dementing disorder. In either case, the depression is treatable, and when appropriate interventions are made, the individual's cognitive functioning can show considerable improvement. We will discuss these issues further in Chapter 11.

The many possible causes of neurocognitive disorder, and the difficulty in distinguishing neurocognitive disorder due to Alzheimer's disease from other forms of cognitive decline, supports the notion that the prevalence of Alzheimer's disease may be overestimated, particularly with the rise in obesity in the United States, which presents a significant risk factor for certain forms of neurocognitive disorder.

Clearly, Alzheimer's disease and the variety of neurocognitive disorders described here are major potential limitations on the lives of older adults. Contrary to the impression given by the media, they afflict a minority of older people. Nevertheless, breakthroughs in their treatment, along with contributions to understanding other major diseases, will be among the most significant achievements of science in the 21st century.

SUMMARY

1. Diseases in middle and later adulthood can significantly interfere with quality of life. Risk factors for chronic disease include a sedentary lifestyle, smoking, alcohol use, and unhealthy diets. Cardiovascular diseases, in which there are pathological changes in the arteries in the form of arteriosclerosis and atherosclerosis, are the number one cause of death worldwide. Heart disease also includes coronary artery disease, myocardial infarction, hypertension, and congestive heart failure. Cerebrovascular accidents involve a cutting off of blood to the brain and may be acute or transient. Cardiovascular diseases are the leading cause of death in the over-75 population, with men having a higher risk, particularly Black men. Behavioral risk factors include a sedentary lifestyle, smoking, high BMI, and excessive alcohol intake. Metabolic syndrome refers to the cluster of symptoms including abdominal obesity, high blood fats, abnormal levels of blood cholesterol, hypertension, and high glucose associated with high risk factors for cardiovascular diseases. Preventive medication, diet, and exercise are advised to reduce or prevent the prevalence of heart disease.

2. Cancer is a group of diseases in which there is abnormal cell growth. Skin cancer is the most prevalent form of cancer in the United States in the adult population. Breast cancer is the most frequent cancer in women, but lung cancer is the deadliest for men and women. There are many behavioral risk factors for cancer, including smoking, sun exposure, and lack of control over diet. Environmental toxins can increase cancer risk. Cancer treatment includes surgery, radiation therapy, chemotherapy, and biological therapy.

3. Several musculoskeletal disorders are more common in older adults than in the younger population. Osteoarthritis is a degenerative joint disease in which the cartilage deteriorates. Osteoporosis is an extreme loss of bone mineral content that primarily affects women. Preventative steps include calcium intake, vitamin D, exercise, dietary control, and estrogen-replacement therapy.

4. Type 2 diabetes is an increasingly common chronic disease in older adults caused by a defect in metabolizing glucose; estimates suggest that 21% of the over-60 population are afflicted. Prevention and treatment involve weight control, exercise, and medication.

5. Respiratory diseases, including chronic obstructive pulmonary disease, chronic emphysema, and chronic bronchitis, are thought to be caused primarily by cigarette smoking. They have no cure at present.

6. Dementia is a clinical condition involving loss of memory and other cognitive functions. Alzheimer's disease is the most common form of dementia, affecting an estimated 7% of the over-65 population. Biological changes include development of amyloid plaques and neurofibrillary tangles. Alzheimer's disease is thought to have genetic causes, possibly involving abnormalities

on the ApoE, APP, and presenilin genes that lead to formation of plaques and tangles. The caspase theory focuses on the neurotoxic role of amyloid. Diagnosis of Alzheimer's disease can be made only from autopsy, but there are improved methods such as those involving brain scans. Medical treatments being tested include anticholinesterases and memantines.

Psychosocial treatments attempt to control behaviors and to provide support to caregivers. Other forms of dementia are vascular dementia, fronterotemporal dementia, Parkinson's disease, Lewy body dementia, and Pick's disease. There are also reversible dementias, including pseudodementia, which, if treated, can lead to a return to normal cognitive functioning.

6

Basic Cognitive Functions: Information Processing, Attention, and Memory

Mastering the Fine Art of Multitasking

How many windows are open on your computer right now? If you're like most of us, we'd venture a guess that you're running a couple of Internet sites (at least), not to mention your e-mail, social media, and maybe a few other software applications. Close by, your cell phone buzzes with incoming texts while your iPad is paused on a game of *Words with Friends*. Do you like having all these multiple sources of connectivity but still worry that they will hamper your productivity? Cheer up! There are actually many advantages to splitting your mental resources, as long as you do it correctly.

It may be hard for you to believe that multitasking could ever have benefits. The experts widely agree, and often with good reason, that we should not let anything distract us from driving. Many states ban cell phone use in the car even with hands-free technology. The claim is that talking on the phone is inherently more distracting than talking to a real person who is in the same car. However, there are no laws against, say, eating a pizza while driving. Nor is there a ban against listening to the radio or even adjusting the heat or windshield wipers. We can poke away at our GPSs with reckless abandon and not break any laws. Yet, all of these activities have the potential to cause us to take our eyes off the road.

However, because our brains can handle multiple tasks at once, dividing our consciousness is not an inherently dangerous activity. The risk seems to come into play when we place too many demands on our cognitive resources. Cell phone use, for whatever reason, has the potential to place such heavy demands on our resources, creating unique problems for drivers. In many situations, however, we have ample cognitive resources to complete the tasks of our daily lives. If we multitask under those conditions, we can actually improve our mental efficiency. For many well-practiced and routine tasks, it's not worth spending the mental effort. If a task requires only 10% of our resources, why not put that other 90% to good use?

Furthermore, playing an hour of online games isn't a particularly good way to maximize your productivity; however, you may actually benefit from a brief mental break while you're plugging away at your desktop. Even a brief walk in the park can help you recharge your brain's batteries. You're also more likely to catch an error if you take your eyes away from the document you're working on and return to it after a slight shift of mental focus. Go ahead and update your Facebook status (quickly!). If you're feeling frustrated, you may get a little uplift from checking in with friends and family, if only for a moment.

Posted by Susan Whitbourne and Stacey Whitbourne

Cognition refers to the way the mind works; specifically, the processes of attention, memory, intelligence, problem solving, and the use of language. We know that aging affects each of these areas of functioning, leading to important changes in many of people's ability to carry out their everyday activities.

PROCESSING SPEED AND ATTENTION

One of the most widely studied areas in cognition and aging, **processing speed** is the amount of time it takes for an individual to analyze incoming information from the senses, formulate decisions, and then prepare a response on the basis of that analysis. Researchers believe that psychomotor speed reflects the integrity of the central nervous system (Madden, 2001).

Reaction Time

The basic measure of processing speed is **reaction time**. To measure reaction time, researchers ask their participants to complete an action such as pushing a computer key when the screen flashes a particular stimulus, known as a target. Stimuli that do not fit the criteria for the target are called distractors.

In **simple reaction time tasks**, participants are instructed to make a response such as pushing the key as soon as they see the target, such as a red circle appearing on the screen in front of them. In **choice reaction time tasks**, participants must make one response for one stimulus and another response for a different stimulus. For example, they would push the "F" button for a red circle and the "J" button for a blue circle.

In some studies, participants see a cue prior to the target's presentation. This cue directs them to look in a particular area of the computer screen. The cue may or may not direct them to the where the actual target will appear. Researchers use such misleading or irrelevant cues to determine how distracting information alters the individual's responses.

Researchers know with certainty that the reaction time of a young adult will be lower (i.e., the person will be quicker) than when that individual gets older. The question is, by how much and under what circumstances will it increase? The documented changes in reaction time with age in adulthood are typically a matter of several hundreds of milliseconds, not enough to be particularly noticeable in everyday life, but enough to be significant under the scrutiny of the laboratory researcher.

People vary greatly in the rate at which they experience a slowing in reaction time. Despite this increasing variability in reaction times with age, overall, the net effect of the changes are negative across adulthood, particularly for choice reaction time tasks (Der & Deary, 2006).

Why do reaction times slow as people age? According to the **general slowing hypothesis**, the increase in reaction time reflects a general decline of information processing speed within the nervous system of the aging individual (Salthouse, 1996). The **age-complexity hypothesis** proposes, furthermore, that through a slowing of central processes in the nervous system, age differences increase as tasks become more complex and the older adult's processing resources are stretched more and more to their limit (Cerella, Poon, & Williams, 1980).

You can clearly visualize the pattern of age differences in reaction time by looking at Figure 6.1. In this graph, called a **Brinley plot**, the reaction times of older groups of adults are plotted against the times of younger adults. If you look closely at this graph, you can see that in the 500 ms range (half a second), older and younger adults have similar performance. These are the tasks that are relatively easy; this is why they are performed so quickly. However, on tasks that take longer for young adults to complete (1,000 ms or 1 second), older adults take proportionately longer (1,500–2,000 ms) than they do on the 500 ms tasks. The hardest tasks take young adults about 2,500 ms to complete, but take older adults as long as 4,000 ms.

The general slowing hypothesis is consistent with a large body of data on reaction time performance in adulthood. This hypothesis does not identify any particular stage or component of information processing as the culprit for causing age differences in reaction time, though there is the assumption that the slowing reflects a lack of efficiency in the nervous system. As we will see later, the general slowing hypothesis is also used to explain age differences in memory. A loss of speed leads to memory impairments, as a backlog develops in cognitive processes calling for multiple operations to be completed simultaneously or within a limited time.

Attention

The slowing of reaction time with age may be attributed to many factors. One that has intrigued researchers is the hypothesis that older adults are particularly disadvantaged in the attentional stage of information processing. **Attention** involves the ability to focus or concentrate on a portion of experience while ignoring other features of that experience, to be able to shift that focus as demanded by the situation, and to be able to coordinate information from multiple sources. Once your attention is focused on a

FIGURE 6.1

Brinley Plot

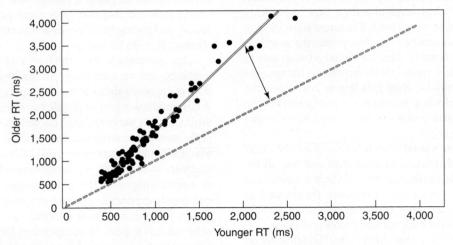

Deviation of dots from the diagonal line shows the extent to which older adults are disproportionately slower as the task becomes more challenging for young adults.

Source: Sliwinski, M. J., & Hall, C. B. (1998). Constraints on general slowing: A meta-analysis using hierarchical linear models with random coefficients. *Psychology and Aging, 13,* 169. American Psychological Association. Reprinted with permission.

piece of information, you are then able to perform further cognitive operations, such as those needed for memory or problem solving.

If you have difficulty concentrating or focusing your attention for long periods of time, you are certainly aware of how frustrating it can be to miss important information or details when you divert your mental resources away from the task. Persistent and serious attentional problems characterize people with attention deficit disorder who, as a result, may have difficulty learning new information or performing more than one task at a time. The attentional deficits associated with the normal aging process can involve deficits of a similar nature, particularly when individuals have to make complex decisions within a short period of time.

Types of Attentional Tasks. Studies of attention are important for understanding the cognitive functions of adults of varying ages and their abilities to function in various real-life situations in which cognitive resources must be focused on some target or goal. Researchers approach these issues by breaking down the attentional tasks involved in everyday life into components to examine in the laboratory. For the most part, these studies suggest that people become less efficient in the use of attentional processes as they get older.

Two methods used in studies on attention and aging involve **visual search tasks** which require that the observer locate a specific target among a set of distractors. In **simple visual search** (Figure 6.2), the target differs from the other stimuli by only one feature, such as shape, color, or size. For example, the target may be a red circle and the

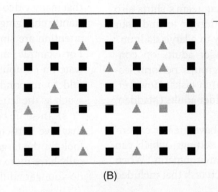

FIGURE 6.2

Types of Visual Search Tasks.
(A) Simple (B) Conjunction

(A)   (B)

distractors are all blue circles. Participants push a key as soon as they determine whether or not the target is present.

Participants completing tests of simple visual search can generally reach high levels of performance very quickly across the trials of an experiment. The target starts to "pop out" among the distractors. At that point, the search is said to become automatic. Because the target is so easy to detect, reaction time tends not to increase as the number of items in the stimulus array gets larger. There could be 10 or 50 blue circles but, as long as the participant can see all the stimuli, participants will find it easy to see if that red circle is there or not.

In **conjunction visual search** (Figure 6.2), the target differs from the distractors in more than one way. If the target is a red circle, the distractors could be red squares and blue circles. To register a correct response, the respondent must indicate that the target is present only when the field contains a stimulus of both the same color and shape.

Researchers propose that simple visual search relies on parallel processing, meaning that you can scan the whole array at once, just looking for the one feature that matches that of the target. It's as if you were at a home basketball game and wanted to spot your friend, a fan of the visiting team, in the large crowd. If all the home fans were wearing the school colors (e.g., maroon), your friend's light blue shirt would easily jump out at you. Older and younger adults perform at similarly high levels in simple visual search tasks, finding the targets quickly and accurately (Whiting, Madden, Pierce, & Allen, 2005).

Conjunction search relies on the more time-consuming task of serial processing because each stimulus must be examined to determine whether it has all the qualities of the target. In the case of the red circle among red squares and blue circles, you must first determine if the stimulus matches one of the target's features, such as color. Then you must determine if the stimulus matches the other feature, such as shape. After that, you integrate the two features and then inspect each stimulus to determine whether or not it is a match. The larger the number of stimuli to scan, the longer the participant will take to decide whether the target is present or not. In the case of your friend at the basketball game, should the visiting team's shirts also be maroon, it would take you much longer to find your friend's face among the fans, especially in a large stadium.

Comparisons of older and younger adults on conjunction search show that both age groups perform less efficiently than they do on simple search tasks. However, the cost to performance is higher for older adults (Madden, Pierce, & Allen, 1996).

On the other hand, older adults have greater experience in making decisions in real-life settings, which can benefit them when they scan actual environments. When compared to younger adults on a search task that included

context to guide their attention, older adults were more likely than younger adults to benefit from background cues (Neider & Kramer, 2011). Furthermore, older adults can benefit from training that gives them practice and guidance in performing even very difficult conjunction searches (Neider, Boot, & Kramer, 2010).

One particularly important area of attentional performance, known commonly as "multitasking," involves studying people's ability to monitor multiple input sources. While multitasking, most people pay a price in terms of the quality of their performance. This includes lower academic performance in college students who go on Facebook or who text while in class (Junco, 2012). It is not only college students. Most people are disadvantaged when it comes to multitasking, and the disadvantages of multitasking that people experience increase progressively in older age groups (Kramer & Madden, 2008). To a certain extent, older adults appear to compensate for the attentional deficits they experience while multitasking by shifting the regions of the brain they activate while attending to more than one input.

A number of investigators who study attention and aging are interested in the way that older adults mentally juggle the information coming in from different sources. In particular, researchers try to determine whether older adults have difficulty turning off one response while performing another in what is called **inhibitory control**. One of the best known inhibitory attention tasks is the Stroop test, in which you are told to name the color of ink in which a word is printed. In the critical trials on the Stroop test, your response time and accuracy are compared when the color and the word match (e.g., the word "red" printed in red) with your performance when the color and the word do not match ("red" is printed in green). People with good inhibitory control are able to turn off the naming of the color based on the word rather than the naming of the color based on the ink.

In a **sustained attention** task, participants must respond when they see a particular target appear out of a continuous stream of stimuli. This is the type of attention that many video games require when players monitor a constantly changing visual array. Laboratory tasks of sustained attention are similar in principle, though not as elaborate. For example, in a typical experimental task, participants watch a computer screen with a series of stimuli; they're told to respond only when the target stimulus appears (such as the letter "X" moving onto a screen containing all "Y"s). In some conditions, the experimenter provides cues that give participants notice about whether and where to look for the target just before it appears. Older adults typically have more difficulty on sustained attention tasks than do younger adults (Dennis, Daselaar, & Cabeza, 2007).

Studies on aging and attentional performance suggest that not all abilities decline. For example, although older adults are typically slower when processing information from visual displays, they can remember the location of an item presented in a visual display and may be even be more efficient at this task than are younger adults (Kramer et al., 2006). Additionally, healthy older adults, with practice, can activate different areas of the brain than can younger adults to raise their performance on the Stroop task to comparable levels (Schulte et al., 2009). Such results support models proposing that aging involves a degree of neural plasticity.

Theories of Attention and Aging.   We will focus on two approaches to understanding age differences in attentional tasks (see Figure 6.3). The **attentional resources theory** regards attention as a process reflecting the allocation of cognitive resources. When you must focus on a particular object, you must dedicate a certain proportion of your mental operations to that object. According to this theory, older adults have greater difficulty on attentional tasks because they have less energy available for cognitive operations than do their younger counterparts (Blanchet, Belleville, & Peretz, 2006). Tasks that require high attentional demands are subject to reduced performance among older adults, compared with tasks that require little attention that remain intact. Although this theory seems rational, little empirical research is available to support its existence (Glisky, 2007).

The second theory of attention and aging, the **inhibitory deficit hypothesis**, suggests that aging reduces the individual's ability to inhibit or tune out irrelevant information (Butler & Zacks, 2006). As we discussed earlier, one important feature of attention is the ability to focus on one element of a stimulus array while ignoring others. If older adults cannot ignore irrelevant information, their attentional performance will suffer.

The inhibitory deficit hypothesis is widely supported by a variety of studies based on psychological and electrophysiological methods. For example, on measures of **event-related potentials (ERPs)**, which measure the brain's pattern of electrical activity in response to stimuli, older adults are less able to block out distracting stimuli when completing a task. Their pattern of response suggests that they experience deficits in the prefrontal cortex, the area of the brain involved in the control of inhibiting irrelevant information (West & Schwarb, 2006). For example, when younger and older participants are asked to observe sequences presented in a randomized order and measured using EEG, older adults are less likely to suppress irrelevant information resulting in both increased frontal activity and poorer memory performance compared with younger adults (Gazzaley et al., 2008).

The inhibitory deficit hypothesis implies that middle-aged and older adults perform best when they have few distractions. One source of such distraction may be their own concern over how they are performing, which therefore may cause them to perform even more poorly than they otherwise would. Imagine that you are a computer programmer anxious about the possibility of being laid off or reassigned because you are not as quick as you once were in your job of inspecting arrays of new data. The more you worry about how you are performing, the less able you are to concentrate on your task. Your performance deficits might ultimately lead you to lose your job or be reassigned to other duties. Thus, people who are worried about the aging of their cognitive abilities may be more likely to engage in identity accommodation (the "over-the-hill" mentality), a process that will ultimately contribute to poorer performance.

However, older adults are not entirely disadvantaged in inhibitory attentional tasks. As we noted earlier, they can benefit from practice with the Stroop test in ways similar to younger adults (Davidson, Zacks, & Williams, 2003), suggesting that performance on certain types of attention can be improved regardless of age. Additionally, changes related to color perception with age may account for some of the age differences in the Stroop task (Ben-David & Schneider, 2009). For example, younger adults perform consistently with older adults when presented with a desaturated Stroop task (Ben-David & Schneider, 2012).

Experience can compensate for age-related changes in sustained attention. In a simulated air-traffic control experiment, older adults who showed deficits on laboratory attentional tasks were able to perform well on the complex tasks required in the situations they encountered on the

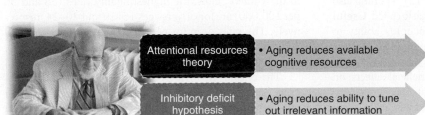

| Attentional resources theory | • Aging reduces available cognitive resources |
| Inhibitory deficit hypothesis | • Aging reduces ability to tune out irrelevant information |

Willie B. Thomas/iStockphoto

FIGURE 6.3

Theories of Attention and Aging

job on a daily basis (Nunes & Kramer, 2009). Education and verbal experience may also protect against increases in distraction while reading (McGinnis, 2012).

Video Games and Attention

With the increasing popularity of video games, many of which demand quick decisions and response speed, researchers are beginning to explore their use as laboratory tasks and as platforms for intervention studies. In action video games, such as first-person shooter games (*Call of Duty, Halo*, and *Battlefield*) or third-person shooter games (*Grand Theft Auto, Gears of War*), the player must have excellent hand-eye coordination, play at a fast pace, and track multiple inputs. The aggressive content of these games aside, their cognitive benefits are becoming well established.

Young adults who play action video games have improved attentional capacity (Green & Bavelier, 2003). Experienced players have more efficient eye movements (West, Al-Aidroos, & Pratt, 2013) and scan a display more quickly, automatically appraising such features as the number of items in a display without having to count (Riesenhuber, 2004). Action video games speed up the player's reaction time while preserving the accuracy of performance, abilities that could have real-world benefits in areas such as driving.

Players of these games also have more attentional resources that they can devote to rapidly changing inputs, meaning that they will make finer-grained distinctions and, therefore, better decisions. They are also better able to focus their attention and ignore distracting or irrelevant information. These effects are not only due to self-selection (i.e., people with better attentional resources are more likely to play these games) but have also been backed up by experimental training studies (Achtman, Green, & Bavelier, 2008).

Experimental studies using action video games as a training tool show that they can enhance a variety of skills, including peripheral attention (seeing a target at the outer edges of a display), ability to process a rapidly changing stream of information, and keeping track of multiple targets (Bavelier, Green, Pouget, & Schrater, 2012). Training also seems to improve the driving-relevant task called **Useful Field of View (UFOV)**, which tests people's ability to respond to stimuli appearing in the periphery of their vision (Green & Bavelier, 2006).

If video games can have these beneficial effects on young adults, it would make sense that they could also improve the attentional abilities of older adults (Dye, Green, & Bavelier, 2009). Studies going back to the early 1990s show that among older adults, training in video games

can improve speeded performance (Dustman, Emmerson, Steinhaus, & Shearer, 1992; Goldstein et al., 1997).

With the continued development of personal computer–based video games, researchers are able to investigate the effects on attention and speeded performance in a wider variety of formats. Older adults do not prefer to play first-person shooter games (McKay & Maki, 2010) but are instead drawn to casual video games played on a personal computer (De Schutter, 2010). These ordinary computer games, as well as those specifically intended to improve cognition in older adults ("brain training"), appear to have beneficial effects on focused and sustained attention (Peretz et al., 2011).

DRIVING AND AGING

The ability to drive is undoubtedly one of the most important functional areas of an adult's life, particularly for people who live in areas that are not well served by public transportation. Changes in basic cognitive functions threaten to impair the older adult's ability to perform this vital task. Furthermore, as we saw in Chapter 4, there are also a number of changes in the visual system that can impair the performance of older drivers, including loss of visual acuity, increased sensitivity to glare, and difficulty seeing in the dark. Physical changes may also limit the older driver's ability to get in and out of a car, fasten a seat belt, change the seat position, turn the steering wheel, or cope with a breakdown (Arbesman & Pellerito, 2008). Finally, many medications used to treat chronic conditions in older adults can impair their driving ability due to side effects such as drowsiness, confusion, and dizziness (Sargent-Cox, Windsor, Walker, & Anstey, 2011).

Despite the media reports that follow each fatal accident involving an older driver, age alone does not determine whether an older adult is safe behind the wheel (Donorfio, D'Ambrosio, Coughlin, & Mohyde, 2008). The effects of age on vision and cognition do not necessarily translate into higher accident rates of older drivers compared to some of their younger counterparts. According to the National Highway Traffic Safety Administration (2012), in the United States, the highest fatality rates (38 and 36 per 100,000) are for drivers ages 16–19 and 20–24, respectively. The rates drop for people 65–74 (18 per 100,000) and even in the 75 and older age group (28 per 100,000), are still lower than the fatality rates for young adults.

The crashes involving older drivers occur at intersections, particularly when the driver is making a turn that must take them across traffic—namely a left-hand turn in the United States and a right-hand turn in countries such as Australia, where people drive on the left (Braitman, Kirley,

Chaudhary, & Ferguson, 2006). Older drivers also have more difficulty when they are required to merge or yield to oncoming traffic (Richardson & Marottoli, 2003).

As we reported in Chapter 1, drivers under the age of 25 are also far more likely than older drivers to drink and drive (see Figure 6.4). Younger drivers are also more likely to drive while distracted, particularly by talking or text messaging on a cell phone. Research suggests that even hands-free devices (such as a Bluetooth earpiece) do not improve driving performance (Ishigami & Klein, 2009). In other words, any type of talking on the phone while driving is unsafe.

Counteracting the effects of age on rapid, complex, decision making is the fact that older adults avoid many of the causes of motor vehicle accidents that injure, or take the lives of, younger adults. Many older drivers are able to self-regulate their behaviors to compensate for the changes they experience in their visual and cognitive abilities. They avoid driving at night, on interstate highways, or situations in which they must make risky left-hand turns (Okonkwo, Crowe, Wadley, & Ball, 2008).

In addition, older drivers have decades of experience behind the wheel that can compensate for their slower reaction times, particularly if they don't need to make a response within a fraction of a second. Under icy conditions, for example, experienced older drivers know how to control the car to avoid a spinout. They may also be better able to predict what other drivers will do in certain situations, such as whether someone will pull out of a parking spot without signaling.

Driving provides a perfect example of the importance of adopting a biopsychosocial perspective to understand the aging process. Biology (changes in vision and reaction time) and psychology (internal distractions causing anxiety) each play important roles. The sociocultural component of the equation provides further insight into this comprehensive model. Driving is necessary in order to live independently in many regions of the United States and in other countries that lack comprehensive public transportation. Older adults who live in suburban or rural areas with limited or no public transportation lose an important connection to the outside world and risk becoming housebound and socially isolated.

Incorporating these factors into a model of driving self-regulation, Donofrio and colleagues (2009) propose that whether older adults continue to drive depends heavily on a number of psychological factors, including their feelings of self-confidence, desire to get out of the home, their need for independence, the importance of driving to their self-worth, and their perceived health. Sociocultural factors also come into play in terms of whether the older adult can get rides with others, has access to public transportation, and lives alone or with others. The question is not whether older adults should drive, but what driving means to their sense of self and identity as well as their ability to stay connected to the outside world.

Older adults may also incorporate social attitudes about aging and driving that serve to impair their performance beyond what would occur due to the normal aging process. Older adults who doubt themselves more frequently will hesitate before making a response due to worries about their abilities, or may suffer internal distractions because they are so preoccupied with their own concerns. Prejudice against them by younger people can exacerbate whatever

FIGURE 6.4

Percent of Drivers Involved in Fatal Accidents with Blood Alcohol Levels of 0.08% or Greater, U.S., 2009

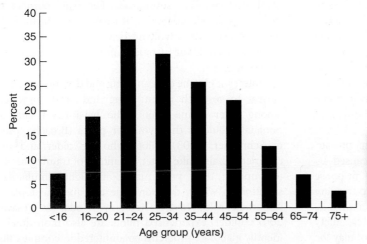

Blend Images/Alamy

Source: http://www.census.gov/compendia/statab/2012/tables/12s1113.pdf

The lights and the signs at this intersection on the University of Massachusetts campus present a complex visual array and may create confusion in older drivers.

Courtesy Susan Whitbourne

fears and concerns older drivers already have about their changing abilities. They may hear derogatory phrases such as "driving while old" or "gray head" and become even more concerned and hence distracted.

As the number of older drivers continues to grow—due to the increased longevity of the Baby Boomer generation—appropriate safeguards, such as driving tests and safety classes, are being considered for them by public officials. Highway safety experts are also exploring alternatives to the traditional intersection, such as substituting well-designed roundabouts for the type of complex junction that can cause so many accidents while turning. Older drivers can also benefit from easy fixes to their automobiles, such as adjusting the head restraints, steering wheel tilt, and mirror. In one survey of aging drivers, researchers found that over half needed to have their head restraints readjusted to provide proper support. Furthermore, through new technologies, such as collision avoidance systems, automobiles will eventually become better adapted to the needs of older drivers (Arbesman & Pellerito, 2008).

Nevertheless, there is value to maintaining precautions that protect all drivers from accidents caused by distracted driving, visual losses, or slowing of response speed. Current licensing policies and procedures are not well equipped to handle the influx of older drivers. Recommendations to address this growing public safety concern include identifying older drivers who may be

medically at-risk and impaired rather than restricting all older drivers (Dobbs, 2008). Rather than only screen for vision, drivers should also be assessed for cognitive status (Ross et al., 2009) (see Table 6.1).

It's also worthwhile to consider that speed is not everything when it comes to navigating your way around the highways and byways of your community. Allowing more time for older drivers to get where they are going might not be such a bad idea and could even make the roads safer for everyone. It is also important to remember that prevention efforts should focus on the avoidable fatalities involving younger drivers who are under the influence of alcohol or other substances. The real "number one killer"—in the United States, at least—is not heart disease but fatal accidents involving drivers who are under the influence: people die at much younger ages than biology would dictate.

Interestingly, the data on aging and driving correspond closely to research about aging and crash prevalence among older airline pilots, who have fewer fatal and nonfatal accidents than younger pilots (Broach, Joseph, & Schroeder, 2003). Pilots who are older and more experienced also take better advantage of training sessions to improve their performance in flight simulators; a situation in which decision time and judgment play an important role (Taylor, Kennedy, Noda, & Yesavage, 2007). Older, experienced pilots are also more likely to identify elaborate problems encountered in complex flight

TABLE 6.1
American Automobile Association Self-Assessment of Driving Abilities

Rate yourself on each of these items using this scale:

1. Always or Almost Always	2. Sometimes	3. Never or Almost Never

☐ I signal and check to the rear when I change lanes.

☐ I wear a seat belt.

☐ I try to stay informed on changes in driving and highway regulations.

☐ Intersections bother me because there is so much to watch from all directions.

☐ I find it difficult to decide when to merge with traffic on a busy interstate highway.

☐ I think I am slower than I used to be in reacting to dangerous driving situations.

☐ When I am really upset, I show it in my driving.

☐ My thoughts wander when I am driving.

☐ Traffic situations make me angry.

☐ I get regular eye checks to keep my vision at its sharpest.

☐ I check with my doctor or pharmacist about the effects of my medications on driving ability. (If you do not take any medication, skip this question.)

☐ I try to stay informed of current information on health and wellness habits.

☐ My children, other family members, or friends are concerned about my driving ability.

Rate yourself on each of these items using this scale:

1. None	2. One or Two	3. Three or More

☐ How many traffic tickets, warnings, or "discussions" with officers have you had in the past two years?

☐ How many collisions (major or minor) have you had during the past two years?

Source: American Automobile Association. (2013). Drivers 65 plus: Suggestions for improvement, from https://www.aaafoundation.org/drivers-65-plus-suggestions-improvement

situations compared with younger inexperienced pilots (Morrow et al., 2009). Similarly, the greater experience of older air traffic controllers seems to benefit their performance (Nunes & Kramer, 2009).

MEMORY

One of the changes people fear the most about aging is that they will lose their memory. The data on the effects of aging on memory suggest that the aging process indeed has negative effects on many aspects of memory. However, as was true for attention, not all aspects of memory are affected in the same way by aging, nor is everyone affected the same way by the aging process.

Working Memory

Working memory keeps information temporarily available and active in consciousness. You use your working memory when you are trying to learn new information or bring to mind information you learned previously that you are trying to recall. Working memory and attention are closely linked, as controlled attention is required to juggle multiple thought processes.

Researchers assess working memory by assigning a task to participants that prevents them from consciously rehearsing the information they are supposed to remember. The "n-back" task, a commonly used working memory test, requires you to repeat the "nth" item back in a list of items presented to you in serial order. For example, you would see a series of visual stimuli, such as a yellow triangle, a red square, a green circle, and a blue diamond. In each instance, you are asked whether the stimulus is new or one previously seen. In the "1-back" task, you are shown the yellow triangle followed by the red square followed by the yellow triangle and asked to remember the stimulus shown prior to the red square (the yellow triangle). The further back in the series (for example, in the "3-back"), the harder the task because more demands are placed on working memory.

FIGURE 6.5

Example of an N-Back Working Memory Task

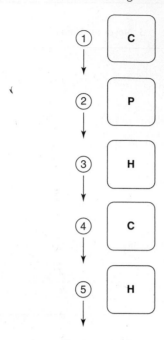

You can see an example of an n-back working memory task in Figure 6.5. The C would be a 3-back task and the H would be a 2-back task.

According to Baddeley (2003), there are four components to working memory. Auditory memory (memory for what you hear) is held within what he called the phonological loop. This information can be rehearsed by repeating the material over and over again such as when you try to remember a phone number and have no way to write it down. Memory for information that you see is maintained within the visuospatial scratch pad. You use the visuospatial scratch pad when you are trying to remember the route home from a store you have visited once by imagining it in your mind. The third component of working memory, the episodic buffer, is responsible for recalling information you already have within long-term memory by bringing it temporarily into working memory. The central executive, the fourth component of working memory, integrates the other three components of working memory. You rely on the central executive when you decide how to allocate cognitive resources to a particular task.

The components of working memory seem to be linked to particular cortical brain regions. Through neuroimaging studies that connect how individuals perform on memory tasks to patterns of their brain's activity, researchers are beginning to understand the structural basis for the effects of aging on working memory. These studies look not just at what individual brain regions do during cognitive tasks, but also at how these brain regions communicate with each other through networks.

While at rest, the brain shows activation in what is known as the **default network**, a circuit in the brain that is active when the brain is at rest while processing internal stimuli. The default network includes the hippocampus, parts of the prefrontal cortex, the parietal lobe, the temporal lobe, and part of the cingulate cortex involved in visualization. During tasks such as those involved in working memory, other areas become activated and the default network becomes deactivated (Buckner, Andrews-Hanna, & Schacter, 2008).

Older adults show decreased activation of the default network compared to younger adults (Andrews-Hanna et al., 2007). They are also less able to deactivate the network during memory tasks, when they need to focus on the incoming input (Hafkemeijer, van der Grond, & Rombouts, 2012). This would mean that they would have fewer resources to devote to the information they need to retain.

There is some evidence, however, that normal aging preserves the default network's ability to deactivate during working memory tasks. In the only longitudinal study to date, there were no changes over an 8-year period in the brain activation patterns of a sample of 32 healthy older adults (Beason-Held, Kraut, & Resnick, 2009). Furthermore, high-functioning older adults may actually draw on the default network to augment their performance in working memory tasks (Sala-Llonch et al., 2012).

Effects of Aging on Long-Term Memory in Adulthood

We turn next to **long-term memory**, the repository of information that is held for a period of time ranging from several minutes to a lifetime. Long-term memory contains information that includes the recent past, such as remembering where you put your cell phone half an hour ago, to information from many years ago, such as what happened at your fourth birthday party. The processes of long-term memory include encoding, storage, and retrieval. We encode information when we first learn it, keep it in long-term storage, and retrieve it when we need to use it on a subsequent occasion.

The "Aging and Long-Term Memory Score Card" in Figure 6.6 summarizes the effects of aging on the various types of long-term memory.

Episodic memory is long-term memory for events ("episodes"). Research suggests that older adults experience impairments in episodic memory, both in encoding and retrieving information (Old & Naveh-Benjamin, 2008a).

FIGURE 6.6

The Aging and Long-Term Memory Scorecard

Abilities that decline	Abilities that do not decline
Episodic memory	Flashbulb memory
Source memory	Semantic memory
False memory	Procedural memory
Tip-of-the-tongue (names)	Implicit memory
Prospective memory	Autobiographical memory ("reminiscence bump")

image100/Age Fotostock America, Inc.

Episodic memory also depends on the integrity of connections among the frontal cortex, temporal and parietal lobes, and areas of the subcortex, including the thalamus. Age-related damage to the white matter, which shows up as white matter hyperintensities, may be associated with memory changes in these regions (Lockhart et al., 2012).

However, in normal aging, these structural changes in areas of the brain involved in working memory are compensated by heightened activation of the prefrontal cortex (Park & Reuter-Lorenz, 2009). According to **scaffolding theory**, older adults are able to recruit alternate neural circuits as needed by task demands to make up for losses suffered elsewhere in the brain. Thus, working memory may decline in later adulthood, but individuals can circumvent these declines by bringing compensatory mechanisms into play. This theory, like the HAROLD and PASA models we described in Chapter 4, builds on the concept of neuroplasticity.

Remote memory involves the recall of information from the distant past. In general, information stored and not accessed from remote memory becomes increasingly difficult to retrieve with passing years. A popular myth is that older people can remember information from many years in the past better than they can remember more recent information. However, this myth is not supported by data on remote memory (Piolino, Desgranges, Benali, & Eustache, 2002). In one study, older adults were asked to recall events from television shows. Their memory for recent programs was superior to their ability to remember programs from many years ago (Squire, 1989).

The exception to this research on remote memory occurs in the area of **autobiographical memory**, or the recall of information from your own past. Many people seem to experience a **reminiscence bump** of very clear memories for the ages of from about 10 to 30 years (Rubin,

Rahhal, & Poon, 1998), an effect that is particularly strong for happy memories (Gluck & Bluck, 2007). Researchers believe that these memories are preserved in part because they are central to identity (McLean, 2008). Remote memories that are not as personally relevant fade with the passage of time.

Flashbulb memory is the recall of important and distinctive events that stand out from other memories of past events. For example, you may remember where you were and what you were doing on December 14, 2012, when 20 schoolchildren and six teachers were fatally wounded in the Newtown, Connecticut, elementary school shooting. When older adults form such memories, they are as likely as younger adults to recall them correctly, as evidenced by research assessing recall of source memory for the news of the September 11, 2001 terrorist attacks (Davidson, Cook, & Glisky, 2006).

In contrast to episodic memory, there are no declines in normal older adults in **semantic memory**, or the ability to recall word meanings and the factual information. Semantic memory is also spared from the negative effects of the aging process (Wiggs, Weisberg, & Martin, 2006). Older adults are able to remember word meanings and a broad array of factual information on a comparable level with younger adults.

Long-term memory also includes your ability to remember actions. **Procedural memory** is recall of the actions involved in particular tasks, such as sewing on a button, playing the piano, and riding a bike. Like semantic memory, procedural memory holds up well with age. In one particularly impressive study, a sample of approximately 500 adults ranging from 18 to 95 years were tested on their ability to learn a fine motor task in which they had to use their fingers to slide a small metal nut off a rod as quickly as possible. Not only did older adults show significant improvement in performance over a series of five learning trials, but they retained their memory for the task for as long as 2 years later with no drop-off in performance (Smith et al., 2005). It's not only humans who have this ability.

The motor learning task study was replicated in a sample of young and old rhesus monkeys tested over a 2-year period. The findings were comparable to those for humans (Walton, Scheib, McLean, Zhang, & Grondin, 2008). So there is truth to the saying that "old monkeys," if not dogs, can learn new tricks.

A well-maintained procedural memory contributes to the ability of older adults to compensate for some of their loss of speed and working memory in diverse areas including bridge playing, chess, reading, cooking, gardening, and typing (Mireles & Charness, 2002). The experienced bridge player, for example, is able to examine a round of cards without giving each individual card a great deal of thought or study. Through years of playing, many of the choices about which card to play follow established conventions and rules, so that the older bridge player does not have to remember as much about each of the hand of 13 cards they are dealt for each round of play.

Implicit memory is long-term memory for information that people acquire without intending to do so. It is another long-term memory process that does not appear to be affected by the aging process (Old & Naveh-Benjamin, 2008b). In testing implicit memory, researchers present participants with a task that involves manipulating but not necessarily remembering information. For example, you might be presented with a list of words and asked to place them into categories, but not to recall them. Later, you would be asked to remember the words you had previously only been told to categorize. Another way to test implicit memory is through priming. Here you are shown information that leads you to think of a certain thing, topic, or situation. For instance, you may see a list of words containing the word "apple." Then the researcher shows you a word fragment such as "a—p—— " and asks you to fill in the remaining three blanks. Implicit memory is demonstrated when your response is "apple" rather than "ample."

Remembering where you heard or saw something is sometimes as important as remembering the information itself. **Source memory** is the recall of where or how an individual acquires information. In everyday life, you use source memory when you are trying to remember which of your friends said she would give you tickets to an upcoming concert or which professor hinted at an impending pop quiz.

Older adults seem to have greater difficulty on source memory tasks when they must judge where they saw an item on a previous occasion (Thomas & Bulevich, 2006). They also are more susceptible to false or illusory memories in which they say they remember something that never happened (Dodson, Bawa, & Slotnick, 2007). They may think that one person said something when in reality it was said by someone else or perhaps not said at all.

An ingenious test of false memory is called the Deese–Roediger–McDermott (DRM) paradigm. In the DRM paradigm, individuals are presented with a list of words (such as cake, honey, candy, etc.; in other words, food that is sweet). However, the word "sweet" is not included in the initial list. The critical trial occurs in the recognition test where the experimenter presents the category name (sweet) along with words from the original list (e.g., cake) as well as distractor words not on the original list (e.g., water). Most people think that they were presented with the word "sweet" because the other words in the category primed them to think of things that were sweet. Very few people are immune from this effect, but when warned, younger participants are better able than older adults to avoid the false memory implantation.

Sometimes you need to remember what to do, rather than what you have done. **Prospective memory** encompasses the recall of events to be performed in the future. In prospective memory, you must remember your intention to perform an action, such as calling that friend who promised the tickets to decide where to meet.

Older adults commonly complain (and you may too) that they cannot remember what they were supposed to get when they went into a room. Although a nuisance, this type of forgetting is not as detrimental as the type of forgetting involved in not taking a medication at a certain time. Older people do indeed appear to have more prospective memory slips than do younger adults. In one study involving a simulated shopping task, older adults forgot more items on their grocery list than did younger adults (Farrimond, Knight, & Titov, 2006).

Neuropsychological evidence suggests that the more heavily a prospective memory task involves planning, and hence the frontal lobes, the more disadvantaged older adults seem to be (McDaniel & Einstein, 2011). Fortunately, if they are aware of their prospective memory problems, older adults can take advantage of reminders through notes, date books, and cell phones, all of which have so far been demonstrated to work effectively for adults in the young-old age category (Schnitzspahn & Kliegel, 2009).

The tip-of-the-tongue phenomenon, more formally known as **retrieval-induced forgetting**, is another source of frequent memory complaints. This is what happens to you when you are unable to remember information that you knew at one time. You are most likely to have a tip-of-the-tongue experience when you are trying to remember the name of the 2005 movie in which the protagonists came uninvited to a family event (answer: *Wedding Crashers*).

The tip-of-the-tongue effect is observed more in older adults in both laboratory and everyday life situations. Young adults occasionally experience this effect when they are trying to retrieve an abstract word, but older people are more likely to forget a person's name (Shafto, Burke, Stamatakis, Tam, & Tyler, 2007), particularly when the person has a name that sounds similar to someone else's (O'Hanlon, Kemper, & Wilcox, 2005). Evidence from imaging studies suggests that the area of the brain used for phonological production is subject to age-related neural declines, a fact that might explain this form of retrieval failure in older adults (Shafto, Stamatakis, Tam, & Tyler, 2009).

Identity, Self-Efficacy, Stereotype Threat, and Control Beliefs

The empirical evidence we have just covered supports in part the commonly held belief that at least some forms of memory suffer as people get older—what varies is perhaps how much, exactly which type, and when. However, countervailing data suggests that how you think about your memory may play just as important a role as your actual age. We summarize the results of research on these important topics in Figure 6.7.

First we will look at the role of identity in memory performance and aging. People who fall prey to the "over-the-hill" form of identity accommodation are more likely to succumb to society's negative stereotypes about aging and suffer more severe age effects than people who are able to maintain a positive view of their abilities using identity assimilation. The "over-the-hill" believers start on a downward spiral that causes them to be painfully aware of each instance of forgetting and to become even more pessimistic about their memory performance in the future. We know that middle-aged adults are highly sensitive to age-related changes in memory (Whitbourne & Collins, 1998), but how does this sensitivity affect their actual performance?

FIGURE 6.7

Identity, Self-Efficacy, Stereotype Threat, and Control Beliefs

- Higher identity accommodation related to lower memory control beliefs
- Higher self-efficacy related to higher performance
- Higher memory control beliefs related to better strategy use leading to better memory
- Stereotype threat reduces memory performance

DNY59/iStockphoto

Memory self-efficacy is a form of self-efficacy that refers to the confidence you have in your memory; specifically, the degree to which you feel that you can successfully complete a memory task. The higher your memory self-efficacy, the greater the likelihood that you will perform to your maximum ability. With increasing age, people feel less and less confident about their memory and consequently, their self-efficacy suffers (West, Thorn, & Bagwell, 2003). They are affected by the so-called "implicit theory" about aging and memory: namely, that memory functioning suffers an inevitable decline in later life (McDonald-Miszczak, Hertzog, & Hultsch, 1995).

An impressive display of the power of memory self-efficacy comes from a 6-year longitudinal study conducted in the Netherlands of a healthy community sample of more than 1,800 individuals aged 55 and older (Valentijn et al., 2006). Individuals with a lower sense of memory self-efficacy, particularly with regard to the belief that their memory had declined, showed poorer memory performance over the course of the study. Whether their lower self-efficacy caused their poorer performance or whether it reflected actual negative changes was impossible to determine. However, other investigations suggest that lower memory self-efficacy may turn into a self-fulfilling prophecy.

Stereotype threat is a concept drawn from research on the standardized test performance of African Americans suggesting that people perform in ways consistent with negative stereotypes of the group to which they see themselves as belonging (Steele, Spencer, Aronson, & Zanna, 2002). Research on stereotype threat and aging suggests that the older person's self-identification as "old" contributes to lower memory test scores. Because older adults are stereotyped as having poorer memories, this belief causes poorer performance. Although older adults can overcome stereotype threat through identity assimilation (Whitbourne & Sneed, 2002), it is difficult to be impervious to society's negative views about aging and memory (Cuddy, Norton, & Fiske, 2005).

Researchers in the area of stereotype threat and aging propose that identification with negative images of aging interferes with memory performance in older adults by lowering their feelings of self-efficacy. Ultimately, they become less able to take advantage of mnemonic strategies (systematic procedures designed to enhance memory, such as ROY G. BIV to remember the colors in the rainbow) (Hess, Auman, Colcombe, & Rahhal, 2003). However, in keeping with the premise of identity process theory, people vary in the way they respond to stereotype threat; sometimes the oldest participants are the least rather than the most affected by stereotype threat. Supporting this view, one study of aging and stereotype threat showed that the oldest participants (those in their 80s) were least affected by these negative unconscious attitudes (Hess & Hinson, 2006). Although identity processes were not investigated in this particular study, the investigators proposed that individual differences in response to threat may mediate the way that older individuals react to negative information about aging and memory.

We might hypothesize that identity assimilation can protect older adults from the harmful effects of believing that aging is associated with inevitable memory loss. Conversely, identity accommodation about memory performance, known to be higher in midlife adults (Whitbourne & Collins, 1998), could also account for the finding that stereotype threat regarding memory performance on the basis of age is higher among middle-aged compared to older adults (O'Brien & Hummert, 2006).

Some may go so far as to say that there is no way of knowing just how much stereotype threat could account for many of the findings on aging and memory. The slightest hint of a memory test can be enough to activate stereotype threat, ultimately leading to poorer performance by older adults. In a study comparing traditional and nontraditional instructional conditions in relation to memory for trivia, age differences were observed in the traditional, but not nontraditional, instructional condition (Rahhal, Colcombe, & Hasher, 2001). A similar explanation could account for the age differences observed in explicit but not implicit memory tasks.

Memory controllability refers to beliefs about the effects of the aging process on memory, such as the extent to which the individual believes that memory decline is inevitable with age (Lachman, 2006). Older people who rely heavily on identity accommodation are more likely to hold negative beliefs about their ability to control their memory as they age (Jones, Whitbourne, Whitbourne, & Skultety, 2009). In turn, older people who believe they cannot exert control over loss of memory do perform more poorly on memory tests (Riggs, Lachman, & Wingfield, 1997). If people believe that they can control their memory, then they are more likely to take advantage of the strategies to ensure they actually do achieve higher performance (Lachman & Andreoletti, 2006).

Memory and Health-Related Behaviors

Given the relationship of various health-related behaviors to the functioning of the central nervous system, as we discussed in Chapter 4, it should be no surprise that memory in later adulthood is also related to health-related behaviors (see Figure 6.8). For example, cigarette smoking is known to cause deleterious changes in the brain. One longitudinal study conducted in Scotland provided impressive

FIGURE 6.8

Lifestyle Factors and Memory

- Avoid smoking
- Dietary control
- Maintain physical activity
- Avoid stress
- Practice using memory skills

Simone van den Berg/Alamy

data showing that people tested as children who eventually became smokers had significantly lower memory and information processing scores when followed up at ages 64 and 66 years, controlling for early life intelligence (Starr, Deary, Fox, & Whalley, 2007).

A second health-related behavior relevant to memory involves diet and specifically the consumption of fish. You have probably heard the saying that fish is "brain food," and evidence suggests that it can be, particularly fish high in omega-3 fatty acids (such as salmon or tuna). Participants in the large-scale Chicago Health and Aging Study (with over 3,700 participants) were followed over a 6-year period during which they were asked to report their food consumption. Approximately 20% of the sample ate two or more meals containing fish per week. Controlling for a host of relevant factors, the rate of cognitive decline in individuals who consumed one or more fish meals a week was reduced by 10 to 13% per year (Morris, Evans, Tangney, Bienias, & Wilson, 2005). A subsequent study of nearly 900 older adults from England and Wales showed that socioeconomic status may also play a role in affecting the relationship between cognitive performance and fish consumption, in that people with higher social status are more likely to include fish in their regular diets (Dangour et al., 2009).

Investigators have established a link between enhanced memory performance in older adults and other dietary components, including vitamin B12, vitamin B6, and folate (Smith & Refsum, 2009). Conversely, homocysteine, an amino acid found in the blood and acquired mainly from eating meat, is negatively related to memory performance (van den Kommer, Dik, Comijs, Jonker, & Deeg, 2008). Vitamin D is another dietary component thought to be linked to cognitive functioning (Wilkins, Sheline, Roe, Birge, & Morris, 2006). Flavonoids, found in certain foods ranging from fruits and vegetables to red wine and dark chocolate, can also have a beneficial influence on cognition. In a longitudinal study conducted in France over a 10-year period, high levels of flavonoid intake were associated with significantly lower memory declines (Letenneur, Proust-Lima, Le George, Dartigues, & Barberger-Gateau, 2007).

In contrast to the documented effects of these substances, one popular natural memory "cure" shows no beneficial effects. Findings from a large, randomized, double-blind, placebo-controlled study of more than 3,000 adults ranging in age from the 70s to the 90s challenge the claims of gingko biloba's effectiveness. Over a period of approximately 6 years, twice-daily doses produced no significant improvements in cognitive functioning (Snitz et al., 2009).

In Chapter 4, we saw that aerobic exercise can contribute to increases in brain areas involved in cognition. Older people who are aerobically fit are not only physically but also mentally healthier (Newson & Kemps, 2006). Research on exercise and cognition repeatedly illustrates that attention, memory, accuracy, and information processing all improve with each heart-pumping activity session, although the mechanisms by which these improvements occur remain unclear (Erickson et al., 2009; Marks, Katz, & Smith, 2009). Moderate- to high-intensity strength training contributes to increased information processing (Chang & Etnier, 2009) and executive functioning (Liu-Ambrose et al., 2010). Accompanying these findings is research demonstrating that strength training through weight lifting can also improve the memory performance of older adults (Lachman, Neupert, Bertrand, & Jette, 2006).

Additionally, research on exercise self-efficacy and control beliefs among a group of older adults engaged in a strength training intervention demonstrated that higher exercise beliefs during the intervention were related to higher levels of resistance and maintenance of exercise after the intervention (Neupert, Lachman, & Whitbourne, 2009).

Health may also play a role in cognition through the route of metabolic factors. As we saw in Chapter 5, people with metabolic syndrome are at increased risk for Alzheimer's disease. Impaired glucose tolerance, a component of metabolic syndrome, shows a clear relationship to cognitive functioning in normal aging individuals (Di Bonito et al., 2007). Older adults with type 2 diabetes are more likely to experience slowing of psychomotor speed as well as declines in executive functioning (Yeung, Fischer, & Dixon, 2009). Even impaired glucose tolerance, a condition known as prediabetes, can be a risk factor for greater declines in cognition. High-fat diets appear to play an important role in this process (Devore et al., 2009).

One possible route through which metabolic factors can affect psychomotor slowing and memory involves the hormone insulin growth factor-1 (IGF-1). As part of the Nurses' Health Study, a nationwide investigation involving more than 120,000 registered female nurses studied from midlife on, researchers obtained blood samples and then several years later conducted telephone interviews of cognitive functioning from a sample of 590 women 70 years of age and older. After adjusting for possible confounding factors (such as education, smoking history, alcohol use, and BMI), the women with low levels of IGF-1 showed slower decreases with age in cognitive functioning than women with high levels of this substance (Okereke et al., 2007).

As we also discussed in Chapter 5, health-related behaviors include those that are involved in the management of stress. Given that stress takes its toll on health and emotions, it makes sense that it would also affect cognitive functioning. You undoubtedly have had the experience of forgetting something important when you were preoccupied with other concerns such as financial strains, increased demands at school or work, or problems in your close relationships. Researchers investigating this issue have provided support for the notion that stress can interfere with memory performance among older adults. In one intriguing investigation, a sample of more than 300 older adults in the Veterans Affairs Normative Aging Study were asked to keep a daily diary of their interpersonal stressors and their memory failures. By tracking the relationship of stressful experiences to memory on a daily basis, researchers were able to establish the lagged effect showing that stressors on one day predicted memory failures on the next (Neupert, Almeida, Mroczek, & Spiro, 2006).

Interference of emotions, such as feelings of depression, may also contribute to poorer performance in older adults by depleting valuable cognitive resources (Meijer, van Boxtel, Van Gerven, van Hooren, & Jolles, 2009). A prospective longitudinal study of widows (begun before the widows lost their husbands), confirmed this idea among older women. Independent of the effect of losing a spouse on depressive symptoms, women in the Longitudinal Aging Study Amsterdam were found to have lower memory performance at the end of a 6-year period. Although the women who eventually lost their husbands started out with lower memory scores, even after controlling for this difference, the widows showed greater memory loss than did the nonwidows over the course of the study (Aartsen, Van Tilburg, Smits, Comijs, & Knipscheer, 2005).

Looking directly at memory performance and its relationship to stress, another group of investigators provided impressive evidence to support the idea that the deficit shown by older adults on working memory tasks can be accounted for in part by the experience of daily stressors (Sliwinski et al., 2006). In this study, a group of more than 100 older community-living adults with intact mental status were compared to young adults on the n-back working memory task. The amount of daily stress in their lives was determined through an interview in which participants were asked questions such as, "Did you have an argument or disagreement with anyone?" and "Did anything happen to a close friend or relative that turned out to be stressful for you?" Testing occurred over six occasions, allowing the investigators to examine within-person variations in the relationship between stress and memory as well as between-person age group differences.

Interestingly, the young adults in the sample were more likely to say "yes" to these and the other four questions assessing interpersonal stress. For instance, young adults said they had an argument on 26% of the days on which a given stressor occurred compared to 5% for older adults. The study's main finding was that on days in which people experienced stress, the performance of people in both age groups was significantly poorer. Emotional strains can interfere with memory in anyone regardless of age.

Why does stress have this impact on memory? Sliwinski and his colleagues (2006) maintain that preoccupation with stress occupies attentional resources that could otherwise be devoted to the memory task. There is evidence that older adults are perhaps more anxious than younger adults about their memory performance and therefore their memories are more vulnerable to this emotional interference (Andreoletti, Veratti, & Lachman, 2006).

A final factor to consider in understanding the relationship between memory and health is that of sleep. In young adults, long-term memory is strongly linked to slow-wave sleep. Experimental participants allowed to sleep in between learning and testing consistently achieve better memory performance than participants who spend an equivalent period of time awake (Diekelmann, Biggel, Rasch, & Born, 2012). However, neither middle-aged nor older adults show a similar benefit (Scullin, 2012). It is possible that the lack of sleep benefits to people in the middle and later adult years may contribute to age-related changes in memory performance, or that other sleep phases may be more beneficial.

Memory Training Studies

One mission of aging and memory research is to find ways to help older adults offset deleterious changes in memory. Many researchers in this field are true "gerontological optimists" who believe that their work can help improve cognitive functioning in older adults. They have established, for example, the fact that even simple practice can produce significant improvements in memory task performance, offsetting the negative effects of mental inactivity. Interventions aimed at improving episodic memory can be beneficial even for individuals suffering from the clinical condition known as mild cognitive impairment (MCI) (Belleville et al., 2006). A review of nonpharmacological interventions aimed at enhancing memory function among individuals with MCI suggests that cognitive interventions may prove beneficial in improving memory function (Teixeira et al., 2012).

Although the simple task of practice can result in enhanced memory performance, there are advantages to encouraging strategy use among older adults. Providing training intended to improve the memories of older adults also has the benefit of increasing feelings of the individual's self-efficacy (West, Bagwell, & Dark-Freudeman, 2008). When this training is provided in a group setting, it can be particularly effective in boosting not only self-efficacy but also memory performance (Hastings & West, 2009).

Older adults can also benefit from interventions that provide them with additional support during the encoding stage, while they are inputting information into long-term memory (Craik & Rose, 2012). This support can take the form of additional cues such as having them see pictures as well as words when learning a word list. Older adults would benefit, according to this approach, by using "deep" processing, in which they think about the meaning of the information they are trying to remember rather than simply repeating information by rote.

Another form of memory support takes into account the older adult's expertise. People who have spent their lives working with numbers will benefit from memory training that uses numerical, versus verbal, types of cues (Craik & Rose, 2012). Any training that benefits an individual's ability to encode will also help that person during the retrieval phase of long-term memory because the information will be more accessible. As you know from your own test-taking experiences, you can't recall material you haven't properly learned.

In one novel training study, virtual reality was used to create experiences that simulated walking through various destinations, while listening to soothing, calming music. The older adults who received this training showed improvement in long-term memory; specifically, verbal memory for stories (Optale et al., 2010).

One of the most ambitious cognitive training interventions is a multisite study known as Advanced Cognitive Training for Independent and Vital Elderly (ACTIVE) that was carried out over a 2-year period on more than 2,800 adults 65 to 94 years of age (Ball et al., 2002). Training consisted of 10 one-hour sessions over a 5- to 6-week period. The participants were trained in one of three types of cognitive skills—memory, reasoning, or speed of processing—while a control group received no training. These cognitive functions were selected because they show the most improvement in laboratory work and are related to everyday living tasks (e.g., telephone use, shopping, food preparation, housekeeping, laundry, transportation, medication use, and management of personal finances). For

Virtual reality training, used by Optale et al. (2010) can help older adults improve their long-term memory.
Source: Optale, G., Urgesi, C., Busato, V., Marin, S., Piron, L., Priftis, K., . . . Bordin, A. (2010). Controlling memory impairment in elderly adults using virtual reality memory training: A randomized controlled pilot study. *Neurorehabilitation and Neural Repair, 24,* 348–357. doi: 10.1177/1545968309353328. Reprinted by Permission of SAGE Publications.

instance, those who received memory training were taught ways to remember word lists and sequences of items, text, and the main ideas and details of stories. Training in the area of reasoning involved learning how to solve problems that follow patterns, such as reading a bus schedule or filling out an order sheet. Training in the speed of processing involved learning how to identify and locate visual information quickly for use in tasks such as looking up a phone number, finding information on medicine bottles, and responding to traffic signs.

Testing conducted at the end of the training period demonstrated that the majority of participants in the speed (87%) and reasoning (74%) groups showed improvement; about one-quarter (26%) in the memory group showed improvement. Two years later, the gains were still evidenced, although these were larger for participants who participated in booster sessions.

Memory training can not only improve an individual's performance, but can even alter the brain. In a study carried out in Norway, middle-aged and older adults learned to use the "method of loci" (associating words with rooms in your home). They were given intensive training, involving 25-minute sessions, five days a week, for eight weeks. Compared to a control group, the training group showed increased white matter density, a change that would help them process new information more quickly and efficiently (Engvig et al., 2012).

In conclusion, attentional and memory processes in adulthood play vital roles in life. Older adults appear to suffer deleterious changes, but these changes are neither universal nor irreversibly negative. Identity and other memory-related beliefs play an important role in determining whether individuals are able to take advantage of compensatory strategies. Future research will help uncover more of these personality—memory linkages as well as to identify which strategies can be most effective in maximizing cognitive performance throughout middle and later adulthood.

SUMMARY

1. Cognition refers to the way the mind works, including the processes of attention, memory, intelligence, problem solving, and the use of language. Aging affects each of these areas, leading to changes in many of people's ability to carry out everyday activities. Processing speed, measured by reaction time, is an important variable in research on cognitive aging. There is a consistent increase of reaction time throughout adulthood. The general slowing hypothesis explains this increase as a decline of information processing speed, and the related age-complexity hypothesis proposes that the loss is greater for more difficult tasks.

2. Attention involves the ability to focus while ignoring other features, to shift that focus, and to coordinate information from multiple sources. Laboratory studies suggest that people become less efficient in the use of attentional processes with age. Multitasking involves the ability to monitor multiple input sources, with older adults experiencing greater disadvantages. Inhibitory control refers to the process of turning off one response

while performing another, and is often measured using the Stroop test. Studies on aging and attentional performance suggest that not all abilities decline. Two approaches to understanding age differences in attentional tasks include the attentional resources theory and the inhibitory deficit hypothesis. Experience can compensate for age-related changes in sustained attention. Based on research suggesting the attentional benefits video games offer to younger adults, researchers are beginning to explore the use of video games in interventional studies as training tools to enhance attentional skills among older adults. Older adults prefer computer games rather than first-person shooter video games, which may benefit focused and sustained attention.

3. Challenges facing older adult drivers include age-related increases in reaction time and changes in visual functioning. However, accidents are higher among younger drivers, perhaps due in part to increased rates of drinking and driving and engaging in distracting behaviors. Older adults compensate for changes in driving ability by modifying behaviors and relying on experience.

4. One of the greatest fears about aging is the loss of memory and indeed, data suggests that the aging process has negative effects on many, but not all, aspects of memory. A working memory, which keeps information temporarily available and active, is significantly poorer in older adults. However, individuals can compensate for these declines by activating different neural circuits.

5. Long-term memory refers to information that is held from several minutes to a lifetime and includes various types; these are impacted by age differently. Episodic, remote, and autobiographical memory are sensitive to age effects, with the exception of a phenomenon known as the reminisce bump, the period of time between the ages of 10 and 30. Flashbulb memory and semantic memory are not affected by the normal aging process. Procedural memory is also retained in older adults, as is implicit memory. However, older adults have more difficulty with tasks involving source memory and prospective memory.

6. Researchers are investigating the interaction of memory changes with changes in self-efficacy, control beliefs, and identity. The concept of stereotype threat implies that older adults may perform more poorly on memory tasks that activate negative stereotypes about aging and memory.

7. Memory in later adulthood is related to a variety of health-related behaviors, including cigarette smoking, consumption of fish high in omega-3 fatty acids, vitamin B12, vitamin B6, folate, and flavonoids. Aerobic exercise can contribute to increases in brain areas involved in cognition. Health may also play a role through the route of metabolic factors. Impaired glucose tolerance, a component of metabolic syndrome, shows a clear relationship to cognitive functioning in normal aging individuals. Stress can also interfere with memory performance.

8. Interventions aimed at improving episodic memory can be beneficial, particularly those that teach strategy use among older adults. One of the most ambitious cognitive training interventions was a multisite study known as Advanced Cognitive Training for Independent and Vital Elderly (ACTIVE), which found that training in memory and reasoning improved the performance of older adults on daily living tasks.

7

Higher-Order Cognitive Functions

Get Ready for the Real Battle of the Sexes

The question of whether men and women differ in cognitive abilities such as intelligence wages on in psychology. Though we are far from a resolution, you can provide your own test data with some help from the fascinating and important theory of multiple intelligences. Developed by Harvard psychologist Howard Gardner (1983), this theory proposes that we have not one, not two, but eight (at least) different types of intelligence. Claims of one person or group's overall superiority over another's now shifts to the more realistic approach in which people's strengths and weaknesses are seen as falling along a set of distinct domains. Multiple intelligences theory is important because it changes the question from "who is smarter" to "how are you smart?"

In the traditional male–female ability war, men are seen as dominating in math and spatial skills and women as having the edge with words. However, this overly-simplistic dichotomy is now discredited because it fails to capture the fact that people of each gender can outperform the other gender on any given task. Surely, you've known plenty of females who can perform complex math calculations in their head and plenty of males who can't divide 100 by 11 without using a calculator. This situation is clouded further by the many confounding factors, not the least of which is the self-handicapping that people engage in if they buy into traditional gender stereotypes. This is one reason that, as psychologists observed for many decades, girls seem to "lose" their math abilities once they reach adolescence and realize that it's not "feminine" to be good at high school algebra.

In a study of 318 Americans and 253 Britons, University College London psychologist Adrian Furnham and collaborators (2002) asked participants to rate themselves, their romantic partner, and several famous people (e.g., Bill Gates) on overall intelligence and 10 (rather than the usual 8) of Gardner's multiple intelligences. As was found in other studies of self-rated intelligence, men believed themselves to be smarter than did women with estimates of 115 vs. 110 (the population mean IQ is set at 100 on most tests). Men have no problem seeing themselves as much smarter than the average person. More important, for our purposes, are the perceived sex differences in scores along the multiple intelligence dimensions.

Men gave themselves higher ratings on several of the components of multiple intelligences theory, including logical, spatial, and naturalistic intelligence. They rated their female partners as higher on verbal, musical, bodily, and interpersonal. People's estimates of themselves and their partners parallel if not actual ability differences, then perceptions of ability differences. Interestingly, Americans rated Prince Charles as higher in intelligence than did Britons, but that's another story. Looking at intelligence as a more multifaceted quality than a simple math–verbal distinction can help us understand each individual's strengths. We can only hope that in intelligence, at least, we turn the battle into détente.

Posted by Susan Whitbourne and Stacey Whitbourne

Information processing and memory are basic cognitive operations that make it possible for you to perform a variety of critical adaptive functions in your everyday life. They also form the basis for your ability to analyze, reason, and communicate with others.

Researchers are interested in understanding higher-level cognitive functions in adulthood and later life for a number of reasons (Salthouse, 2012). First, these functions play a major role in such areas as health, occupational performance, and even in relationships. Second, information on thinking and learning in later adulthood can provide a greater understanding of the potential for "lifelong learning." With many adults retooling in order to find new positions in the rapidly changing labor market, determining the factors that contribute to the most effective training strategies is crucial to helping people find and keep their jobs. Finally, an understanding of these functions is useful in informing our grasp of how to diagnose and treat the cognitive disorders that can develop in middle and later adulthood.

EXECUTIVE FUNCTIONING AND ITS MEASUREMENT

The higher-order cognitive skills needed to make decisions, plan, and allocate mental resources to a task are called executive functioning. Specifically, an individual's executive functioning draws upon several abilities, including working memory, selective attention, mental flexibility, and the ability to plan and inhibit distracting information (Miyake et al., 2000).

Clinicians and researchers are particularly interested in learning how aging affects executive functioning because it is central to so many activities that older adults need to use in order to be able to care for themselves. Even a task such as driving, which depends heavily on speed, has a strong executive functioning component. You need to use your executive functions to determine the route to take to your destination, alternate between input from the road and that of your vehicle's dials and instruments, and make any changes in your route to account for traffic, construction, or obstacles in the road. Studies on aging and executive functioning and aging are also increasingly focusing on interventions that can protect and maximize these important skills.

Intelligence Tests

The higher-order cognitive functions that make up executive functioning contribute, at least in part, to an individual's overall intelligence. An **intelligence test** provides an assessment of an individual's overall cognitive status along a set of standardized dimensions. The scores on an intelligence test may be used in a research context, particularly when investigators are seeking to understand the effects of aging. They are also used by clinicians as part of a larger neuropsychological evaluation in which clinicians need to establish a diagnosis of a neurological or psychiatric disorder. Psychologists working in human resource departments may also use intelligence testing as part of a larger process of personnel selection or evaluation.

Through intelligence testing, psychologists obtain a set of standardized scores that allow them to evaluate the cognitive strengths and weaknesses of their research subjects, clients, or personnel. The most commonly used intelligence tests in clinical settings are on a one-to-one basis, providing a comprehensive view of the client's abilities to perform a range of perceptual, memory, reasoning, and speeded tasks.

The most well-known individual test of adult intelligence is the **Wechsler Adult Intelligence Scale (WAIS)**. Originally developed in 1939 by David Wechsler as the Wechsler–Bellevue test, the WAIS, first published in 1955, is now in its fourth edition (WAIS-IV) (Wechsler, 2008). Wechsler originally sought to develop a tool that he could use in a psychiatric capacity, particularly to assist in diagnosis of psychological disorders. He constructed two sets of scales, putting them into the categories of "Verbal" and "Performance" intelligence (or "IQ"). As the terms imply, Verbal IQ tests knowledge of such areas as vocabulary and general information. Performance IQ tests measure nonverbal abilities such as spatial relationships and reasoning. In providing these estimates, examiners compare a person's raw score on each of the various scales to scores for that person's age group. This permits the examiner to provide a so-called "deviation IQ," which is based on a normal distribution of scores that have a mean of 100 and a standard deviation of 15.

In the versions prior to the WAIS-IV, people received Verbal and Performance IQ scores along with an overall IQ. However, the test developers of the WAIS-IV decided to revise the scoring to reflect developments in the fields of neuropsychology and cognitive psychology. They also felt that some of the test items were becoming outdated, such as the 1940-ish cartoon figures shown on the test called "Picture Arrangement." The WAIS-IV includes new test items, several new tests, and a completely different scoring system (see Table 7.1).

The four indexes that the WAIS-IV produces, as you can see from this table, are Verbal Comprehension, Perceptual Organization, Working Memory, and Processing Speed. There are 10 standard tests, and five optional tests, which the examiner may give depending on the specific purpose of

TABLE 7.1
Scales on the Wechsler Adult Intelligence Scale-IV (WAIS-IV)

Scale	Subtest	What is Tested
Verbal Comprehension	Similarities	Abstract reasoning
	Vocabulary	Vocabulary
	Information	Cultural information
	Comprehension	(Supplemental)
Perceptual Reasoning	Block design	Spatial perception
	Matrix reasoning	Inductive reasoning
	Visual puzzles	Non-verbal reasoning
Working Memory	Digit span	Attention, concentration
	Arithmetic	Concentration while manipulating mental information
Processing Speed	Symbol search	Visual perception, speed
	Coding	Visual-motor coordination

Source: Adapted from Wechsler, D. (2008). Wechsler Adult Intelligence Scales-IV. Retrieved from http://www.pearsonassessments. com/HAIWEB/Cultures/en-us/Productdetail.htm?Pid=015-8980-808

the assessment. The Full Scale IQ reflects general cognitive functioning but is perhaps less informative than the four index scores, each of which captures a different facet of the individual's strengths and weaknesses.

In addition to providing these scores, examiners using the WAIS-IV take note of behaviors that might be relevant to understanding the individual's performance. These include the test taker's fluency in English; physical appearance; problems with vision, hearing, or motor behavior; difficulties with attention and concentration; and motivation for testing. These observations would be particularly helpful for interpreting the scores of an older adult, which may be affected by physical or sensory limitations.

Although not currently in use by clinicians, another intelligence test is worth noting because of its extensive use in research on aging. The **Primary Mental Abilities Test (PMAT)** assesses the seven abilities of Verbal Meaning, Word Fluency (the ability to generate words following a certain lexical rule), Number (arithmetic), Spatial Relations, Memory, Perceptual Speed, and General Reasoning. Unlike the WAIS-IV, psychologists administer the PMAT in a group format rather than an individualized manner, which also makes it more practical for research purposes. The PMAT's scales roughly parallel at least some of those included in the WAIS-IV, such as Memory and Working Memory, and Perceptual Speed and Processing Speed.

Neuropsychological Assessment

There are a variety of specialized tests that can evaluate an individual's executive functioning. The process of **neuropsychological assessment** involves gathering information about a client's brain functioning from a series of standardized cognitive tests. In cases involving older adults with cognitive deficits, in particular, neuropsychologists may adapt their assessment to try to target the specific area in the brain that they believe has suffered damage or decline. The assessment is conducted individually rather than in group format.

Tests of executive functioning are typically part of the total process of neuropsychological assessment. However, most neuropsychological assessments of older adults also include other measures of cognitive functioning and may incorporate some we have already discussed as part of intelligence testing. There are enough available neuropsychological tests within each category so that if a clinician wishes to investigate one area in depth for a particular client, then he or she will be able to probe into the individual's possible disorder by administering more tests from that category.

You might be surprised to learn that there is no one set procedure for conducting a neuropsychological assessment. In fact, particular neuropsychologists may have preferences for certain tests, especially if they tend to see the same type of client in their practice or their area of research expertise. In clinical settings, though, neuropsychologists are expected to have training in enough types of tests to be able to adapt the assessment to the individual's symptoms. In working with older adults, neuropsychologists are also expected to be familiar with the tests that are appropriate for people in this age group rather than those used in diagnosing a child or adolescent.

Several neuropsychological tests are either derived from or the same as tests from the WAIS-IV, such as Digit Span (used to assess verbal recall and auditory attention) and Similarities (used to assess verbal abstraction abilities).

Other tests, such as the Trail Making Tests, also called "Trails," were developed specifically to assess the individual's so-called "frontal lobe functioning," which includes attention, the ability to scan visual stimuli, and follow a sequence of numbers. The examiner shows the test taker a pattern of numbered circles, with the instructions to draw lines to connect the circles in order. Another variant of the Trail Making Test displays a pattern of numbered circles and letters, and the test taker's job is to connect them in order, from 1 to A to 2 to B, and so on. The Wisconsin Card Sorting Test (WCST) measures the individual's ability to form mental sets in categorizing cards with related features, such as number of items, color, or shape.

The WCST is now administered on a computer rather than with physical cards, reflecting a growing trend in neuropsychology to use computerized test batteries. In addition to the convenience factor, computerized testing allows the psychologist to administer an adaptive test, in which the client's responses to earlier questions determine subsequent questions. For example, the Cambridge Neuropsychological Testing Automated Battery (CANTAB) consists of 22 subtests that assess visual memory, working memory, executive function and planning, attention, verbal memory, and decision making and response control. Having these tests on a laptop or tablet device has clear advantages to having to carry all 22, or more, physical tests. However, there may be drawbacks to the use of computerized assessment for current cohorts of older adults who may have limited experience taking tests in this format, the psychologist must take this into account when evaluating the results.

Aging and Executive Functioning

Researchers conducting laboratory studies that examine the relationship between age and executive functioning may draw from the intelligence and neuropsychological tests we have just discussed. Additionally, they may employ specific measures designed to pinpoint a particular type of executive functioning. For example, they may use the task-switching method, in which participants respond to one type of stimulus in one set of trials (judging if a number is odd) and the opposite in the next set of trials (judging if a number is even). In the first set of trials, participants adopt a certain mental set which needs to change in the second set of trials.

Another experimental task measures verbal fluency, a form of executive functioning that depends on the individual's ability to generate multiple items meeting a single criterion (Kemper & McDowd, 2008). Tests of verbal fluency ask participants to produce as many items as possible in response to one stimulus, such as listing as many possible words that begin with the letter "K" in a set amount of time.

Scores on measures of executive functioning appear to show steady declines in later adulthood; researchers show that these declines are important because they are related to negative changes in a number of everyday cognitive functions needed for daily life (Vaughan & Giovanello, 2010). Interestingly enough, however, the same older adults experiencing these declines do not perceive themselves to be affected by these changes in their own self-reports of their ability to manage daily tasks (Tucker-Drob, 2011). It is possible that this self-perception reflects the process of identity assimilation due to older adults' desire to see themselves as cognitively in control of their lives.

Nevertheless, these changes in executive functioning do seem to occur and seem to be related to underlying age-related brain changes. In one investigation using the Wisconsin Card Sorting Task, for example, researchers in Germany found that performance on the executive functions in this task and reductions was correlated with the thickness of the cortex in the brain regions that the test seems to tap (Burzynska et al., 2012).

On tests of verbal fluency, older adults show a greater tendency to perseverate, meaning that they continue to produce the same words, such as "king," "keel," "kept," "king," and "kite," where "king" counts as a perseveration. However, the tendency to perseverate is less evident in people with larger vocabularies (Henry & Phillips, 2006).

Fortunately, there are ways that older adults can perhaps compensate for these changes in executive functioning. Following similar models as studies on brain plasticity, researchers are showing that physical exercise can benefit executive functioning in older adults. Not only do people who exercise have better executive functioning, but experimental studies show that aerobic exercise training improves performance on tests of mental flexibility, attention, and inhibitory control (Guiney & Machado, 2012).

Video game playing also benefits executive functioning in such areas as task switching (Strobach, Frensch, & Schubert, 2012), reasoning (Basak, Boot, Voss, & Kramer, 2008), and trail making (Nouchi et al., 2012). It is possible that these results are due to increases in brain volume in areas of the brain involved in video game play (Basak, Voss, Erickson, Boot, & Kramer, 2011). Players who spontaneously take advantage of tile-matching puzzle games also seem to have improved verbal intelligence, visual memory, and nonverbal working memory (Thompson, Barrett, Patterson, & Craig, 2012).

However, the question remains of how well changes in the tasks specific to the video games used in these training studies transfers to real-world abilities (Boot et al., 2010). Some studies show limited transfer in the executive functions of inhibition, inductive reasoning, and attentional focus (van Muijden, Band, & Hommel, 2012). It is likely that whether transfer occurs depends on the type of training method used (Ackerman, Kanfer, & Calderwood, 2010).

Nevertheless, research on video game training and executive functioning is expanding, and it is likely that as the training tasks become better understood, more robust transfer to everyday abilities will be demonstrated. There is also intriguing evidence that video game play can have beneficial effects on the executive functioning needed to perform certain jobs. In one study, novice surgical students who were trained in a first-person shooter game showed improved performance on a virtual reality endoscopy test compared to a control group trained with a video chess game (Schlickum, Hedman, Enochsson, Kjellin, & Fellander-Tsai, 2009).

LANGUAGE

The use of language involves a wide range of cognitive functions, including comprehension, memory, and decision making. As we discussed in Chapter 6, many of these functions are negatively affected by the aging process. However, the majority of researchers believe that the average healthy older adult does not suffer significant losses in the ability to use language effectively under normal speaking conditions (Hoyte, Brownell, & Wingfield, 2009). The basic abilities to carry on a conversation, read, and write remain intact throughout later life. The "Language and Aging Score Card" in Table 7.2 summarizes this research.

Cognitive Aspects of Language

Although many cognitive functions relevant for language are preserved in older adults, the scorecard shows that there are changes that can have a detrimental effect on the older adult's ability to use and maximize language most effectively. For example, even older adults with normal age-related vision read at slower rates compared to younger adults (Nygaard, Echt, & Schuchard, 2008). Their slower processing speeds may affect their comprehension while reading (Federmeier, Kutas, & Schul, 2010). For example, younger adults typically make predictions about what a sentence will say as soon as they start reading it. Older adults take longer to make these predictions, which also means that they are slower to gain information from the context of what they are reading (Wlotko, Federmeier, & Kutas, 2012).

While reading, older adults may have greater difficulty forming visual images to accompany concrete words, a process that can benefit the memory of younger adults for written material (Huang, Meyer, & Federmeier, 2012). They may also have difficulty tracing character development in reading fiction, particularly when a new character is introduced within a story line about another character (Noh & Stine-Morrow, 2009). This may be because they find it more difficult to switch their attentional focus. On the positive side, however, older adults do maintain the ability to attend selectively to the text of what they are reading (Price & Sanford, 2012).

As we saw in Chapter 4, changes in hearing and speech perception have the potential to influence the ability to comprehend spoken language. For example, older adults may find it more difficult to hear all the words spoken in a conversation; they then must work harder to make sense out of what other people are saying (Janse, 2009).

In using written language, older adults may experience deficits in retrieval that can lead to spelling errors for words they once knew (Burke, 1997). You can most likely

TABLE 7.2
Language and Aging Scorecard

Factors that contribute to decline	Factors that contribute to preservation
Slower reading rate	Semantic memory is retained or improved
Changes in hearing and speech perception	Able to get the "gist" of a story
Slowing of cognitive functions	No problem with paralinguistic elements of speech
Retrieval deficits	Activate the right hemisphere more
Simpler grammatical structures	Greater experience with language
Working memory deficits	More cognitive complexity

relate to this problem if you have ever looked at a word you have just written that has multiple letters (such as "recommendation") and wondered whether there are one "c" or two.

Adults' slower cognitive processes may also have an effect on the complexity of grammatical structures that they use. As you form sentences, you must keep one clause in mind while you compose the next one, a process that places demands on your working memory. As we saw in Chapter 6, working memory undergoes significant changes with age. Consequently, compared with young adults, older adults speak in simpler sentences (Kemper, Marquis, & Thompson, 2001). Their writing also becomes simpler, in both the expression of ideas and the use of grammatical complexity (Kemper, Greiner, Marquis, Prenovost, & Mitzner, 2001). Thus, although older adults retain their knowledge of grammatical rules (a form of semantic memory), declines in working memory can cause older adults to lose track of what they mean to say while they are saying it, especially when the language they are producing requires thought and preparation (Harley, Jessiman, & MacAndrew, 2011).

On the positive side, older adults' greater experience with language gives them the potential to compensate for other cognitive changes that affect their ability to produce and understand speech. Most older adults retain the ability to understand individual words (James & MacKay, 2007). They can grasp and remember the descriptions provided in language relating to the thoughts and actions of a character in a story (Stine-Morrow & Miller, 1999). Older adults are also able to use strategies effectively to maximize their comprehension of written text (Stine-Morrow, Milinder, Pullara, & Herman, 2001). They can also put together the structure of the sentence with the speaker's emphasis (Titone et al., 2006).

Neuroimaging evidence suggests that older adults compensate for deficits in one area of the brain by recruiting alternative brain regions in the processing of speech (Wong et al., 2009), unless the task depends heavily on semantic memory (Kahlaoui et al., 2012). Consistent with the HAROLD model, older adults seem able to activate the right hemisphere of the brain when they are processing speech, a reversal of the left hemispheric dominance typically seen in younger adults (Tyler et al., 2010). They also increase activation in frontal regions of the brain typically not activated in younger adults, consistent with the PASA model (Peelle, Troiani, Wingfield, & Grossman, 2010).

Experience is another way that older adults compensate for changes in memory and speed. This is particularly true for highly educated older adults, whose extensive vocabularies allow them to take advantage of the context in language (Osorio, Ballesteros, Fay, & Pouthas, 2009).

In general, though, older adults also have a rich backlog of experiences from which to draw when they listen or read. Even if they are unable to hear each word, they are often able to derive the meaning of words used in a straightforward conversation (Stewart & Wingfield, 2009). They can also take advantage of interpreting the paralinguistic aspects of speech, including gestures and facial expressions. You have likely encountered this experience of filling in missing information in speech that is directed toward you. Someone approaches you at a loud party, and it is probably safe to assume, even if you are unable to hear, that he or she is saying "Hello" or "What's up?" You are pretty safe in returning the greeting.

The advantage of greater experience also manifests itself in reading. Older adults are able to glean information more quickly, particularly if the material is of a relatively familiar nature. Consequently, they can skim for information rather than stop and examine every word or phrase.

Thus, older adults have well-developed structures of information that allow them to anticipate and organize information that may typically overwhelm a novice. Even in situations that do not involve expert knowledge of a skill, previous experience can make up for slower processing of new linguistic information. For example, an avid soap opera watcher can anticipate what the characters will say (and often do) rather than needing to hear every single spoken word in a particular interchange between characters. When reading magazines or newspapers, a knowledgeable older reader is able to make up for changes in working memory by relying on more effective structures for retrieving related information from written text (Stine-Morrow, Soederberg Miller, Gagne, & Hertzog, 2008).

Social Aspects of Language

Corresponding to changes in language use and comprehension throughout adulthood are changes in the way that older adults use language socially. Perhaps most striking is the tendency of older adults to reminisce with others about experiences from the past. As they do so, they often polish and refine their storytelling so that by the time their reminiscences have been practiced and rehearsed, the stories have considerable impact on the listener. In your own family you may have heard an older relative tell the same story over and over again so often that you can repeat it by heart. Watching the reaction of your friends when they first hear the same story may cause you to realize that it is a pretty good story after all. This is perhaps one reason why comedians in their 60s, 70s, and beyond have become such masters of the punch line.

Reminiscences about the past may also serve a function for older adults in solidifying relationships and building shared identities with others from their generation. As they do so, they can enhance and strengthen their relationships with their long-time friends and family members.

Younger adults may become annoyed with the older adults they know well and feel that the older people's speech is too repetitive or focused on the past (Bieman-Copland & Ryan, 2001). At times, older adults may also speak more off-topic, particularly when they are giving instructions about how to perform an action. Younger adults seem to be better able to focus their speech in such situations (Trunk & Abrams, 2009). In a related vein, older adults may experience "mental clutter" due to an inability to inhibit irrelevant information. This tendency causes their speech to become somewhat rambling. However, these slight changes seem more related to altered executive functioning than to age, per se, because we know that inhibition is a key component of frontal lobe control over behavior.

The problem of intergenerational communication is made worse if the older person tends to focus on his or her current disabilities or health limitations. Talking extensively about a topic in which the listener has no interest or that makes the listener uncomfortable can have an effect opposite to that intended and possibly isolate the older individual. Such examples highlight the downside to changes in these conversational patterns when they have the unintended effect of turning off the listener.

Intergenerational communication can take a decidedly nasty turn. **Elderspeak** is a speech pattern directed at older adults similar to the way people talk to babies. If you have ever heard an older adult referred to as "cute," or being called "honey," or "sweetie," you have heard one form of

elderspeak. More generally, elderspeak involves simplifying your speech much as you would talk to a child by leaving out complex words or talking in a patronizing or condescending tone of voice. Younger people who speak in this manner do so because, either consciously or unconsciously, they equate the older and perhaps frailer adult as being equal in status to a child. Offering unnecessary help, making personal comments about clothing or appearance, or talking in short, simple sentences are just some examples of this type of speech pattern.

Researchers investigating elderspeak have proposed that its use fits into the **communication predicament model** of aging. The predicament is that older adults are thought of as mentally incapacitated, leading younger people to speak to them in a simplified manner; over time, this can reduce the older adult's actual ability to use language. (See Figure 7.1.) In addition, failure to encourage independent behaviors in the older person, a part of the communication predicament, leads to a further spiraling downward of the older person's abilities (Ryan, Hummert, & Boich, 1995).

The communication predicament model is part of a larger phenomenon known as infantilization, in which the older person loses the incentive to attempt to regain self-sufficiency in the basic activities of daily life (Whitbourne, Culgin, & Cassidy, 1995; Whitbourne & Wills, 1993). Moreover, when older adults in a residential facility are treated by younger staff in an infantilizing manner, they lose the desire to socialize with each other, potentially leading to social isolation (Salari & Rich, 2001). The self-fulfilling nature of infantilization can also increase the older person's awareness of age stereotypes, causing a self-fulfilling

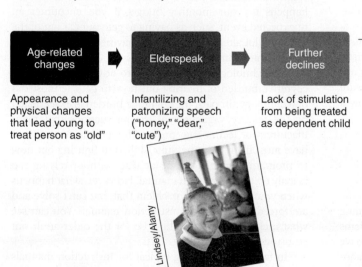

Appearance and physical changes that lead young to treat person as "old"

Infantilizing and patronizing speech ("honey," "dear," "cute")

Lack of stimulation from being treated as dependent child

Jason Lindsey/Alamy

FIGURE 7.1

Social Elements of Language: The Communication Predicament Model

Source: Adapted from Ryan, E. B., Hummert, M. L., & Boich, L. H. (1995). Communication predicaments of aging: Patronizing behavior toward older adults. *Journal of Language and Social Psychology, 14*, 144–166.

prophecy to spread across a wide domain of areas of functioning. If you think you are unable to carry out a task because you are too old, infirm, or feeble, then the chances are you will eventually lose the ability to carry out that task.

Because infantilization results in a loss of independence, researchers believe that it is important to sensitize those who work with older adults so that they avoid falling into this pattern. These programs have started, at least within assisted living facilities (Williams & Warren, 2009), but clearly more work in this area would have wide-ranging benefits.

Bilingualism and Aging

In contrast to common belief, being able to speak and think in two languages benefits the individual. This advantage begins in infancy and continues through old age (Bialystok, Craik, Green, & Gollan, 2009). Even if the speaker no longer relies on one of the languages, that second language remains active. This means that the bilingual speaker must add the step of deciding which language to use in a given situation depending on its context. As a result, bilingual individuals continually practice and therefore build their executive functions. This constant strengthening of their executive functioning may result in protection against the effects of Alzheimer's disease (Bialystok, 2011).

It is interesting to think that the use of two languages benefits executive function tasks, such as task-switching, that do not depend on verbal skills. Imaging studies suggest that the advantage conferred to bilinguals reflects better connectivity among networks in the brain (Luk, Bialystok, Craik, & Grady, 2011).

The advantage of bilingualism does not extend to all cognitive tasks. In working memory tasks, however, bilingual older adults seem to have greater difficulty with verbal than spatial stimuli, even after controlling for vocabulary (Luo, Craik, Moreno, & Bialystok, 2012). In a comparison of bilinguals to monolinguals on the Stroop interference task, which may be considered at least in part a measure of executive functioning, older bilinguals did not show a performance advantage (Kousaie & Phillips, 2012).

EVERYDAY PROBLEM SOLVING

From figuring out why your computer is freezing up the night before a paper is due to managing your dwindling bank account, you must constantly deal with problems requiring solutions in your daily life. Researchers have increasingly moved these daily challenges into the laboratory to evaluate the ability of older adults to manage such everyday tasks as handling their personal finances,

maintaining their medication schedules, and monitoring their diets (Allaire & Marsiske, 2002). Ultimately, it is performance on tasks such as these that helps to contribute to an older person's quality of life (Gilhooly et al., 2007) and may even predict mortality independently of basic cognitive abilities (Weatherbee & Allaire, 2008).

Characteristics of Problem Solving

Psychologists approach the topic of problem solving by identifying types of problems and the stages involved in successfully approaching and resolving them. Essentially, problem solving involves the steps of assessing a current situation, deciding on a desired end-state, and finding ways of transforming the current into the desired state. The final step is evaluating the outcome of the solution to determine its efficacy. For example, when you are planning your budget for the month, you begin by assessing how much money is in your account (current state). You then decide how much money to allocate for food, entertainment, and transportation based on your desired end-state (having money left at the end of the month). At the end of the month, you assess whether your plan worked out and if not, revise your strategy and hope it works out better than the one you just used.

Problems vary tremendously in their structure and complexity. This example of a monthly budget is one that is fairly well structured in that the constraints are clear (there is only so much money in your account) and there is a fairly clear set of steps that you must follow to achieve a solution. With problems that lack clear goals or involve necessary steps that are difficult to discern, an increased cognitive burden is placed on the individual. This is what happens to your monthly budget if you encounter an unexpected event, such as paying to get your car out of the impound lot after it was towed or having to lend your best friend some money.

As technology has continued to advance, so has the cognitive burden of figuring out how to get the most out of technology. In part, the cognitive burden is exacerbated by the relative vagueness of the instructions that manufacturers of technology provide for people to use. You have most likely become quite skilled in figuring out how to program your cell phone or iPad without relying too heavily on the instruction manual. However, what happens when you come across a problem that you can't solve and are forced to consult an instruction manual? You can see what a challenge this might pose for the older adult not accustomed to high-tech gadgets.

In fact, it is becoming typical for instruction manuals to exist only in a downloadable form. If you are trying to set up a printer that comes without a manual, you might be forced to go online where, ironically enough, you would be expected to print the instructions. Making matters worse is the notoriously cryptic nature of such instructions. Even if a manual comes with the product, it is difficult to read because it is printed in tiny font on thin paper and with as few words as possible.

Complexity and vagueness in instructions is not limited to high-tech areas, though. Cooking recipes often are based on the assumption that you know whether to grease a pan before adding dough, what "simmer" means, and whether a piece of meat is truly "brown" or onions are "wilted." Prescription bottles have warning labels that instruct the patient to take the medication with "plenty of water" but also may indicate not to eat or drink before or after taking the medication.

Problem Solving in Adulthood

As we have just noted, everyday problems are multidimensional, and the steps in solving them are not always clear. Taking these factors into account, **everyday problem solving** involves situations that typically occur in people's daily lives, can be solved in more than one way, and require the problem solver to decide which strategy will lead to the desired result (Thornton & Dumke, 2005). Table 7.3 summarizes the negative and positive effects of aging on problem-solving abilities.

As people get older, they gain in some problem-solving skills at the expense of others. They may become slower and have more memory lapses; however, if they are very familiar with a problem or a type of problem, they can get to a solution more quickly and effectively than can a novice. If you have stood by in awe as your grandmother produced a perfectly formed piecrust in less than 2 minutes while your own dough sticks hopelessly to the rolling pin, then you can relate to this observation. Indeed, researchers have found that the more extensive experience of older adults can enhance not only their problem-solving performance (Crawford & Channon, 2002) but also their feelings of self-efficacy (Artistico, Cervone, & Pezzuti, 2003).

Because middle-aged and older adults have acquired expertise through their years of exposure to certain kinds of problems associated with their jobs, hobbies, or daily routines, they have many advantages in everyday problem solving. They develop the ability to scan quickly for the important factors in a problem and avoid those that are irrelevant. As a result, expert problem solvers avoid information overload by honing in on specific areas that experience has taught them are important to consider. For example, in the area of medical decision making, older people were found in one study to weigh a number of factors and make complex choices more quickly than could young adults when presented with a similar problem (Meyer, Talbot, & Ranalli, 2007).

Older adults may also make choices that are better founded and less subject to extraneous factors. One study on decision making found that, in general, older adults avoid what is known as the "attraction effect." In tests of

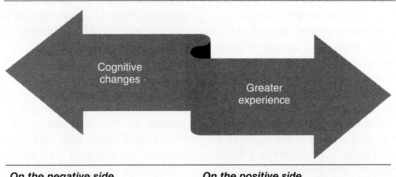

TABLE 7.3
Problem Solving Changes in Adulthood

On the negative side	On the positive side
Young and middle-aged adults outperform older adults (beginning at age 70)	Age differences minimized when problems are interpersonal
Older adults less effective in their analytic strategies	Older adults better at heuristics (mental short-cuts)

the attraction task, participants must choose from either two (A vs. B) or three (A vs. B vs. C) alternative options. For example, option A may represent a product of medium quality costing $30, while option B is a product of somewhat higher quality costing $40. These two options are about equal in their desirability. Researchers then present a different group of participants with three choices. A and B remain the same, but C is the least desirable of all three ($100 for a product of only slightly higher quality than B). The addition of choice C should have no effect on people's decision to choose either A or B, but it does. Even though no one would choose C, its presence drives them to be more likely to pick the alternative between A and B that seemed the closest to C (choice B in this example).

A comparison of older and younger adults in the case of shopping for groceries showed a greater susceptibility of younger adults to demonstrate the attraction effect, meaning that their choices were less rational than those of older adults (Tentori, Osherson, Hasher, & May, 2001). In a follow-up study (Kim & Hasher, 2005), researchers tested the possibility that older adults were less vulnerable to the attraction effect because they had more experience with grocery shopping. The actions of younger and older adults were compared on an additional task that would be more typical for college students, namely, a choice between options for extra experimental credit. Younger adults showed the attraction effect once again in the grocery shopping case, but not in the experimental credit case. Older adults, though less familiar with the ins and outs of experimental credits, nevertheless did not show the attraction effect in either situation.

These studies are particularly interesting because they relate to behavioral economics, an emerging field that investigates the illogical choices that consumers make in everyday situations. According to the results of the attraction effect study, then, older adults should be wiser consumers.

Increased experience enhances problem solving in the later years by allowing older adults to sift quickly through information, honing in on what is relevant and arriving at a solution. As we have just seen, this ability to mobilize a familiar strategy can have advantages but can create difficulties in some situations, particularly when it is important to look at possible alternative approaches. For example, an automobile mechanic who goes directly to the distributor as the source of a stalled engine may not notice a more serious wiring flaw elsewhere. Older problem solvers may think that they are doing a better job at solving the problem but, by objective criteria, they may not be considering alternative solutions as effectively as do younger adults and therefore can make an erroneous decision (Thornton & Dumke, 2005). In a comparison of young, middle-aged, and older adults on ill-defined problems, older adults

were found to generate the fewest possible solutions, even when the problems were ones for which their greater experience should have proved helpful (Thornton, Paterson, & Yeung, 2013).

Memory problems can also contribute to difficulties in problem solving. If you are unable to remember the steps you've taken to try to solve a problem, you'll be more likely to repeat ineffective solutions. This was the pattern of results observed in a study of Japanese monkeys (Kubo, Kato, & Nakamura, 2006). Their task was to find which of nine small openings in a panel contained food. In the experimental condition, the food was hidden behind white plastic circles, so the monkeys had to move the plate to see what was behind it. In the control condition, the food was visible through clear plastic plates. The older monkeys in the experimental condition were hampered in their problem-solving abilities because they went back and checked behind plates they had already moved.

Making up for losses in their strategic planning ability, older problem solvers have the advantage of more experience and more access to information that could help them in a larger variety of situations. As we have already pointed out, people with experience have well-organized storehouses of knowledge that they can easily access and put to use. You may have an older relative who likes to travel abroad and can quickly tell you the pros and cons of a trip you are planning to a foreign country that you have never visited. After years of traveling internationally, this sage advisor can give you knowledge about the country's hotels, places of interest, weather patterns, and the best travel deals. Sports trivia buffs have a similar mastery of large amounts of content matter because they have that knowledge organized into systematic units, such as which 16 teams are in the U.S. American Football Conference versus the 16 in the National Football Conference. These are good people to know if you are looking for information, but not good people to challenge in a trivia contest: you will undoubtedly lose.

Research on the speed at which adults make decisions confirms that older people are able to reach answers more quickly than younger people who either lack the knowledge or the ability to categorize that knowledge. However, older persons are also more apt to make quicker decisions in areas in which they may not have expertise. Furthermore, they are less likely to seek additional information once their decision has been made. It is possible that the rapid problem solving shown by older adults reflects the fact that their experience gives them an advantage in the many areas of decision making. Therefore, they are not as dependent on incoming information as younger adults. The other possibility is that older adults are less able to organize multiple sources of information, leading their decisions to be based on prior experience rather than on new data related to the problem (Marsiske & Margrett, 2006).

The finding that older adults are faster at solving problems conflicts with the majority of research on adult development and cognition. The types of measures and outcomes used in studies of problem solving do not always capture timed responses, as is true for studies of psychomotor speed. Rather, studies of problem solving involve measures based on the amount of information that the participant gathers prior to making a decision, and these measures are not as sensitive to small changes in reaction time.

Supporting the findings from studies of aging and cognition are results from neuropsychological testing. Performance on the Wisconsin Card-Sorting Task appears to be maintained through midlife (Garden, Phillips, & MacPherson, 2001), though age-related effects are apparent in older adults (Head, Kennedy, Rodrigue, & Raz, 2009).

Not all older adults experience similar changes in everyday problem-solving ability, though. For example, older adults with more education have higher scores on the Everyday Problems Test (EPT) (Burton, Strauss, Hultsch, & Hunter, 2006) (see Figure 7.2), a measure designed to replicate the steps used to solve problems encountered in daily life. For example, the EPT assesses the ability to read and comprehend instructions for thawing a turkey or determining the best long-distance telephone plan. Poorer performance on the EPT is related to slower and inconsistent reaction times for older adults (Burton, Strauss, Hultsch, & Hunter, 2009). Among African Americans, in particular, health status plays a role in influencing the quality of decisions they make on this task (Whitfield, Allaire, & Wiggins, 2004).

When it comes to making practical decisions in situations with which they are familiar, then, middle-aged and older adults may have an advantage. This possibility was tested in a study on decision making comparing younger and older adults in a task where a prior choice was either relevant or not to the opportunity to receive future rewards (Worthy, Gorlick, Pacheco, Schnyer, & Maddox, 2011). Younger adults earned more points when the best strategy was to select which of two cards per trial would pay off with the higher reward and when there was no carryover from trial to trial. Older adults, in contrast, earned more points when the value of the reward on each trial depended on the sequence of choices made on prior trials. The findings support the idea that older adults are more likely to base their decisions on the knowledge they develop from prior experience.

As a result of their greater experience and expertise in terms of content and process, older adults may be better able than their younger peers to enact the stages of problem solving in which they appraise the problem, come up with a strategy, and then carry out that strategy. However, when a familiar dilemma appears with a new twist, or when a premature decision leads to avoiding important information, older adults are relatively disadvantaged. Young problem solvers may suffer from their lack of familiarity with many situations, but because they can process larger amounts of information in a shorter time, they may avoid some of the traps of failing to see alternatives that befall their elders.

Indications: Temporarily Relieves Cough Due to Minor Throat and Bronchial Irritation as May Occur With a Cold.

DIRECTIONS: Follow dosage below:
Do Not Exceed 4 Doses in a 24-Hour Period.

 ADULT DOSE (and children 12 years and over): 2 teaspoonfuls every 6 to 8 hrs.

CHILD DOSE
 6 yrs. to under 12 yrs.
1 teaspoonful every 6 to 8 hrs.

 2 yrs. to under 6 yrs.
1/2 teaspoonful every 6 to 8 hrs.
Under 2—Consult Your Doctor

1. What is the maximum number of teaspoons an adult should take in 24 hours?

2. Mr. Jones smokes and has smoker's cough. What is the maximum number of doses he should take per day?

Warnings—A persistent cough may be a sign of a serious condition. If cough persists for more than 1 week, tends to recur, or is accompanied by fever, rash, or persistent headache, consult a doctor. Do not take this product for persistent or chronic cough such as occurs with smoking, asthma, emphysema, or if cough is accompanied by excessive phlegm (mucus) unless directed by a doctor.

FIGURE 7.2

Sample Item From the Everyday Problems Test

Source: Willis, S. L., & Marsiske, M. (1997). Everyday Problems Test. Retrieved from http://geron.psu.edu/sls/(101)EPT%20%20open%20ended%20I.pdf.

Yuri Arcurs/Age Fotostock America, Inc.

Working together to solve problems, these older adults seem to be enjoying both the opportunity for mental challenges and socializing. Perhaps they are updating a Facebook page.

Adult Learners

The literature on problem solving in adulthood emphasizes the ability to come to a resolution when dealing with a dilemma. However, the ability to "find" problems seems to be an equally compelling aspect of adult cognition. Research and theory on this aspect of adult cognition were stimulated, in part, by Swiss psychologist Jean Piaget's concept of **formal operations**, the ability of adolescents and adults to use logic and abstract symbols in arriving at solutions to complex problems. Adult developmental researchers have proposed that there is a stage of **postformal operations**, referring to the way that adults structure their thinking over and beyond that of adolescents (Commons, Richards, & Armon, 1984; Sinnott, 1989).

Thinking at the postformal operational level incorporates the tendency of the mature individual to use logical processes specifically geared to the complex nature of adult life. The postformal thinker is also able to judge when to use formal logic and when, alternatively, to rely on other and simpler modes of representing problems. For example, you do not need to use the rules of formal logic to unplug a stopped drain. Hands-on methods are generally suitable for dealing with practical situations like this one involving actions in the physical world.

Related to the postformal stage of cognitive development is **dialectical thinking**, which is an interest in and appreciation for debate, arguments, and counterarguments (Basseches, 1984). Dialectical thinking involves the recognition that often the truth is not "necessarily a given," but that common understandings among people are a negotiated process of give and take. People may not be able to find the ideal solution for many of life's problems, but through the process of sharing their alternative views with each other, most reasonable adults can at least come to some satisfactory compromises. Although you may not agree with some of your friends who have vastly different political opinions than your own, you have learned to respect their viewpoints, no matter how difficult it may be for you to do so and remain on speaking terms.

On a daily basis, average adults face many ambiguities and uncertainties in dilemmas ranging from how to resolve conflicts with their friends to how to make the best choices for their children's education. Many people actively seek out the opportunity to engage others in dialogue and intellectual engagement. The ability to integrate diverging viewpoints as well as see the advantages to different points of view may be the key to understanding the way that adults think (Kallio, 2011).

These ideas about adult cognition present interesting implications about adults as thinkers, problem solvers, and, particularly, learners. Adult learners are increasingly becoming part of the concerns of those who teach at the college level. In 2009, 16% of the undergraduate population was age 35 or older (U.S. Bureau of the Census, 2010c). As of 2005, 44% of all U.S. adults aged 17 and older were involved in some form of adult education, including 49% of adults 35 to 49 years old and 22% of those aged 70 and older. The largest percent of working-age adults were taking courses relevant to their jobs (27%). Personal interest courses were the second most frequent form of adult education, accounting for the majority of people aged 60 and older (National Center for Education Statistics, 2013). The economic downturn of the late 2000s seems to have prompted more adults to follow through on their plans to pursue higher education in order to keep their current jobs or improve their prospects for better jobs (Kimmel, Gaylor, Ray Grubbs, & Bryan Hayes, 2012).

In the classroom, adult learners may attempt to master the material through using strategies such as taking more copious notes and relying on them more heavily as they are trying to acquire new information (Delgoulet & Marquie, 2002). The adult learner is also more likely to challenge the instructor to go beyond the information and explore alternative dimensions. Such tendencies, though fascinating in the classroom, can lead to problems when it comes to evaluation. For a person who can see all the alternate angles to a standard multiple-choice exam question, it can be very difficult to arrive at the correct answer because more than one has virtues that merit attention. The adult thinker and learner may find it equally fascinating to ponder ambiguities rather than settle on one choice even though only one choice is graded as correct.

The preference that many adult learners have for applying their real-world experiences to what they gain from the classroom suggests that instructors should incorporate problem-centered teaching as much as possible (Papa & Papa, 2011). Flexible models of instruction that allow learners to apply what they are learning to their own lives through active decision making can also fit well with the learning style of nontraditional adult students (Cornelius, Gordon, & Ackland, 2011).

Educators must also adapt their methods of instruction to accommodate the learning styles and preferences of adult students at different levels of ability and literacy. For example, in the case of second language learning, students with low literacy skills and less prior education in their home countries behave differently in the classroom than students who already have more classroom experience. They are less likely to ask for help and participate in classroom interactions. To reach these students, instructors may adopt methods such as asking the students with more education and classroom experience to mentor them, starting with oral exercises before moving to written exercises, and encouraging them to use language in new ways (Ramírez-Esparza et al., 2012).

INTELLIGENCE

If you were asked to define the term "intelligence," you would probably guess that it represents the quality of a person's ability to think. In the most general sense, psychology defines **intelligence** as an individual's mental ability. We know that "some people are cleverer than others" (Deary, 2012, p. 454); the question is why, and how this cleverness changes over adulthood.

The existence of age effects on intelligence in adulthood has many practical and theoretical ramifications. For practical reasons, it is important to find out the relative strengths and weaknesses of younger versus older workers. As we noted earlier in our discussion of problem solving, there appear to be fairly distinct differences in the styles that adults of different ages use when making decisions. Employers in the public and private sectors can put to practical use the data that psychologists produce from studies using standard intelligence test scores. From a theoretical standpoint, research on intelligence in adulthood has provided new perspectives on the components of thought. This research has also provided insight into the perennial question of how mental processes are affected by "nature versus nurture," as researchers have continued to exploit and explore the application of complex research designs to data on intelligence test scores in adulthood.

Just as physical abilities partially define a person's identity, intelligence serves as an attribute of the person that forms part of the sense of self. People have a good idea of whether they are "smart" or "not as bright," a self-attribution that they can carry for years (Leonardelli, Hermann, Lynch, & Arkin, 2003). If you're one of these people, you value the products of the mind, such as your ability to solve tough crossword puzzles and score well in games against your friends. As a result, you may be more vigilant for changes in intelligence associated with aging than people who take pride in their physical strength or dexterity. In some cases, these changes may be more imagined than real, particularly as people age and begin to believe the media images portraying older adults as losing their mental abilities. When the changes are not just imaginary, however, this may prove to be a tough change to acknowledge.

The earliest findings on adult intelligence proposed that age differences across adulthood followed the **classic aging pattern** of an inverted U-shape, with a peak in early adulthood followed by steady decline (Botwinick, 1977). Results from the Wechsler scales, which supported the view that intelligence generally erodes over successive decades in adulthood, contrasted a smaller but uniform body of evidence from longitudinal studies. When samples of adults were followed through repeated testings using the Wechsler scales or other standardized tests, the finding was either no decline or a decline that did not become apparent until very late in life.

Theories of intelligence differ in the number and nature of abilities proposed to exist. Fortunately, researchers working in the field of adult development and aging have come to a resolution, in theory if not practice, of how best to characterize the nature of adult intelligence. Most believe that there are two main categories of mental abilities corresponding roughly to verbal and nonverbal intelligence.

Theoretical Perspectives on Adult Intelligence

The earliest theory of intelligence, that proposed by British psychologist and statistician Charles Spearman (1904, 1927), proposed the existence of **g or general factor**, defined as the ability to infer and apply relationships on the basis of experience. According to Spearman, g could not be directly observed, but could be estimated through tests that tap into specific mental abilities. Psychologists now find it more useful to divide intelligence into a set of multiple components. Raymond B. Cattell and John L. Horn proposed **fluid-crystallized theory (Gf-Gc)**, the view that intelligence should be divided into two distinct factors (Cattell, 1963; Horn & Cattell, 1966). **Fluid reasoning (Gf)** is the individual's innate ability to carry out higher-level cognitive operations (Cattell, 1971). Originally called **crystallized intelligence**, **comprehension knowledge (Gc)** represents the acquisition of specific skills and information that people gain as the result of their exposure to the language, knowledge, and conventions of their culture. These broad abilities each reflect distinct abilities that are measured by specific tests.

In addition to these two factors, the "extended" Gf-Gc theory proposes that there are eight other broad factors that incorporate cognitive skills such as memory, speed, sensory processing, reading, writing, and mathematical knowledge. Each of these broad factors is measured by a specific test or tests that tap narrower, related, abilities. In the extended Gf-Gc model, each broad ability has its own predictive power rather than each reflecting different aspects of g.

Although Cattell and Horn regarded Gf and Gc as being distinct factors, his own analysis of the available studies at the time led educational psychologist John B. Carroll to propose that intelligence is organized into a three-level structure (Carroll, 1993). Combining these theories, the **Cattell-Horn-Carroll (CHC) model of intelligence** proposes that there is a three-tier structure to intelligence (see Table 7.4). At the bottom of the structure are the individual abilities (shown in the right-hand column), such

as inductive reasoning or spatial relations. These make up the second level of abilities (the left-hand column), which includes Gf and Gc. The third level in the CHC model is g, or general ability.

Researchers testing the CHC model have used a variety of measures to test its structure. Using the WAIS-IV standardization sample of 2,200 participants ages 16–90 years old, Benson and colleagues (2010) identified areas of overlap with the CHC abilities. Gc is reflected in all four scales of the Verbal Comprehension Index. All three scales on the Processing Speed Index relate to Gs. The Perceptual Reasoning Index assesses a combination of Gv and Gf, because Block Design, Visual Puzzles, and Picture Completion tap Gv but Matrix Reasoning and Figure Weights reflect Gf. The Working Memory Index reflects Gsm, as would be expected, but the Arithmetic scale also reflects a combination of Gf and Gq in addition to Gsm.

Knowledge of these correspondences is helpful to know, because given the WAIS-IV's widespread use, particularly in clinical practice, there is value to understanding its structure. The Benson et al. study also provides weighted formulas that both researchers and clinicians can use to calculate the CHC composites of Gv, Gf, and Gq from the WAIS-IV scale scores.

Research on Adult Intelligence

What happens to intelligence as you get older? This seemingly simple question is hotly debated in the literature on adult development and aging. Some researchers claim that intelligence starts to dip as early as the 20s; others are convinced by their data that the changes only become noticeable after the decade of the 60s.

The most comprehensive study of adult intelligence was conducted by K. Warner Schaie. Begun in the 1950s, what is now known as the Seattle Longitudinal Study (SLS) has produced extensive information about what happens to people's intellectual skills as they age. In addition to providing a picture of how age alters intelligence, the SLS also has provided important evidence about how cohort and time of measurement influence patterns of performance on basic intellectual abilities.

When he began the SLS, Schaie's intention was to conduct a one-time cross-sectional study in which he would compare 500 people divided into 10 five-year age intervals or cohorts in their performance on the PMAT. His participants were drawn from the insured members of a prepaid medical plan. Schaie decided to expand on the study several years later, when he instituted a series of follow-ups that he then went on to conduct every seven years. As a result of adopting this method, Schaie was able to analyze

TABLE 7.4
Structure of Intelligence According to the CHC Model

Broad ability	Definition	How specific abilities are measured
Fluid reasoning (Gf)	Use of deliberate and controlled mental operations that can be performed automatically	Deductive reasoning, inductive reasoning, Piagetian reasoning, speed of reasoning
Comprehension knowledge (Gc)	Knowledge of a culture that individuals gain through acculturation	Language development, general information, vocabulary, foreign language knowledge
Short-term memory (Gsm)	Ability to apprehend and maintain awareness of a limited number of elements in a situation that occurred within the past 30–60 seconds	Memory span, working memory
Visual processing (Gv)	Ability to generate, store, retrieve, and transform visual images	Visualization, spatial relations, visual memory, length estimation
Auditory processing (Ga)	Abilities that depend on sound as input, including ability to interpret and organize sounds	Memory for sound patterns, musical discrimination, sound localization
Long-term storage and retrieval (Glr)	Ability to store and consolidate new information in long-term memory and retrieve it for minutes, hours, weeks, or longer	Free recall memory, ideational fluency, word fluency, figural fluency, associative memory
Processing speed (Gs)	Ability to perform automatically and fluently relatively easy or elementary cognitive tasks, especially when attention and focused concentration is required	Perceptual speed, number facility, speed of reasoning, writing speed, reading speed
Reaction and decision speed (Gt)	Ability to perform simple and complex decisions at the onset of simple stimuli	Simple reaction time, choice reaction time, semantic processing speed
Quantitative knowledge (Gq)	Breadth and depth of person's acquired store of mathematical knowledge	Mathematical knowledge, mathematical achievement
Reading and writing (Grw)	Breadth and depth of person's acquired store of reading and writing knowledge and skills	Reading comprehension, verbal language comprehension, reading speed, writing speed

Source: Adapted from McGrew, K. S. (2009). CHC theory and the human cognitive abilities project: Standing on the shoulders of the giants of psychometric intelligence research. *Intelligence*, 37(1), 1–10. doi: 10.1016/j.intell.2008.08.004

the data in a series of sequential studies. This made it possible for him to test the effects of age as distinct from time of measurement and cohort. Schaie's foresight in planning a study that would make possible the sophisticated developmental research designs described in Chapter 3 has provided a wealth of information on intelligence in adulthood and the factors that affect its fluctuations.

The first set of findings the SLS produced was based on the cross-sectional analyses comparing all 10 cohorts on the PMAT at one point in time. Replicating the classic aging pattern, the scores of the older adults were lower than those of the younger adults. It was not until 7 years later that Schaie was able to show that the classic aging pattern reflected not the effect of age changes, but the combined effects of age, cohort, and time of measurement. For most

abilities, even the oldest age group increased or showed no change between the first and second testings. The stage was set for what has now become a 40-year-plus exploration for the factors accounting for why people change, or not, across the adult years.

The findings that Schaie and his collaborators published in a comprehensive review (2006) showed distinct patterns of age changes across the primary abilities. Vocabulary, a measure of Gc, showed the least amount of change, holding up fairly steadily until the age of 74. The largest drop in scores occurred on Numeric Ability, which in the CHC model represents Gq (quantitative knowledge). Supporting these findings are analyses from the University of Manchester Longitudinal Study, conducted over a 20-year period on over 6,000 middle-aged and older adults

(Ghisletta, Rabbitt, Lunn, & Lindenberger, 2012). In this study, tests measuring Gf declined at a faster rate than did those of Gc. However, confirming findings from the SLS, there were large individual differences, particularly during the midlife years.

Despite the compelling nature of these findings, Salthouse concluded from his own analysis of cross-sectional data that the "decline" occurs in intelligence starting at age 20 (2009). Schaie (2009), arguing that cross-sectional data cannot prove or disprove the existence of age changes, regards this assertion as unfounded. Moreover, challenging Salthouse's treatment of intelligence as a unitary quality, others maintain that not only do people vary from each other in the rate and extent of change (interindividual change), but also within themselves and their own abilities (intraindividual change) (Nilsson, Sternäng, Rönnlund, & Nyberg, 2009).

In an analysis specifically investigating differences between earlier- and later-born cohorts in the SLS data, a team headed by Gerstorf (2011) showed that some abilities seem particularly sensitive to cohort effects. Figure 7.3 shows the changes in PMAT scores from ages 50 through 80 in two cohorts. The later-born cohort had higher scores throughout the entire age range on all abilities except number. Moreover, the earlier cohort also had lower rates of decline.

Why would there be such powerful cohort influences on the rates of cognitive change in later adulthood? Gerstorf et al. (2011) controlled for such possible contributors as years of education and disease (cardiovascular and cancer). The remaining effects may be due to differences in the quality of education (i.e., discovery vs. rote learning), exposure to technology, the increasing complexity of work environments, and changes in gender roles associated with greater labor force participation among women. The authors concluded, essentially, that their findings support the common belief now that "60 is the new 40," or at least "the new 50."

Another important factor that affects intelligence test scores is an individual's health status. As we saw in Chapter 3, retrospective studies show that people close to death show diminished intellectual functioning. Findings from the SLS suggest that health status is indeed related to intelligence test performance. Arthritis, cancer, and osteoporosis are health conditions associated with intelligence test scores (Schaie, 1996), as is metabolic syndrome (Akbaraly et al., 2009). These effects are not limited to Western countries; similar findings were reported among a study of more than 3,200 Chinese age 60 and older, even after controlling for age, smoking, hypertension, and diabetes (Liu et al., 2009).

Taking advantage of the types of healthy behaviors we discussed in Chapter 1 also seems to help preserve "executive function," or the ability to allocate cognitive resources. The Whitehall II study showed greater declines in this type of intellectual ability among those in the sample who smoked, abstained entirely from alcohol, did not participate in exercise, and consumed low amounts of fruits and vegetables (Sabia et al., 2009). Not surprisingly, these were also the individuals who showed the largest increase in BMI over adulthood (Sabia, Kivimaki, Shipley, Marmot, & Singh-Manoux, 2009) (see Table 7.5).

Though for the most part it would make sense that lifestyle choices would have an impact on intellectual functioning, it is also possible that the cause of poorer lifestyle choices is related to poorer intellectual functioning (Elovainio et al., 2009). As we noted earlier, metabolic syndrome is associated with fluid intelligence; however, after controlling for education, this relationship becomes much less significant (Akbaraly, Singh-Manoux, Marmot, & Brunner, 2009).

Whatever the contribution of lifestyle and diet to fluid intelligence, there is increasing evidence showing a relationship between measures of brain activation and test scores. Activation of the prefrontal cortex seems to play a role in fluid intelligence among both older and younger adults even when memory performance is controlled (Waiter et al., 2010). Variations in neurological abilities may also account for findings that older individuals with lower fluid intelligence also show greater fluctuations in scores over time (Ram, Rabbitt, Stollery, & Nesselroade, 2005). Perhaps these older individuals are more vulnerable to the physiological changes that can exacerbate the aging of the abilities that underlie fluid intelligence. In fact, researchers in the Canadian Study of Health and Aging have observed a predictive effect of low fluid intelligence test scores in a higher rate of mortality in older adults (Hall, Dubin, Crossley, Holmqvist, & D'Arcy, 2009).

Another important source of individual differences is gender; differences between men and women are indeed observed in intelligence tests performance in adulthood. Men outperform women on numerical skill, the crystallized ability of knowledge of general information, and spatial orientation. In general, women tend to decline earlier

TABLE 7.5

Factors That Affect the Aging of Intelligence

Factor	Type of Effect
Smoking	Cigarette smokers show greater IQ declines
Obesity	Among men, obesity predicts lower IQ scores
Lifestyle	People with more active engagement show less of an intelligence decline

<u>FIGURE 7.3</u>

Data From the SLS Showing Cohort Differences in Patterns of Change Between Ages 50 Through 80 on Five Primary Abilities

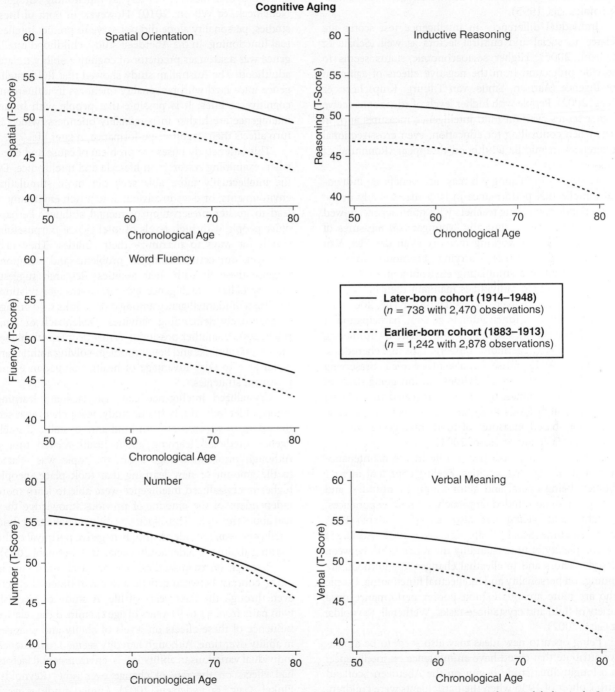

Cognitive Aging

Source: Gerstorf, D., Ram, N., Hoppmann, C., Willis, S. L., & Schaie, K. W. (2011). Cohort differences in cognitive aging and terminal decline in the Seattle Longitudinal Study. *Developmental Psychology*, 47(4), 1026–1041. doi: *10.1037/a0023426*

across the lifespan on fluid abilities, whereas men show earlier losses on crystallized abilities (Dixon & Hultsch, 1999). However, women receive higher scores on the fluid intelligence measure of Digit Symbol (Kaufman, Kaufman, McLean, & Reynolds, 1991; Portin, Saarijaervi, Joukamaa, & Salokangas, 1995).

Individual differences in intelligence test scores are related to social and cultural factors as well (Schaie & Zanjani, 2006). Higher socioeconomic status seems to provide protection from the negative effects of aging on intelligence (Aartsen, Smits, van Tilburg, Knipscheer, & Deeg, 2002). People with higher levels of education receive higher scores even on fluid intelligence measures and, in fact, when controlling for education, even cross-sectional differences in middle adulthood disappear (Ronnlund & Nilsson, 2006).

Having a stimulating job may also benefit an individual's intellectual performance in later life. A study in the Netherlands comparing teachers with nonteachers showed that teachers were technically "younger" on measures of verbal fluency and working memory (Van der Elst, Van Boxtel, & Jolles, 2012). Carrying this notion forward, being exposed to a stimulating environment after retirement can also help individuals maintain their intellectual abilities (Schaie, Nguyen, Willis, Dutta, & Yue, 2001). As is true for cognitive functioning in general, participation in exercise training can also benefit intelligence by promoting brain plasticity (Eggermont, Milberg, Lipsitz, Scherder, & Leveille, 2009). Expertise may also play a role in preserving an individual's intellectual abilities. An intriguing study of players of the Chinese game "Go" revealed that among those with high levels of expertise, the expected decline in memory-based measures of fluid intelligence was not observed (Masunaga & Horn, 2001).

Personality may also play a role in the maintenance or decline of cognitive abilities. Feeling confident in your abilities, being liberal and autonomous in attitudes, and having an open-minded approach to new experiences, thoughts, and feelings are also related to higher PMA scores over time (Schaie, Willis, & Caskie, 2004). Adding to the complexity of understanding the relationship between lifestyle factors and intellectual changes in adulthood are findings on personality and intellectual functioning. People who are more anxious exhibit poorer performance on a variety of fluid and crystallized tasks (Wetherell, Reynolds, & Gatz, 2002).

Being open to new ideas may also seem to be a positive attribute that could have an influence on intelligence. In a longitudinal study begun on the Aberdeen Scotland Birth Cohort of 1936 when the participants were children, those high in the personality trait of openness to experience had higher scores on measures of reading ability in their

mid-60s (Hogan, Staff, Bunting, Deary, & Whalley, 2012). Similarly, an Australian study on adults ages 74 to 90 years of age found that participants higher on one aspect of openness to experience (enjoyment of fantasy) had higher Gf, Gc, and scores on a measure of everyday functioning (Gregory, Nettelbeck, & Wilson, 2010). However, in both of these studies, personality alone did not serve to predict intellectual functioning. In the Aberdeen study, childhood intelligence was a stronger predictor of cognitive ability in later adulthood. The Australian study showed that fluid intelligence interacted with personality openness in influencing cognitive abilities. It is possible that people with higher intelligence are higher in personality openness, which in turn affects their cognitive performance in later life.

This latter study raises the problem of cause and effect when examining research on lifestyle and intelligence. Do the intellectually more able seek out more stimulating environments, or does involvement in a rich environment lead to greater preservation of mental abilities? Perhaps older people with high levels of intelligence purposefully search for ways to maximize their abilities. They may also seek out certain complex problems and situations because these fit with their abilities. Research suggests that crystallized intelligence exhibits a stronger relationship than fluid intelligence among older adults who engage in cognitively demanding activities (Dellenbach & Zimprich, 2008). Another possibility is that people with higher intellectual abilities and better problem-solving abilities are better able to take advantage of health maintenance and treatment strategies.

Crystallized intelligence can also facilitate learning among older individuals. In one study, researchers assessed the extent to which scores on fluid and crystallized intelligence predicted learning about health-related topics. Although prior knowledge about the topic was related to the amount of new learning that took place, people higher in crystallized intelligence were able to learn more independent of the amount of previous knowledge they had about the topic. Thus, focusing only on deficits in fluid intelligence can provide an unduly negative portrayal of the learning abilities of older adults (Beier & Ackerman, 2005).

Research on twin studies provides a classic example of the contrast between genetic and environmental effects even through the later years of life. A study of Swedish twin pairs from 41 to 91 years of age examined the relative influence of these effects on levels of ability and changes in ability over time. Although heredity seemed to influence individual variations in ability levels, environmental factors had effects on the rate of change over time (Reynolds, Finkel, Gatz, & Pedersen, 2002). Similar findings were obtained in a study of Danish twins, who were measured using a cohort-sequential design and retested every 2 years for up to four testings. As with the Swedish study, overall intellectual ability appeared to be a function of genetics, but the rate of change over time was a function of environmental influences (McGue & Christensen, 2002).

Training Studies

Researchers have for decades tried to develop effective intervention strategies to examine ways to counteract the effects of age on intelligence. There is a long tradition within the developmental perspective advocated by Schaie, Baltes, and Willis of seeking ways to help preserve people's functioning as strongly and as for long as possible (Willis & Schaie, 2009).

The underlying theoretical and philosophical perspective for this approach evolved from some of the earliest work in this area by Baltes and Schaie (1976): "Our central argument is one for plasticity of intelligence in adulthood and old age as evidenced by large interindividual differences, multidirectionality, multidimensionality, the joint significance of ontogenetic and historical change components, and emerging evidence on modifiability via intervention research" (p. 724). To put it more simply, Baltes and Schaie argued for the need to see intelligence as "plastic" or modifiable rather than simply an attribute that declines with age. Much like the debate between the neuronal fallout and plasticity models of aging of the central nervous system, the view of intelligence as "plastic" assumes that declines are not inevitable even though some resources may be sensitive to the effects of aging. The basic assumption that adult intelligence is responsive to interventions was a driving force behind later research, particularly for training studies carried out within the SLS (Willis et al., 2009).

Underlying the plasticity model is the idea that older adults possess **reserve capacity**, abilities that are there to be used but are currently untapped (Staudinger, Marsiske, & Baltes, 1995). You can think of reserve capacity as your ability to perform to your highest level when you are positively motivated by a teacher, coach, competitor, or friend. You may not have even imagined that such a strong performance was possible until you completed it successfully. Training studies operate according to the same principle. Tapping into an individual's reserve capacity involves **testing the limits**, the process of continuing to train people until they show no further improvements (Baltes & Kliegl, 1992).

The earliest studies to demonstrate plasticity were conducted in the early 1970s at Penn State University by Baltes, Willis, and their colleagues. These studies demonstrated that, given practice and training in test-taking strategies, older adults could improve their scores on tests of fluid

FIGURE 7.4

Conceptual Model of ACTIVE Trial

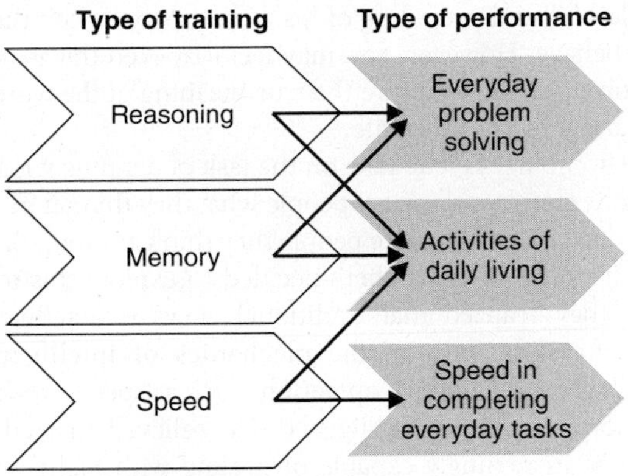

Source: Adapted from Willis, S. L., Tennstedt, S. L., Marsiske, M., Ball, K., Elias, J., Koepke, K. M., … Wright, E. (2006). Long-term effects of cognitive training on everyday functional outcomes in older adults. *Journal of the American Medical Association, 296*, 2805–2814.

intelligence (Hofland, Willis, & Baltes, 1980; Plemons, Willis, & Baltes, 1978; Willis, Blieszner, & Baltes, 1981). Keeping in mind that fluid intelligence is theoretically intended to be a "pure" measure of ability, educational experiences should not have had an impact on the scores of older adults. Applying these methods to individuals in the SLS sample, the Penn State group was able to show that training in fluid intelligence tasks such as inductive reasoning could produce gains that lasted for at least seven years (Schaie, 1994).

Most recently, the ADEPT findings were expanded in ACTIVE, the large multisite intervention study we described in Chapter 6, which showed a positive impact of training on the cognitive functions of memory, reasoning, and speed of processing. In an innovative variant on the overall training paradigm, the ACTIVE researchers investigated the impact of training in these areas on actual abilities to maintain functional independence in everyday life. Training in the area of reasoning had a significantly positive impact on the ability of the older adults in the study to manage their daily activities, an effect that was maintained over a 5-year period (Willis et al., 2006). (See Figure 7.4.) These types of findings provide hope that cognitive training can enable older adults to live independent lives and prevent functional disability.

THE PSYCHOLOGY OF WISDOM

Some might argue that the most advanced form of cognition is the capacity for wisdom. Unlike the ability to score well on a traditional intelligence test, wisdom reflects a far less quantifiable phenomenon. If you were asked to define wisdom, you might come up with a meaning that incorporates the individual's knowledge of the ways of the world and understanding of how other people feel, think, and behave. However, you may feel that even this general definition doesn't capture the true meaning of the word as you use it in your own life.

Psychologists who take on the task of defining wisdom actually start by asking lay people what they think it means and, further, to nominate people they think are wise. Baltes and his team of researchers decided to explore this topic after they realized that traditional views of intelligence were focusing only on the **mechanics of intelligence**, which involve cognitive operations such as speed, working memory, and fluid intelligence. He believed that adults become increasingly capable of dealing with higher-level conceptual issues, and that conventional tests, by measuring the mechanics of intelligence, fail to capture these abilities. The central element of the Baltes wisdom model proposes that wise people are experts in the **pragmatics of intelligence**, meaning that they can apply their abilities to the solution of real-life problems. According to Baltes, cognitive development in adulthood involves growth in this ability to provide insight into life's many dilemmas, particularly those that are psychosocial or interpersonal.

According to the **Berlin Wisdom Paradigm**, wisdom is a form of expert knowledge in the pragmatics of life (Baltes & Smith, 2008). For many people, wisdom evolves in the later years of life as they become aware of the role of culture in shaping their lives and personalities (called "life span contextualism"). Wise people become less likely to judge others and have a greater appreciation for individual differences in values, life experiences, and beliefs ("value relativism"). People who are wise also have a rich base of factual or declarative knowledge and an extensive background of procedural knowledge, meaning that they know how things work (Baltes, Staudinger, Maercker, & Smith, 1995). Finally, another quality, not always emphasized in the more cognitive approaches to wisdom, is the ability of wise people to recognize and manage uncertainty as a fact of life (Ardelt, 2004).

These conclusions about wisdom developed through studies identifying the characteristics of people nominated by others to be wise who were then asked to comment about another person's personal difficulties. Research using this method did not find consistent support for an age-related growth of wisdom (Baltes & Smith, 2008; Baltes & Staudinger, 2000), perhaps reflecting the selected nature of the samples (e.g., clinical psychologists) and the brevity of the task.

Building on the Baltes Wisdom Paradigm, Grossmann and his colleagues developed a longer task, which they administered to a larger and more representative sample (Grossmann et al., 2010). Participants read stories involving social problems, such as conflict between different ethnic groups or individuals. The researchers then rated their responses along six dimensions, including being able to see multiple points of view, recognizing that knowledge of any situation is limited, making multiple predictions of how the situation may unfold, and trying to resolve the conflict through compromise. A group of professional counselors and wisdom researchers validated these rating scales. The findings supported the view that, relative to middle-aged and younger adults, older adults are better able to take multiple perspectives, try to forge compromises, and recognize the limitations of knowledge. The same individuals who received higher scores on the wisdom ratings had also received lower scores on a measure of fluid intelligence, supporting the Baltes distinction between pragmatics and mechanics.

Cultural influences also play a role in the development of wisdom over the adult years. Using the same wisdom scenarios, a subsequent study showed that young and middle-aged Japanese adults had responses that were wiser than those of their American counterparts. For the older adults in the sample, however, the Japanese–American differences were weaker. In fact, older Americans gave responses that were considered wiser than their Japanese counterparts for conflicts involving groups rather than individuals (Grossmann et al., 2012).

Wisdom may also play a role in facilitating the individual's own adjustment to life. Older adults who scored higher on the wisdom ratings using the scenario measure had higher life satisfaction, lower negative affect, less of a tendency to have depressive thoughts, and better social relationships. Five years after participating in the study, the wisest participants also were most likely to still be alive, even after controlling for other factors such as gender, social class, income, perceived health, and verbal abilities (Grossmann, Na, Varnum, Kitayama, & Nisbett, 2012).

Gardner's **theory of multiple intelligences**, which we discussed in the Aging Today section of the chapter, has unfortunately not served as much of a testing ground for studies on intelligence in adulthood. His proposal, that intelligence includes several traditional abilities (logical/mathematical, verbal, visual/spatial) as well as others not usually tapped in intelligence tests (naturalistic, interpersonal, intrapersonal, musical, bodily "kinesthetic," or athleticism), would seem to be an ideal way to capture the complexity of intelligence required for adaptation to daily life. In this sense, wisdom might be seen as most relevant to the domains of interpersonal (knowledge of others) and intrapersonal (knowledge of self), paralleling the distinction between mechanics and pragmatics of intelligence.

We might hope that future researchers will explore these alternate, and important forms of ability that clearly impact many areas of functioning throughout the adult years.

SUMMARY

1. The higher cognitive functions include language, problem-solving ability, and intelligence. Changes in memory contribute in part to age-related losses in language, such as the ability to derive meaning from spoken or written passages, spell, and find words. As a result, older adults use simpler and less specific language. However, many language abilities are maintained, and older adults are able to use nonlanguage cues to help them derive meanings from language. The way that younger persons speak to older adults can also be problematic if this involves elderspeak, which is patronizing and infantilizing speech directed at an older person. The communication predicament describes the negative effects on cognition and language when older people are communicated to in this manner.

2. Throughout the adult years, there is a trade-off in the factors affecting everyday problem solving between alterations in speed of processing and working memory and gains in experience as individuals encounter a wider variety of problems as well as more depth in their own fields of expertise. However, because experienced problem solvers tend to seek answers to familiar problems by seeking familiar solutions, they may miss something important that is unique to a particular problem. In addition to focusing on one solution rather than considering others, older adults may also tend to stick with one pattern of responding when the situation calls for being able to call on a range of ideas.

3. There are a number of theories of intelligence, but the majority of research on adult intelligence is based on the fluid-crystallized theory. Studies on the primary mental abilities support the theory's proposal that fluid (unlearned, nonverbal) abilities decrease gradually throughout adulthood. By contrast, the crystallized abilities that are acquired through education and training steadily increase through the 60s and show a decrease only after that point. Other conceptions of intelligence, including the theory of multiple intelligences and triarchic theory, have not been tested yet on adults of varying ages but hold potential to offer a broader view of intelligence.

4. The most extensive study of adult intelligence is the Seattle Longitudinal Study, in which sequential methods have been applied to the Primary Mental Abilities test. In addition to providing data on age patterns in intelligence test scores, this study has highlighted relationships with intelligence among health, personality, lifestyle, and sociocultural factors.

5. Intervention studies in which older adults are given training in the abilities tapped by intelligence test scores have yielded support for the notion of plasticity. Even 5 hours of training can result in improved scores across tests for as long as a 7-year period. Following from these training studies, researchers have proposed establishing the reserve capacity of older adults not demonstrated in ordinary life by using a method known as testing the limits.

6. Many older adults turn to the pragmatics of intelligence, or the practical use of knowledge, and away from the mechanics of intelligence, or the skills typically measured on tests of ability. The quality of wisdom in later life develops as individuals become more interested in developing their abilities in the pragmatics of life.

8

Personality

AGING TODAY

The Neuroticism Paradox

No one wants to be neurotic. In ancient times, Hippocrates described the "melancholic" temperament as suffering from chronically disturbed bodily fluids. In modern psychology, Freud identified the neurotic personality as the prototype of psychopathology. Over the millennia, people who are anxious, worried, and depressed have been regarded as suffering from undesirable attributes that diminish their life quality and make them difficult, if not miserable, to be around. Mental health professionals long ago abandoned the phrase "neurosis" to describe the syndrome of extreme sadness and worry. Instead, psychological disorders involving depressed moods and highly anxious states fall into several categories of the diagnostic nomenclature system.

Yet, poking through the heaps of data proclaiming the dangers of sad moods and high neuroticism were always a few glimmers of hope for those with a chronically dim view of the world. For example, researchers in the late 1970s began to talk about the virtues of "depressive realism": the more honest perceptions of self and world in people who typically feel unhappy. In one landmark experimental study (Alloy & Abramson, 1979), nondepressed undergraduates were more likely than the depressed to think that they were in control of a random event (the turning on and off of a light bulb). The term "sadder but wiser" aptly captured the essence of this effect. In contrast, the nondepressed tend to overemphasize their own role in the events in their lives, part of a general tendency for nondepressed people to view themselves in an unrealistically positive light.

If being depressed is related to a tendency to analyze self and the world more critically, the costs of lower self-esteem and feelings of helplessness, of course, can be very high. However, the slight benefit of being more realistic might be considered a strength. Extrapolating to people high in neuroticism, whose mood tends to be more negative, we see that there can be some hidden advantages.

Nevertheless, should you feel that your own personality traits are inhibiting your enjoyment of life, there are ways you can make positive changes to increase your fulfillment:

1. Don't be worried about worrying. If your reasons are realistically tied to what's happening in your life, don't add guilt over feeling negative to your existing feelings of sadness or anxiety.
2. When real worries come your way, take practical steps to turn things around. You can change your mood by changing your thoughts, one step at a time.
3. Use depressive realism to your advantage. Although people with clinical depression have great difficulty seeing the positive in life, going overboard in the opposite direction also carries risks. Take a good hard look at the situations you can control and those you can't, and work to change what you can control.

The moral of the story is that being in a bad mood isn't always a bad thing. Sometimes you may even be able to see yourself and your life in a clearer and more honest light.

Posted by Susan Whitbourne and Stacey Whitbourne

In everyday language, people use the term "personality" to describe a person's characteristic way of feeling or behaving. For example, you might say that someone does you a favor because that person is "nice," "generous," or "friendly." Although psychologists use a variety of ways to define personality, there is no one consistent meaning that all psychologists use. Instead, psychologists who study personality approach its definition from the vantage point of their particular theoretical preference.

PSYCHODYNAMIC PERSPECTIVE

Freud is credited with having "discovered" the unconscious in psychology because of the importance he attached to hidden motives and feelings within the mind. His approach, called the **psychodynamic perspective**, emphasizes the ways in which unconscious motives and impulses express themselves in people's personalities and behavior. Current theories of adult development and personality based on the psychodynamic perspective continue to emphasize such Freudian ideas as the importance of early development and the ways in which people cope with such emotions as fear, anxiety, and love. However, the methods used to study these phenomena are far different than the clinical approach of the traditional Freudians.

Although he left a rich body of work that later theorists would subsequently revise and reshape, many believe that Freud's legacy in the area of adult development and aging was to make the unfounded claim that personality does not change after early childhood. According to Freud, the major tasks of personality development are completed by the time the child turns 5 years old. Some changes continue to occur through adolescence, but by early adulthood, the individual's psychological development is essentially over. As a result, according to this traditional Freudian view, therapy is of little value to individuals over the age of 50, who he believed had personalities so rigidly set that they could not be radically altered.

Contemporary followers of traditional Freudian thinking share his emphasis on early development but do not share the pessimistic view that adults are incapable of change. Freudian theory today as applied to adult development is divided into three main branches, as shown in Figure 8.1. This framework will help you keep the differences among these three branches straight while also seeing their common basis in the psychodynamic perspective.

Ego Psychology

According to Freud's theory, the mind is made up of three structures that he named id, ego, and superego.

FIGURE 8.1

Branches of Psychodynamic Theory

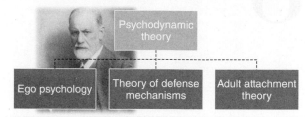

Time & Life Pictures/Getty Images, Inc.

As you might recall from your introductory psychology course, the id refers to the individual's biological instincts, which include the needs for food, sex, and water. Id instincts can also include the need to hurt, kill, and exert power over others. The superego attempts to control the id's irrational instincts in part through imparting society's moral standards (the conscience) and in part by providing the individual with an image of goodness to which the individual can aspire (the ideal self).

In Freudian theory, the **ego** is the part of the mind that controls rational thought. Its job is to negotiate a way for people to meet their biological needs without putting themselves at risk of violating society's expectations or falling short of their ideals. Although Freud regarded the ego as acting in the service of the id, other theorists propose that the ego is the central part of the mind and carries out the important functions of helping people find a balance between expressing their inner selves while finding ways to adapt to the world's demands. Psychologists in the area of **ego psychology** believe that the ego plays a central role in actively directing behavior.

Erikson's theory of psychosocial development proposes that it is the ego that matures throughout life as the individual faces particular biological, psychological, and social forces. He defined each point in the ego's development in terms of a push and pull that leads the individual toward a favorable outcome (such as attaining a sense of identity) or an unfavorable outcome (such as not attaining a sense of identity). As each stage is navigated, the individual moves on to the next set of issues following the epigenetic principle, as each stage unfolds in a predetermined order. Although the theory proposes that particular issues are most likely to arise at particular ages, earlier issues may arise at a later point in life, and the later stages may move to the forefront in earlier periods if conditions develop that stimulate the individual to confront those issues. Research based on Erikson's theory includes studies that cover a single stage and those that incorporate all or most of the stages. Of all eight stages, identity and generativity receive the greatest attention, particularly among researchers whose work covers adolescence, emerging adulthood, and midlife.

Identity. Erikson's conception of the stage of identity achievement vs. identity (or role) diffusion portrays adolescents as struggling to define themselves in the face of physical changes associated with puberty, cognitive changes, and particularly role changes where they are expected to find a place for themselves in society.

Starting with this conceptual view, James Marcia (1966) developed the **identity status interview**, which examines the degree of commitment held by the individual to identity issues and the degree of exploration the individual used to arrive at this commitment. The individual is grouped into one of four identity statuses on the basis of this interview: Identity Achievement (strong commitments following a period of exploration), Foreclosed (strong commitments without a period of exploration), Moratorium (actively exploring different commitments), and Identity Diffuse (no strong commitments with or without a period of exploration). The identity status interview expanded on Erikson's theory by showing that people could have strong identities without having given their roles much thought. For example, they may have taken on the views of their parents in religion, politics, or even their choice of career.

Marcia's work on the identity statuses has yielded a wealth of research that elaborated on his initial framework, including hundreds of studies that detail the personalities and behavioral profiles of emerging adults in each of the identity statuses (Kroger & Marcia, 2011). For example, people in the identity achievement status tend to be balanced in their thinking, mature in their relationships to others, and thoughtful about their life options. People in the moratorium status tend to be open and curious, on the positive side, but also anxious, depressed, and low in self-esteem. Individuals who are in the foreclosed status appear to be higher in self-esteem but closed-minded and rigid. Those who are identity diffuse are more likely to engage in delinquent and drug-related behaviors as well as having low self-esteem. Within the identity diffuse statuses, however, there are further distinctions that can be made between the "carefree" diffuse, who do not care about identity issues, and the undifferentiated, who are trying unsuccessfully to arrive at a set of commitments (Schwartz et al., 2011). College-age individuals involved in identity exploration may, at least temporarily, engage in high-risk sexual and driving-related behaviors (Ritchie, Meca, Madrazo, Schwarz, et al., 2013).

The identity status model is a useful one for helping to understand the identity formation process during adolescence and emerging adulthood. However, it is less clear how it can be applied to adults in midlife and beyond. Technically, using the identity status framework,

you could be considered "identity achieved" if you went through a period of exploration during your college years or even your early teens. Some 30 years later, would it still be appropriate for you to retain that same set of commitments despite the many opportunities for change that would have ensued since then? The identity process model, by looking at adult development in terms of identity accommodation, identity assimilation, and balance, makes it possible to describe the adult's position on issues relevant to the sense of self at any point in life. People who retain their adolescent commitments without questioning or challenging them, in this framework, are not identity achieved but instead considered high on identity assimilation (Sneed & Whitbourne, 2003).

Generativity. Midlife adults must also come to terms with issues relating to generativity, according to Erikson's theory. Because Erikson defined generativity as showing care and concern for guiding the next generation, it would follow that parents would be higher in generativity than nonparents. However, not just having children but also successfully parenting them seems to be more consistent with Erikson's views. Peterson et al. (2006) found that, indeed, parents higher in generativity not only felt closer to their college-age children but also had children who were happier, more likely to be able to plan for the future, higher in prosocial personality attributes, and higher in social interest as indicated by their interest in politics (Peterson, 2006), a feature of generative midlife adults as well (Hart, McAdams, Hirsch, & Bauer, 2001). Grandparenting is another way to express generativity, not only by the fact of having grandchildren, but also being involved in mentoring, spending time with them, and strengthening the bonds of mutual family ties (Hebblethwaite & Norris, 2011).

Generativity is not completely selfless, however. According to McAdams (2008), generative behaviors also expand and enrich one's own ego in a process he calls the "redemptive self." By being generative, in other words, you are benefiting your own development as well as the people you are helping. In truly generative behavior, though, the balance shifts more toward concern about others rather than concern about your own personal accomplishments. Along the same lines, Bauer (2008) talks about the "noisy ego" versus the "quiet ego." Bauer proposes that people high on generativity have moved past the phase when their "noisy" ego causes them to focus on their own self-interest and can instead have a "quiet" enough ego to allow them to hear what others need and help without thought or concern of how these actions will benefit them.

Although people high in generativity may be better parents, at least according to some criteria, the idea of the redemptive self suggests that generativity goes beyond even good parenting to extend to concern with larger society. If this is true, then it seems that people high in generativity should also show greater interest in and concern for helping others beyond their own families, such as participating in volunteer work in their communities; in this regard, generativity shares certain features with altruism (Agostinho & Paço, 2012). In research testing whether people who are committed to environmental causes (which may also be seen as reflecting care toward future generations), Matsuba et al. (2012) found that both college students and midlife adults high in generativity were also more likely to be concerned with environmental issues. Similarly, people scoring high on generativity are more likely to believe in, and engage in, environmentally responsible behavior (Urien & Kilbourne, 2011).

Overall Psychosocial Development. Researchers also approach studying Erikson's theory by measuring development along all eight stages simultaneously. In contrast to studies that focus on specific stages, the broad-spectrum approach examines individual differences both in levels of psychosocial development and in the relationships among the stages. According to Erikson, anyone can confront any psychosocial issue at any point in life. Measuring individual differences on all stages at once allows researchers to test this notion.

One of the earliest measures used to investigate psychosocial development across a range of stages was the Inventory of Psychosocial Development (IPD) (Constantinople, 1969), the questionnaire used in the Rochester Adult Longitudinal Study (RALS). The original sample of more than 300 students in the classes of 1965–1968 was followed up in 1977, when they were in their early 30s.

At the same time, a new sample of 300 undergraduates entered the study, making it possible to conduct sequential analyses (Whitbourne & Waterman, 1979). Both of these samples participated again in 1988–1989, when the third undergraduate sample was added. At this point, the sample contained three cohorts of college students and two cohorts of adults in their early 30s (Van Manen & Whitbourne, 1997; Whitbourne, Zuschlag, Elliot, & Waterman, 1992). The most recent follow up took place in 2000–2002 (Whitbourne, Sneed, & Sayer, 2009), when the two oldest cohorts were in their 40s and 50s (Sneed, Whitbourne, Schwartz, & Huang, 2012).

The latest follow-up of the RALS used hierarchical linear modeling (HLM), making it possible to look at how individuals changed over time relative to themselves and to others in the sample. Previous follow-ups relied on comparing the entire sample's means, obscuring those individual change curves. By using HLM, it was possible not only to see how much change occurred but also who was most and who was least likely to change.

One question was whether people who were in a committed relationship right after college would show more or less growth of intimacy in the ensuing decades. As it turned out, those who became involved in marriage or a cohabiting relationship after the age of 31 started out with lower intimacy scores in college. However, over the subsequent two decades, these late-bloomers showed a steeper growth curve than did the individuals who married or cohabited within a few years of college graduation.

Moreover, as you can see in Figure 8.2, the individuals in the 1946 Cohort (who were in college in the 1960s)

FIGURE 8.2

Rochester Adult Longitudinal Study Results on Intimacy vs. Isolation by Relationship Status at Age 31

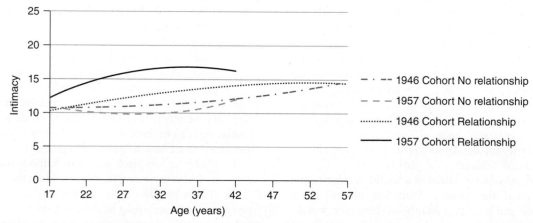

Source: Adapted from Whitbourne, S. K., Sneed, J. R., & Sayer, A. (2009). Psychosocial development from college through midlife: A 34-year sequential study. *Developmental Psychology, 45*, 1328–1340.

showed a different pattern than those in the 1957 Cohort (in college in the 1970s). Within the 1946 cohort, those in a relationship by age 31 started out with higher intimacy scores in college than did those not in a relationship. However, those not in relationships by age 31 showed a steeper growth curve and therefore had reached the same intimacy level as their peers. These trends also occurred for the younger cohort but to an even greater degree.

Similar patterns of "catching up" occurred for people who got a later start in their careers. During college, they had low scores on the Eriksonian quality of industry (identifying with a work ethic); however, in the subsequent 20 years, they showed a steeper increase and eventually caught up with their higher-achieving counterparts.

Figure 8.2 also provides an example of the advantage of conducting sequential analyses. Had only the 1946 cohort been tested over this age span, the results would have looked very different than if the 1957 cohort was tested as well. The data are superior to what would have been obtained through traditional longitudinal methods because they were based on the study of more than one cohort over more than one test occasion.

These findings from the RALS show that continued personality development is not only possible but predictable. Even the psychosocial stages associated with childhood showed continued gains for many of the RALS members during adulthood. The RALS data did not, unfortunately, include the kind of rich personal narratives that investigators can obtain when they test their participants in face-to-face interviews. However, the questions that participants answered about their work and family histories provided descriptive information that could supplement the survey scores. By studying the patterns of life changes, the first author extracted enough descriptive material to identify five patterns of "life pathways" (Whitbourne, 2010). (See Table 8.1.) Others have also used the pathways metaphor to capture the variations that people's lives take as they develop over time (Friedman & Martin, 2011). Clearly, there are times when test scores are unable to capture the complexities of lives as they are lived, a point we will return to later.

The five pathways have a connection to the identity processes we described in Chapter 2 and to which we return later in this chapter. In identity assimilation, individuals attempt to maintain a consistent view of themselves over time. Like those on the Straight and Narrow pathway, people who use identity assimilation also fear change and prefer to think of themselves as stable even when situations might require that they change. Identity accommodation is to the Meandering Way because this identity process involves excessively changing in response to experiences when it would be preferable to maintain some consistency. Identity balance is very much like the Authentic Road; people who use identity balance are able to change flexibly in response to experiences but still maintain consistency of their sense of self over time.

A second longitudinal study of college students, this one focusing on women, began in the 1950s to 1960s

TABLE 8.1
Five Pathways Through Adulthood

Frances Twitty/iStockphoto

Pathway	Description
Authentic road	Achieves solid identity commitments through exploration and change
Triumphant trail	Overcomes challenges Is resilient
Straight and narrow way	Maintains consistent life pattern Is defensive about change
Meandering way	Fails to settle on a course in life Constantly searches for identity
Downward slope	Shows self-defeating behavior Makes poor decisions

Source: Adapted from Whitbourne, S. K. (2010). The search for fulfillment. New York: Ballantine.

by Ravenna Helson and her colleagues at Mills College, a private school in California. Although not originally intended as a study of Eriksonian development, a number of the findings were interpreted in terms of his theory. The study's founders originally intended to study leadership and creativity among college women (Helson, 1967) but, like the RALS, the study's scope continued to expand and it has now included five follow-ups of the sample, who are now about 70 years old.

The findings reported by Helson and her team in the early years presented evidence for considerable personality stability. However, there were several notable exceptions. The Mills women increased in the qualities of assurance, independence, and self-control and decreased on a scale measuring their perceived femininity. There was also evidence of substantial individual differences in personality change patterns, which the investigators linked to variations in level of ego development and identity. For example, women higher in identity at age 43 were more likely to have achieved higher levels of generativity at age 48 (Vandewater, Ostrove, & Stewart, 1997). Similar findings were obtained in a later analysis in which the identity of a woman at age 43 served to predict her well-being at the age of 60 (Helson & Srivastava, 2001). Social roles also influenced the development of women in this sample through late midlife of such qualities as dominance, masculinity/femininity, flexibility, and achievement (Helson & Soto, 2005).

Ego Development.   Closely related to Erikson's notion of psychosocial development is Jane Loevinger's (1976) view of the ego, which incorporates how people think as well as the structure of personality (see Figure 8.3). Loevinger defined the ego as the structure within personality that attempts to synthesize, master, and interpret experiences. She regarded the ego as involved in the ability to regulate impulses, relate to others, achieve self-understanding, and think about experiences. The development of the ego proceeds in a series of stages that move from lower to higher levels in these characteristics.

FIGURE 8.3

Stages in Loevinger's (1976) Theory

- Conformist stage
- Conscientious-
  conformist level
- Conscientious stage
- Individualistic level
- Autonomous stage
- Integrated stage

Kyu Oh/iStockphoto

Individuals in the first, or Conformist, stage have only a very basic understanding of themselves, other people, and the reasons for following society's rules. They have simple views of right and wrong, and it is hard for them to understand why others think and feel the way they do. Loevinger believed that most adults fall into the second stage, known as the Conscientious-Conformist stage. Developmentally, this is the stage when people first have an internalized sense of right and wrong and are able to be aware of their own motives as well as those of other people. Next is the Conscientious stage, when people develop a true conscience, one that is an internalized understanding of society's rules and the reasons for those rules. People in the Conscientious stage are also able to have insight into their own emotions as well as the emotional needs of others.

The final three stages involve an increasing sense of individuality and self-determination. In the Individualistic stage, an appreciation and respect for individuality emerges. Next, people in the Autonomous stage have even more clearly articulated inner standards. They recognize and appreciate the complexities of their own behavior and that of others. People in the Autonomous stage are also better able to live with uncertainty (somewhat like those in the postformal stage, which we described in Chapter 7). Finally, the Integrated stage, which Loevinger proposed would be reached by relatively few people, is one in which the individual has a clear sense of self, is able to recognize inner conflicts, and highly values individuality. In this stage, the individual is able to achieve the expression of the true "inner self," much as proposed by Maslow in his conception of self-actualization (Pfaffenberger, 2007).

To measure ego development, Loevinger devised the Sentence Completion Test (Hy & Loevinger, 1996), which contains 36 sentence openings (e.g., "Raising a family … ", "When a child will not join in group activities … "). A trained rater, using a manual that lists matches for each stage, scores each item individually before arriving at a composite score. This means that the items are assessed independently from each other rather than, as in other approaches to ego development, considering how they relate to each other (Thorne, 1993).

Loevinger's theory combines ego psychology with moral development, and in that sense is not a "typical" psychodynamically based theory (Westen, 1998). In fact, scores on Loevinger's measure of ego development have a strong cognitive component. Researchers conducting a large-scale analysis of studies on more than 5,600 participants found that there were strong correlations between ego level and intellectual abilities. People at higher levels of ego development, according to Loevinger's theory, are also more likely to have high scores on personality variables such as assertiveness, conformity, and fearfulness (Cohn &

Westenberg, 2004). However, relatively few people reach the highest stages, at least as judged by the Sentence Completion Test (Pfaffenberger, 2011).

Vaillant's Theory of Defense Mechanisms

The psychodynamic theory proposed by George Vaillant (2000) emphasizes the development of defense mechanisms over the course of adulthood (see Table 8.2). As we mentioned earlier, intended to help protect the conscious mind from knowing about unconscious desires, defense mechanisms are strategies that people use almost automatically as protection against morally unacceptable urges and desires.

Unlike Freud, who proposed that personality is invariant after childhood, Vaillant regards the ego defense mechanisms as becoming increasingly adaptive in adulthood, helping people cope with life's challenges ranging from stress at work to discrimination to marital unhappiness. Over time, Vaillant proposed, people use increasingly mature and adaptive defenses and fewer immature and maladaptive ways of minimizing anxiety. Immature defense mechanisms include acting out and denial.

You can understand these differences by considering these two scenarios. In acting out (an immature defense), you react when you are angry by throwing something, slamming a door, or hitting your fist against a wall. These actions may temporarily relieve your anger but can also cause you (or your possessions) harm. You also will look quite ridiculous to your friends if you throw such a fit of rage in front of them. Using a more mature defense mechanism, such as humor in the face of anger, would help you feel better and avoid the social and practical costs of rash action.

The use of immature defense mechanisms becomes rarer with age, as Vaillant discovered in his Study of Adult Development (1993). In this study, Vaillant and his research team investigated the use of defense mechanisms in three diverse samples of individuals. The first consisted of men in what was known as the Harvard Grant Study. Begun in 1938, this study was intended to characterize the physical and psychological functioning of Harvard undergraduates on a wide variety of measures. Over the course of the subsequent decades, it continued to follow the men as they made their way through the early and middle years of life. Men in the second group, called the Core City sample, were a socioeconomically and racially diverse group chosen as a comparison to the Harvard men. In order to extend the findings beyond men, Vaillant eventually recruited a sample of women from a study originally focused on gifted children. The women in this sample were interviewed again for the purpose of the defense mechanism study when they were in their late 70s.

The initial set of findings provided evidence within each of the three samples for a positive relationship between maturity of defenses and various outcome measures. For instance, Core City men who used immature defenses (such as acting out) were more likely to experience alcohol problems, unstable marriages, and antisocial behavior (Soldz & Vaillant, 1998).

Other longitudinal investigations support these findings. Cramer (2003) conducted a 24-year longitudinal

TABLE 8.2
Categories of Defense Mechanisms Identified by Vaillant

Category	Examples
Psychotic	*Delusional projection*—attributing one's own bizarre ideas and feelings to others *Denial*—disclaiming the existence of a feeling, action, or event *Distortion*—significantly exaggerating and altering the reality of feelings and events
Immature	*Projection*—attributing unacceptable ideas and feelings to others *Hypochondriasis*—expressing psychological conflict as exaggerated physical complaints *Acting out*—engaging in destructive behavior that expresses inner conflicts
Neurotic	*Displacement*—transferring unacceptable feelings from the true to a safer object *Repression*—forgetting about a troubling feeling or event *Reaction formation*—expressing the opposite of one's true feelings
Mature	*Altruism*—turning unacceptable feelings into behavior that is helpful to others *Sublimation*—expressing unacceptable feelings in productive activity *Humor*—being able to laugh at an unpleasant or disturbing feeling or situation

Source: Adapted from Vaillant, G. E. (2000). Adaptive mental mechanisms: Their role in a positive psychology. *American Psychologist, 55*, 89–98.

study in which she followed more than 150 men and women from early to middle adulthood. As in the Vaillant studies, age was associated with the use of more mature defenses. In the subsequent 20 years from middle to later adulthood, Cramer and her colleagues found that the maladaptive defense mechanisms used by people with a narcissistic personality (whose gratification depends on the admiration of others) became less psychologically healthy (Cramer & Jones, 2008). Consistently, these studies show that older adults are able to manage their emotions through the use of mature defense mechanisms that involve the control of negative emotions or trying to put the situation into perspective (Diehl, Coyle, & Labouvie-Vief, 1996; Labouvie-Vief & Medler, 2002).

The general pattern that emerges is that older adults cope with anxiety, stress, or frustration by reacting in less self-destructive or emotional ways than they would have when they were younger. Rather than getting frustrated and giving up on a solution, older adults are more apt to try and understand the situation and figure out a way around it. They can suppress their negative feelings or channel them into productive activities. By contrast, younger people (including adolescents and young adults) are more likely to react to psychologically demanding situations by acting out against others, projecting their anger onto others, or regressing to more primitive forms of behavior.

Consistent gender differences have also emerged in studies of defense mechanisms and coping (Diehl, et al., 1996; Labouvie-Vief & Medler, 2002). Regardless of age, women are more likely to avoid unpleasant or stressful situations, to blame themselves when things go wrong, and to seek the support of others. Men are more likely to externalize their feelings and to use reaction formation, a defense mechanism in which people act in a way that is opposite to their unconscious feelings.

Adult Attachment Theory

Adult attachment theory proposes that the early bond between the infant and caregiver set the stage for all of the individual's later significant relationships. Through interactions with their caregivers (usually the mother), infants develop **attachment styles** that are mental representations or frameworks about what to expect in a relationship. These mental representations form models not only of relationships, but also of the self, and so they are important for understanding both an individual's personality and close relationships.

According to adult attachment theory, if people feel safe and cared for, they will carry forward into their adult relationships a **secure attachment style** in which they feel confident about themselves and confident that others

Rafal Strzechowski/Age Fotostock America, Inc.

People who are insecurely attached may continue to experience relationship difficulties in adulthood.

will treat them well. People who were either abandoned as infants or felt that they would be, develop an **anxious attachment style** in which they imagine that their adult partners will also abandon them. Being neglected in infancy may also produce adults who show the **avoidant attachment style** with a fear of abandonment so intense that they stay away from close relationships altogether.

There is very little research specifically on aging and adult attachment style in samples, in part because it is seen as a theory about how people choose and relate to romantic partners relatively earlier in adulthood. In fact, we will explore the implications of attachment style for long-term relationship satisfaction in Chapter 9.

Older adults do appear less likely to experience anxious types of attachment in comparison with younger adults (Segal, Needham, & Coolidge, 2009). Moreover, older adults who reported secure attachment with their parents state that they are currently happier on a daily basis than those who reported less secure attachment (Consedine & Magai, 2003). Although attachment style might seem to be a stable feature of personality, there is evidence that it can change even in as short a period as a few years (Zhang & Labouvie-Vief, 2004).

Looking at attachment from a different perspective, Cicirelli (2010) examined the numbers of individuals that older adults named as serving attachment-related functions in their lives. These functions include being protected from harm, providing emotional security, and serving as a "safe haven" during times of stress. Older adults may have fewer attachment figures in their social networks, according to this study, but those they have fit into a wider range of roles. Rather than seeing only their spouses or partners as serving these attachment functions, older adults turn to adult children, deceased spouses, in-laws, physicians, caregivers, clergy, and animals.

TRAIT APPROACHES

When you think about how to describe the personality of a friend, relative, or coworker, you most likely begin by listing a set of a characteristics or qualities that seem to fit the person's observable behavior. These characteristics typically take the form of adjectives such as "generous," or "outgoing," or perhaps, "quiet" and "unfriendly." Trait theories of personality propose that adjectives such as these capture the essence of the individual's psychological makeup based on the concept of the **trait**, which is a stable, enduring disposition that persists over time.

The **trait perspective** in personality is based on the assumption that the organization of the personal dispositions known as traits guide the individual's behavior. Trait theory is also increasingly viewed in terms of genetic theories of personality, which suggest that the enduring nature of personality traits over time reflect the fact that they are at least partially inherited (Bouchard, 2004).

The most generally accepted trait theory in the field of personality and aging is based on Costa and McCrae's proposal that there are five major dimensions to personality (Figure 8.4). The **Five-Factor Model (FFM)** (sometimes called the "Big Five") is a theory intended to capture all the essential characteristics of personality in a set of five broad dispositions. Each disposition has six subscales or "facets." To characterize an individual completely requires knowing how that person rates on each of these 30 facets. The tool used to test the FFM is the **Neuroticism-Extraversion-Openness Personality Inventory–Revised (NEO-PI-R)**, a questionnaire containing 240 items measuring the 30 facets (Costa & McCrae, 1992). Clinicians may use the NEO-PI-R to supplement other diagnostic instruments because it provides a measure of personality separate from psychopathology. Researchers use the NEO-PI-R to chart changes in personality over time, or to study the relationship between personality and other behaviors, including those relevant to health status.

The five traits in the FFM are neuroticism, extraversion, openness to experience (or "openness"), agreeableness, and conscientiousness (you can remember these as spelling "OCEAN" or "CANOE"). Each trait name closely fits its meaning in everyday conversation—people high in neuroticism tend to worry a great deal, those who are extraverted are outgoing and sociable, being open to experience means that you are willing to entertain new ideas, having high agreeableness means you get along well with others, and being conscientious means that you attend to detail and tend not to procrastinate.

Within the trait categories, where you stand within the six facets can make a difference in how your personality is reflected in your behavior. For example, within the extraversion trait, people can be either high or low in the facet of warmth, and high or low on the facet of gregariousness. Being high on both would mean you genuinely like to be around people and relate easily to others. Being low on warmth but high on gregariousness would mean that you seek out being with others but that people find it hard to get to know you very well.

Research on Aging and the Five-Factor Model

Studies based on the scales of the Five-Factor Model and aging show a high degree of consistency over time throughout adulthood, with greater consistency among increasingly older groups of adults. However, the consistency between scores obtained at different measurement points becomes smaller the longer the time interval between them (Roberts & DelVecchio, 2000). This means that people maintain their relative positions along the traits in comparison to their age peers; the "highs" stay high and the "lows" stay low. If you had high neuroticism scores as a young adult, you would continue your high levels of worry, anxiety, and general malaise throughout your midlife years and beyond.

Although people may maintain their relative positions along each of the traits, their mean scores may undergo change across adulthood. In a meta-analysis of 92 longitudinal studies, Roberts (2006) reported that individuals increase in social dominance, conscientiousness, emotional stability (the opposite of neuroticism), social vitality (a facet of extraversion) and openness to experience through age 40. Social vitality and openness decreased after this point, but agreeableness increased. These findings are consistent

Ikon Images/Alamy

FIGURE 8.4

Five-Factor Model of Personality

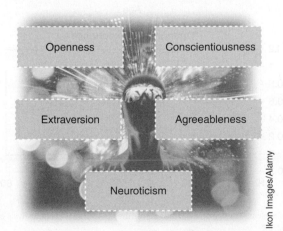

Openness · Conscientiousness · Extraversion · Agreeableness · Neuroticism

with the often-cited comment by early psychologist William James (1842–1910) that personality is "set in plaster" by the age of 30. However, the meta-analysis also showed that four out of the six traits continued to change in middle and later adulthood (see Figure 8.5). The authors concluded that "this meta-analysis clearly contradicts the notion that there is a specific age at which personality traits stop changing" (p. 14).

It is also important to understand how people's personalities influence their life choices, which in turn affect their personalities. According to the **correspondence principle**, people experience particular life events that reflect their personality traits; once these events occur, they further affect people's personalities (Roberts, Donnellan, & Hill, 2013). A person who is high on extraversion is more likely than a person who is more introverted to choose

FIGURE 8.5

Results of Meta-Analysis Conducted by Roberts et al. (2006) on Six Personality Traits

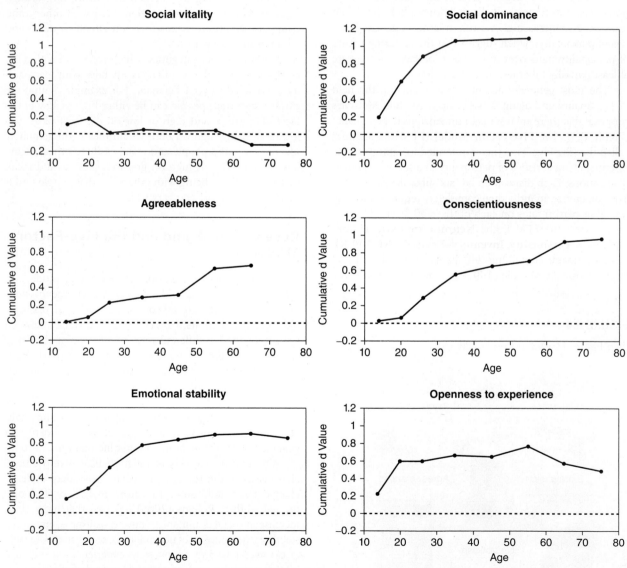

Source: Roberts, B. W., Walton, K. E., & Viechtbauer, W. (2006). Patterns of mean-level change in personality traits across the life course: A meta-analysis of longitudinal studies. *Psychological Bulletin, 132*(1), 1–25. doi: 10.1037/0033-2909.132.1.1

social pursuits at night or on weekends. Being in these social situations may, in turn, promote further growth in extraversion. According to this principle, then, personality stability is enhanced by the active choices that people make rather than by any intrinsic likelihood of traits remaining static over time.

Health and Personality Traits

The idea that personality traits could be related to significant health problems and health-related behaviors originated when researchers discovered what became known as the **Type A behavior pattern**, a collection of traits that include being highly competitive, impatient, feeling a strong sense of time urgency, and highly achievement-oriented. First identified by cardiologists Meyer Friedman and R.H. Rosenman (1974), the Type A behavior pattern became known as a major risk factor for heart disease, particularly when people high in the Type A behavior pattern also had high levels of hostility (Suarez, Williams, Kuhn, & Zimmerman, 1991).

The Type A–hostility–cardiovascular disease connection was for many years considered a case of correlation not equaling causation. It was only when researchers obtained longitudinal data that they were able to overcome the limitations of correlational approaches to the problem. In one important study, researchers followed over 300 healthy men for a 10-year period, measuring their hostility, depression, and anger as well as physiological risk factors for heart disease (Boyle, Jackson, & Suarez, 2007). The men higher in hostility and more prone to experience anger also showed increases in coronary heart disease risk.

High levels of anxiety may also serve as risk factors for cardiovascular disease. In comparing the personality factors of anxiety, general levels of distress, and anger, researchers investigating predictors of cardiovascular heart disease over a 14-year period found that, in particular, people high in the trait of anxiety also were more likely to develop subsequent illness, even taking into account their other risk factors such as smoking, cholesterol, BMI, and blood pressure (Kubzansky, Cole, Kawachi, Vokonas, & Sparrow, 2006).

The relationship between personality and health may go back as far as childhood. Researchers have observed relationships between low scores in childhood on the trait of conscientiousness and higher death rates in adulthood (Friedman et al., 1995). Being low in conscientiousness might lead people to be more careless about many aspects of life, including control over diet and exercise patterns, leading them to develop higher BMIs. In turn, they are more likely to gain weight during adolescence and early

adulthood (Pulkki-Raback, Elovainio, Kivimaki, Raitakari, & Keltikangas-Jarvinen, 2005).

The trait of conscientiousness continues to relate to greater weight gains during adulthood, particularly in women, placing them at risk for weight-related diseases. One 14-year longitudinal study showed a relationship between women's scores on neuroticism and weight gains (Brummett et al., 2006). People low in conscientiousness and high on neuroticism also have higher likelihoods of cigarette smoking (Terracciano & Costa, 2004). High neuroticism scores, particularly on the facet of vulnerability, relate to high rates of heroin and cocaine use among adults. Marijuana users, particularly young adults, score high on openness to experience and low on agreeableness and conscientiousness (Terracciano, Löckenhoff, Crum, Bienvenu, & Costa, 2008).

Conscientiousness continues to play a role in mortality in later adulthood as well. Among a sample of more than 1,000 Medicare recipients ranging from 65 to 100 years of age followed over a 3- to 5-year period, conscientiousness, particularly self-discipline (a facet of conscientiousness), predicted lower mortality risk over a 3-year period. As the study's authors point out, it is possible that high levels of self-discipline relate to a greater tendency to be proactive in engaging in behaviors that are protective of health and to avoid those behaviors that are damaging to health (Weiss & Costa, 2005). Reinforcing these findings, research from a large sample of Italian adults found that lower levels of conscientiousness (including impulsivity) were associated with lower levels of high-density lipoprotein (the "good" cholesterol) (Sutin et al., 2010) and interleukin-6, a protein that you have already learned is important to bolstering immune function (Sutin et al., 2009). Similarly, research from the National Survey of Midlife Development in the United States (MIDUS) showed that people high in conscientiousness and neuroticism were likely to have low IL-6 levels at least in part due to their lower rates of obesity (Turiano, Mroczek, Moynihan, & Chapman, 2013). Being high on neuroticism may, then, have health benefits when paired with high levels of conscientiousness.

Conscientiousness may, then, exert its positive effect on health through its link with prevention-related behaviors. Lodi-Smith et al. (2010) used structural equation modeling to analyze the relationships among conscientiousness as rated by the participant and someone close to the participant ("observer-rated"), and self-reported engagement in preventive and risky health-related behaviors, education, and self-reported health. People higher in conscientiousness engaged in more preventive behaviors and fewer high-risk health behaviors (smoking, excessive drinking). Because self-report bias may lead people to rate themselves high in conscientiousness and positive health-related behaviors, the observer ratings were an important data source in this study. In fact, people high in observer-rated conscientiousness actually did engage in fewer risky health-related behaviors.

Lower mortality is also related to other personality traits. In a sample of more than 2,300 individuals followed since 1958 in the Baltimore Longitudinal Study of Aging, longevity was associated with high scores on conscientiousness, low scores on neuroticism, and high scores on the activity facet of extraversion (Terracciano, Löckenhoff, Zonderman, Ferrucci, & Costa, 2008). High levels of openness, particularly emotional awareness and curiosity, also seem related to lower mortality rates, even after controlling for educational levels (Jonassaint et al., 2007). Insight into these findings came from a study examining personality traits and medical care utilization. Among older adults, rates of admission to hospital emergency departments were higher for individuals who were less agreeable and more extraverted (Chapman et al., 2009).

Openness to experience also relates to early life experiences. In one study, young adults high in openness reported a higher number of stressful life events in childhood. However, individuals with high openness scores showed less physiological reactivity to a laboratory stressor in which they were asked to discuss a recent highly stressful event. Unlike their low openness peers, those high in openness even showed a slight boost in positive affect while experiencing the stressor (Williams, Rau, Cribbet, & Gunn, 2009).

Personality traits may also be related to risk of developing cognitive disorders, including Alzheimer's disease (see Figure 8.6). An investigation of nearly 1,000 Catholic nuns and priests indicated that high conscientiousness while alive correlated with lower rates of Alzheimer's disease. Even among those whose brains showed a high degree of

pathology upon autopsy, high levels of conscientiousness seemed to serve as a protective factor against the experience of cognitive symptoms associated with the disease (Wilson, Schneider, Arnold, Bienias, & Bennett, 2007). High levels of neuroticism in midlife also appear to be predictive of an earlier onset of the disease but only in women (Archer et al., 2009).

High levels of hostility in early adulthood may pose a risk factor not only for heart disease but for the development of depression during the ensuing years. Alumni of the University of North Carolina tested in college were followed up when they averaged of 47 years old. College students with high hostility scores who remained high in hostility were at a significantly greater risk for developing depression in midlife. Higher hostility in college was also associated with riskier health-related behaviors, including smoking and drinking. Those students also were more likely to experience negative changes in family life. Changes in hostility over the study period also predicted obesity, failure to exercise, high-fat diets, social isolation, poor health, and, for women, lower income (Siegler et al., 2003).

Clearly, personality factors are integral aspects of the biopsychosocial model of development in adulthood and old age. Traits and behavior patterns that have their origins in inherited predispositions or through early life experiences influence the health of the individual through a variety of direct and indirect pathways. However, although personality traits may be an inherent part of "who" you are, they can modulate and change over adulthood (Staudinger & Kunzmann, 2005) even as they influence some of the most basic components of your ability to remain healthy.

SOCIAL COGNITIVE APPROACHES

As we have just seen, personality psychologists focus in large part on how people's adaptation and dispositions change through life. There is also growing interest in the factors that cause people to feel emotions such as happiness or sadness. Researchers also investigate the "whys" of behavior, or motivation. Traditionally, emotion and motivation have long captured the attention of psychologists, and the area of social cognition and aging is no exception.

Some of the growing interest in emotions stems from a desire to help people feel better about themselves and their experiences, and some is based on a resurgence of a topic that has always been within the domain of psychology. In looking at aging and emotions in particular, researchers are also gaining an increased appreciation for the ways that older adults are able to focus their attention on the positive, rather than negative, aspects of their daily lives. Research on motivation and aging helps provide insight into people's goals, desires, and needs and how they change through life.

FIGURE 8.6

Relationship Between Personality and Health

- Cardiovascular risk factors related to Type A behavior and anxiety
- Lower BMI related to higher levels of conscientiousness
- Drug use and smoking related to lower levels of conscientiousness
- Lower mortality related to higher levels of openness
- Higher risk of Alzheimer's disease related to low conscientiousness and high neuroticism

John Slater/Photodisc/ Getty Images, Inc.

FIGURE 8.7

Socioemotional Selectivity Theory

Informational rewards (gain knowledge)

Sense that time is running out

Emotional rewards (maximize positive feelings)

Daniel Bendjy/iStockphoto

According to one viewpoint in adult development and aging, emotions and motivation are intimately linked. **Socioemotional selectivity theory** proposes that throughout adulthood, people structure the nature and range of their relationships to maximize gains and minimize risks (see Figure 8.7) (Charles & Carstensen, 2010). According to this theory, people look for different rewards from their interactions with others as they approach the later years of their lives.

Essentially, this theory proposes that there are two types of functions served by interpersonal relationships. One is an informational function. Relationships that serve this function provide you with important knowledge that you would not otherwise have. For instance, when you moved into your college dormitory, you probably sought out the people who seemed to know the most about where to buy the items needed for your new life, such as textbooks, school supplies, and the cheapest and best cup of coffee. These friends served an informational function in your life. The second role of relations with others is emotional. Relationships that serve this function contribute to your sense of well-being. In your friendships that serve a relational function, you seek to find people who help you feel good about yourself and your life. These are the people you turn to when you're feeling lonely, depressed, or stressed in hopes that they will make you feel better. In psychological terms, we would say that through this process you are engaging in **affect regulation**, or increasing your feelings of happiness and well-being.

Socioemotional selectivity theory proposes that as people grow older, they become more focused on the emotional functions of relationships and less interested in the informational function. They want to spend time with the people who make them feel good. This shift, according to the theory, occurs as people become increasingly sensitive to the inevitable ending of their lives and recognize that they are "running out of time." It is not aging so much as this recognition of less time left to live that triggers the shift in what people want out of their interactions. Young adults, when placed either under artificial time constraints through experimental manipulations or under real time constraints, show similar preferences toward the emotional functions of social interactions as do older adults (Carstensen, Isaacowitz, & Charles, 1999).

Endings of any kind, whether the end of life or the end of a chapter in your life, bring out strong emotions and cause you to want to spend time with the people who have been closest to you. Think of times when significant life events have come to an end, such as when you graduated from high school and said goodbye to your classmates. Knowing that you did not have much time left to spend with these people, you wanted to make the most out of the time you did have.

Similarly, the desire to maximize emotional rewards leads adults increasingly to prefer spending time with people who are familiar to them rather than seeking out new friends and acquaintances. Family and long-time friends are the people who will serve these positive emotional functions of self-validation and affect regulation. Older adults are less interested in meeting new people and broadening their social horizons because they prefer to maximize the emotional and minimize the information functions of their relationships (Lang & Carstensen, 2002).

As you think about this theory, it may be helpful to reflect on your own friendship patterns. You may be at a point in your life right now where spending time with friends and acquaintances is more important than spending time with your family. Your number of Facebook friends may well be over 500 and include many people you have not spoken with for months, even years. As you navigate your way through your postgraduate years, you will most likely find that the number of people in your social network dwindles, and you are left with a much smaller network of close friends and family. As part of this transition, you will go through a "weeding out" process where you focus on maintaining the positive relationships and removing (or "unfriending") the negative ones.

One intriguing approach to testing socioemotional selectivity is taken by Isaacowitz and his colleagues, who use eye-tracking instruments to examine the way in which older and younger adults approach stimuli varying in their positive emotional value. In one investigation (Isaacowitz, Wadlinger, Goren, & Wilson, 2006), older and younger adults were compared in their eye movements when viewing faces conveying happy, sad, and neutral emotional expressions. Older adults were less likely than younger adults to look at parts of the face conveying anger and

According to socioemotional selectivity theory, older adults prefer to spend time with the people close to them in their lives.

sadness, and more likely to look at the parts conveying happiness. This study's findings imply that older adults would prefer, literally, to "accentuate the positive" when it comes to reading other people's facial expressions. Subsequent research has shown that older adults with higher levels of cognitive functioning are more likely to focus on positive images in an experimental manipulation that put them in a bad mood (Isaacowitz, Toner, & Neupert, 2009).

The findings on socioemotional selectivity are not consistent, however, in supporting the idea of a "positivity bias" among older adults. In a meta-analysis of a large number of studies comparing younger and older adults, Murphy and Isaacowitz (2008) observed that both older and younger adults showed a preference for positive emotional stimuli. Consistent with the theory, older adults were more likely to avoid negative emotional stimuli. There may also be cultural factors involved in the relationship between age and a positivity bias. Among a Chinese sample, older adults looked away from, not toward, happy faces (Fung et al., 2008).

It is also possible that although older adults may prefer looking at positive images, their attempts at affect regulation are not always successful. Older adults may display this positive-looking bias, but not experience positive affect. Consequently, SST may not be able to explain entirely which factors account for the experience of positive emotional states in older adults (Isaacowitz, 2012).

We do know that the intensity of emotion experienced by an individual does not change over adulthood (Carstensen & Turk-Charles, 1994). Older adults can experience strong emotions when prompted with relevant stimuli. In one investigation of age differences in emotional reactivity, older adults were compared with younger adults in their reactions to movies with specific, age-relevant themes intended to provoke sadness (Kunzmann & Gruhn,

2005). Older adults felt appropriate levels of sadness as acutely as did young adults to the depiction of situations appropriate for their age group, such as loss associated with bereavement and chronic illness.

Nevertheless, it seems that older adults have an advantage in that they seem to react more slowly in emotionally provoking situations (Wieser, Muhlberger, Kenntner-Mabiala, & Pauli, 2006). Rather than fly into a fit of rage when irked, an older adult may be more likely to think twice and maintain emotional control (Charles & Carstensen, 2010). This may be because older adults are better able to regulate their emotions after being exposed to negative stimuli more quickly than are younger adults (Larcom & Isaacowitz, 2009). They may also be less likely to report negative affect, as suggested by a longitudinal study of more than 2,800 adults studied from 1971 to 1994 (Charles, Reynolds, & Gatz, 2001).

Being less perturbed by emotional stimuli may also help older adults maintain their cognitive focus (Samanez-Larkin, Robertson, Mikels, Carstensen, & Gotlib, 2009). If you are better able to think logically and maintain your "cool," you will be less likely to forget something or slip up and make a mistake. Older adults have perhaps learned through the years that there is value in stepping back and not becoming highly aroused when something upsetting has happened (Magai, Consedine, Krivoshekova, Kudadjie-Gyamfi, & McPherson, 2006).

As is true for identity assimilation, a process that causes people to minimize negative information, the desire to focus on the positive implied in socioemotional selectivity theory can have undesirable consequences. There are times when it is necessary to focus on the possibility of negative outcomes, particularly in the area of health. If you just refuse to think about the need to change your health habits when your medical provider tells you to do so, you are likely to run into problems. It does appear, however, that older adults can switch their focus when failing to make the right health-related decision could have unfavorable consequences (Luckenhoff & Carstensen, 2007).

COGNITIVE PERSPECTIVE

The cognitive perspective views people as driven by the desire to predict and control their experiences. Emerging from this perspective are cognitive self theories, which propose that people regard events in their lives from the standpoint of how relevant these are to their own sense of self. The concept of self-efficacy is an example of the cognitive perspective. People high in self-efficacy believe that they can be successful, and this belief can stimulate them to higher performance than they would otherwise show.

Ryan McVay/Getty Images, Inc.

Possible selves

• We are motivated to achieve a hoped-for self and avoid a feared self

Coping and control

• Older adults may be more rather than less capable of coping with stress

Identity process theory

• Identity balance and assimilation help older adults maintain self-esteem
• Identity accommodation is related to poorer self-esteem and cognitive performance

FIGURE 8.8

Theories Within the Cognitive Perspective

Cognitive perspective theories also place emphasis on coping, the mechanisms that people use to manage stress (see Figure 8.8).

Specific theories about aging and personality based on the cognitive perspective place importance on the ways that people interpret their experiences and understand themselves over time. An important principle of the cognitive perspective is the idea that people do not always view themselves realistically. In part, this is because people strive to maintain a sense of themselves as consistent (Baumeister, 1996, 1997). In other words, most people prefer to see themselves as stable and predictable (even if they are not). Another basic tendency is for people to view their abilities and personal qualities in a positive light (Baumeister, Bratslavsky, Finkenauer, & Vohs, 2001). These ideas are important to keep in mind as you read about the views about aging represented by the cognitive perspective.

Possible Selves Theory

The **possible selves** model proposes that the individual's view of the self, or self-schema, guides the choice and pursuit of future endeavors (Markus & Nurius, 1986). The possible self means literally just that: what are you now, and what *could* you be in the future? These thoughts about the self can motivate you to act in certain ways so that you achieve your "hoped-for" possible self, or the person you would like to be. These self-conceptions about the person you will be in the future continue to shift as you develop throughout adulthood. People can remain hopeful of change until well into their later years (Smith & Freund, 2002). Increasingly important as you get older is your health-related possible self, meaning your hope that you will remain in good shape and free of disease (Frazier, Johnson, Gonzalez, & Kafka, 2002; Hooker & Kaus, 1994). A dreaded possible self is the opposite of the hoped-for possible self. With regard to health, most people

would rather not become ill and so they will take action to avoid that outcome.

According to possible selves theory, people are motivated to strive for a hoped-for possible self and will attempt to avoid a dreaded or feared possible self. To the extent that they are successful in this process, positive feelings of life satisfaction are theorized to emerge. People think of themselves in a negative light and view their lives negatively when they are unable to realize a hoped-for possible self or to avoid the dreaded possible self. For instance, you probably feel better when your grades confirm your possible self as a good student and study harder to avoid the dreaded self of a person who fails out of college.

However, people have ways to protect themselves from these negative self-evaluations. One tactic is to revise the possible self to avoid future disappointment and frustration if experiences suggest that the possible self may not be achievable. You may realize that you will not be a straight A student if your grades include a mix of As and Bs (or lower grades), so you revise your possible self accordingly. You will probably feel better about yourself in the long run if you do so even though you may continue to strive for good grades. A similar process seems to be at play for older adults. In one study, those older adults who underestimated their future selves (in both the physical and social domains) had higher well-being a year later than those who overestimated their future selves (Cheng, Fung, & Chan, 2009). By lowering their expectations, they evaluated more positively the outcomes they did achieve.

Coping and Control

Adult development researchers are interested in the field of aging and sense of personal control in part, based on a popular belief that adults undergo a loss of the feeling that they control what happens to them as they with age. Studies carried out within the National Survey of Midlife

Development in the United States (MIDUS) showed that contrary to the popular myth, older adults retain the feeling of being in control of their lives despite being aware of the constraints they may encounter. They do so by viewing their resources and potential positively rather than focusing on losses (Plaut, Markus, & Lachman, 2003).

The cognitive approach to stress emphasizes the role of perceptions as determining whether an event will be viewed as a threat which, in turn, determines whether it is viewed as stressful. The experience of **stress** occurs when you perceive that the situation overwhelms your ability to manage effectively in that situation. **Coping** refers to the actions people take to reduce stress. There are two main forms of coping. In **problem-focused coping**, people attempt to reduce their stress by changing something about the situation. Conversely, in **emotion-focused coping**, people attempt to reduce their stress by changing the ways they think about the situation. Other methods of coping fall in between these two, such as seeking social support, a coping method that involves both taking action (by talking to other people) and attempting to feel better (which may result from talking to other people).

There is no one best way to cope, because for situations that cannot be changed, people only become more stressed if they keep trying to use problem-focused coping, particularly as their efforts deplete their coping resources. For situations that can be changed, however, using emotion-focused coping would mean that you fail to take advantage of steps to improve the situation that would cause it to be less of a problem in the future. For example, if you have a number of pressing deadlines, simply wishing they would go away will not be an effective means of coping, because by missing the deadlines, you create further problems for yourself.

When you cope successfully with a stressful situation, your mood improves and you have a higher sense of well-being (Lachman, Rosnick, Röcke, Bosworth, & Hertzog, 2009). The process seems to be reciprocal—people who feel better also cope more successfully. One longitudinal investigation of coping in midlife adults followed over a 10-year period found that people who were less depressed are more likely to resolve problematic situations successfully.

Being in good health and having extensive social networks also contribute to successful coping (Brennan, Schutte, & Moos, 2006). It is not only the number of people in their social network, but also the quality of social support that can help older people feel more satisfied with their lives (Berg, Hassing, McClearn, & Johansson, 2006). Think of how this process applies in your own life; by having others regard you positively, it is likely that you will develop an enhanced sense of self-esteem, which in turn has positive effects on your subjective health, which in turn enhances your well-being, and so on.

Thus, social support and relationships with others have an influence on feelings of well-being by reinforcing the view that you are valued. At the same time, being concerned about family and having a sense of responsibility for children and other family members seems to have additional adaptive value. In one investigation of Australians ranging from 61 to 95 years of age, sense of belonging and concern about family predicted high scores on a measure assessing reasons for living (Kissane & McLaren, 2006). Sense of mastery, particularly for men, also seems to play a key role in influencing the relationship between social support and perceived stress (Gadalla, 2009).

The objective nature of people's life circumstances may place constrain people's coping abilities, such as in cases when people are unable to afford their basic life necessities (Diener, Oishi, & Lucas, 2003). However, coping can help individuals to withstand even very stressful life events such as personal illness and death or illness of a friend or family member (Hardy, Concato, & Gill, 2004).

People who are characteristically able to cope with challenging life events are said to be high in **resilience**, or the ability to recover from stress. This point was demonstrated among a sample of older adult widows and widowers followed intensively over a 6-week period while they rated their daily experiences of stressful events and emotional reactions (Ong, Bergeman, Bisconti, & Wallace, 2006). The measure of resilience used in this study tapped such qualities as the respondent's ability to overcome negative emotions and adapt to new situations. The more resilient individuals were able to maintain a positive mood even on days when they experienced high degrees of stress.

Furthermore, the type of coping people use may reflect their perceived sense of the ability to reduce stress. Older individuals with higher levels of self-efficacy are more likely to use problem-focused coping, compared to those who use emotion-focused coping, who are more likely to rate themselves high both in social support and perceived stress (Trouillet, Gana, Lourel, & Fort, 2009).

Religion also plays a role in adapting to difficult life circumstances, serving as another important coping resource for many older adults (Van Ness & Larson, 2002). Furthermore, cultures and nations vary in their norms or expectations for experiencing emotions. For example, people in China have the lowest frequency and intensity of both positive and negative emotions compared to people living in the United States, Australia, and Taiwan (Eid & Diener, 2001).

Although some discussions of coping in later life regard older adults as passive rather than active copers, it is not necessarily a given that as people get older they adopt a fatalistic approach to managing their fortunes or that they become ineffective copers. A study of the victims of the 2005 Hurricane Katrina that devastated New Orleans showed that older and younger adults were equally effective in engaging in coping strategies to manage their responses to the disaster (Cherry, Silva, & Galea, 2009).

Thus, older adults can show initiative in managing their situations and making efforts to alter the course of events in their lives. People who show this type of initiative strongly wish to maintain a feeling of independence, even if they have been forced to relinquish some of their actual independence due to functional changes in their abilities (Duner & Nordstrom, 2005). The ability to take charge of potentially stressful situations, before they become problems, was found in one study of community-dwelling, active, older adults to be related to fewer health-related stressful situations (Fiksenbaum, Greenglass, & Eaton, 2006).

That aging may bring with it more effective ways of coping with stress was illustrated in one intriguing study comparing learning under stress between older and younger rats. The stress in this experiment consisted of being kept in restraint for a period of 21 days. The younger rats were more impaired while stressed in their ability to learn and remember than were the older animals (Bowman, 2005). Along similar lines, researchers comparing the cardiovascular reactivity of older and younger humans during a stressful laboratory task found that the blood pressure of older adults actually increased more in response to stress than did the blood pressure of their younger counterparts. However, the older adults managed to keep their negative emotions in check, even when it was apparent that their bodies were registering heightened levels of stress (Uchino, Berg, Smith, Pearce, & Skinner, 2006).

Researchers in this area regard it as a given that social support is an important resource for people of any age to have when faced with stressful experiences. Everyone knows how important it is to be able to talk to someone who can, if not help, at least hear you out when you have had something bad happen to you. Loss of functional abilities is certainly one important stressful area for older adults. In investigating responses of anxiety, depression, and self-esteem to loss of abilities in married older adults, one set of researchers found that high levels of marital closeness were a protective factor for psychological problems. Older adults with functional losses were able to maintain positive mood and self-regard if they were in marital relationships characterized by such factors as feeling loved, understood, and able to communicate (Mancini & Bonanno, 2006).

Identity Process Theory

According to identity process theory, the goal of development is optimal adaptation to the environment through establishing a balance between maintaining consistency of the self (identity assimilation) and changing in response to experiences (identity accommodation). The actions people take upon the environment reflect attempts to express their sense of self by engaging in the activities they regard as important and worthwhile. Through identity assimilation, people interpret events in a way that is consistent with their present identity. If an event occurs that is so discrepant a person cannot interpret it in terms of identity at the moment, identity accommodation comes into play.

Most people have fairly positive views of themselves, but as they get older, more and more experiences occur that can potentially erode self-esteem. However, research on identity processes shows that adults increasingly rely on identity assimilation, and this is how older people are able to maintain a positive self-esteem. The edge that assimilation has over accommodation is theorized to be just enough to maintain this positive view without leading individuals into self-views that are so off base as to be completely out of sync with experiences.

The multiple threshold model, which we described in Chapter 2, predicts that individuals react to specific age-related changes in their physical and psychological functioning in terms of the identity processes. This model was tested out in a study of nearly 250 adults ranging in age from 40 to 95 years (Whitbourne & Collins, 1998). Individuals who used identity assimilation with regard to these specific changes (i.e., they did not think about these changes or integrate them into their identities) had higher self-esteem than people who used identity accommodation (i.e., became preoccupied with these changes). A certain amount of denial, or at least minimization, seems to be important with regard to changes in the body and identity.

Later studies have examined the relationship between identity and self-esteem more generally and found self-esteem to be higher in people who use both identity balance and identity assimilation (Sneed & Whitbourne, 2003). Identity accommodation, by contrast, is related to lower levels of self-esteem throughout adulthood. However, men and women differ in their use of identity processes in that women use identity accommodation more than do men (Skultety & Whitbourne, 2004). In addition, some women who use identity assimilation may claim that they use identity balance to appear as though they are flexible and open to negative feedback when in reality, they prefer not to look inward and perhaps confront their flaws (Whitbourne, et al., 2002).

That there may be an advantage to identity assimilation in terms of health and mortality is supported by research on self-perceptions of aging and longevity (Levy, Slade, Kunkel, & Kasl, 2002). Older adults who managed to avoid adopting negative views of aging (which may be seen as a form of identity assimilation) lived 7.5 years longer than those individuals who did not develop a similar resistance to accommodating society's negative views about aging into their identities. The advantage of denial against negative self-evaluations associated with aging (a form of identity assimilation) also was demonstrated in a long-term longitudinal investigation in which people who used denial had better psychological health (Cramer & Jones, 2007). Conversely, relying primarily on identity accommodation is associated with the experience of depressive symptoms (Weinberger & Whitbourne, 2010).

The tendency to use identity assimilation when thinking back on your life and how you have changed is a general bias that pervades the way people recall their previous experiences. The **life story** is the individual's inner personal narrative of the past events in his or her life (Whitbourne, 1985). This tendency was demonstrated in one study investigating retrospective reports of personality change in a sample of nearly 260 men and women in their early 60s. Men, in particular, were likely to see themselves as having gained in such attributes as "confident power" between their 20s and 60s (Miner-Rubino, Winter, & Stewart, 2004).

Identity assimilation may also serve a protective function in other contexts in which older adults are faced with potentially negative information about their abilities. One group of researchers used a novel opportunity to study this process among older drivers referred to driver education classes due to a history of auto accidents. Those older drivers who overestimated their driving abilities became less depressed after receiving feedback about their actual driving abilities than older drivers who took a more pessimistic view of whether their driving abilities had changed (De Raedt & Ponjaert-Kristoffersen, 2006).

However, there may be cultural biases in the tendency to use identity assimilation or identity accommodation. A cross-national study comparing Dutch and American older adults showed that maintaining a youthful age identity mediates the link between identity processes and self-esteem. However, this mediation effect was stronger in the Americans than the Dutch, reflecting cultural differences in views of aging (Westerhof, Whitbourne, & Freeman, 2012). People in the U.S. are more likely to be focused on maintaining a youthful identity compared to people living in the Netherlands, which has strictly enforced mandatory retirement at age 65.

As personality research, with its focus on individual differences, continues to be integrated into studies within the field on topics as diverse as health, cognition, reactions to life events, and physical changes, greater understanding will be gained about how people vary in their reactions to the aging process. Such work will help further the development of the field in terms of biopsychosocial processes, leading both to a richer theoretical understanding of aging and practical implications for intervention.

MIDLIFE CRISIS THEORIES AND FINDINGS

The **midlife crisis** refers to a period of self-scrutiny and reevaluation of goals triggered by the individual's entry into middle age. Derived from an age-stage approach to personality in adulthood, the midlife crisis had its origins in psychodynamic theory but has spread far beyond its original meaning to become a catch-all term for any changes that people experience between the ages of 30 to 60. In this section of the chapter, we'll examine the evidence, pro and con, to see whether the midlife crisis deserves its place in the scientific literature, if not popular lore.

Theory of the Midlife Crisis

It is safe to say that most people in contemporary American society are familiar with the term "midlife crisis." The topic of the midlife crisis has become a permanent fixture in popular psychology. A recent search of a popular commercial website revealed more than 100 books on the topic, and there is no sign of diminishing interest in the foreseeable future. It may therefore surprise you to learn that the concept is largely discounted in academic psychology.

The term midlife crisis was coined by psychoanalyst Elliot Jaques (1965) in a paper outlining the role of fear of mortality as prompting life crises in well-known historical figures. The term remained relatively obscure until it was picked up by journalist Gail Sheehy (1974), whose popular book called *Passages: Predictable Crises of Adult Life* placed it front and center in the psychological life of 40-something adults. Sheehy's book was based on research being conducted by others, including Yale psychologist Daniel Levinson, who would later publish his own bestseller called *The Seasons of a Man's Life* (Levinson, Darrow, Klein, Levinson, & McKee, 1978). The Levinson/Sheehy approach emphasizes strict age-based turning points in adulthood, of which the midlife crisis was just one. In his subsequent publication on women, which was greeted with far less attention in the popular press, Levinson claimed that similar alternations between change and stability characterize adult women (Levinson & Levinson, 1996).

Levinson's publication itself was based on interviews with a small sample of 40 men ranging in age from the mid-30s to mid-40s. The men in the sample were intended to represent men from diverse backgrounds, with 10 from each of the following occupations: business executive, academic biologist, blue-collar worker, and novelist. In addition to these interviews, the authors included informal analyses of the biographies of famous men and the stories of men portrayed in literature.

Although the midlife crisis was the common notion to emerge from Levinson's work, his study went beyond age turning points in proposing the changes that occur throughout the midlife years. Levinson proposed that development involves primarily changes in the **life structure**, or the way that the individual's life is patterned at a given point in time. Your life structure includes your involvement in family, work, leisure, friendships, and religion, and takes into account your ethnicity. It is influenced by your conscious and unconscious sense of self but also by the social and cultural environment in which you are living.

The idea of the life structure is certainly consistent with other views of development in midlife, including that of the life story and changes in identity. What distinguishes Levinson's theory was his proposal that the life structure evolves through an orderly series of universal stages in adulthood. He proposed that these stages alternate between periods of tranquility and periods of transition, with each

stage having a specific focus. You can see the stages and their associated ages in Figure 8.9.

Levinson believed that during periods of stability, the man builds his life structure around the decisions he made in the previous stage. If he chose to pursue a certain career path, he continues in that path throughout the period of stability. However, as the period reaches its close, the man becomes driven by both internal and external factors to question his previous set of commitments. For the next 4 or 5 years, during the transitional period that ensues, he explores different alternatives and seeks a new life structure or a modification of the existing one. Levinson believed that these transitional periods are inevitable. Choices are always imperfect, and as the outcome of one set of choices plays itself out, the individual begins to experience regrets and a desire for change. As stated by Levinson (p. 200), "no life structure can permit the living out of all aspects of the self."

The period called the midlife transition has a special quality compared to other transitional periods because

<u>FIGURE 8.9</u>

Stages of Adult Development According to Levinson

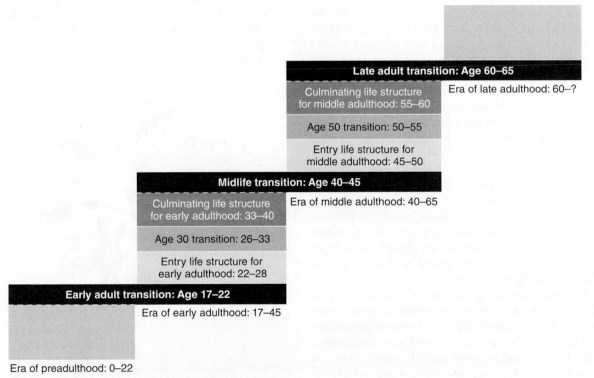

Levinson proposed that there are three important transitions in adulthood, with the midlife transition serving as the basis for the "midlife crisis."

Source: Levinson, D. J., Darrow, C. N., Klein, E. B., Levinson, M. H., & McKee, B. (1978). *The seasons of a man's life*. New York: Alfred A. Knopf. Copyright © 1978 by Daniel J Levinson. Reprinted by permission of Alfred A Knopf, a Division of Random House Inc.

it involves the most significant shift, from early to middle adulthood. As shown in Figure 8.9, the period of the midlife transition ("crisis") is targeted as 40 to 45. However, its beginning can occur anywhere between 38 and 43, and its ending can occur anywhere between the years of 44 to 47.

The first theme of the midlife crisis is overcoming disillusionment due to failure to achieve the dreams of youth that inevitably cannot be fully realized. The individual must then establish a new set of more realistic aspirations. The second theme of the midlife crisis involves making decisions about how to pursue the life structure during middle adulthood. During this time, the man questions his marriage, comes to grips with the maturing of adolescent children, handles promotions or demotions at work, and reflects on the state of the nation and the world. He may begin to establish mentoring relationships with younger persons so that he may pass along the torch of what was handed to him during his early adulthood. Finally, the man must resolve the polarities of his personality involving masculinity and femininity, feelings about life and death, and the needs for both autonomy and dependence on others.

Although Levinson's theory predicts that the stage sequences are universal, it does allow for variations in progress through the late 30s that would affect the specific nature of the midlife crisis. In the most frequently observed pattern reported in the sample, a man advances steadily through a stable life structure but then encounters some form of failure. Usually, this need not be a catastrophic loss, such as getting fired or facing divorce, but it may be simply a perceived failure to achieve some particular desired goal by a certain age. For instance, he may not have won an award or distinction for which he was striving, such as the biologist who knows he will never win a Nobel Prize. Most people would not be distraught over such a "failure," particularly if they were generally well regarded in their profession or community. However, if this goal was part of an individual's "dream," it can lead to serious disappointment and self-questioning. Some men in the sample did in fact realize their dreams, others failed completely, and still others decided to change their life structures entirely out of boredom.

The characteristics of the midlife crisis are by now well known through their representation in contemporary literature, theater, movies, and song. For many people, they seem almost synonymous with the particular characteristics of the Baby Boomers, whom current society regards as being obsessed with aging, determined to stay young, and selfishly concerned with their own pleasure. However, this is not what Levinson believed. He regarded the midlife crisis to be a virtually universal process that has characterized human existence for at least 10,000 years.

Critiques and Research on the Midlife Crisis

Apart from the original investigation by Levinson and colleagues, little to no empirical support has been presented for the existence of the midlife crisis as a universal phenomenon (Lachman, 2004). Even before the data were available, however, psychologists in the adult development field expressed considerable skepticism about the concept of the midlife crisis based on what at the time appeared to be extrapolation far beyond the available evidence (Brim, 1976; Whitbourne, 1986).

One of the most significant criticisms of the midlife crisis was the fact that Levinson (and Sheehy) relied too heavily on age as a marker of development. As you've already learned, chronological age is not necessarily an accurate indicator of an individual's psychological status or even physical functioning. However, adding to this problem is the fact that Levinson and other midlife crisis writers contradicted each other on exactly when this age was supposed to be. Some said 40 to 45, others 38 to 47, others exactly the age of 43. Because of this lack of clarity, the midlife crisis term can be used for any situation in which a person feels stressed, unhappy, or preoccupied with feelings of failure. We will return to this point shortly.

The Levinson study itself was also flawed in that the original sample was hardly representative enough to support claims of universality. Of the 40 men that Levinson and his team interviewed, half were from the highly

This cartoon depiction of a middle-aged businessman illustrates the variety of issues supposedly confronting men as they go through the midlife crisis.

educated and intellectually oriented strata of society. Another one-quarter of the sample consisted of successful business executives. The concerns of the men in this sample, such as running companies, publishing novels, and competing for Nobel Prizes, are hardly those of the average man (or woman).

There were other problems with the study as well (Whitbourne, 2010). Levinson himself seemed to lack objectivity, given his stated goal of writing the book: "The choice of topic also reflected a personal concern: at 46, I wanted to study the transition into middle age in order to understand what I had been through myself" (p. x). He speculated that perhaps the study's results reflected the "unconscious fantasies and anxieties" (p. 26) of himself and his middle-aged male colleagues. Compounding this problem was the fact that the study's investigators never clearly stated their procedures for conducting the ratings of life stages. They did not even publish the interview questions, as is typical for a study such as this one.

One of the first empirical challenges to the midlife crisis concept actually came from the laboratories of McCrae and Costa, who used their extensive database on personality at the time to test several specific predictions (McCrae & Costa, 2003). The easiest process was to plot the scores on the NEO scales by year across the supposed midlife crisis peak years. However, the scores were essentially flat; in fact, neuroticism was lower by a very small amount in the 43-year-olds.

Having explored this indirect approach, McCrae and Costa created what they called a "Midlife Crisis Scale" and administered it to 350 men ages 30 to 60 years. Items on this scale asked participants to rate themselves on emotions related to the midlife crisis such as feelings of meaninglessness, turmoil, and confusion, job and family dissatisfaction, and fear of aging and death. If any questions had detected a midlife crisis, these surely would have. Yet they did not, either on the initial sample or in a different group of 300 men tested with a slightly shorter version (Costa & McCrae, 1978). The most telling data of all, however, emerged in this second study on the Midlife Crisis Scale. The data were from men participating in the Department of Veterans Affairs Normative Aging Study, one of the longitudinal personality investigations that eventually became part of the basis for the Five-Factor Model. Men who had received higher scores on the neuroticism factor 10 years earlier were the ones who received higher scores on the Midlife Crisis Scale. This finding suggests that people with chronic psychological problems are more likely to experience a phenomenon such as the midlife crisis.

The majority of all the data contradicting the existence of the midlife crisis are from the laboratories of McCrae

and Costa. There is ample documentation, however, from many other sources. One was a study conducted by the first author on nearly 100 adult men and women between the ages of 24 and 61 (Whitbourne, 1986). Among the extensive interview data collected on identity and life histories, none of the participants, even those in their 40s, fit the criteria for a midlife crisis even when they were asked specifically about the impact of aging on their identities. A second interview and questionnaire study conducted on another sample of more than 300 men ranging from age 38 to 48 ("prime time" for the midlife crisis) yielded similar findings (Farrell & Rosenberg, 1981).

The National Survey of Midlife Development in the United States (MIDUS) added another nail in the coffin to the midlife crisis concept (Wethington, Kessler, Pixley, Brim, & Ryff, 2004) (see Figure 8.10). Only 26% of respondents reported that they had experienced a midlife crisis, hardly the 100% that midlife crisis theory would predict. However, even this percentage is most likely an exaggeration, because those who reported having a midlife crisis included the general experiences that everyone has in life of being aware that time is passing. Even so, when the researchers categorized these responses by age, they could detect no particular peak in the mid-40s. Some of the women in the sample even declared that the age of their midlife crisis was over 60, hardly considered "midlife" by any stretch of the imagination.

More recently, McFadden and Rawson Swan (2012) reviewed studies on midlife crisis vs. midlife transition among women, including participants in the 10-year Melbourne Longitudinal Study. Their analysis showed that, once again, stages in midlife did not predict any of the well-being outcome measures, including self-esteem, life satisfaction, depression, and marital satisfaction.

We hope that you see that the midlife crisis simply fails to withstand multiple tests as a scientifically useful concept. By now, you must surely be wondering why a concept so thoroughly debunked by the data continues

FIGURE 8.10

Results of MIDUS Survey on the Midlife Crisis

- 26% stated they had one
- However, this included "awareness of the passage of time"
- No peak occurred among people in their 40s
- Even people in their 60s reported currently having a midlife crisis

cogal/iStockphoto

to remain alive and debated, nearly 50 years after Jaques coined the term.

Some argue that the idea of a midlife crisis makes a "good story" (Rosenberg, Rosenberg, & Farrell, 1999). People in their middle years, settled into stable patterns of both personality and social roles, find it exciting to think about getting that proverbial red sports car or leaving their jobs behind them and moving to some exotic new place. The now-classic 1999 movie, *American Beauty*, reinforced the idea in the minds of the public that the average man becomes obsessed with youth and tries to keep himself young not only with a new sports car, but also with the young cheerleader who lived next door. Sensational events such as hurricanes, tornadoes, and other disasters capture media attention, as do celebrity meltdowns. The idea that personality is subject to major upheavals in the middle years seems to capture this disaster mentality.

In summary, personality is characterized in multiple ways in psychology. Studying how personality develops over adulthood may lead to the realization that you need not become hardened into a rigid pattern of set dispositions. Change is possible throughout your life, if not in predictable stages, at least in ways that allow you to feel better about yourself as you grow older. As researchers explore relationships between health and personality, they will continue to provide greater understanding of how to maximize the chances of maintaining physical functioning as well.

SUMMARY

1. Studies of personality in adulthood are based on theories that attempt to define the nature and structure of personality. Within psychodynamic theory, ego psychology focuses on the role of the ego, the structure in personality that is theorized to perform the executive functions of personality. Ego psychologists include Erikson, Loevinger, and Vaillant. Several major longitudinal studies have provided tests of ego psychology theories. Psychosocial development from college to midlife was the focus of the Rochester Adult Longitudinal study, which also examined the relationship of life experiences to personality among men and women. In the Mills study, college women were followed using measures testing Erikson's and Loevinger's theories as well as the interaction of personality and social context. The Vaillant study examined the use of ego defense mechanisms

in three samples of adults. Coping and defense mechanisms have also been examined in several large national samples. Together, the findings from this research suggest that through middle age and beyond, individuals become more accepting of themselves and better able to regulate their negative feelings. Social context also affects the course of development, and personality in turn affects the way individuals select and react to their experiences.

2. Attachment theory proposes that the earliest interactions with caregivers relate to adult personality and relationships. Studies on adult age differences in attachment style show that older adults are less likely to be anxiously attached and more likely to be dismissive compared with younger adults. Older adults may have fewer attachment figures in their social networks, but those they have fit into a wider range of roles.

3. Within the trait perspective, the Five-Factor Model (FFM) has stimulated a large body of longitudinal and cross-sectional studies on personality in men and women throughout the adult age range. The five traits in the FFM include neuroticism, extraversion, openness to experience, agreeableness, and conscientiousness. There are also important individual differences in changes in personality over time: many of them are related to health and behavioral risk patterns, such as the Type A behavior pattern.

4. Socioemotional selectivity theory proposes that, over the course of adulthood, individuals select social interactions that will maximize the emotional rewards of relationships. Older adults appear better able than their younger counterparts to regulate negative affect.

5. Cognitive self theories propose that individuals view the events in their lives from the standpoint of the relevance of these events to the self. Identity process theory and the possible selves model fit into this category of theories.

6. According to the midlife crisis theory, there is a period in middle adulthood during which the individual experiences a radical alteration in personality, well-being, and goals. Midlife crisis theory was developed by Levinson and colleagues through an interview study of 40 adult males and has gained strong support in popular culture. However, subsequent researchers using a variety of empirical methods have failed to provide support for this theory, and it is generally disregarded within the field of adult development.

9

Relationships

AGING TODAY

The Language of Love in Close Relationships

The three magic words, "I love you," can mean all kinds of things in a long-term relationship. They can be a way for you to bond emotionally with your partner, to initiate intimacy, or to make amends for past wrongs. However, most couples look beyond these magic words to the way that their partners behave. It's all very well and good to say you care, but if you don't provide concrete clues to your partner, chances are that your relationship will be headed for trouble.

In a long-term study of marriage, Huston and colleagues examine the daily behaviors of 168 couples studied over a 13-year period to find out which behaviors provide the key to relationship success. In a 2012 study, the day-to-day behaviors of these couples were examined and how they showed affection to each other in both words and deeds (Schoenfeld, Bredow, & Huston, 2012).

The study's couples reported on how they expressed love in their daily routines, data that allowed Schoenfeld and colleagues to gain insight into the existence of, and reasons for, sex differences in communicating affection. They predicted that women would be more predisposed to be warm and nurturing and that men would suppress their loving emotions. Carrying this one step further, the researchers also predicted that wives would be more likely to avoid being openly antagonistic to their husbands. The women should, according to previous research, be more likely to engage in self-sacrifice, especially the wives who were more in love with their husbands. For their part, husbands should, according to previous research, be more likely to express their love through initiating sex.

The findings showed that love and sexual intimacy were more closely connected for the husbands than for the wives. Husbands in love draw on a wide range of behaviors to show their love, both by expressing their affection and by pursuing joint activities.

The take-home message of this study is that the three little words can do relationships a lot of good. It's likely that people in good relationships spontaneously tell each other how they feel. However, it's also possible that expressing love on a daily basis can jump-start a relationship and make it more fulfilling.

Posted by Susan Whitbourne and Stacey Whitbourne

Your relationships with others are essential to your existence throughout life. From your intimate partners to your family, friends, and the broader community, your social connections are a crucial part of who you are and how you feel on a day-to-day basis. It is difficult to capture the central qualities and complexities of these many relationships, and it is perhaps even more challenging to study the way these relationships interact with developmental processes within the individual over time. Yet researchers must be able to translate that intuitive sense of the importance of relationships into quantifiable terms that can demonstrate the nature and impact of social processes in adulthood.

Changes in the broader society of the country and world heavily impact the nature of individual relationships. You can see from even brief glances at news stories in the media that patterns of marriage and family life change significantly with each passing year. In the United States at least, fewer people marry today, and those who do are waiting longer than previous generations. Family compositions are continually changing as people leave and reenter new long-term relationships, often involving their children and extended families as well. In this chapter, we examine these changing family patterns and try to provide an understanding of what theorists say about the qualities of close relationships and how they interact with the development of the individual.

MARRIAGE AND INTIMATE RELATIONSHIPS

The marital relationship has come under intense scrutiny in today's world. The union between two adults is thought to serve as the foundation of the entire family hierarchy that is passed along from generation to generation. You hear about the death of marriage as an institution, yet interest in marriage itself never seems to wane in the popular imagination, the media, and professional literature. The decision to marry involves a legal, social, and, some might say, moral commitment in which two people promise to spend the rest of their lives together. Furthermore, as states in the United States arrive at positions on the legality of gay marriage, with even the Supreme Court weighing in on the issue in the spring of 2013, it seems clear that marriage is still a very relevant social institution.

Even as the definition of marriage continues to evolve, the statistics on its success rate prove to be as discouraging as ever for those who contemplate legalizing their own relationship with a partner. Given the current divorce statistics, you know that many people are not able to maintain the hopeful promises they make to each other in their wedding vows. What factors contribute to a successful marital relationship and what might lead to its demise? Social scientists are nowhere near finding answers to these questions, but as we will see shortly, there is a plethora of theories.

Marriage

In the year 2012, 123.6 million adults were married and living with their spouse, a number that represents 55% of the population age 18 and older (see Table 9.1). Among the entire 18 and older population, the percentage of those who have ever been married is far higher—approximately 74% (U.S. Bureau of the Census, 2013a). Between the years 2006–2010, the median age of marriage was 25.8

Digital Vision/SUPERSTOCK

The wedding day is a momentous occasion celebrated by couples as the beginning of their new life together.

TABLE 9.1
Some Facts About Marriage

What is the...?	Fact
Percent in U.S. population currently married	55%
Percent married at least once by age 55	74%
Median age of marriage	Men = 28.3 Women = 25.8
Rates of marriage by race/ethnicity	Asians highest (64%) Blacks lowest (34%)
Number of same-sex couples Number of same-sex couples reporting that they are married	780,000 150,000

Geckly/iStockphoto

for women and 28.3 for men. Although the age of first marriage is on the increase, by the age of 40, 84% of all women are married, a percentage that has not changed since 1995 (Copen, Daniels, Vespa, & Mosher, 2012).

There are differences by race and ethnicity in marriage statistics. Among all adults 18 and older, over half of non-Hispanic Whites (58%) are married, as are nearly half (49%) of Hispanics. Asian-Americans (64%) are most likely to be currently married and living with a spouse, and Blacks (34%) the least (U.S. Bureau of the Census, 2013a).

As a social institution, **marriage** is defined as a legally sanctioned union between a man and a woman (in most U.S. states). People who are married often pay joint income tax returns and are given virtually automatic privileges to share the rest of their finances as well as other necessities such as health care and housing. They often share a last name, usually the husband's, although many wives never change their names, a practice that seems to be on the rise. In the 1970s, couples began to create a new hyphenated last name, a trend that now appears to have decreased in popularity.

Generally, marital partners are entitled to retirement, death, and health insurance benefits as well as the entire portion of the estate when one partner dies. Although marriages need not legally conform to the statutes of a particular religion, they are often performed in a religious context.

Having explained the legal definition of marriage, you can clearly see what and who is excluded. People who are not legally married are not automatically entitled to the benefits available to those who are. Individuals living within a committed and long-term relationship not sanctioned by the law must seek exceptions to virtually all of the conditions that are set forth for married people unless their employers provide these benefits. Individuals who are of the same sex and living within a committed homosexual relationship face additional barriers to the benefits granted to married persons if living in a state where gay marriage is not legal. This was true in states with legalized gay marriage until the Supreme Court ruled part of the Defense of Marriage Act unconstitutional in June 2013.

Obviously, the legal definition of marriage includes no mention of the partners' emotional relationship with each other. People can be legally married and live apart, both literally and figuratively. Most social scientists distinguish between an intimate and a marital relationship because the two need not exist within the same couple. The legal commitment of marriage adds a dimension to an intimate relationship not present in a nonmarital close relationship in that ending a marital relationship is technically more difficult than ending a nonmarital one. Furthermore, many people view a legalized marriage as a moral and spiritual commitment that they cannot or will not violate.

Definitional concerns aside, there is a body of evidence on marriage in adulthood suggesting that married adults have many advantages compared with those who are unmarried. Researchers analyzing the findings of over 50 studies, including those based on more than 250,000 older adults from a variety of countries, showed a 9 to 15% reduction in mortality risk for married men and women (Manzoli, Villari, Pirone, & Boccia, 2007). This protective effect of marriage was greater in countries from Europe and North America compared to studies from Asia and the country of Israel. Marriage also confers with it greater happiness and a variety of other benefits to the quality of life, a fact that had come into question (particularly for women) in the 1980s, but that is now accepted as well established (Wood, Goesling, & Avellar, 2007).

Among people 65 and older in the United States, a higher percentage of men (72%) than women (45%) are married and living with a spouse (U.S. Bureau of the Census, 2013a). Consequently, women over the age of 65 are almost twice as likely (37%) as men (19%) to be living alone (Administration on Aging, 2012). Therefore, older women are at greater risk for some of the disadvantages that come with single status, including fewer financial resources, access to care, and social support.

The percentage of older adults living with a spouse varies by age, sex, and race/ethnicity. As you can see from Figure 9.1, women are more likely than men not to live with a spouse, with the lowest percentage (4.2%) being Black women 85 and older. The highest percentage of men living with a spouse are those who are non-Hispanic Whites in the 65 to 74 age bracket. Because living with a spouse typically provides emotional and financial resources, these figures suggest that Black women 85 and older are at greatest risk for living without adequate support within the home.

Cohabitation

Living in a stable relationship prior to or instead of marrying is referred to as **cohabitation**. Since the 1960s, there has been a steady increase in the number of couples who choose this lifestyle. In 1960, an estimated 439,000 individuals in the United States reported that they were cohabitating with a person of the opposite sex. By 2011, this number was estimated at about 7.7 million (Lofquist, Lugaila, O'Connell, & Feliz, 2012). From 50 to 60% of all marriages are now preceded by cohabitation (Stanley, Amato, Johnson, & Markman, 2006); looking at the data on couples who cohabitate, approximately 28% of women 44 and under who cohabitate eventually marry their partner (National Center for Health Statistics, 2010).

Though the commonsense wisdom is that the experience of living together contributes positively to the success of a marriage, the opposite seems to be true, at least in part. Data on divorce patterns show that there is a greater risk of marital breakup among people who cohabitated before they became engaged. The greater likelihood of divorce among couples who cohabitate before becoming engaged is referred to as the **cohabitation effect** (Cohan & Kleinbaum, 2002).

One explanation for the cohabitation effect is that couples who would not have gotten married "slide" into marriage through inertia; in other words, the fact that they were already living together becomes the basis for entering into marriage even if the fit between the two partners is not all that good. Eventually they divorce due to the

FIGURE 9.1

Percent Married With Spouse Present

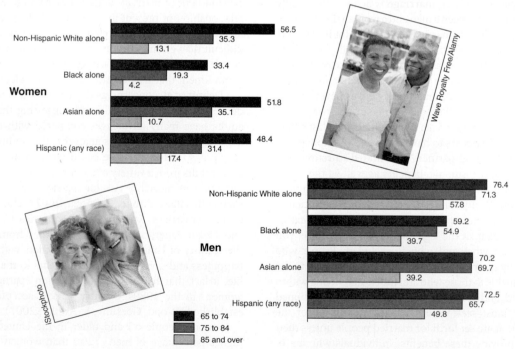

Source: He, W., Sangupta, M., Velkoff, V. A., & DeBarros, K. A. (2005). *65+ in the United States: 2005.* Current Population Reports Special Studies. U.S. Census Bureau, Current Population Reports, P23-209. Washington DC: U.S. Government Printing Office.

fact that they were not well matched at the outset. Not only are they more likely to divorce, but people with this relationship history experience greater unhappiness during the period in which they remain under the same roof after their marriage (Rhoades, Stanley, & Markman, 2009).

To try to tease out the causal links involved in the cohabitation effect, Lu and colleagues (2012) evaluated the likelihood of a cohabiting relationship's ending after controlling for demographic characteristics of the partners prior to their cohabitation. Rather than compare cohabiting with noncohabiting partners, they separated out individuals who had engaged in "serial" cohabitation, meaning that they had lived with more than one partner in a cohabiting relationship. This turned out to be an important control. People who had cohabited only with their spouse prior to marriage did not show the cohabitation effect. It was only those serial cohabitators who showed higher rates of marital disruption. The cohabitation effect does not appear to apply equally to all couples.

Along with a rise in the overall numbers of couples who cohabitate is a parallel increase in the number of cohabitating adults with children under the age of 15. In 1960, this number amounted to 197,000, but by 2011, it was estimated to have increased greatly to the present estimated level of 1.5 million (U.S. Bureau of the Census, 2010a).

Most investigations of cohabitation involve younger adults, but older adults also enter into cohabiting relationships. As of 2010, 366,000 adults 65 and older were reported to be living in a cohabiting relationship, amounting to 5% of all cohabiting couples in the U.S. (Lofquist et al., 2012). One study investigating cohabitation in older adults suggests that the unions they form tend to persist longer than those formed by younger adults. Using data from the Health and Retirement Study, a longitudinal sample of over 21,000 adults 50 and older followed from 1998 to 2006, Brown et al. (2012) reported that among the 4% who entered into cohabitation, only 18% ended in separation, and most people remained together either until one of them died or the study was over. Compared to younger adults, older adults seem to be more likely, then, to view cohabitation as an alternative to marriage.

Same-Sex Couples

Gay marriage was first legalized in the United States by the Commonwealth of Massachusetts in 2004, and as of late 2013 has since been legalized in 13 other states, including Vermont, Connecticut, Delaware, Hawaii, New York, Rhode Island, the District of Columbia, Iowa, Maine, Maryland, Washington, Minnesota, and New Hampshire. California, having legalized gay marriage through a state Supreme Court ruling in 2008, subsequently rejected its legality in a contentious 2008 ballot known as Proposition 8.

Around the world, gay marriage is considered legal in 11 countries (as of mid-2013), including the Netherlands, Belgium, Spain, Canada, South Africa, Norway, Portugal, Iceland, Argentina, Denmark, and France. Other states in the U.S. are considering similar legislation as are other nations around the world. Clearly, based on the extent of debate about this issue in on a global scale, it is a topic that will remain on political agendas in the coming years.

The U.S. Census bureau estimates that there are as many as 780,000 same-sex households in the U.S. of whom nearly 150,000 report themselves as same-sex spouses. The largest percentage (1.6%) of same-sex partners involved people of two or more races. San Francisco, Seattle, and Portland, Oregon, were the cities with the highest numbers of same-sex partnerships. Later in the chapter we will discuss the dynamics of same-sex couples with children.

In a comprehensive review of the characteristics of same-sex couples, Peplau and Fingerhut (2007) concluded that, compared with heterosexual couples, there are many similarities in the dynamics of the relationship. One notable exception, however, is a greater sharing of household tasks among lesbian and gay couples.

Although there is little research on the factors contributing to the longevity of these relationships and partner satisfaction, the available evidence suggests that because most of the individuals living in these relationships are not legally bound to each other, they are more likely to dissolve when the partnership is not working out. A large study carried out in the U.K. of two birth cohorts (1958 and 1970) following same- and opposite-sex cohabitations showed that same-sex cohabiting couples were more likely to dissolve than opposite-sex couples (Lau, 2012).

Divorce and Remarriage

Approximately 10% of the adult population in the United States is divorced (U.S. Bureau of the Census, 2012c). Taking into account all marriages that end in divorce, the average length of first marriage prior to divorce is about 8 years (Kreider & Ellis, 2011). Divorce statistics also show important variations by race. Black women between the ages of 25 and 44 have higher divorce rates than White or Hispanic women (National Center for Health Statistics, 2010). Research on children of divorced parents suggests that for women, but not men, parental divorce is a stronger indicator of a lack of commitment and confidence in the marriage (Whitton, Rhoades, Stanley, & Markman, 2008).

Divorce rates have been declining since reaching a peak in 1980. Many factors combine to account for this decreasing divorce rate. One is that people are marrying at later ages; the older a woman at marriage, the lower the probability that she will become divorced (Bramlett & Mosher, 2002). Second, the previously skyrocketing divorce rates increased consciousness in society about the need for prevention. Suggesting that such efforts can pay off, a study of over 2,200 households in the Midwest of the United States showed that couples who participated in premarital education had higher levels of marital satisfaction, lower levels of conflict, and reduced odds of divorce (Stanley et al., 2006). Research on second marriages suggests that couples are less likely to engage in premarital education compared with couples entering into first marriages—a trend linked to decreased marital happiness and increased rates of divorce (Doss, Rhoades, Stanley, Markman, & Johnson, 2009).

The dissolution of a marriage is ordinarily perceived by those involved as a disappointment and a sad if not tragic event (see Figure 9.2). One or both of the partners may be relieved to see the end of an unsuccessful relationship, but they are nevertheless affected in many ways by the inevitable consequences of the divorce on their daily lives, the lives of children, and the lives of extended family members. The couple must resolve a range of practical issues, such as changes in their housing and financial affairs— but the greatest toll is the emotional one. For many couples, child custody arrangements present the most significant challenge caused by their altered status as a family.

Studies on divorced (compared with married) individuals show that they have lower levels of psychological well-being, poorer health, higher mortality rates, more problems with substance abuse and depression, less satisfying sex lives, and more negative life events (Amato, 2000). The negative consequences of divorce are more severe for individuals who have young children, especially women (Williams & Dunne-Bryant, 2006). These effects may persist for many years, particularly for individuals who remain psychologically attached to their ex-partner, experience

FIGURE 9.2

Psychological Aspects of Divorce

- Practical consequences
- Child custody
- Lower psychological health
- Poorer health
- Problems with substance abuse
- More negative life events

iStockphoto

conflict in coparenting, or who have unusual difficulty in living on their own (Sweeper & Halford, 2006). Divorced or widowed adults who do not remarry are in poorer health (including chronic conditions and depressive symptoms) than those who remarry (Hughes & Waite, 2009). Divorce in older adults has negative effects on health in that newly divorced older adults experience more physical limitations in their daily lives (Bennett, 2006).

Although technically divorce rates in the population as a whole have declined, the media frequently cite the disturbing statistic that one out of every two marriages will end in divorce. However, the divorce statistics are much more complicated than this simple formula would imply. Those who divorce in a given year are generally not the same people as those who have gotten married, so the number of divorces cannot simply be compared with the number of marriages to determine the odds of divorcing. Furthermore, the divorce rate in any given year includes those people who are divorcing for a second or third time and people who tend to have a higher divorce rate than those who are getting a first divorce. Including these individuals in the divorce statistics artificially inflates the divorce rate for all marriages.

Another factor influencing the divorce rate is the number of people in the population of marriageable age, which itself is influenced by birth and death rates. In the United States, approximately 18% of all marriages are second marriages, and 4% are third marriages. The average duration of a second marriage that ends in divorce is about the same as that for a first marriage (Kreider & Ellis, 2011). The probability of a second marriage ending in divorce after 10 years is 0.39, slightly higher than that of the ending of a first marriage, which is 0.33 (Bramlett & Mosher, 2002).

People who are more likely to contemplate divorce when their marriage is in trouble are said to be high on **divorce proneness**. These individuals are also more likely to have an extramarital affair (Previti & Amato, 2004). Those high in divorce proneness may have a long history of difficulties in the area of intimacy. Data from the RALS (described in Chapter 8) showed that women who in college had low intimacy scores were more likely to have divorced by their late 50s; the same was not true for men (Weinberger, Hofstein, & Whitbourne, 2008).

Separated and divorced individuals often cite infidelity as the cause of their breakup. Data from a national U.S. survey conducted between 1991 and 2008 reveal that more than half of men and women who engage in extramarital affairs also become separated or divorced from their spouses (Allen & Atkins, 2012). People who are in a troubled marriage may become unfaithful because they are unhappy with their spouses. For these individuals, the extramarital affair provides the final push toward seeking a divorce, particularly if it is the other partner who has the affair. By the same token, people who engage in an affair and then say their marriage was unhappy may be using identity assimilation, seeking to protect their identities as good spouses.

Identity may also play a role in how individuals cope emotionally with divorce. There are a wide range of negative emotional outcomes associated with divorce. People who are divorcing experience such feelings as loss of trust, low self-esteem, anxiety, worry about being hurt in future relationships, anger, depression, and preoccupation with what other people think. For some individuals, however, divorce provides relief from a highly conflictual situation.

You might think that the initiator would have fewer negative emotions than the noninitiator, but the individual's role in the divorce does not clearly relate to the emotional outcome. Some divorced couples seem to transition well into postdivorce relationships in which they remain friends or share in parenting or operating a joint business. Examining these factors in divorce, Frisby et al. (2012) proposed that one of the most difficult aspects of divorce is loss of "face," meaning that divorce represents a threat to the individual's identity. Individuals divorced within the prior 2 years had more positive emotions if they were able to see the divorce as allowing them to gain independence and were supported by their partner in protecting their identities.

Of the nearly 74 million children under 18, approximately 9%, or 6.6 million, are living in the home of a divorced parent (U.S. Bureau of the Census, 2012c). As difficult as it is for children to be caught in between parents who are divorced, it may be just as hard, if not harder, to be caught in between parents who are in a high-conflict marriage. In one longitudinal study of marriage, children 19 years of age and older were asked to state whether they felt they had been caught in between parental arguments. The children of parents whose marriages were characterized by a high degree of conflict were most likely to feel caught in the middle. Not surprisingly, these feelings were related to lower subjective well-being and poorer relationships with their parents. Thus, in some ways, the children were better off when their parents divorced than if the parents had remained together in an unhappy marriage (Amato & Afifi, 2006).

Among divorced couples, mediation is increasingly being seen as an effective means of reducing conflict and hence improving children's adjustment. Mediation is based on a model of cooperative dispute settlement rather than the more adversarial approach that occurs when lawyers become part of the scene. In one 12-year longitudinal study, divorced couples were randomly assigned to either mediation or legal assistance. Conflict significantly declined, particularly in the first year after divorce, among couples who participated in mediation (Sbarra & Emery, 2008).

Widowhood

The death of a spouse is regarded as one of the most stressful events of life, and for many older adults, widowhood involves the loss of a relationship that may have lasted 50 years or more. As we shall see, however, the effect of widowhood on the bereaved individual varies greatly according to the circumstances surrounding the spouse's death and the nature of the couple's relationship (McNamara & Rosenwax, 2010).

In the United States, there are currently approximately 14 million widowed adults ages 18 and older; 76% of these are 65 and older. The majority (80%) of the over-65 widowed adults are women. By the age of 85 and older, the majority of women are widows (73%), about double the rate for men (36%) (U.S. Bureau of the Census, 2012b). The highest rate of widowhood is among Black women 85 and older (76.2%).

Widows who experienced extensive caregiver burden at the end of their spouse's life no longer face these duties (Ferrario, Cardillo, Vicario, Balzarini, & Zotti, 2004). This relief from the burdens of caregiving may alleviate the symptoms of depression and stress present during the spouse's dying months or years (Bonanno, Wortman, & Nesse, 2004).

In general, men seem particularly vulnerable to depression after the death of their wives (Bennett, Smith, & Hughes, 2005). Without remarriage, their levels of well-being may not return to preexisting levels even for as long as 8 years after the spouse has died (Lucas, Clark, Georgellis, & Diener, 2003). Among both men and women, anniversary reactions occur in which the bereaved experience a renewal of their feelings at or around the time of the spouse's death. These reactions may continue for 35 years or longer (Carnelley, Wortman, Bolger, & Burke, 2006), signifying that people may not completely ever "work through" their grief, as we will discuss in Chapter 13.

In what is called the **widowhood effect**, there is a greater probability of death in those who have become widowed compared to those who are married. Widowed men have the highest mortality rates. Figure 9.3 illustrates the widowhood effect with data from a study involving nearly 6,000 older adults studied over an 11-year period (Williams et al., 2011). Even after controlling for various health risks or causes of death, widowed individuals have a higher risk of mortality than the nonwidowed. Their higher mortality is not due to cardiovascular disease but appears to be mediated by such conditions as depression, psychosocial stress, chronic economic hardship, and loss of social support

FIGURE 9.3

The Widowhood Effect Showing Higher Risk of Mortality for Widows Compared to Married Men and Women

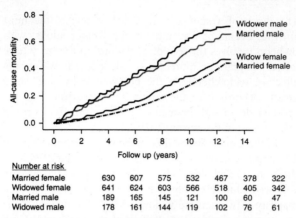

Number at risk							
Married female	630	607	575	532	467	378	322
Widowed female	641	624	603	566	518	405	342
Married male	189	165	145	121	100	60	47
Widowed male	178	161	144	119	102	76	61

Source: Williams, B. R., Zhang, Y., Sawyer, P., Mujib, M., Jones, L. G., Feller, M. A., … Ahmed, A. (2011). Intrinsic association of widowhood with mortality in community-dwelling older women and men: Findings from a prospective propensity-matched population study. *The Journals of Gerontology: Series A: Biological Sciences and Medical Sciences*, 66A, 1360–1368, by permission of Oxford University Press. doi: 10.1093/gerona/glr144 p. 1364

and environmental resources. As a result, they suffer from physical and emotional declines that led to their relatively earlier death compared to their married counterparts.

Several studies support the notion that the widowed suffer more health problems, particularly in the period shortly after they lose their spouses. They may engage in riskier behaviors such as eating fewer fruits and vegetables and foods with higher fat content and engaging in less physical activity. They are more likely to drink alcohol (Stroebe, Schut, & Stroebe, 2007) and more likely to smoke (Wilcox et al., 2003). Women who remarry after becoming widows are favored in a number of ways over women who remain widows. The remarried ones have fewer depressive symptoms, worry less about money, and

have higher incomes than women who remain widowed (Moorman, Booth, & Fingerman, 2006).

In a major prospective study of more than 200 widows, Bonanno and his collaborators (2002) followed women for 18 months after the death of their husbands. The majority showed relatively little distress following their loss, in a pattern called "resilient grief." However, some widows experienced chronic grief that did not subside during the study period, and some showed high levels of depression prior to and after the loss. Studies such as these underscore the notion that widowhood is not a unitary process and that there are multiple factors influencing reactions to the loss of a spouse.

Psychological Perspectives on Long-Term Relationships

Throughout the vicissitudes of marriage, divorce, remarriage, and widowhood, most adults actively strive to maintain gratifying interactions with others on a day-to-day basis. Furthermore, for many adults, the feeling of being part of a close relationship or network of relationships is the most salient aspect of identity (Whitbourne, 1986). Whether this relationship is called "marriage," "family," "friendship," or "partnership" is not as important as the feeling that one is valued by others and has something to offer to improve the lives of other people.

Poets, philosophers, playwrights, and novelists, among others, have attempted for centuries to identify the elusive qualities of "love" (see Table 9.2). Although they have not been around for as long, psychologists and sociologists have also contributed their share of theories to account for why people develop close, loving relationships and what factors account for their maintenance or dissolution over time (see Table 9.2).

The earliest sociological explanations of relationship satisfaction across the years of marriage attempted to relate the quality of marital interactions to the presence of children in the home and their ages. As relationships in the real world have seemed to become more complicated, however,

TABLE 9.2

Perspectives on Long-Term Relationships

Perspective	How Applied to Relationships
Socioemotional selectivity theory	People prefer long-term relationships to maximize their positive affect
Social exchange theory	Relationships are evaluated according to costs and benefits
Equity theory	Balance is sought between what each contributes to the relationship
Similarity	Couples who are similar are happier
Need complementarity	Couples who are different are happier
Behavioral approach	The behaviors couples engage in affect their relationship satisfaction

so have the theories, and there is now greater recognition of the multiple variations that are possible when adults form close relationships. The emotional factors involved in long-term relationships are also gaining greater attention, as it is realized that some characteristics of human interactions transcend specific age- or gender-based boundaries.

Socioemotional selectivity theory, which we described in Chapter 8, implies that older adults would prefer to spend time with their marital partner (and other family members) rather than invest their energies in meeting new people. They should regard the long-term marital relationship as offering perhaps the most potential to serve emotional functions because their experience together over the years has allowed them to understand and respond to each other's needs. Indeed, research suggests that older adults are more likely to keep sight of the positive aspects of their relationships even when they have disagreements (Story et al., 2007). In addition, if older adults are better able to control their emotions, particularly the negative ones, they should get along better with their partner because each is less likely to irritate the other one. Finally, because older adults do experience strong feelings, their affection for one another should not fade.

Social exchange theory attempts to predict why some relationships succeed and others fail in terms of whether the relationship's rewards exceed the costs of alternatives to that relationship. The rewards of marriage include love, friendship, and feelings of commitment. When considering a breakup, partners weigh these benefits against legal, financial, social, and religious barriers or constraints. Children will also factor into this equation, adding both to the perceived benefits such as co-parenting and to the costs, which include child custody. When the balance shifts so that rewards no longer outweigh the costs, one or both partners will initiate a breakup. Over time, exchange theory predicts that the intrinsic rewards of being in the relationship, including the reliance the partners develop toward each other, increase to the point that the attractiveness of alternatives tends to fade.

In support of the notion of social exchange as a factor in relationship formation, researchers find that the earning potential of young women is becoming more important in determining their desirability as mates. With women making strides in the labor market, their income is now being seen by husbands as an important asset in their own movement up the occupational career ladder (Sweeney & Cancian, 2004).

However, there are still some very traditional determinants of what makes men happy, at least in the early years of marriage. In a 3-year longitudinal study of characteristics important in a mate, men were found to place higher value on good looks, a pleasing disposition, and a dependable character over time rather than financial prospects or favorable social status (Shackelford, Schmitt, & Buss, 2005).

For cohabitating couples, at least, sexuality seems to follow the principles of social exchange theory. In one study, comparisons of relationship dissolution among cohabitating and married couples showed that cohabitators were more likely to end relationships in which the partners only rarely engaged in sex. Presumably, those who are cohabitating perceive fewer barriers to ending a relationship if the sexual dimension of the relationship no longer proves to be satisfactory (Yabiku & Gager, 2009).

Similar to exchange theory, **equity theory** proposes that partners are satisfied in a relationship if they feel they are getting what they deserve (Walster, Walster, & Berscheid, 1978). This means that they seek getting no more, and certainly no less, than they put into the relationship (Hatfield & Rapson, 2012). Equity theory seems to apply particularly well for couples in the early stages of a relationship when couples are deciding whether to build further ties with each other (Hatfield, Rapson, & Aumer-Ryan, 2008).

Two theories contrast the adages about relationships known as "like attracts like" with "opposites attract." The **similarity hypothesis** proposes that similarity of personality and values predicts both initial interpersonal attraction and satisfaction within long-term relationships (Gaunt, 2006). Sometimes the similarity may be more apparent than real, however. In one 13-year longitudinal study of marital relationships, researchers found that couples who perceived each other as higher in agreeableness than they actually were in reality were more in love during the early stages of marriage and more likely to remain in love over time (Miller, Niehuis, & Huston, 2006). Partner perceptions also play a role in marital satisfaction, particularly for wives; if they perceive their husband as being supportive, they rate their satisfaction with their marriage as higher (Priem, Solomon, & Steuber, 2009).

The **need complementarity hypothesis**, in contrast, proposes that people seek and are more satisfied with marital partners who are the opposite of themselves (Winch, 1958). Despite the anecdotal evidence you may have about this viewpoint from observing your extraverted cousin happily engaged to a shy introvert, the evidence seems to favor the opposite point of view. This is true particularly in the sensitive area of finances within relationships. People who like to spend money may be attracted to those who like to save, but over the long-term, their high level of conflict will detract from the relationship's likelihood of survival (Rick, Small, & Finkel, 2011).

The **behavioral approach to marital interactions** emphasizes the actual behaviors that partners engage in with each other during marital interactions as an influence on marital stability and quality (Karney & Bradbury, 1997). According to this perspective, people will be more satisfied in a long-term relationship when their partners engage in positive or rewarding behaviors (such as expressing affection) and less satisfied with they are critical or abusive. Conflict increases when a partner either turns away from or turns against a partner who is trying to make an emotional connection (Gottman & Driver, 2005).

Sexuality remains an important component of happy relationships throughout adulthood. Although you may imagine that older adults lose interest in sex, those who are in good physical health seem to maintain a virtually lifelong desire to engage in sexual relations (Lindau & Gavrilova, 2010). You can see in Figure 9.4 that over 40% of women and men in the 75–84 age range who are living with a partner engaged in intercourse at least once in the previous year. Even those older adults not living with a partner engage in at least yearly (if not more) sexual intercourse. Furthermore, a considerable number were engaged in some form of sexual activity on a much more frequent basis, with over half of women and men (54%) in the 75–85 year old age bracket having sex two to three times a month, or more.

Approximately one-third in this age group also engaged in oral sex (Waite et al., 2009b).

Thus, sexuality remains important to older adults in the context of their intimate relationships. We know that midlife, and particularly older, adults experience physical changes that could affect their ability to engage in some form of sexual activity, as we discussed in Chapter 4. However, it appears that the majority of adults in their mid-50s and above find ways to incorporate sexuality into their lives on a regular basis, particularly if they are in an intimate relationship.

Returning to the question of satisfaction in marriage, obviously there is more to long-term enjoyment of relationships than expressing sexuality. Alternative theories to marital satisfaction each have their own set of predictions about who will be happiest in a long-term relationship. Unfortunately, studies of marriage suffer from the obvious disadvantage in that they only include couples who remain married. The truly dissatisfied ones leave the relationship, and therefore make it impossible to know which factors either predicted their unhappiness or would have characterized them over time if they had stayed together.

FIGURE 9.4

Percent of Older Men and Women Who Had Intercourse in the Previous Year

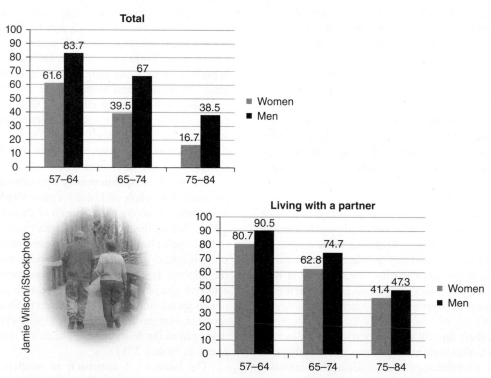

Source: Waite, L. J., Laumann, E. O., Das, A., & Schumm, L. P. (2009). Sexuality: Measures of partnerships, practices, attitudes, and problems in the National Social Life, Health, and Aging Study. *Journals of Gerontology Series B: Psychological Sciences and Social Sciences*, 64 Supplement 1, 156–166.

Nevertheless, a 13-year longitudinal study by University of Texas family psychologist Ted Huston and his collaborators (Huston, 2009) provides some useful insights into the course of long-term marriages.

The surprising feature of Huston's work was his discovery that the seeds of marital bliss, or trouble, are sown even before the couple walk down the aisle. In the **enduring dynamics pathway**, the way a couple interacts early in their relationship will characterize the course of the relationship over time. They either get along well with each other and resolve conflict easily, or they don't.

There are, however, couples whose problems evolve over time. Those who fit the **emergent distress pathway** develop relationship problems over time as they find that they are unable to cope with the inevitable arguments that occur when people live together. Instead of resolving their problems with such adaptive tactics as communicating openly and working out compromises, they become defensive, withdraw, stonewall and become blatantly vicious toward each other. It's not clear whether their distress causes these dysfunctional coping methods or whether their ineffective ways of handling problems leads to distress. The upshot is that these couples become increasingly unhappy over time until they finally decide to end things entirely.

Like couples who experience emergent distress, those who fit the **disillusionment pathway** start out happy and in love when they first tie the knot. Over time, they gradually fall out of love and start to develop mixed feelings about their partner. Part of what happens with these couples is that they take each other for granted. They become less and less interested in seeking their partner's love and approval than they were at the beginning, and as the patina fades, they drift further and further apart.

Both the emergent distress and disillusionment models assume that couples start out as hopeful and optimistic that their relationship will work out; it is only after the months or years go by that they find themselves arguing constantly or just losing interest.

After following their couples 2 and 13 years after marriage, Huston and his team concluded that their data gave the most support to the enduring dynamics model of distress. Rather than newlyweds being head over heels in love, only to have the relationship unravel over time, the dynamics that characterize the beginning of a relationship persisted over time. Two key features seemed to differentiate the happy from the unhappy couples: positive expressions of affection and love, and negative behaviors of being critical, angry, and impatient toward the partner. The happy couples expressed their love through affectionate behaviors, enjoyed being together, and made sure they spent time together. The unhappy ones created a negative emotional climate and avoided being with each other. The

more in love the couple were, the more they expressed their positive feelings toward each other, including initiating sexual activity (Schoenfeld et al., 2012).

Such marital discord for unhappy couples takes its toll on well-being. Couples in their later years who are constantly in conflict are at risk of experiencing higher levels of depression and anxiety and lower levels of self-esteem and life satisfaction (Whisman, Uebelacker, Tolejko, Chatav, & McKelvie, 2006).

For couples who want to work on a troubled relationship, couples therapy is a known effective method for promoting positive change (Davis, Lebow, & Sprenkle, 2012). Although couples therapy shares many features of individual therapy, there are important differences. Couples therapists are trained to examine the types of interactive patterns that lead couples into conflict and then, more importantly, to help them break these dysfunctional patterns. They tend to be more "take charge" than individual therapists, actively intervening when they see problems unfolding before them during therapy sessions. As the couple learn to see their strengths and feel that change is possible, they can come to new understandings of themselves and their relationship (Benson, McGinn, & Christensen, 2012).

FAMILIES

The transformation of a marriage into a "family" traditionally is thought to occur when a child enters the couple's life on a permanent basis. Most of the psychological literature on children and families focuses not on the parents but on the children and their adjustment to the various arrangements for living worked out by their parents (Hetherington & Kelly, 2002). Here, we will examine areas of research specific to studies of adult development and aging.

Despite population trends toward more single-parent and cohabiting families, the large majority of households in the United States consist of people living together as a family. In 2010, there were 116.7 million households in the United States, of whom 32.9 million consisted of married couples without their own children (28.2%). The average family size is 3.14 (U.S. Bureau of the Census, 2012b). Over the past 20 years, fewer households include husband and wife families, with increases in the percent of one-person households, and either one or two people sharing their household with nonfamily members (see Figure 9.5) (Lofquist et al., 2012).

Parenthood

The birth of a couple's first child ushers in the **transition to parenthood (TtP)**, the period of adjustment to the new family status represented by the presence of a child in the home. From a biopsychosocial perspective, the TtP involves biological changes (when the mother bears the child) as her body adapts to rapid hormonal and other physiological alterations. Both parents experience psychological changes including the emotional highs and lows associated with this new status. At the same time, each individual's identity shifts as the parents begin to incorporate their new status in life into their sense of self. They also undergo social changes due to this new role that alters their status with other family members and the community. Their new role brings changes in what society expects of them, expectations that typically reflect social norms for men and women as fathers and mothers.

In the United States in 2009, there were 4.1 million births, which represented a decline of 3% from just the year before (Martin et al., 2011). However, this decline in births affected women 15–39 years of age; women in their 40s and older either rose slightly or remained stable.

FIGURE 9.5

Changes in Family Household Composition From 1990–2010

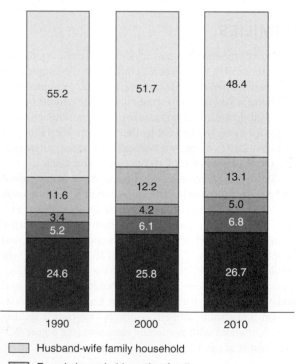

Researchers initially became interested in the TtP because they had consistently found (mainly through cross-sectional studies) that marital satisfaction dips during the child-rearing years, a drop-off particularly marked for women. Researchers now use a prospective design, studying couples before and after the child's birth. The majority of these involve studies of the couple after the mother becomes pregnant.

In a meta-analysis of studies using this design, Mitnick and her collaborators (Mitnick, Heyman, & Smith Slep, 2009) identified 37 studies with sample sizes ranging from 23 to 400 on individuals who were, on average, in their late 20s. Although most of the studies they analyzed showed a slight decline in relationship satisfaction, this was comparable to that of nonparents together for similar lengths of time as the new parents. The meta-analysis only was able to show an overall effect, however, and did not take into account individual differences or variations in patterns of relationship such as those suggested in Huston's longitudinal studies of couples. Although the TtP is not a universal crisis, there are several factors that increase the risk of a couple's experiencing major relationship problems when their child is born. We have summarized these in Figure 9.6.

Typically, the division of labor in the home becomes more traditional after children are born. Working women without children already perform more household duties than men do, but after becoming mothers, the situation is exacerbated (Coltrane, 2000). Mothers assume more of the stereotypically female roles of performing household duties such as laundry, cooking, and cleaning, in addition to providing the bulk of the child care. Men increase their involvement in paid employment outside the home after the child enters the family (Christiansen & Palkovitz, 2001). In part, these changes reflect policies in the workplace as well as the beliefs family responsibilities should be more equitably divided (Singley & Hynes, 2005).

In some cases, marital satisfaction is affected by the process referred to as **doing gender**, a term that refers to the tendency of women and men to behave in stereotypically gendered ways. Parenthood sets up a dynamic which leads the parents to feel that they are now a "traditional" family (Vespa, 2009). For a couple who may have shared housework in a more egalitarian fashion before the child was born, this shift into gendered roles can place strain on the relationship (Grote, Clark, & Moore, 2004).

With changes in legal status for same-sex marriages, an increasing number of gays and lesbians are becoming parents, either through artificial insemination, adoption, or surrogacy. Approximately 14% of male–male and 27% of female–female households include children (Krivickas & Lofquist, 2011). These couples share many of the experiences of heterosexual couples (Goldberg & Sayer, 2006).

FIGURE 9.6

Predictors of Women's Dissatisfaction During the Transition to Parenthood

- Younger age, non-white race/ethnicity, short relationship duration prior to pregnancy
- Poor relationships with own parents
- Unplanned pregnancy
- Impulsivity
- Greater centrality of work
- Newborns who are female or with difficult temperaments
- Psychological characteristics including high levels of neuroticism, insecure attachment style, or psychological disorder

age fotostock/SuperStock

However, the social context seems to have a significant impact on same-sex parents. Those who experience homophobia, live in states with unfavorable legal climates regarding adoption by gays, and receive less support from their friends and families are more likely to feel depressed and anxious (Goldberg & Smith, 2011). Despite the strains they may experience, however, same-sex parents provide care for their children that is of comparable quality to that provided by opposite-sex parents (Biblarz & Stacey, 2010).

Fatherhood is increasingly being studied as an aspect of identity in adulthood, in part reflecting the increasing role of fathers in the raising of their children (Marsiglio, Amato, Day, & Lamb, 2002). Becoming a first-time father can significantly influence a man's patterns of social interaction outside the home. A 7-year longitudinal study of nearly 3,100 fathers of children under the age of 18 described the "transformative" process that occurs as new fathers become more involved with their own parents, grandparents, and other relatives. Fathers also become more involved with service-oriented groups and church. These effects occur along with the birth of each child but are particularly pronounced at the time of the first child's birth (Knoester & Eggebeen, 2006).

Men who feel that they will be better fathers during the transition to parenthood also become more involved in parenting. Moreover, the way that mothers perceive their husbands in the father role can help shape the way that fathers see themselves. A short-term longitudinal study of 183 Canadian couples studied over the first 18 months of first-time parenthood showed that the confidence that men had in their parenting was shaped by how competent their wives viewed them which, in turn, shaped both their self-perceptions and their involvement with their infants (Tremblay & Pierce, 2011).

The extent to which a single father is able to adjust to the role of solo parent is affected by the characteristics of the children, including their age and gender, and his own characteristics, including his age and educational level. The father's adjustment to this role is also affected by his ability to juggle the roles of parent and worker and maintain a relationship with his ex-wife or partner as well as by his original desire to have custody (Greif, 1995). Overall, however, single fathers spend less time caring for their children than do single mothers, but more than do married fathers (Hook & Chalasani, 2008).

Changes in the family living situation in recent decades are often discussed in terms of **blended families**, also known as reconstituted families. Within these family situations, at least one adult is living with a child who is not a biological child of that adult. Often these family situations develop after a divorce and remarriage (or cohabitation), in which two adults establish a household together. The dynamics within these relationships, though the subject of many fictional accounts, are only beginning to receive empirical attention in the literature. Some evidence suggests that these relationships are more stressful in the case of mothers and stepchildren than between fathers and stepchildren (Ward, Spitze, & Deane, 2009).

The Empty Nest

We have examined the factors that influence the transition of a couple that occur when their first child is born. Now we will take a look at what happens during the reverse process. The **empty nest** describes the period in a couple's life that occurs when their children permanently depart from the home.

For many years, the common belief was that the empty nest would be an unwelcome change, particularly for women. However, the reality that the empty nest may be a positive step in a couple's relationship is becoming more and more apparent. Much of the research on the empty nest dates back to earlier decades, when women were less likely to maintain continuous employment outside the home than is currently true. Furthermore, much of the earlier research was conducted at a time when children were more clearly launched, as compared to the present, in which children often take longer to leave the parental home and may "boomerang" back when their economic circumstances take a turn for the worse. Many parents then, if not now, regard their children's leaving to be a mark of their success in preparing them for adulthood.

With the children gone from the home, couples potentially have the opportunity to enjoy more leisure-time activities together, a change that should bring them closer together (Gagnon, Hersen, Kabacoff, & Van Hasselt, 1999). Being able to spend time with each other may also allow them to enjoy greater marital satisfaction and also improved sexual relations. An intensive study of a small sample of Canadian women married after the age of 50 found a shift away from an emphasis on sexual intercourse to greater valuing of other expressions of intimacy, such as cuddling, companionship, and affection. These women still felt that they had strong sexual chemistry with their husbands, even though the expression of that chemistry had changed from the passion of youth (Hurd Clarke, 2006).

Perhaps for these reasons, the empty nest may have some advantages in helping keep a couple's sexual relationship alive. When children do return home for whatever reason, the quality of a couple's sexual relationship may decline at least in terms of frequency of sexual activities (Dennerstein, Dudley, & Guthrie, 2002). In fact, a survey of more than 15,000 midlife Canadian women showed that the predictors of sexual activity within the past 12 months included age, marital status, race, income, alcohol use, smoking, and empty nest status (Fraser, Maticka-Tyndale, & Smylie, 2004). Women whose children were still living in the home were less likely to have intercourse than women who were empty nesters.

However, among certain couples, the empty nest can pose challenges. Mitchell and Lovegreen (2009) identified a pattern they called the "Empty Nest Syndrome" (ENS) in an interview study they conducted of 300 empty nest parents from four cultural groups living in Vancouver, British Columbia. The interviews showed that mothers were slightly more likely than fathers to report ENS; however, the percentages of despondent parents were very low overall, ranging from 20 to 25% in most of the groups studied. Parents of Indo/East Indian ethnicity, whose culture emphasizes continuing bonds between parents and adult children, had far higher rates of ENS (50 and 64% for fathers and mothers) than the parents of Chinese or southern European or British ancestry.

In addition to the role of culture, the Vancouver study identified key social psychological factors that seemed to place these midlife parents at risk of experiencing ENS. These include having an identity that is wrapped up in their parent role, feeling that they are losing control over their children's lives, having few or only children, and lacking a support network. Parents who worried about their children's safety and well-being in the world outside the home also were more vulnerable to ENS. For the most part, however, it's important to remember that the parents in this study were more likely than not to adapt well to the empty nest transition.

Although the empty nest is viewed as the norm when discussing adult children and their parents, there are a growing number of adult sons and daughters living with their parents (ages 25 to 34 years old), a situation referred to by the slang term "boomerang" children in the United States and "kids in parents' pockets eroding retirement savings" (KIPPERS) or "kidults" in the United Kingdom. In part, the return of children back into the empty nest is associated with the economic downturn of the late 2000s (Palmer, 2009).

As is true for the empty nest, there is surprisingly little research on this popular topic. One Canadian survey reported cultural differences in the tendency of parents and young adult children to live together, with Asian and Latin American born parents most likely to host their 20- to 24-year-old children (Turcotte, 2006). Parents with live-in children were more likely than parents whose children did not live at home to experience feelings of frustration over the time spent taking care of their adult children, but the percentage of these negative feelings was very low (8% with live-in children vs. 4% whose children did not live at home). The parents of children living at home also reported more conflict about money, the children themselves, and the distribution of labor in household responsibilities.

The situation seems more negative with boomerang children compared with children who had never left the home, particularly as mothers are likely to resent the fact that they are losing some of the freedom they gained when their children initially left the home. These parents are less likely to say that their children made them happier (57%) than the parents of nonboomerang children (68%). On the other hand, a larger percentage of parents of children living at home (64%) say they are satisfied with the amount of time they spend with their offspring than are parents whose children had moved out (49%).

Parents and children transition together, then, over the course of their relationship, from the children's entrance into the home until their eventual exit, whether permanent or not. The dynamics of these relationships over time may be understood both in terms of identity and in terms of sociocultural factors. Many parents highly value their identities as parents and therefore see the development of their children as reflections of their own competence. At the same time, children try to dissociate from their parents in order to establish their own identities. All of these changes happen in a sociocultural context which, as we have seen in the empty nest research, may affect the normative expectations that parents and children have regarding their positions in the family. We will see later that the dimensions of intergenerational relationships are complex and multifaceted, reflecting these intersecting forces.

Parent–Adult Child Relationships

As children move through the years of adulthood, many facets of their relationships with their own parents undergo change. For example, as children have their own families, they begin to gain greater insight into the role of being a parent. On the one hand, the children may now appreciate what their parents did for them; on the other hand, they may resent their parents for not having done more. Another changing feature of the relationship stems from the child's increasing concern that parents will require help and support as they grow older. Adult children and their parents may also find that they do not agree on various aspects of life, from an overall philosophy and set of values (such as in the area of politics) to specific habits and behaviors (such as methods of food preparation). Whether parents and their adult children live in the same geographic vicinity and actually see each other on a frequent basis must also be added into the equation.

There are several key concepts that can help you gain insight into parent–adult child relationships (see Table 9.3). **Filial maturity** occurs when children reach the age of relating to their parents as equals (Blenkner, 1963; Fingerman, 1996). **Filial anxiety** is the fear of having to take care of an aging, infirmed parent (Cicirelli, 1988). **Filial obligation** describes the cultural values that adult children are expected to care for their parents, including having them live in their homes. Filial obligation is more likely to occur in African American (Wilson, 1986), Hispanic (Keefe, Padilla, & Carlos, 1979), and Asian American families (Velkoff & Lawson, 1998). Filial obligation is also known as **filial piety** in China, represented by the character 孝 (*xiao*).

The **intergenerational solidarity model (ISM)** summarizes the six relevant dimensions of families that span at least two generations (Bengtson & Schrader, 1982; Silverstein & Bengtson, 1997). According to this model (see Figure 9.7), six independent dimensions of solidarity characterize adult family relationships: associational (frequency of interaction), affectual (feelings), consensual (agreement in values, beliefs, and lifestyles), functional (help exchange), normative (commitment to fulfill family obligations), and structural (availability in terms of distance and health).

Each of the ISM dimensions runs along a continuum from positive to negative. For example, the positive pole of the affectual dimension would describe families high in intimacy, and the negative pole would capture families that are emotionally distant. These poles apply to the family as it exists, not to the satisfaction or dissatisfaction that the family may have with where their family ranks on the dimension. A family may see each other only relatively infrequently (i.e., be low on the associational dimension) but not be dissatisfied if they prefer not to see each other very often (Bengtson, Giarrusso, Mabry, & Silverstein, 2002).

In addition to differing in the six solidarity dimensions, families may also vary in their levels of ambivalence (Lüscher, 2002). Not only does this mean that families may have ambivalent feelings toward each other, a possibility that the ISM would allow for, but also that they may not be sure exactly how to interact with each other. **Structural ambivalence** in family relations means that society's structures do not make clear how family members should behave (Connidis & McMullin, 2002). Family members then face contradictory sets of expectations based on such factors as their age and their gender. The uncertainty they face may then produce psychological ambivalence, in which an adult child feels both love and annoyance at a parent.

Tensions between parents and their adult children can increase the extent to which they experience ambivalence, which in turn lowers their affectual solidarity (Birditt, Miller, Fingerman, & Lefkowitz, 2009). According to some researchers, these tensions are almost automatically built into the parent–adult child relationship by virtue of the fact that the parents are more emotionally invested in their children than children in their parents. The **intergenerational stake hypothesis** proposes that parents are higher in affectual solidarity toward their children than children

TABLE 9.3
Concepts in Adult Parent–Child Relationships

Concept	Meaning
Intergenerational stake	Older generations value relationship with adult children more than children value relationships with parents
Developmental schism	Gap between parents and children in how much they value the relationship and seek independence
Role reversal	Discredited view that parents and children switch roles
Filial maturity	Developmental changes in children
Filial anxiety	Worry about being forced to take on care of parents
Filial obligation (piety)	Feeling of commitment that the child should care for the parent

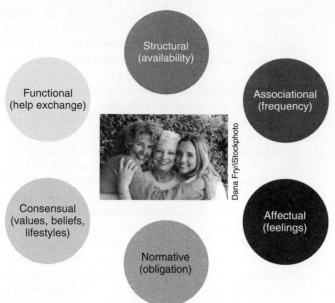

Functional (help exchange)

Structural (availability)

Associational (frequency)

Consensual (values, beliefs, lifestyles)

Normative (obligation)

Affectual (feelings)

Dana Fry/iStockphoto

FIGURE 9.7

The Six Dimensions of the Intergenerational Solidarity Model

are toward their parents. In other words, parents feel more positively about their children than do their children about them. Consequently, parents are likely to try to resolve conflicts with their children through methods that are as constructive as possible (Birditt, Rott, & Fingerman, 2009).

Although originally proposed as a feature of parents and their adult children only, the intergenerational stake also applies to three-generation families. Grandmothers report lower negative quality in their relationship than do their middle-aged children, who in turn report lower negative quality in the relationship than do their own children (Birditt, Tighe, Fingerman, & Zarit, 2012).

Parents and their adult children also differ in their developmental needs resulting, in some cases, in another set of intergenerational tensions. The **developmental schism** occurs when there is a gap between the two generations in how much they value the relationship and whether they wish to be independent (Birditt, Miller, et al., 2009; Fingerman, 2001). One manifestation of the developmental schism is the mother's tendency to regard her daughter as more important than the daughter does the mother, and for the daughter to regard the mother as more intrusive than the mother does the daughter. Mothers are also more likely to regard their daughters as confidants than daughters do their mothers.

Another contributor to the developmental schism occurs when the daughter still seeks the approval of the mother and feels guilty when she feels that she is not living up to her mother's expectations for her. Because of intergenerational stake, when conflicts occur, parents are more likely than are their children to try to resolve conflicts

using constructive strategies in which they attempt to maintain and build a positive relationship (Birditt, Rott, et al., 2009). Despite these problems, the majority of adult children (56%) state that they feel close to their parents. Another large group (38%) see their relationships as ambivalent. Fortunately only a small minority (6%) see them as problematic (Fingerman, Hay, & Birditt, 2004).

For older adults, adult parent–child relationships can play a vital role in well-being, particularly with regard to the development of generativity, and particularly for women (An & Cooney, 2006). Aging parents who have good relationships with their adult children are less likely to feel lonely or depressed (Koropeckyj-Cox, 2002). At the same time, adult children who retain strong attachment ties to their parents also experience psychological benefits (Perrig-Chiello & Höpflinger, 2005).

Part of the intergenerational stake involves concern over the welfare of one's children. When their children succeed, parents can benefit in life satisfaction and well-being; when problems befall their children, parents can suffer ill consequences as well. In a longitudinal study carried out in the Netherlands, Kalmijn and colleagues (2012) found that the divorce of children produced an increase in depressive symptoms among parents, particularly for mothers. On the other hand, when children married and became parents, their own parents also showed a boost in feelings of well-being.

The term **role reversal** refers to the family situation in which adult children take over in the role as parent because the parents are unable to care for themselves. Although this is a term we hear about in the popular literature, the data on intergenerational support present a more complicated picture (Blieszner, 2006), suggesting that much of the flow is downstream from parents to children.

According to the intergenerational solidarity model and the intergenerational stake hypothesis, parents should be more invested in providing support for their adult children than vice versa. However, parents may also provide help to their children because they perceive that the children need this support, which is what **contingency theory** proposes. It is only when the parents of middle-aged adults become infirmed that the direction of support would shift the other way. A survey of over 600 middle-aged adults showed that parents indeed are more likely to support their children than their parents, but also respond when needed to intervene in crises in each generation (Fingerman et al., 2010). Moreover, when parents do experience declines in health, it seems that the norms of filial responsibility lead to mutual adaptations between children and parents (Silverstein, Gans, & Yang, 2006). One in-depth study of a small group of adult children highlighted the concern that children had for respecting the autonomy of their parents within the context of filial obligation (Funk, 2010). In other words, children wanted to take care of their parents but not impinge on their independence.

The potential difficulties between adult children and their parents, particularly for women, are thought to rise to the point of crisis when there is the need to provide caregiving to the parent. Caregiving, which we introduced in Chapter 5, consists of providing assistance in carrying out the tasks of everyday life to an infirm older adult. A large body of evidence has accumulated on this topic since the early 1980s, most of it cross-sectional. Based on this research, it was considered a foregone conclusion that the caregiving role was a traumatic one for the adult child. The daughters in this situation were referred to as "women in the middle" or the **sandwich generation**, meaning that midlife caregivers are sandwiched between their aging mothers and their teenaged children. However, because disability rates of older adults are declining, less than 20% of families in the U.S. are involved at any one point in time in providing care for a parent (Grundy & Henretta, 2006). Moreover, despite the belief that one child (the daughter) has sole responsibility for caregiving, spouses tend to share caregiving roles even when in dual-earner situations (Henz, 2010).

There can be risks, however, experienced by middle-aged adults who serve as caregivers, at least for the time that they are engaged in these roles. In a large longitudinal study of nearly 5,000 Midwest adults, researchers found that both men and women were less likely to engage in a range of healthy behaviors, from using a seat belt, to choosing healthy foods based on their content, to smoking (Chassin, Macy, Seo, Presson, & Sherman, 2010).

A relatively recent trend in parenting literature describes the behavior of **helicopter parents**, those who supposedly smother and overprotect their overly dependent children (regardless of the age of the child). As we have seen, middle-aged parents are likely to provide whatever support they can to adult children who are in need of financial help. Moreover, parents benefit from their relationships with their adult children as do children from their relationships with parents. The question is: How much is too much?

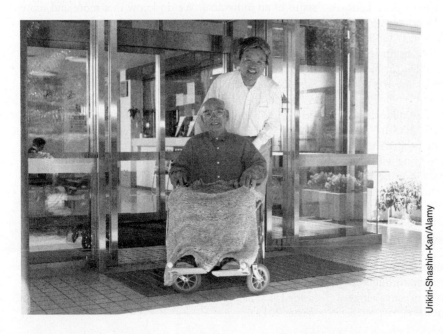

Urikiri-Shashin-Kan/Alamy

This son assisting his father may be expressing a sense of filial obligation.

Fingerman and colleagues (2012) interviewed middle-aged parents with at least one child over the age of 18 and also interviewed up to three of their children. Both parents and children rated the extent of support, and indicated whether the amount provided was too little or too much. Approximately one-fifth of children and nearly 30% of parents reported "intense" support (i.e., too much). However, rather than being detrimental to the child's well-being, young adults whose parents provided a wide range of support ranked higher in life satisfaction. Their parents did not particularly suffer from the support they provided unless they thought their children needed "too much" support, perhaps reflecting what they perceived as their own failure to live up to the ideal identity of a parent.

Clearly, the area of parent–adult child relationships reflects many complex and interacting factors. From a biopsychosocial perspective, we can understand these relationships as involving biological processes pertaining to the aging and health of parents; psychological processes relating to such areas as emotions, identity, and closeness; and social expectations for normative parent–child relationships in one's culture and historical era.

Siblings

The sibling relationship has many unique features within the constellation of family interactions (Van Volkom, 2006). Those who are siblings by birth share a genetic background; those who have been raised together share many experiences dating to early childhood. By the time siblings reach later adulthood, it is quite possible that they are the only remaining members of their original family and have known each other longer than anyone else they have known in their entire lives. As is true for adult child–parent relationships, the sibling relationship is not one of choice; to be sure, many people allow their connections with brothers and sisters to fall by the wayside. However, even if they do not stay in frequent contact, they may still maintain the relationship and tend to value it in a positive manner (Bedford, Volling, & Avioli, 2000).

The potential exists for the sibling relationship to be the deepest and closest of an adult's life and to bring with that closeness both shared joy and shared pain. For the most part, it appears that these relationships tend to be positive in middle and later adulthood (Gold, 1989). Nevertheless, siblings may carry with them into midlife the perception that either they or their sibling was differentially favored by their parents. When this happens, they experience high levels of tension in their relationship (Suitor et al., 2009). The sibling relationship can fluctuate throughout adulthood, however. Increased closeness between siblings is associated with a number of significant life events, such

as marriage, the birth of children, divorce and widowhood, and the development of health problems or death of a family member (Connidis, 1992). The role of parental support in the sibling tie also appears to be a factor in maintaining relationships between siblings but perhaps in unexpected ways. In a test of the intergenerational solidarity model within a Netherlands sample, researchers found that the poorer the relationship with parents, the more support siblings provide for each other. Thus, siblings may turn to each other to compensate for the failure to connect with parents (Voorpostel & Blieszner, 2008).

Grandparents

For many older adults, the rewards of family life begin to grow much richer when they reach the status of grandparents. At this point, they are in a position to be able to enjoy the benefits of expressing their generativity through interacting with the youngest generation. At the same time, grandparents can avoid the more arduous tasks of parenthood.

Many people still think of grandparents as the warm, generous, older adults portrayed in storybooks: kindly relatives who have ample time to spend with their families and want to do so. However, variations in patterns of grandparenting, along with a rapidly increasing growth in the number of grandparents in the population, may require a change in this image.

There may be as many as 70 million grandparents in the United States according to popular estimates; there are no official data in the U.S. Census on the grandparent status of an individual. We do know that more and more grandparents are involved in some form of caregiving of their grandchildren, with an estimated 22% in the U.S. (Fuller-Thomson & Minkler, 2001) and slightly more in Europe (33% of grandmothers and 26% of grandfathers) (Hank & Buber, 2009).

A substantial number of children are raised entirely by their grandparents, with an estimated 2.9 million in 2011 living in the homes of grandparents without the presence of their own parents (U.S. Bureau of the Census, 2013a). The term **skip generation family** refers to the family living situation in which children live with their grandparents and not their parents. The skip generation family may occur when there is substance abuse by parents; child abuse or neglect by parents; teenage pregnancy or failure of parents to handle children; and parental unemployment, divorce, AIDS, or incarceration. African American and Hispanic children are more likely to grow up in a skip generation family or to be part of a multigeneration household headed by their grandparent (Luo, LaPierre, Hughes, & Waite, 2012).

This grandfather is enjoying his relationship with his grandchildren as they share storytelling time.

Although only a small percentage (14%) of grandparents in skip generation households are over the age of 60 years, substantial percentages live in poverty (Economist, 2007). Many have a disability. However, on the positive side, the role of surrogate parent can contribute positively to the grandparents' sense of identity, particularly for African American grandmothers (Pruchno & McKenney, 2002). Feeling that others are supportive can help ameliorate the negative effects of the stress and strain of caring for the grandchild (Musil, Warner, Zauszniewski, Wykle, & Standing, 2009).

Grandparents vary in the extent to which they become involved in the lives of their grandchildren. The classic study of grandparenting conducted by Neugarten and Weinstein (1964) identified five types of grandparents. The first type, the formal grandparent, follows what are believed to be the appropriate guidelines for the grandparenting role. Formal grandparents provide occasional services and maintain an interest in the grandchild but do not become overly involved. By contrast, the second type, the fun seeker, prefers the leisure aspects of the role and primarily provides entertainment for the grandchild. The surrogate parent is the third type; as the name implies, takes over the caretaking role with the child. Fourth, the reservoir of family wisdom, which is usually a grandfather, is the head of the family, who dispenses advice and resources but also controls the parent generation. Finally, the distant figure is the fifth type of grandparent; he or she has infrequent contact with the grandchildren, appearing only on holidays and special occasions.

Other attempts to characterize or delineate styles or categories of grandparenting have followed a similar pattern, with distinctions typically being made among the highly involved, friendly, and remote or formal types of grandparents (Mueller, Wilhelm, & Elder, 2002). The "remote-involved" dimension is one that seems to resonate in the attitudes that grandchildren have toward their grandparents as well (Roberto, 1990). The symbolic value of the grandparent in the family lineage, or the "family watchdog" (Troll, 1985), is another central component identified in several classifications. There is evidence that the role of grandparent is more central in the lives of grandmothers than grandfathers (Pollet, Nelissen, & Nettle, 2009).

Although these variations may exist in patterns of grandparenting, it is safe to say that the role of grandparent is an important one for the older adult (Harwood, Sultzer, & Wheatley, 2000) and that grandparent identity is an important contributor to well-being (Reitzes & Mutran, 2004). Grandparents feel a strong sense of connection to the younger generation (Crosnoe & Elder, 2002) and may play an important role in mediating relationships between parents and grandchildren during conflicts (Werner, Buchbinder, Lowenstein, & Livni, 2005).

Contact with their grandchildren declines steadily through the grandchildren's early adulthood, particularly when they leave the home of their parents and start an independent life of their own (Geurts, Poortman, van Tilburg, & Dykstra, 2009). Those grandparents who get along with their own children are more likely to maintain contact with their grandchildren throughout this period (Dunifon & Bajracharya, 2012). Research shows that such contact may be important to the mental health of the older generation. Grandparents who are unable to maintain contact with their grandchildren due to parental divorce or disagreements within the family are likely to suffer a variety of ill consequences, including poor mental and physical health, depression, feelings of grief, and poorer quality of life (Drew & Smith, 2002). However, as their grandchildren get older, many grandparents are able to stay in touch and even to consider their grandchildren as part of their social network (Geurts, van Tilburg, & Poortman, 2012).

FRIENDSHIPS

Of the areas of relationships examined in this chapter, oddly enough, friendship has probably received the least attention regarding its function, meaning, and changes over the course of adulthood. Yet, everyone can attest to the importance of friends in their own life, and the many roles that friends play in providing many forms of support and boosting one's emotional well-being.

Theoretical Perspectives

From a life course perspective, the major dimension that underlies close friendships is reciprocity, or a sense of mutuality (Hartup & Stevens, 1997). The fundamental characteristic of reciprocity is that there is give and take within the relationship at a deep, emotional level involving intimacy, support, sharing, and companionship. At the behavioral level, reciprocity is expressed in such actions as exchanging favors, gifts, and advice.

Close friends in adulthood confide in each other, help each other in times of trouble, and attempt to enhance each other's sense of well-being. Although there may be developmental differences across the life span in the expression of reciprocity, the essence of all friendships remains this sense of deep mutuality. Another important function of friendships is socializing, or helping each other through life transitions in other spheres, such as changes in health, marital relationships, residence, and work.

FIGURE 9.8

Characteristics of Friendships in Adulthood

- Follow a trajectory from formation to dissolution
- May be distinguished in terms of closeness
- Vary in terms of friendship styles
- Throughout adulthood are related to well-being and self-esteem

Nicholas Monu/iStockphoto

Patterns of Friendships

Although people's lives change substantially throughout the vicissitudes of adulthood, many people remain close to their "best" friends. According to a 2002 survey (Fetto, 2002), 65% of American adults have known their best friends for at least 10 years, and 36% for 20 years or more. Nearly all (91%) said they would take a vacation with their best friend.

This tendency to stick with their best friends occurs despite the pressures of people's jobs, children, and romantic partners. In fact, as people enter long-term intimate relationships, many engage in **dyadic withdrawal**, which is the process of reducing the individual friendships of the couple and increasing the joint friendships (Kalmijn, 2003). Overall this means a decline will occur in a person's total number of friends. On the other hand, as couples share social networks, they expand their own friendship circles and also strengthen their own relationship (Cornwell, 2012). Part of this may occur through "platonic couple love" in which couples who are best friends also emulate the desirable qualities of the other couple (Greif & Deal, 2012).

Friendship patterns at any age may be seen as following a developmental trajectory from formation to dissolution (see Figure 9.8) (Adams & Blieszner, 1994). You have probably experienced this trajectory with your own friends. The stage of friendship formation involves moving from being strangers to acquaintances to friends. The maintenance phase encompasses what is usually thought of as "friendship," during which friends sustain an active interest and involvement with each other. They may evaluate the quality of the friendship periodically during this phase, deciding to increase or decrease their level of involvement. In terms of Hartup's framework, it would be during the maintenance phase that reciprocity levels are highest. Friendships may remain in the maintenance phase for years, even decades, at varying levels of closeness. The end of a friendship, which occurs during the dissolution phase, may be hard to identify. A friendship may end gradually over a period of time as feelings of reciprocity dwindle and the relationship essentially falls by the wayside. Friendships may also end through a conscious decision based on insurmountable disagreements and conflict.

Friendships in adulthood may also be distinguished in terms of the closeness of the relationship, which may or may not change over time. People may maintain **peripheral ties**, which are not characterized by a high degree of closeness, for many years (Fingerman & Griffiths, 1999). Peripheral ties include people such as neighbors, coworkers, professional contacts, gym buddies, friends of friends, or the parents of one's children's friends. These relationships may be amicable and cordial but never progress beyond this level. Other peripheral ties may be those that are in the friendship formation stage and will later progress to close friendships. A third type of peripheral tie is one that was formerly a close friendship and has now moved to the dissolution/disinterest stage.

There may also be variations in friendship patterns in adulthood based on individual differences in approaches toward friends, called **friendship styles** (Matthews, 1986). Individuals who have an independent friendship style may enjoy friendly, satisfying, and cordial relationships with people but never form close or intimate friendships. The type known as discerning individuals are extremely selective in their choice of friends, retaining a small number of very close friends throughout their lives. Finally, people with an acquisitive friendship style are readily able to make and retain close friendships throughout their lives and therefore have a large social network.

People tend to choose as friends other people who are similar in gender, socioeconomic status, and ethnicity (Adams & Blieszner, 1994). Throughout adulthood, close social ties serve as a buffer against stress and are related to higher levels of well-being and self-esteem. Relationships with friends may even be more predictive of high levels of self-esteem than income or marital status (Siebert, Mutran, & Reitzes, 2002). For people who have no family members, friendships serve as an important substitute for keeping an individual socially active (Lang & Carstensen, 1994). Moreover, friendships play a particularly important role in the lives of older gay men and lesbians, who have considerably more elaborated conceptions of their friendship ties than do heterosexual individuals (De Vries & Megathlin, 2009).

Friends are an important influence on you throughout your life. Although you may not realize it, they contribute to our personal narratives, sense of self, and even important life choices (Flora, 2013). The nature of your friendships may change over time, but they continue to serve as a source of self-definition and support.

As you have learned in this chapter, close social ties play an important role in development. Even as relationships respond to a changing social context, they continue to influence people's well-being and adaptation. There continue to be areas of research that need further work, however, particularly in the areas of grandparenting, siblings, and friendships. From a biopsychosocial perspective, this research will provide greater understanding of the interactions among health, personality, and social context.

SUMMARY

1. Close relationships form an important component of adult life. Development in adulthood and later life interacts in important ways with the ties that people have with others. Societal changes impact the nature of individual relationships. The large majority of adults get married. Although marriage rates are decreasing and people are waiting longer to get married than in previous decades, the majority of adults are living in a marital relationship.

2. Cohabitation rates have been increasing in recent decades. According to the cohabitation effect, people living together before marriage are more likely to divorce. Approximately 10% of the adult population in the United States is divorced. The divorce rate is highest among men in their 50s. Taking into account all marriages that end in divorce, the average length of first marriage prior to divorce is about 8 years. Divorce statistics also show important variations by race.

3. Birthrates have decreased over the past 20 years, and women are having children at later ages. Most women, however, have their first child before the age of 30. Women who have a child after age 30 are more highly educated and have higher incomes but also have a higher risk of encountering medical complications. Men with higher education and occupation are more involved in raising their children but spend less time in providing care. The number of single fathers is increasing, but there are also more fathers who have no contact with children.

4. Widowhood is a stressful event for men and women; however, men are more likely to show the widowhood effect of increased mortality after becoming a widow. The effects of widowhood can persist for many years, and many people report various forms of attachment to their deceased spouse.

5. Studies of the transition to parenthood indicate that decreases in marital satisfaction are especially likely to occur when the division of labor assumes more traditional lines in the household. The study of adult child–parent relationships reveals a number of important phenomena related to changes in roles and their altered views of each other. Although caregiving is usually thought of in negative terms, there is some evidence of positive outcomes. The intergenerational solidarity model proposes six dimensions to characterize the cohesiveness of these relationships.

6. Siblings are another important family tie in adulthood. Closeness between siblings varies over the adult years along with other family and life events.

7. The majority of older adults are grandparents, a relationship that tends to be positive. There is a trend toward grandparents raising grandchildren in a "skip generation" (no parents present) household. Theoretical explanations of grandparenting focus on the remote-involved dimension, and various categorization schemes are based on this concept.

8. Friendships are another source of important close relationships in adulthood. Even if individuals are not involved in tight-knit friendships, they may have many important peripheral ties.

10

Work, Retirement, and Leisure Patterns

AGING TODAY

That Delicate Work–Family Balance and How to Have It All

In March 2013, Yahoo!'s CEO, Marissa Mayer, took one giant leap backward for womankind, if not mankind, when she announced the family-unfriendly policy that "Yahoos" (as employees are called) could no longer work from home. This was not Mayer's first foray into the Mommy/Daddy wars. Soon after giving birth to her son, she returned to the Yahoo! helm, installing a nursery (at her own expense) in her office. Not remarkably, she later announced that having a baby was "way easier than everyone made it out to be." No irony here. She didn't work from home, she just moved part of her home to her office. As *New York Times* columnist Maureen Dowd noted: "The fear that this might set an impossible standard for other women—especially women who had consigned "having it all" to unicorn status"—reverberated. Even the German family minister, Kristina Schröder, chimed in: "I regard it with major concern when prominent women give the public impression that maternity leave is something that is not important."

The truth is that Mayer likely got it wrong about flexible schedules. When companies create family-friendly environments, their employees work harder, feel better about the company, and feel better about their lives. Research on male and female employees shows clearly that there are major impacts on a number of outcome variables related to productivity, life satisfaction, and satisfaction with their roles at home and at work.

In role enrichment, your "experiences in one role improve the quality of life in the other role" (Greenhaus & Powell, 2006a, p. 73). You may have limited time and energy, but the skills, feelings, and values you develop in one sphere help you perform better in the other. Role enrichment occurs because we can transfer our skills from one sphere to the other.

The upshot is that, as you will learn, if you have not already, you don't have to give up your work for your family life, or your family life for your work. There may be tough times when things go badly. Babysitters become unavailable, children get sick, school beckons you to parent–teacher meetings, work deadlines get shortened, you need to put in extra hours, etc. However, when you can draw on the resources in both areas of your life, shore up your coping strategies and—most importantly—be lucky enough to have understanding colleagues and supervisors, you can enjoy a fulfilling and enriching life in both spheres.

Posted by Susan Whitbourne and Stacey Whitbourne

The majority of adults are involved in productive activities in some form of paid employment. For people who are fortunate enough to be in a job they enjoy, the experience of work is positive and fulfilling and allows them to express their personal interests and abilities. Other workers view their job as a means of supplying income that enables them to support themselves and most likely their families. Yet others struggle to find employment, a concern for many Americans given the economic climate following the 2008 economic downturn.

Whatever a person's current job situation, work provides the primary focus of his or her life. Work will dominate your life from your 20s onward, until either you retire or become too ill to continue. The type of job you have, the amount of money you make, and the conditions in which you work carry over to virtually every other area of your life. If you're like most people, you will come to define your identity in terms of your job title, prestige, security, and status.

In this chapter, we will talk about work in terms of vocational development, satisfaction, and performance. We will conclude the chapter with an extensive look at how retirement affects people in terms of their finances, life satisfaction, and leisure pursuits. Although the thought of retirement may seem very far away to you now, as you will

learn, it's never too early to start planning for it. Before we get to that section, however, we'll explore the ways that you can lead a fulfilling work life.

WORK PATTERNS IN ADULTHOOD

We will start with some basic concepts and statistics about work before we explore the psychological aspects of work in adulthood. The **labor force** includes all civilians in the over-16 population who live outside of institutions (prisons, nursing homes, residential treatment centers) and have sought or are actively seeking employment. They are not necessarily the people who are employed.

In 2012, the total civilian, noninstitutionalized population over the age of 16 was 243.3 million people; nearly two-thirds (64%) of this group were in the labor force. Reflecting the downturn in the U.S. economy beginning in late 2008, 92% of the labor force were employed in 2012, down from 96% in 2007 but up from 90% in 2010.

As you can see from Figure 10.1, the labor force is increasingly consisting of workers 55 and older (Toossi, 2012). These shifts reflect the continued aging of the Baby Boomer generation, whose influence will continue to have an impact despite the fact that the oldest members will no

FIGURE 10.1

Labor Force by Age, 2000, 2010, and Projected 2050

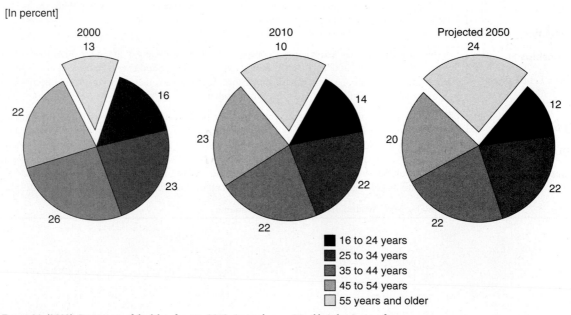

[In percent]

16 to 24 years
25 to 34 years
35 to 44 years
45 to 54 years
55 years and older

Source: Toossi, M. (2012). Projections of the labor force to 2050: A visual essay. *Monthly Labor Review,* from http://www.bls.gov/opub/mlr/2012/10/art1full.pdf

longer be in the population. In 2018, nearly 80% of the 55- to 59-year-old population will still be in the labor force, an all-time high (Toossi, 2009).

Whites, Blacks, and Hispanics have similar labor force participation rates, meaning that they are employed or seek employment to the same extent. However, in 2011, although the average unemployment rate was 8.9%, the rates among Blacks (15.8%), American Indians and Alaska Natives (14.6%), and Hispanics (11.5%) far exceeded those of Whites (7.9%) and Asians (7%) (U.S. Department of Labor, 2013).

People with a college education are far more likely to be employed than people with a high school education or less (Bureau of Labor Statistics, 2013b). In 2012, people with less than a high school education had an unemployment rate of 12.4%, those with a high school education had an unemployment rate of 8.3%, and those with a bachelor's degree or higher had an unemployment rate of 4.0%. However, even among college graduates, there are racial and ethnic disparities in the unemployment rate. Blacks with a college degree or higher had an unemployment rate

of 6.3%, and those of Hispanic or Latino ethnicity had an unemployment rate of 5.1%.

In 2011, 58.1% of women were in the labor force (Bureau of Labor Statistics, 2013d). The great majority of mothers with children under 18 years old were in the labor force (70.9%), but mothers with children 6 to 17 years old were more likely to be in the labor force (76.5%) than were mothers with children under 6 (64.2%).

Despite their increasing involvement in the labor force, however, women still earn less than men. We call this the **gender gap**: it is expressed as a proportion of women's to men's salaries. As of 2011, full-time employed women earned a median of $684 per week, which was 82% of the median for men (Bureau of Labor Statistics, 2013d). The gender gap is more pronounced among Asians (77%) and Whites (82%), and lowest among Blacks and Hispanics (91%).

Part of the reason for the gender gap is that women are less likely than men to be employed in high-paying sectors of the market. Although women outnumber men in the professional and related occupations (see Figure 10.2),

FIGURE 10.2

Distribution of Full-Time Wage and Salary Employment by Sex and Major Occupation Group, U.S., 2011

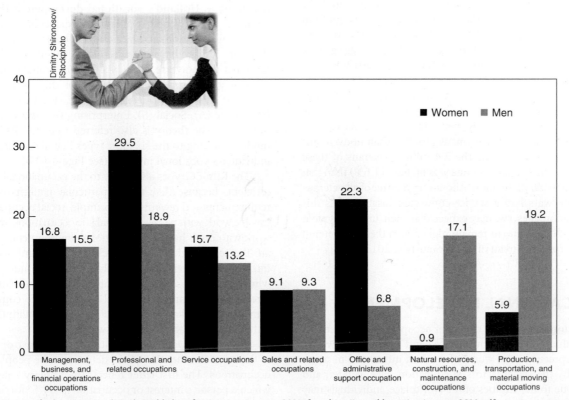

Source: Bureau of Labor Statistics. (2012). Highlights of women's earnings in 2011, from http://www.bls.gov/cps/cpswom2011.pdf

they are more likely to be employed in the lower-paying fields of education and healthcare (69%) than professional men (30%). By contrast, 8% of professional women were employed in the higher-paying computer and engineering fields, compared with 44% of male professionals.

Although students about to graduate from college often worry about whether they will get a job, a college degree is a benefit when it comes to occupational level and, ultimately, lifetime earning potential. Statistically speaking, your income is likely to rise with each increase in your educational level. In 2012, college graduates in the U.S. earned $1,066 per week compared to the $652 earned by high school graduates (Bureau of Labor Statistics, 2013a).

However, even for college graduates in the U.S., there are disparities according to racial and ethnic minority status. For example, in 2012, among men with a bachelor's degree or higher, Black men earned 73% of the income of Whites, and Hispanic college graduates earned 82% of the income of White men. This disparity remains approximately the same even at the advanced graduate degree levels (Bureau of Labor Statistics, 2013c).

Educational levels within the United States vary considerably by age group. In general, there has been an increasing trend over the past 40 years for older adults to have higher levels of education, with more individuals ages 65–74 having a college diploma (14.1%) than was true in 1985 (9.4%). This trend is certain to continue, as is evident from the fact that the 25- to 34-year-old age bracket now includes the highest percentage of college graduates of all age groups of adults (24%) (U.S. Bureau of the Census, 2012c).

The unemployment rate for young male U.S. veterans (18–24) of the wars in Iraq and Afghanistan as of 2011 is far higher (29.1%) than that of nonveterans (17.6%) from the same age group. Similarly, male veterans 25 to 34 years of age had higher unemployment (13.4%) than nonveterans (9.5%). Overall, among the 2.4 million veterans of these wars, the unemployment rate was higher (11.6%) than that of the general population. About one-quarter of all veterans of these wars had a service-connected disability. As this population ages, we may expect that their unemployment rates will continue to remain higher than their nonveteran counterparts (Bureau of Labor Statistics, 2012).

VOCATIONAL DEVELOPMENT

Vocation is a person's choice of occupation. It reflects the individual's personal preferences and interests. However, development in the world of work is influenced in many ways by the social factors of education, race, gender, and age. Due to the realities of the workplace, individuals may not be able to find a job that best matches their vocational interests. Nevertheless, vocational development theories are based on the premise that people are able to choose the career they wish to pursue.

Thinking about your own desire to enter a given field, it is likely that you chose your career path and hence college major because of your vocational interests. You decided at an earlier point in your life that you wanted to pursue a given field, whether it was music, psychology, nursing, or social work, because it suited your personality, values, and skills. These are the factors that vocational development theories take into account when they attempt to explain the career choices that people make and determine people's levels of happiness and productivity once they have acted on those choices.

The basis of vocational development theories is the concept of **career**, which is the term that captures the unique connection between individuals and social organizations over time. Many factors shape the individual's career, including personal development, the specific organization for which the person works, and the profession or occupational category that describes the individual's occupation.

Holland's Vocational Development Theory

According to **Holland's vocational development theory** (Holland, 1997), people express their personalities in their vocational aspirations and interests. Holland proposed that there are six fundamental types (also called codes) that represent the universe of all possible vocational interests, competencies, and behaviors. Each of the six types is identified by its initial letter: Realistic (R), Investigative (I), Artistic (A), Social (S), Enterprising (E), and Conventional (C). The theory is also referred to as the **RIASEC model**, referring to the six basic types that characterize an individual's vocational interests (see Figure 10.3).

The RIASEC types also apply to the occupational environment, because they reflect particular patterns of job requirements and rewards. For example, social occupations involve work with people, and realistic occupations involve work with one's hands. Occupational environments, then, are the settings that elicit, develop, and reward specific interests, competencies, and behaviors of the individuals who work in those environments. If you are working in a realistic environment, you will be expected to complete activities that make use of your ability to work with things rather than your ability to work with people.

Vocational psychologists typically combine two or three of the initials in the RIASEC model to describe people and occupations. The first letter reflects the primary type into which a person's interest or occupation falls ("S" for Social, for example). The second and third letters allow for a more

FIGURE 10.3

Holland's RIASEC Model

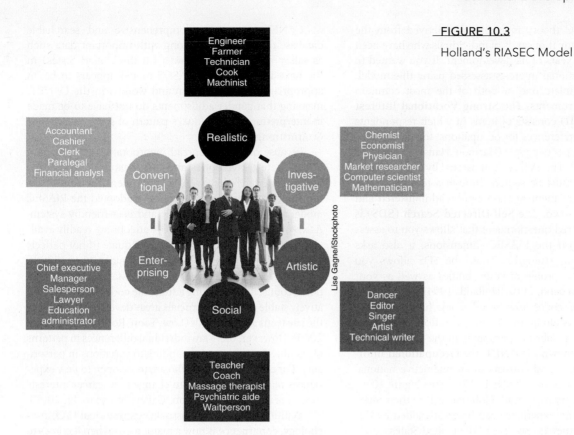

Lise Gagne/iStockphoto

accurate and differentiated picture of the individual or occupation. Both a construction worker and a corrections officer are R code occupations, and both have the RE code designation. They differ in their third code, which is C for the construction worker and S for the corrections officer.

From a personality perspective, the RIASEC types as applied to individuals are very much like traits (Armstrong & Anthoney, 2009). Putting the two together, researchers have suggested that there are three underlying dimensions: interest in people versus things, preference for abstract versus concrete ideas, and striving for personal growth versus striving for accomplishment. However, personality traits do not completely map to vocational interests (Mount, Barrick, Scullen, & Rounds, 2005).

The six RIASEC types are organized within the individual in a hexagonal structure. This structure implies that the types have a relationship to each other based on their distance from each other on the structure. Types that are most similar (such as R and C) are closest; those that are the most dissimilar (such as C and A) are farthest away from each other.

The notion of the hexagon is an important one because it helps define the way that your interests correspond to your environments. You will be most satisfied in your job

if you are in an environment that fits your personality type. **Congruence** or "fit" occurs when your vocational type matches your occupational environment.

Not only does congruence make you feel happier, but it also influences your ability to be effective on the job. According to vocational development theory, if you are happy, you will also be most productive. Unfortunately, people cannot always find jobs congruent with their interests, particularly in a tough economy. In these situations, the RIASEC model predicts that people will experience low job satisfaction and a high degree of instability until they can find fulfilling work environments. When they are unable to do so, their work productivity may suffer.

Supporting this idea, researchers have found that individuals with Artistic interests working in Realistic environments, for example, have lower work quality than people whose interests match their environments (Kieffer, Schinka, & Curtiss, 2004). Again, when jobs are scarce, people may have to take whatever work they can find and seek congruence elsewhere through leisure pursuits. The Artistic type in the Realistic job may wait out the hours until the workday is over and then rush home to work on crafts, play a musical instrument, or go to a pottery studio.

The RIASEC theory is empirically derived from the responses of many thousands of individuals who have been tested over the years of its development. If you wanted to have your vocational interests assessed using this model, you could complete one or both of the most common assessment instruments. The **Strong Vocational Interest Inventory (SVII)** consists of items in which respondents indicate their preferences for occupations, topics of study, activities, and types of people (Harmon, Hansen, Borgen, & Hammer, 1994). The SVII is administered by a professional counselor and must be scored through a testing service. The second assessment method can be administered and scored on your own. The **Self-Directed Search (SDS)** is a self-administered questionnaire that allows you to assess where you fit on the RIASEC dimensions; it also asks you to rate your strengths. Thus, the SDS allows you to determine the profile of your abilities as well as your interests (Gottfredson, 2002; Holland, 1994).

The RIASEC codes now have become fully integrated into an online system in use by many vocational placement agencies and state labor departments in the United States. This system is known as **O*NET**, the **Occupational Information Network**, and consists of an interactive national database of occupations (O*NET, 2010) (see Figure 10.4). People who are trying to find a job that will fit their interests, training, and experience can be greatly aided by this system, even if they do not live in the United States.

O*NET provides a comprehensive and searchable database of occupations, along with important data such as salary and expected growth (in the United States) in the next 10 years. The RIASEC model appears to be an appropriate fit for both men and women in the O*NET, meaning that gender adjustments do not have to be made in interpreting an individual's pattern of scores (Anthoney & Armstrong, 2010).

Because of its widespread incorporation into occupational interest inventories and classification schemes, the RIASEC model is likely to be prominent for some time to come. Vocational counselors have adopted the RIASEC model as an easily interpretable and user-friendly system. Assessment tools for both people and jobs are readily available and inexpensive, and there is adequate (if not perfect) empirical support for it from large-scale studies (Smith, Hanges, & Dickson, 2001). From the standpoint of vocational counseling for young adults, the codes seem to be relatively stable during the crucial career development years of the late teens and early 20s (Low, Yoon, Roberts, & Rounds, 2005). However, there are individual differences in patterns of stability, possibly corresponding to variations in personality. For example, people who are more open to new experiences may be more likely to change their career interests over time (Rottinghaus, Coon, Gaffey, & Zytowski, 2007).

Within the field of industrial-organizational (I/O) psychology, congruence is now a major focus when it comes to

FIGURE 10.4

The O*NET OnLine Website

the business of matching people to jobs. At the same time, as anyone who has spent time in a workplace would attest to, it is also important to determine the fit or match among individuals working together as a team (Muchinsky, 1999). Does an RCE type get along better with another RCE, or would their similar styles lead to narrow thinking and lack of productivity among members of a work unit? Perhaps the RCE should be working alongside an SAI, whose "people" orientation will complement the "thing"-oriented approach of the Realistic individual.

The notion of congruence between people and jobs has received considerable empirical support, not only in terms of job ratings but also in terms of career change behavior. All other things being equal, people will tend to move out of incongruent jobs and into positions more suited to their interests (Donohue, 2006). Unfortunately, for many people, factors outside their control, such as race and ethnicity, limit these choices. For individuals whose vocational situations are affected by such constraints, the role of identity and the possibility for realizing one's true vocational interests are far less significant than the reality of these sociocultural factors.

Super's Life-Span Life-Stage Theory

As individuals traverse the various stages of their vocational development, their sense of self also undergoes changes. **Super's life-span life-stage theory** focuses on the role of the self and proposes that people attempt to realize their inner potential through their career choices (Super, 1957; Super, 1990). If you see yourself as an artist, then you will desire work in which you can express that view of yourself.

In contrast to Holland's theory, which emphasizes vocational preferences (the fact that you prefer artistic work), Super's theory places the focus on the occupation that you see as most "true" to your inner self. Super's theory also takes into account the fact that the constraints of the marketplace mean that people are not always able to achieve full realization of their self-concepts. In a society with relatively little demand for artists, the person with the artistic self-concept will need to seek self-expression in a job that allows for a certain degree of creativity but will also bring in a paycheck. Such an individual may seek a career in computer graphic design, for example, because that is a more viable occupation than that of an oil painter.

According to Super, the expression of self-concept through work occurs in a series of four stages that span the years from adolescence to retirement (see Figure 10.5). In the exploration stage (teens to mid-20s), people explore career alternatives and select a vocation that they will find to express their self-concept. By the time they reach the establishment stage (mid-20s to mid-40s), people are focused

FIGURE 10.5

The Stages in Super's Self-Concept Model

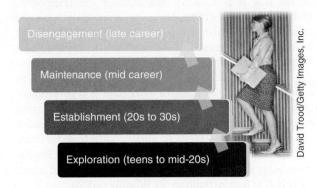

on achieving stability and attempt to remain within the same occupation. At the same time, people seek to move up the career ladder to managerial positions and higher. In the maintenance stage (mid-40s to mid-50s), people attempt to hold onto their positions rather than to seek further advancement. Finally, in the disengagement stage (mid-50s to mid-60s), workers begin to prepare for retirement, perhaps spending more time in their leisure pursuits.

When Super first wrote about career development, the job market was much more stable than today. In the 1950s, many people were employed by one company for their entire careers. Climbing up the career ladder was seen as a fairly typical goal, particularly for workers in white-collar occupations, but also for blue-collar workers employed in such industries as steel or car manufacturing. This model began to change substantially in the 1980s, when large corporations began programs of downsizing, particularly after the advent of computerized technology.

The modern workplace is likely to promote **recycling**, the process through which workers change their main field of career activity partway into occupational life (Sullivan, Martin, Carden, & Mainiero, 2003). In recycling, middle-aged workers may find themselves once again in the establishment stage they thought they had left behind in their late 20s. People can continue to recycle back through Super's stages several times throughout their work lives (Hall, 1993).

People may also experience **career plateauing**, in which they remain static in their vocational development. They may experience structural plateauing, in which they do not advance up to higher-level positions, or content plateauing, in which they feel that they have mastered their work and no longer see it as a challenge (Lapalme, Tremblay, & Simard, 2009).

People may reach their plateau at a young age if they enter a so-called dead-end job, or if their moves within or between companies involve lateral changes rather than vertical advancement. At that point, the individual may decide that it is time to seek another job (Heilmann, Holt, & Rilovick, 2008). However, some employees are content to remain in the status quo, particularly if they have achieved success and are satisfied with their current positions (Smith-Ruig, 2009).

There are strategies for those workers who wish to combat plateauing. A study of more than 300 government employees showed that workers who reported serving as a mentor were less likely to experience the negative effects of plateauing (Lentz & Allen, 2009). In some cases, multiple mentors can help individuals continuously acquire knowledge that will help them achieve personal and career success (De Janasz, Sullivan, & Whiting, 2003).

Occupation as Calling

The role of the self in vocational development forms the core of theories that emphasize people's desires both to achieve self-expression through their work and to contribute to the larger good. A **calling** is an individual's consuming passion for a particular career domain that serves people in some capacity and contributes to a sense of personal meaning and purpose (Duffy, Allan, Autin, & Bott, 2013).

Ultimately, your choice of a vocation may reflect a feeling that you are drawn to a particular line of work, either because of the job tasks it entails, the personality needs it fulfills (as in the RIASEC model), or because it serves a socially useful purpose. In addition, the notion of calling implies that the individual feels the need to pursue the occupation in order to contribute to the larger social good (Dik, Eldridge, Steger, & Duffy, 2012).

Examples of calling items would include "being passionate" about your work, enjoying your work more than anything else, being willing to sacrifice everything to do this job, having this job being on your mind in some way at all times, and finding the experience of performing your work to be deeply gratifying (Dobrow & Tosti-Kharas, 2011).

A calling is related to identity in that when a person pursues a calling, he or she is attempting to express a central feature of the self. A job that fulfills the criteria for a calling has the potential to provide an individual with one of the deepest forms of satisfaction (Hall & Chandler, 2005). People who feel that they are pursuing a calling feel more engaged in their work and experience more positive outcomes as a result of this engagement (Hirschi, 2012).

For people to experience the benefits of a calling, however, they must actually be living the calling, not just dreaming about it. When they feel that their job fulfills the criteria for a calling, they will feel more committed to their work and derive more meaning from it, which will ultimately benefit their overall satisfaction (Duffy, Bott, Allan, Torrey, & Dik, 2012).

In order to identify a calling, however, individuals must go through intense reflection about their values and priorities in life. They can promote this process through meditation, introspection, and reflection. Ultimately, people's ability to pursue a calling requires self-understanding, an adaptability to changing economic and social circumstances, and the belief that they can be successful at their chosen career path (Hall & Chandler, 2005).

Variations in Vocational Development

Recent approaches within the vocational developmental literature increasingly concentrate on the **boundaryless career**, or a career that crosses the boundaries of an employer or organization (Arthur & Rousseau, 1996). Many workers who, in the past, were restricted by the opportunities presented to them by their organization are now progressing through their careers at their own pace. People who have the boundaryless career mindset seek opportunities for development in their jobs and when they do not receive it, may feel less psychologically invested in the organization that employs them (Briscoe & Finkelstein, 2009). However, there is a reality to the notion of a boundaryless career in that employees may not feel that they have the luxury to contemplate switching employers in a tight job market (Inkson, Gunz, Ganesh, & Roper, 2012).

A related concept is the **protean career**, in which individuals are both self-directed and driven internally by their own values (Hall & Briscoe, 2004). In the protean career, the individual seeks personal growth through self-reflection and self-learning. Instead of focusing on external criteria for success, the individual following the protean career has internal standards for success that will enhance his or her identity. People seeking a calling may follow the protean career, but it is also possible for individuals to follow the protean career without seeing their occupation as a true calling (Hall & Chandler, 2005). A protean career attitude can help individuals gain insight into what is driving their career and ultimately to achieve career success (De Vos & Soens, 2008).

Although the boundaryless and protean careers have some overlap, they are empirically distinct (Briscoe, Hall, & Frautschy DeMuth, 2006) and may provide an alternative to the traditional notion prevalent for so many years in the vocational literature of the "one life, one career" mentality. As changes continue to occur in the workplace and society leading to greater deviation from the standard organizational framework of the mid-20th century, vocational counselors will increasingly offer workers ideas about ways to manage their own careers around internal rather than external goals and employer-developed criteria (Raabe, Frese, & Beehr, 2007).

Having the boundaryless mindset and protean career attitude appear to be particularly important for women seeking greater flexibility and self-direction in their career development (Cabrera, 2009). Looking at career paths in a more fluid and flexible manner is also becoming increasingly important for those employed in knowledge-based occupations—such as information technology—because their career paths tend to be more fragmented than are those of people in other professions (Donnelly, 2009).

VOCATIONAL SATISFACTION

As we have just discussed, the most fulfilling work may be that in which people feel they can express their identities. The concept of **vocational satisfaction** refers to the extent to which people find their work to be enjoyable. For our purposes, we will consider vocational satisfaction to be equivalent to job satisfaction, as both terms are used in the literature.

We can assume that workers who are satisfied are more committed to the organizations for which they work (Hoffman & Woehr, 2006). Therefore, both employees and employers benefit when workers are high in vocational satisfaction.

Intrinsic and Extrinsic Factors

People can be satisfied with their jobs either because they love the work that they perform, they value the salary and other perks it provides, or both. **Intrinsic factors in vocational satisfaction** refer to the tasks required to perform the work itself. The central defining feature of an intrinsic factor is that it cannot be found in precisely the same fashion in a different type of job. For example, the sculptor engages in the physical activities of molding clay or stone, and the accountant must perform the mental activities of manipulating numbers. Although each job involves other activities, these are the ones that serve to define the work required to perform each.

Intrinsic factors involve or engage your sense of identity in that the work directly pertains to your feelings of competence, autonomy, and stimulation of personal growth. Your ability to express autonomy and self-direction in the daily running of your job are also part of the intrinsic aspects of work because these factors are directly tied to your sense of self. Having work that is a calling fulfills your intrinsic motivation, but you can have intrinsic motivation for your work without feeling that it is a calling.

Extrinsic factors in vocational satisfaction are the features that accompany the job but are not central to its performance. You can receive extrinsic satisfaction from many different jobs regardless of the work tasks they require. The easiest extrinsic factor to understand is salary. Although some jobs earn more than others, you can earn the same amount of money by performing very different work tasks. A professional athlete and an oil magnate may earn the same six- or seven-figure paycheck for performing a very different set of job activities. Therefore, salary is not intrinsic to work.

There are a number of additional extrinsic factors associated with the conditions of work, such as the comfort of the environment, demands for travel, convenience of work hours, friendliness of coworkers, amount of status associated with the job, and adequacy of the company's supervision and employment policies. These aspects of work do not directly engage your sense of personal identity and competence. Although a high salary may certainly reinforce your sense of worth (particularly in Western society), you can earn that high salary in many ways that are not necessarily tied to your true vocational passions. The racial climate is another important condition of the workplace that can affect worker satisfaction but is not intrinsic to the job itself (Lyons & O'Brien, 2006).

At this point in your life, you may or may not have had a job yet that you felt was intrinsically satisfying. However, you can probably think of people you know who do feel connected to their work at an intrinsic level. Perhaps you have encountered a customer service representative who seemed genuinely interested in helping you solve a problem and was willing to work with you until you found the satisfactory solution. This may have been an employee who found the job to be intrinsically rewarding, feelings that she expressed in the apparent pride that she took in helping you with your situation.

Intrinsic factors give you a sense of active engagement in your work and contribute to your sense of self. The customer service representative who provided you with such kind and gracious help may not see her job as one that represents her life's work; however, she may nevertheless enjoy the part of her job that allows her to get people what they need. You can see a summary of the intrinsic and extrinsic factors in Figure 10.6.

There are motivational qualities to the intrinsic and extrinsic features of jobs. According to the **two-factor motivational theory** (Herzberg, Mausner, & Snyderman, 1959), intrinsic and extrinsic factors play different roles in contributing to vocational satisfaction. When workers are motivated for intrinsic reasons ("job motivators"), they are more likely to achieve self-actualization. Extrinsic factors, also called "hygiene factors," do not play a central role

<u>FIGURE 10.6</u>

Intrinsic and Extrinsic Factors in Vocational Satisfaction

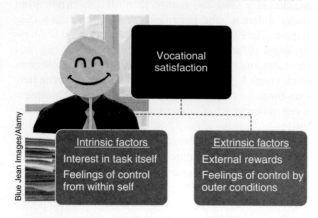

in vocational satisfaction. Favorable hygiene factors can prevent the development of job dissatisfaction, but they cannot promote it. Growth, self-fulfillment, and feelings of achievement can only come from the fulfillment of job motivators, not from the hygiene factors (Herzberg, Mausner, & Bloch Snyderman, 2005).

Self-determination theory focuses on the amount of control that workers have over their jobs as influences on vocational satisfaction (Deci & Ryan, 2008). Workers are most satisfied when they are able to fulfill their intrinsic needs for self-expression and autonomy in the job. If they are working solely for the extrinsic rewards of salary and other benefits, their job satisfaction suffers. However, extrinsic motivation in self-determination theory has several levels involving differing amounts of control over the conditions of work. In the most extreme form of extrinsic motivation, workers have practically no control over their work conditions and choices of how to spend their time. Less extreme forms of extrinsic motivation engage more and more of the worker's ability to make decisions and feel in control of the conditions of work (Gagne & Deci, 2005). The more workers see themselves as in control of what they do on the job, the more the work engages their sense of identity.

At its most extreme, work that you perform for extrinsic reasons can have the paradoxical effect of lowering your productivity by diminishing your intrinsic interest in the work. The situation known as **motivation crowding out** describes the situation in which people's intrinsic motivation decreases when they receive extrinsic rewards to do work they enjoy, leading them to be less productive than they would otherwise be (James, 2005).

Obviously, everyone works for the extrinsic reward of money, and a theory that ignores this fact is bound to fall short of the mark (Bassett-Jones & Lloyd, 2005). The key

to understanding self-determination theory is to recognize its central proposal that to be maximally motivating, the work that you do must be an expression, at least in part, of your identity. If you can feel that your paid work gives you the opportunity to develop your innermost goals and desires, you will perform at higher levels of persistence and discipline.

Positive and Negative Moods

Job satisfaction can be affected not only by the motivation to work, but also by people's feelings about their jobs. You can have feelings on the job (such as being excited about the upcoming weekend) and feelings about the job (such as liking your job activities). According to **affective events theory**, events at work lead individuals to experience affective reactions, and these in turn influence attitudes toward work and performance (Weiss & Cropanzano, 1996).

There are many factors that can affect your mood, and ultimately, your satisfaction at work. For example, if you experience positive events at work, such as being complimented by a supervisor, you will have a positive emotional experience; if you experience negative events, such as conflict with a coworker, your emotions will be negatively affected (Fisher, 2002). Your mood when you wake up in the morning can also affect the way you feel about your work as you go throughout the day.

In a study of 29 customer service representatives employed at a call center of an insurance company, researchers tracked mood changes throughout the day, the affective display of their customers, and the employee's affect subsequent to the call. The organization measured the productivity of the employees. The call center employees who started the day in a bad mood rated their customers more negatively. After talking to a customer who displayed positive affect, the employees themselves felt better. In contrast, after talking to a customer who displayed negative affect, the employees felt no worse themselves, but their productivity suffered in that they were more likely to take a break after such a call. The findings suggest that start-of-the-day mood plays an important role in affecting how employees feel throughout the day and, ultimately, how well they perform (Rothbard & Wilk, 2011).

Job satisfaction and positive emotions are also related to such job characteristics as autonomy, participation in the organization, supervisory support, and concern by supervisors for employee welfare. Conversely, the stress of feeling overloaded can trigger negative emotions in employees (Wegge, von Dick, Fisher, West, & Dawson, 2006).

Personality traits can also influence the ways in which people interpret what happens to them at work. Affective events theory predicts that people will differ in their reactions to daily work experiences on the basis of their personality traits (Weiss & Cropanzano, 1996). You might think that people high in agreeableness would be better able to bounce back from negative interactions at work. However, in a study of university employees, researchers found that those high in agreeableness actually had more negative affect following interpersonal conflict than those low in agreeableness. Highly agreeable employees were also more likely to experience negative affect when they perceived their work environments to be low in social support (Ilies, Johnson, Judge, & Keeney, 2011).

In general, it appears that high subjective well-being predicts job satisfaction. In a meta-analysis testing the relationship over time between overall well-being and job satisfaction, researchers found more support for the direction from subjective well-being to job satisfaction than vice versa. Consistent with other research on overall mood, it appears that people high in subjective well-being tend to experience more positive emotions that carry over into their work lives (Bowling, Eschleman, & Wang, 2010).

Personality traits may also interact with changes in job satisfaction over time. Looking at the intrinsic–extrinsic dimension of vocational satisfaction, researchers have found that people with high neuroticism scores are less likely to feel that their jobs are intrinsically rewarding. Perhaps for this reason, neuroticism is negatively related to job satisfaction; by contrast, people high in the traits of conscientiousness and extraversion are more satisfied in their jobs (Furnham, Eracleous, & Chamorro-Premuzic, 2009; Judge, Heller, & Mount, 2002; Seibert & Kraimer, 2001).

Similarly, in one longitudinal study of adults in Australia, although personality changes were found to predict changes in work satisfaction, changes in personality were also found to result from higher job satisfaction. Over time, workers who were more satisfied with their jobs became more extraverted (Scollon & Diener, 2006).

Person–Environment Correspondence

We have seen that Holland's vocational development theory proposes that people seek to find congruence between their personalities and the characteristics of the job. According to **person–environment correspondence theory**, people are most satisfied when their workplaces respond to their needs. In contrast to Holland's congruence model, person–environment correspondence theory focuses on needs rather than interests (Dawis, 2002).

Person–environment correspondence theory stresses the role of values in promoting job satisfaction. **Occupational reinforcement patterns (ORPs)** are the work values and needs likely to be reinforced or satisfied by a particular occupation. The six ORPs are (1) achievement: using one's abilities and feeling a sense of accomplishment; (2) altruism: being of service to others; (3) autonomy: having a sense of control; (4) comfort: not feeling stressed; (5) safety: stability, order, and predictability; and (6) status: being recognized and serving in a dominant position.

Reflecting the importance of ORPs, O*NET incorporates ORPs into its job search system. Each occupation can be identified by a particular pattern of ORPs that it satisfies, making it possible for job seekers to match their personal values with those likely to be met by the job. The addition of values to the usual assessment of interests and skills can provide a useful perspective both for employees and career counselors (Smith & Campbell, 2006).

Work Stress

Work stress can be a major threat to people's feelings of well-being and can eventually take its toll on physical health as well. There are many forms that work stress can take, as we have already seen, ranging from negative interactions with coworkers to difficulties dealing with clients, customers, and supervisors. People may also experience stress when they feel that their job is not compatible with their needs, interests, values, and personal dispositions. Therefore, work stress is a very broad category. For our purposes, we will turn here to studies that specifically examine ratings of stress as reported by employees in specific situations.

Emotional labor is the requirement of service-oriented jobs in which workers must smile and maintain a friendly attitude regardless of their own personal feelings or emotions. Performing emotional labor can be stressful to those service employees who feel that they must constantly put on an act in order to carry out their job successfully. In a study of hotel service employees in the U.S., Chu et al. (2012) found, as would be expected, that workers who are higher in negative affect working in service settings where they are expected to show positive emotions were more emotionally drained. They can alleviate this stress by learning how to engage in "deep acting," in which they generate thoughts, images, and memories that can put them in the right mood.

A large study carried out in Denmark on over 1,000 workers from 55 workplaces investigated the impact of workplace bullying, a form of stress in which individuals are exposed over a lengthy period to negative interpersonal acts on the job which they cannot cope with or control. Workers rated the extent to which they experienced workplace bullying in the form of social isolation, direct harassment, intimidating behavior, work-related criticism, and physical violence. They rated stress in terms of intrusive thoughts, avoidance, and hyperarousal and also provided saliva samples that were used to measure cortisol (the stress hormone). All forms of workplace bullying were stressful, particularly direct harassment and intimidating behavior (Hogh, Hansen, Mikkelsen, & Persson, 2012). Thus, individuals exposed to work-related bullying become traumatized in ways that can lead to both psychological and physiological consequences.

The Whitehall II study provided compelling data to show the links between work-related stress and the risk of metabolic syndrome (Chandola, Brunner, & Marmot, 2006). Carried out over five phases from 1985 to 1997, the study included measurements of stress, social class, intake of fruits and vegetables, alcohol consumption, smoking, exercise, and obesity status at the start of the study. Holding all other factors constant and excluding participants who were initially obese, men under high levels of work stress over the course of the study had twice the risk of subsequently developing metabolic syndrome. Women with high levels of stress had over five times the risk of developing this condition.

More recent research suggests that Whitehall II men who reported higher justice at work (such as perceived job fairness) had a far lower risk of metabolic syndrome compared with men who experienced lower work justice (Gimeno et al., 2010). For women, stress encountered at work independently predicted type 2 diabetes, even after controlling for socioeconomic position and stressors unrelated to work (Heraclides, Chandola, Witte, & Brunner, 2009).

Physiological data obtained in the form of cortisol levels from Whitehall II also illustrates the impact on health of social position within the workplace (Kumari et al., 2010). Daily assessments of cortisol, the hormone involved in the response to stress and anxiety, were taken from an older Whitehall cohort six times throughout the day. Men in lower employment grades showed higher cortisol levels early in the morning, levels that remained higher throughout the day than for men in higher employment grades. These higher levels could be explained not only by higher levels of stress during the day but also by poorer quality of sleep at night.

Thus, maximizing workplace satisfaction, in addition to helping maintain worker productivity, can make a key difference in promoting the health and long-term well-being of the individual (Olsson, Hemstrom, & Fritzell, 2009).

Relationships Between Work and Family Roles

One of the great challenges of adult life is dividing your time, energy, and role involvement across your many commitments. The two areas that many people find most difficult to integrate in terms of competing demands are occupation and family life. Both carry with them major obligations and responsibility, and both contribute heavily to the individual's sense of identity. However, they do not necessarily need to be in conflict, as research is increasingly demonstrating.

According to the **work–family enrichment model**, experiences in one role improve the quality of life in the other. This model is based on the theory of conservation of resources, which proposes that organizations can protect their workers against stress by providing them with support to maintain both their work and family roles (Hobfoll, 2002).

As shown in Figure 10.7, there are five categories of resources that people can acquire through their role experiences that can improve performance in the other area (Greenhaus & Powell, 2006b). For example, parents may gain networking experience with other parents who help them on their job. Researchers also use the term "positive spillover" to describe this transfer of skills from one domain to the other (Masuda, McNall, Allen, & Nicklin, 2012). Role experiences can also prove enriching through their

FIGURE 10.7

Components of Work-Family Enrichment

- Skills and perspectives: Interpersonal skills, coping skills, respect for individual differences

- Psychological and physical resources: Self-efficacy, hardiness, optimism

- Social capital resources: Networking, information

- Flexibility: Flexible work arrangements

- Material resources: Money, gifts

Ocean/Corbis

effect on mood. If you have a good day at work, you bring your good mood home with you. In addition, according to social exchange theory, employees who feel that their work supports their ability to carry out their family roles, according to this model, feel more obligated to reciprocate with favorable attitudes toward their job and their company.

In a meta-analysis testing the work-family enrichment model, McNall and colleagues (2010) tested the two directions of work-family enrichment, from work to family (WFE) and family to work (FWE) on the criterion variables of job satisfaction, affective commitment (emotional attachment to the organization), turnover intentions, family satisfaction, life satisfaction, and physical/mental health across a total of 46 studies (encompassing 111 correlations). Both WFE and FWE were positively associated with the work-related outcomes of job satisfaction and affective commitment. WFE had a positive influence on the nonwork-related outcomes of family and life satisfaction. FWE had a positive relationship with family satisfaction. Both forms of enrichment were related to physical and mental health. The findings also showed stronger effects for women than men, reflecting the fact that women are more likely to integrate the two sets of roles.

Alternatively, the **work–family conflict model** proposes that people have a fixed amount of time and energy to spend on their life roles. This model is based on a scarcity perspective (Edwards & Rothbard, 2000): the more time and energy people invest in one area, the less they have for the other set of demands and activities. The workaholic, according to this view, has little energy or time for family relationships. Conversely, high involvement with family should preclude total commitment to the job.

When work–family conflict does occur, it takes its toll on the individual's physical and mental health, causing emotional strain, fatigue, perception of overload, and stress (van Hooff et al., 2005). There are variations in the extent and impact of work–family conflict, however, and not all workers feel the same degree of conflict. Conflict is most likely to occur among mothers of young children, dual-career couples, and those who are highly involved with their job. Workers who devote a great deal of time to their job at the expense of their families ultimately pay the price in terms of experiencing a lower overall quality of life (Greenhaus, Collins, & Shaw, 2003). There are higher levels of work–family conflict among those employed in the private sector than those employed in the public sector (Dolcos & Daley, 2009).

Age also plays into the work–family conflict equation. Younger workers (under age 45) typically experience more conflict than older workers (46 and older); though when older workers experience conflict, the effects seem to be stronger (Matthews, Bulger, & Barnes-Farrell, 2010). However, there are individual differences in personality that affect the work–family balance, such as dispositional affectivity as well as variations on a day-by-day basis in levels of positive and negative affect that the person experiences (Eby, Maher, & Butts, 2010).

Organizations are increasingly recognizing the importance to their workers of providing a "family-friendly" environment, which may include support and schedule control (McNall, Masuda, & Nicklin, 2010). There are tangible benefits to these situations. When managers provide support to employees through such measures as accommodative work schedules, employees actually become more productive and are less likely to leave the organization (Odle-Dusseau, Britt, & Greene-Shortridge, 2012). In addition, when workers feel a strong sense of engagement with their jobs in family-friendly organizations, their work-family enrichment increases (Siu et al., 2010). Conversely, a strong family identity can promote feelings of satisfaction and commitment to the job (Wayne, Randel, & Stevens, 2006). Social support from an individual's workgroup also plays a role, because many potentially positive or negative interactions at work, as we pointed out earlier, involve coworkers (Bhave, Kramer, & Glomb, 2010). Moreover, supervisors who themselves experience work-to-family enrichment promote similar outcomes in their subordinates.

Age and Vocational Satisfaction

Throughout this chapter, we have assumed that vocational satisfaction is an important part of every worker's life. In this section, we will look explicitly at whether and how change in their attitudes toward their jobs impacts vocational satisfaction.

The motivation to work varies greatly among workers. For some, the thought of retiring may be greatly appealing. Retirement will provide them with release from the daily grind. On the other hand, older workers might feel more satisfied than younger workers because they have been able to advance through seniority and promotions. The question of whether job satisfaction increases, decreases, or stays the same over adulthood is a surprisingly difficult one to answer. This is because, as you learned earlier, more and more working adults recycle through their jobs. As a result, it is **job tenure**, the length of time a person has spent in the job, rather than age that may relate to job satisfaction. Gender, level of employment, and salary also interact with age differences in job satisfaction (Riordan, Griffith, & Weatherly, 2003).

In a meta-analysis of 802 empirical articles that included many studies from outside the U.S., Ng and

Feldman (2010) examined the relationships between age and 35 different measures of job attitudes. Across these studies, age was related only weakly (with correlations averaging about 0.20) to overall job satisfaction, satisfaction with the work itself, satisfaction with pay, job involvement, and intrinsic work motivation. However, the relationships were stronger for older workers with more tenure in the organization, minorities, and workers without a college education. Interestingly, the authors concluded that there were no differences in levels of work commitment between Baby Boomers and those in Gen X, who many social commentators believe are less diligent than their parents.

Identity processes may come into play as adults evaluate their vocational satisfaction. Researchers investigating job satisfaction in adulthood have begun to discuss the construct of **core self-evaluations**, which represents a person's appraisal of people, events, and things in relation to oneself. The core self-evaluation is composed of self-esteem, generalized self-efficacy, high emotional stability, and the belief that you control your fate (Judge, Locke, Durham, & Kluger, 1998). Core self-evaluations can influence vocational satisfaction to the extent that these self-perceptions influence the opportunities people seek in the workplace. For example, women may perceive themselves according to traditional stereotyped views that lead them to be seen as less assertive and competitive than their male counterparts (Furnham, Miller, Batey, & Johnson, 2011).

Another factor that may affect the older worker's commitment and involvement in the job is exposure to age discrimination in the workplace. Although older workers are protected by federal law prohibiting discrimination (see below), as we saw in Chapter 1, negative stereotypes about the abilities and suitabilities of older persons in the workplace persist (Rupp et al., 2006). Older workers may begin to disengage mentally when they feel that they are subject to these age stereotypes, pressures to retire in the form of downsizing, and the message that their skills are becoming obsolete (Lease, 1998). These pressures can lead older workers to be less likely to engage in the career development activities that would enhance their ability to remain on the job or find a new one when their job is eliminated due to downsizing. (In the next section, we will look specifically at age stereotypes about performance in the workplace.)

Level of occupation is yet another factor to be considered in vocational satisfaction, as a person in a managerial position who is earning a high salary has the resources to invest time and energy in nonwork options. Of course, a higher level of employment may involve higher daily job demands, leading to less time for leisure pursuits. Individual differences in the extent to which an adult believes in the "work ethic" may also interact with the age–job satisfaction relationship. The work commitment of individuals with strong work ethic values may never taper off, even if the commitment of these people does not translate into higher financial rewards.

Support from employers is a key factor in the relationship between age and job satisfaction. Older workers can also be more fully engaged in their job and hence achieve higher satisfaction if they feel that their employer values their contributions. Providing training and development programs specifically geared for older workers is a part of this process. Particularly important to keeping the older worker motivated and satisfied is providing job assignments to keep the work fresh and interesting (Armstrong-Stassen & Ursel, 2009).

Age-related changes in physical and cognitive functioning must also be taken into account. If these changes interfere with the ability to perform the job satisfactorily, then the older worker will be unable to perform his or her duties or may only be able to do so with difficulty. If the aging process alters the degree of person–environment fit between the individual and the job, the worker will feel increasingly dissatisfied and unfulfilled. The role of the supervisor may be particularly important in this regard. For example, a manager who is sensitive to an older worker's mobility problems may be able to lessen the demands for physical movement placed on the employee.

AGE AND VOCATIONAL PERFORMANCE

We've seen how individuals feel about their jobs throughout the years of adulthood. Now it's time to evaluate how well people perform in these jobs. As you might imagine, there are a host of variables to consider in addition to age, including education, occupational status, health, cognitive functioning, and personality. Although we may not be able to tease these variables apart, this discussion should help you gain insight both into what we know about aging workers and what questions remain left to address in future research.

In Figure 10.8, we show the three main characteristics of older workers and how they intersect with influence job performance. As you can see in the figure, older workers have slightly lower core work performance, although the effect of age on work performance varies with the nature of the task (Warr, 1994). For example, workers in jobs that require crystallized intelligence (which does not decrease until well past retirement) and depend on experience theoretically should show improved performance in later adulthood. Older workers in jobs with high crystallized

FIGURE 10.8

Characteristics of the Older Worker

Golden Pixels LLC/Alamy

components should be strongly motivated to put in the effort they need to perform well on the job because they realize that their efforts will most likely meet with success.

By contrast, if the job is highly dependent on strength, speed, or working memory, older workers will be less able to perform well and at the same time will be less motivated to put in effort that they believe may not pay off (Kanfer & Ackerman, 2004). One area in which older adults may perform more poorly involves shift work, in which the individual's work hours change from daytime hours to evenings or nights. Although these schedules present a challenge for workers of all ages, they are particularly difficult for older workers (Bonnefond et al., 2006).

On the positive side, older workers show fewer counterproductive work behaviors, such as voluntary absenteeism. They are also more likely to engage in good "citizenship," meaning that they participate in more voluntary activities. They also tend to be safer in that they take fewer risks on the job. Of course, some of these factors relate to survival effects in that the unhealthy, uncooperative, and risky workers tend to be the ones who do not last on the job as long.

Some older workers focus on maintaining their current employment status and plan how to end their careers without jeopardizing this status. Others may have already experienced some disability and attempt to compensate for their losses while still maintaining their position at work. Many older workers, however, do not experience a loss in work functioning and are able to maintain high levels of performance until they retire (Ng & Feldman, 2012).

Injuries are a second area of investigation in understanding the relationship between age and job performance. Overall, workers over the age of 55 are nearly half as likely to suffer a nonfatal injury as those who are 35 years and

younger, and about half as likely to suffer death due to a work-related injury. However, when older workers (ages 55–64) must miss work due to injury or illness, they spend twice as many days away from work (12) per year than do younger workers (ages 25–34) (Bureau of Labor Statistics, 2010). Driving-related accidents in the transportation industry have the highest fatality rate of all U.S. industries, and it is in this job that older workers have the highest rate of dying as well (Pegula, Marsh, & Jackson, 2007).

With regard to overall physical fitness, decreases in strength and agility can certainly have a negative influence on job performance in some areas of employment, particularly when physical exertion is involved (Sluiter & Frings-Dresen, 2007). However, workers of any age can suffer from conditions that impair their performance, such as a cold or muscle ache. Furthermore, as pointed out by Warr (1994), every worker has restrictions in the kind of work that he or she can perform. The fact that older workers may have some limitations due to physical aging changes does not mean that they cannot achieve adequate performance on all types of jobs. People learn to cope with their limitations and gravitate to jobs they are able to perform (Daly & Bound, 1996). If they become disabled enough, they will leave the job market altogether.

Passage of the **Age Discrimination in Employment Act (ADEA)** in 1967 made it illegal to fire or not employ workers on the basis of their age. This legislation was intended to provide protection for older workers (over 40) from discrimination by employers who would otherwise seek to replace them with younger, cheaper, and presumably more productive employees. For example, potential employers in most jobs cannot ask a job seeker for his or her age or even questions that would give away the job seeker's age, such as year of college or high school graduation.

However, the ADEA does not protect workers in occupations in which age has a presumed effect on the performance of critical job tasks. For example, the ADEA does not cover police officers and firefighters, on the grounds that their occupations require that they be able to protect the public by engaging in highly demanding physical activity. Airline pilots are another group not protected by the ADEA, as they face mandatory retirement at age 65 (see Figure 10.9).

The ADEA resulted in settlements amounting to approximately $72.1 million in the year 2009 alone. However, despite the reach of ADEA to many areas of the U.S. workplace, ageism still exists and can take many forms, ranging from biases against the abilities of older workers to stereotyped beliefs about their personalities and work attitudes (Ng & Feldman, 2012). As their self-image and abilities change, older workers can begin to doubt their self-efficacy; in terms of the identity model, they

FIGURE 10.9

Areas of Protection Under the Age Discrimination in Employment Act

- Apprenticeships
- Job notices and ads
- Pre-employment inquiries (except for lawful purpose)
- Benefits
- Mandatory retirement

iStockphoto

overaccommodate to the view that aging causes a loss of essential job skills. A self-fulfilling prophecy can develop, resulting in their further losing their ability to keep up with new technologies.

According to Maurer (2001), self-efficacy on the job reflects the effects of direct or vicarious rewards, learning, persuasion, and changes in physiological functioning and health. Workers with a stronger sense of self-efficacy will be more likely to seek out opportunities to get additional training. Thus, supervisors who intervene by building the self-efficacy of their older workers can ultimately help them retain, if not improve, their job skills.

The findings on age and job performance, like those in the area of vocational satisfaction, point to the importance of applying knowledge about adult development and aging in general to specific questions relating to older workers. From a human resources perspective, managers need to attend to the varying capabilities of workers of different ages and also to take into account age dynamics as they play out in the workplace, balancing the complementary strengths of workers of younger and older ages (Brooke & Taylor, 2005). In such environments, all workers can achieve their maximum performance while also feeling that they have something worthwhile to contribute in the workplace.

RETIREMENT

Retirement may be the furthest thing from your mind if you are a college student in your late teens or early 20s. You are most likely concentrating on finding a job rather than retiring from one. Ideally, you will find a job that you enjoy and that will also give you a solid basis for being able to spend 10 or 20 years (or more!) enjoying your retirement years.

Many people think of retirement as an event that is marked by a ceremony such as the proverbial "gold watch"

given to the retiree as thanks for years of loyal service. This traditional image of retirement was never really true, however. Even when careers had more predictable trajectories, people often continued to maintain some type of employment after they had retired from their primary job. The definition of retirement is becoming even murkier with current changes in labor force participation by individuals in their middle and later years, as you will soon learn.

The economy's health affects not only the financial security of the employed, but also the financial security of the retired. Interest rates, tax policies, inflation, and the overall growth of the economy are some of the factors that determine the amount of money that retired individuals receive from their various sources of income. Policies being decided upon now by governments around the world will affect billions of older individuals in the decades to come. You might feel as though you are years away from retirement and therefore are not affected by these debates, but they are affecting your current paycheck now and will continue to have an impact on your financial stability throughout the rest of your life.

Definitions of Retirement

Retirement is defined simply as the withdrawal of an individual in later life from the labor force. However, for most workers, retirement occurs in a series of phases through which they progress at least once, if not several, times throughout their lives.

Because retirement is not simply an event with a defined start and end point, it is best conceptualized in terms of a period of adjustment (Wang & Shultz, 2010). The retirement process occurs over five phases, as shown in Figure 10.10 (Sterns & Gray, 1999). People experience an anticipatory period that may last for decades. Eventually, they make the decision to retire. After their last day of work in the particular job (the act of retirement), workers go through an initial adjustment period followed, ultimately, by a more or less final restructuring of their activity patterns.

Complicating this picture is the fact that fewer and fewer workers are showing the **crisp retirement pattern**, in which they leave the labor force in a single, unreversed, clear-cut exit. More typically, retirees show the **blurred retirement pattern**, in which they exit and reenter the labor force several times. Some accept **bridge employment**, which is when retirees work in a completely different occupation than they had during most of their adult life. For example, an insurance agent may retire from the insurance business but work as a crossing guard or server at a fast-food restaurant. Other workers may retire from one job in a company and accept another role in the same company.

FIGURE 10.10

Phases of Retirement

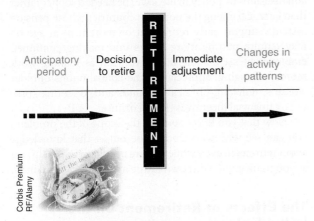

Corbis Premium
RF/Alamy

In general, involvement in bridge employment is strongly related to financial need. Workers who have a long, continuous history of employment in private sector jobs tend not to seek bridge employment because they typically have sufficient financial resources (Davis, 2003).

Ultimately, the criteria for retirement are met when an individual in later life with a cohesive past work pattern has not worked for a sustained period of time and is not psychologically invested in work any longer (Beehr, Glazer, Nielson, & Farmer, 2000).

Facts About Retirement

Even though they may arrive there in phases, by the age of 65, the large majority of Americans are no longer in the labor force. At present, 18.5% of the 65 and older population are still considered to be in the labor force, meaning that they are either working or actively seeking employment, and virtually all of those 75 years and older (92.4%) have ended their full-time participation in the nation's workforce (Bureau of Labor Statistics, 2013b). However, many remain employed on a part-time basis; as of 2006 (the latest statistics available), 34% of those 65 and older worked 34 hours per week, and 13% worked 1 to 14 hours per week (Holder & Clark, 2008).

Retirement is in many ways a 20th-century phenomenon (Sterns & Gray, 1999). Throughout the 1700s and mid-1800s, very few people retired—a trend that continued into the 1900s; in 1900, about 70% of all men over 65 years were still in the labor force. The jobs held by older workers often held high status and prestige. The wisdom and experience of older workers were valued, and it was considered a benefit to society to have them continuing to contribute to the workplace. However, by the early 1930s, pressures on the economy in combination with the growth

of unions led to the first instance in the United States of compulsory retirement (in the railroad industry). Because older workers were forced to retire but did not receive retirement benefits, they lived in poverty.

In 1935, spearheaded by President Franklin D. Roosevelt, the U.S. Congress passed the **Social Security Act**, federal legislation that guarantees income for retirees and others who are unable to work as well as a lump sum in death benefits for survivors. By 1940, the number of older workers in the labor force had dropped to slightly over 40%; this number has continued to decrease. Social Security payments are divided into Old-Age and Survivors Insurance (OASI) and Disability Insurance (DI). **Old Age and Survivors Disability Insurance (OASDI)** combines OASI and DI.

As of 2013, 38.5 million people in the U.S. over the age of 65 were receiving Social Security benefits (Social Security Administration, 2013). The average monthly Social Security benefit for a retired worker through 2012 was $1,241. As of 2010, 37% of the income of Americans 65 and older came from Social Security. The remaining income came from earnings (30%), assets such as interest income (11%), and either private (9%) or government (9%) pensions (Social Security Administration, 2012).

Political leaders in the U.S. are struggling with the economic ramifications brought about by the growth of the older population. Social Security benefits continue to rise, placing greater strain on the economy as a whole. Medical insurance, which is also paid out by the Social Security Administration, is also rising at astronomical rates. To understand how this crisis came about, you need to know how Social Security is funded.

The OASDI trust fund receives its income from Social Security payroll taxes on current U.S. workers. It is a "pay-as-you-go" system, which sounds like it might mean that you personally invest in your own retirement benefits. However, it actually means that workers pay into the system to pay for current retirees (and some for their own future as the trust fund accumulates). The only disbursements that the OASDI trust fund can make are direct payments to beneficiaries and administrative costs. Federal law mandates that all excess funds are invested in interest-bearing securities backed by the U.S. The balance in the OASDI trust fund at any one moment is like your bank account. You pay in from your wages, salary, loans, or parental support and take out what you need for your expenses. You then save everything you do not spend, which then accumulates over time.

Similarly, the OASDI trust fund includes the accumulated value, including interest, of all prior surpluses and deficits paid into and out of it from previous years. The current Social Security crisis can be translated, then, into simple mathematical terms. As the balance of retired to employed workers continues to shift, the amount to be paid to retirees will increase faster than the income that will be paid into the OASDI trust fund. At that point, the only way that the government can pay out benefits is to dip into the trust fund assets, which then run the risk of being depleted. As with your personal bank account, if your income falls below your expenses, you eventually will have to dig into your savings; you will then run the risk of spending down until nothing is left and you are forced to borrow more.

In 2011, the OASI trust fund had $2.4 trillion in assets. It took in $699 billion and paid out $604 billion, leaving about $95 billion to be added to the fund's assets. You would probably be quite delighted to have this much in your own bank account, but considering the amount paid out each year to retirees alone, over time the entire fund will be depleted.

One way to view the rising costs is to view them in terms of the total gross domestic product (GDP), which is the total output of the U.S. economy. In 2012, OASDI is at 5% of the GDP, a drastic rise from 3% in 1970 and 4.2% in just 2006. By 2036, it will reach a peak of nearly 6.4%, after which it will hover at about 6% through 2086. Another way to look at the problem is to compare income with payments from the OASDI trust fund. In 2012, 12.9% of worker's earnings were going toward OASDI, and 13.8% were needed to pay out in benefits. The tax base will remain at about 13% through the foreseeable future, but cost rates will increase up to slightly more than 17%. By 2021, OASDI benefits will need to be paid out of the trust fund, and by 2033, all funds will be depleted.

These demographic and economic shifts are raising questions about Social Security reform, although no answers have yet even come close to acceptance. Similarly, the European Union (EU) countries such as France, Germany, Italy, and Greece are grappling with an aging population that will need to be supported by a smaller workforce. In addition, however, EU countries face the challenge presented by the fact that member nations themselves have wildly varying economies even as their workforces shrink and their retired population grows. To keep the weaker countries from defaulting on their debts, the richer nations need to provide support, but even these economically stronger nations are forced to reckon with their own aging populations. A number of these European countries already have high levels of funding going to social services, meaning that their economies become even further strained. As a result, EU nations are beginning to examine stronger incentives to reduce early retirement and keep more older workers in the labor force (European Union, 2010).

Changing demographics are clearly putting pressure on the global economy to ensure the financial security of retired individuals. It is likely that a combination of later retirement, longer involvement in the workforce, and difficult decisions by policy makers will be needed sooner rather than later. Changing the norms in countries whose pension systems support early retirement or retirement at age 65 may require putting more efforts into making continued employment seem more attractive such as making work more challenging, appreciating the contributions of older workers, reducing physical demands and, of course, providing financial incentives (Rijs, Cozijnsen, & Deeg, 2012).

Now that you know some of the scope of the problem, you can see why we stated at the outset that knowledge about retirement even while you are in college may help you as you think about your own future and that of your family.

The Effects of Retirement on the Individual

Until the 1960s, most American workers resisted the idea of retiring because they believed that retirement would place their financial security at risk. However, succeeding generations of workers are viewing retirement more positively. In part, this is because their retirement earnings are higher than was true for past older Americans. In addition, older workers have greater freedom than they did in the past to continue working past the traditional retirement age of 65. The passage of the ADEA in 1967 meant that U.S. workers in the 40- to 65-year age range were legally protected from age discrimination. An amendment to the ADEA in 1978 eliminated mandatory retirement before the age of 70, and in 1986 mandatory retirement was eliminated altogether from most occupations.

With these changes in U.S. retirement laws, it has also become easier for workers to continue in the jobs they have held throughout their lives or to find new employment even while they earn retirement benefits from their previous occupations. These changes have also eased the potential stress of the transition, so that retired individuals no longer necessarily experience the poor health, low income, and loss of status that was associated with exit from the labor force earlier in the 1900s.

The view that retirement is an unwanted life change fits most closely with the **role theory of retirement**, which proposes that retirement has deleterious effects because the loss of the work role loosens the ties between the individual and society (see Table 10.1).

The **continuity theory of retirement** proposes that retired individuals maintain their self-concept and identity over the retirement transition. Even though they are no longer reporting for work on a daily basis, they are able to engage in many of the same activities they did when they were working. In addition, a retired person remains

TABLE 10.1
Theories of Retirement and the Individual

Theory	Proposed effects of retirement
Role theory	Roles provide source of fulfillment Loss of work role is harmful
Continuity theory	Retirees maintain previous sense of identity Retirement is not a crisis
Life course perspective	Normative timing of events Retirement stressful only when unexpected
Resource model	Adjustment to retirement reflects physical, cognitive, motivational, financial, social, and emotional resources The more resources, the more favorable will be the individual's adjustment

Steve Cole/iStockphoto

a retired "X" in his or her community, a status conferred officially in some professions as in retired professors who are referred to as "emeritus." These two theories focus on retirement as an isolated event.

The **life course perspective on retirement** proposes that changes in the work role in later life are best seen as logical outgrowths of earlier life events. The factors that shaped the individual's prior vocational development will have a persisting influence throughout retirement.

According to the **resource model** of retirement, the individual's adjustment to retirement reflects his or her physical, cognitive, motivational, financial, social, and emotional resources; the more resources, the more favorable will be the individual's adjustment at any one point through the retirement transition (Wang, 2007). The resource model fits well with the biopsychosocial perspective, as shown in Figure 10.11.

The majority of people adjust well to retirement, if not immediately after they transition out of their work role, then within a period of a few years (Wang, 2007). In general, supporting the resource model, having a diverse

set of physical, psychological, and social resources seems to ease the transition to retirement, even among individuals who initially experience poor adjustment (Wang, Henkens, & van Solinge, 2011).

FIGURE 10.11

Biopsychosocial Model of Retirement

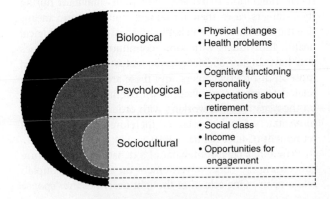

People also adjust better to retirement if they retire in an "on-time" rather than "off-time" manner (Gill et al., 2006). Voluntarily retiring, instead of being forced to retire through downsizing, also promotes better adaptation (Clarke, Marshall, & Weir, 2012). The amount of time allowed for retiring is another related factor. A minimum of 2 years' planning prior to early retirement is related to a positive retirement experience compared with a decision made 6 months or less prior to retirement (Hardy & Quadagno, 1995). As important as length of time, however, is the quality of retirement planning, which should include not only financial planning but also adequate discussion with the individual's spouse or partner (Noone, Stephens, & Alpass, 2009).

Socioeconomic status is another influence on retirement adjustment. People at the high end of the social class scale are less likely to retire than people at the lower end and retire at a later age. However, when they do retire, they tend to be in better health than are people at lower socioeconomic levels and also have longer life expectancy (Majer, Nusselder, Mackenbach, & Kunst, 2011). Their advantaged economic security also means that they are better able to take advantage of the opportunities that retirement offers them to engage in productive and enjoyable leisure activities, such as involvement in retirement learning communities and the opportunity to travel. Individuals with higher levels of education and previous experience in managerial or professional positions may be better able to find part-time employment after retirement if they desire it. Past experience in community organizations and activities may also make it easier for such individuals to find rewarding opportunities for unpaid volunteer work and participation in clubs, organizations, and informal networks.

The continuity of an individual's work career is a further influence on the impact of retirement. Those in orderly careers spend the majority of their employed years in a series of related occupations. The higher the extent of orderliness in people's careers, the higher their attachments to their communities, friends, and social activities. The social integration that these individuals maintain during their careers eases their retirement transition and means that they are likely to be in better physical and psychological health. Individuals with more continuous work histories also have higher socioeconomic status and income than those in disorderly careers, and these are factors generally related to greater satisfaction with retirement. However, on the negative side, workers with orderly careers may be more attached to their jobs and therefore less satisfied with retirement (Gee & Baillie, 1999).

There has been somewhat of a debate in the literature concerning the effect of retirement on a married couple's relationship. One school of thought describes the "spouse underfoot syndrome," whereby partners are more likely to experience conflict now that they are in each other's presence for most of the daytime and nighttime hours (the spouse who is underfoot is typically the husband). However, there is a contrasting view of retirement as a second honeymoon, in which couples are now free to enjoy each other's company on a full-time basis, without the constraints presented by having to leave home for 8 or more hours a day. As with much of the data on retirement, there is no simple answer. The transition itself from work to retirement seems to take its toll on marital satisfaction when partners have high levels of conflict. The greatest conflict is observed when one partner is working and the other has retired. Eventually, however, these problems seem to subside; after about 2 years of retirement for both partners, levels of marital satisfaction once again rise (Moen, Kim, & Hofmeister, 2001).

The factors that influence retirement adjustment do appear to differ between women and men. Men operate according to the "usual" mode of retirement view, in which decisions regarding retirement do not involve the family. According to the **new mode of retirement** perspective, the characteristics of the person's spouse and lifelong family responsibilities play a role in retirement decisions and adjustment. Current cohorts of older women are more likely to operate according to the new modes of retirement: they are more likely than men to be influenced by the health, financial security, and work status of their spouses. However, among couples raised with more egalitarian values, both are likely to be influenced increasingly by the work status of their spouses (Pienta, 2003).

As we can see, work and retirement are broad and fascinating areas of study in the field of adult development and aging. Research from a developmental perspective has been somewhat slow to get off the ground. However, increasing information on the topics of vocational satisfaction and retirement adjustment, and their interaction with personality and social structural factors, are providing greater clarification about this component of adult life.

LEISURE PURSUITS IN LATER ADULTHOOD

Throughout adulthood, people express themselves not only in their work lives, but also through their hobbies and interests. Occupational psychologists and academics studying the relationship between job characteristics and satisfaction often neglect the fact that, for many adults, it is the off-duty hours rather than the on-duty hours that contribute the most to identity and personal satisfaction. In contrast, marketers recognize the value of developing promotional campaigns that appeal to the aging Baby Boomers who potentially have resources to spend on leisure pursuits (Ferguson & Brohaugh, 2010).

As people move through adulthood and into retirement, it becomes more crucial for them to develop leisure interests so that they will have activities to engage in during the day to provide focus and meaning to their lives. In addition, leisure pursuits can serve important functions by helping older adults maintain their health through physical activity and their cognitive functioning through intellectual stimulation. The social functions of leisure are also of potential significance, particularly for people who have become widowed or have had to relocate due to finances, a desire for more comfortable climates, or poor health.

Researchers who study leisure time activities in later adulthood find strong evidence linking leisure participation to improvement in feelings of well-being, particularly among older adults who are trying to overcome deficits in physical functioning or social networks (Silverstein & Parker, 2002). Furthermore, cognitively challenging leisure activities can be at least as, if not more beneficial than, physical exercise to help individuals maintain their intellectual functioning, including lowering the risk for vascular dementia (Verghese, Wang, Katz, Sanders, & Lipton, 2009).

Regular leisure-time physical activity can have important health consequences. A longitudinal study in Sweden followed men over five time points (Byberg et al., 2009). Participants were asked about their level of physical activity with questions such as, "Do you often go walking or cycling for pleasure?" People who engaged in physical activity in their leisure time died at later ages than those who did not over the 35-year period of the study (see Figure 10.12). Another follow-up in Sweden of over 1,800 men and women ages 75 and older showed that the protective effect of physical activity on mortality continued into the 90s, an effect enhanced by engaging in other healthy lifestyle behaviors, particularly not smoking (Rizzuto, Orsini, Qiu, Wang, & Fratiglioni, 2012).

As we discussed in Chapter 5, older adults are less likely than younger people to engage in physical activities as leisure-time pursuits. They may also not be aware of the potential benefits that mental and physical activity can provide. A study of the protective effects of exercise on immune functioning in nearly 750 adults showed that the older adults at greatest risk were unaware of how much they could reduce their chances of developing cardiovascular and cognitive disorders by engaging in mental and physical activity. The authors concluded that not only can engaging in active leisure pursuits help to preserve cognitive function and maintain cardiovascular health, but individuals can also benefit from the stress-reducing effects of engaging

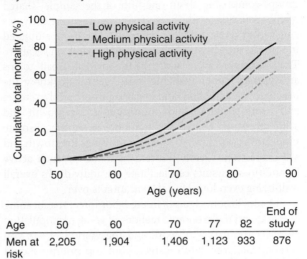

Source: Reproduced from Total mortality after changes in leisure time physical activity in 50 year old men: 35 year follow-up of population based cohort, Byberg, L., Melhus, H., Gedeborg, R., Sundström, Ahlbom, A., Zethelius, B., ... Michaëlsson, K., *British Medical Journal*, 338, 2009 with permission from BMJ Publishing Group Ltd.

in enjoyable leisure-time pursuits (Lin, Friedman, Quinn, Chen, & Mapstone, 2012).

One way to improve participation in active leisure-time pursuits is to help individuals find activities that they find truly enjoyable. Researchers have found that the Holland RIASEC model, for example, can be applied to leisure activities in older adults (Kerby & Ragan, 2002). Just as people can be counseled to seek a person–environment fit for vocations, they might also be advised to find the leisure pursuit that will keep them motivated and, hence, active in a pursuit that will ultimately have value in maximizing their functional abilities.

Another approach to understanding the satisfaction older adults can obtain from leisure activities comes from "Innovation Theory." According to this view, older adults who become involved with a new leisure activity may experience a range of psychological benefits, including enhanced sense of meaning in life and well-being and even a feeling of self-reinvention.

Travel is a leisure activity that often takes people out of their comfort zone and can therefore stimulate these benefits. Using responses from Israeli participants in a mail-in survey reporting on their most recent vacations involving travel, Nimrod and Rotem (2012) defined a group of "absolute" innovators (the most extreme) who were most likely to say that they took the trip in order to participate in new activities, try new food, learn something new about their relationships, gain a new skill, and learn something new about themselves and life in general. This group, comprising about one-fifth of the sample, shared many similarities with the non-innovators in the activities engaged in while traveling. However, the groups differed in some of the activities they engaged in while on vacation. The innovators were more likely to visit small towns and villages rather than big cities, getting to know the local people, gambling, and engaging in physical exercise, and using travel to find opportunities for growth and self-expression. Unlike the noninnovators, the absolute innovators used travel to find opportunities for growth and self-expression. Clearly, retirement involving such active leisure-time pursuits can facilitate the individual's overall well-being even long after the vacation is over.

In conclusion, changes in the labor force, the meaning of work, and the economic realities of an aging population all affect the nature of work and the workplace. As you contemplate your future career, your top priority should be thinking about what you will find to be most fulfilling.

SUMMARY

1. Work is a major focus of adult life from the 20s until retirement and beyond. Labor force age dynamics have shifted with movement of the Baby Boom generation and the aging of the labor force. There are disparities by race and gender in income levels, even controlling for educational attainment.

2. Contemporary vocational psychology is oriented primarily around Holland's RIASEC theory of vocational development, which is the basis for O*NET, a comprehensive catalog of occupations. The highest level of worker satisfaction and productivity is theorized to occur when there is congruence between persons and their environments. Super's self-concept theory proposes that individuals move through several stages of career development, in which they attempt to maximize the expression of their self-concept in their work. Rather than proceed straight through these stages, however, individuals may plateau at the maintenance stage

or recycle through earlier stages after a career change. The boundaryless career captures the concept that individuals direct their own career progression.

3. Theories and research on vocational satisfaction attempt to determine the relative influence of intrinsic and extrinsic factors on a worker's happiness and productivity in a job. Occupational reinforcement patterns are the work values and needs that are likely to be satisfied in a job, and if these are present, the individual will be more satisfied. Self-determination theory proposes that in the highest form of extrinsic motivation, people's jobs become the basis for their identities. Conflict between work and family is a source of potential vocational dissatisfaction. Researchers have not established whether age is related to vocational satisfaction because the influence of job tenure must also be taken into account.

4. The question of whether older workers are as productive as younger workers is another focus of occupational research. Older workers are relatively advantaged in jobs that rely on experience and perform more poorly in jobs that demand speed. Older workers have fewer fatalities on the job as well as lower absentee rates. Passage of the ADEA in 1967 offered protection to workers over 40 from discrimination by employers, although several occupations are excluded from this legislation.

5. Retirement is defined as the individual's withdrawal from the labor force in later life. Rather than being a discrete event, however, for most people it spans a process that may last for years. Most retired people do not suffer a loss of health, either mental or physical, but some do experience the transition as stressful. The resource model of retirement proposes that people will be most satisfied in retirement if they can draw on physical, psychological, and social sources of support.

6. Leisure activities can serve a variety of important functions for adults throughout their working lives, but particularly in later adulthood after retirement. Researchers have identified positive effects of leisure involvement on physical functioning, well-being, and ultimately, mortality.

11

Mental Health Issues and Treatment

AGING TODAY

Shedding Light on Psychology's Dark Triad

Lurking beneath the surface of people who use others to their own advantage is psychology's "Dark Triad." Defined as a set of traits that include the tendency to seek admiration and special treatment (otherwise known as narcissism), to be callous and insensitive (psychopathy), and to manipulate others (Machiavellianism), the Dark Triad is rapidly becoming a new focus of personality psychology.

Researchers are finding that the Dark Triad underlies a host of undesirable behaviors, including aggressiveness, sexual opportunism, and impulsivity. Until recently, the only way to capture the Dark Triad in the lab was to administer lengthy tests measuring each personality trait separately. With the development of the "Dirty Dozen" scale, however, psychologists Peter Jonason and Gregory Webster (2010) are now making it possible to spot these potentially troublesome traits with a simple 12-item rating scale.

People who score high on the traditional Dark Triad measures that test each of the three qualities separately show a pattern of behavior that in fact combines the worst of all worlds. They seek out multiple casual-sex partners. When someone gets in their way, they act out aggressively to take what they want. Oddly enough, although their self-esteem doesn't seem to be either higher or lower than others, people who score high on the Dark Triad qualities have an unstable view of themselves. Perhaps reflecting the aggressiveness inherent in the Dark Triad, these tendencies are more likely to be shown by men, particularly those who are high on psychopathy and Machiavellianism.

What does it mean to possess high levels of the Dark Triad qualities? In an investigation of how others perceive these traits, Austrian psychologists John Rauthmann and Gerald Kolar (2012) asked nonuniversity adults ranging from 18 to 75 years of age to judge the perceived "darkness" of each Dark Triad quality. Of the three, narcissism was judged to be the "brightest." People who are high on psychopathy and Machiavellianism can cause you harm, but many narcissists only harm themselves. However, other studies suggest that over time, the initial glow of the narcissist's bright qualities does tend to fade. People who interact with narcissists like them less and less the more time they spend with them.

As we know from other research, psychopathy and narcissism aren't single, unitary traits. It may not even be possible to capture the self-ratings of people on psychopathy scales, given the propensity of psychopaths to lie. Furthermore, there's more than one kind of narcissist—the grandiose and the vulnerable. The Dirty Dozen scale clearly doesn't capture these subtleties.

To sum up, the Dirty Dozen scale is—just that—a little dirty. Its main advantage is that it's quick and easy to complete. If you sense that someone (or you) might have the Dark Triad traits, consider yourself warned.

Posted by Susan Whitbourne and Stacey Whitbourne

Up until this point in the book, we have focused primarily on people who fit the definition of "normal" as they navigate the adult years. We will now turn our focus to psychological disorders and how they affect individuals throughout their lives. By some accounts, over half of the entire adult population struggle with the symptoms of one or another disorder. In this chapter, we focus our discussion on the most common disorders affecting people in adulthood and later life; however, it is important to keep in mind that the difference between normal and abnormal is often a matter of degree.

Furthermore, psychological disorders reflect developmental processes that continue throughout life. The balance of risk and protective factors as they evolve earlier in life have a cumulative impact in later adulthood (Whitbourne & Meeks, 2010).

PSYCHOLOGICAL DISORDERS IN ADULTHOOD

The criteria used to judge behavior as " abnormal" include feeling personal or subjective distress, being impaired in everyday life, causing a risk to the self or other people, and engaging in behavior that is socially or culturally unacceptable (Whitbourne & Halgin, 2013). **Psychological disorders** include the range of behaviors and experiences that fall outside of social norms, create adaptational difficulty for the individual on a daily basis, and put the individual or others at risk of harm. People who have a hobby of collecting coins would not be considered abnormal, for example, because they are engaging in a behavior that does not hurt them or others and is culturally

acceptable. By contrast, consider people known as "hoarders," who collect old newspapers, magazines, and cereal boxes to the point that their homes become virtually uninhabitable. These individuals might very well be considered to have a psychological disorder: they are not only engaging in behavior that is outside the norm but may also be putting themselves and others at risk for fire, injury, or disease due to the dirt and debris that have accumulated in their home.

Specific sets of behaviors that meet the conditions of abnormality are given a diagnosis according to the criteria set forth in the **Diagnostic and Statistical Manual (DSM)**, which is the major reference used by mental health professionals in the United States and Canada to diagnose people with psychological disorders. Outside the United States and Canada, clinicians and researchers use the **International Statistical Classification of Diseases and Related Health Problems (ICD)**, the reference guide to all medical illnesses, including psychological disorders.

The most recent edition of the DSM is the DSM-5 (American Psychiatric Association, 2013). To assign a diagnosis, the clinician must determine whether the client meets the minimum number of specific criteria that is required. In addition, the clinician rates the disorder's severity in the individual. Clinicians may also perform separate ratings to indicate how much stress the individual is experiencing and what overall level of functioning he or she demonstrates at the time of the evaluation.

Table 11.1 lists the major disorders from DSM-5 that are relevant to understanding older adults. When reading about these disorders, it is important for you to understand that we are listing their major features in abbreviated fashion. In a real-world setting, clinicians must go carefully through each of the criteria to ensure that the individual

Roger Bamber/Alamy

This man, an example of a hoarder, shows the thousands of possessions he has collected over many decades of never throwing anything away.

TABLE 11.1
Selected Diagnoses in the DSM-5 as Observed in Older Adults

Category	Description	Examples of Specific Disorders	Important Considerations for Older Adults
Depressive disorders	Prolonged sad mood	Major depressive disorder, persistent depressive disorder	Depression may appear as cognitive impairment or physical symptoms
Anxiety disorders	Intense anxiety, worry, or apprehension	Generalized anxiety disorder, panic disorder, specific phobia, social anxiety disorder, agoraphobia	Symptoms of anxiety disorders may present or coexist with medical symptoms
Obsessive-compulsive and related disorders	Obsessions (repeated thoughts) and compulsions (urges)	Obsessive-compulsive disorder, body dysmorphic disorder, hoarding disorder	
Schizophrenia spectrum and other psychotic disorders	Psychotic symptoms such as distortion of reality and serious impairment in thinking, behavior, affect, and motivation	Schizophrenia, schizoaffective disorder, catatonia disorder, delusional disorder, brief psychotic disorder, schizotypal personality disorder	In schizophrenia, likelihood of complete remission is 20–25%; the 10% who continue to experience symptoms have higher suicide rates than other older adults
Neurocognitive disorders	Significant loss of cognitive functioning as a result of neurological dysfunction or medical illness	Delirium, major and mild neurocognitive disorder	Delirium may be misdiagnosed as dementia
Substance-related and addictive disorder	Use, intoxication, or withdrawal of psychoactive substances	Alcohol use disorder, sedative-, hypnotic-, or anxiolytic-related disorders	Older adults are more at risk than is often thought

actually should receive the diagnosis. In general, these criteria involve a fairly high degree of severity and a persistence of symptoms over a period of time that is usually no less than 2 weeks. In other words, just because a person may seem to be depressed or anxious does not mean that the person should be diagnosed with the disorder on the spot.

Major Depressive Disorder

Individuals who experience prolonged and extreme sadness may be diagnosed with a form of depressive disorder, depending on the length and nature of the symptoms. In **major depressive disorder**, the major symptom is an extremely sad mood that lasts most of the time for at least 2 weeks and is not typical of the individual's usual mood. The individual may also experience other symptoms including appetite and sleep disturbances, feelings of guilt, difficulty concentrating, and a low sense of self-worth.

Over the course of adulthood, 16.6% of adults are estimated to meet the diagnostic criteria for major depressive disorder. This figure represents the lifetime prevalence, meaning that it includes anyone who has ever received this diagnosis. Each year, 6.7% of the adult population receives

a diagnosis of major depressive disorder, with clinicians classifying 30.4% of these cases (2.0% of the adult population) as severe. Women are 70% more likely than men to experience major depressive disorder at some point in life. Compared to adults 60 years of age and older, adults 59 years of age and younger are approximately twice as likely to have experienced major depressive disorder. Looking only at 12-month prevalence, 18- to 29-year-olds are 200% as likely as adults 60 and older to have experienced this disorder. The average age of onset of the disorder is 32 years old (Kessler et al., 2005).

Though the prevalence of a diagnosable mood disorder is lower in older than in younger adults, many older adults report symptoms of depressive disorders. Among a sample of nearly 2,000 women aged 60 to 91 years, the rates of subclinical depression were estimated at 20%. However, among those seen in medical settings, such as inpatient hospitals or clinics, the rates of depressive symptoms can reach as high as 30% (Whitbourne & Meeks, 2010). Moreover, although women are more likely to experience the diagnosable condition of major depressive disorder, depressive symptoms are higher in men between the ages of 60 and 80. By that point, the rates of depressive symptoms in women and men are roughly equal (Barefoot, Mortensen, Helms, Avlund, & Schroll, 2001).

There are age differences in the symptoms of depression, and what appears as a depressive symptom for a younger adult may not appear as one in an older adult. The traditionally recognized "psychological" symptoms of depression, such as **dysphoria** (sad mood), guilt, low self-esteem, and suicidal thoughts, are less likely to be acknowledged by older adults. Rather than seeking treatment for these psychological symptoms, older people are more likely to seek treatment for physical symptoms, such as pain and abdominal disturbances (Amore, Tagariello, Laterza, & Savoia, 2007).

Health care professionals are not well trained in recognizing the signs of depression in their older clients (Charney et al., 2003). In part, this is because older adults do not necessarily report their symptoms in a manner that allows for accurate diagnosis. In addition, health care providers are not attuned to diagnosing psychological disorders in their older clients. Complicating the situation further, physicians spend less time per visit with an older patient than they do a younger patient.

Many insurance companies reimburse for a mental health diagnosis and intervention at a lower rate than for a physical disorder, adding to the likelihood that an older adult will not seek treatment for psychologically based symptoms. The situation has improved for recipients of the government's health insurance for older adults. In 2008, the U.S. Congress approved an important revision to Medicare, the government insurance program for people 65 and older. Known as "parity," people on Medicare can now pay the same out-of-pocket expense for mental health that they would for medical care (Medicare Improvements for Patients and Providers Act of 2008).

Other deterrents to an appropriate diagnosis of depressive disorders in older adults relate to attitudes toward depression among mental health professionals. Some may assume that depression is a natural consequence of aging and therefore pay less attention to its symptoms. Alternatively, a psychologist or physician may wish to avoid stigmatizing older clients by diagnosing them with a psychological disorder (Duberstein & Conwell, 2000). Misdiagnosis may also occur because the symptoms of mood disorders occur in conjunction with a medical condition, leading to the physician's failure to detect the mood disorder or to misattribute the symptoms to a physical cause (Delano-Wood & Abeles, 2005). Careful diagnosis with attention to possible underlying medical conditions or dementia is therefore vital (Small, 2009).

When trying to determine the cause of an older adult's depression, it is important for health care workers to look for possible contributing psychosocial factors. These additional factors include functional limitations (Okura et al., 2010), sensory impairments (Dillon, Gu, Hoffman, & Ko, 2010), the inability to provide basic self-care tasks (Yong, 2006), and pain (McCarthy, Bigal, Katz, Derby, & Lipton, 2009b). Institutionalization presents another risk factor, as do changes in cognition and personality, particularly among the oldest-old (Margrett et al., 2010). Psychosocial issues such as bereavement, loneliness, and stressful life events can also serve as risk factors for depressive disorders in both middle (Kendler, Myers, & Zisook, 2008) and later adulthood (Holley & Mast, 2007).

An inability to employ successful coping strategies to deal with late-life stressors can also increase the individual's risk of developing depression. In one study covering a 10-year period, older adults who used ineffective coping methods, such as avoidance, were more likely to develop symptoms of depression compared with their age peers who attempted to handle their problems through direct, problem-focused coping methods (Holahan, Moos, Holahan, Brennan, & Schutte, 2005).

Medical disorders also present significant risk factors for depression (Sneed, Kasen, & Cohen, 2007); specifically, arthritis-related activity limitations (Shih, Hootman, Kruger, & Helmick, 2006), hip fracture (Lenze et al., 2007), diabetes (Campayo et al., 2010), metabolic syndrome (Almeida, Calver, Jamrozik, Hankey, & Flicker, 2009), stroke (Santos et al., 2009), and hypertension (Garcia-Fabela et al., 2009). Apart from these major medical conditions, there are some less obvious but still noteworthy contributors to late-life depression involving physical health. As we pointed out in Chapter 4, tooth loss is a condition that affects a substantial number of older adults. Perhaps not surprisingly, researchers have found that depressed older adults are more likely to have experienced tooth loss (Hugo, Hilgert, de Sousa Mda, & Cury, 2009). Another potentially overlooked risk factor is the lack of sufficient vitamin D, which may also present a risk factor for cognitive impairment (Barnard & Colon-Emeric, 2010). Interventions that help to address these conditions could potentially spare many older adults unnecessary emotional suffering.

Not only do physical conditions increase the risk of major depressive disorder, but older adults become more likely to suffer further impairments in physical and cognitive functioning when their psychological symptoms are untreated (Boyle, Porsteinsson, Cui, King, & Lyness, 2010). Depressive symptoms predict mortality in older adults (St. John & Montgomery, 2009), perhaps indirectly by weakening the individual's immune system. Depression may activate cytokines that eventually increase the risk of cardiovascular disease, osteoporosis, arthritis, type 2 diabetes, cancers, periodontal disease, frailty, and functional decline (Kiecolt-Glaser & Glaser, 2002). In addition, major depressive disorder and chronic depression can increase an individual's risk of developing a neurocognitive disorder (Byers, Covinsky, Barnes, & Yaffe, 2012).

Bipolar Disorder

Bipolar disorder is diagnosed in people who have experienced one or more manic episodes during which they feel elated, grandiose, expansive, and highly energetic. Formerly called manic-depression, people with bipolar disorder may or may not have experienced a period of significant depression along with being manic for at least a week (bipolar I) or may have experienced depression and at least one "hypomanic" episode, in which their manic symptoms lasted for less than a week (bipolar II).

Bipolar disorder has a lifetime prevalence rate of 3.9% in the U.S. population and a 12-month prevalence of 2.6%. Of those diagnosed with bipolar disorder in a given year, nearly 83% (2.2% of adult population) have cases classified as "severe." At least half of all cases begin before a person reaches the age of 25 (Kessler, Chiu, Demler, Merikangas, & Walters, 2005).

Researchers know considerably less about bipolar disorder in later life than they do about major depressive disorder. Rates of bipolar disorder are lower in older adults than in the younger population (Depp & Jeste, 2004). There may be neurological contributions, as suggested by the fact that bipolar disorder in older adults is related to a higher risk for cerebrovascular disease (Subramaniam, Dennis, & Byrne, 2006) and white matter hyperintensities (Zanetti, Cordeiro, & Busatto, 2007).

Bipolar disorder exacts a high psychosocial cost on those who have experienced its symptoms throughout their lives. For example, older adults with a lifetime history of "rapid cycling," in which their symptoms alternate frequently between depression and mania, feel that their life goals were significantly interfered with if not entirely derailed (Sajatovic et al., 2008). Nevertheless, approximately 60% of all individuals with bipolar disorder can live symptom-free if they receive adequate treatment (Perlis et al., 2006).

Anxiety Disorders

The main characteristic of an **anxiety disorder** is anxiety, a sense of dread about what might happen in the future. In addition to having the unpleasant feelings associated with anxiety, people with anxiety disorders go to great lengths to avoid anxiety-provoking situations. As a result, they may have difficulty performing their jobs, enjoying their leisure

pursuits, or engaging in social activities with their friends and families.

Anxiety disorders are the most highly prevalent of all psychological disorders, with the exception of substance abuse disorders. They have a lifetime prevalence of 28.8% and an overall 12-month prevalence of 18.1%. Of all 12-month prevalence cases, nearly 23% are classified as severe. The percentage of people reporting lifetime prevalence across all anxiety disorders peaks between the ages of 30–44, with a sharp drop-off to 15.3% among people 60 years and older (Kessler, Chiu, et al., 2005). Older adults are less likely (7%) than young adults (21%) and middle-aged adults (19%) to be diagnosed with an anxiety disorder. Older women are nearly five times more likely than men to be diagnosed with an anxiety disorder (Gum, King-Kallimanis, & Kohn, 2009).

It is possible that the lower diagnosis of anxiety disorders in general among older adults reflects their greater resilience. It is also possible that, as with depressive disorders, health care professionals are not well trained in recognizing and diagnosing anxiety disorder symptoms in their older clients (Scogin, Floyd, & Forde, 2000). Similar to mood disorders, the symptoms of an anxiety disorder may present or coexist with medical symptoms (Mehta et al., 2007), particularly for some forms of anxiety disorders, including panic attacks and agoraphobia (which we discuss below) (Sareen, Cox, Clara, & Asmundson, 2005). As we also have seen, health practitioners may not be attuned to diagnosing psychological symptoms in an older individual with physical health problems. Consequently, the practitioner may miss the diagnosis of an anxiety disorder, along with an opportunity to intervene. The implications of failing to diagnose anxiety disorders can be serious, as older adults with anxiety symptoms have higher rates of mortality, particularly among African American older adults (Brenes et al., 2007).

In the anxiety disorder known as **generalized anxiety disorder**, the individual experiences an overall sense of uneasiness and concern without a specific focus. People who have this disorder are very prone to worrying, especially over minor problems. They may also have additional symptoms, such as feeling restless and tense, having trouble concentrating, being irritable, and having difficulty sleeping. Generalized anxiety disorder has a lifetime prevalence of 5.7%. Over a 12-month period, the prevalence is reported to be 3.1%; of these, 32% are classified as severe (Kessler, Chiu, et al., 2005).

Medical patients have higher rates (8%) of generalized anxiety disorder than do individuals in the general population (Wittchen, 2002). Among older adults, the 6-month prevalence (those who reported symptoms in the past 6 months) is 2%, and the lifetime prevalence is estimated to be 3.6%, with a median age of onset at 31 (Kessler, Berglund, et al., 2005). However the prevalence rates are higher among certain minority groups; older Latina/o immigrants to the United States seem to be particularly at risk (Jimenez, Alegria, Chen, Chan, & Laderman, 2010).

The form of anxiety disorder known as **panic disorder** involves the experience of panic attacks, in which people have the physical sensation that they are about to die (e.g., shortness of breath, pounding heart, sweating palms, and so on). People who suffer from a panic disorder may have these episodes at unpredictable times. Individuals may also experience **agoraphobia**, the fear of being trapped or stranded during a panic attack in a public place. Their fear of having a panic attack leads them to avoid places such as elevators, shopping malls, or public transportation, where escape during an attack would be difficult.

Panic attacks are estimated to occur in 20% or more of adult samples; panic disorder has a much lower lifetime prevalence of between 3 and 5% (Wittchen, Gloster, Beesdo-Baum, Fava, & Craske, 2010). The prevalence of agoraphobia is estimated to be much lower than panic disorder, affecting up to 1.4% of the adult U.S. population (Kessler et al., 2006). Agoraphobia is also less common among older adults than among adults in their 30s to 60s (Kessler, Berglund, et al., 2005). Unlike younger adults, who may develop agoraphobia following a panic attack, it is more likely that this condition in older adults is related to fear of harm or embarrassment (Scogin, et al., 2000).

The diagnosis of **specific phobia** is based on the individual's having an irrational fear of a particular object or situation. This disorder is the most commonly observed form of anxiety disorder in older adults. Among all adults, the lifetime prevalence rate is estimated at 12.5%; among adults 60 and older, the prevalence is also fairly high with estimates at 7.5% (Kessler, Berglund, et al., 2005).

Almost any object or situation can form the target of a specific phobia. People can have phobias of anything from driving to syringes. The four categories of specific phobias include animals, the natural environment (storms, heights, fires), blood-injection-injury (seeing blood, having an invasive medical procedure), and engaging in activities in particular situations (driving, flying, being in an enclosed space). A fifth category of specific phobias includes a variety of miscellaneous stimuli or situations, such as a child's fear of clowns or an adult's fear of contracting a particular illness.

Overall, the lifetime prevalence for specific phobia is 12.5% (Kessler, Chiu, et al., 2005). The highest lifetime prevalence rates of specific phobias involve fear of natural situations, particularly heights, estimated to be between 3.1 and 5.3%. Animal phobia ranges in prevalence of from 3.3 to 7%. That these are the two most common forms of specific phobia is indicated by the fact that among people with any form of specific phobia, 50% have a fear of animals or a fear of heights (LeBeau et al., 2010).

In **social anxiety disorder**, the individual experiences extreme anxiety about being watched by other people. The term, which was formerly called social phobia, is somewhat misleading in that it is not literally a fear of other people but a fear of being publicly embarrassed or made to look foolish. In some cases, the individual becomes anxious at the thought of eating in the presence of other people.

The lifetime prevalence of social anxiety disorder is 12%, making it the second most common form of anxiety disorder. Its prevalence peaks among adults in their 30s. Of the 6.8% who develop this disorder over a 12-month period, nearly 30% are classified as severe. Women are more likely to suffer from this disorder than men (Kessler, Chiu, et al., 2005).

Obsessive-Compulsive and Related Disorders

People who experience **obsessive-compulsive disorder** suffer from obsessions, or repetitive thoughts (such as the belief that one's child will be harmed) and compulsions, which are repetitive behaviors (such as frequent hand washing). The obsessions and compulsions are unrelenting, irrational, and distracting.

The most common compulsions involve repeating a specific behavior, such as washing and cleaning, counting, putting items in order, checking, or requesting assurance.

Compulsions may also take the form of mental rituals, such as counting up to a certain number every time an unwanted thought intrudes. In general, there appear to be four major dimensions to the symptoms of OCD: obsessions associated with checking compulsions, the need to have symmetry and to put things in order, obsessions about cleanliness associated with compulsions to wash, and hoarding-related behaviors (Mataix-Cols, Rosario-Campos, & Leckman, 2005).

In the related disorder known as **hoarding**, people collect and store seemingly useless items that they cannot discard. The items can be as insignificant as outdated newspapers, mail, shopping bags, empty food containers, and even food remnants. People with hoarding disorder cannot dispose of these items because they are convinced that they will need them later, even though they have no clear utility. Their homes become cluttered with these objects, to the point of becoming virtually uninhabitable.

OCD has a lifetime prevalence of 1.6%. The 12-month prevalence is slightly lower, 1%; of these, about half are classified as severe (Kessler, Chiu, et al., 2005). The lifetime prevalence among older adults is estimated at

0.7% (Kessler, Berglund, et al., 2005). Unfortunately, in part because they may not spontaneously seek help, older adults with this disorder may escape detection and therefore not receive treatment (Ayers, Saxena, Golshan, & Wetherell, 2010).

Trauma and Stress-Related Disorders

Exposure to trauma such as an earthquake, fire, physical assault, and war can lead individuals to experience symptoms that may last for a prolonged period of time, even after the trauma subsides. These symptoms include intrusion of distressing reminders of the event, dissociative symptoms such as feeling numb or detached from others, avoidance of situations that might serve as reminders of the event, and hyperarousal, including sleep disturbances or irritability. People are diagnosed with **acute stress disorder** if they experience these symptoms for up to a month after the trauma. The diagnosis of **post-traumatic stress disorder (PTSD)** is given to people whose symptoms persist for more than a month.

The lifetime prevalence of PTSD is 6.8% with a yearly prevalence of 3.5%. Of those who develop PTSD within a given year, 37% experience severe symptoms (Kessler, Chiu, et al., 2005). Among Army soldiers returning from Afghanistan, 6.2% met the PTSD diagnostic criteria, with more than double that rate, 12.9%, among soldiers returning from Iraq (Hoge et al., 2004). As combat has continued in these two war zones, the number of soldiers developing mental health problems, particularly PTSD, has continued to climb. It is estimated that nearly 17% of Iraq war veterans meet the screening criteria for this disorder (Hoge, Terhakopian, Castro, Messer, & Engel, 2007).

The symptoms of PTSD and related disorders, such as depression, can persist for many years. Survivors of the North Sea oil rig disaster in 1980 continued to experience symptoms of PTSD along with anxiety disorders (not including PTSD), depressive disorders, and substance use disorders that were significantly higher than those of a matched comparison group (see Figure 5.2).

It is likely that the rates of PTSD among the older adult population will grow in future years due to the aging of Vietnam veterans. Estimates are that at the age of 19, the prevalence of PTSD among Vietnam soldiers was 15%. Because PTSD can arise many years after exposure to trauma, these numbers may well continue to increase (Department of Health and Human Services, 1999). Exposure to the terrorist attacks in the United States of September 11, 2001, led to greater likelihood of PTSD among older adults (DiGrande et al., 2008). Furthermore, as younger and middle-aged adults serving in the Iraq and Afghanistan Wars grow older, the incidence of PTSD

will likely increase substantially in coming decades (Chan, Cheadle, Reiber, Unutzer, & Chaney, 2009).

Severe health problems, such as heart disease, can increase the individual's risk of developing PTSD after exposure to combat (Spindler & Pedersen, 2005). PTSD, in turn, can also increase an individual's risk of developing heart disease. A longitudinal study of nearly 2,000 veterans in the Normative Aging Study revealed that, even after controlling for a number of risk factors, men who had experienced higher levels of PTSD were more likely to have heart attacks or develop coronary heart disease (Kubzansky, Koenen, Spiro, Vokonas, & Sparrow, 2007).

Late-onset stress symptomatology (LOSS) refers to a phenomenon observed in aging veterans who were exposed to stressful combat situations in young adulthood. Symptoms related to the combat experiences (such as an increase in memories about the trauma) begin to emerge in later life, perhaps as a function of exposure to stresses associated with aging, such as retirement and increased health problems (Davison et al., 2006). Symptoms of LOSS are similar to those of PTSD, but the progression is distinct in that it develops later in life. Researchers at the VA Boston Healthcare System have developed a survey designed to identify LOSS among older veterans, thereby allowing mental health professionals to help treat the symptoms and offer the needed support (King, King, Vickers, Davison, & Spiro, 2007).

Schizophrenia and Other Psychotic Disorders

The term **schizophrenia** refers to a disorder in which individuals experience distorted perception of reality and impairment in thinking, behavior, affect, and motivation. Individuals with schizophrenia do not experience these symptoms continuously, but to receive the diagnosis, they must have displayed them for a significant period of time during a one-month period.

The types of symptoms people with schizophrenia experience include delusions (false beliefs), hallucinations (false perceptions), disorganized and incoherent speech, very abnormal motor behavior, and what are called the "negative" symptoms of apathy, withdrawal, and lack of emotional expression. While their symptoms are active, they are unable to get or hold onto a job, hold onto a relationship, or take care of themselves. These symptoms must have lasted for 6 months or more, and the individual must not have another diagnosis (such as drug or alcohol abuse) that could better explain the symptoms. In addition to providing the overall diagnosis, clinicians use rating scales that are new to the DSM-5 in which they evaluate the severity of each of these types of symptoms.

Epidemiologists estimate that 1% of the population has schizophrenia at some point in their lives, with higher rates for adults 30 to 44 (1.5%) than people older than 65 (0.2%) (Keith, Regier, & Rae, 1991). The 1-year prevalence is estimated at 0.5% in the United States (Wu, Shi, Birnbaum, Hudson, & Kessler, 2006). In part, the apparent decrease in older age groups reflects the fact that people with this disorder do not survive until old age.

People with schizophrenia have a higher rate of cardiovascular and metabolic disorders, either because of their lifestyle habits or the medications they must take to control their symptoms (Protopopova, Masopust, Maly, Valis, & Bazant, 2012). In addition, the nature of this disturbance and its association with other illnesses and substance abuse mean that a person with schizophrenia experiences feelings of isolation and an identity as being "different" (Quin, Clare, Ryan, & Jackson, 2009). Perhaps as a consequence, older adults with schizophrenia have higher suicide rates than older adults in the community who do not have this diagnosis (Cohen, Abdallah, & Diwan, 2010). As many as 15% of individuals with schizophrenia die as a result of suicide, and up to 50% make a suicide attempt at some point in their lives (Harvey & Bowie, 2013).

On the positive side, older adults who have suffered from schizophrenia for many years develop a wide range of coping skills (Solano & Whitbourne, 2001). Those naturally developing mechanisms can be augmented with clinical interventions that focus on methods to cope with everyday life problems.

Compared to other psychological disorders, the course and outcome of schizophrenia are poorer (Jobe & Harrow, 2010). During the first 10 to 15 years, people with schizophrenia have more recurrent episodes and their chances of completely recovering, even after the first 10 years, are worse than those of people with other disorders. Most people continue to experience psychotic symptoms and disordered thinking, as well as negative symptoms. They are less able to obtain or keep a job. On the positive side, however, if they receive treatment during their acute phase, over 40% can recover (i.e., they have no symptoms or hospitalizations and have at least part-time work) for one or more years at a time. Some people with schizophrenia can even show complete recovery for the remainder of their lives (Meeks, 2000).

For years, clinicians referred to a condition known as **late-onset schizophrenia**, a form of the disorder that was thought to originate in adults over the age of 45 years (Jeste et al., 1997). However, this condition is now thought not to be schizophrenia but rather some other phenotype of psychotic disorder, the risk factors for which may include sensory deficits, some forms of neurocognitive

disorder, social isolation, and substance abuse (Whitbourne & Meeks, 2010).

Substance-Related Disorders

In 2011, illicit drugs were used by an estimated 22.5 million persons 12 years and older in the United States, representing 8.7% of the population (Substance Abuse and Mental Health Services Administration, 2012). The majority of adults who abuse or are dependent on alcohol or illicit drugs are in their late teens and early 20s; however, the overall numbers and percentages of older adults are on the rise with the aging of the Baby Boom generation. The legal use of medical marijuana may also change patterns of substance use among middle-aged and older adults in the coming years.

As of 2008, the last year for which data on older adults are available, an estimated 4.3 million adults aged 50 and older (4.7%) had used an illicit drug within the past year (see Figure 11.1). Older adults are particularly at risk for abuse of prescription drugs, as 36% of the medications used in the United States are taken by adults over the age of 65 years. Nonmedical use of prescription drugs is the most common form of illicit drug abuse among people 65 and older with an estimated prevalence of 0.8% (double the percentage who abuse marijuana) (Substance Abuse and Mental Health Services Administration, 2009).

FIGURE 11.1

Past Illicit Drug Use Among Adults 50 or Older

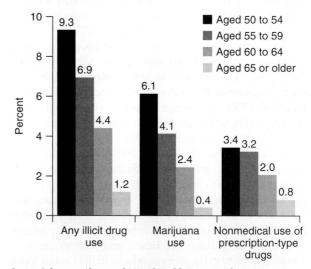

Source: Substance Abuse and Mental Health Services Administration. (2009). Illicit drug use among older adults. Findings from the SAMHSA 2006 to 2008 National Surveys on Drug Use and Health (NSDUHs), Retrieved from http://www.oas.samhsa.gov/2k9/168/168OlderAdultsHTML.pdf

Attention has only recently been drawn to the problems of older drinkers. In part, this is because people who use alcohol to excess tend not to live past their 60s and 70s. By the time they reach the age of 70, they have either become abstinent or died from excessive alcohol use or from related high-risk behaviors such as smoking (Vaillant, 2003).

Symptoms of alcohol dependence are thought to be present in as many as 14% of older adults who receive medical attention in hospitals and emergency rooms. Alcohol use is also thought to be relatively prevalent in settings in which only older adults live, such as nursing homes and retirement communities. People with a history of problem drinking and those who retired involuntarily seem most likely to abuse alcohol after they enter retirement (Kuerbis & Sacco, 2012).

The risks of alcohol abuse among older adults range from cirrhosis of the liver (a terminal condition) to heightened rate of injury through hip fractures and motor vehicle accidents. Alcohol may also interact with the effects of prescription medications. Other health problems that can develop in older drinkers are increased risk of diabetes, high blood pressure, congestive heart failure, osteoporosis, and mood disorders. Alcohol also interacts badly with common medications, including aspirin, acetaminophen, cold and allergy medication, sleeping pills, pain medication, and antianxiety medications and antidepressants (National Institute on Alcohol Abuse and Alcoholism, 2013).

Even without a change in drinking patterns, an older person may experience difficulties associated with physiological changes in the kidneys that affect tolerance. Long-term alcohol use may also lead to changes in the frontal lobes and cerebellum, exacerbating the effects of normal aging on cognitive and motor functioning. In severe and prolonged alcohol abuse, neurocognitive disorders can develop, leading to permanent memory loss and early death (as we discussed in Chapter 5).

There are treatment approaches that can be effective in reducing alcohol consumption among those older adults who continue to struggle with abuse and dependence. Participation in Alcoholics Anonymous, receiving support from family and friends, and using adaptive coping mechanisms can be effective methods of reducing an older adult's reliance on alcohol. As is true for younger people, the context of drinking is important. One of the most effective treatments may be finding a new network of friends who do not engage in or approve of drinking (Moos, Schutte, Brennan, & Moos, 2004).

Personality Disorders

A **personality disorder** is a long-standing pattern of inner experience and behavior that has maladaptive qualities.

Personality disorders are estimated to be found among 9% of the general population (Samuels et al., 2002), an overall rate that is fairly steady across adulthood (Abrams & Horowitz, 1999). In later life, people with personality disorders experience significant deleterious effects on their psychological functioning and relationships with others (Segal, Coolidge, & Rosowsky, 2006). Here, we will look at the personality disorders that have received the most attention in studies on adult development and aging.

Antisocial personality disorder is characterized by **psychopathy**, a set of traits that include lack of remorse and an impulsive lifestyle. The traits associated with psychopathy fall into two dimensions (Hare & Neumann, 2006). Factor 1 is a cluster of traits that represent disturbances in the capacity to experience emotions such as empathy, guilt, and remorse. This cluster also includes manipulativeness, egocentricity, and callousness. Factor 2 incorporates the unstable and impulsive behaviors that contribute to the socially deviant lifestyle of the individual with this disorder.

Studies of the relationship between age and antisocial personality disorder provide support for the notion that psychopathy is highly stable over time (Harpur, Hart, & Hare, 2002). One large-scale study conducted on nearly 900 male prisoners between the ages of 18 and 89 showed that there were no age differences on Factor 1, which represents the "personality" contribution to the disorder. By contrast, scores on the Factor 2 items that reflect socially deviant and impulsive behaviors decrease dramatically across age groups. This characterization corresponds closely to data on the numbers of prisoners by age reported by the U.S. Department of Justice. The rate of imprisonment drastically decreases after the age of 45 (Harrison & Beck, 2005).

Changes over adulthood in the impulsive and antisocial element of psychopathy may reflect a number of influences other than changes in the personality disorder itself, however. Once again we return to an explanation involving survivor or attrition effects. The apparent decrease in antisocial behavior may reflect the fact that people who were high on Factor 2 (impulsivity) of psychopathy are no longer alive. In addition to having been killed in violent crime or as the result of drug or alcohol abuse, such individuals also have a higher than expected mortality rate due to poor health habits (Laub & Vaillant, 2000).

Another personality disorder studied in later adulthood is **borderline personality disorder**, a diagnosis given to people who show symptoms that include extreme instability in sense of self and relationships with others, sexual impulsivity, fear of abandonment, repeated suicide attempts, and difficulties controlling their emotions. Along with high levels of neuroticism, scoring high on a measure of borderline personality disorder may make older individuals more likely to experience "stress generation," meaning that they create more negative events in their lives, as we reported in Chapter 8 (Gleason, Powers, & Oltmanns, 2012).

According to the **maturation hypothesis**, people who have personality disorders that involve "immature" symptoms such as acting out, being entitled, and having an unstable sense of self improve or at least become more treatable later in life (see Figure 11.2). By contrast, people who fit the symptom picture of the "mature" personality disorders that involve being perfectionistic, cold and distant, and distrustful of others become more symptomatic over time (Engels, Duijsens, Haringsma, & van Putten, 2003).

There are many possible explanations for the maturation hypothesis, including brain injury, disease, and life stresses. It is also possible that older adults with longstanding personality disorders become better at coping with their symptoms, particularly those that involve acting out (Segal, Hook, & Coolidge, 2001). Furthermore, a point we will return to when we cover assessment, many personality disorder diagnostic instruments were designed for younger populations and therefore do not capture accurately the symptoms as they appear in older adults (Oltmanns & Balsis, 2011).

Overall, however, having a personality disorder in later life does not bode well for the individual's ability to navigate the aging process. Even when controlling for current health problems, depression, and health-related behaviors, people in their late 50s and early 60s with personality disorders are more likely to require more medical care. People with borderline personality, in particular, reported experiencing higher levels of pain and fatigue and more negative perceptions of their general levels of physical health (Powers & Oltmanns, 2012).

ELDER ABUSE

A condition that may become one of serious clinical concern is the abuse of an older adult through the actions taken by another person, or through self-neglect that leads to significant loss of functioning. The term **elder abuse** is used to refer to a large category of actions taken directly against older adults that inflict physical or psychological harm. To protect vulnerable adults, Adult Protective Services (APS) were mandated by Title XX of the Social Security Act in 1975. Although a federal program, there is little or no funding attached to it. This means that the states are responsible for enforcing the regulations and as a result, there is considerable variation in the definitions and reporting mechanisms for abuse.

Elder abuse is a notoriously difficult behavior to document, because it is one surrounded by guilt, shame, fear, and the risk of criminal prosecution. Victims are afraid to report abuse because they are afraid of being punished by their abusers, and the perpetrators obviously do not wish to reveal that they are engaging in this socially unacceptable if not criminal activity.

There are five types of elder abuse: physical abuse, sexual abuse, psychological abuse, financial exploitation, and neglect (National Center for Elder Abuse, 2013) (see Table 11.2). Individuals may also experience self-neglect, which occurs when their own behavior puts them at risk, and although there is no perpetrator, this form of abuse can be equally serious. Examples of self-neglect include situations when vulnerable older adults fail or refuse to address their own basic physical, emotional, or social needs. Examples of self-neglect in vulnerable older adults include failing to engage in self-care tasks such as nourishment,

FIGURE 11.2

Maturation Hypothesis of Personality Disorders in Later Adulthood

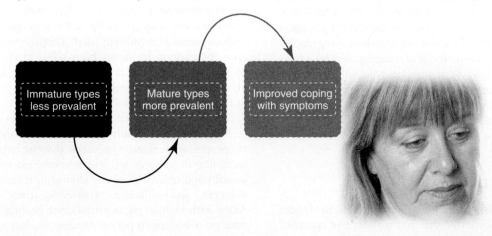

iStockphoto

TABLE 11.2
Types of Elder Abuse

Type	Description	Examples
Physical abuse	Use of physical force against an older adult that may result in bodily injury, physical pain, or impairment	Striking with an object, hitting, pushing, shoving, etc.
Sexual abuse	Nonconsensual sexual contact of any kind with an older adult	Unwanted touching, rape, sodomy, coerced nudity, etc.
Psychological abuse	Infliction of anguish, pain, or distress on an older adult through verbal or nonverbal acts	Verbal assaults, insults, threats, intimidation, humiliation, and harassment
Financial exploitation	Illegal or improper use of an older adult's funds, property, or assets	Cashing an older adult's checks without authorization. Forging an older adult's signature. Misusing or stealing an older adult's money or possessions
Neglect	Refusal or failure to fulfill any part of a person's obligation or duties to an older adult	Refusing or failing to provide an older audult with such necessities as food, water, clothing, shelter, personal hygiene, medicine, comfort, personal safety, and other essentials

Source: National Center on Elder Abuse http://www.ncea.aoa.gov/

clothing, hygiene, and shelter; misusing of medications; and managing or administering finances without appropriate help or consultation from others (Centers for Disease Control and Prevention, 2013).

Given its potential to cause significant psychological (Yan & Sokum, 2001) and physical harm (Dong et al., 2009) to older adults, there is surprisingly little research on the topic of elder abuse. According to a survey in the U.S. of nearly 5,800 respondents 60 and older, 14.1% experience some form of abuse with 4.6% suffering emotional abuse, 1.6% being victimized by physical abuse, and 5.2% being financially exploited (Acierno et al., 2010). These may be underestimates, because surveys do not get an adequate sampling of highly cognitively impaired older adults. Furthermore, in minority communities, cultural sensitivities may limit individuals from reporting instances of abuse of elders in the family (Dong, 2012).

Targeting their caregivers, and providing them with better coping skills as well as adequate reimbursement and social support, are important preventative strategies to reduce the incidence of this very tragic situation (Nadien, 2006). However, if elder abuse is to be stemmed, changes must occur at the larger societal level. A report by the U.S. Government Accountability Office (Government Accountability Office, 2011) proposes that more funding of state Adult Protective Services (APS) agencies is needed to support both reporting and prevention. Federal law mandates that elder abuse be reported through the state APS, but these agencies are underfunded. In fiscal year 2009, only $11.9 million was budgeted for all activities related to elder

abuse, and little of this went to fund APS. Moreover, states vary widely in their laws regarding who is mandated to report abuse. Delaware and Florida are 2 of the 14 states that mandate everyone from physicians to bank officers to report elder abuse to the APS. New York State, North and South Dakota, and Colorado have no mandated reporting whatsoever (Government Accountability Office, 2011).

SUICIDE

Although suicide is not a diagnosis in the DSM-5, suicide is related to psychological disorders that are diagnosable (National Institute of Mental Health, 2013) (see Figure 11.3). Among people who committed suicide in 2010, 33% tested positive for alcohol, 23% for antidepressants, and 21% for opiates, including heroin and prescription pain killers (Centers for Disease Control and Prevention National Center for Injury Prevention and Control, 2012).

In 2010, suicide was the 10th leading cause of death in the U.S., taking its toll on 38,364 adults, the majority of whom were between the ages of 25 to 54 (National Center for Vital Statistics, 2013). Among individuals 15 to 24 years of age, however, suicide was the third leading cause of death, accounting for 20% of deaths in that age group. The age-adjusted suicide rate in the United States of all age, race, and sex groups is highest for all demographic categories among males ages 75 and older, at 16.3 per 100,000 suicide deaths per in the population (Centers for Disease Control and Prevention National Center for Injury

- Depression and other psychological disorders
- Substance abuse disorder or combination of substance abuse with another disorder
- Prior suicide attempt
- Family history of psychological disorder or substance abuse
- Family violence, including physical or sexual abuse
- Firearms in the home
- Incarceration
- Exposure to the suicidal behavior of others

However, many people have these risk factors but are not suicidal

Sheryl Griffin/iStockphoto

FIGURE 11.3

Facts About Suicide in Older Adults

Prevention and Control, 2012). This translates to a total of about 2,500 individuals, roughly divided up between the years of 75 to 79, 80 to 84, and 85 and older, with about 800 in each grouping (Centers for Disease Control and Prevention National Center for Injury Prevention and Control, 2013b).

Although statistically it is difficult to predict who will commit suicide at any age, because the rates in the population are so low, there are several known risk factors for older adults (Conwell, Van Orden, & Caine, 2011). Psychiatric illness is present in 71 to 97% of suicides in older adults, particularly depressive disorders. Additional risk factors are physical illness and limitations in functioning, chronic pain, and deficits in cognitive functioning. Social isolation and stressful life events are further risk factors. Thus, suicide can be understood as a biopsychosocial phenomenon contributed to by factors that are biological (functional losses and illness), psychological (cognitive changes and depression), and sociocultural (stress and isolation).

One key symptom to identifying an older person at risk of suicide is a history of previous suicide attempts (Murphy et al., 2012). However, the older adult contemplating suicide may not appear, even to a trained clinician, to be severely depressed. Instead, the suicidal older adult may outwardly show only mild to moderate symptoms of depression. As a result, suicides are much more difficult for health care workers to detect (Duberstein & Conwell, 2000). Other subclinical symptoms shown by suicidal older adults include hostility, sleep difficulties, anxiety, and depression (Liu & Chiu, 2009).

Given the difficulty of diagnosing depression among older adults, it would seem particularly important for health care providers to be aware of suicide risk factors when working with older adults. Sadly, it is estimated that

between 43 and 76% of all suicide victims had seen a health care provider within a month of their death (Duberstein & Conwell, 2000). Greater sensitivity to symptoms of mood disorders in conjunction with more thorough evaluation of the additional psychological and medical risk factors through multidisciplinary training can prove helpful in identifying and managing suicide risk in older adults (Huh et al., 2012).

TREATMENT ISSUES IN MENTAL HEALTH CARE

With the aging of the Baby Boom generation, mental health researchers are turning their attention with great concern toward the need for more research and training in providing services to older adults. Clearly, more training will be needed both for practitioners currently in the field and those who will be entering the ranks of therapists and other mental health care workers (Qualls, Segal, Norman, & Gallagher-Thompson, 2002).

The publication of the *APA Guidelines for Psychological Practice with Older Adults* (American Psychological Association, 2004) led to the development of training models in the emerging field of **professional geropsychology** (Knight, Karel, Hinrichsen, Qualls, & Duffy, 2009), the application of gerontology to the psychological treatment of older adults (see Figure 11.4). Clinicians are increasingly being trained according to these guidelines, following what is known as the **Pikes Peak Model of Geropsychology**, a set of competencies that professional geropsychologists are expected to have when working with older adults (Karel, Knight, Duffy, Hinrichsen, & Zeiss, 2010). Clinicians can now assess themselves in these competencies to determine

FIGURE 11.4

Selected Items from the APA Geropsychology Guideliness

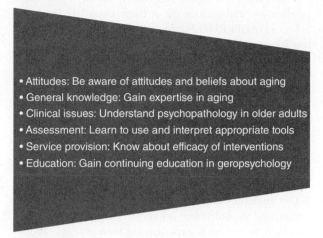

- Attitudes: Be aware of attitudes and beliefs about aging
- General knowledge: Gain expertise in aging
- Clinical issues: Understand psychopathology in older adults
- Assessment: Learn to use and interpret appropriate tools
- Service provision: Know about efficacy of interventions
- Education: Gain continuing education in geropsychology

Source: Adapted from American Psychological Association. (2004). Guidelines for psychological practice with older adults. *American Psychologist, 59*, 236–260.

in which areas they require further training (Karel et al., 2012).

The psychological disorders we have discussed in this chapter involve a variety of potential causes and, therefore, may be treatable by a variety of approaches. Clinicians who work with adult populations recognize the need to differentiate the approaches they take to young and middle-aged adults from the approaches they take to older adults (Zarit & Zarit, 2007).

In addition to potentially different etiologies for disorders at different points in adulthood, clinicians must take into account the possible effects of chronic medical conditions as well as normal age-related changes in physical, cognitive, and social functioning (Hinrichsen & Dick-Siskin, 2000). The client's ethnic and minority status must also be taken into account, particularly as these interact with age-related changes, health, and the individual's cultural values (Ferraro, 2002; Lau & Gallagher-Thompson, 2002).

Assessment

A **psychological assessment** is a procedure in which a clinician provides a formal evaluation of an individual's cognitive, personality, and psychosocial functioning. Clinicians conduct assessments under a variety of conditions. In many cases, they use the assessment process to provide a diagnosis. However, clinicians may also use assessment for a variety of other purposes, such as determining an older adult's legal competence or to assist in planning appropriate levels of care.

Clinicians should tailor each assessment they conduct to the physical and cognitive needs of their clients which, in the case of older individuals, should take into account certain accommodations. Clients should be made to feel comfortable and relaxed and given sufficient time to ask questions about the procedure, which may be unfamiliar and hence stressful. There are also practical concerns that psychologists should address, such as making sure that the people they are testing have the correct eyeglasses and hearing aids, if necessary. The clinician may also have to take into account physical limitations due to arthritis and the potential for older adults to require rest periods or breaks during lengthy testing sessions.

Throughout the assessment process, clinicians should look for changes in sensory abilities, motor functions, and cognitive processes that may hamper the older client's understanding of problems or questions given during the assessment process. The materials themselves may need to be adapted to changes in vision and hearing, although clinicians cannot change items on standardized measures. For example, the clinician should speak in a clear voice and make sure there is adequate lighting. In addition, the room should be free of distractions, such as the hum of a computer or outside noise, which may compromise an older adult's performance (Edelstein, Martin, & McKee, 2000). It is also important to be sensitive to cultural or language differences between clinician and client, regardless of the age of the client (Edelstein, Martin, & Gerolimatos, 2013).

A typical assessment incorporates multiple approaches, allowing the clinician to get a full picture of the individual's psychological functioning. Many clinicians begin their assessment with a **clinical interview**, a series of questions that they administer in face-to-face interactions with the client. The clinical interview has the advantage of being somewhat flexible as well as providing clinicians with insights they could only gain by directly observing how the client behaves.

The second component of assessment that is particularly important in working with older adults is a **mental status examination**, which assesses a client's current state of mind. In conducting a mental status examination, the clinician assesses such qualities of the client as appearance, attitudes, behavior, mood and affect, speech, thought processes, content of thought, perception, cognition, insight, and judgment. The outcome of the mental status examination is a comprehensive description of how the client looks, thinks, feels, and behaves. The mental status examination also typically includes a measure of **orientation**, which reflects whether examinees know where they are (orientation to place), what time it is (orientation to time), and who they are (orientation to person).

The **Mini-Mental State Examination (MMSE)** is a brief structured tool that clinicians use as a screening device to assess dementia (Folstein,1975). Widely used today, most clinicians supplement it with more comprehensive tests, particularly if a client receives a poor score. Figure 11.5 contains sample items from the MMSE.

The MMSE is quick and relatively easy to administer, making it useful as a screening instrument, which is how it was intended to be used. However, it cannot identify the type of neurocognitive disorder an individual has, and is not specific enough to be able to provide even a tentative diagnosis. Another problem with the MMSE is that it is sensitive to the individual's educational background and ethnicity (Espino, Lichtenstein, Palmer, & Hazuda, 2004; Mast, Fitzgerald, Steinberg, MacNeill, & Lichtenberg, 2001). Given these and other limitations of the MMSE, geropsychologists are increasingly turning to the types of neuropsychological measures we discussed in Chapter 7.

Researchers and clinicians alike also make use of measures targeted toward specific symptoms in older adults. Several of these focus on depression, which, as we discussed in Chapter 5, may coexist, mask, or be the result of a neurocognitive disorder. The **Geriatric Depression Scale (GDS)** is a screening tool that asks individuals to answer a true–false set of questions about their symptoms, and is well established for use with older adult populations (Nyunt, Fones, Niti, & Ng, 2009). The **Center for Epidemiological Studies Scale for Depression (CES-D)** is a 20-item questionnaire that screens for depressive symptoms (Radloff, 1977). Other assessments for mood and anxiety symptoms are completed not by the individual, but by a researcher or clinician, and include the Anxiety Disorders Interview Schedule (ADIS-R) (DiNardo & Barlow, 1988), the Hamilton Rating Scale of Depression (Hamilton, 1967) and the Hamilton Anxiety Rating Scale (Hamilton, 1959).

A key area of differential diagnosis is distinguishing between dementia and other psychological disorders, particularly depression. As we saw in Chapter 5, depression can cause pseudodementia and can lead the clinician to inaccurately diagnose a neurocognitive disorder when the client's symptoms represent a disturbance of mood. However, there are important differences in the symptom pattern of individuals with these disorders (Small, 2009). In depression, the symptoms of dysphoria are more severe, and the individual is likely to exaggerate the extent to which he or she is experiencing memory loss. People who have dementia tend, in contrast, to be overconfident about their cognitive abilities. They may show very wide variations in performance from one test to another; however, older adults with dementia show a progressive loss of cognitive abilities that tends to affect them across the board. The timing of symptoms is another diagnostic key, because older adults with depression experience cognitive symptoms prior to depressive symptoms. If the

---

Time orientation

Ask:

What is the year _____ (1), season _____ (1),

month of the year _____ (1), date _____ (1),

day of the week _____ (1)?

Drawing

Say: Please copy this design.

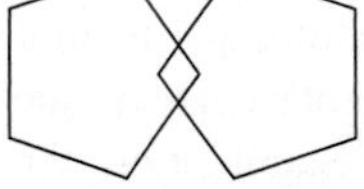

Registration of three words

Say: Listen carefully. I am going to say three words. You say them back after I stop. Ready? Here they are. Pony (wait 1 second), Quarter (wait 1 second), Orange (wait 1 second). What were those words?

_____ (1)

_____ (1)

_____ (1)

Give 1 point for each correct answer, then repeat them until the patient learns all three.

FIGURE 11.5

Sample Items From the Mini-Mental State Exam (MMSE)

Source: Folstein, M. F., Folstein, S. E., & McHugh, P. R. (1975). © 1975, 1998 MiniMentalLLC. "MINI-MENTAL STATE." A PRACTICAL METHOD FOR GRADING THE COGNITIVE STATE OF PATIENTS FOR THE CLINICIAN. *Journal of Psychiatric Research*, 12(3): 189–198, 1975.

cognitive symptoms persist after the depression has been treated, then the dementia is more likely the cause (Wilkins, Mathews, & Sheline, 2009).

Differences between depression and dementia are important for clinicians to note in their assessment of older adults. As we pointed out in Chapter 5, if the depression is caught in time, there is a good chance of successful treatment, whereas if the individual's symptoms are due to a neurocognitive disorder, the clinician will take another approach to intervention.

In addition to these psychological assessment tools, clinicians evaluating older adults also measure their ability to perform activities of daily living (ADLs) and instrumental ADLs (IADLs). These provide important information that can be used in treatment planning, especially if it appears that the client might be best served in an institutional setting. Moreover, clinicians also track changes in the ADLs and IADLs over time to determine whether changes are needed in the client's placement status, perhaps corresponding to changes in cognitive functioning.

Clinicians typically complete their assessment of a client before they go on to adopt a treatment strategy, although they continue to assess their clients throughout the course of therapy. Ongoing evaluations allow clinicians to use information gathered from treatment to help refine their initial diagnoses and to monitor the progress of their clients as they proceed through treatment.

Treatment

Following the assessment phase, clinicians embark on a program of treatment intended to provide the client with relief from his or her symptoms. The best mental health treatment follows a biopsychosocial model in which clinicians take into account the complex interactions among the client's physical symptoms and health, cognitive abilities, emotional strengths, personality, sense of identity, and social support network.

As is true for medical care, clinicians in the field of mental health also strive to work with professionals in other disciplines, allowing the older client to benefit from an integrated approach that brings together nursing, physical therapy, occupational therapy, psychotherapy, medical care, and input from family. Models other than the traditional provision of psychotherapy are clearly becoming seen as viable alternatives for work with older adults. Care managers can be used to coordinate services to individual clients, offering services through primary care physicians to ensure that the clients maintain their involvement in treatment. One study investigating this type of comprehensive model showed significant reductions in suicidal thinking and depressive symptoms in a sample of over

9,000 individuals 60 and older maintained over a 2-year period (Alexopoulos et al., 2009).

Medical interventions.   Clinicians tend to approach therapy with clients of any age from the standpoint of their own theoretical perspective, training, and experience. Many in the mental health field operate from the **medical model**, a perspective that focuses primarily on the physiological causes of a psychological disorder. In the medical model, the primary line of defense against psychological disorders involves using **psychotherapeutic medications**, which attempt to reduce an individual's psychological symptoms. These medications cannot cure the disorder, but they can alleviate the client's distress from its most prominent symptoms.

In many cases, clinicians test out the effectiveness of one medication; if it fails to produce relief, they will test others until they find one that helps the client's symptoms subside. For older adults, this process may be a challenge because many psychotherapeutic medications interact with other medications that these clients take for their chronic diseases. Moreover, because older adults typically see multiple health professionals, they are great risk for these unintended consequences. A physician might prescribe a sleeping medication to an older adult patient who is already taking an antianxiety or cardiac medication, potentially causing the older adult to become suicidal due to the interaction of the medications. Consequently, clinicians who work with older adults must take detailed and careful histories. The need to avoid dangerous interactions among medications is another reason that integrative health care is so important for older adults.

In addition to taking precautions against drug interactions, clinicians must be familiar with the medication's side effects for older adults, which may differ from those seen with younger adults. Unless the clinician prescribes them in lower doses, older adults are at risk of accumulating toxic levels in the blood because aging increases the time that medications take to clear the excretory system of the kidneys.

For older clients with major depressive disorder, medications known as antidepressants are highly effective, particularly what are called selective serotonin reuptake inhibitors (SSRIs). These drugs help restore normal levels of serotonin (a neurotransmitter involved in mood) (Klysner et al., 2002; Mottram, Wilson, Ashworth, & Abou-Saleh, 2002). In cases of severe depression, individuals may undergo **electroconvulsive therapy** (ECT), a method of treatment in which an electric current is applied through electrodes attached across the head. ECT can be effective for older adults, but it is only used when they have not responded to other forms of treatment (O'Connor et al., 2010). One risk of ECT is short-term memory loss, which also makes ECT a less than desirable treatment for older adults.

SSRIs may also be used to treat people with anxiety disorders. However, their effectiveness vs. placebo in older adults with anxiety disorders is not well established (Lenze et al., 2009). There are a number of other antianxiety medications available for use with older adults, including the effective, but potentially addictive, category known as benzodiazepines. These medications require higher and higher doses to obtain their intended outcome, and when discontinued, they are likely to lead to significant withdrawal symptoms. Older adults are particularly vulnerable to these effects and, furthermore, may experience a number of additional potentially dangerous side effects, such as unsteadiness, daytime sleepiness, impaired cognitive functioning, and slowed reaction time resulting in increased risk of falling (Woolcott et al., 2009). The medication buspirone has fewer of these side effects but is not as effective in treating generalized anxiety disorder and cannot be prescribed for individuals who also have symptoms of depression (Flint, 2005).

Other medications useful in treating anxiety in older adults are beta blockers, which reduce anxiety by lowering sympathetic nervous system activity. However, older adults with cardiovascular disease cannot use this medication, making it a less desirable treatment approach.

Medications for the treatment of schizophrenia include the antipsychotic medications known as **neuroleptics**. These medications alter dopamine activity and are effective in reducing delusions and other forms of thought disorder as well as lowering the chance of an individual's experiencing a relapse. People with early-onset schizophrenia are often maintained on these medications for many years, allowing them to live independently in the community. Older adults who develop late-life schizophrenia also seem to respond to neuroleptics. However, there are potent side effects, including confusion and agitation, dizziness, and motor disturbances. Some of these motor disturbances can resemble those of Parkinson's disease.

The most serious side effect of neuroleptic medication is tardive dyskinesia, which involves involuntary, repetitive movements, particularly in the muscles of the face. These movements include chewing, moving the jaw from side to side, and rolling the tongue. Older adults are more likely than younger adults to experience tardive dyskinesia, even after they stop taking these medications. In fact, these medications are the second most common cause of Parkinsonian symptoms in older adults (Thanvi & Treadwell, 2009). Medications that alter serotonin functioning used for treatment of schizophrenia (clozapine and resperidone) do not produce these effects on motor functioning. However,

clozapine can have fatal side effects and must be carefully monitored, particularly in older adults (Kelly et al., 2010).

Psychotherapy. Because older adults typically see a medical professional before they consult a mental health professional, they may never be able to receive the benefits of psychosocial interventions. Current cohorts of middle-aged individuals are more comfortable with seeking psychotherapy for psychological symptoms than older adults, who may be skeptical about the therapy process, having been less socialized than younger cohorts to accept the need for psychological interventions. Part of therapy may involve educating older adult clients to feel less embarrassed or stigmatized by the process. This seems particularly important in the case of older African Americans, who are less likely than older adult Whites to use psychotherapy when it is offered (Joo, Morales, de Vries, & Gallo, 2010). Regardless of age, race, or ethnicity, men attribute a greater stigma to psychotherapy than do women (Pepin, Segal, & Coolidge, 2009).

Just as older adults may have negative attitudes toward therapy, older therapists may harbor negative views about aging that inadvertently affect the way they approach their older clients. For this reason, gerontologists feel it is important to help educate current mental health professionals about the need to be sensitive to potentially ageist attitudes.

Once they are in therapy, however, older adults can benefit from the wide range of treatment models shown to be effective for reducing symptoms of the major disorders experienced by older adults. In a review of five randomized clinical trials involving psychotherapy for people over 50 with subclinical depression, Lee et al. (2012) concluded that psychotherapy is effective, safe, and cost-effective.

Figure 11.6 illustrates the major forms of psychotherapy showing, in addition, how they may be integrated in working with older adults. Although clinicians tend to operate primarily within a perspective they favor, integrative approaches are increasingly being used that match the client's disorder with the treatment shown to be most effective. The principles of **Evidence-Based Practice in Psychology** propose that clinicians should integrate the best available research evidence and clinical expertise in the context of the cultural background, preferences, and characteristics of clients (American Psychological Association Presidential Task Force on Evidence-Based Practice, 2006). In work with older adults, then, clinicians must incorporate knowledge of age-related physical, psychological, and social changes into their work.

Across theoretical models, clinicians recognize the importance of the therapeutic alliance that they establish with their clients. This means that they work to establish a collaborative relationship in which the client feels invested

FIGURE 11.6

Models of Psychotherapy With Older Adults

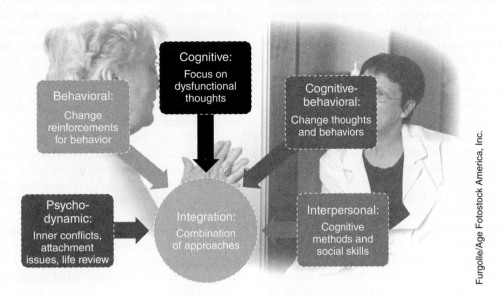

in the process. The therapeutic alliance can help clinicians in their work with older adults, establishing an atmosphere of trust in which clients feel that they will be understood (Hyer, Yeager, Hyer, & Scott, 2010).

Traditional **psychodynamic therapy** focuses on the client's underlying conflicts, but these traditional models are changing, and therapists working from this framework may emphasize other issues such as the client's attachment style (Van Assche et al., 2013). Within the psychodynamic framework, clinicians are also incorporating the method known as **life review therapy**, which involves helping the older adult rework past experiences, both pleasant and unpleasant, with the goal of gaining greater acceptance of the past (Butler, 1974). Particularly useful in life review therapy is having the opportunity to reframe past events that were once viewed negatively in a positive light, allowing the individual to gain a sense of mastery over his or her life (Korte, Westerhof, & Bohlmeijer, 2012).

At the opposite end of the theoretical spectrum, clinicians working from the perspective of **behavioral therapy** intervene by changing the reinforcements associated with the individual's behavior. In the case of depression, where behavioral therapy has been successfully applied to older adults (Teri, 1994), this approach is based on the notion that the client's symptoms are due to decreases in pleasant events in their lives associated with physical changes, loss of friends, and loss of rewarding social roles. Treatment involves having the client identify events that are positively

reinforcing and then completing "homework" in which the client engages in more of these events.

Treatment with **cognitive therapy** is based on the theory that clients develop psychological disorders because they have maladaptive thought processes. As we saw in Chapter 8, cognitive theories of personality and aging emphasize the thoughts that people have about themselves and their life situations. As a theory of psychopathology, the cognitive approach maintains that people's emotions follow from their thoughts. Depressive symptoms such as sadness, according to this view, occur because individuals believe that they have lost something of importance to them. Cognitive therapists help their clients reframe their thoughts about their experiences which then should help them develop more adaptive emotions.

The combination of behavioral and cognitive approaches forms the basis for **cognitive-behavioral therapy**, an approach in which the clinician encourages clients to develop more adaptive behaviors and ways of thinking about their experiences. This approach appears to have considerable relevance to work with older depressed clients, particularly for those who have a tendency to focus excessively on what they believe they are losing in the way of age-related changes in physical functioning, memory, and health.

In treating clients with depression, for example, cognitive-behavioral therapists use several elements of behavioral therapy, including instructing clients to keep track of their pleasant and unpleasant events and helping them understand the relationship between their mood and these behaviors. The cognitive piece involves teaching their clients to be alert to and try to change their negative thoughts about the self (Satre, Knight, & David, 2006).

Cognitive-behavioral therapy works well with older adults who have a depressive disorder (Samad, Brealey, & Gilbody, 2011). Even as few as seven sessions can produce positive results (Serfaty et al., 2009). Furthermore, cognitive behavioral therapy can be successfully used in treating suicidal older adults (Bhar & Brown, 2012). For older adults with schizophrenia, cognitive-behavioral therapy serves as a useful adjunct to medications, helping clients learn how to monitor and control their behavior in social situations (Patterson et al., 2003).

Increasingly, cognitive-behavioral therapy is being seen as an effective alternative to antianxiety medications in treating anxiety disorders in older adults (Mohlman & Price, 2006), although not for certain subgroups such as older individuals high in neuroticism and self-perceived health problems (Schuurmans et al., 2009). It can also be targeted to specific issues that impair quality of life in older adults, such as activity restrictions due to fear of falling (Zijlstra et al., 2009b). Cognitive-behavioral therapy can also be useful in reducing symptoms of insomnia and pain from osteoarthritis (Vitiello, Rybarczyk, Von Korff, & Stepanski, 2009). Relaxation training, a component of cognitive-behavioral therapy, can also be an effective intervention for older adults with generalized anxiety disorder (Ayers, Sorrell, Thorp, & Wetherell, 2007).

Aiming at social relationships more specifically is **interpersonal therapy (IPT)**, which helps clients learn to understand and change their relationships with others. Clinicians using interpersonal therapy train their clients in social skills, interpersonal relationships, and methods of conflict resolution. IPT has been shown to be an effective treatment method for older adults, particularly those coping with bereavement issues (Miller & Reynolds, 2012) and for those at risk for suicide (Heisel, Duberstein, Talbot, King, & Tu, 2009).

One advantage of cognitive-behavioral therapy for treating older adults is that it can be adapted to a variety of settings, including physician's offices and even the telephone (Arean & Ayalon, 2005). Telepsychology, in which treatment is provided over the Internet, is also becoming increasingly accepted in the field of psychology, and is particularly beneficial for older adults (Brenes, Ingram, & Danhauer, 2012). Not only can this benefit clients who have mobility issues that make it difficult for them to travel to a clinician's office, but telepsychology can also be used in rural areas or parts of the country in which there are few clinicians trained in geropsychology.

There are, then, encouraging results from studies investigating psychotherapy effectiveness in later life. However, psychotherapy with older individuals presents a number of challenges. These involve factors that alter both the nature of psychological difficulties experienced by older adults and the nature of the therapeutic process (Hinrichsen & Dick-Siskin, 2000). Older adults, particularly those over the age of 75, have a greater probability of physical health impairments that can compromise the effectiveness of therapy because these conditions represent a significant threat to quality of life (Licht-Strunk, van der Windt, van Marwijk, de Haan, & Beekman, 2007). Changes in identity associated with these impairments can themselves stimulate the need for psychotherapy. However, by boosting the older adult's sense of mastery, the older adult can overcome even physical limitations and experience an improvement in mood (Steunenberg, Beekman, Deeg, Bremmer, & Kerkhof, 2007). Reducing symptoms of depression through psychotherapy can in turn lead to improvements in perceptions of disability (Karp et al., 2009) and health-related perceived quality of life (Chan et al., 2009).

Based on the belief that mental health is linked to physical health (Galper, Trivedi, Barlow, Dunn, & Kampert, 2006), researchers are exploring the use of exercise as a therapeutic tool in the treatment of psychological disorders in later adulthood to supplant or replace medications (Blake, Mo, Malik, & Thomas, 2009). Older adults with depressive symptoms who do not meet the criteria for major depressive disorder seem particularly amenable to exercise as a form of intervention, including video game forms of exercise (Rosenberg et al., 2010). Meditation is another alternative approach that builds on the known association between pain and depressive symptoms in older adults. In one innovative investigation, both mindfulness meditation and education served to reduce pain and improve psychological functioning that was maintained for at least 4 months after treatment (Morone, Rollman, Moore, Li, & Weiner, 2009).

Psychosocial issues involving relationships with family may also confront an older adult and should be taken into account by clinicians providing psychotherapy (Knight & Kellough, 2013). These issues include death of family and friends, changes in relationships with children and spouses, and the need to provide care to a spouse or parent. Finally, the social context can play an important role in influencing the outcome of treatment. Just as there are relationships between mental health and SES, there is a link between the effectiveness of antidepressant treatment and social class. In one study, older adults from lower social classes were found to be less likely to respond over the course of a 20-week period to a combination of psychotherapy and

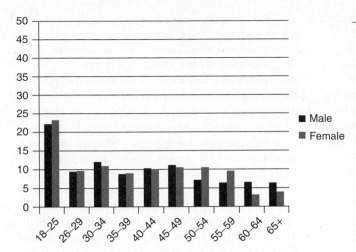

Source: Substance Abuse and Mental Health Services Administration (2012). Results from the 2010 National Survey on Drug Use and Health: Mental health detailed tables. Rockville, MD: Substance Abuse and Mental Health Services Administration. http://www.samhsa.gov/data/NSDUH/2k10MH_Findings/2k10MH_DTables/TOC.htm

FIGURE 11.7

Percentage of Adults by Age Group With Serious Mental Illness 2010

medication than individuals in middle- and high-income brackets (Cohen et al., 2006).

Family issues may, however, be alleviated through the provision of therapy for older adults experiencing symptoms of depression. Researchers investigating the impact of interventions, including both medication and interpersonal therapy, observed favorable effects on perceived burden among caregivers of the patients whose symptoms responded to treatment (Martire et al., 2010).

Although therapy can have many beneficial effects, equally important as treatment is prevention. Targeting specific older adults at risk, such as those who have become bereaved and have experienced illness or disability, can help to reduce not only the need for treatment but also to maximize the psychological functioning of older adults who might otherwise develop disorders such as depression (Schoevers et al., 2006).

SERIOUS MENTAL ILLNESS

Though we have focused in this chapter on psychological disorders in older adults, it is important to remember that despite the presence of chronic physical health conditions, the majority of older adults do not experience significant distress. This fact is borne out by the Substance Abuse and Mental Health Services Administration (SAMHSA), which tracks the incidence of serious mental illness. Survey after survey in this series consistently reports lower rates of serious mental illness within the past year for adults 65 and older (see Figure 11.7). These results are not limited to the United States. A large-scale investigation of nearly 7,500 adults in Australia ages 20 to 64 showed lower rates of anxiety and psychological distress among the older age groups (Jorm et al., 2005).

Clearly, although older adults are at higher risk in an objective sense for experiencing psychological disorders, a combination of selective survival, enhanced use of coping mechanisms, and an ability to maintain an optimistic attitude toward adversity seem to offer significant protective factors against psychological problems in later adulthood. Increasingly, new methods of treatment are becoming available to provide services to those older adults who need assistance in these adaptive processes.

In summary, when we think of the aging process, we are likely to anticipate a number of negative changes that would have adverse mental health effects. By contrast, the facts reveal that older adults are highly resilient to the physical, psychological, and social changes involved in the aging process. It is nevertheless true that there will be an increasing need for mental health workers in the coming decades trained in diagnosis, assessment and treatment, and there will also be an increased need for research on effective treatment methods for aging individuals in need of intervention.

SUMMARY

1. Psychological disorders are those behaviors that significantly alter the individual's adaptation. The DSM-5 contains descriptions of the disorders that can affect children and adults and is used by clinicians to assign diagnoses based on specific criteria.

2. The main symptom of major depressive disorder is an extremely sad mood that lasts most of the time for at least 2 weeks and that is not typical of the individual's usual mood. Although the prevalence of a diagnosable mood disorder is lower in older than in younger adults, many older adults report symptoms of depressive disorders. Health care professionals may not be attuned to

diagnosing depressive symptoms in older adults. Medical conditions increase the risk for depression, including hip fracture, stroke, hypertension, and diabetes. A diagnosis of bipolar disorder occurs in individuals who have experienced one or more manic episodes during which they feel elated, grandiose, expansive, and highly energetic. Rates of bipolar disorder are lower among older adults compared with younger adults. Individuals diagnosed with anxiety disorders experience a sense of dread about what might happen in the future and will avoid anxiety-provoking situations. Anxiety disorders are more common in younger rather than older adults as well as among women. Types of anxiety disorders include generalized anxiety disorder, panic disorder, agoraphobia, specific phobias, and social anxiety disorder. People who experience obsessive-compulsive disorder suffer from unrelenting, irrational, and distracting obsessions and compulsions. Although the lifetime prevalence among older adults is extremely low, rates of detection may also result in lack of treatment.

3. Exposure to traumas can lead individuals to experience a variety of symptoms that may last for a prolonged period of time and can include acute stress and post-traumatic stress disorder. It is thought that PTSD prevalence in the over-65 population will increase as Vietnam veterans become older. Individuals diagnosed with schizophrenia experience distorted perception of reality and impairment in thinking, behavior, affect, and motivation. The decrease in schizophrenia seen with age is likely an artifact of survival into older adulthood. Substance-related disorders are more likely to occur in younger adults. However, alcohol abuse and dependence are becoming an area of concern for the over-65 population, as are disorders related to the use of prescription medications. Personality disorders are characterized by a long-standing pattern of inner experience and behavior that has maladaptive qualities. According to the maturation hypothesis, adults with personality disorders in the immature category experience fewer symptoms in later life.

4. Two additional topics of concern in the area of mental health and aging are elder abuse and suicide. According to survey research, the incidence of elder abuse may be as high as 14% of older adults; unfortunately, the large majority of cases normally escape detection. Age-adjusted rates of suicide indicate that males aged 75 and older account for the highest number of suicides per year. Risk factors for suicide among older adults include the presence of a psychiatric illness, physical illness, and limitations in functioning, chronic pain, and cognitive functioning deficits.

5. The field of clinical geropsychology involves the provision of psychological services to older adults. Treatment begins with a thorough assessment. A number of tools are available that can be applied specifically to persons in later life. These tools range from clinical interviews to structured self-report inventories. Assessment of people within this age group requires that the clinician adapt the test materials and the testing situation to the specific needs and cognitive or sensory limitations of the older adult. Therapy methods range from somatic treatments, such as ECT and medications, to psychotherapy. Cognitive and interpersonal therapy methods appear to hold considerable promise for treatment of older adults.

6. Despite the many threats to positive mental health, the majority of older adults do not report elevated levels of serious mental illness.

12

Long-Term Care

AGING TODAY

Family Caregiving Across the Generations

With nearly one-third of the U.S. adult population providing medical care for a relative, the chances are good that you or someone you know is a family caregiver. Having to decide which relatives will provide which caregiving roles can place stress on extended families, particularly when family members are spread far and wide geographically and across multiple generations.

Fortunately, there are several excellent online resources, including the American Psychological Association's (APA) "Caregiver Briefcase." This publication addresses the challenges that caregivers encounter that can affect their own mental and physical health. The APA report points out that most caregivers are female, which is probably not a surprise. What many people don't know is that nationwide, 1.3 to 1.4 million caregivers are children and teens between the ages of 8 and 18. Many of these children care for a parent with a disability.

Family caregivers are the lynchpin of the health care system. Without family caregivers, the medical costs of patients would rise even higher than they are now. The APA report cites the extensive evidence showing that family caregiving reduces hospital stays, Medicare inpatient expenditures, and the costs of home health and nursing home care.

Many experts recommend that caregivers join a support group. Caregivers may think that they can't afford the time to participate in one of these groups. However, joining such a group is probably the most consistent advice about alleviating caregiver burden provided to individuals. Other people in a similar situation are perhaps the best able to provide support, not to mention practical advice. Respite care may also be located while participating in a caregiver support group.

All caregivers need to maintain their own emotional health in order to continue in their demanding role. Psychologists know that coping "self-statements" can help lower stress in any situation. The NIA guide suggests certain phrases that caregivers can repeat to themselves when they're feeling particularly stressed, such as "I'm doing the best I can," "I can't control some things that just happen," and "Sometimes I just need to do what works for right now." The NIA guide also emphasizes the importance of getting support from other caregivers, even if it's in online form rather than in a face-to-face context.

Moving beyond caregivers of people with Alzheimer's disease, though, the APA Caregiving Briefcase addresses many types of caregiving situations. People are able to determine where they fit into the spectrum of caregivers and check out resources specific to themselves and loved ones. Whether or not you need these caregiving resources at the moment, it's important to know where to go to look for information if and when this happens to you. Or, you may pass this information along to relatives who are caregivers now. These guides will help you and those in need of support.

Posted by Susan Whitbourne and Stacey Whitbourne

Have you ever lived in an institution? Your first response may be to answer "no," unless you have been hospitalized for a physical or psychological disorder. However, think about the question in a slightly different way. Dormitory residents live under one roof, are not related to each other, and are there because they share a similar position in life. In a dormitory, as in a hospital setting, residents must deal with problems that come with communal living, such being unable to control many aspects of the environment, needing to answer to people in charge, being served food prepared for a large number of people, and being assigned to live with a stranger. Now imagine what it would be like adapting to these problems if you were infirm and limited in your freedom to come and go as you please.

For the purposes of this chapter, an **institutional facility** is a group residential setting that provides individuals with medical or psychiatric care. Hospitals are short-term institutional facilities to which people are admitted with the understanding that they will be discharged when they no longer need round-the-clock treatment. At the other end of the spectrum are long-term institutional facilities into which an individual moves permanently after losing the ability to live independently.

Closely related to the issue of institutional care is that of the funding for health care, another topic we cover in this chapter. Individuals hospitalized for physical and psychological problems in later life are increasingly confronting the rising cost of health care as a barrier to the effective resolution of their difficulties. In addition to the problems that result from the failure to receive proper treatment, this situation creates considerable stress and anguish for the older individual.

Although you may not spend much time thinking about the health care coverage available to you in your later years, you are surely aware of the hotly debated discussions about the state of health care in the coming decades. From offering public options for health insurance to making prescription medications more affordable for older adults, health care is one of the most crucial issues facing the United States as well as many other countries. Following along the lines of our coverage of Social Security, we will examine the impact that recent policy changes to the structure and funding of health care may have on older adults.

INSTITUTIONAL FACILITIES FOR LONG-TERM CARE

People with chronic disabilities, cognitive disorders, or physical infirmities that keep them from living independently may receive treatment in one of a variety of institutional long-term care settings. These institutions range

FIGURE 12.1

Types of Institutional Facilities for Older Adults

Directphoto.org/Alamy

from hospital-like facilities to living situations that are more like independent residences, providing minimal food and services (see Figure 12.1).

Nursing Homes

For individuals whose illness or disability requires daily nursing care as well as other support services, nursing homes provide comprehensive care in a single setting. A **nursing home** is a type of medical institution that provides a room, meals, skilled nursing and rehabilitative care, medical services, and protective supervision. The care provided in nursing homes includes treatment for problems that residents have in many basic areas of life, including cognition, communication, hearing, vision, physical functioning, continence, psychosocial functioning, mood and behavior, nutrition, and dental care. To manage these problems, residents typically need to take medications on a regular basis. Residents of nursing homes may also receive training in basic care as well as assistance with feeding and mobility, rehabilitative activities, and social services.

Typically, nursing homes are thought of as permanent residences for the older adults who enter them. However, about 30% of those who enter a nursing home are discharged and able to move back into the community (Sahyoun, Pratt, Lentzner, Dey, & Robinson, 2001). Many nursing homes are actually called rehabilitation centers, and specifically focus on short-term stay residents who need care immediately following hospitalization, after which they can return to their homes with supportive services until they are restored to their previous level of functioning. We will talk more about these services later in the chapter.

Nursing homes are certified by state and federal government agencies to provide services at one or more levels of care. A **skilled nursing facility** is a type of nursing home that provides the most intensive nursing care available outside of a hospital. Nurses and other health care workers in this type of facility can apply dressings or bandages, help residents with daily self-care tasks, and provide oxygen therapy. They are responsible for taking vital signs of their patients, including their temperature, pulse, respiration, and blood pressure.

In an **intermediate care facility**, individuals who do not require hospital or skilled nursing facility care but do require some type of institutional care receive health-related services. These facilities provide health and rehabilitative services as well as food, but do not have intense nursing care services available.

Nursing home services have become a big business in the United States. In the year 2011, nursing home expenditures were estimated to be $149.3 billion, or about 6% of the total U.S. health care expenditures (Center for Medicare and Medicaid Services, 2013d). The cost of nursing home care is rising faster than the cost of other medical care goods and services, with the yearly average private-pay facility costing slightly over the equivalent of $60,000 U.S. based on 2004 rates. (Stewart, Grabowski, & Lakdawalla, 2009).

As of 2010, slightly fewer than two-thirds (63%) of residents have their nursing home expenses paid for by Medicaid, slightly over one-fifth (22%) pay for nursing homes themselves through their own funds or other forms of insurance, and the remainder (14%) have their nursing home expenses paid for by Medicare (Harrington, Carrillo, Dowdell, Tang, & Blank, 2011). Although quality control is intended to provide comparable care to all residents, those who pay for their own nursing home care are afforded a greater range of facilities, better accommodations, and higher staff-to-patient ratios compared to those who are funded through Medicaid (Donoghue, 2006).

As of 2011, there were approximately 15,700 nursing homes in the Unites States with a total of over 1.7 million beds (National Center for Health Statistics, 2011). The large majority of nursing homes (80%) have between 50

and 199 beds (Center for Medicare and Medicaid Services, 2010b). The average size of a certified facility in 2010 was 108; about half are owned by national chains (Harrington et al., 2011).

Two-thirds of nursing homes in the United States fall into the category of "for-profit" facilities, meaning that they seek to have their revenue exceed their expenses. Nonprofit facilities, which include primarily those run by religious organizations, constitute the second largest group (27%), and government-owned facilities, primarily those run by the Veterans Administration, compose the remainder (6%). Therefore, most nursing homes are run like a business with the goal of making a profit (Center for Medicare and Medicaid Services, 2010b).

Perhaps because they are less oriented toward the "bottom line," not-for-profit nursing homes have higher quality ratings than their for-profit counterparts (Comondore et al., 2009). Related to this issue is the payment mode of residents. When nursing homes have more private-pay patients, they are able to provide better care because the rates for these patients are higher than the reimbursement rates that facilities receive from governmental subsidies.

The numbers of residents have remained steady at about 1.3 to 1.4 million since 1995 despite increases in the older adult population. Thus, the percentage of older adults in nursing homes declined in the 20 years between 1985 and 2004 (see Figure 12.2), reflecting increases in home health services and generally better health of the over-65 population. Almost twice as many women (65.4%) as men (34.6%) live in nursing homes (Center for Medicare and Medicaid Services, 2010b).

Among the 65 and older population, about 7% have at least one nursing home stay within the calendar year. This rises to 21.5% for the 85 and older population. Nearly two-thirds of nursing home residents have some cognitive impairment, though only about 10% are severely impaired. However, about half require assistance in activities of daily

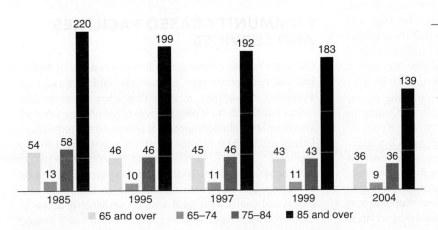

Source: http://www.cdc.gov/nchs/data/nnhsd/ Estimates/nnhs/Estimates_Demographics_Tables. pdf#Table02.

FIGURE 12.2

Rate of Nursing Home Residence Among People 65 and Older (per 1,000 Population)

living (Center for Medicare and Medicaid Services, 2010b), and half are bedfast or chairbound (Harrington et al., 2011).

Mood and anxiety disorders are present in nearly one-quarter of all older adults living in these settings. Over half (65%) of all residents receive psychotropic medications, including antidepressants, antianxiety drugs, sedatives and hypnotics, and antipsychotics (Harrington et al., 2011). Though having more functional limitations than older adults living in their own homes, nursing home residents have more depressive symptoms and lower self-rated quality of life (Karakaya, Bilgin, Ekici, Kose, & Otman, 2009).

Residential Care Facilities

An alternative to a nursing home is a **residential care facility**, which provides 24-hour supportive care services and supervision to individuals who do not require skilled nursing or health-related care. They provide meals, housekeeping, and assistance with personal care such as bathing and grooming. Some residential care facilities may provide other services, such as management of medications and social and recreational activities.

As of 2010, there were approximately 733,000 people living in residential care facilities in the U.S. Their median length of stay was just under 2 years. The majority were non-Hispanic white, female, and ages 85 and older. More than half (57%) had a diagnosis of high blood pressure, and a large percentage (42%) had a diagnosis of Alzheimer's disease. However, most residents had more than one chronic condition, with about one-quarter having 4 to 10 diagnoses, and half having 2 to 3. A large percentage (40%) had difficulty completing three or more activities of living. This population, then, has a high burden of functional and cognitive impairment (Caffrey et al., 2012).

A board and care home is a group living arrangement designed to meet the needs of people who cannot live on their own in the community and who also need some nursing services. Typically, these homes provide help with activities of daily living such as bathing, dressing, and toileting. Although the name may imply that these homes provide a "homelike" setting, research refutes this idea. A survey conducted by the Institute of Medicine determined that board and care homes are typically understaffed by workers who are not required to receive training (Wunderlich, Kohler, & Committee on Improving Quality in Long-Term Care, 2001).

Housing complexes in which older persons live independently in their own apartments are known as **assisted living facilities**. The residents of these facilities pay a regular monthly rent that usually includes meal service in communal dining rooms, transportation for shopping and appointments, social activities, and housekeeping services.

These facilities are professionally managed and licensed and may represent one of several levels of care provided within the same housing community, including health care services, in some cases. The cost for living in an assisted living facility may range from hundreds to thousands of dollars a month. In some states, funds may be available through government support programs for those who cannot afford to live in these facilities on their own. However, most residents pay the rental and other fees out of their own funds.

The philosophy of assisted living is to allow residents to live in private apartments but to receive high levels of service so that they can continue living in the same facility even if they experience changes in their physical or cognitive functioning. However, many facilities do not achieve the goal of providing high levels of service, particularly those facilities that are on the lower end of the cost spectrum (Wunderlich et al., 2001).

Older adults may also choose to live in group homes, where they can share a house and split the cost of rent, housekeeping services, utilities, and meals, sometimes under the supervision of a manager who assists them in some home maintenance tasks. Another arrangement involves adult foster care, in which a family provides care in their home for one or more older adults. The foster family may provide the older adult with meals and housekeeping and help with dressing, eating, bathing, and other personal care. These settings offer some advantages because of their homelike feeling, but because they are small and rely on a live-in caregiver for help with personal care, cooking, housekeeping, and activities, that caregiver's resources may be spread thin. If one resident becomes ill and requires more nursing care, other residents may suffer from lack of attention. Another problem in adult foster care is lack of privacy compared to a residential care setting (Wunderlich et al., 2001).

COMMUNITY-BASED FACILITIES AND SERVICES

Older adults who choose not to live in a residential facility but still need some type of care can take advantage of a number of support services that allow them to live independently in their own homes. Some of these services are offered by volunteer groups at no cost to the individual. Others are fee-based, some of which may be paid for by Medicare.

The residential environment of the older adult can be conceptualized along four dimensions, including the aesthetics and safety of the local area, convenience of access to shops and services, positive regard and mutual help among neighbors, and the attractiveness and ease of accommodation within the home. Each of these represents qualities of the physical environment, rather than the perceived environment. Research evaluating their contribution to the older adult's adaptation to the community suggests that the reality of the environment plays a crucial role in influencing well-being and satisfaction (Rioux & Werner, 2011).

The concept of **aging in place** refers to the principle that with appropriate services, older adults can remain in their own homes, or at least in their own communities (Pynoos & Nishita, 2007). Taking advantage of the same multidisciplinary focus so important for institutional care, older adults can benefit from interventions that allow them to maintain their autonomy and previous patterns of living (Szanton et al., 2011).

Home Health Services

Bringing services into the home is the focus of **home health services**, which provide assistance to older adults within their own private residences. Some of these services are free, or offered at a minimum price. These include "Meals on Wheels," the provision of a hot meal once a day; so-called "friendly visiting," in which a volunteer comes to the home for a social visit; and assistance with shopping. Other home-based services provide assistance with light housekeeping, such as laundry, cooking, and cleaning.

Home health care services may also include the types of restorative services that nursing homes provide, such as physical therapy, speech therapy, occupational therapy, rehabilitation, and interventions targeted at particular areas of functional decline. The home health care worker comes right into the individual's home, bringing along equipment as necessary. The advantage to home health care over institutional care is that the older adult can remain at home, staving off institutionalization or emergency room care (Tinetti et al., 2002). Moreover, home health care workers can teach older adults in their care how to maximize their mobility through such measures as fall prevention, muscle strength training, and home safety (Gitlin et al., 2009). However, home health care workers cannot provide skilled nursing to their clients nor can they perform heavy maintenance or assistance in areas outside of health services, such as paying bills.

The most recent figures on home health care services come from the 2004 National Nursing Home and Hospice Care Survey, which reported that nearly 1 million persons 65 years of age and over are home health care patients (Centers for Disease Control and Prevention, 2004). In the year 2011, $74.3 billion was spent in the United States on home health care; 80% of these costs were publicly funded (Center for Medicare and Medicaid Services, 2013c).

Nursing and assisted living are often provided within the same institution as in this Masonic facility in Minnesota.

Day Treatment Services

Older adults who do not need to be in an institution on a 24-hour basis can receive support services during the day from community services specifically aimed at their needs. A **geriatric partial hospital** provides older adults living in the community who need psychiatric care with a range of mental health services. In **adult day care**, older adults who need assistance or supervision during the day receive a range of services in a setting that is either attached to another facility, such as a nursing home, or is a standalone agency. Depending on the site, the services provided can include medication management, physical therapy, meals, medical care, counseling, education, and opportunities for socialization.

These services may fall into the category of **respite care**, which provides family caregivers with a break while allowing the older adult to receive needed support services. Being able to bring their relatives to these services for help during the day allows caregivers to maintain their jobs or spend time taking care of their own household or personal needs.

Community Housing Alternatives

Other alternatives in community care involve the provision of housing in addition to specialized services that can maintain the person in an independent living situation. **Government-assisted housing** is provided for individuals with low to moderate incomes who need affordable housing or rental assistance. People using government-assisted housing typically live in apartment complexes and have access to help with routine tasks such as housekeeping, shopping, and laundry.

An **accessory dwelling unit**, also known as an "in-law apartment," is a second living space in the home that allows the older adult to have independent living quarters, cooking space, and a bathroom. People living in these units may also take advantage of day treatment services to receive support when the rest of the family is at work or school.

A **continuing care retirement community (CCRC)** is a housing community that provides different levels of care adjusted to the needs of the residents. Within the same CCRC, there may be individual homes or apartments in which residents can live independently, an assisted living facility, and a nursing home. Residents move from one setting to another based on their needs but continue to remain part of their CCRC community. CCRCs typically are on the expensive side. Many require a large down payment prior to admission and also charge monthly fees. Some communities, however, allow residents to rent rather than buy into the facility.

Residents moving into CCRCs typically sign a contract that specifies the conditions under which they will receive long-term care. One option provides unlimited nursing care for a small increase in monthly payments. A second type of contract includes a predetermined amount of long-term nursing care; beyond this the resident is responsible for additional payments. In the third option, the resident pays fees for service, which means full daily rates for all long-term nursing care.

If the older adult can afford this type of housing, there are definite advantages to living in CCRCs. In addition to the relative ease of moving from one level of care to another, the CCRCs provide social activities, access to community facilities, transportation services, companionship, access to health care, housekeeping, and maintenance. Residents may travel, take vacations, and become involved in activities outside the community itself.

THE FINANCING OF LONG-TERM CARE

The financing of long-term care is currently undergoing intense scrutiny in every nation of the world. The economic issues involved in health care, particularly as the Baby Boomers grow older, are prompting discussions about how to provide care in a cost-effective and humane manner.

Within the U.S., changes in health maintenance organizations (HMOs) have wreaked havoc in many sectors of the health care industry, causing great anxiety among the public, politicians, and health care professionals. In many ways, the U.S. health care financing crisis is a function of the huge expenses associated with the long-term care of older adults. Insecurity over the financing of health care can constitute a crisis for adults of any age, but particularly so for older persons with limited financial resources. The ability to receive proper treatment for chronic conditions is therefore a pressing social and individual issue.

Long-term health care financing has a history dating back to the early 1900s and the first attempts in the U.S. to devise government health insurance programs. In the ensuing century, as these programs became established, their benefits structure and financing grew increasingly complex and diversified. Throughout this process, the developers of these plans, which involve state and federal agencies along with private insurance companies, have attempted to respond to the rapidly changing needs of the population and the even more rapidly changing nature of the nation's economy. Outside the U.S., developed countries such as Canada and many European nations have worked out different solutions than those existing in the United States and are also encountering challenges to their economy as their populations grow older.

As you will see shortly, the nursing homes and other facilities in which older adults receive treatment that we just described are subject to strict federal and state requirements to ensure that they comply with the standards set forth in the legislation that created the funding programs. The intimate connection between financing and regulation of these long-term care facilities has provided the incentive for nursing homes to raise their level of care so that they can qualify for this support.

Medicare

Title XVIII of the U.S. Social Security Act, passed and signed into law by President Lyndon B. Johnson in 1965, created the federal health care funding agency known as **Medicare**, designated as "Health Insurance for the Aged and Disabled" (see Figure 12.3).

Like OASDI, Medicare has a pay-as-you-go system that seemed sound when it was first put into effect because workers paid into a system that supports current beneficiaries. Medicare's funding structure is different from Social Security's in that current beneficiaries pay premiums, just as they do for other health insurance. Medicare has a trust fund of its own that is separate from the one for OASDI.

Medicare has grown enormously since its inception. In 1966, Medicare covered 19.1 million people at a cost of $1.8 billion. By 2012, 41.9 million Americans 65 and

FIGURE 12.3

Structure of Medicare

- Part A: Hospital insurance
- Part B: Medical insurance
- Part C: Medicare advantage plans
- Part D: Prescription drug coverage

older were covered (Center for Medicare and Medicaid Services, 2013b). Nursing homes received $32.2 billion from Medicare. The total benefits paid out by Medicare in 2011 totaled over $558 billion, or 3.7% of the gross domestic product. By 2083, Medicare spending is expected to reach 11.4% of the gross domestic product (Center for Medicare and Medicaid Services, 2010a).

In the mid-1960s, there were far more employed workers than people 65 and older needing health care, and it appeared that by taxing the employed workers to pay for those requiring care, the system would maintain itself indefinitely. There was apparently little reason at that time to be concerned about what would ultimately become a perfect storm of a rapid increase in life expectancy combined with an even more rapid increase in costs associated with health care.

The trustees of the Social Security trust fund (2012) project that by the year 2024, the Medicare trust fund will be completely exhausted. The gap between expenditures and revenue will continue to increase steadily through at least the year 2081. The situation was considered grave enough so that in its annual report of 2007, the Social Security trustees issued their first-ever warning that the program is on its way to becoming unsustainable. This impending crisis became the immediate impetus for the **Patient Protection and Affordable Care Act (PPACA)** (P.L. 111-148), legislation signed into law by President Barack Obama in the spring of 2010 that is intended to expand health care insurance to all Americans and reform Medicare spending.

Since it first became law, Medicare has been subject to numerous legislative and administrative changes designed to improve health care services to older adults, the disabled, and the poor. In 1973, the program was expanded to broaden eligibility to citizens already receiving Social Security benefits, people over 65 who qualify for Social Security benefits, and individuals with end-stage renal disease requiring continuous dialysis or a kidney transplant.

The Department of Health and Human Services (DHHS) has the overall responsibility for administration of the Medicare program, with the assistance of the Social Security Administration (SSA). In 1977, the Health Care Financing Administration (HCFA) was established under the DHHS to administer Medicare and Medicaid; it was replaced in July 2001 by the **Centers for Medicare and Medicaid Services (CMS)**, the U.S. government agency responsible for the formulation of policy and guidelines, oversight and operation of contracts, maintenance and review of records, and general financing. State agencies also play a role in the regulation and administration of the Medicare program in consultation with CMS.

Medicare Part A (Hospital Insurance, or HI) coverage includes all medically necessary services and supplies provided during a patient's stay in the hospital and subsequent rehabilitation in an approved facility. This includes the cost of a semiprivate hospital room, meals, regular nursing services, operating and recovery room, intensive care, inpatient prescription drugs, laboratory tests, X-rays, psychiatric hospital, and inpatient rehabilitation. Luxury items, cosmetic surgery, vision care, private nursing, private rooms (unless necessary for medical reasons), and rentals of television and telephone are not included in coverage.

Coverage in a skilled nursing facility is included in Part A if it occurs within 30 days of a hospitalization of 3 days or more and is certified as medically necessary. Part A of Medicare covers rehabilitation services and appliances (walkers, wheelchairs) in addition to those services normally covered for inpatient hospitalization. Patients must pay a copayment for days 21–100 of their care in this setting.

Home health services are also included in Part A of Medicare for the first 100 visits following a 3-day hospital stay. Respite periods are also covered for some forms of end-of-life care to allow a break for the patient's caregiver. In 2009, opponents to health care reform stated that the changes would include "death panels" to decide who would and who would not qualify for end-of-life care; however, within existing Medicare legislation, this care was already fully insured, covering pain relief, supportive medical and social services, physical therapy, nursing services, and symptom management.

For most people, Medicare Part A is free, but people who were self-employed or paid Medicare taxes for less than 10 years combined must pay a monthly fee. This amounted to $441 per month in 2013. Hospital stays are free for the first 60 days (the "benefit period"), and then from 61 to 90 days are $296 per day. After 90 days, the amount goes up to $592 per day, up to a maximum of 60 days for an individual's entire lifetime. However, each new stay "resets" the benefit period, as long as the individual was out of the hospital for 60 consecutive days. Moreover, there is a deductible of $1,184 (in 2013) for each benefit period, meaning that a person could pay that deductible several times within a given year.

Medicare Part B provides benefits for a range of medical services available to people 65 and older. The amount an individual pays varies according to his or her income. Part B services include preventive treatments, including glaucoma and diabetes screenings as well as bone scans, mammograms, and colonoscopies. Other covered services include laboratory tests, chiropractor visits, eye exams, dialysis, mental health care, occupational therapy, outpatient treatment, flu shots, and home health services. A one-time physical examination is also included in Part B.

FIGURE 12.4

Standard Medicare Prescription Drug Benefit in 2013

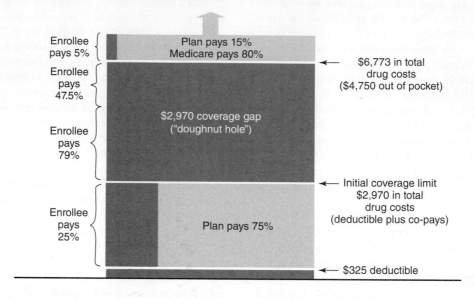

The premium for Medicare Part B varies by a person's yearly income, with those earning $85,000 or less paying $104 per month. The monthly premiums increase until they reach a maximum of $335 per month for individuals making $214,000 per year. Couples simply double their income level values such that the $104.90 would be payable by each member of a couple in which their total combined income was $170,000 or less. In 2013, the Part B deductible was $147 per year.

Part C of Medicare, also called Medicare Advantage, provides coverage in conjunction with private health plans. Individuals who have both Part A and Part B can choose to get their benefits through a variety of risk-based plans, including health maintenance organizations (HMOs), preferred provider organizations (PPOs), private fee-for-service plans, and a health insurance policy administered by the federal government.

Established by the Balanced Budget Act of 1997 (Public Law 105-33), Part C first became available to Medicare recipients in 1998. Beginning in 2006, PPOs began to serve beneficiaries on a regional basis. HHS identified 26 regions across the nation in which PPO plans compete to provide services in order to ensure that all Medicare beneficiaries, including those in small states and rural areas, would have the opportunity to enroll in a PPO as well as to encourage private plans to participate. As of 2013, most people pay a monthly premium of $104.50.

Part D of Medicare is a prescription drug benefit plan that provides coverage for a portion of the enrollee's costs

(see Figure 12.4). First available in 2006, through passage of the 2003 **Medicare Modernization Act (MMA)**, there were 31.5 million Americans who had enrolled in Part D by 2012. People who wish to receive Part D coverage pay a monthly premium that varies by plan and income. In 2013, the average monthly premium was $39, with a range from $11.60 to $66.60 on top of a medical plan premium (Center for Medicare and Medicaid Services, 2013a).

Though providing welcome relief for Medicare recipients, as originally passed, the effectiveness of Part D was severely limited by what turned out to be a huge catch. There is a coverage gap in Part D benefits known as the **donut hole**, in which the enrollee's coverage drops and out-of-pocket expenses rise. As of 2013, Medicare pays 75% of drug costs between a deductible of $325 and $2,970. Once the $2,970 is reached, enrollees start to pay a larger portion of their drug costs. When their drug costs for the year exceed $6,773 (the starting point for catastrophic coverage), their plan pays 95% of all their drug costs.

Despite these problems, Part D is becoming increasingly popular, in part because Congress has begun to reduce the size of the donut hole (and will close it entirely by 2020). The other reason Part D is gaining in popularity is because prescription drug costs are becoming increasingly prohibitive in price. The only way that people can afford their medications is to have some type of insurance, and Medicare coverage is both widely available and may be relatively less expensive than the alternatives—even with the donut hole. Consequently, the costs of Part D to Medicare

are escalating rapidly (Kaiser Family Foundation, 2010a), accounting for about 15% of health care expenditures in the U.S. Total drug spending in the U.S. was $320 billion in 2011 (IMS Institute for Healthcare Informatics, 2012).

Medicaid

Title XIX of the Social Security Act of 1965, known as **Medicaid**, is a federal and state matching entitlement program that provides medical assistance for certain individuals and families with low incomes and resources. Initially, Medicaid was formulated as a medical care extension of federally funded programs providing income assistance for the poor, with an emphasis on dependent children and their mothers, the disabled, and the over-65 population. More people are now eligible for Medicaid, including low-income pregnant women, children living in poverty, and some Medicare beneficiaries who are not eligible for any cash assistance program. Legislative changes are also providing increased and better medical care, enhanced outreach programs, and fewer limits on services.

Medicaid services for older adults cover inpatient and community health care costs not included in Medicare, such as skilled nursing facility care beyond the 100-day limit covered by Medicare, prescription drugs (without a premium), eyeglasses, and hearing aids. Although intended to provide support for individuals living at, close to, or below the poverty level, older adults receiving long-term care who are not otherwise poor may be eligible for Medicaid when their benefits have run out and they cannot afford to pay their medical expenses. Many states have a medically needy program for such individuals, who have too much income to qualify as financially needy. This program allows them to spend down their assets to the point of being eligible for Medicaid by paying medical expenses to offset their excess income. Medicaid then pays the remaining portion of their medical bills by providing services and supplies that are available under their state's Medicaid program. This means that individuals will not go into debt in order to pay their medical bills.

Unfortunately, each state has different regulations governing Medicaid eligibility, including those that govern the spend down clause. Couples may also have different rules governing spend down requirements than individuals. Prior to becoming in need of services, then, individuals who wish to protect their assets should receive financial counseling in order to determine the best plan for their situation.

The largest source of funding for medical and health-related services for those in need of assistance, Medicaid provided health care assistance to 4.8 million older adults (8.8% of all Medicaid beneficiaries) in 2011. Compared to the average costs of $2,851 per child, the average costs for an older adult was $15,931. In 2009, Medicaid paid out $50.1 billion to nursing homes for more than 1.6 million beneficiaries (Center for Medicare and Medicaid Services, 2012).

Medicaid also paid for at least some of the care given to patients in residential care facilities (19%). Among those aged 65–74 living in these facilities, 39% received Medicaid payments. The percentages were lower for residents aged 75–84 (16%) and 85 and older (10%). The mean total monthly charge for residents of these facilities was $3,165 as of 2010 (Caffrey et al., 2012).

As shown in Figure 12.5, there is considerable variation by state in the amount spent on long-term care. On average, states spend 41.2% of Medicaid funding on nursing facilities. Louisiana has the highest percentage in the United States at 26.6%, and New Mexico the least (1.6%) (Kaiser Family Foundation, 2010b).

LEGISLATIVE LANDMARKS IN THE LONG-TERM CARE OF OLDER ADULTS

The regulation of nursing homes and community-based services for older adults and the disabled is a major focus of U.S. health policy and legislation in the United States. It is only through such legislation that quality standards for health care facilities can be enforced. Unfortunately, the process of ensuring quality long-term care has been a difficult one marked by a series of regulatory efforts that failed because they were not properly enforced. The system only now seems to be coming under control after nearly 30 years of active reform efforts.

1987 Omnibus Budget Reconciliation Act of 1987 (OBRA 1987)

The current U.S. laws governing the operation of institutional facilities have their origins in a report completed by the prestigious Institute of Medicine in 1986 called "Improving the Quality of Care in Nursing Homes." This report recommended to Congress major changes in the quality and nature of services provided to nursing home residents. The outcome of the report was passage of the Omnibus Budget Reconciliation Act of 1987 (OBRA 1987). This budget bill included a number of pieces of legislation, including the **Nursing Home Reform Act (NHRA)**, a U.S. federal law that mandated that facilities must meet physical standards, provide adequate professional staffing and services, and maintain policies governing their administrative and medical procedures.

FIGURE 12.5

Medicaid Spending on Long-Term Care by State

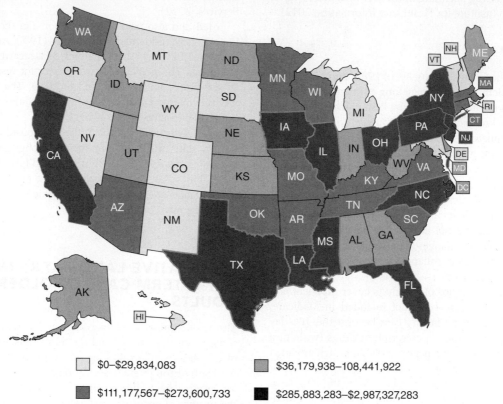

☐ $0–$29,834,083	☐ $36,179,938–108,441,922
☐ $111,177,567–$273,600,733	☐ $285,883,283–$2,987,327,283

Source: Kaiser Family Foundation. (2010). State health facts. Retrieved from http://www.statehealthfacts.org/savemap.jsp?typ=4&ind=180&cat=4&sub=47.

A significant component of NHRA was that it provided safeguards to ensure the quality of care and protection of residents' rights. Each resident must be provided with services and activities to attain or maintain the highest practicable physical, mental, and psychosocial well-being possible for that person. Facilities are required to care for residents in a manner and an environment that promotes, maintains, or enhances quality of life.

The conditions of NHRA specify that nursing homes must be licensed in accordance with state and local laws, including all applicable laws pertaining to staff, licensing, registration, fire, safety, and communicable diseases. They must have one or more physicians on call at all times, 24-hour nursing care services (including at least one full-time registered nurse), a range of rehabilitation and medical services, and activity programs. In terms of administration, they must have a qualified administrator, a governing body legally responsible for policies, and confidential record-keeping procedures. The facility must admit eligible patients regardless of race, color, or national origin.

In addition to specifying requirements for nursing homes to be licensed, NHRA mandated a set of resident rights regarding their treatment, including the ability to choose their own physicians, to have their needs and preferences, and to refuse medications and treatments. Their physical safety and dignity are protected by the right to be treated with respect, to be free from physical and mental abuse, to be afforded privacy and treatment, to voice their grievances, and to transfer or leave the facility should they so desire. The nursing home must inform residents in writing about services and fees prior to admission, and residents have the right to manage their own money (or choose someone to do so). They must be able to keep personal belongings and property to the extent that these do not interfere with the rights, health, or safety of others.

NHRA also established procedures to ensure that all conditions are met for maintaining compliance with the law. These procedures included monitoring of the performance of facilities by outside survey agencies to determine whether they comply with the federal conditions of

Family members hold personal pictures of their loved ones on January 17, 2009, who were allegedly abused in a nursing home in Albert Lea, Minnesota.

Brie Cohen/Albert Lea Tribune/©AP/Wide World Photos

participation. Unfortunately, 10 years after the NHRA regulations were put into effect, it became clear that there were still serious problems with nursing home quality. Some regulations were never implemented, and others were not enforced.

In 1997, the U.S. Senate Committee on Aging received reports that documented inadequate care in California nursing homes had caused widespread death and suffering of residents. These reports triggered a hearing in 1998 by the U.S. Senate Special Committee on Aging regarding the substandard quality of care in California nursing homes. The report's title was "Betrayal: The Quality of Care in California Nursing Homes." This report revealed that 98% of nursing homes had minimal (35%), substandard (33%), or serious (30%) deficiencies.

In response to these findings, the Clinton administration announced the **1998 Nursing Home Initiative**. This was intended to improve enforcement of nursing home quality standards, including altering the timing of nursing home inspections to allow for more frequent inspections on weekends and evenings as well as weekdays (when many of the abuses occurred); conducting background checks on workers; and establishing a national registry of nursing home aides. States were given the authority to impose immediate sanctions and monetary penalties on nursing homes that continued to violate the rights of residents.

1999–2000 Congressional Hearings on Nursing Home Abuse

Despite the best intentions of the Nursing Home Initiative, hearings on nursing home quality held by the Senate Committee on Aging just a short time later, in 1999 and 2000, revealed that nursing home abuse was still rampant.

Nationwide, 27% of nursing homes were cited with violations causing actual harm to residents or placing them at risk of death or serious injury; another 43% were cited for violations that created a potential for more than minimal harm.

The Senate hearings also revealed flaws in the surveys. Inspectors often missed significant problems such as pressure sores, malnutrition, and dehydration. In some cases, nursing homes were cited because a member of the nursing staff had committed acts of physical, sexual, or verbal abuse against residents. Formal complaints made by residents or families were uninvestigated.

Making the problem worse was the fact that the state governmental agencies discouraged the filing of complaints because they did not have the resources to follow through on them. The Senate Committee also found that the majority (54%) of nursing homes were understaffed, putting residents at increased risk of hospitalization for avoidable causes, pressure sores, and significant weight loss months (Minority Staff Special Investigations Division Committee on Government Reform U.S. House of Representatives, 2001).

2002 Nursing Home Quality Initiative

In November 2002, the federal government introduced another initiative intended to correct the problems identified in the 2000 reports. The **2002 National Nursing Home Quality Initiative** combined new information for consumers about the quality of care provided in individual nursing homes with resources available to nursing homes to improve the quality of care in their facilities. Quality improvement organizations (QIOs) were contracted by the federal government to offer assistance to skilled nursing facilities to help them improve their services. The 2002 Initiative also included a provision to train volunteers to serve as ombudspersons. The role of the ombudspersons is to help families and residents on a daily basis to find nursing homes that provide the highest possible quality of care and to give consumers the tools they need to make an informed, educated decision on selecting a nursing home.

The 2002 initiative should have done a considerable amount to improve the quality of care in nursing homes, but like its predecessors, it was ineffective in achieving its goals. In 2007, the GAO issued a major report analyzing the effectiveness of the online reporting system based on data from 63 nursing homes in California, Michigan, Pennsylvania, and Texas, institutions that had a history of serious compliance problems (see Figure 12.6). From this analysis, the GAO concluded that, once more, efforts to strengthen federal enforcement of sanctions had not been effective.

The 2007 report showed that nursing homes that committed violations of patient care or rights were often given leeway, either in terms of the amount they were penalized or the length of time they were granted before being required to pay the penalty. Even those that were penalized simply made temporary changes—only to slide back down until they were sanctioned again. Meanwhile, the residents of these homes continued to suffer abusive treatment

FIGURE 12.6

2007 GAO Report on Nursing Home Abuse

because the administrators did not correct the fundamental problems (Government Accountability Office, 2008).

As you will learn shortly, deficiencies in nursing homes remain a significant problem, severely limiting the quality of care that many residents receive. Continued reporting of these deficiencies, monitoring by government agencies, and involvement of family members advocating for residents are important safeguards. If you have a relative in a nursing home, it is important for you to be aware of these problems and stay vigilant in order to prevent them from affecting your relatives. Whether or not these abuses affect you personally, they have tragic consequences for older adults. Fortunately, there are many nursing homes that maintain the highest of standards. Families must learn how to find these nursing homes for their older relatives, as well as to manage paying for the services they provide.

THE QUALITY OF LONG-TERM CARE

Information about nursing homes and nursing home residents comes from the Online Survey, Certification, and Reporting system (OSCAR). The OSCAR system collects information from state surveys of all the certified nursing facilities in the United States, which is entered into a uniform database. Surveyors assess both the process and the outcomes of nursing home care in 15 major areas. Each of these areas has specific regulations, which state surveyors review to determine whether facilities have met the standards. When a facility fails to meet a standard, a deficiency or citation is given. The deficiencies are given for problems that can result in a negative impact on the health and safety of residents. Similarly, home health agencies are mandated to submit data on their effectiveness through a survey tool called the Outcomes Assessment and Information Set (OASIS). Unfortunately, as reported by CMS, nursing homes are becoming more and more likely to receive at least one health deficiency in these annual surveys, although these deficiencies are becoming less likely to involve serious harm to residents.

Consumers can also find information about nursing home quality through the *U.S. News & World Reports* rankings (U.S. News and World Reports, 2012). The rankings take into account the results compiled by CMS, state survey health inspections, nurse-to-resident ratios, and quality measures based on the health status of residents.

As the U.S. government attempts to improve the quality of care provided by nursing homes, yearly monitoring continues through the listing of deficiencies as reported to OSCAR (see Figure 12.7). In the years between 2005 and 2010, the average number of deficiencies per facility was 9.37, an increase over previous years; this

FIGURE 12.7

Top Ten Deficiencies in Nursing Homes, 2010 by Percent

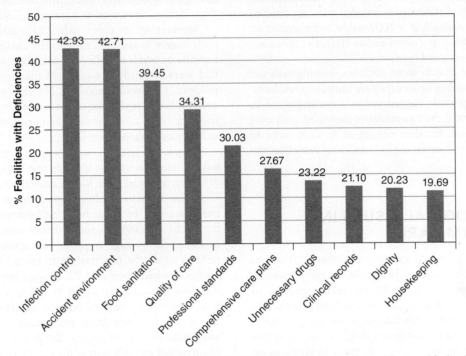

Source: Harrington, C., Carrillo, H., Dowdell, M., Tang, P. P., & Blank, B. W. (2011). Nursing facilities, staffing, residents, and facility deficiencies, 2005 through 2010, from http://www.theconsumervoice.org/sites/default/files/OSCAR-2011-final.pdf

demonstrates that the quality of care within nursing homes is on a steady decline. In 2010, 23% of the nation's nursing homes received deficiencies for poor quality of care. However, the average number of deficiencies varied substantially across the states. In 2010, the state with the highest number of deficiencies was West Virginia: 54% of facilities received a deficiency for actual harm or jeopardy to residents (Harrington et al., 2011).

Deficiencies that cause harm or immediate jeopardy to residents are considered the most serious of all. In 2010, lack of infection control was the number one deficiency, occurring in 43% of all U.S nursing homes. The District of Columbia (DC) had the highest percentage of homes with this deficiency (89%); in fact, DC had the most deficiencies in each of the top 10 areas of deficiency.

Some other areas of concern also deserve mention. For instance, continence (control over elimination of urine and feces) is a highly sensitive and personal area of life. Though training programs exist that are designed to help residents gain and maintain continence through use of diet, fluids, and regular schedules, these are rarely used; as of 2010, these programs were available to only 7% of residents, despite the fact that 56% were reported to have urinary incontinence. Bowel incontinence occurred in 43% of all residents, but bowel training was available to just 4% (Harrington et al., 2011).

Clearly, when continence training is a need that is unmet, this can detract from the quality of an individual's life as well as the quality of the life of the staff. Worsening continence is one of the top reasons that older residents of nursing homes become socially disengaged (Dubeau, Simon, & Morris, 2006). Continuing education that addresses knowledge, beliefs, and attitudes may help ultimately in encouraging nursing staff to work on restoring continence in their patients (Saxer, de Bie, Dassen, & Halfens, 2009).

The use of physical and chemical (drug) restraints to keep residents from being aggressive is another key area of deficiency. In 2010, about 8% of nursing homes inappropriately employed physical restraints (Harrington et al., 2011). However, in one New York state study, researchers found that African Americans living in nursing homes with a high percentage of White residents were more likely to be placed in restraints than African Americans living in homes that were largely African American (Miller, Papandonatos, Fennell, & Mor, 2006). The problem is not limited to the U.S. A Swedish study estimated that as many as 18% of residents in Sweden were reported to be physically restrained in a 2007 study, representing an increase from 16% just 7 years earlier (Pellfolk, Sandman, Gustafson, Karlsson, & Lövheim, 2012).

It is possible that in some contexts, nursing staff use restraints because they believe they are protecting residents. In a focus group study carried out in a nursing home in Finland, nurses and their supervisors expressed guilt over using restraints but felt they needed to do so in order to keep the residents from falling or wandering away (Saarnio & Isola, 2010).

PSYCHOLOGICAL ISSUES IN LONG-TERM CARE

The psychosocial needs of residents and strategies that can be implemented to enhance the quality of life in nursing homes became a focus early in the reform process of OBRA 1987. Unfortunately, change is slow to come about. Researchers still believe that nursing homes in the United States had not, at least as of the late 1990s, made significant changes in the freedom of choice afforded to residents on a day-to-day basis (Kane et al., 1997).

In terms of the rhythm of life in the average nursing home, although deficiencies in activities exist in less than 10% of nursing homes, there still remains a good deal of room for improvement. A study of the daily life of residents conducted in 2002 revealed that, as was the case in the 1960s, residents spent almost two-thirds of the time in their room, doing nothing at all (Ice, 2002). Thus, for many residents, there are simply not enough activities in the average nursing home (Martin et al., 2002). At the same time, the training of specialists to work with the nursing home population is lagging; social workers are not given sufficient educational preparation to work in these challenging and often stressful settings (Allen, Nelson, & Netting, 2007).

Models of Adaptation

Theoretical models attempting to provide insight into the adaptation of the individual to the institutional environment of a long-term care facility began to develop in the 1970s with the increasing attention in gerontology given to ecological approaches to the aging process. In part, this interest developed in response to practical concerns about the best ways to minimize behavioral disturbances and maximize adaptation of older adult residents to institutional settings. Many researchers studying institutionalization

believed that it was important to find ways to maximize the resident's ability to maintain independence even while having to adjust to an environment that inevitably fostered dependence (Gottesman & Bourestom, 1974).

Maximizing an older individual's adaptation to the environment is also tied in with the challenges that large institutions (such as college dorms) face in attempting to find ways to satisfy the needs of the so-called "average" resident. The average resident, like the "average" college student, is a hypothetical construct. When trying to satisfying the needs of everyone, administrators of institutions will inevitably satisfy very few.

To put this issue in very concrete terms, consider the issue of temperature. For some people, a room temperature of 68 degrees is just right, but for others, 76 is the ideal place to set the thermostat. Most institutions must regulate the temperature of the entire building, however, because they do not have individual room thermostats. In attempting to please the average resident, the administrator would need to adjust the temperature to the mean of these two numbers, which would be 72. Neither group of residents will find this temperature to be a comfortable one, yet according to the "average," it is the correct level.

As you can see from this example, in predicting adaptation to the institution, the actual qualities of the environment are only part of the equation. Researchers are interested in learning how residents perceive the institution's physical qualities and relating these perceptions to their adaptation (Sloane et al., 2002).

As important as the physical environment is to adaptation, the psychosocial needs of the residents also play a crucial role. These needs may have more to do with the amount of control people feel they have over their environments than with the physical characteristics of the institution. Feeling that you can control the temperature in your room if you want to may be even more important to your satisfaction than the actual temperature. This possibility was tested in an interview study of residents of nursing homes in Victoria, British Columbia. Scenarios were presented of vignettes in which residents were asked to make decisions such as what time to go to bed, what medicines to take, whether to move to a different room, and what type of end-of-life care to receive. Not everyone wished to have control over these decisions, though. Older adults with more years of education and a greater number of chronic illnesses were likely to state that they wished to be able to make these decisions themselves rather than have them made for them by nursing home staff (Funk, 2004).

Empirical interest in the institutionalization process has dwindled somewhat from the 1970s, when several teams of researchers were actively investigating environmental models and aging (Nehrke et al., 1981). However, one of these models offers some useful concepts for predicting how well people will adapt to an institutional setting. This model, the **competence-press model** (Lawton & Nahemow, 1973), predicts an optimal level of adjustment that institutionalized persons will experience on the basis of their levels of competence (physical and psychological) compared with the demands or "press" of the environment, or the demands it places upon individuals.

As you can see in Figure 12.8, there is balance between competence and press. In the optimal situation, there is a match between an individual's abilities and the environment's demands. A small degree of discrepancy is acceptable, but when the mismatch goes outside this range, the individual will experience negative affect and maladaptive behaviors. For example, the intellectually competent older resident (high competence) will do well in a setting in which autonomous decisions are expected (high press), but a person with a significant cognitive impairment will adapt maximally when the environment is very structured (low press).

By considering the interaction between the individual and the environment of the institution, the competence–press model makes it possible to provide specific recommendations to institutions about how best to serve the residents. The model is essentially a biopsychosocial one, allowing room for multiple dimensions of competence and press to be considered when evaluating older adults (Lichtenberg, MacNeill, Lysack, Bank, & Neufeld, 2003). Competence may be defined in terms of biological and psychological characteristics, such as mobility and cognitive resources. The social factors in this model are incorporated into the level of press in the

FIGURE 12.8

Competence–Press Model of Adaptation

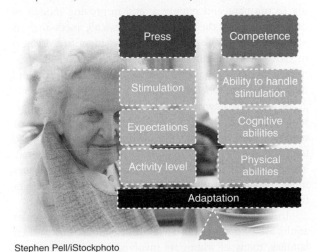

Stephen Pell/iStockphoto

environment, which include the expectations of staff and amount of stimulation provided by other residents.

Suggestions for Improving Long-Term Care

Clearly the environment plays an important role in affecting the individual's health, both inside and outside an institutional environment. Within the institutional setting, the implications of the competence–press model are that the needs of individuals should be met to the greatest extent possible. Innovations in nursing home care are being developed with the goal of maximizing the fit between the person and environment. For example, bathing, a situation that can be distressing when conducted in a way that embarrasses or exposes the resident, can be treated in a more individualized manner, making it a less aversive experience (Camp, Cohen-Mansfield, & Capezuti, 2002). Even a change as simple as switching from individually plated to "family style" meals can have a beneficial effect on resident adjustment as measured by perceived quality of life, physical performance, and increases in body weight (Nijs, de Graaf, Kok, & van Staveren, 2006).

Nurses aides, who increasingly are managing many of the daily living activities of residents (Seblega et al., 2010), can be taught to use behavioral methods to help residents maintain self-care and, hence, independence (Burgio et al., 2002). Such interventions can also benefit staff–resident relationships. Because satisfaction with treatment by staff is such a significant component of satisfaction with the institution (Chou, Boldy, & Lee, 2002), any intervention that maximizes positive interactions between staff and residents is bound to have a favorable impact on the sense of well-being experienced by residents. Such training, even with patients who have severe dementia, can help reduce dependence on psychotropic medications (Fossey et al., 2006).

New models for nursing home design attempt to break up the monotony to create a heightened feeling of a community or neighborhood. Nursing stations are removed from view, allowing residents and staff to share lounges. Hallways have alcoves that can store medicine carts and nursing stations. Small group living clusters, improved interior design, and access to gardens can help maintain independence in residents whose autonomy would otherwise be threatened (Regnier & Denton, 2009).

Other models of change stress new ways of allocating staff to meet the care needs of residents. In one such model, rather than basing staff assignments on the completion of specific tasks for all residents (bathing, changing dressings, administering medications), staff are assigned to meet all the needs of a particular group of residents. Although such a system increases the staffing requirements, overall the

Courtesy of the Leonard Florence Center for Living, Chelsea, MA

The Leonard Florence Center for Living in Chelsea, Massachusetts, is based on the Green House model. Composed of ten homes, each containing ten private bedrooms and baths, the Center serves 100 residents within a six-story condominium-style complex.

institutions reduce their expenses in the areas of restraints and antipsychotic medications. Hospitalization rates, staff turnover, and success in rehabilitation also improve as does the satisfaction that residents express about their care. Another improvement involves the use of a team approach to providing mental health services. When staff work as a multidisciplinary team, residents receive better services; at the same time, staff are more informed and perform more effectively in their jobs (Bartels, Moak, & Dums, 2002).

Another factor to consider in understanding the psychological adaptation of the older adult to the institutional environment is the possibility that a nursing or residential care home may represent an improvement over a private residence. Researchers in Finland found that nursing home residents were higher in sense of well-being than those living at home, many of whom were no longer able to care for themselves. Because many residential facilities for older adults have long waiting periods, particularly the better ones, older adults may be relieved to be admitted where they know they will no longer suffer the burden of living on their own (Böckerman, Johansson, & Saarni, 2012).

The **Green House model** offers an alternative to the traditional nursing homes by offering older adults individual homes within a small community of 6 to 10 residents and skilled nursing staff. The Green House residence is designed to feel like a home; medical equipment is stored away from sight, the rooms are sunny and bright, and the outdoor environment is easily accessible. Self-reports of quality of life among Green House residents are higher in comparison to traditional nursing homes (Kane, Lum, Cutler, Degenholtz, & Yu, 2007). Additionally, research evaluating the Green House model to traditional nursing programs suggests that family members are more satisfied

with the care provided by the Green House model (Lum, Kane, Cutler, & Yu, 2008).

These reforms in institutions can bring about much needed changes in the care of older adults. However, the broadest proposal for sweeping changes in the health care system in the United States goes beyond changes in institutional models. The Institute of Medicine (2008) issued a mandate for retooling the health care workforce to take into account the increase in older adults needing services at all levels. As we show in in Figure 12.9, there is a growing gap between the number of filled positions in geriatric psychiatry and the number of available positions, which in 2007 amounted to a discrepancy of nearly 70 unfilled positions nationwide.

The Institute of Medicine report focuses on three key areas: enhancing competence in geriatric care, increasing recruitment and retention, and improving models of care. Supporting these ideas, a large-scale meta-analysis of more than 2,700 published articles identified 15 new models of care ranging from acute care in patient homes, nurse–physician teams for nursing home residents, and models of comprehensive care in hospitals (Boult et al., 2009). Clearly, new ideas are needed to revamp the current health care system for the aging Baby Boomers, whose numbers, lifestyles, and values will almost invariably lead to challenges of the status quo of care now being offered. These aging Baby Boomers will want to hear Rolling Stones music playing in the corridors of their care facilities, not the quiet and soothing strains of a string orchestra.

In conclusion, the concerns of institutionalized older adults are of great importance to individuals and to their families, many of whom are involved in helping to make

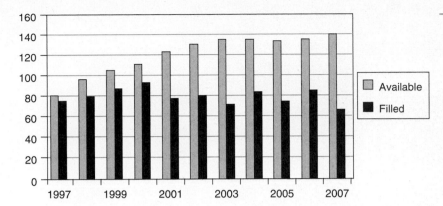

FIGURE 12.9

Discrepancy Between Available and Filled Positions in Geriatric Psychiatry

Source: Institute of Medicine. (2008). Retooling for an aging America: Building the healthcare workforce. Retrieved from http://www.iom.edu/Reports/2008/Retoolingfor-an-Aging-America-Building-the-Health-Care-Workforce.aspx.

long-term care decisions for their older relatives. The dignity and self-respect of the resident, which is fortunately now being regulated by state and federal certification standards, can best be addressed by multidimensional approaches that take into account personal and contextual factors. Interventions based on these approaches will ultimately lead to a higher quality of life for those who must spend their last days or months in the care of others.

SUMMARY

1. A wide range of long-term care settings are available that are specifically designed for older adults, such as nursing homes and residential care facilities. The percentage of older adults in these institutions with cognitive deficits is relatively high; the use of psychotropic medications is also common. Increasing attention is being given to home health care to allow older adults who need some level of care to remain living independently, a concept referred to as aging in place. Other residential sites include special housing that is designed for older adults.

2. Medicare, a pay-as-you-go system, is designed to provide hospital insurance and supplemental medical insurance. Other forms of insurance attached to Medicare are becoming increasingly available to older adults. Medicaid is intended to reduce the burden of health care costs among those who need help paying for medical services, but individuals receiving this assistance must "spend down" to eliminate their assets. The cost of Medicare is expected to skyrocket over the coming decades; this will lead to the bankruptcy of the Social Security Trust fund unless preventive measures are taken.

3. The rights of nursing home residents became protected with the passage of the Nursing Home Reform Act in 1987. Complaints about nursing home care have decreased since that time. However, problems in areas such as food sanitation remain a concern, as do the use of restraint as a means of controlling resident behavior and abuse. Care in nursing homes is an area needing continued monitoring, as was evident by the findings obtained in the 2002 General Accountability Office report on nursing home abuse and more recently by the 2007 General Accountability Office's review of the enforcement of violations in nursing home standards.

4. Psychological issues in long-term care focus on the provision of an adequate environment that will maximally meet the needs of residents. The competence–press model proposes an ideal relationship between how demanding an environment is and the abilities of the resident to meet those demands. The neighborhoods where older adults live are also of concern to researchers attempting to understand the relationship between well-being and feelings of safety and security among the residents.

13

Death and Dying

AGING TODAY

How Our Beliefs Help Us During Hard Times

TOPICS

Themes and issues

Models of development

Methods

Physical changes

Health

Memory and attention

Higher-order cognition

Personality

Relationships

Work and retirement

Mental health

Long-term care

Death and dying

Successful aging

How do you cope with crisis? When faced with a situation that tests you emotionally, can you handle it? How can you come out on the other side of tragedy or loss and manage to resume your previous life? These are among the toughest questions we ever face in life. Some of the best advice for coping with tests of faith comes from studies of how older adults manage the experience of bereavement.

There is surprisingly little research on spirituality and coping, but what evidence exists suggests that our values and beliefs can guide us through difficult losses. Columbia University psychologists Anthony Mancini and George Bonanno propose that resilience comes in several forms, depending on your personality (Mancini & Bonanno, 2009). For some, being adaptive and flexible will help you readjust your life and come to terms with your loss. For others, mental toughness ("repressive coping") provides the route. Being able to maintain your sense of who you are, or identity, may also help you rebound from the loss of someone close to you. Finally, being able to draw upon your positive memories with the deceased can serve as a source of comfort. This last point is particularly important.

Here are some useful suggestions for learning how to cope with the challenges in your life and become more resilient:

1. Don't let despair overwhelm you and don't give in to the temptation to give up and stop moving forward. A little bit of denial, at first, may enable you to get through each day until you can start to absorb the loss.
2. Tell yourself you can do it. Once you perceive that you can cope, you actually can cope better. Positive "self-statements" can shore up your sense of self-efficacy. Measuring your coping success in small steps allows your confidence to build, increasing your coping strengths even further.
3. View the loss as a test of faith, a sign that you can handle adversity, or at least a testament to your ability to see a silver lining in the ugliest circumstance. Our trials are as much a part of our identities as are our successes.

People who survive into their later years, having managed to cope with the many curve balls that life throws their way, can inspire us to learn how better to survive our own challenges.

Posted by Susan Whitbourne and Stacey Whitbourne

For many people, the concept of death is as fascinating as it is frightening. By definition, death remains the great unknown; even individuals who have had so-called near-death experiences cannot claim with certainty that what happened to them is an accurate prediction of what is to come in the future.

If you are in good health, you may not give your own death much thought. However, those who live until the years of later adulthood may find themselves prone to consider the ending of their lives. Even if they do not give attention to the existential questions of their own mortality, they must make practical arrangements, such as planning their funeral or finalizing their will. Perhaps what most people wish for is a long, **healthy life span**, which is the length of time an individual can live without significant disease and disability. In keeping with Erikson's concepts of generativity and ego integrity, many people also wish to leave something behind to be remembered by and to have made an impact on other people's lives.

In keeping with the biopsychosocial perspective, death and dying are best understood in a multidimensional manner. Death is, of course, a biological event, as it is the point in time when the body's functions case to operate. However, this biological fact of life is overlaid with a great deal of psychological meaning, both to the individual and to those in the individual's social network. Socioculturally, death is interpreted in multiple ways varying according to time, place, and culture.

WHAT DO WE KNOW ABOUT DEATH?

From a medical and legal perspective, the technical definition of **death** is the irreversible cessation of circulatory and respiratory functions, or when all structures of the brain have ceased to function (President's Commission for the Study of Ethical Problems in Medicine and Biomedical and Behavioral Research, 1981). The term **dying** refers to the period during which the organism loses its vitality. These terms, as you will learn, are not always clear-cut, particularly with advances in life support technology that allow people to be kept alive almost indefinitely after an organ vital to survival has failed.

Medical Aspects of Death

Although the death experience varies from person to person, there are some commonalities in the physical changes shown by a person whose functions are deteriorating to the point that death will occur within a few hours or days. In a dying person, the symptoms that death is imminent include being asleep most of the time, being disoriented, breathing irregularly, having visual and auditory hallucinations, being less able to see, producing less urine, and having mottled skin, cool hands and feet, an overly warm trunk, and excessive secretions of bodily fluids (Gavrin & Chapman, 1995). An older adult who is close to death is likely to be unable to walk or eat, recognize family members, suffer constant pain, and feel that breathing is difficult.

There are many variations in the dying process, a concept captured by the term **dying trajectory**, or the rate of decline in functioning prior to death (Glaser & Strauss, 1968). There are two major features of a dying trajectory—duration and shape. Those who die suddenly function normally and then show a precipitous descent. These would be people with no prior knowledge of illness, perhaps the victim of sudden cardiac failure, or people who die in accidents. The second and third trajectories include individuals who have advance warning of a terminal illness and who experience a lingering period of loss of function. A steady downward trajectory applies to people whose disease causes them to undergo a continuous and predictable decline, a process that characterizes many people who die of cancer (see Figure 13.1). The third trajectory characterizes people who go through a generally downward course that is marked by a series of sharp drops. Eventually their death occurs during a crisis related to their illness or due to another fatal cause during which their functional abilities suddenly decrease. Such individuals are likely to be dying from cardiovascular or Alzheimer's disease (Teno, Weitzen, Fennell, & Mor, 2001).

Apart from the three dying trajectories, there are other patterns shown by people near the end of life. Some individuals are statistically at increased risk of dying, though technically they do not have a terminal disease. One set consists of individuals in their 80s or older who are in good health but have limited physical reserves. They may die from complications associated with an acute condition such as influenza or a broken hip due to a fall. In other cases, people whose organ systems are gradually deteriorating may slowly lose the ability to care for themselves while at the same time developing an acute illness such as renal failure or pneumonia that eventually leads to death. This pattern may characterize individuals in the later stages of Alzheimer's disease. The immediate cause of death may be the acute illness, but it has occurred against a backdrop of general loss of function.

A common syndrome observed at the end of life is the **anorexia-cachexia syndrome**, in which the individual loses appetite (anorexia) and muscle mass (cachexia). The

FIGURE 13.1

Dying Trajectories

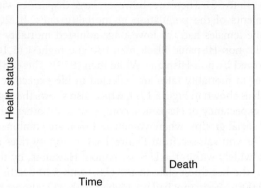

A. Sudden death from an unexpected cause

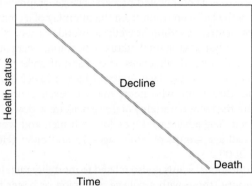

B. Steady decline from a progressive disease with a "terminal" phase

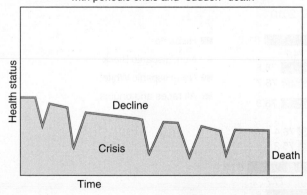

C. Advanced illness marked by slow decline with periodic crisis and "sudden" death

Source: Field, M. J., Cassel, C. K., & Committee on Care at the End of Life. (1997). *Approaching death: Improving care at the end of life*, Institute of Medicine, Division of Health Care Services. Washington, DC: National Academy Press.

majority of cancer patients experience cachexia, a condition also found commonly in patients who have AIDS and neurocognitive disorder. Patients who are dying are also likely to experience nausea, difficulty swallowing, bowel problems, dry mouth, and edema, or the accumulation of liquid in the abdomen and extremities that leads to bloating. Anxiety, depression, confusion, and memory loss are also common psychological symptoms that people experience in their final days and hours (Field, Colditz, Willett, Longcope, & McKinlay, 1994).

Obviously the symptoms experienced by dying individuals involve pain and suffering, not only for the patients themselves but also indirectly for their family members. However, those who work with the dying observe that against this backdrop, the final period of life can also involve emotional and spiritual growth (Field, Cassel, & Committee on Care at the End of Life, 1997). As we will see later, the notion of "acceptance" as the final stage of dying implies an ability to transcend these painful physical symptoms.

Death by the Numbers

Mortality data provide a fascinating picture of the factors within a given population that influence the course of human life. By knowing how to interpret statistics about death, you can gain a great deal of insight into the factors that contribute to living a long life.

The quickest way to gauge the health of a given region of the world or period in history is to find out who dies and when. The **crude death rate** is simply the number of deaths divided by population alive during a certain time period. This number can be multiplied by 1,000 to give the number of deaths per thousand in the population, or 100,000 to give the number of deaths per 100,000. An **age-specific death rate** is the crude death rate for a specific age group. The age-specific death rate only discloses the likelihood of people dying within their own age group. When researchers or health policy experts want to gauge the "health" of a population, they often use a statistic that adjusts the crude death rate for the number of people in the population within a given age group. They therefore calculate the **age-adjusted death rate**, a statistic that combines all the age-specific death rates within groups of the population. There will automatically be more deaths in the older age groups within the population (currently about half of all deaths occur after at 75), but there are fewer of those individuals in the population. The age-adjusted death rate takes that factor into account (see Figure 13.2).

In 2010, there were 2,468,435 deaths in the U.S., which translates to a crude death rate of 799.5 per 100,000

FIGURE 13.2

Age-Specific and Age-Adjusted Death Rate

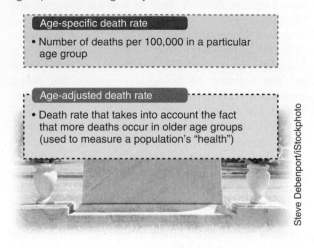

Age-specific death rate

- Number of deaths per 100,000 in a particular age group

Age-adjusted death rate

- Death rate that takes into account the fact that more deaths occur in older age groups (used to measure a population's "health")

Steve Debenport/iStockphoto

in the population, and an age-adjusted death rate of 746.2 (MInino & Murphy, 2010). The age-adjusted death rate is lower than the crude death rate because more of the deaths occurred disproportionately to that smaller population base of people 75 and older. Just 10 years earlier, fewer Americans had died (about 2.4 million). The age-adjusted death rate at that time was 860. As you can see, then, although fewer people died in 2000, the U.S. was statistically unhealthier then because the age-adjusted death rate was so much higher than it was 10 years later. In general, the age-adjusted death rate in the U.S. has been declining steadily.

Deaths due to heart disease have dropped precipitously in the past 10 years (from 257 to 179), as have deaths due to cancer (200 to 173), stroke (61 to 39), and COPD. However, suicides (10 to 12) and accidental deaths are on the rise (35 to 38). There are, however, large disparities within segments of the population in mortality rates. In 2010, White females had the lowest age-adjusted mortality rate (631); non-Hispanic Black men had the highest (1,104), followed by non-Hispanic White men (879). These differences in mortality rates are reflected in life expectancy at birth as shown in Figure 13.3, which also shows the higher life expectancy of Hispanics, compared to all other ethnic and racial groups, when women and men are combined.

As you can see from Figure 13.4, mortality rates also vary widely within the U.S. by region. Hawaii is, by these data, the healthiest state in the U.S., with 590 deaths per 100,000; Mississippi had the highest with 962, almost 30% higher than the overall U.S. death rate.

Teasing apart the various contributions to mortality rate differences is a complicated process. The geographic variations in the U.S. can result from the interplay of a complex host of factors, including race/ethnicity and sex, as we have just seen, but also marital status, education, occupation, stress, and cultural influences on diet and lifestyle.

People who have been married have a lower mortality rate than those who never married, even taking into account the higher mortality of those who are widowed and divorced. The advantage holds for both men and women across all age groups of adults ages 15 and older (Heron et al., 2009).

Educational status is also related to mortality rate. In all age groups, those with a college education or better have

FIGURE 13.3

Life Expectancy at Birth, by Hispanic Origin, Race, and Sex U.S. 2010

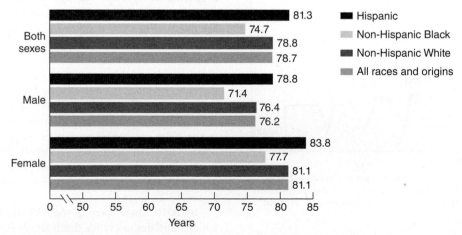

Both sexes: Hispanic 81.3, Non-Hispanic Black 74.7, Non-Hispanic White 78.8, All races and origins 78.7

Male: Hispanic 78.8, Non-Hispanic Black 71.4, Non-Hispanic White 76.4, All races and origins 76.2

Female: Hispanic 83.8, Non-Hispanic Black 77.7, Non-Hispanic White 81.1, All races and origins 81.1

- ■ Hispanic
- Non-Hispanic Black
- Non-Hispanic White
- All races and origins

Years

Source: Miñino, A. M. and S. L. Murphy (2010). "Deaths in the United States, 2010." NCHS data brief, no. 99.

FIGURE 13.4

Age-Adjusted Death Rates by State, United States, 2010

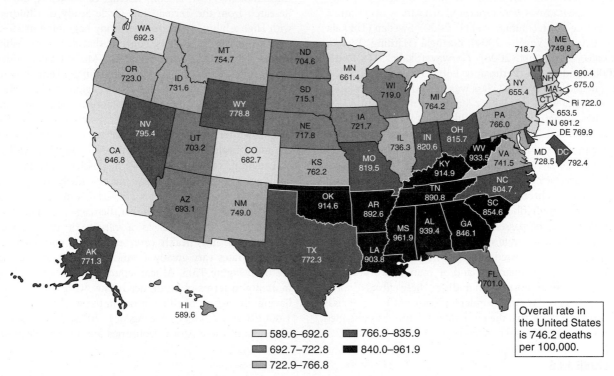

☐ 589.6–692.6	■ 766.9–835.9
■ 692.7–722.8	■ 840.0–961.9
☐ 722.9–766.8	

Overall rate in
the United States
is 746.2 deaths
per 100,000.

Source: Kindig, D. A., Seplaki, C. L., & Libby, D. L. (2002). Death rate variation in U.S. subpopulations. Bulletin of the World Health Organization, 80, 9–15. Figures 1 and 2. http://www.who.int/bulletin/archives/80(1)9.pdf

lower mortality rates. These findings on education relate to the well-established relationship between social status and mortality (Adler et al., 1994). Since the mid-19th century, men in laboring and trade occupations are known to have higher death rates than those of the professional class (Macintyre, 1997). Data from the Whitehall II study show why. Men in lower employment grades have higher risk of coronary heart disease compared with men in higher employment grades (Marmot, Shipley, Hemingway, Head, & Brunner, 2008). Men and women from Whitehall II in lower socioeconomic positions had a 1.60 times higher risk of death compared with those in higher socioeconomic positions (Marmot et al., 2008). People in lower socioeconomic classes are also more likely to suffer from communicable diseases, exposure to lead, and work-related injuries (Pamuk, Makuc, Heck, Reuben, & Lochner, 1998). These results also apply to women from lower socioeconomic classes (Langford & Johnson, 2009), who are more likely to be obese (Hart, Gruer, & Watt, 2011).

Not only the level of occupation but also the pattern of jobs people hold throughout adulthood are related to mortality rates. The risk of mortality is lower in men who move up from manual to professional or managerial-level occupations (House, Kessler, Herzog, & Mero, 1990; Moore & Hayward, 1990). Men who hold a string of unrelated jobs have higher rates of early mortality than those with stable career progressions (Pavalko, Elder, & Clipp, 1993).

Although at one time the class disparity in mortality rates was considered to be due to poorer sanitation, nutrition, and housing, current explanations focus on psychosocial factors as well. Stress is an important part of this equation. Researchers in the United States have established that people who report higher levels of subjective distress have higher mortality rates (Pratt, 2009). On-the-job stress is a major contributor to overall distress, particularly job stress in the form of lack of control over work conditions (Magnusson Hanson, Theorell, Oxenstierna, Hyde, & Westerlund, 2008). Workers in jobs who lack control over the pace and direction of what they do with their time (as is true in an assembly-line or migrant farming job) are at higher risk of dying from cardiovascular disease. In a 25-year follow-up study of more than 12,500 male workers (aged 25 to 74), exposure to even 5 years of assembly-line work increased the risk of dying from heart disease. Assembly-line workers had an 83% higher mortality risk than would be expected on the basis of their age (Johnson, Stewart, Hall, Fredlund, & Theorell, 1996).

These findings were replicated in a variety of countries, including Spain (Muntaner et al., 2009); Sweden (Tiikkaja, Hemstrom, & Vagero, 2009); Portugal (Harding, Teyhan, Rosato, & Santana, 2008); Norway (Skalicka & Kunst, 2008); and Russia (Perlman & Bobak, 2009). In addition, in Finland, lower social class was related to higher suicide risk among women (Maki & Martikainen, 2009).

Researchers suggest that lifelong exposure to social inequality is a key element of the income–mortality link. Such inequality incorporates a host of factors, including exposure to environmental health hazards, inequalities in health care, lack of social support, loss of a sense of mastery and control, chronic exposure to discrimination, and an impoverished childhood. These social class influences on mortality may be passed along from generation to generation. A 39-year longitudinal follow-up of nearly 4,100 Swedish adults showed that individuals whose parents were divorced, unmarried, and/or manual workers had increased risk of mortality in midlife. These effects of social class influenced mortality independently of the social class and marital status that the participants themselves obtained during midlife (Fors, Lennartsson, & Lundberg, 2011).

People who are involved in organized religion may, regardless of social class, have lower rates of mortality (McCullough, Hoyt, Larson, Koenig, & Thoresen, 2000). Research from the Terman Life-Cycle Study of Children with High Ability, a longitudinal study beginning in 1940 with numerous follow-ups, suggests that this relationship may be particularly true for women (McCullough, Friedman, Enders, & Martin, 2009). Women in the Terman sample who were identified as the least religious had a higher risk of dying compared with the more religious women. This finding is consistent with other research showing that people with higher religious involvement report higher self-rated health and fewer depressive symptoms (Idler, McLaughlin, & Kasl, 2009). It is possible that lack of faith has an effect on mortality, but also likely that people involved in organized religion also have a more extensive social network which helps buffer them against stress.

Reflecting differences in a variety of psychosocial factors, including health care, education, and lifestyle, mortality rates vary greatly around the world, as you can see from Figure 13.5. African countries have the highest mortality in terms of crude death rate, with South Africa having the highest of all countries in the world (17.23 per 1,000) (Central Intelligence Agency, 2012). The majority of deaths in these African countries are due to infectious

FIGURE 13.5

Crude Death Rates Around the World, 2006

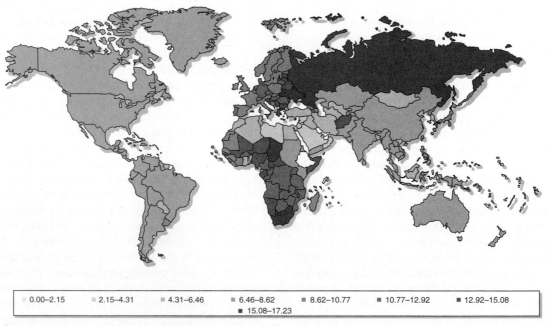

▪ 0.00–2.15	▪ 2.15–4.31	▪ 4.31–6.46	▪ 6.46–8.62	▪ 8.62–10.77	▪ 10.77–12.92	▪ 12.92–15.08
			▪ 15.08–17.23			

There are large variations around the world in death rates as can be seen from this figure. Death rates are given per 1,000 in the population.

Source: CIA, The World Factbook, available at: https://www.cia.gov/library/publications/the-world-factbook/ (Retrieved from http://www.globalhealthfacts.org/data/topic/map.aspx?ind=90#notes)

or parasitic diseases. Across all countries studied by the World Health Organization, the poor are over four times as likely to die between the ages of 15 and 59 as are the non-poor (World Health Organization, 2009). Cardiovascular disease, in contrast, takes its toll in Kazakhstan, Ukraine, and Afghanistan, all of whose rates of death due to this disease are far higher than any state in the United States, including those with highest cardiovascular death rates.

SOCIOCULTURAL PERSPECTIVES ON DEATH AND DYING

As we pointed out earlier, death and dying are best viewed from a biopsychosocial perspective. From the biological and medical perspectives, death is an event that can be defined by a set of physical changes within the body's cells. From a sociocultural perspective, death derives its meaning from the way that a society or culture interprets the processes through which life ends. Awareness of the end of life is a uniquely (so we think) human characteristic, as is the ability to endow this event with meaning. People then imbue that meaning on the basis of the prevailing philosophy, economics, and family structure of their culture.

According to the sociocultural perspective, people learn the social meaning of death from the language, arts, and death-related rituals of their cultures. A culture's **death ethos**, or prevailing philosophy of death, can be inferred from funeral rituals, treatment of those who are dying, belief in the presence of ghosts, belief in an afterlife, the extent to which death topics are taboo, the language people use to describe death (through euphemisms such as "passed away"), and the representation of death in the arts. Death may be viewed as sacred or profane, as an unwanted extinction of life or a welcome release from worldly existence (Atchley, 2000).

Throughout the course of Western history, cultural meanings and rituals attached to the process of death and to the disposition of dead bodies have gone through remarkable alterations. The ancient Egyptians practiced what are perhaps the most well known of all death rituals. They believed that a new, eternal life awaited the dead and that the body had to be preserved through mummification in order to make it the permanent home for the spirit of the deceased. The mummies were buried in elaborate tombs, where they were decorated and surrounded by valued possessions. Family members would visit the tombs to bring offers of food to sustain the dead in the afterlife. The *Book of the Dead* contained magic spells intended to guide the departed through the underworld and into the afterlife.

Mummification was practiced in many cultures, including South America, where the Incans were known to have preserved their dead until as recently as 500 years ago.

People can still request that their bodies be mummified today, with services provided by a firm in Salt Lake City for the cost of $35,000 to $60,000 (Dickinson, 2012).

Cultural views within Western society toward death and the dead have undergone many shifts from ancient times to the present. In Figure 13.6, we summarize three of the most significant developments identified in the work of writer Phillipe Aries (1974, 1981). For many centuries until the early Middle Ages, the prevailing view was of **tamed death**, in which death was viewed as familiar and simple, a transition to eternal life. Death and dying were events that involved the entire community, supported by specific prayers and practices that "tamed" the unknown.

Over the next several decades, this view of death as a natural process began to be replaced in a cultural shift to a view of death as the end of the self, something to be feared and kept at a distance. For a period in the 1800s, death and dying became glorified, and it was considered noble to die for a cause (the "beautiful death"). Gradually, Western attitudes have shifted once again into what Aries called **invisible death**, the preference that the dying retreat from the family and spend their final days confined in a hospital setting. These attitudes become translated into **social death**, the process through which the dying become treated as nonpersons by family or health care workers as they are left to spend their final days in the hospital or nursing home.

As death has become removed from the everyday world, it has acquired more fear and mystery. Instead of developing our own personal meanings, we are at the mercy of the many images of death we see in the media. News sources expose us to stories of death from the massive

FIGURE 13.6

Shifts in Death Ethos From Ancient Times to the Present

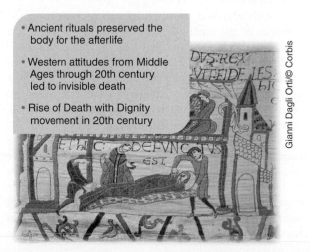

- Ancient rituals preserved the body for the afterlife
- Western attitudes from Middle Ages through 20th century led to invisible death
- Rise of Death with Dignity movement in 20th century

Gianni Dagli Orti/© Corbis

The popularity of the TV series *Dexter*, which features a serial killer who targets criminals, underscores the cultural preoccupation with death.

scale of natural disasters to school shootings and terrorist attacks. The death of one famous person may preoccupy the American or European media for weeks, as was the case in the deaths of such celebrities as Princess Diana (1997), John F. Kennedy, Jr. (1999), Michael Jackson (2009), and Whitney Houston (2012). Some of the most popular movies and television shows focus exclusively on homicide, often taking us step-by-step through the grisliest of tales involving serial killers.

At the same time, medical advances make it possible to keep people alive under far less tenable circumstances than they could in the past, and they can restore life to a person who has, temporarily, ceased to breathe or sustain a heartbeat. Issues of organ and tissue transplants further cloud the boundary between life and death. Related trends in attitudes toward death emphasize the quality of the death experience and the fear of enduring a prolonged period of terminal decline.

Amid the growing institutionalization of death and the attempts by the medical establishment to prolong life, a small book published in 1969 was to alter permanently Western attitudes toward and treatment of the dying. This book, by Elisabeth Kübler-Ross (1969), called *On Death and Dying*, described five **stages of dying** considered to occur universally among terminally ill patients: denial, anger, bargaining, depression, and acceptance.

Unfortunately, the original views of Kübler-Ross became distorted as the book's popularity grew. The five stages began to be interpreted as a series of steps that must be followed by each dying patient. If a patient refused to engage in "bargaining," for instance, then it must mean something was wrong with the way that person was handling the terminal illness. The Kübler-Ross formulation also ignores other emotions that dying individuals may experience, such as curiosity, hope, relief, and apathy.

The critical point that Kübler-Ross attempted to make in her writing is that to reach acceptance of a fatal illness, the dying person must be allowed to talk openly with family members and health care workers. Rather than hide the diagnosis or pretend that everything will be all right, those who interact with the dying individual need to give that person a chance to express the many emotions that surface, ranging from fury to dejection. Along with the work of cultural anthropologist Ernest Becker, whose book *The Denial of Death* (Becker, 1973) drew attention to Western culture's unwillingness to face the reality of mortality, these writings set the stage for a major shift in cultural attitudes and medical practice for the dying.

Most importantly, the idea of **death with dignity** proposed that the period of dying should not subject the individual to extreme physical dependency or loss of control of bodily functions (Humphrey, 1991). This idea now lies behind efforts in the medical community for dying patients and their families to bring death back into the home. Similarly, patients are being offered the opportunity for a **good death**, in which they can have autonomy in making decisions about the type, site, and duration of care they receive at the end of life (Carr, 2012).

Thus, medicine is making great strides in keeping people alive using artificial means. Patients and their loved ones, however, are increasingly looking for ways to make death once again a more natural way to bring those lives to a humane ending.

PSYCHOLOGICAL PERSPECTIVES ON DEATH AND DYING

From a psychological standpoint, death and dying carry many layers of meaning. Toward the end of their lives, individuals may begin to shift their identities to incorporate the reality that faces them. As with changes they experience throughout life, people use identity assimilation to minimize if not deny, as much as possible, this coming reality. At some point, however, they must accommodate the fact that their life will be ending, at which point the process of identity balance may start to allow them to face this fact with equanimity.

The way in which a person dies can become a part of the individual's identity, at least when the individual becomes aware that death is imminent. Your life develops an ending that may cause you to think of yourself differently than you did prior to having that knowledge, a fact which may also help you ease your own death anxiety (Wojtkowiak & Rutjens, 2011). Furthermore, when you reach that point, you may wish to take steps to leave a legacy that will continue to define you after you are gone, a process called **legitimization of biography**. Through this process, people attempt to see what they have done as having meaning, and they prepare the "story" of their lives by which they will be remembered in the minds of others (Marshall, 1980). Some individuals may put their memoirs in writing, and others achieve an internal reckoning in which they evaluate their contributions as well as their shortcomings.

Psychologically, the dying process can begin well before the individual is in any real physical jeopardy. People first start to think about their own mortality when they reach the point called **awareness of finitude**, which is when they pass the age when other people close to them had themselves died (Marshall, 1980). For example, if a man's father died at the age of 66, a kind of counting-down process begins when the son reaches that age. He anticipates the end of life and understands that life really will end.

The notion that the awareness of life's end triggers an intense period of self-evaluation is also an important component of Erikson's concept of ego integrity, as we discussed in Chapter 8. Erikson emphasized that during this period of life, individuals deal with mortality and questions related to the ending of their existence by attempting to place their lives into perspective. Presumably, this process may occur at any age, as the dying individual attempts to achieve a peaceful resolution with past mistakes and events that can no longer be made up for or changed. As we pointed out in Chapter 11, life review therapy may be useful for older adults who might not spontaneously engage in this potentially important process.

Terror management theory also proposes that when people's thoughts of death are activated, either consciously or unconsciously, they can experience a wide range of beneficial effects. They may adopt better health habits, be more focused on intrinsic rather than extrinsic goals, show more compassion, and be more motivated to have close interpersonal relationships. People may even be more creative, less likely to hold stereotypes, and feel greater attachment to their community. The recognition that your life is finite may stimulate you, no matter what your age, to focus on what is really important and adopt a broader perspective in your beliefs, attitudes and values (Vail et al., 2012).

ISSUES IN END-OF-LIFE CARE

Improvements in medical technology along with changes in attitudes toward death and dying are leading clinicians to become far more sensitive to the emotional and physical needs of dying patients. At the same time, legislation and social movements that advocate for the rights of dying patients are making progress in allowing them to preserve their dignity and autonomy.

Advance Directives

One of the most significant changes to take place in medical treatment of the dying, the **Patient Self-Determination Act (PSDA)** of 1990 guarantees the right of all competent adults to have an active role in decisions about their care. The PSDA guarantees that prior to becoming ill, an individual can put in writing his or her wishes regarding end-of-life treatment.

The patient's wishes for end-of-life care take the form of an **advance directive (AD)**, also called a living will, which is a written order that stipulates the conditions under which a patient will accept or refuse treatment. Another component of an AD is for patients to make a **durable power of attorney for health care (DPAHC)** appointment, also known as a health care proxy, to make decisions to act on their behalf should they become incapacitated. Not only are advance directives useful in ensuring that patients play an active role in deciding on their treatment, but they also facilitate communication among patients, health care staff and families; protect an individual's resources; alleviate anxiety; and reduce the chances of the patient's being maltreated (The President's Council on Bioethics, 2005).

In Table 13.1 we have included an example of a type of living will that people can construct themselves (AgingwithDignity.org, 2010).

ADs specify the code status, or the conditions under which dying patients wish to be treated. Full code means that there should be no limit on life-sustaining treatment; in other words, the patient requests to be intubated or ventilated and resuscitated with CPR after fatal cardiac or pulmonary arrest. A **do not resuscitate (DNR) order** directs health care workers not to use resuscitation if the patient experiences cardiac or pulmonary arrest.

Patients may also request **palliative care**, which will provide them with relief from symptoms such as nausea, pain, and dyspnea as well as some services such as physical and occupational therapy. According to the World Health Organization (2002b), palliative care should neither hasten nor postpone the end of life. **Overtreatment** occurs when patients request palliative care but instead receive active life support that includes resuscitation.

The PSDA mandates that health care professionals receive education about ADs as well as provide information to patients as they are being admitted to the hospital. The existence of an AD must be documented in the medical record. Each state is permitted to establish and define its own legislation concerning advance directives, but the basic federal requirements must be met in all Medicare- and

TABLE 13.1

Five Wishes to Express in an Advance Directive

Wish	Example of How Wish Is Honored
The person I want to make care decisions for me when I can't	List names of health care agents
My wish for the kind of medical treatment I want or don't want	Specifies situations in which life-support or resuscitation should be provided
My wish for how comfortable I want to be	How much and what kind of pain medication and treatment should be provided
My wish for how I want people to treat me	Whether to die at home and to have others present
My wish for what I want my loved ones to know	Wish to be buried or cremated, desire to be remembered in specific way

Source: Adapted from Agingwithdignity.org

Medicaid-funded facilities in order for them to continue to receive funding.

Various safeguards are in place to protect against abuse of the process, such as the requirement for witnesses and the requirement that more than one physician provide a diagnosis for a condition. In addition to documenting the patient's wishes, the PSDA was intended to ensure more active involvement in planning and treatment by patients and to uphold the principles of respect for their dignity and autonomy.

Studies on the effectiveness of the PSDA show that health care providers do not always communicate with dying patients or alleviate their pain (Bakitas et al., 2008). Nursing home staff often have not developed procedures to communicate either among themselves or with patients to determine at what point in the resident's illness palliative care should begin (Travis et al., 2002). Hospital patients do not consistently receive the opportunity to complete an AD, leading the bereaved family to feel that the patient's wishes were not respected (Teno, Gruneir, Schwartz, Nanda, & Wetle, 2007). There are racial disparities in the provision of ADs, with African Americans and Hispanics less likely to have ADs in their medical files (Degenholtz, 2002). Patients who are White, have greater access to resources, better health care, and better education are more likely to die in their own homes than in nursing homes (Gruneir et al., 2007).

Because there is no one scenario that best describes the type of ending that they envision, individuals must be given the opportunity to make the choice that best fits their values and desires (Vig, Davenport, & Pearlman, 2002). Often, these values and desires stem from their religious beliefs. A study of nearly 350 patients in the U.S. with advanced

cancer showed that those who used religion as a way to cope with their illness were more likely than their nonreligious counterparts to choose mechanical ventilation to prolong their life (Phelps et al., 2009). In an interview study of older Chinese adults living in Canada, their beliefs in Eastern religions led them to be less accepting of Western medicine and the provision of ADs (Bowman & Singer, 2001). It is therefore necessary to understand the patient's cultural background when providing end-of-life care (Crawley, Marshall, Lo, & Koenig, 2002). If possible, options should be discussed with family members (Haley et al., 2002; Hickman, 2002).

However, for those older adults who do prepare an AD, their end-of-life experience is more likely to conform to their preferences (Silveira, Kim, & Langa, 2010). Coordinated patient care palliative services can improve patients' perceived quality of life, even when they experience significant pain (Bakitas et al., 2009). As with the provision of good nursing home care, an interdisciplinary approach can help to overcome the problems of lack of coordination and communication among health care workers (Connor, Egan, Kwilosz, Larson, & Reese, 2002).

Families who are involved in the process of end-of-life care planning also benefit in that they experience less emotional strain before and after their relative's death. A controlled study in Australia showed that bereaved relatives given this opportunity experienced significantly greater satisfaction and less stress, anxiety, and depression (Detering, Hancock, Reade, & Silvester, 2010). Involving families in the process of planning palliative care can also reduce their emotional burden (Radwany et al., 2009). Families who experience the death of their relative as a time of "peaceful awareness" rate the overall quality of the experiences significantly higher (Ray et al., 2006) and are better able to recover during the bereavement period (Akiyama, Numata, & Mikami, 2010).

Physician-Assisted Suicide and Euthanasia

Patients can write an AD in order to specify the level of care they want to receive at any point in time, including well before they become terminally ill. In **physician-assisted suicide (PAS)**, terminally ill individuals make the conscious decision, while they are still able to do so, that they want their lives to end before dying becomes a protracted process. Patients themselves receive from their physicians the medical tools necessary to end their lives. In contrast, physicians performing **euthanasia** take the actions that cause the patient to die, with the intention of preventing the suffering associated with a prolonged ending of life (see Figure 13.7).

The leading proponent of PAS was Dr. Jack Kevorkian. In 1989, he built what he called a "suicide machine," which he then used in 1990 on his first patient, a 54-year-old woman with Alzheimer's disease. Throughout the 1990s, he conducted more than 100 assisted suicides. In a highly controversial televised segment on the program *60 Minutes*, aired in November 1998, Kevorkian ended the life of a 52-year-old Michigan man suffering from a terminal neurological disease. Because this procedure was illegal (and was flagrantly performed in front of millions of TV viewers), Kevorkian was arrested and subsequently convicted on second-degree murder charges. In 2007, Kevorkian was released from prison after serving 8 years of a 10- to 25-year sentence; he died in 2011 shortly after the release of an award-winning HBO documentary about his life called *You Don't Know Jack*.

Oregon and Washington are currently the only two states in the U.S. that permit physician-assisted suicide, but euthanasia is illegal in all states. Voluntary active euthanasia, which occurs when terminally ill patients request the physician to end their lives, is legal in Switzerland, the Netherlands, and Belgium. Patients who request physician-assisted suicide cite as their main reason the desire to die with dignity (Georges et al., 2007). However, a relatively small number of terminally ill patients actually choose to end their lives in this manner (Hedberg, Hopkins, & Kohn, 2003).

Those who oppose physician-assisted suicide regard as primary the physician's ethical code to "do no harm" and do not wish to present options to patients that they do not find morally acceptable (Curlin, Lawrence, Chin, & Lantos, 2007). Empirical data suggest that dying patients who are suicidal may have treatable psychological symptoms that, when addressed properly, lead them to regain the will to live. They may vary considerably on a day-to-day basis in their feelings about assisted suicide (Pacheco, Hershberger, Markert, & Kumar, 2003). However, as the disease progresses, they may decide to "let go" once they are able to work through their depression (Nissim, Gagliese, & Rodin, 2009).

Another argument against euthanasia and physician-assisted suicide is the one offered by opponents of health care reform in the United States during the year 2009, when talk of "death panels" was used as an argument against changes specifically to Medicare. According to this view, physicians and other health care providers would decide to end a patient's life prematurely as a cost-saving measure. However, a survey of physicians conducted in the United Kingdom suggests that costs are not the primary consideration in these situations. Instead, physicians regarded pain in the patient, no expectation for improvement, and expectation of further suffering as the main reasons to consider ending a patient's life (Seale, 2009).

There are ways that euthanasia and physician-assisted suicide can be humanely managed within a larger palliative approach. A study of nearly 1,700 patient deaths in Belgium showed that patients were more likely to choose to end their lives in palliative care settings where they could also receive spiritual care (Van den Block et al., 2009).

Hospice Care

Increasingly, the provision of end-of-life care is the domain of a **hospice**, a site or program that provides medical and supportive services for dying patients. Within the hospice environment, dying patients are attended to with regard to their needs for physical comfort and psychological and social support and given the opportunity to express and have their spiritual needs met. The care is palliative, focusing on controlling pain and other symptoms, and

<u>**FIGURE 13.7**</u>

Difference Between Physician-Assisted Suicide and Euthanasia

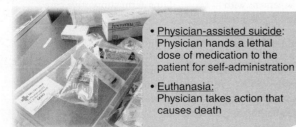

- <u>Physician-assisted suicide:</u> Physician hands a lethal dose of medication to the patient for self-administration

- <u>Euthanasia:</u> Physician takes action that causes death

ETIENNE ANSOTTE/AFT/Getty Images, Inc.

FIGURE 13.8

Illness Timeline and Type of Care

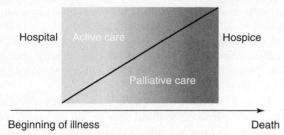

This figure shows the timeline of care provided to dying patients. As the illness progresses, active treatment is reduced and palliative care is increased. Toward the end of illness, hospice care replaces palliative care until death occurs.

Source: Field, M. J., & Cassel, C. K. (Eds), & Committee on Care at the End of Life, Institute of Medicine. (1997). Approaching death: Improving care at the end of life. The National Academies Press. Reprinted with permission from the National Academies Press, Copyright 1997, National Academy of Sciences.

it is likely to take place within the home, beginning when the patient no longer wishes to receive active disease treatment. Physicians supervise the care of the patients, working closely with spiritual and bereavement counselors. Hospice services fit closely with expressed patient needs of obtaining adequate pain control and symptom management, avoiding an extended period of dying, achieving a sense of personal control, relieving the burden they place on others, and strengthening ties with those who are close to them (Kelly et al., 2002).

Figure 13.8 illustrates a model showing how hospice care falls in the continuum of an individual's illness timeline. At the beginning of the illness, the patient is treated entirely with active care in a hospital. As the illness

progresses, the ratio of palliative to active care increases steadily until by the end, the patient receives palliative care only.

The first well-known hospice was St. Christopher's in London, which opened in 1967. The hospice movement spread to the United States in the 1970s. In 1982, hospice benefits were made available to persons on Medicare who had a life expectancy of less than 6 months. By 2007, there were 2,200 hospices in the U.S. and an additional 1,400 home health care agencies that provided hospice services (Centers for Disease Control and Prevention, 2012).

Improving Health Care and Mental Health Services to Dying Patients

Research on end-of-life care, including studies of the needs of and services preferred by dying patients and their families now provides the basis for improved training of health care professionals. One of the largest research projects carried out on the effectiveness of ADs was known as "SUPPORT" ("Study to Understand Prognoses and Preferences for Outcomes and Risks of Treatments") (Lynn et al., 1997). Its authors concluded that the best end-of-life care is adapted to the nature of the patient's needs, rhythms, and situations as these vary over the dying trajectory (Dy & Lynn, 2007) (see Table 13.2).

Professional organizations are increasingly incorporating principles of good end-of-life care into their policy as well as providing suggested training curricula. In 1997, the American Medical Association (AMA) approved a set of guidelines to establish quality care for individuals at the end of life (American Medical Association, 1997). These include providing patients with the opportunity to discuss and plan for end-of-life care, assurance that attempts will be made to provide comfort and respect

TABLE 13.2

Getting Services for the Dying "Right"

	Trajectory		
	Rapid decline over a few weeks or months before death	**Chronic illness with intermittent exacerbations**	**Very poor function with long, slow decline**
Model of Care	Integration with hospice or palliative care	Disease management with education and rapid intervention	Long-term supportive care
Specific Care Needs	Maximize continuity	Provide education on self-care	Plan for long-term care and future problems
	Plan for rapid decline, changing needs, and death	Attempt to avoid hospitalization when possible	Avoid non-beneficial and harmful interventions
	Manage patient's symptoms at home	Assist in decision-making about interventions that might not work	Provide support and assistance for long-term caregivers
	Provide support for caregiver	Plan for potential of sudden death	Provide reliable institutional care when necessary

Source: Adapted from Dy, S., & Lynn, J. (2007). Getting services right for those sick enough to die. *BMJ: British Medical Journal, 334*, 511–513.

the patient's end-of-life wishes, assurance of dignity, and attention to the individual's goals. These rights also include minimizing the burden to the family and assisting the bereaved through the stages of mourning and adjustment.

Several years later, the American Psychological Association passed its own set of guidelines for end-of-life care (American Psychological Association, 2001). These include promoting quality end-of-life care, support for terminally ill people and family members, accurate assessment of depression and cognitive capabilities of dying persons, and assistance with end-of-life decision making. Psychologists are also encouraged to be aware of their own views about the end of life, including recognizing possible biases about providing services based on a patient's disability status, age, sex, sexual orientation, and ethnicity. In addition, the guidelines support access to, and reimbursement for, professional mental health services for seriously ill individuals and their families and promoting and supporting public policies that provide for the psychosocial services for dying individuals and their families. The guidelines also encourage psychologists to work cooperatively with caregivers, medical providers, and multidisciplinary teams to enhance understanding of the psychological aspects of dying and death and to improve quality of care for the dying.

BEREAVEMENT

Bereavement is the process during which people cope with the death of another person. A process that can affect anyone, regardless of age, bereavement is more likely to take place in later adulthood when people have an increased risk of losing their spouse, siblings, extended family, friends, colleagues, and neighbors.

Like the processes of death and dying, we can best understand bereavement as a biopsychosocial process. Physiologically, bereavement places stress on the body, leading to a series of physical symptoms, such as tightness in the chest, shortness of breath, loss of energy and strength, sleep problems, digestive symptoms, and decreased immune system resistance. As we saw in Chapter 9, these symptoms can be severe enough to increase risk of dying in widowed spouses. Emotionally, bereaved individuals experience a range of feelings including anger, depression, anxiety, feelings of emptiness, and preoccupation with thoughts of the deceased. Cognitive changes can also occur in some bereaved individuals, including impaired attention and memory, a desire to withdraw from social activities, and increased risk of accidents. Socioculturally, the loss of a spouse alters the individual's position in the family and community and status within society and may also place the individual at risk of an increasing financial burden. Loss of other family members, friends, and neighbors can dramatically change the individual's support network.

Jeremiah Deasey/iStockphoto

This woman mourns the loss of her husband after his funeral. Adjustment to widowhood can be a long and difficult process.

Losses that fall outside the category of family and friends can also create bereavement reactions. Individuals whose job places them in situations where they work with dying persons may experience severe anxiety symptoms that interfere with their daily lives and ability to perform their jobs. For example, not only survivors but also some recovery workers in a disaster site experience lingering effects of trauma. Those with a history of depression, generalized anxiety disorder, or post-traumatic stress disorder are particularly vulnerable to these effects (Evans, Patt, Giosan, Spielman, & Difede, 2009).

Of all forms of bereavement, the loss of an adult child is perhaps the most devastating. The grief a parent experiences over a child's death is highly intense and is associated with increased risk of depression, guilt, and health complaints lasting for many years (Rogers, Floyd, Seltzer, Greenberg, & Hong, 2008). Moreover, bereaved parents are themselves at higher risk of mortality. A longitudinal study carried out in Sweden showed that mothers of children 18 and under were themselves at greater risk of dying than their nonbereaved counterparts. In this study, although the risk of dying was lower in mothers of children 18 and older, it remained elevated for at least 8 years following the child's death (Rostila, Saarela, & Kawachi, 2012). An Israeli study on an older sample of adults between 75 and 94 years of age showed the effects of parental bereavement can continue for as long as 20 years, even after controlling for age, gender, education, and widowhood status. The effect was more pronounced for mothers than fathers (Cohen-Mansfield, Shmotkin, Malkinson, Bartur, & Hazan, 2013), replicating the findings of the Swedish study.

Bereaved parents may eventually find a sense of meaning and purpose in life, however difficult this may be (Wheeler, 2001). Furthermore, parents may be able to compensate through providing specific forms of coping support to each other during the grieving process (Wijngaards-de Meij et al., 2008).

Religious teachings can provide comfort to the dying and bereaved through their emphasis on the existence of an afterlife and the belief that human events occur because of some higher purpose. The loss of a loved one, particularly when it occurs "prematurely" (i.e., before old age), may be seen as a test of one's faith. Grieving families and friends comfort themselves with the knowledge that they will be reunited in heaven with the deceased, where they will spend eternity together. Another belief in which people may find comfort is that death is a blessed relief from a world of trouble and pain. Bereaved individuals may also seek solace in the belief or perception that they can sense the presence of departed loved ones. As the bereaved or terminally ill attempt to come to grips with the ending of a life, they rely on these beliefs to make sense out of the death or achieve some kind of understanding of its meaning.

Conventional and professional wisdom regarding bereavement was based on the assumption that the survivor must "work through" the death of the deceased (see Figure 13.9). According to this view, the individual must experience a period of mourning, but after that, it is time to move on and seek new relationships and attachments. In part, this view was based on the assumption within psychodynamic theory that to resolve grief normally, emotional bonds to the loved one must be broken (Bowlby, 1980).

Researchers and theorists now recognize that the bereaved can benefit from the continuing bond they feel toward those they have lost; what we call the **attachment view of bereavement** in Figure 13.9. In contrast to the conventional view that the bereaved should eliminate all of the departed person's possessions from the home, the attachment view of bereavement proposes that the bereaved can

continue to benefit from maintaining emotional bonds to the deceased individual. This means that the survivor can hold onto at least some of the spouse's possessions because of their symbolic value without ever having to dispose of them. Similarly, the bereaved individual can benefit from holding onto thoughts and memories of the deceased (Field, Gal-Oz, & Bonanno, 2003). In some ways, the deceased person becomes a part of the survivor's identity.

In some cases, however, the bereaved individual develops a major depressive disorder following the loss. Previous to the publication of the DSM-5, mental health professionals excluded the bereaved from a diagnosis of depression for a 2-month period following the death of the loved one. The DSM-5, like the ICD, no longer contains the bereavement exclusion. Thus, an individual whose reaction to the loss meets the criteria for a major depressive episode, after a two-week period, would receive this diagnosis. The reasoning behind the change in DSM5 is that bereavement-related depression is not a special category and can be diagnosed and treated in similar ways as major depressive disorder (Zisook et al., 2012). The DSM-5 will include another condition, known as persistent complex grief disorder, as a diagnosis for further study.

The **dual-process model of coping with bereavement** proposes that the practical adaptations to loss are as important to the bereaved person's adjustment as the emotional (Stroebe, Schut, & Boerner, 2010). The practical adaptations include the set of life changes that accompany the death, including taking on new tasks or functions, called the "restoration" dimension. The "loss dimension" involves coping with the direct emotional consequences of the death.

One memorable example of restorative coping comes from the main character in the movie *Up*. The main character, Carl Fredericksen, has lost his beloved wife of many years, Ellie. He is embittered and miserable, though determined to go through on his plans he had had with Ellie to revisit South America. However, he becomes transformed through his relationship with Russell, a Boy

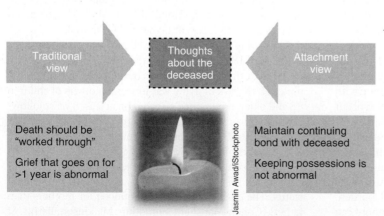

Jasmin Awad/iStockphoto

FIGURE 13.9

Theories of Bereavement

Scout who literally wanders into his life and helps Carl to learn once more how to experience positive emotions.

According to the dual-process model, people are able to adjust to bereavement by alternating between the two dimensions of coping. At times, it is best to confront the emotional loss of the individual; at other times, it is most advantageous to avoid confronting these emotions and instead attempt to manage the practical consequences (Stroebe, Schut, & Stroebe, 2005). People seem to vary in their response to loss, according to this model, on the basis of their attachment style. Securely and insecurely attached individuals show different patterns of mourning and require different types of help to be able to adapt to the loss (Stroebe et al., 2010).

Focusing specifically on personality factors as predictors of reactions to bereavement, Mancini and Bonanno (2009) propose that people who are best able to cope with loss are able to use flexible adaptation—the capacity to shape and adapt behavior to the demands of the stressful event. At other times, though, it is more beneficial to use "repressive coping," in which the painful event is expunged from conscious awareness. Other personal qualities that can help people cope with significant losses, such as widowhood, include optimism, the capacity for positive emotions, and ability to maintain a sense of continuity over time.

The idea that denial may be adaptive, at least for a time, fits well with identity process theory. Let us consider the example of widowhood. Identity assimilation may be a preferable approach during the early days and weeks after the loss of the spouse. Being able to avoid focusing on or ruminating over the loss, as in the healthy denial component of assimilation, may allow individuals to remain optimistic and feel a greater sense of personal control. They may also be better able to carry out the restoration dimension of adapting to the practical changes in their living situation, as stated in the dual process model.

For example, widows who wear their wedding rings and refer to themselves as "Mrs. X" for a time after their husband's death are displaying this type of adaptation. Continuing to identify with their role as wife may help them retain this valued part of their sense of who they are within their families and communities. Over time, through identity accommodation, they may be able to establish greater identity balance by gradually incorporating the notion of themselves as widows into their sense of self.

There are lessons to be learned from the experience of people as they cope with death, dying, and bereavement. In particular, older adults have a remarkable ability to manage the fear of death that causes younger people to react with anxiety and efforts at denial. It may be the ability to move ahead without losing the memory of the departed individuals in one's life that long-lived individuals possess and make it possible for them to survive repeated losses in later adulthood. These individuals have developed ways of integrating the pain of multiple losses into their lives and are able to take their lives in positive new directions. In the future, this process may be made that much less painful by the understanding among mental health professionals of the need that the bereaved have to retain rather than abandon the emotional ties of attachment.

SUMMARY

1. Death is defined as the point of irreversible loss of bodily functions, although this state may be difficult to determine as a result of the advent of life support systems that can keep people alive longer. At the end of life, individuals experience a number of physical changes, many of which are physically uncomfortable, in addition to involving a great deal of pain. Dying trajectories take into account variations in the dying process.

2. Mortality data provide insight into the variations by age, sex, and race in the causes of death. Mortality rates differ according to variables such as ethnicity, geographic variations, marital status, education, and occupation. Mortality rates are decreasing around the world, primarily because of a decrease in infant mortality. However, mortality reductions vary according to the level of a country's economic development. The poor are disproportionately more likely to die in all countries around the world, particularly where there is inadequate health care.

3. A culture's death ethos is reflected in the traditions established by that culture in funeral rituals, belief in the afterlife, and the language used to describe death. Western attitudes toward death have undergone major shifts throughout history. Contemporary American attitudes regard death in a sensationalistic way, but there is a predominant tendency to institutionalize death and make it "invisible." The death with dignity movement has attempted to promote the idea that the individual should have control over the conditions of death. The dying process may occur through one of several dying trajectories, or rate of decline in functioning prior to death.

4. Issues in end-of-life care focus on the extent to which dying patients can exert control over their medical care. As a result of the Patient Self Determination Act, individuals can establish advance directives that indicate whether they wish to extend their lives through artificial means prior to needing to make this decision. The

SUPPORT study on end-of-life care revealed a number of serious weaknesses in the medical care of dying patients in the United States. Many were in pain, felt their preference for palliative care was not respected, and did not believe that they had an adequate opportunity to discuss their preferences with their health care providers. Physician-assisted suicide is a controversial issue that is now legal in the states of Oregon and Washington. Hospices are settings that provide medical and supportive services for dying patients, allowing them to receive personal attention and maintain contact with family.

5. Bereavement is the process of mourning the loss of a close person. The death of a spouse is the most severe loss an individual can experience, but the death of other family members, especially children, causes extreme and long-lasting distress. In the past, theories of grief resolution focused on the need to "work through" a death. Current views emphasize an alternative in which the bereaved are more accepting of the sad feelings accompanying the loss.

14

Successful Aging

AGING TODAY

How to Become an Age Buster

TOPICS

Themes and issues

Models of
 development

Methods

Physical changes

Health

Memory and attention

Higher-order
 cognition

Personality

Relationships

Work and retirement

Mental health

Long-term care

Death and dying

Successful aging

Nobel Prize winners seem to be getting older, according to the Nobel Prize Internet Archive. How do some people manage to remain creative and productive into their 80s, 90s, and beyond? There are many notable examples, such as John Glenn, who resumed his career as an astronaut at the age of 77 when he rode in the space shuttle *Discovery*. Glenn, who famously said, "Too many people, when they get old, think that they have to live by the calendar," personifies age busting.

Glenn provides an example of one of the many people who fit the criteria of being an "age buster;" a person who defies age by not fitting the "typical" pathway for achievement in his or her field. For example, according to one formula used by psychologist Harvey Lehman, composers reach their peak of productivity in their early adult years. Using that criterion, Giuseppe Verdi, who composed his last opera, *Falstaff*, at the age of 80, clearly bucked that productivity curve. There are plenty of modern examples of age busters, including older actresses with leading roles—even though actresses over 30 are often considered "over the hill." Consider Helen Mirren (born in 1945), and Katharine Hepburn, who won three Oscars after she turned 60. For many, the exercise and nutrition guru Jack LaLanne (perhaps best known for his power juicer infomercials) was the ultimate age buster.

How do they do it? John Glenn may have gotten it right when he decided not to think about his age and instead focus on his goals and aspirations. Often the most satisfied and successful older adults are those who don't pay attention to their age, their physical changes (within reason), or the stereotypes about age that are prevalent in our society.

Age busters may be born with an edge that allows them to remain creative and productive throughout their lives. The most highly creative people who continue to blaze trails well into their 80s and 90s were highest in the ability to generate new ideas. They started their productivity early in life and maintained it right up until the end. Michelangelo and Pablo Picasso both started their upward trend of productivity in their youth and continued straight through to midlife and well beyond into their late 80s. Unfortunately, some who are on track to become age busters don't live long enough to fulfill their high creative potential: Mozart and Van Gogh are two such examples. We will never know how long they would have remained productive; however, we can venture a guess that they would have kept going for decades longer than their untimely ends.

Posted by Susan Whitbourne and Stacey Whitbourne

Many people assume that at the end of life, people experience a precipitous drop in their well-being and adjustment. However, as you have learned by now, survival into the later years of adulthood requires that individuals can negotiate the many threats presented to living a long life. As we stated at the outset of this book, to get old you have to not die; to age successfully requires additional adaptive qualities. Because older adults have managed to avoid so many threats that could have ended their lives at a younger age, there may be some special quality about increasingly older individuals that can account, in part, for their having reached this point in their lives.

In this final chapter, we will explore the topics of psychological growth and creativity in the later adult years. Successful agers not only "survive" but also achieve heightened levels of personal expression and happiness. We hope these inspirational qualities can guide and sustain your optimism and hope about your own future adult years.

WHAT IS SUCCESSFUL AGING?

As we discussed in Chapter 1, the process of optimal aging refers to age-related changes that improve the individual's functioning. Throughout this book, we have identified numerous instances in which the loss–gain ratio favors older adults. Here we will try to pinpoint the factors that coalesce in certain older adults to give them an edge and permit them to hold onto their abilities until the very end of their lives.

An Overview of Successful Aging

Let us begin by asking you to think of people you would nominate as successful, or optimal, agers. Do you have a grandmother who you have difficulty keeping up with when the two of you go for a walk? Is there a great-uncle in your family who can beat everyone at word games? How about your mother's cousin, who backpacks around the world for 3 or 4 weeks a year? Perhaps your 80-year-old neighbor has never worn glasses and can hear better than you can. Now, think about well-known older individuals who became cultural icons. Perhaps you have come up with Betty White, the American television comedian and star of television's legendary sitcom about older women, *Golden Girls*. White skyrocketed to popularity in 2010 when a Facebook-inspired movement led the producers of *Saturday Night Live* to invite the 88-year-old to host the show, a performance that garnered her an Emmy Award.

The most widely researched model of optimal aging, proposed by Rowe and Kahn (1998), serves as the theoretical foundation of their work on the MacArthur Foundation Study of Aging in America. As distinct from "usual" aging (i.e., primary), the **Rowe and Kahn definition of successful aging** regards the optimum state to be the absence of disease and disability, high cognitive and physical functioning, and engagement with life.

Subsequent investigators, examining the range of studies falling into the domain of successful aging, have critiqued the Rowe and Kahn definition as being unclear, overly focused on physical and cognitive health, and lacking psychological traits such as spirituality and well-being. A review of the successful aging literature showed that the majority of studies did not use all three criteria in their definitions of successful aging (Depp & Jeste, 2006).

More recently, data from the Health and Retirement Study (HRS), a longitudinal investigation of adults ages 51 and older, was used to develop a successful aging measure incorporating the criteria of no major disease, no limitation in activities of daily living, the ability to perform a variety of physical tasks (such as walking one block), and a telephone-based assessment of cognitive functioning. Participants rated their degree of active engagement by reporting whether they had worked; volunteered; cared for grandchildren; and interacted with a spouse, friends, or neighbors (McLaughlin, Connell, Heeringa, Li, & Roberts, 2010). The HRS measures were assessed over four time intervals from 1998 to 2004.

The participants of the HRS sample who met all four criteria for successful aging decreased during the six years of the study from about 12% to 11% from the first until the fourth time period. These low percentages reflected the fact that the Rowe and Kahn criteria exclude from the definition of successful agers people with health conditions. Roughly half of the sample met the criteria for successful aging across the entire 6-year period in terms of active engagement, high cognitive functioning, and high physical functioning. Approximately 80% met the criterion of no disability, even by the end of the period. However, only 43% reported having no disease at the beginning of the study, and even fewer (37%) did by the point of the final data collection. The criteria are even more restrictive when used with ethnic and minority elders. Comparing self-rated and objectively rated successful aging among a sample of urban African American older adults, Cernin et al. (2011) concluded that self-ratings of successful aging were more strongly related to a wider variety of variables (such as engagement in exercise) compared to the objectively determined ratings that an outsider might make based on the Rowe and Kahn definition.

These findings make sense: even when you think of the successful agers you have either known or seen in the media, some may very well have one or more age-related limitations. That sprightly grandmother may have a few memory lapses now and then, or perhaps she has had cataract surgery. That backpacking mother's cousin may need to use a cane as she navigates her way around the world. You may also know other individuals who have an age-related physical disability that severely limits their mobility, but whose sense of optimism and hope rivals yours, even on your best days.

The Rowe and Kahn definition of successful aging has also been criticized on the grounds that it does not take into account the individual's social context in the form of cultural norms, or life-span constraints on educational and occupational opportunities. Supporting this idea was the fact that in the HRS, successful agers were more heavily represented among Whites and among those with a college education or higher (McLaughlin et al., 2010). The Survey of Health, Aging and Retirement in Europe (SHARE) on 22,464 men and women in 13 European countries averaging 63 years old found important contributors to successful aging of early childhood conditions, including parental social class and income (Brandt, Deindl, & Hank, 2012). Thus, successful aging is best viewed as a lifelong process reflecting the influence of multiple factors, including favorable or unfavorable childhood conditions.

A model that focuses on a broader range of influences is the **World Health Organization (WHO) definition of active aging**, which encompasses the process of optimizing opportunities for health, participation, and security in order to enhance quality of life as people age (World Health Organization, 2002a). Figure 14.1 shows the WHO model of active aging which, in many ways, is like that of the Bronfenbrenner (1994) ecological perspective in that it specifies a role for social, health care, and economic determinants as well as pointing to the importance of the physical environment. Noteworthy is the fact that WHO makes explicit the role of autonomy and independence, placing greater emphasis on the individual's ability to get around in the environment, rather than on whether the individual needs physical accommodations due to disability.

It was with these criticisms in mind, then, that University of California at San Diego researchers embarked on a project to overcome the limitations that they identified in the Rowe and Kahn model (Vahia, Thompson, Depp, Allison, & Jeste, 2012). They administered several standardized measures to nearly 1,950 women participating in the San Diego site of the Women's Health Initiative (WHI) Study in an attempt to predict self-rated successful aging. These participants had been part of a longitudinal study that had followed them for 7 years between 1994 and 2005. The successful aging sample women ranged from 60 to 89; at the start of the study, all were postmenopausal, free of substance-abuse disorders, and relatively healthy (i.e., without known terminal illnesses).

Vahia and colleagues measured a range of qualities that they believed would relate to successful aging, including self-efficacy, optimism, attitudes toward aging in general, attitudes toward one's own aging, resilience, the endorsement of physical and emotional symptoms, depression (using the CES-D), and a test of cognitive functioning (orientation, crystallized knowledge, and spatial skills). Using a method similar to path analysis, they found that the women highest in subjectively rated successful aging had high scores in what they called psychological protective factors of resilience, self-efficacy, and optimism; were high in positive emotional functioning (low in CES-D and self-rated emotional symptoms); and rated themselves low in physical symptoms, although physical symptoms were not as strongly related to successful aging as the resilience and emotional factors. Performance on the cognitive tests did not predict self-rated successful aging in these women.

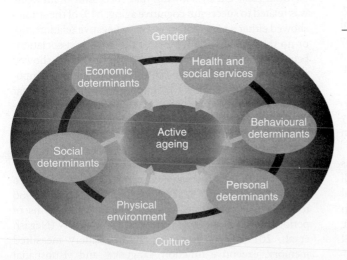

FIGURE 14.1

World Health Organization Model of the Determinants of Active Ageing

Source: World Health Organization (2002). *Active ageing: A policy framework.* Geneva, Switzerland, World Health Organization. http://whqlibdoc.who.int/hq/2002/WHO_NMH_NPH_02.8.pdf

The Vahia et al. (2012) study's findings support the contention that the Rowe and Kahn definition of successful aging is overly narrow and that psychological resilience and optimism are more important contributors to the older individual's own sense of aging well than are objective determinants. Building on these strengths, older adults may employ a range of active coping methods to help them achieve their desired goals which, as they think toward their future, can include preparing for potential stressors. Through proactive coping, successfully aging older adults can anticipate events that they believe represent a threat to their well-being and then engage in mental preparation to reduce the impact of the stress when it occurs. When the stressful event does occur, it will drain less of their coping resources (Ouwehand, de Ridder, & Bensing, 2007).

Sexuality is another component of successful aging, known to play a role in overall health and well-being in the midlife and later years (Lindau & Gavrilova, 2010). The women participating in the San Diego WHI also provided information about their current levels of sexuality, allowing the researchers to evaluate the contributions of involvement in sexual relations in the context of the larger study. They were asked to report on whether sex was still a "part of your life" in the last 6 months, with or without a partner; to rate their levels of sexual desire, arousal, and satisfaction; to indicate their frequency of reaching orgasm; and their level of sexual dysfunction (pain, need for lubrication, tightness). Although sexual activity and functioning were negatively correlated with age, there was no relationship between age and sexual satisfaction. The overall scores of these women on the successful aging measures were related to sexual satisfaction but, again, not related to actual sexual activity.

Actual physical health, then, appears to be less important in predicting successful aging, even in an area of functioning as important to overall well-being as sexuality. Specifically addressing disability's role in the successful aging model, researchers conducting a large-scale study of over 2,200 adults 61 to 85 years old carried out in Australia developed a structural equation model in which they predicted successful aging from a variety of physical, psychological, and social measures (Parslow, Lewis, & Nay, 2011). In their final model, health behaviors, particularly physical exercise, predicted successful aging to an even greater extent than did social support or social contact.

Thus, these findings reinforce the fact that exercise is an important preventative measure in predicting overall well-being. However, even those highest on the successful aging factor reported that they had several chronic health conditions. From this, we can infer that people with chronic disease need not be prevented from enjoying a high level of quality of life.

Successful Cognitive Aging

A number of investigators are exploring the notion that successful aging in the cognitive sense remains an important topic in its own right. As we have explored in earlier chapters, there are large interindividual differences in cognitive functioning, so we know that some people maintain higher levels of performance than do others. Moreover, an individual's cognitive functioning plays an important role in the ability to adapt to the demands of everyday life, as we saw in Chapter 7. Many older adults, as we have also seen, regard cognitive functioning as central to their identities; this is one reason that they so greatly fear developing Alzheimer's disease and other forms of neurocognitive disorder.

In keeping with this focus, then, **successful cognitive aging** can be defined as cognitive performance that is above the average for an individual's age group as objectively measured (Fiocco & Yaffe, 2010). A sample of "Superagers," defined as individuals 80 and older with superior episodic memory (i.e., comparable to that of middle-aged adults), were found by Harrison and colleagues (2012) on MRIs to have thicker cerebral cortex volume. Their memory performance, in turn, was correlated positively with the cortical thickness. They also showed greater volume of the cingulate cortex, an area that may be involved in preventing episodic memory loss.

However, the sheer size of a brain region may not be as important as the way that brain region is organized or functions. In a review of 80 studies comparing brain function and cognitive performance in older adults, Eyler and colleagues (2011) looked for relationships between MRI and PET scan activity in the cortical lobes and subcortical areas involved in movement, sensory processing, and the insula, located deep within the cortex. The findings were far from clear-cut in showing that successful brain aging was related to successful cognitive aging: 61% of the studies showed either a mixed relationship, a negative relationship, or no relationship at all. More of the positive associations between brain activity and cognitive performance showed up for the frontal cortex (35%). In the medial temporal lobe, which includes the hippocampus, there were far fewer significant relationships (20%). Consistent with the HAROLD and PASA compensation models (see Chapter 4), it is possible that the successful brain agers are most likely to show greater abilities to take advantage of brain plasticity (Greenwood, 2007).

A longitudinal investigation carried out on 560 Mayo Clinic patients age 65 and older from the years 1986 to 2004 defined successful cognitive aging in terms of performance on a neuropsychological test battery (Negash et al., 2011). The tests used in this battery measured memory, executive function, language, and visuospatial skills. The outcome variables used to define successful cognitive aging were mortality status (remaining alive) and lack of a diagnosis of mild cognitive impairment. Three models of successful aging were compared using differing cutoff points on the neuropsychological tests. The model with the best predictive value identified 56 participants as successful agers with the remaining 504 as "typical agers." In addition to being more highly educated, the cognitively-defined successful agers had scored within the top 10% across all of the tests. This model yielded better predictions than a model based on comparing test scores to the norms of young adults. Thus, cognitive aging may be best understood as maintaining relative superiority to a person's age peers, not to standards based on the performance of young adults.

The factors that predict successful cognitive functioning in older adults may be different than those which predict better functioning among younger adults. C-reactive protein (CRP), a known risk factor for cardiovascular disease in midlife, seems to serve a protective function against neurocognitive disorder for older adults. In a longitudinal study of male veterans and age-matched community volunteers and their first-degree relatives, the individuals with the highest CRP levels were least likely to develop neurocognitive disorders over the 6-year period of the study (Silverman et al., 2012).

There is also support for the idea in successful aging models of remaining engaged with life (Reichstadt, Depp, Palinkas, Folsom, & Jeste, 2007). Older adults with social support (Bowling, Banister, Sutton, Evans, & Windsor, 2002), particularly support from family (Kissane &

McLaren, 2006), are most likely to have high ratings of successful aging.

Unfortunately, many younger people have a tendency to view the happy and productive older person as an anomaly. Cultural icons such as Jack LaLanne and Betty White are beloved by the young in part because they seem so atypical of their age group. Many people automatically assume that aging inevitably brings about depression and hopelessness, so when people do not show these qualities, they must be truly special. However, as we have seen elsewhere in this book, most older people do not become depressed, and personality development in middle and later adulthood appears to be in the positive direction of greater adaptive ability. Most older adults preserve their cognitive abilities to a very large degree. Studies of centenarians (Motta, Bennati, Ferlito, Malaguarnera, & Motta, 2005) and super-centenarians (those over 110) show that those who live to these advanced ages are sturdy both cognitively and physiologically (Schoenhofen et al., 2006).

Factors That Promote Successful Aging

As we have just seen, people may age successfully even if they have a number of chronic health conditions. Older adults are also less likely to experience serious mental illness, as you learned in Chapter 12.

Interest in successful aging fits more generally within the larger field of **positive psychology**, which seeks to provide a greater understanding of the strengths and virtues that enable individuals and communities to thrive. Within this tradition, **life satisfaction** is the overall assessment of an individual's feelings and attitudes about one's life

David Crausby/Alamy

Members of the Red Hat Society at the Lord Mayor's parade in London on New Year's Day. The Red Hat Society is an organization of women 50 and older who get together for tea wearing red hats and purple dresses.

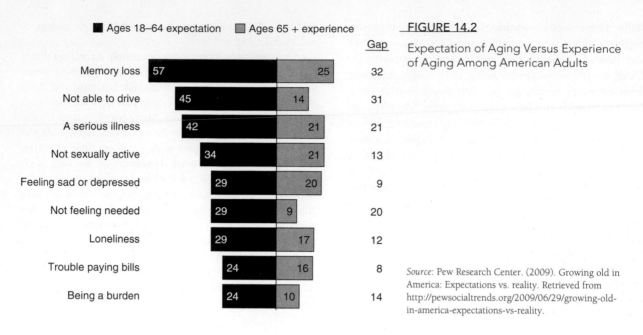

Ages 18–64 expectation   Ages 65 + experience

		Gap
Memory loss	57 / 25	32
Not able to drive	45 / 14	31
A serious illness	42 / 21	21
Not sexually active	34 / 21	13
Feeling sad or depressed	29 / 20	9
Not feeling needed	29 / 9	20
Loneliness	29 / 17	12
Trouble paying bills	24 / 16	8
Being a burden	24 / 10	14

FIGURE 14.2

Expectation of Aging Versus Experience of Aging Among American Adults

Source: Pew Research Center. (2009). Growing old in America: Expectations vs. reality. Retrieved from http://pewsocialtrends.org/2009/06/29/growing-old-in-america-expectations-vs-reality.

at a particular point in time. **Subjective well-being** is the individual's overall sense of happiness. These two terms clearly are related; however, somewhat separate research traditions have developed around their use, so it is helpful to treat them as distinct. One difference is that life satisfaction may be more of a cognitive evaluation, but subjective well-being is more affective or emotional. Together, they represent a complete picture of a person's well-being (Diener, 1999). Therefore, unless we specify otherwise, we will focus on subjective well-being as a way to understand the paths that people take toward successful aging in the adult years.

One of the great puzzles for researchers who study successful aging is to explain why so many adults are able to remain positive in their approach to life despite their accumulating chronic health conditions, normal age-related changes, and alterations in their social roles and financial security. The **paradox of well-being** refers to the well-established finding that older adults maintain high subjective well-being despite facing challenges from their objective circumstances.

One reason that the successful ager is thought of as the miraculous exception rather than the rule is that many theorists, researchers, and laypeople believe in the **social indicator model** (Mroczek & Kolarz, 1998). According to this model, demographic and social structural variables, such as age, gender, marital status, and income, account for individual differences in levels of well-being. Because by demographic standards older individuals are in a disadvantaged position on these indices, they should therefore be less happy than the young. When an older adult is able to avoid becoming depressed by the potentially disturbing circumstances of poor health, widowhood, and low income, then that person seems deserving of some kind of special recognition.

Judged solely by the standards of being able to avoid the despair brought about by lower status on important social indicators, however, there would in fact be many successful agers. A national survey by the Pew Research Center (2009) of almost 3,000 Americans showed that most older adults manage to enjoy relatively high subjective well-being on a variety of indices. Among respondents 75 and older, 81% said they were "very" or "pretty" happy, and only 19% rated themselves as "not too happy." Interestingly, as we show in Figure 14.2, most older adults rated their own experience of aging more favorably than younger adults would expect along a variety of dimensions from extent of memory loss to the feeling of being a burden on others.

The question is whether older adults have developed a set of coping skills over their lifetimes that allow them to frame events that younger adults would consider detrimental to their own well-being or even that the older adults would have found challenging when they themselves were younger. It is also possible that cohort effects lead current generations of older adults to feel higher levels of subjective well-being because they grew up with different expectations about what their lives would be like than is true for current cohorts of young adults. Another possibility is that the paradox of well-being reflects a survival effect, and that the older adults who are still alive and available to be tested are hardier and more optimistic than those who are either no longer in the population or unwilling to be sampled. Perhaps these individuals were always inclined to view the world in a positive way, and the fact that they are the ones left standing at the end of life reflects their particular optimistic bias.

A far clearer understanding of the competing effects of age and cohort comes from findings reported by Baird, Lucas, and Donnellen (2010), who used a cohort sequential design and multilevel modeling to analyze the data from two large European national surveys. The German Socio-Economic Panel Study was begun in 1984 with a full sample of over 40,000 participants. The original participants were asked to rate their happiness on an 11-point scale. They were followed over time, but at each testing occasion, new samples were added, making it possible for the researchers to follow distinct cohorts over the course of time. The final sample available for analysis consisted of nearly 21,000 adults who had participated an average of eight times.

After controlling for the effects of cohort, time of measurement, and number of test occasions, Baird et al. (2010) concluded that the course of life satisfaction across adulthood was relatively stable until the very oldest ages, dropping slightly after the age of 70 and then more steadily in the 80s. The researchers' confidence in this picture was enhanced by the fact that they were able to control for so many competing interpretations. However, when they

conducted similar analyses on the British Household Panel Study (BHPS) (see Figure 14.3), they found a different pattern. Life satisfaction among this sample decreased early in adulthood, increased from mid to late adulthood, and then declined at the very end of life. In both cases, however, the results seemed to contradict predictions from socioemotional selectivity theory of a general upturn in satisfaction among the oldest-old. Furthermore, they make the paradox of well-being a little less paradoxical. It appears that at the very end of life, individuals may be influenced by objective life circumstances and, on average, show a gradual decline of their overall well-being.

It is still possible that those people who remain happier longer are the ones who view the world in an optimistic manner, which, in turn, allows them to remain high in life satisfaction when their age peers are not. The **set point perspective** proposes that people's personalities influence their level of well-being throughout life. For example, in a study of 2,000 German emerging adults, university students higher in neuroticism were found to have experienced more negative life events. These negative events, in turn, could further influence their levels of well-being (Lüdtke, Roberts, Trautwein, & Nagy, 2011). Conversely, children high in self-esteem in childhood seem have higher self-esteem throughout their lives, which could further influence their levels of well-being (Robins & Trzesniewski, 2005).

It appears that personality traits may change in tandem with changes in well-being throughout adulthood. Using MIDUS data, Hill et al. (2012) found that people higher

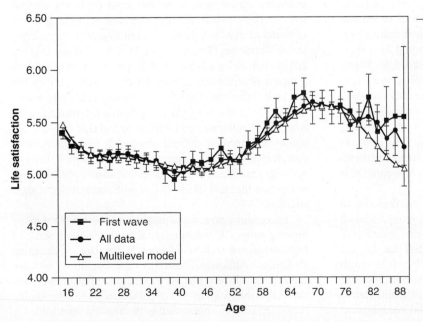

FIGURE 14.3

Results From Baird, Lucas, and Donnellen (2010) on Life Satisfaction in Adulthood

Source: Baird, B. M., Lucas, R. E., & Donnellan, M. B. (2010). Life satisfaction across the lifespan: Findings from two nationally representative panel studies. *Social Indicators Research, 99,* 183–203. doi: 10.1007/s11205-010-9584-9

on the positive poles of the FFM traits had higher levels of well-being. Over time, positive changes in these traits correlated with further increases in well-being. The study's findings suggest that personality appears to act as more than a set "point" in that its relationship to changes in well-being continues to evolve.

That being said, however, there are connections between objective social indicators and subjective well-being. Studies of older adults show positive associations between feelings of well-being and personal resources, including physical functioning and adequacy of financial support (Katz, 2009). Not only physical functioning, but participation in physical activity also contributes to the subjective well-being of older adults (Mhaoláin et al., 2012). Education level, in turn, predicts high levels of physical and cognitive functioning, which also predict high levels of subjective well-being (Jang, Choi, & Kim, 2009).

As we have noted many times throughout the book, there are advantages to having higher educational levels and income in terms of health status although money and status cannot guarantee happiness, they can help to resolve many of the challenges that people at the lower end of the income spectrum experience (Deacon, 2008). Even after adjusting for medical conditions, lower socioeconomic status is related to depression and poorer health-related status (Rostad, Deeg, & Schei, 2009).

That subjective well-being reflects an individual's evaluation of his or her life circumstances was suggested by McAdams, Lucas, and Donnellen (2012), who examined data from the BHPS from 1996 to 2004. They were able to determine the extent to which overall life satisfaction related to satisfaction in domains, including health, income, housing, spouse or partner, job, social life, and the amount and use of leisure time. If the set point perspective determined well-being, then happier people should have rated each domain more positively. However, instead, McAdams et al. found that the life-span patterns of change on the specific subdomains differed considerably. The data suggested that when people arrive at their sense of overall well-being, they do so by mentally combining all the specific domains. Life satisfaction in older adults will be high if the positives outweigh the negatives, but low if they experience themselves more negatively in the subdomains that contribute to overall well-being.

Satisfaction with health was one of the domains to show an accelerated decline in the oldest groups studied by McAdams et al. As we noted earlier, however, individuals may be in poor health objectively but still feel that they are aging successfully. As a result, self-rated physical health may differ from a more objective measure of physical functioning. Researchers believe that older adults derive their self-rated health ratings through **social comparison**, the process that occurs when people rate themselves relative to their primary reference group. If people in the older adult's reference group are in poorer health, then the individual's self-rated health will be higher than if the comparison group is in better health.

Using data from the HRS, Yin et al. (2011) found that physical functioning had a decreasing relationship to self-rated health as individuals grew older. However, there were differences within the older groups in the physical functioning-health ratings relationship. Whites were more likely to have their actual physical functioning affect their self-rated health, as were older adults with advanced educational degrees. Thus, older adults from non-White racial/ethnic groups and less education whose health is disadvantaged may be more likely to compare themselves to members of a group which, like theirs, is in poor health. As a result, they may not show decreases in ratings of their own health.

Subjective well-being in later life also seems related to the tendency that people have over the years of adulthood to create and embellish their **life story** or narrative view of the past in which they express their identities over the course of time (Whitbourne, 1985). Although individuals may differ in their narrative styles (Goodson, 2013), the process of constructing a life story continues throughout life and can serve a variety of adaptive functions (McAdams, 2011). Older adults seem to benefit from a life story that emphasizes their achievements and experiences that reflect favorably on their identity, altering the way that they interpret events that might otherwise detract from their self-esteem (Whitbourne et al., 2002). Emerging adults seem to benefit from exploring alternatives as they arrive at identity commitments as long as this exploration does not involve a high degree of rumination and self-criticism (Ritchie, Meca, Madrazo, Schwartz et al., 2013). For older adults, identity processes may provide a means of maintaining high levels of well-being in the face of less than satisfactory circumstances. Identity assimilation allows them to place a positive interpretation on what might otherwise cause them to feel that they are not accomplishing their desired objectives. Eventually, however, they may come to experience declines which they can no longer minimize and at that point, identity balance can bring their life story closer in line with the realities of their situation.

Successful aging is a complex process involving many moving parts. Older adults are able to develop a sense of high subjective well-being even in the face of daunting challenges. Although researchers are beginning to view subjective well-being as subject to potential threats very late in life, the vast majority of older adults avoid becoming depressed or even dissatisfied with their life situations.

CREATIVITY AND AGING

Successful aging is more than a state of mind. Individuals who age optimally not only feel good, they are capable of producing good work. You do not have to be a creative genius to age successfully, but the older adults who have become the creative geniuses of the past and present can inspire you to think about the aging process in ways you never thought imaginable.

What Is Creativity?

A creative person is conventionally thought of as someone who has the ability to produce a notable or extraordinary piece of work; however, more generally, researchers define **creativity** as the ability to generate products or ideas that are original, appropriate, and have an impact on others. Appropriateness in this context means that other people appreciate the work and may want to purchase or use it. Creativity may describe the work of an eminent genius, but it can also apply to everyday behaviors exhibited in the individual's life space, including cooking, scrapbooking, taking photographs, and even wearing different hairstyles (Ivcevic & Mayer, 2009). To distinguish eminent creativity from everyday creativity, researchers talk about "Big C" (eminent) and "little c" (everyday); individuals may also show "mini-C" creativity, which refers to creativity in constructing personal, or self, understanding (Beghetto & Kaufman, 2007).

Neuroscientists are attempting to learn what happens during the brain while the individual is engaged in the creative process by comparing brain scans of individuals involved in creative activities compared to everyday thinking. Some of the tasks investigated include analogies (thinking of novel relations between words), metaphors (making up a concrete representation of an abstract concept) (Vartanian, 2012), and thinking of alternative uses of objects, also called conceptual expansion (Abraham et al., 2012). It appears that the entire brain is activated during creative activity, not just the right side, contradicting the myth that creativity is a right-hemisphere process. Moreover, the areas involved in creative thought are not necessarily any different than those involved in everyday tasks. It is likely that creativity emerges from a complex set of interrelated processes within the brain (Sawyer, 2011).

Based on the idea that the personality trait of openness to experience would be related to cognitive flexibility, another index of creativity, researchers studied the correlation between brain activation and scores on this measure among older men and women tested 2 years apart. For men, higher openness scores were related to the activation of the anterior cingulate cortex (involved in monitoring processes). Prefrontal activation (reflecting flexibility) was related to women's openness scores; for both sexes, openness was also related to frontal lobe activation (Sutin, Beason-Held, Resnick, & Costa, 2009). Thus, the brains of individuals who may be more creative dispositionally may differ in important ways in later life.

Personality openness may, in turn, be a protective factor against mortality. In a longitudinal study of aging veterans, Turiano and colleagues (2012) found a positive association between scores on the creativity facet of openness to experience and lower risk of mortality. The protective effects of personality creativity remained statistically significant even after the researchers controlled for other correlates of mortality including age, education, health status, and health risk behaviors.

Creativity is likely to be highest when the prefrontal cortex has sufficiently matured so that people are able to be flexible but at the same time have had sufficient training in their area of expertise so that they can put that flexibility to good use (Dietrich, 2004). Presumably, this happy coincidence occurs about 20 years into the career, when most people are in midlife (Feist, 2006). If not, people can also enhance their creativity by exercising these areas of the brain through mental activity. Involvement in challenging mental exercise can not only stimulate cognitive functioning and well-being but also illustrates the ability of older adults to engage creatively with life. McFadden & Basting (2010, p. 154) point out that when it comes to creativity, "what's good for the person is usually good for the brain."

Creative Older Adults

This conceptual background to understanding creativity shows that creativity may involve many of the same features of successful aging. Among the ranks of the eminently creative (who are creative with a "capital C") are highly successful artists, musicians, writers, and performers who continued to produce highly acclaimed works well into their later decades. Outside of the arts, older adults continue to make important contributions to the world in everything from politics to science.

The first systematic effort to identify age trends in productive accomplishments was Lehman's 1953 book *Age and Achievement* (1953). Lehman analyzed the quantity and quality of creative products by age and discipline and concluded that the peak of productivity in the adult years tends to occur prior to the age of 40, often between 30 and 35. However, Lehman found that earlier peaks are reached in the sciences and in fields in which success was dependent on intellectual imagination and physical ability. Later this observation was dubbed the **Planck hypothesis** after the brilliant German scientist Max Planck, to refer to the tendency of peak scientific productivity to occur in early adulthood (Dietrich, 2004).

Lehman claimed that older adults have the edge in fields that rely on experience and judgment, such as politics and diplomacy. Authors write their "best books" in between these extremes, for an author's success involves imagination, discipline, and the philosophical perspectives gained from experience. He also noted that some artists who lived until very old age produced their best works very late in life, as did other notable individuals in virtually every field of accomplishment.

Dennis (1966) examined the total output, regardless of the quality of work, by contributors to seven domains within the arts and sciences. As you can see from Figure 14.4, although there is a rather steep decline after the peak age in the arts, and somewhat less so in the sciences, scholarly productivity is steady throughout later adulthood, with even a slight peak in the 60s. Dennis attempted to compensate for the differential ages that creators lived to be (which would obviously cut down on productivity in the later years), by limiting his sample to people who lived to be at least 80 years old.

So far, we can summarize the studies by Lehman and Dennis as depicting an average curve showing a rapid increase in creative output that reaches a career peak in the late 30s or early 40s, after which a steady decline begins. The peak and rate of decline vary by discipline, but the decline occurs nevertheless. Based on this research, one would have to argue that creative productivity is unlikely to be a component of successful aging.

Simonton (1997) approached the issue of age and creativity by developing a mathematical model to calculate

FIGURE 14.4

Age and Productivity by Discipline as Judged by Dennis (1966)

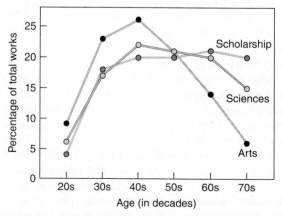

Source: Dennis, W. (1966). Creative productivity between the ages of 20 and 80 years. *Journal of Gerontology, 21*, 1–8.

age's relationship to creativity while controlling for some possible confounding factors such as at what age creative individuals began their careers and how long they live. Instead of using chronological age, Simonton based his model on **career age**, which is the age at which an individual begins to embark on his or her career. On the average, according to Simonton's model, productivity in later life is higher among people who begin their careers at a later age.

However, an individual's productivity also reflects **creative potential**, which is the total number of works that a person could hypothetically produce in a life span with no upper limits. A person with high creative potential might produce thousands of works of art during his or her career, but a person with low creative potential may produce 10, 20, or perhaps just 1 (a "one-hit wonder").

You can see how creative potential and career age combine in Table 14.1 to produce different patterns of age and achievement. Laurie London was a young one-hit wonder who never again wrote a hit song; Margaret Mitchell was an older one-hit wonder. Mitchell would qualify for writing her "best book" at the age of 37, but had she started earlier, it is not clear whether she would have produced many more. In contrast, Jane Austen, who died at the age of 41, produced one major novel a year in the 7 years before her death at the age of 41.

Pablo Picasso and Anna Marie Robertson both produced notable works in old age. We can assume that Anna Mary Robertson, who started painting in her 70s (and lived to 101) had high creative potential by virtue of the fact that she produced thousands of paintings during her lifetime. However, because she started late in life, none of her accomplishments would count toward the productivity score for early adulthood. Conversely, Wolfgang Amadeus Mozart began his career in childhood, writing at least 600 pieces of music before his death at the age of 35. Therefore, his productivity in old age cannot be calculated.

There is some connection between the quantity and quality of an individual's creative productivity. The **equal odds rule** predicts that creative individuals who produce more works are more likely to produce one or more of high quality than are those who produce fewer works. If this sounds familiar, it is because it is the same as the law in sports that "If you don't shoot, you can't score." The equal odds rule implies that people are most likely to produce their best work during their peak period of productivity on the basis of probability alone. Verdi composed his first operatic masterpiece at the age of 29 and his last at the age of 80. He had a relatively high probability of creating a masterwork during his late career because he continued to produce such a large number of pieces of music right up until the end.

TABLE 14.1
Examples of High and Low Creative Potential and Career Onset

Creative potential	Career age	Example
Low	Younger	Laurie London ("He's Got the Whole World in His Hands" recorded at age 13)
Low	Older	Margaret Mitchell ("Gone With the Wind" at age 37)
High	Younger	Pablo Picasso
High	Older	Anna Mary Robertson ("Grandma Moses")

Imo/iStockphoto

Contemporary older adults have an even better chance of remaining productive throughout their later years than those living in previous centuries. As Simonton points out (2012), as life expectancy continues to increase with improvements in health care and other living conditions, older adults are likely to have a longer empty nest period after their children leave the home. Modern technology also makes more resources available on the Internet so that the artist need not be the "lone genius" of years past. With more leisure time, the older artist also has the chance to pursue multiple interests, making it possible to continue to develop the personality openness that fosters creativity. Improved communication also means that artists, scientists, writers, and creative individuals from many fields can collaborate to cross-foster new ideas and projects. Older and younger collaborators can further enhance each other's productivity, leading both to improve the quality and quantity of their output.

- **Old age style**– simpler and more powerful (including "swan song")
- **Lastingness**– endurance over time
- **Integration and synthesis**– incorporate complex and multiple features
- **Willingness to criticize**– see own work objectively

Adam Berent/iStockphoto

Characteristics of Last Works

The creative works produced by older adults possess special qualities not observed earlier in adulthood, as you can see from Figure 14.5. You almost certainly recognize the famous statue of Abraham Lincoln that sits within the Lincoln Memorial in Washington, D.C. This statue was created by Massachusetts sculptor Chester French when he was 70 years old. To many, its power exemplifies key components of the types of work that creative individuals can produce late in life by virtue of their experience, perspective, and desire to leave a permanent impact on the world.

The **old-age style** is an approach to art that eliminates the fine details and instead presents the essence of the work's intended meaning (Lindauer, 1998). When you see a creation produced by an older artist showing the old age style, you are likely to have a strong emotional reaction. This is because the artist has moved away from a precise and objective rendering of the image that focuses

FIGURE 14.5

Characteristics of Last Works

on formal perfection. The work has an impact on you because the artist intentionally sought to share his or her subjective experience. In a painting, the artist may eliminate almost everything except color and shape. A sculptor may concentrate more on the form and underlying emotion of the subject of the piece rather than on representing each and every detail, such as each hair on the head or nail on the hand. If you look carefully at the sculpture of Lincoln, you notice the strong eyes, cheekbones, and hands because French carved those out in bold relief.

The emergence of an old age style can be seen in the works of history's most famous artists, including Michelangelo, Rembrandt, Renoir, Matisse, Degas, Georgia O'Keeffe, and Picasso. Henri Matisse explicitly talked about this change in his own perspective as a "distillation of form. I now keep only the sign which suffices, necessary for its existence in its own form, for the composition as I conceive it" (Brill, 1967). Another excellent example of the old age style is provided by the work of Michelangelo, who sculpted a Pietà late in his life (the Pietà Rondanini), less detailed than the more meticulously sculpted iconic Pietà in the Vatican for which he is much more famous. Some art historians regard the later work as more emotionally charged and hence effective.

Older artists often focus their work on topics related to aging and death. It is not necessarily that the work has become morbid or depressing, but that it presents the reality of the artist's life and impending death in a manner that may have particular clarity and a strong impact on the viewer. Writers become more reflective, introspective, and subjective (Lubart & Sternberg, 1998). They may portray the characters in their novels more realistically but also with greater empathy, and they come to take on greater complexity and a sense of timelessness (Adams-Price, 1998).

As a preface to the old age style, creativity may be expressed in midlife as "paring down life to the essentials." Midlife may bring with it not a crisis involving confrontation with mortality, but a heightened sense of urgency to create a lasting legacy. Strenger (2009), from this vantage point, analyzed the productive works of a 20th-century educator in the business field, Charles Handy. At the age of 49, Handy left behind a prestigious position in industry because he felt he had lost touch with his sense of inner purpose. He started a new life as an author and, having written 17 books between the ages of 50 and 75, sought and eventually found new meaning in life.

Related to old age style is the **swan song**, a creative work produced at the very end of an artist's life (Simonton, 1989). In music, a swan song has shorter main themes and simpler melodies than the prior works of the composer. As

Michelangelo's Pieta di Rondanini, one of his last sculptures, is thought to represent the essence of the old age style with its lack of detail and focus on raw emotions. It therefore contrasts dramatically with his early Pieta in the Sistine Chapel.

a result, the swan song is evocative and easy to remember. Simonton considers the best example of the swan song to be "Lachrymosa," from Mozart's last work, the Requiem in D Minor. Although Mozart was not old when he died, he knew that his death was imminent and fittingly wrote a piece of music intended to honor the dead. Centuries later, this melody was to be the music played in the funeral scene of the movie, *Amadeus*, creating the emotionally compelling backdrop to the burial of Mozart's body in a pauper's grave.

As in Mozart's case, artists may produce swan songs because they are aware that they are at the end of their lives. The swan song is the ultimate expression of old age style as the artist seeks to produce a work for the ages. These works often become some of the most successful that the composer produces, and thus in many ways may grant the composer a certain immortality.

Perhaps because of their simplicity and emotional power, the work of older artists also demonstrates **lastingness** in that they persist over time; "that which does not end" (Delbanco, 2011, p. 244). Creative older adults experience a deep sense of gratification and experience the process as rewarding regardless of the result. However, works that endure nevertheless resonate and touch the lives of others.

Along these lines, older creative adults may become better at critiquing their own work. An intensive study of Beethoven's letters and notes from conversations with others showed that as he aged, he was able to make more "accurate" assessments of the quality of his works, as judged by the frequency with which his works were subsequently performed and recorded (Kozbelt, 2007).

The work of scientists and academicians may show a different set of changes as they age. According to the Planck hypothesis, the work of young scientists is more innovative than that of older scientists. Perhaps reflecting in part the nature of scientific discovery, and in part the greater experience they gain in their field, older scientists shift their priorities. The aging scientist may become more involved in the writing of texts and integrative review articles rather than in conducting research to produce new scientific discoveries. If they work in academic settings, they may move up the administrative hierarchy to a position of authority, meaning that they have less time for their own research.

Some aging academicians turn to the subject of aging; this was true for B. F. Skinner, who wrote *Enjoy Old Age: A Practical Guide* (Skinner & Vaughan, 1983) toward the end of his life. In fact, the first geriatrics text was written by Sir John Floyer in the early 1700s when he was 75 years old. An aging inventor may start to address age-related concerns, as was the case for Benjamin Franklin, who fabricated the first known pair of bifocals when he was 78 years old, well past the age when most people start to need them.

The old age style may be stimulated by proximity to death, a desire to leave behind a legacy, or perhaps age-related changes or health problems. Beethoven became deaf in his later years, and his musical style also changed. For example, in his late string quartets, he became more expressive and less bound by conventional forms. Blindness forced changes in the painting of a number of well-known older artists, including Georgia O'Keeffe, Mary Cassatt, Edgar Degas, and Claude Monet. Henri Matisse suffered from stomach cancer and was confined to a wheelchair at the end of his life. Despite these severe limitations, these artists continued to produce great works until or nearly until their last years of life.

In the case of the artist Monet, cataracts caused changes not only in the clarity of his vision but in his ability to see colors. When he developed cataracts, he was literally unable to see the colors on the canvas that he knew appeared in nature. Even special glasses (colored yellow) could not correct this defect. The paintings of water lilies he created at this time were shaded in reds, oranges, and yellow instead of blue, green, and purple. It was not until he had successful cataract surgery at the age of 85 that his color vision was restored. His final work, an enormous series of water lilies, was installed in a Paris museum after his death. The colors in these final paintings were as vibrant as they had been in his earlier work. In 1908, he wrote, "These landscapes of water and reflections have become an obsession, it is beyond the strength of an old man, and yet I want to succeed in portraying what I feel. I have destroyed some, I have started all over again, and I hope that something will emerge from so much effort."

Similarly, unable to paint due to the discomfort of his illness, Matisse changed his medium to paper sculptures, which have since become some of the classic instances of this master's life contributions. Demonstrating the same phenomenon but in another creative medium was the poet William Carlos Williams. He suffered a stroke in his 60s, after which he became severely depressed. Following treatment for depression, he went on to produce some of his greatest works, including the Pulitzer Prize–winning *Pictures from Bruegel*, published when he was 79.

The limitations caused by physical and sensory age-related changes suffered by some of these artists were not necessarily met with equanimity. Michelangelo, for example, attempted to destroy his last sculpture, actually hacking off one hand; fortunately, however, one of his apprentices stopped him before it was too late to save it. Similarly, Monet destroyed many of the canvases he produced during the years he suffered from cataracts. Picasso's self-portrait *Facing Death* portrays a stark image of a man painted in broad brushstrokes, staring unflinchingly at the viewer, refusing to accept his own physical aging. Georgia O'Keeffe, who lived to the age of 98, was similarly frustrated with her inability to see in her last decade of life, when she could only produce pottery. Nevertheless, all of these individuals lived very long lives, and despite their personal frustrations, found ways to express their creative potential right up until the very end.

Sociocultural Perspectives on Creativity and Aging

These models of successful aging and creativity are useful and inspiring, but one important shortcoming seen by some critics is that they fail to take sufficient account of sociocultural context. Socioeconomically and racially disadvantaged individuals have a much lower chance of ever reaching old age, much less "successful" old age, as traditionally defined within psychology or the arts. Certain sectors of the population, particularly minorities from low-income backgrounds, do not have the opportunity to achieve good health and full expression of their innate abilities. Everyone we have talked about up to now came from a relatively advantaged background or at least achieved material success. For many talented individuals who are not afforded the benefits of higher levels of education and income, the creative process faces more challenges. Education and income remain lower among Blacks in the United States, and even a college education does not protect a person from career discrimination, as we noted in Chapter 10.

A second critical fact in analyses of successful aging regards the definition of eminence as used in studies of aging and creativity. Women are far less likely than would be expected on the basis of chance to appear in lists of the creative and productive at any age. For example, it is only within the area of children's literature that Lehman (1953) listed women as constituting anywhere near 50% of the notable contributors. A total of only 20 women were listed in the Lehman work as "worthy of mention" (p. 91).

Little, if any, mention in the analysis of productivity is made of Blacks. Simonton (1998) explored the question of whether assessments of creative output among historical figures would show evidence of bias against members of minority cultures. Specifically, he examined whether African Americans who had achieved recognition within reference works specific to Black scholarship would also be mentioned in reference works of the White majority culture. Although there was considerable convergence between the minority and majority reference works, one-fifth of African Americans who had achieved eminence in the minority reference works were not mentioned in any of the majority indices of eminence. Furthermore, certain areas of accomplishment within Black culture were not recognized within the majority reference works, including law, education, religion, classical music, and the sciences. White reference works gave higher ratings to African Americans in the fields of athletics and in jazz and blues music, but African American sources gave greater recognition to those who achieved eminence in the civil rights movement.

These differential patterns of recognition point to distinct opportunities that affect an individual's ability to achieve career recognition, if not personal fulfillment. Clearly, differences in educational opportunities as well as cultural values play a role in determining the ultimate achievements of people from nonmajority backgrounds. Those who do manage to break through cultural barriers are likely to receive considerable recognition within their own as well as the majority culture.

Some examples of eminent minority productive agers are Jackie Robinson, the first African American to play major league baseball; Booker T. Washington, the first to receive an honorary degree from Harvard; and William Grant Still, the first to conduct a major symphony orchestra and to have his own composition performed by a major American orchestra. These "famous firsts" seem particularly important within African American reference works

of eminence because they attest to the ability of highly talented and persistent individuals to overcome the effects of discrimination. That their work has until recently been overlooked in studies of aging and creativity limits the generalizability of current models of successful aging.

SUCCESSFUL AGING: FINAL PERSPECTIVES

People in later life appear not only to manage to feel satisfied with their lives but also to be able to achieve new forms of creative expression. Many scientists, artists, writers, and political leaders have produced notable contributions in their later adult years. The accomplishments of these unusual individuals adds to the literature on subjective well-being as well as the framework proposed by Erikson and colleagues of "vital involvement" to add support to the concept of successful aging.

As we showed in the analysis of Simonton's model of creative productivity, people who begin their careers with a high degree of creative potential are likely to maintain higher creative output well into their 60s, 70s, and beyond. Where does this creative potential come from? In part, the level of talent needed to sustain such a long and productive career may have a neurological basis. Personality may also play a role. There is evidence from an unusual 45-year longitudinal study of men originally tested as graduate students that the personality qualities of openness and flexibility predict creativity and success in later adulthood. Those men with the highest numbers of awards and notable publications at age 72 were higher on scales of tolerance and psychological-mindedness at age 27 (Feist & Barron, 2003).

Analyzing the lives of a set of six highly creative older adults (including Grandma Moses), Antonini and colleagues (2008) identified a passionate commitment to pursuit of their discipline as the common thread. These individuals also shared the trait of flexibility or plasticity and, rather than dwell on their accomplishments of the past, looked forward to new goals and new creative enterprises. They maintained their curiosity and, similar to the quality of openness to experience, were able to keep up with their times and adapt to changing circumstances. Part of a "successful" life narrative may involve coming to grips with the recognition of how cultural constraints have affected your ability to realize the hopes and dreams of youth. Yet, people must also strive to transcend these constrictions and arrive at a personal sense of meaning in life that rises above the boundaries of culture and time. As you continue to develop and navigate through your adult years, we hope that you will find your personal sense of meaning to accompany a long and successful life.

SUMMARY

1. The process of successful aging involves being able to overcome the threats to physical and psychological well-being presented by the aging process. Successful aging also involves the ability to become engaged with life in terms of both relationships and productive activity; successful cognitive aging refers to individuals who perform above average compared to their age group. Subjective well-being, a component of successful aging, is higher in older adults, a phenomenon referred to as the paradox of well-being. There are several possible mechanisms through which higher subjective well-being is achieved, including coping mechanisms, overall happiness, life satisfaction, social comparison, and the use of identity assimilation in forming a life story.

2. Creativity includes the work of geniuses as well as everyday behaviors. Brain scans of individuals engaged in creative tasks suggests that not only is the entire brain involved during creative endeavors, but that the areas activated are the same across all types of activities. Research on productivity and creativity has involved attempts to determine whether older individuals are more or less able to maintain the quality and quantity of works produced when younger. Variations by discipline were observed in early studies in which peak ages were reached earlier for areas in which imagination and physical ability are required. However, the findings of various authors indicated overall declines after peaks reached in young adulthood. In some cases, upturns were noted in the productivity of individuals living until the 70s and beyond among exceptionally talented older persons. Many achievements have also been produced by people in advanced old age. This area of research is hampered by the fact that some individuals who may have maintained their productivity do not live until old age. Furthermore, average productivity rates do not take into account the individual variations shown in the quality and quantity of works. Simonton's model of creative productivity describes the relationship between age and production of creative works using a mathematical formula that incorporates creative potential, ideation, and elaboration based on the career age of an individual rather than chronological age. In this model, highly productive individuals begin early and maintain a high production rate long into their careers. Those who are more productive are also more likely to produce works of high quality.

3. The old age style characterizes the works of older artists and musicians. One component of the old age style is simplification of detail and increasing subjectivity. The swan song is a related phenomenon, referring to the tendency of composers to produce very simple themes in their last works. Among scientists and academicians, the old age style refers to a tendency to synthesize, producing works such as texts and reviews that integrate existing knowledge. The old age style may be a reaction to increasing proximity to death or to the presence of age-related changes or health problems.

4. Commonalities between creative older adults include a passionate commitment to pursuit of their discipline, flexibility or plasticity, a sense of looking forward, and adaptation.

GLOSSARY

1998 Nursing Home Initiative: program developed by President Clinton intended to improve enforcement of nursing home quality standards.

2002 National Nursing Home Quality Initiative: federal program that combined new information for consumers about the quality of care provided in individual nursing homes with resources available to nursing homes to improve the quality of care in their facilities.

A board and care home: a group living arrangement designed to meet the needs of people who cannot live on their own in the community and also need some nursing services.

Accessory dwelling unit: also known as an "in-law apartment," this second living space in the home allows the older adult to have independent living quarters, cooking space, and a bathroom.

Accommodation: when people change their schemas in response to new information about the world.

Acetylcholinesterase: the enzyme that normally destroys acetylcholine after its release into the synaptic cleft; also called cholinesterase.

Activities of daily living (ADL): an individual's ability to complete the tasks of bathing, dressing, transferring, using the toilet, and eating.

Activity theory: the view that older adults are most satisfied if they are able to remain involved in their social roles.

Acute stress disorder: the diagnosis given to an individual whose symptoms persist for up to a month after a trauma and include the intrusion of distressing reminders of an event; dissociative symptoms, such as feeling numb or detached from others; avoidance of situations that might serve as reminders of the event; and hyperarousal, including sleep disturbances or irritability.

Adrenopause: the phenomenon where DHEA, which is higher in males than females, shows a pronounced decrease over the adult years.

Adult attachment theory: proposes that the early bond between the infant and caregiver set the stage for all of the individual's later significant relationships.

Adult day care: older adults who need assistance or supervision during the day receive a range of services in a setting that is either attached to another facility, such as a nursing home, or is a standalone agency.

Adult-onset diabetes or type 2 diabetes: a disease that develops over time and gradually reduces the individual's ability to convert dietary glucose to a form that can be used by the body's cells.

Advance directive (AD): also called a living will, which is a written order that stipulates the conditions under which a patient will accept or refuse treatment.

Aerobic capacity: the maximum amount of oxygen that can be delivered through the blood.

Affect regulation: the ability to increase a person's feelings of happiness and well-being.

Affective events theory: proposes that events at work lead to affective reactions; these in turn influence attitudes toward work and performance.

Age Discrimination in Employment Act (ADEA): passed in 1967, makes it illegal to fire or not employ workers on the basis of their age.

Age: an objectively determined measure that indicates how many years (and/or months or days) a person has lived up to the present moment.

Age-adjusted death rate: a statistic that combines all the age-specific death rates within groups of the population.

Age-as-leveler view: proposes that as people become older, age overrides all other "isms."

Age-complexity hypothesis: proposes that through a slowing of the central processes in the nervous system, age differences increase as tasks become more complex and the older adult's processing resources are stretched more and more to their limit.

Ageism: a set of beliefs, attitudes, social institutions, and acts that denigrate individuals or groups based on their chronological age.

Age-related macular degeneration (ARMD): a condition caused by damage to the photoreceptors located in the central region of the retina known as the macula.

Age-specific death rate: the crude death rate for a specific age group.

Aging in place: the principle that older adults can remain in their own homes, or at least in their own communities, with appropriate services.

Agnosia: the loss of the ability to recognize familiar objects.

Agoraphobia: the fear of being trapped or stranded during a panic attack in a public place.

Alveoli: tiny air sacs in the lungs where exchange of gases takes place.

Alzheimer's disease: a form of neurocognitive disorder in which the individual suffers progressive and irreversible neuronal death.

Amnesia: a condition where the individual has as the main symptom profound memory loss.

Amyloid plaque: the formation of abnormal deposits of protein fragments.

Amyloid precursor protein (APP): a larger protein found in the normal brain.

Androgenetic alopecia: male and female pattern hair loss.

Andropause: age-related declines in the male sex hormone testosterone.

Anorexia-cachexia syndrome: a syndrome observed at the end of life in which the individual loses appetite (anorexia) and muscle mass (cachexia).

Anticholinesterase: treatments that inhibit the enzyme acetylcholinesterase.

Antioxidants: chemicals that prevent the formation of free radicals.

Anxiety disorder: the main characteristic includes anxiety, a sense of dread about what might happen in the future.

Anxious attachment style: individuals imagine that their adult partners will abandon them.

Aphasia: the loss of language ability.

ApoE: a protein that carries cholesterol throughout the body but also binds to beta-amyloid, possibly playing a role in plaque formation.

Apolipoprotein E (ApoE) gene: one of the prime genes thought to be involved in late-onset familial Alzheimer's disease.

Apoptosis: the destruction of neurons.

APP gene: appears to control the production of APP, the protein that generates beta-amyloid.

Apraxia: the loss of the ability to carry out coordinated movement.

Archival method: when investigators use available records to provide data on the hypotheses they wish to test.

Arteriosclerosis: a general term for the thickening and hardening of arteries.

Arthritis: a general term for conditions affecting the joints and surrounding tissues that can cause pain, stiffness, and swelling in joints and other connective tissues.

Assimilation: the way in which people use their existing schemas in order to understand the world around them.

Assisted living facilities: housing complexes in which older persons live independently in their own apartments.

Atherosclerosis: a form of cardiovascular disease where fatty deposits collect at an abnormally high rate within the arteries, substantially reducing their width and limiting the circulation of the blood.

Attachment styles: mental representations or frameworks about what to expect in a relationship.

Attachment view of bereavement: the view that the bereaved can continue to benefit from maintaining emotional bonds to the deceased.

Attention: involves the ability to focus or concentrate on a portion of experience while ignoring other features of that experience, to be able to shift that focus as demanded by the situation, and to be able to coordinate information from multiple sources.

Attentional resources: a theory that regards attention as a process reflecting the allocation of cognitive resources.

Autobiographical memory: the recall of information from a person's own past.

Autoimmune theory: proposes that aging is due to faulty immune system functioning in which the immune system attacks the body's own cells.

Autonomy vs. shame and doubt: stage in Erikson's theory when young children learn ways to be able to act independently from their parents without feeling afraid that they will venture too far off on their own.

Avoidant attachment style: a fear of abandonment so intense that individuals stay away from close relationships altogether.

Awareness of finitude: thoughts about mortality that occur when individuals pass the age when other people close to them had themselves died.

Baby Boom generation: the term used to describe people born in the post–World War II years of 1946 to 1964.

Basal metabolic rate (BMR): the rate of metabolism.

Basic trust vs. basic mistrust: stage in Erikson's theory that involves the infant's establishing a sense of being able to rely on care from the environment (and caregivers).

Behavioral approach to marital interactions: emphasizes the actual behaviors that partners engage in with each other during marital interactions as an influence on marital stability and quality.

Behavioral therapy: an approach that changes the reinforcements associated with the individual's behavior.

Bereavement: the process during which people cope with the death of another person.

Berlin Wisdom Paradigm: proposes that wisdom is a form of expert knowledge in the pragmatics of life.

Beta-amyloid-42: the form of amyloid most closely linked with Alzheimer's disease and that consists of a string of 42 amino acids.

Biological age: the age of an individual's bodily systems.

Biopsychosocial perspective: a view of development as a complex interaction of biological, psychological, and social processes.

Bipolar disorder: diagnosed in people who have experienced one or more manic episodes during which they feel elated, grandiose, expansive, and highly energetic.

Blended families: also known as reconstituted families, family situations where at least one adult is living with a child who is not a biological child of that adult.

Blurred retirement pattern: a pattern of retirement in which workers exit and reenter the workplace several times.

Body mass index (BMI): an index of body fat calculated by dividing weight in kilograms by (height in meters) squared.

Bone remodeling: a process in which old cells are destroyed and replaced by new cells.

Borderline personality disorder: a set of symptoms that include extreme instability in sense of self and relationships with others, sexual impulsivity, fear of abandonment, and difficulties controlling their emotions.

Boundaryless career: a career that crosses the boundaries of an employer or organization; people with this mindset seek opportunities for development in their jobs.

Bridge employment: when retirees work in a completely different occupation than they had during most of their adult life.

Brinley plot: the reaction times of older groups of adults are plotted against the times of younger adults.

Calling: the choice of occupation based on a combination of factors related to career development, job satisfaction, well-being, and personal growth.

Caloric restriction hypothesis: proposes that the key to prolonging life is to restrict caloric intake.

Cardiac output: the amount of blood that the heart pumps per minute.

Cardiovascular disease: a term that refers to a set of abnormal conditions that develop in the heart and arteries.

Career age: the age at which an individual begins to embark on his or her career.

Career plateauing: when people remain static in their vocational development.

Career: the term that captures the unique connection between individuals and social organizations over time.

Caregiver burden: the term used to describe the stress that caregivers experience in the daily management of their afflicted relative.

Caregivers: individuals, usually family, who provide support to people with chronic diseases.

Case report: provides in-depth data from a relatively small number of individuals.

Caspase: proposes that beta-amyloid stimulates the production of substances called caspases—enzymes that are lethal to neurons.

Cataract: a clouding or opacity in the lens.

Cattell-Horn-Carroll (CHC) model of intelligence: proposes that there is a three-tier structure to intelligence.

Centenarians: people who are 100 years old and older.

Center for Epidemiological Studies Scale for Depression (CES-D): a 20-item questionnaire that screens for depressive symptoms.

Centers for Medicare and Medicaid Services (CMS): the U.S. government agency responsible for the formulation of policy and guidelines, oversight and operation of contracts, maintenance and review of records, and general financing.

Cerebrovascular accident: also known as a "stroke" or "brain attack," an acute condition in which an artery leading to the brain bursts or is clogged by a blood clot or other particle.

Choice reaction time tasks: tasks used to measure processing speed in which respondents must make one response for one stimulus and another response for a different stimulus.

Chromosomes: distinct, physically separate units of coiled threads of DNA and associated protein molecules.

Chronic obstructive pulmonary disease (COPD): a group of diseases that involve obstruction of the airflow into the respiratory system.

Chronosystem: from the ecological perspective, changes that take place over time.

Circadian rhythm: the daily variations in various bodily functions.

Classic aging pattern: an inverted U-shaped pattern, with a peak in early adulthood followed by steady decline.

Climacteric: the gradual winding down of reproductive ability in men and women.

Clinical interview: a series of questions that clinicians administer in face-to-face interaction with clients.

Cognition: the way the mind works; specifically, the processes of attention, memory, intelligence, problem solving, and the use of language.

Cognitive therapy: an approach based on the theory that clients develop psychological disorders because they have maladaptive thought processes.

Cognitive-behavioral therapy: an approach in which the clinician encourages clients to develop more adaptive behaviors and ways of thinking about their experiences.

Cohabitation effect: the greater likelihood of divorce among couples who cohabitate before becoming engaged.

Cohabitation: living in a stable relationship prior to or instead of marrying.

Cohort effects: the social, historical, and culture influences that affect people during a particular period of time.

Cohort: a term used to describe the year (or period) of a person's birth.

Cohort-sequential design: method in which cohorts are compared at different ages.

Collagen: the fibrous protein that makes up about one-quarter of all bodily proteins.

Communication predicament model: a predicament where older adults are thought of as mentally incapacitated, leading younger people to speak to them in a simplified manner (using elderspeak). Over time, this can have the effect of reducing the older adult's actual ability to use language.

Competence-press model: predicts an optimal level of adjustment that institutionalized persons will experience on the basis of their levels of competence compared with the demands or "press" of the environment or the demands it places upon individuals.

Comprehension knowledge (Gc): originally called crystallized intelligence, represents the acquisition of specific skills and information that people gain as the result of their exposure to the language, knowledge, and conventions of their culture.

Compression of morbidity: the concept that the illness burden to a society can be reduced if people become disabled closer to the time of their death.

Computed axial tomography (CAT or CT scan): an imaging method that clinicians and researchers use to provide an image of a cross-sectional slice of the brain from any angle or level.

Congestive heart failure (or heart failure): a condition in which the heart is unable to pump enough blood to meet the needs of the body's other organs.

Congruence: occurs when one's vocational type matches one's occupational environment.

Conjunction visual search: the target differs from the distractors in more than one way.

Contextual influences on development: the effects of sex, race, ethnicity, social class, religion, and culture on development.

Contingency theory: proposes that parents may also provide help to their children because they perceive that the children need this support.

Continuing care retirement community (CCRC): a housing community that provides different levels of care based on the needs of the residents.

Continuity principle: the changes that people experience in later adulthood build on what they lived through in their earlier years.

Continuity theory of retirement: proposes that retired individuals maintain the ties they had to society when they were working.

Continuity theory: proposes that whether disengagement or activity is beneficial to the older adult depends on the individual's personality.

Coping: the actions people take to reduce stress.

Core self-evaluations: represents a person's appraisal of people, events, and things in relation to oneself.

Coronary (ischemic) heart disease: a condition caused by atherosclerosis, which blocks the blood supply to the heart muscle.

Correlation: expresses the strength and direction of a relationship between two variables.

Correlational design: a research design in which researchers investigate relationships among two or more variables.

Correspondence principle: people experience particular life events that reflect their personality traits; once these events occur, they further affect people's personalities.

Cortisol: the hormone produced by the adrenal gland.

Creative potential: the total number of works that a person could hypothetically produce in a life span with no upper limits.

Creativity: the ability to generate products or ideas that are original, appropriate, and have an impact on others.

Crisp retirement pattern: a pattern of retirement in which workers leave the workplace in a single, unreversed, clear-cut exit.

Cross-linking theory: proposes that aging causes deleterious changes in cells of the body that make up much of the body's connective tissue.

Cross-sectional design: a research design where groups of people are compared with different ages at one point in time.

Cross-sequential design: method in which cohorts are examined at different times of measurement.

Crude death rate: the number of deaths divided by population alive during a certain time period.

Crystallized intelligence: represents the acquisition of specific skills and information that people gain as the result of their exposure to the language, knowledge, and conventions of their culture.

Daily diary method: a research method in which participants enter data on a daily basis.

Death ethos: the prevailing philosophy of death.

Death with dignity: the idea that death should not involve extreme physical dependency or the loss of control of bodily functions.

Death: the irreversible cessation of circulatory and respiratory functions, or when all the structures of the brain have ceased to function.

Debriefing: a procedure that reveals a study's purpose and answers to the participant after testing has completed.

Default network: a circuit in the brain that is active while the brain is at rest.

Dehydroepiandrosterone (DHEA): a weak male steroid (androgen) produced by the adrenal glands.

Delirium: an acute cognitive disorder that is characterized by temporary confusion.

Dementia: a loss of cognitive abilities.

Deoxyribonucleic acid (DNA): a molecule capable of replicating itself that encodes information needed to produce proteins.

Dependent variable: the outcome that researchers observe.

Dermis: the middle layer of the skin containing protein molecules of elastin and collagen, among which various nerve cells, glands, and the hair follicles reside.

Descriptive research design: a design that provides information about age differences but does not attempt to rule out social or historical factors.

Developmental schism: occurs when there is a gap between the two generations in how much they value the relationship and whether they wish to be independent.

Developmental science: a term replacing "developmental psychology" that expands the focus of life span development to include a broader variety of domains.

Diabetes: a disease where individuals are unable to metabolize glucose, a simple sugar that is a major source of energy for the body's cells.

Diagnostic and Statistical Manual (DSM): the major reference used by mental health professionals in the United States and Canada to diagnose people with psychological disorders.

Dialectical thinking: related to the postformal stage of cognitive development involving an interest in and appreciation for debate, arguments, and counterarguments.

Disengagement theory: the view that the normal and natural evolution of life causes older adults to wish to loosen their social ties.

Disillusionment pathway: relationship type where a couple starts out happy but gradually falls out of love.

Divorce proneness: people who are more likely to contemplate divorce when their marriage is in trouble.

Dizziness: an uncomfortable sensation of feeling lightheaded and even floating.

Do not resuscitate (DNR) order: directs health care workers not to use resuscitation if the patient experiences cardiac or pulmonary arrest.

Doing gender: a term that refers to the tendency of women and men to behave in stereotypically gendered ways.

Donepezil hydrochloride: a generic version of the drug Aricept.

Donut hole: a coverage gap in Medicare Part D in which the enrollee's coverage drops and out-of-pocket expenses rise.

Dual-process model of coping with bereavement: proposes that the practical adaptations to loss are as important to the bereaved person's adjustment as the emotional.

Durable power of attorney for health care (DPAHC): also known as a health care proxy, is appointed to make decisions to act on a person's behalf should that person become incapacitated.

Dyadic withdrawal: the process of reducing the individual friendships of the couple and increasing the joint friendships.

Dying trajectory: the rate of decline in functioning prior to death.

Dying: the period during which the organism loses its vitality.

Dysphoria: sad mood.

Dysthermia: a condition in which the individual shows an excessive raising of body temperature (hyperthermia) or excessive lowering of body temperature (hypothermia).

Early-onset familial Alzheimer's disease: a form of Alzheimer's that strikes at the relatively young age of 40 to 50 years.

Ecological perspective: identifies multiple levels of the environment as they affect the individual's development.

Ego Integrity versus Despair: toward the end of adulthood, when individuals face psychosocial issues related to aging and facing their mortality.

Ego psychology: the belief that the ego plays a central role in actively directing behavior.

Ego: the part of the mind that controls rational thought.

Elastase: an enzyme that breaks down the elastin found in lung tissue.

Elder abuse: a large category of actions taken directly against older adults that inflict physical or psychological harm.

Elderspeak: a speech pattern directed at older adults similar to the way people talk to babies.

Electroconvulsive therapy (ECT): a method of treatment for depression in which an electric current is applied through electrodes attached across the head.

Electroencephalogram (EEG): a brain scanning method that measures electrical activity in the brain.

Emergent distress pathway: couple whose relationship problems develop over time.

Emerging adulthood: the transition prior to assuming the full responsibilities associated with adulthood normally associated with the years 18 to 29.

Emotional labor: the requirement of service-oriented jobs in which workers must smile and maintain a friendly attitude regardless of their own personal feelings or emotions.

Emotion-focused coping: coping in which people attempt to reduce their stress by changing the ways they think about the situation.

Empty nest: describes the period in a couple's life that occurs when their children permanently depart from the home.

Endocrine system: a large and diverse set of glands that regulate the actions of the body's other organ systems.

Enduring dynamics pathway: how a couple interacts early in their relationship will characterize the course of the relationship over time.

Epidemiology: the study of the distribution and determinants of health-related states or events (including disease).

Epidermis: the outermost layer of the skin that protects the underlying tissue.

Epigenetic principle: In Erikson's theory, the proposal that asserts that each stage unfolds from the previous stage according to a predestined order.

Episodic memory: memory for events that took place in the past.

Equal odds rule: the principle that creative individuals who produce more works are more likely to produce one or more of high quality than are those who produce fewer works.

Equilibrium: when assimilation and accommodation are perfectly balanced.

Equity theory: proposes that partners are satisfied in a relationship if they feel they are getting what they deserve.

Erectile dysfunction: a condition in which a man is unable to achieve an erection sustainable for intercourse.

Error catastrophe theory: proposes that the errors that accumulate with aging are ones that are vital to life itself.

Error theories: propose that mutations acquired over the organism's lifetime lead to the malfunctioning of the body's cells.

Ethnicity: captures the cultural background of an individual, reflecting the predominant values, attitudes, and expectations in which the individual has been raised.

Euthanasia: a process where physicians take actions that cause the patient to die, with the intention of preventing the suffering associated with a prolonged ending of life.

Event-related potentials (ERPs): measure the brain's pattern of electricity in response to stimuli.

Everyday problem solving: involves problems that typically occur in people's daily lives, that can be solved in more than one way, and that require the problem solver to decide which strategy will lead to the desired result.

Evidence-based practice in psychology: proposes that clinicians should integrate the best available research evidence and clinical expertise in the context of the cultural background, preferences, and characteristics of clients.

Executive functioning: higher-order cognitive skills, including judgment, knowledge, and decision making.

Exosystem: from the ecological perspective, includes the environments that people do not closely experience on a regular basis but that impact them nevertheless.

Experimental design: research method in which an independent variable is manipulated and scores are then measured on the dependent variable. Involves random assignment of respondents to treatment and control groups.

Extrinsic factors in vocational satisfaction: features that accompany the job but are not central to its performance.

Fat-free mass (FFM): lean tissue.

Fear of falling: the anxiety about the fear of falling; this anxiety can create a vicious cycle in which older individuals increasingly restrict their movement.

Filial anxiety: is the fear of having to take care of an aging, infirmed parent.

Filial maturity: occurs when children reach the age of relating to their parents as equals.

Filial obligation or filial piety: the cultural values that adult children are expected to care for their parents, meaning that they feel committed to taking care of their parents should this become necessary.

Five-Factor Model (FFM): a theory intended to capture all the essential characteristics of personality in a set of five broad dispositions.

Flashbulb memory: the recall of important and distinctive events that stand out from other memories of past events.

Fluid reasoning (Gf): the individual's innate abilities to carry out higher-level cognitive operations involving the integration, analysis, and synthesis of new information.

Fluid-crystallized theory (Gf-Gc): the view that intelligence should be divided into two distinct factors.

Focus group: when respondents meet together and discuss a particular topic that the researcher assigns to them.

Formal operations: the ability of adolescents and adults to use logic and abstract symbols to arrive at solutions to complex problems.

FOXO genes: a group of genes that may operate to influence the rate of cell death.

Free radical theory: proposes that the cause of aging is the increased activity of unstable compounds that compromise the cell's functioning.

Free radicals: unstable compounds produced when certain molecules in cells react with oxygen.

Friendship styles: individual differences in approaches toward friendships.

Frontotemporal neurocognitive disorder (FTD): a neurocognitive disorder that involves specifically the frontal lobes of the brain.

Functional age: age based on performance rather than chronological age.

Functional magnetic resonance imaging (fMRI): a type of scan that can be used to show changes in the brain over the course of a mental activity.

g or general factor: the ability to infer and apply relationships on the basis of experience.

Gender gap: expressed as a proportion of women's to men's salaries.

Gender: an individual's identification as being male or female.

Gene: the functional unit of a DNA molecule carrying a particular set of instructions for producing a specific protein.

General slowing hypothesis: proposes that the increase in reaction time reflects a general decline of information processing speed within the nervous system of the aging individual.

Generalized anxiety disorder: the individual experiences an overall sense of uneasiness and concern without specific focus.

Generativity versus Stagnation: when middle-aged adults focus on the psychosocial issues of procreation, productivity, and creativity.

Genome: the complete set of instructions for "building" all the cells that make up an organism.

Genome-wide association study: a method used in behavior genetics in which researchers search for genetic variations related to complex diseases by scanning the entire genome.

Genome-wide linkage study: a method used in behavior genetics in which researchers study the families of people with specific psychological traits or disorders.

Geriatric Depression Scale (GDS): A depression screening instrument that asks individuals to answer a true–false set of questions about symptoms of depression.

Geriatric partial hospital: provides older adults living in the community who need psychiatric care with a range of mental health services.

Geriatrics: the medical specialty in aging.

Gerontology: the scientific study of the aging process.

Glaucoma: a group of conditions causing blindness related to changes in pressure within the eyeball.

Glucocorticoid cascade hypothesis: the view that increased cortisol levels accelerate neuronal loss in the hippocampus and that repeated (cascading) increases in cortisol over the lifetime lead to further degeneration.

Gompertz function: plots the relationship between age and death rates for a given species.

Good death: the opportunity for patients to have autonomy in making decisions about the type, site, and duration of the care that they receive at the end of life.

Government-assisted housing: provided for individuals with low to moderate incomes who need affordable housing or rental assistance.

Green House model: an alternative to the traditional nursing homes; offers older adults individual homes within a small community of 6 to 10 residents and skilled nursing staff.

Health: a state of complete physical, mental, and social well-being; not merely the absence of disease or infirmity.

Health expectancy: the number of years a person could expect to live in good health if current mortality and morbidity rates persist.

Healthy life span: a term that means that older adults live as long as possible in as healthy a state as possible.

Helicopter parents: parents who are seen as smothering and overprotecting their overly dependent children.

Hemispheric Asymmetry Reduction in OLDer adults (HAROLD) model: model of plasticity in which the brains of older adults become activated in the opposite hemisphere when the original area suffers deficits.

Hierarchical linear modeling (HLM): a statistical methodology where researchers study the patterns of change within individuals over time.

High-density lipoproteins (HDLs): the plasma lipid transport mechanism that carries lipids from the peripheral tissues to the liver, where they are excreted or synthesized into bile acids.

Hippocampus: the structure in the brain responsible for consolidating memories.

Hoarding: people collect and store seemingly useless items that they cannot discard.

Holland's vocational development theory: proposes that people express their personalities in their vocational aspirations and interests.

Home health services: provide assistance to older adults within their own private residences.

Hormone replacement therapy (HRT): a therapeutic administration of lower doses of estrogen than in estrogen-replacement therapy (ERT) along with progestin to reduce the cancer risk associated with ERT.

Hormones: the chemical messengers produced by the endocrine systems.

Hospice: a site or program that provides medical and supportive services for dying patients.

Hypertension: a disease in which an individual chronically suffers from abnormally elevated blood pressure.

Hypothalamus-releasing factors (HRFs): hormones produced by the hypothalamus that regulate the secretion of hormones in turn produced by the anterior pituitary gland.

Identity: a composite of how people view themselves in the biological, psychological, and social domains of life.

Identity accommodation: the process of making changes in identity in response to experiences that challenge people's current view of themselves.

Identity achievement versus identity diffusion: when individuals must decide "who" they are and what they wish to get out of life.

Identity assimilation: the interpretation of new experiences in terms of a person's existing identity.

Identity balance: the dynamic equilibrium that occurs when people tend to view themselves consistently but can make changes when called for by their experiences.

Identity process theory: proposes that identity continues to change in adulthood in a dynamic manner.

Identity status interview: examines the degree of commitment held by the individual to identity issues and the degree of exploration the individual used to arrive at this commitment.

Immune senescence: the belief that there are widespread age-related declines in immune system functioning.

Implicit memory: long-term memory for information that people acquire without intending to do so.

Incidence statistics: data that provide estimates of the percent of people who *first* develop symptoms in a given period.

Independent variable: the factor that the researcher manipulates.

Individuality: a principle of adult development and aging that asserts that as people age, they become more different from each other.

Industry vs. inferiority: stage in Erikson's theory that involves the individual's identifying with the world of work and developing a work ethic.

Informed consent: written agreement to participate in research based on knowing what participation will involve.

Inhibitory control: the process of turning off one response while performing another.

Inhibitory deficit hypothesis: suggests that aging reduces the individual's ability to inhibit or tune out irrelevant information.

Initiative vs. guilt: stage in Erikson's theory when the child becomes able to engage in creative self-expression without fear of making a mistake.

Inoculation hypothesis: the belief that older minorities and women have actually become immune to the effects of ageism through years of exposure to discrimination and stereotyping.

Institutional facility: a group residential setting that provides individuals with medical or psychiatric care.

Instrumental activities of daily living (IADL): the ability to use the telephone, go shopping, prepare meals, complete housekeeping tasks, do laundry, use private or public transportation, take medications, and handle finances.

Intelligence: an individual's mental ability.

Intelligence test: provides an assessment of an individual's overall cognitive status along a set of standardized dimensions.

Interactionist model: the view that not only do genetics and environment interact in complex ways to produce their effects on the individual, but that individuals actively shape their own development.

Intergenerational solidarity model (ISM): summarizes the six relevant dimensions of families that span at least two generations.

Intergenerational stake hypothesis: proposes that parents are higher in affectual solidarity toward their children than children are toward their parents.

Interindividual differences: differences between people.

Intermediate care facility: health-related services are provided to individuals who do not require hospital or skilled nursing facility care but do require some type of institutional care.

International Statistical Classification of Diseases and Related Health Problems (ICD): the reference guide to all medical illnesses, including psychological disorders.

Interpersonal therapy (IPT): an approach that helps clients learn to understand and change their relationships with others.

Intimacy versus Isolation: when individuals are faced with making commitments to close relationships.

Intra-individual differences: variations within the same individual.

Intrinsic factors in vocational satisfaction: the tasks required to perform the work itself.

Invisible death: the current Western attitude of a desire for death to retreat from the family and to be confined to hospitals.

Job tenure: the length of time a person has spent in the job.

Korsakoff syndrome: a form of dementia progressing from Wernicke's disease to a chronic form of alcohol-induced neurocognitive disorder.

Labor force: includes all civilians in the over-16 population who live outside of institutions and have sought or are actively seeking employment.

Laboratory studies: the testing of participants in a systematic fashion using standardized procedures.

Lastingness: the quality of an older artist's work that allows it to persist over time.

Latent variable: a statistical composite of several variables.

Late-onset familial Alzheimer's disease: a form of familial Alzheimer's disease that starts at the age of 60 or 65 years.

Late-onset schizophrenia: a form of schizophrenia that was thought to originate in adults over the age of 45 years.

Late-onset stress symptomatology (LOSS): a phenomenon observed in aging veterans who were exposed to stressful combat situations in young adulthood.

Legitimization of biography: steps to leave a legacy that will continue to define oneself after one is gone.

Life course perspective: the norms, roles, and attitudes about age that have an impact on the shape of each person's life.

Life course perspective on retirement: proposes that changes in the work role in later life are best seen as logical outgrowths of earlier life events.

Life expectancy: the average number of years of life remaining to people born within a similar period of time.

Life review therapy: involves helping older adults rework past experiences, both pleasant and unpleasant, with the goal of gaining greater acceptance of the past.

Life satisfaction: the overall assessment of an individual's feelings and attitudes about one's life at a particular point in time.

Life span: the maximum length of life for a given species.

Life span perspective: the view of development as continuous from childhood through old age.

Life story: the individual's narrative view of his or her own past.

Life structure: the way that the individual's life is patterned at a given point in time.

Logistic regression: a method in which researchers test the likelihood of an individual receiving a score on a discrete yes–no variable.

Longitudinal design: a research design where people are followed repeatedly from one test occasion to another.

Long-term memory: the repository of information that is held for a period of time ranging from several minutes to a lifetime.

Low-density lipoproteins (LDLs): the plasma lipid transport mechanism that transports cholesterol to the arteries.

Lung age: a mathematical function showing how old your lung is based on a combination of your age and a measure obtained from a spirometer called forced expiratory volume.

Macrosystem: from the ecological perspective, includes the larger social institutions ranging from a country's economy to its laws and social norms.

Magnetic resonance imaging (MRI): a brain imaging method that uses radio waves to construct a picture of the living brain based on the water content of various tissues.

Major depressive disorder: the major symptom of which is an extremely sad mood that lasts most of the time for at least 2 weeks and is atypical of the individual's usual mood.

Marriage: defined as a legally sanctioned union between a man and a woman (in most U.S. states).

Maturation hypothesis: the belief that people who have personality disorders that involve "immature" symptoms, such as acting out, being entitled, and having an unstable sense of self, improve or at least become more treatable later in life.

Mechanics of intelligence: involves cognitive operations such as speed, working memory, and fluid intelligence.

Mechanistic model: proposes that people's behavior changes gradually over time, shaped by the outside forces that cause them to adapt to their environments.

Mediation: a method used to compare the correlation between two variables with and without their joint correlation to a third variable.

Medicaid: a federal and state matching entitlement program that provides medical assistance for certain individuals and families with low incomes and resources.

Medical model: a perspective that focuses primarily on the physiological causes of a psychological disorder.

Medicare: the federal health care funding agency passed and signed into law in 1965, designated as "Health Insurance for the Aged and Disabled."

Medicare Modernization Act (MMA): U.S. legislation passed in 2003 that created the prescription drug benefit in Medicare.

Medicare Part A (Hospital Insurance or HI): provides coverage that includes all medically necessary services and supplies provided during a patient's stay in the hospital and subsequent rehabilitation in an approved facility.

Medicare Part B: provides benefits for a range of medical services available to people 65 and older who pay a monthly insurance premium.

Melatonin: the hormone manufactured by the pineal gland responsible in part for the sleep–wake cycles.

Memantine: a type of medication for Alzheimer's disease that targets the excitatory neurotransmitter glutamate.

Memory controllability: beliefs about the effects of the aging process on memory, such as the extent to which the individual believes that memory decline is inevitable with age.

Memory self-efficacy: the degree to which an individual believes he can successfully complete a memory task.

Menopause: the point in a woman's life when menstruation stops permanently.

Mental status examination: assesses such qualities of the client as appearance, attitudes, behavior, mood and affect, speech, thought processes, content of thought, perception, cognition, insight, and judgment.

Mesosystem: from the ecological perspective, the system in which interactions take place among two or more microsystems.

Meta-analysis: a statistical procedure that allows for a combination of findings from independently conducted studies.

Metabolic syndrome: a cluster of symptoms associated with high risk factors for cardiovascular (and other) diseases, including high levels of abdominal obesity, high blood fats, abnormal levels of blood cholesterol, hypertension, and high glucose.

Microsystem: from the ecological perspective, the setting in which people have their daily interactions and that therefore have the most direct impact on their lives.

Midlife crisis: a period of self-scrutiny and reevaluation of goals triggered by the individual's entry into middle age.

Mild cognitive impairment (MCI): a form of neurocognitive disorder that signifies that the individual may be at risk for developing Alzheimer's disease.

Mini-Mental State Examination (MMSE): a brief, structured tool that clinicians use as a screening device to assess dementia.

Moderation: when two variables are believed to have a joint influence on a third.

Modernization hypothesis: proposes that the increasing urbanization and industrialization of Western society is what causes older adults to be devalued.

Most Efficient Design: a set of three designs manipulating the variables of age, cohort, and time of measurement.

Motivation crowding out: describes workers who feel that they cannot fulfill their intrinsic needs because their motivation is controlled entirely by extrinsic factors.

Multidirectionality: the idea that development can proceed in multiple directions within the same person.

Multi-infarct dementia or MID: the most common form of vascular neurocognitive disorder; caused by transient ischemic attacks.

Multiple jeopardy hypothesis: theorizes that older individuals who fit more than one discriminated-against category are affected by biases against each of these categorizations.

Multiple regression analysis: a multivariate correlational research design in which a set of variables is used to predict scores on another variable.

Multiple threshold model: proposes that individuals realize that they are getting older through a stepwise process as aging-related changes occur.

Multivariate correlational design: a research design where researchers simultaneously evaluate the effects of more than two variables.

Mutations: alterations in genes that lead to changes in their functions.

Myocardial infarction: an acute condition in which the blood supply to part of the heart muscle (the myocardium) is severely reduced or blocked.

Need complementarity hypothesis: proposes that people seek and are more satisfied with marital partners who are the opposite of themselves.

NEO-PI-R: a questionnaire containing 240 items measuring the 30 facets of the Five-Factor Model.

Nephrons: cells in the kidneys that serve as millions of tiny filters that cleanse the blood of metabolic waste.

Neurocognitive disorder with Lewy bodies: condition first identified in 1961; similar to Alzheimer's disease in that it causes progressive loss of memory, language, calculation, and reasoning as well as other higher mental functions.

Neurocognitive disorder: a condition where an individual experiences a loss of cognitive function severe enough to interfere with normal daily activities and social relationships.

Neurofibrillary tangles: abnormally twisted fibers within the neurons themselves.

Neuroleptics: antipsychotic medication used to treat schizophrenia.

Neuronal fallout model: proposes that individuals progressively lose brain tissue over the life span because neurons do not have the ability to replace themselves when they die.

Neuropsychological assessment: involves gathering information about a client's brain functioning from a series of standardized cognitive tests.

New modes of retirement: the view that the characteristics of the person's spouse and lifelong family responsibilities play a role in retirement decisions and adjustment.

Niche-picking: the proposal that genetic and environmental factors work together to influence the direction of a child's life.

Nonnormative influences: the random idiosyncratic events that occur throughout life.

Normal aging is different from disease: the principle that growing older does not necessarily mean growing sicker.

Normal-pressure hydrocephalus: a reversible form of dementia that can cause cognitive impairment, dementia, urinary incontinence, and difficulty in walking.

Normative age-graded influences: influences that lead people to choose experiences that their culture and historical period attach to certain ages or points in the life span.

Normative history-graded influences: events that occur to everyone within a certain culture or geopolitical unit (regardless of age).

Nursing Home Reform Act (NHRA): a U.S. federal law mandating that facilities meet physical standards, provide adequate professional staffing and services, and maintain policies governing their administrative and medical procedures.

Nursing home: a type of medical institution that provides a room, meals, skilled nursing and rehabilitative care, medical services, and protective supervision.

O*NET, the Occupational Information Network: consists of an interactive national database of occupations.

Observational method: a way for researchers to conduct a systematic examination of what people do in particular settings.

Obsessive-compulsive disorder: characterized by unrelenting, irrational, and distracting obsessions, or repetitive thoughts and compulsions, or repetitive behaviors.

Occupational reinforcement patterns (ORPs): the work values and needs likely to be reinforced or satisfied by a particular occupation.

Old Age and Survivors Disability Insurance (OASDI): combines Old-Age Survivors Insurance and Disability Insurance.

Old-age style: an approach to art that eliminates the fine details and instead presents the essence of the work's intended meaning.

Oldest-old: a subgroup of older adults between the ages of 85 and older.

Old-old: a subgroup of older adults between the ages of 75 to 84.

Optimal aging: growing older in a way that slows or alters the process.

Organismic model: proposes that heredity drives the course of development throughout life.

Orientation: reflects whether examinees know where they are (orientation to place), what time it is (orientation to time), and who they are (orientation to person).

Osteoarthritis: a painful, degenerative joint disease that often involves the hips, knees, neck, lower back, or the small joints of the hands.

Osteoporosis: a disease that occurs when the bone mineral density reaches the point that is more than 2.5 standard deviations below the mean of young, White, non-Hispanic women.

Overactive bladder: a condition whose symptoms include incontinence and the need to urinate more frequently than normal.

Overtreatment: occurs when patients request palliative care but instead receive active life support that includes resuscitation.

Palliative care: a request by dying patients that will provide them with relief from symptoms such as nausea, pain, and dyspnea as well as with some services such as physical and occupational therapy

Panic disorder: involves the experience of panic attacks in which people have the physical sensation that they are about to die.

Paradox of well-being: the well-established finding that older adults maintain high subjective well-being despite facing challenges from their objective circumstances.

Parkinson's disease: a disease that shows a variety of motor disturbances, including tremors, speech impediments, slowing of movement, muscular rigidity, shuffling gait, and postural instability or the inability to maintain balance.

Part C of Medicare: also called Medicare Advantage; provides coverage in conjunction with private health plans.

Part D of Medicare: a prescription-drug benefit plan that provides coverage for a portion of the enrollee's costs.

Path analysis: a method where researchers test all possible correlations among a set of variables to see if they can be explained by a single model.

Patient Protection and Affordable Care Act (PPACA): legislation signed into law by President Barack Obama in the spring of 2010 intended to expand health care insurance to all Americans.

Patient Self-Determination Act (PSDA): passed in 1990, guarantees the right of all competent adults to have an active role in decisions about their care.

Perimenopause: a 3- to 5-year span in which a woman gradually loses her reproductive ability; it ends in menopause when a woman has not had her menstrual period for 1 year.

Peripheral ties: friendships that are not characterized by a high degree of closeness.

Personal aging: changes that occur within the individual and reflect the influence of time's passage on the body's structures and functions.

Personality disorder: a long-standing pattern of inner experience and behavior that has maladaptive qualities.

Person–environment correspondence theory: people are most satisfied when their workplaces respond to their needs.

Photoaging: age changes caused by radiation.

Physician-assisted suicide (PAS): a process through which terminally ill individuals make the conscious decision, while they are still able to do so, that they want their lives to end before dying becomes a protracted process.

Pick's disease: a form of dementia that involves severe atrophy of the frontal and temporal lobes.

Pikes Peak Model of Geropsychology: a set of competencies that professional geropsychologists are expected to have when working with older adults.

Planck hypothesis: the tendency of peak scientific productivity to occur in early adulthood.

Plasticity in development: the course of development may be altered (is "plastic") depending on the nature of the individual's specific interactions in the environment.

Plasticity model: a view of the aging nervous system that proposes that although some neurons die, the remaining ones continue to develop.

Plaque: hard deposits inside the arterial walls consisting of cholesterol, cellular waste products, calcium, and fibrin.

Polypharmacy: a condition in which an individual takes multiple drugs.

Positive psychology: seeks to provide a greater understanding of the strengths and virtues that enable individuals and communities to thrive.

Positron emission tomography (PET) scan: a brain scan method that shows radioactive compounds in the blood as they pass through the brain.

Possible selves: model proposing that the individual's view of the self, or self-schema, guides the choice and pursuit of future endeavors.

Posterior–Anterior Shift with Aging (PASA) model: proposes that the front (anterior) of the brain in older adults becomes more responsive to make up for the lower responsiveness found in the rear (posterior) of the brain.

Postformal operations: a stage proposed by adult development researchers that refers to the way that adults structure their thinking over and beyond that of adolescents.

Post-traumatic stress disorder (PTSD): the diagnosis given to people whose symptoms persist for more than a month after a trauma and include the intrusion of distressing reminders of an event; dissociative symptoms, such as feeling numb or detached from others; avoidance of situations that might serve as reminders of the event; and hyperarousal, including sleep disturbances or irritability.

Pragmatics of intelligence: an individual's aptitude to apply his or her abilities to the solution of real-life problems.

Presbycusis: an age-related hearing loss due to degenerative changes in the cochlea or auditory nerve leading from the cochlea to the brain.

Presbyopia: the loss of the ability to focus vision on near objects.

Presenilin genes (PS1 and PS2): genes that may lead APP to increase its production of beta-amyloid, which in turn causes neurofibrillary tangles and amyloid plaques.

Prevalence statistics: data that provide estimates of the percentage of people who have ever had symptoms in a particular period.

Primary aging or normal aging: a set of changes built into the hard wiring of an organism that progress at different rates among individuals but are universal, intrinsic, and progressive.

Primary Mental Abilities Test (PMAT): assesses the seven abilities of Verbal Meaning, Word Fluency, Number, Spatial Relations, Memory, Perceptual Speed, and General Reasoning.

Problem-focused coping: coping in which people attempt to reduce their stress by changing something about the situation.

Procedural memory: the recall of the actions involved in particular tasks, such as sewing on a button, playing the piano, and riding a bike.

Processing speed: the brain's efficiency in processing information.

Professional geropsychology: the application of gerontology to the psychological treatment of older adults.

Programmed aging theories: propose that aging and death are built into the hardwiring of all organisms and are therefore part of the genetic code.

Prospective memory: the recall of events to be performed in the future.

Prospective study: a variant of longitudinal design in which researchers sample from a population of interest before they develop a particular type of illness or experience a particular type of life event.

Protean career: a career in which individuals are both self-directed and driven internally by their own values.

Pseudodementia: a condition where cognitive symptoms appear, causing impairment similar to neurocognitive disorder.

Psychodynamic perspective: emphasizes the ways in which unconscious motives and impulses express themselves in people's personalities and behavior.

Psychodynamic therapy: focuses on the client's underlying conflicts; however, these traditional models are changing, and therapists working from this framework may emphasize other issues, such as the client's attachment style.

Psychological age: the performance that an individual achieves on measures of such qualities as reaction time, memory, learning ability, and intelligence.

Psychological assessment: a procedure in which a clinician provides a formal evaluation of an individual's cognitive, personality, and psychosocial functioning.

Psychological disorders: include the range of behaviors and experiences that fall outside of social norms, create adaptational difficulty for the individual on a daily basis, and put the individual or others at risk of harm.

Psychopathy: a set of traits that include a lack of remorse and an impulsive lifestyle.

Psychosocial theory of development: the view proposed by Erikson that at certain points in life, a person's biological, psychological, and social changes come together to influence his or her personality.

Psychotherapeutic medications: an attempt to reduce an individual's psychological symptoms.

Qualitative method: when researchers use a flexible approach to understand the main themes in their data.

Quasi-experimental design: a research design where groups are compared on predetermined characteristics.

Race: defined in biological terms as the classification within the species based on physical and structural characteristics.

Random error theories: hypothesizes that aging reflects unplanned changes in an organism over time.

Reaction time: the basic measure of processing speed.

Reciprocity in development: people both influence and are influenced by the events in their lives.

Recycling: the process through which workers change their main field of career activity part way into occupational life.

Reliability: a measure's consistency and whether it produces the same results each time it is used.

Religion: an individual's identification with an organized belief system.

Reminiscence bump: clear memories from the age of about 10 to 30 years.

Remote memory: involves the recall of information from the distant past in general.

Replicative senescence: the loss of the ability of cells to reproduce.

Reserve capacity: abilities that are there to be used but are currently untapped.

Residential care facility: provides 24-hour supportive care services and supervision to individuals who do not require skilled nursing care.

Resilience: the ability to recover from stress.

Resource model: an individual's adjustment to retirement reflects his or her physical, cognitive, motivational, financial, social, and emotional resources; the more resources, the more favorable will be the individual's adjustment at any one point through the retirement transition.

Respite care: provides family caregivers with a break while allowing the older adult to receive needed support.

Retirement: the withdrawal of an individual in later life from the labor force.

Retrieval-induced forgetting: being unable to remember information that a person knew at one time in the past.

Reversible neurocognitive disorders: disorders due to the presence of a medical condition that affects but does not destroy brain tissue.

RIASEC model: the six basic types that characterize an individual's vocational interests.

Rivastigmine: a generic version of the drug Exelon.

Role reversal: the family situation in which adult children take over in the role as parent because the parents are unable to care for themselves.

Role theory of retirement: proposes that retirement has deleterious effects because the loss of the work role loosens the ties between the individual and society.

Rowe and Kahn definition of successful aging: the absence of disease, high cognitive and physical function, and engagement with life.

Sandwich generation: midlife caregivers are sandwiched between their aging mothers and their teenaged children.

Sarcopenia: a progressive age-related loss of muscle tissue.

Scaffolding theory: proposes that older adults are able to recruit alternate neural circuits as needed by task demands to make up for losses suffered elsewhere.

Schemas: the mental structures we use to understand the world.

Schizophrenia: a disorder in which individuals experience a distorted perception of reality and impairment in thinking, behavior, affect, and motivation.

Secondary aging or impaired aging: changes due to disease.

Secretases: in healthy aging, the part of APP remaining outside the neuron is trimmed by enzymes.

Secure attachment style: individuals feel confident about themselves and confident that others will treat them well.

Selective attrition: the fact that the people who drop out of a longitudinal study are not necessarily representative of the sample that was originally tested.

Selective optimization with compensation model (SOC): proposes that adults attempt to preserve and maximize the abilities that are of central importance and put less effort into maintaining those that are not.

Self-determination theory: focuses on the amount of control that workers have over their jobs as influences on vocational satisfaction.

Self-Directed Search (SDS): a self-administered questionnaire that allows one to assess where one fits on the RIASEC dimensions.

Self-efficacy: a term used in the social psychological literature to refer to a person's feelings of competence at a particular task.

Semantic memory: the ability to recall word meanings and factual information.

Sequential design: designs consisting of different combinations of the variables of age, cohort, and time of measurement.

Set point perspective: the view that people's personalities influence their level of well-being throughout life.

Sex: an individual's inherited predisposition to develop the physiological characteristics typically associated with maleness or femaleness.

Similarity hypothesis: proposes that the similarity of personality and values predicts both initial interpersonal attraction and satisfaction within long-term relationships.

Simple reaction time tasks: tasks used to measure processing speed in which participants are instructed to make a response, such as pushing a key as soon as a target appears.

Simple visual search: the target differs from the other stimuli by only one feature, such as shape, color, or size.

Single nucleotide polymorphisms (SNPs): small genetic variations that can occur in a person's DNA sequence.

Single photon emission computed tomography (SPECT): a brain scan method that detects radioactive compounds as they pass through the brain.

Skilled nursing facility: a type of nursing home that provides the most intensive nursing care available outside of a hospital.

Skip generation family: a family living situation in which children live with their grandparents and not their parents.

Sleep apnea: a disorder in which the individual becomes temporarily unable to breathe while asleep.

Social age: calculated by evaluating where people are compared to the "typical" ages expected for people to be when they occupy certain positions in life.

Social aging: the effects of a person's exposure to a changing environment.

Social anxiety disorder: the individual experiences extreme anxiety about being watched by other people.

Social clock: the expectations for the ages at which a society associates with major life events.

Social comparison: the process that occurs when people rate themselves relative to their primary reference group.

Social death: the process through which the dying become treated as nonpersons by family or health care workers as they are left to spend their final months or years in a hospital or nursing home.

Social exchange theory: predicts why some relationships succeed and others fail in terms of whether the relationship's rewards exceed its costs.

Social indicator model: demographic and social structural variables, such as age, gender, marital status, and income, account for individual differences in levels of well-being.

Social Security Act: federal legislation that guarantees income for retirees and others who are unable to work as well as a lump sum in death benefits for survivors.

Socioeconomic status (SES): or "social class," reflects people's position in the educational and occupational ranks of a society.

Socioemotional selectivity theory: proposes that throughout adulthood, people structure the nature and range of their relationships to maximize gains and minimize risks.

Somatopause of aging: a decline in the somatotrophic axis (GH and IGF-1).

Source memory: the recall of where or how an individual acquires information.

Specific phobia: based on the individual's having an irrational fear of a particular object or situation.

Stages of dying: the process considered to occur universally among terminally ill patients including denial, anger, bargaining, depression, and acceptance.

Stereotype threat: suggests that people perform in ways consistent with negative stereotypes of the group to which they see themselves as belonging.

Stress incontinence: a condition where the individual is unable to retain urine while engaging in some form of physical exertion.

Stress: the perception that a situation overwhelms the individual's ability to manage effectively in that situation.

Strong Vocational Interest Inventory (SVII): consists of items in which respondents indicate their preferences for occupations, topics of study, activities, and types of people.

Structural ambivalence: the idea that society's structures do not make clear how family members should behave.

Structural equation modeling (SEM): a process where researchers test models involving relationships that include latent variables.

Subcutaneous: the bottommost layer of skin, giving the skin its opacity and smoothing the curves of the arms, legs, and face.

Subdural haematoma: a blood clot that creates pressure on brain tissue.

Subjective well-being: an individual's overall sense of happiness.

Successful cognitive aging: defined as cognitive performance that is above the average for an individual's age group as objectively measured.

Super's life-span life-stage theory: focuses on the role of the self and proposes that people attempt to realize their inner potential through their career choices.

Supercentenarians: people who are 110 years old and older.

Survey method: a way to gain information about a sample that can then be generalized to a larger population.

Survivor principle: people who live to old age outlive the many threats that could have caused their deaths at earlier ages.

Sustained attention: when participants completing a task must respond when they see a particular target appear out of a continuous stream of stimuli.

Swan song: a creative work produced at the very end of an artist's life.

Tamed death: the prevailing view until the Middle Ages in which death was viewed as familiar and simple, a transition to eternal life.

Tau: the protein that makes up neurofibrillary tangles.

Telomeres: repeating sequences of proteins that contain no genetic information.

Terminal decline: the gradual loss of cognitive abilities as an individual draws closer to death.

Terror management theory: proposes that people regard with panic and dread the thought of the finitude of their lives.

Tertiary aging: the rapid loss of functions experienced at the very end of life.

Testing the limits: the process of continuing to train people until they show no further improvements.

Tetrahydroaminoacridine (THA): also called tacrine and given the brand name Cognex.

Theory of multiple intelligences: theory that intelligence includes several traditional abilities as well as others not usually tapped in intelligence tests.

Time of measurement: the year or period in which a person is tested.

Time-sequential design: method in which data are organized by age and time of measurement.

Tinnitus: a symptom in which the individual perceives sounds in the head or ear (such as a ringing noise) when there is no external source.

Trait: a stable, enduring disposition that persists over time.

Trait perspective: a theory based on the assumption that the organization of the personal dispositions known as traits guide the individual's behavior.

Transient ischemic attack (TIA): a condition caused by the development of clots in the cerebral arteries; also called a ministroke.

Transition to parenthood (TtP): the period of adjustment to the new family status represented by the presence of a child in the home.

Two-factor motivational theory: proposes that intrinsic and extrinsic factors play different roles in contributing to vocational satisfaction.

Type A behavior pattern: a collection of traits that include being highly competitive, being impatient, feeling a strong sense of time urgency, and being highly achievement-oriented.

Urge incontinence: a form of urinary incontinence in which the individual experiences a sudden need to urinate and may even leak urine.

Useful field of view (UFOV): tests people's ability to respond to stimuli appearing in the periphery of their vision.

Validity: a test's ability to measure what it is supposed to measure.

Variable: a characteristic that "varies" from individual to individual.

Vascular neurocognitive disorder: a progressive loss of cognitive functioning due to damage to the arteries supplying the brain.

Vertigo: the sensation of spinning when the body is at rest.

Visual search tasks: require that the observer locate a specific target among a set of distractors.

Vocation: a person's choice of an occupation.

Vocational satisfaction: the extent to which people find their work to be enjoyable.

Wear and tear theory: proposes that as people age, they believe they are "falling apart."

Wechsler Adult Intelligence Scale (WAIS): the most well-known individual test of adult intelligence.

Wernicke's disease: an acute condition caused by chronic alcohol abuse involving delirium, eye movement disturbances, difficulties maintaining balance and movement, and deterioration of the nerves to the hands and feet.

White matter hyperintensities (WMH): abnormalities in the brain thought to be made up of parts of deteriorating neurons.

Whitehall II: a survey of a large sample of British adults focusing on the relationships among health, social class, and occupation.

Widowhood effect: the greater probability of death in those who have become widowed compared to those who are married.

Work–family conflict model: proposes that people have a fixed amount of time and energy to spend on their life roles.

Work–family enrichment model: proposes that experiences in one role improve the quality of life in the other.

Working memory: keeps information temporarily available and active in consciousness.

World Health Organization definition of active aging: the process of optimizing opportunities for health, participation, and security in order to enhance quality of life as people age.

Young-old: a subgroup of older adults between the ages of 65 to 74.

REFERENCES

Aartsen, M. J., Smits, C. H., van Tilburg, T., Knipscheer, K. C., & Deeg, D. J. (2002). Activity in older adults: Cause or consequence of cognitive functioning? A longitudinal study on everyday activities and cognitive performance in older adults. *Journals of Gerontology Series B: Psychological Sciences and Social Sciences, 57,* P153–162.

Aartsen, M. J., Van Tilburg, T., Smits, C. H., Comijs, H. C., & Knipscheer, K. C. (2005). Does widowhood affect memory performance of older persons? *Psychological Medicine, 35,* 217–226.

Abraham, A., Pieritz, K., Thybusch, K., Rutter, B., Kröger, S., Schweckendiek, J., ... Hermann, C. (2012). Creativity and the brain: Uncovering the neural signature of conceptual expansion. *Neuropsychologia.* doi:10.1016/j.neuropsychologia.2012.04.015

Abrams, R. C., & Horowitz, S. V. (1999). Personality disorders after age 50: A meta-analytic review of the literature. In E. Rosowsky, R. C. Abrams & R. A. Zweig (Eds.), *Personality disorders in older adults: Emerging issues in diagnosis and treatment* (pp. 55–68). Mahweh, NJ: Lawrence Erlbaum.

Achem, S. R., & Devault, K. R. (2005). Dysphagia in aging. *Journal of Clinical Gastroenterology, 39,* 357–371.

Achenbaum, W. A. (1978). *Old age in the new land: The American experience since 1970.* Baltimore: Johns Hopkins University Press.

Achtman, R. L., Green, C. S., & Bavelier, D. (2008). Video games as a tool to train visual skills. *Restorative Neurology & Neuroscience, 26,* 435–446.

Acierno, R., Hernandez, M. A., Amstadter, A. B., Resnick, H. S., Steve, K., Muzzy, W., & Kilpatrick, D. G. (2010). Prevalence and correlates of emotional, physical, sexual, and financial abuse and potential neglect in the United States: The National Elder Mistreatment Study. *American Journal of Public Health, 100,* 292–297. doi:AJPH.2009.163089 pii:10.2105/AJPH.2009.163089

Ackerman, P. L., Kanfer, R., & Calderwood, C. (2010). Use it or lose it? Wii brain exercise practice and reading for domain knowledge. *Psychology and Aging, 25,* 753–766. doi:10.1037/a0019277

Adams-Price, C. (1998). Aging, writing, and creativity. In C. Adams-Price (Ed.), *Creativity and successful aging: Theoretical and empirical approaches* (pp. 289–310). New York: Springer.

Adams, R. G., & Blieszner, R. (1994). An integrative conceptual framework for friendship research. *Journal of Social and Personal Relationships, 11,* 163–184.

Adler, N. E., Boyce, T., Chesney, M. A., Cohen, S., Folkman, S., Kahn, R. L., & Syme, S. L. (1994). Socioeconomic status and health: The challenge of the gradient. *American Psychologist, 49,* 15–24.

Administration on Aging. (2012). A profile of older Americans: 2011. Retrieved from http://www.aoa.gov/aoaroot/aging_statistics/Profile/2011/docs/2011profile.pdf

AgingwithDignity.org. (2010). Five wishes.

Agostinho, D., & Paço, A. (2012). Analysis of the motivations, generativity and demographics of the food bank volunteer. *International Journal of Nonprofit and Voluntary Sector Marketing, 17,* 249–261. doi:10.1002/nvsm.1427

Aimoni, C., Bianchini, C., Borin, M., Ciorba, A., Fellin, R., Martini, A., ... Volpato, S. (2010). Diabetes, cardiovascular risk factors and idiopathic sudden sensorineural hearing loss: A case-control study. *Audiology and Neurootology, 15,* 111–115. doi:000231636 pii:10.1159/000231636

Akbaraly, T. N., Kivimaki, M., Shipley, M. J., Tabak, A. G., Jokela, M., Virtanen, M., ... Singh-Manoux, A. (2009). Metabolic syndrome over 10 years and cognitive functioning in late mid life: The Whitehall II study. *Diabetes Care.* doi:dc09-1218 pii:10.2337/dc09-1218

Akbaraly, T. N., Singh-Manoux, A., Marmot, M. G., & Brunner, E. J. (2009). Education attenuates the association between dietary patterns and cognition. *Dementia and Geriatric Cognitive Disorders, 27,* 147–154. doi:000199235 pii:10.1159/000199235

Akiyama, A., Numata, K., & Mikami, H. (2010). Importance of end-of-life support to minimize caregiver's regret during bereavement of the elderly for better subsequent adaptation to bereavement. *Archives of Gerontology and Geriatrics, 50,* 175–178. doi:S0167-4943(09)00077-6 pii:10.1016/j.archger.2009.03.006

Alameel, T., Andrew, M. K., & Macknight, C. (2010). The association of fecal incontinence with institutionalization and mortality in older adults. *American Journal of Gastroenterology.* doi:ajg201077 pii:10.1038/ajg.2010.77

Aldwin, C. M., & Gilmer, D. F. (1999). Health and optimal aging. In J. C. Cavanaugh & S. K. Whitbourne (Eds.), *Gerontology: Interdisciplinary perspectives* (pp. 123–154). New York: Oxford University Press.

Alexandersen, P., Karsdal, M. A., & Christiansen, C. (2009). Long-term prevention with hormone-replacement therapy after the menopause: Which women should be targeted? *Womens Health (Lond Engl)*, 5, 637–647. doi:10.2217/whe.09.52

Alexopoulos, G. S., Reynolds, C. F., III,, Bruce, M. L., Katz, I. R., Raue, P. J., Mulsant, B. H., … Ten Have, T. (2009). Reducing suicidal ideation and depression in older primary care patients: 24-month outcomes of the PROSPECT study. *American Journal of Psychiatry*, 166, 882–890. doi:appi.ajp.2009.08121779 pii:10.1176/appi.ajp.2009.08121779

Allaire, J. C., & Marsiske, M. (2002). Well- and ill-defined measures of everyday cognition: Relationship to older adults' intellectual ability and functional status. *Psychology and Aging*, 17, 101–115.

Allen, E. S., & Atkins, D. C. (2012). The association of divorce and extramarital sex in a representative U.S. sample. *Journal of Family Issues*, 33, 1477–1493. doi:10.1177/0192513x12439692

Allen, K. R., & Walker, A. J. (2000). Qualitative research. In C. Hendrick & S. S. Hendrick (Eds.), *Close relationships* (pp. 19–30). Thousand Oaks, CA: Sage Publications.

Allen, P. D., Nelson, H. W., & Netting, F. E. (2007). Current practice and policy realities revisited: Undertrained nursing home social workers in the U.S. *Soc Work Health Care*, 45, 1–22.

Alloy, L. B., & Abramson, L. Y. (1979). Judgement of contingency in depressed and nondepressed students: Sadder but wiser? *Journal of Experimental Psychology: General*, 108, 441–485.

Almeida, O. P., Calver, J., Jamrozik, K., Hankey, G. J., & Flicker, L. (2009). Obesity and metabolic syndrome increase the risk of incident depression in older men: The health in men study. *American Journal of Geriatric Psychiatry*, 17, 889–898. doi:10.1097/JGP.0b013e3181b047e3 pii:00019442-200910000-00010

Alonso-Fernandez, P., Puerto, M., Mate, I., Ribera, J. M., & de la Fuente, M. (2008). Neutrophils of centenarians show function levels similar to those of young adults. *Journal of the American Geriatrics Society*, 56, 2244–2251. doi:JGS2018 pii:10.1111/j.1532-5415.2008.02018.x

Alsantali, A., & Shapiro, J. (2009). Androgens and hair loss. *Current Opinions in Endocrinology, Diabetes, and Obesity*, 16, 246–253.

Alzheimer's Association. (2010). 2010 Alzheimer's disease facts and figures. Retrieved from http://www.alz.org/national/documents/report_alzfactsfigures2009.pdf

Amato, P. R. (2000). The consequences of divorce for adults and children. *Journal of Marriage and the Family*, 62, 511–521.

Amato, P. R., & Afifi, T. D. (2006). Feeling caught between parents: Adult children's relations with parents and subjective well-being. *Journal of Marriage and Family*, 68, 222–235.

American Cancer Society. (2013). Cancer facts and figures 2013.

American Medical Association. (1997). Caring to the end: Conscientious end-of-life care can reduce concerns about care of the terminally ill. *American Medical News*.

American Psychiatric Association. (2000). *DSM-IV: Diagnostic and statistical manual of mental disorders text revision*. Washington DC: American Psychiatric Association.

American Psychiatric Association. (2013). *DSM-5 Diagnostic and statistical manual of mental disorders 5*. Washington DC: American Psychiatric Association.

American Psychological Association. (2001). APA resolution on end-of-life issues and care. Retrieved from http://www.apa.org/about/policy/end-of-life.aspx

American Psychological Association. (2003). Ethical principles of psychologists and code of conduct. Retrieved from http://www.apa.org/ethics/code2002.html#8_02

American Psychological Association. (2004). Guidelines for psychological practice with older adults. *American Psychologist*, 59, 336–265.

American Psychological Association Presidential Task Force on Evidence-Based Practice. (2006). Evidence-based practice in psychology. *American Psychologist*, 61, 271–285. doi:10.1037/0003-066x.61.4.271

Amore, M., Tagariello, P., Laterza, C., & Savoia, E. M. (2007). Beyond nosography of depression in elderly. *Archives of Gerontology and Geriatrics*, 44 Suppl 1, 13–22.

An, J. S., & Cooney, T. M. (2006). Psychological well-being in mid to late life: The role of generativity development and parent-child relationships across the lifespan. *International Journal of Behavioral Development*, 30, 410–421.

Ancoli-Israel, S., & Cooke, J. R. (2005). Prevalence and comorbidity of insomnia and effect on functioning in elderly populations. *Journal of the American Geriatrics Society*, 53, S264–271.

Andreoletti, C., Veratti, B. W., & Lachman, M. E. (2006). Age differences in the relationship between anxiety and recall. *Aging and Mental Health*, 10, 265–271.

Andrew, M. K., Freter, S. H., & Rockwood, K. (2006). Prevalence and outcomes of delirium in community and non-acute care settings in people without dementia: A report from the Canadian Study of Health and Aging. *BMC Medicine*, 4, 15.

Andrews-Hanna, J. R., Snyder, A. Z., Vincent, J. L., Lustig, C., Head, D., Raichle, M. E., & Buckner, R. L. (2007). Disruption of large-scale brain systems in advanced aging. *Neuron*, 56, 924–935. doi:10.1016/j.neuron.2007.10.038

Angelucci, L. (2000). The glucocorticoid hormone: From pedestal to dust and back. *European Journal of Pharmacology*, 405, 139–147. doi:S0014299900005471 pii:S0014-2999(00)00547-1

Anger, J. T., Saigal, C. S., & Litwin, M. S. (2006). The prevalence of urinary incontinence among community dwelling adult women: Results from the National Health and Nutrition Examination Survey. *Journal of Urology*, 175, 601–604. doi:S0022-5347(05)00242-9 pii:10.1016/S0022-5347(05)00242-9

Anthoney, S. F., & Armstrong, P. I. (2010). Individuals and environments: Linking ability and skill ratings with interests. *Journal of Counseling Psychology*, 57, 36–51.

Antonini, F. M., Magnolfi, S. U., Petruzzi, E., Pinzani, P., Malentacchi, F., Petruzzi, I., & Masotti, G. (2008). Physical performance and creative activities of centenarians. *Archives of Gerontology and Geriatrics, 46,* 253–261.

Aoi, W. (2009). Exercise and food factors. *Forum in Nutrition, 61,* 147–155. doi:000212747 pii:10.1159/000212747

Arbesman, M., & Pellerito, J. M., Jr., (2008). Evidence-based perspective on the effect of automobile-related modifications on the driving ability, performance, and safety of older adults. *American Journal of Occupational Therapy, 62,* 173–186. doi:10.5014/ajot.62.2.173

Archer, N., Brown, R. G., Reeves, S., Boothby, H., Lovestone, S., & Nicholas, H. (2009). Midlife neuroticism and the age of onset of Alzheimer's disease. *Psychological Medicine, 39,* 665–673.

Ardelt, M. (2004). Wisdom as expert knowledge system: A critical review of a contemporary operationalization of an ancient concept. *Human Development, 47,* 257–285.

Arean, P. A., & Ayalon, L. (2005). Assessment and treatment of depressed older adults in primary care. *Clinical Psychology: Science and Practice, 12,* 321–335.

Aries, P. (1974). *Western attitudes toward death: From the middle ages to the present.* Baltimore: Johns Hopkins University Press.

Aries, P. (1981). *The hour of our death.* New York: Alfred A. Knopf.

Armstrong-Stassen, M., & Ursel, N. D. (2009). Perceived organizational support, career satisfaction, and the retention of older workers. *Journal of Occupational and Organizational Psychology, 82,* 201–220.

Armstrong, P. I., & Anthoney, S. F. (2009). Personality facets and RIASEC interests: An integrated model. *Journal of Vocational Behavior, 75,* 346–359.

Arnett, J. J. (2000). Emerging adulthood: A theory of development from the late teens through the twenties. *American Psychologist, 55,* 469–480.

Arnold, J. T., Liu, X., Allen, J. D., Le, H., McFann, K. K., & Blackman, M. R. (2007). Androgen receptor or estrogen receptor-beta blockade alters DHEA-, DHT-, and E(2)-induced proliferation and PSA production in human prostate cancer cells. *Prostate, 67,* 1152–1162. doi:10.1002/pros.20585

Arthur, M. B., & Rousseau, D. M. (Eds.). (1996). *The boundaryless career: A new employment principle for a new organizational era.* New York: Oxford University Press.

Artistico, D., Cervone, D., & Pezzuti, L. (2003). Perceived self-efficacy and everyday problem solving among young and older adults. *Psychology and Aging, 18,* 68–79.

Atchley, R. C. (1989). A continuity theory of normal aging. *Gerontologist, 29,* 183–190.

Atchley, R. C. (2000). *Social forces and aging* (9th ed.). Belmont CA: Wadsworth Thomson Learning.

Ayers, C. R., Saxena, S., Golshan, S., & Wetherell, J. L. (2010). Age at onset and clinical features of late life compulsive hoarding. *International Journal of Geriatric Psychiatry, 25,* 142–149. doi:10.1002/gps.2310

Ayers, C. R., Sorrell, J. T., Thorp, S. R., & Wetherell, J. L. (2007). Evidence-based psychological treatments for late-life anxiety. *Psychology and Aging, 22,* 8–17.

Baan, R., Grosse, Y., Straif, K., Secretan, B., El Ghissassi, F., Bouvard, V., ... Cogliano, V. (2009). A review of human carcinogens—Part F: Chemical agents and related occupations. *Lancet Oncology, 10,* 1143–1144.

Baddeley, A. (2003). Working memory: Looking back and looking forward. *Nature Reviews Neuroscience, 4,* 829–839.

Baird, B. M., Lucas, R. E., & Donnellan, M. B. (2010). Life satisfaction across the lifespan: Findings from two nationally representative panel studies. *Social Indicators Research, 99,* 183–203. doi:10.1007/s11205-010-9584-9

Bakitas, M., Ahles, T. A., Skalla, K., Brokaw, F. C., Byock, I., Hanscom, B., ... Hegel, M. T. (2008). Proxy perspectives regarding end-of-life care for persons with cancer. *Cancer, 112,* 1854–1861. doi:10.1002/cncr.23381

Bakitas, M., Lyons, K. D., Hegel, M. T., Balan, S., Brokaw, F. C., Seville, J., ... Ahles, T. A. (2009). Effects of a palliative care intervention on clinical outcomes in patients with advanced cancer: The Project ENABLE II randomized controlled trial. *Journal of the American Medical Association, 302,* 741–749. doi:302/7/741 pii:10.1001/jama.2009.1198

Baliunas, D. O., Taylor, B. J., Irving, H., Roerecke, M., Patra, J., Mohapatra, S., & Rehm, J. (2009). Alcohol as a risk factor for type 2 diabetes: A systematic review and meta-analysis. *Diabetes Care, 32,* 2123–2132. doi:dc09-0227 pii:10.2337/dc09-0227

Ball, K., Berch, D. B., Helmers, K. F., Jobe, J. B., Leveck, M. D., Marsiske, M., ... Willis, S. L. (2002). Effects of cognitive training interventions with older adults: A randomized controlled trial. *Journal of the American Medical Association, 288,* 2271–2281.

Baltes, P. B. (1979). Life-span developmental psychology: Some converging observations on history and theory. In P. B. Baltes & J. O. G. Brim (Eds.), *Life-span development and behavior* (Vol. 2, pp. 255–279). New York: Academic Press.

Baltes, P. B., & Baltes, M. M. (1990). Psychological perspectives on successful aging: A model of selective optimization with compensation. In P. B. Baltes & M. M. Baltes (Eds.), *Successful aging: Perspectives from the behavioral sciences* (pp. 1–34). New York: Cambridge University Press.

Baltes, P. B., & Graf, P. (1996). Psychological aspects of aging: Facts and frontiers. In D. Magnusson (Ed.), *The lifespan development of individuals: Behavioral, neurobiological, and psychosocial perspectives* (pp. 427–460). New York: Cambridge University Press.

Baltes, P. B., & Kliegl, R. (1992). Further testing of limits of cognitive plasticity: Negative age differences in a mnemonic skill are robust. *Developmental Psychology, 28,* 121–125.

Baltes, P. B., & Schaie, K. W. (1976). On the plasticity of intelligence in adulthood and old age: Where Horn and Donaldson fail. *American Psychologist, 31,* 720–725.

Baltes, P. B., & Smith, J. (2008). The fascination of wisdom: Its nature, ontogeny, and function. *Perspectives on Psychological Science, 3,* 56–64.

Baltes, P. B., & Staudinger, U. M. (2000). Wisdom: A meta-heuristic (pragmatic) to orchestrate mind and virtue toward excellence. *American Psychologist, 55,* 122–136. doi:10.1037/0003-066x.55.1.122

Baltes, P. B., Staudinger, U. M., Maercker, A., & Smith, J. (1995). People nominated as wise: A comparative study of wisdom-related knowledge. *Psychology and Aging, 10,* 155–166.

Bandura, A. (1977). Self-efficacy: Toward a unifying theory of behavioral change. *Psychological Review, 84,* 191–215.

Banks, J., Marmot, M., Oldfield, Z., & Smith, J. P. (2006). Disease and disadvantage in the United States and in England. *Journal of the American Medical Association, 295,* 2037–2045.

Baquer, N. Z., Taha, A., Kumar, P., McLean, P., Cowsik, S. M., Kale, R. K., … Sharma, D. (2009). A metabolic and functional overview of brain aging linked to neurological disorders. *Biogerontology, 10,* 377–413. doi:10.1007/s10522-009-9226-2

Barefoot, J. C., Mortensen, E. L., Helms, M. J., Avlund, K., & Schroll, M. (2001). A longitudinal study of gender differences in depressive symptoms from age 50 to 80. *Psychology and Aging, 16,* 342–345.

Barnard, K., & Colon-Emeric, C. (2010). Extraskeletal effects of vitamin D in older adults: Cardiovascular disease, mortality, mood, and cognition. *American Journal of Geriatric Pharmacotherapy, 8,* 4–33. doi:S1543-5946(10)00008-5 pii:10.1016/j.amjopharm.2010.02.004

Bartels, S. J., Moak, G. S., & Dums, A. R. (2002). Mental health services in nursing homes: Models of mental health services in nursing homes: A review of the literature. *Psychiatric Services, 53,* 1390–1396.

Bartzokis, G., Beckson, M., Lu, P. H., Nuechterlein, K. H., Edwards, N., & Mintz, J. (2001). Age-related changes in frontal and temporal lobe volumes in men: A magnetic resonance imaging study. *Archives of General Psychiatry, 58,* 461–465.

Basak, C., Boot, W. R., Voss, M. W., & Kramer, A. F. (2008). Can training in a real-time strategy video game attenuate cognitive decline in older adults? *Psychology and Aging, 23,* 765–777.

Basak, C., Voss, M. W., Erickson, K. I., Boot, W. R., & Kramer, A. F. (2011). Regional differences in brain volume predict the acquisition of skill in a complex real-time strategy videogame. *Brain and Cognition, 76,* 407–414.

Basseches, M. (1984). *Dialectical thinking and adult development.* Norwood NJ: Ablex.

Bassett-Jones, N., & Lloyd, G. C. (2005). Does Herzberg's motivation theory have staying power? *Journal of Management Development, 24,* 929–943.

Bauer, J. J. (2008). How the ego quiets as it grows: Ego development, growth stories, and eudaimonic personality development. In H. A. Wayment & J. J. Bauer (Eds.), *Transcending self-interest: Psychological explorations of the quiet ego.* (pp. 199–210). Washington, DC: American Psychological Association.

Baumeister, R. F. (1996). Self-regulation and ego threat: Motivated cognition, self deception, and destructive goal setting. In P. M. Gollwitzer & J. A. Bargh (Eds.), *The psychology of action: Linking cognition and motivation to behavior* (pp. 27–47). New York, NY: Guilford Press.

Baumeister, R. F. (1997). Identity, self-concept, and self-esteem: The self lost and found. In R. Hogan, J. A. Johnson & S. R. Briggs (Eds.), *Handbook of personality psychology* (pp. 681–710). San Diego, CA: Academic Press.

Baumeister, R. F., Bratslavsky, E., Finkenauer, C., & Vohs, K. D. (2001). Bad is stronger than good. *Review of General Psychology, 54,* 323–370.

Bavelier, D., Green, C. S., Pouget, A., & Schrater, P. (2012). Brain plasticity through the life span: Learning to learn and action video games. *Annual Review of Neuroscience, 35,* 391–416. doi:10.1146/annurev-neuro-060909-152832

Beason-Held, L. L., Kraut, M. A., & Resnick, S. M. (2009). Stability of default-mode network activity in the aging brain. *Brain Imaging and Behavior, 3,* 123–131. doi:10.1007/s11682-008-9054-z

Bechtold, M., Palmer, J., Valtos, J., Iasiello, C., & Sowers, J. (2006). Metabolic syndrome in the elderly. *Current Diabetes Reports, 6,* 64–71.

Becker, E. (1973). *The denial of death.* New York: Free Press.

Bedford, V. H., Volling, B. L., & Avioli, P. S. (2000). Positive consequences of sibling conflict in childhood and adulthood. *International Journal of Aging & Human Development, 51,* 53–69.

Beehr, T. A., Glazer, S., Nielson, N. L., & Farmer, S. J. (2000). Work and nonwork predictors of employees' retirement ages. *Journal of Vocational Behavior, 57,* 206–225.

Beeri, M. S., Schmeidler, J., Sano, M., Wang, J., Lally, R., Grossman, H., & Silverman, J. M. (2006). Age, gender, and education norms on the CERAD neuropsychological battery in the oldest old. *Neurology, 67,* 1006–1010.

Beghetto, R. A., & Kaufman, J. C. (2007). Toward a broader conception of creativity: A case for 'mini-c' creativity. *Psychology of Aesthetics, Creativity, and the Arts, 1,* 73–79. doi:10.1037/1931-3896.1.2.73

Beier, M. E., & Ackerman, P. L. (2005). Age, ability, and the role of prior knowledge on the acquisition of new domain knowledge: Promising results in a real-world learning environment. *Psychology and Aging, 20,* 341–355.

Belleville, S., Gilbert, B., Fontaine, F., Gagnon, L., Ménard, É., & Gauthier, S. (2006). Improvement of episodic memory in persons with mild cognitive impairment and healthy older adults: Evidence from a cognitive intervention program. *Dementia and Geriatric Cognitive Disorders, 22,* 486–499.

Bellipanni, G., Bianchi, P., Pierpaoli, W., Bulian, D., & Ilyia, E. (2001). Effects of melatonin in perimenopausal and menopausal women: A randomized and placebo controlled study. *Experimental Gerontology, 36,* 297–310.

Ben-David, B. M., & Schneider, B. A. (2009). A sensory origin for color-word Stroop effects in aging: A meta-analysis. *Neuropsychol*

Dev Cogn B Aging Neuropsychol Cogn, 16, 505–534. doi:911771785 pii:10.1080/13825580902855862

Ben-David, B. M., & Schneider, B. A. (2012). A sensory origin for color-word Stroop effects in aging: Simulating age-related changes in color-vision mimics age-related changes in Stroop. *Aging, Neuropsychology, and Cognition, 17*, 730–746.

Bengtson, V., Giarrusso, R., Mabry, J. B., & Silverstein, M. (2002). Solidarity, conflict, and ambivalence: Complementary or competing perspectives on intergenerational relationships? *Journal of Marriage and Family, 64*, 568–576. doi:10.1111/j.1741-3737.2002.00568.x

Bengtson, V. L., & Schrader, S. S. (1982). Parent-child relations. In D. J. Mangen & W. A. Peterson (Eds.), *Research instruments in social gerontology*, Vol 2 (pp. 115–185). Minneapolis: University of Minnesota Press.

Benloucif, S., Orbeta, L., Ortiz, R., Janssen, I., Finkel, S. I., Bleiberg, J., & Zee, P. C. (2004). Morning or evening activity improves neuropsychological performance and subjective sleep quality in older adults. *Sleep, 27*, 1542–1551.

Bennett, D. A., Schneider, J. A., Tang, Y., Arnold, S. E., & Wilson, R. S. (2006). The effect of social networks on the relation between Alzheimer's disease pathology and level of cognitive function in old people: A longitudinal cohort study. *Lancet Neurology, 5*, 406–412.

Bennett, K. M. (2006). Does marital status and marital status change predict physical health in older adults? *Psychogical Medicine, 36*, 1313–1320.

Bennett, K. M., Smith, P. T., & Hughes, G. M. (2005). Coping, depressive feelings and gender differences in late life widowhood. *Aging and Mental Health, 9*, 348–353.

Benson, L. A., McGinn, M. M., & Christensen, A. (2012). Common principles of couple therapy. *Behavior Therapy, 43*, 25–35. doi:10.1016/j.beth.2010.12.009

Benson, N., Hulac, D. M., & Kranzler, J. H. (2010). Independent examination of the Wechsler Adult Intelligence Scale—Fourth Edition (WAIS-IV): What does the WAIS-IV measure? *Psychological Assessment, 22*, 121–130. doi:10.1037/a0017767

Berg, A. I., Hassing, L. B., McClearn, G. E., & Johansson, B. (2006). What matters for life satisfaction in the oldest-old? *Aging and Mental Health, 10*, 257–264.

Betik, A. C., & Hepple, R. T. (2008). Determinants of VO2 max decline with aging: An integrated perspective. *Applied Physiology, Nutrition, and Metabolism, 33*, 130–140. doi h07-174 pii:10.1139/h07-174

Bhar, S. S., & Brown, G. K. (2012). Treatment of depression and suicide in older adults. *Cognitive and Behavioral Practice, 19*, 116–125. doi:10.1016/j.cbpra.2010.12.005

Bharucha, A. E., & Camilleri, M. (2001). Functional abdominal pain in the elderly. *Gastroenterol Clin North Am, 30*, 517–529.

Bhave, D. P., Kramer, A., & Glomb, T. M. (2010). Work–family conflict in work groups: Social information processing, support, and demographic dissimilarity. *Journal of Applied Psychology, 95*, 145–158.

Bialystok, E. (2011). Reshaping the mind: The benefits of bilingualism. *Canadian Journal of Experimental Psychology/Revue canadienne de psychologie expérimentale, 65*, 229–235. doi:10.1037/a0025406

Bialystok, E., Craik, F. I. M., Green, D. W., & Gollan, T. H. (2009). Bilingual minds. *Psychological Science in the Public Interest, 10*, 89–129. doi:10.1177/1529100610387084

Biblarz, T. J., & Stacey, J. (2010). How does the gender of parents matter? *Journal of Marriage and Family, 72*, 3–22. doi:10.1111/j.1741-3737.2009.00678.x

Bieman-Copland, S., & Ryan, E. B. (2001). Social perceptions of failures in memory monitoring. *Psychology and Aging, 16*, 357–361.

Binkley, N. (2009). A perspective on male osteoporosis. *Best Practices in Research on Clinical Rheumatology, 23*, 755–768. doi:S1521-6942(09)00115-6 pii:10.1016/j.berh.2009.10.001

Birditt, K. S., Miller, L. M., Fingerman, K. L., & Lefkowitz, E. S. (2009). Tensions in the parent and adult child relationship: Links to solidarity and ambivalence. *Psychology and Aging, 24*, 287–295. doi:10.1037/a0015196

Birditt, K. S., Rott, L. M., & Fingerman, K. L. (2009). "If you can't say anything nice don't say anything at all": Coping with interpersonal tensions in the parent–child relationship during adulthood. *Journal of Family Psychology, 23*, 769–778.

Birditt, K. S., Tighe, L. A., Fingerman, K. L., & Zarit, S. H. (2012). Intergenerational relationship quality across three generations. *The Journals of Gerontology: Series B: Psychological Sciences and Social Sciences, 67B*, 627–638. doi:10.1093/geronb/gbs050

Bischoff-Ferrari, H. A., Kiel, D. P., Dawson-Hughes, B., Orav, J. E., Li, R., Spiegelman, D., … Willett, W. C. (2009). Dietary calcium and serum 25-hydroxyvitamin D status in relation to BMD among U.S. adults. *Journal of Bone and Mineral Research, 24*, 935–942. doi:10.1359/jbmr.081242

Blake, H., Mo, P., Malik, S., & Thomas, S. (2009). How effective are physical activity interventions for alleviating depressive symptoms in older people? A systematic review. *Clinical Rehabilitation, 23*, 873–887. doi:0269215509337449 pii:10.1177/0269215509337449

Blanchet, S., Belleville, S., & Peretz, I. (2006). Episodic encoding in normal aging: Attentional resources hypothesis extended to musical material. *Aging, Neuropsychology and Cognition, 13*, 490–502.

Blenkner, M. (1963). Social work and family relations in later life with some thoughts on filial maturity. In E. Shanas & G. F. Streib (Eds.), *Social structure and the family: Generational relations* (pp. 46–59). Englewood Cliffs, NJ: Prentice-Hall.

Blieszner, R. (2006). A lifetime of caring: Dimensions and dynamics in late-life close relationships. *Personal Relationships, 13*, 1–18.

Bloom, H. G., Ahmed, I., Alessi, C. A., Ancoli-Israel, S., Buysse, D. J., Kryger, M. H., … Zee, P. C. (2009). Evidence-based recommendations for the assessment and management of sleep disorders in older persons. *Journal of the American Geriatrics Society, 57*, 761–789.

Blum, S., Luchsinger, J. A., Manly, J. J., Schupf, N., Stern, Y., Brown, T. R., ... Brickman, A. M. (2012). Memory after silent stroke: Hippocampus and infarcts both matter. *Neurology, 78,* 38–46.

Boards of Trustees of the Federal Hospital Insurance and Federal Supplementary Medical Insurance Trust Funds. (2012). 2012 Annual report of the Boards of Trustees of the Federal Hospital Insurance Trust Fund and the Federal Supplementary Medical Insurance Trust Fund. Retrieved from http://www.cms.gov/Research-Statistics-Data-and-Systems/Statistics-Trends-and-Reports/ReportsTrustFunds/Downloads/TR2012.pdf

Böckerman, P., Johansson, E., & Saarni, S. (2012). Institutionalisation and subjective wellbeing for old-age individuals: Is life really miserable in care homes? *Ageing & Society, 32,* 1176–1192. doi:10.1017/s0144686x1100081x

Bodner, E. (2009). On the origins of ageism among older and younger adults. *International Psychogeriatrics, 21,* 1003–1014.

Boling, M. C., Bolgla, L. A., Mattacola, C. G., Uhl, T. L., & Hosey, R. G. (2006). Outcomes of a weight-bearing rehabilitation program for patients diagnosed with patellofemoral pain syndrome. *Archives of Physical Medicine and Rehabilitation, 87,* 1428–1435.

Bonanno, G. A., Wortman, C. B., Lehman, D. R., Tweed, R. G., Haring, M., Sonnega, J., ... Nesse, R. M. (2002). Resilience to loss and chronic grief: A prospective study from preloss to 18-months postloss. *Journal of Personality & Social Psychology, 83,* 1150–1164.

Bonanno, G. A., Wortman, C. B., & Nesse, R. M. (2004). Prospective patterns of resilience and maladjustment during widowhood. *Psychology and Aging, 19,* 260–271.

Bonnefond, A., Härmä, M., Hakola, T., Sallinen, M., Kandolin, I., & Virkkala, J. (2006). Interaction of age with shift-related sleep-wakefulness, sleepiness, performance, and social life. *Experimental Aging Research, 32,* 185–208.

Boot, W. R., Basak, C., Erickson, K. I., Neider, M., Simons, D. J., Fabiani, M., ... Kramer, A. F. (2010). Transfer of skill engendered by complex task training under conditions of variable priority. *Acta Psychologica, 135,* 349–357. doi:10.1016/j.actpsy.2010.09.005

Borges, R., Temido, P., Sousa, L., Azinhais, P., Conceicao, P., Pereira, B., ... Sobral, F. (2009). Metabolic syndrome and sexual (dys)function. *J Sex Med, 6,* 2958–2975. doi:JSM1412 pii:10.1111/j.1743-6109.2009.01412.x

Bortz, W. M. (2005). Biological basis of determinants of health. *American Journal of Public Health, 95,* 389–392.

Botwinick, J. (1977). Intellectual abilities. In J. E. Birren & K. W. Schaie (Eds.), *Handbook of the psychology of aging* (pp. 580–605). New York: Van Nostrand Reinhold.

Bouchard, T. J. J. (2004). Genetic influence on human psychological traits: A survey. *Current Directions in Psychological Science, 13,* 148–151.

Boult, C., Green, A. F., Boult, L. B., Pacala, J. T., Snyder, C., & Leff, B. (2009). Successful models of comprehensive care for older adults with chronic conditions: Evidence for the Institute of Medicine's "Retooling for an aging America" report. *Journal*

of the American Geriatrics Society, 57, 2328–2337. doi:JGS2571 pii:10.1111/j.1532-5415.2009.02571.x

Boustani, M., Baker, M. S., Campbell, N., Munger, S., Hui, S. L., Castelluccio, P., ... Callahan, C. (2010). Impact and recognition of cognitive impairment among hospitalized elders. *Journal of Hospital Medicine, 5,* 69–75. doi:10.1002/jhm.589

Bowlby, J. (1980). *Attachment and loss, Vol. 3: Loss, sadness and depression.* London: Hogarth.

Bowling, A., Banister, D., Sutton, S., Evans, O., & Windsor, J. (2002). A multidimensional model of the quality of life in older age. *Aging and Mental Health, 6,* 355–371.

Bowling, N. A., Eschleman, K. J., & Wang, Q. (2010). A meta-analytic examination of the relationship between job satisfaction and subjective well-being. *Journal of Occupational and Organizational Psychology, 83,* 915–934. doi:10.1348/096317909x478557

Bowman, K. W., & Singer, P. A. (2001). Chinese seniors' perspectives on end-of-life decisions. *Social Science and Medicine, 53,* 455–464.

Bowman, R. E. (2005). Stress-induced changes in spatial memory are sexually differentiated and vary across the lifespan. *Journal of Neuroendocrinology, 17,* 526–535.

Boylan, S., Welch, A., Pikhart, H., Malyutina, S., Pajak, A., Kubinova, R., ... Bobak, M. (2009). Dietary habits in three Central and Eastern European countries: The HAPIEE study. *BMC Public Health, 9,* 439. doi:1471-2458-9-439 pii:10.1186/1471-2458-9-439

Boyle, L. L., Porsteinsson, A. P., Cui, X., King, D. A., & Lyness, J. M. (2010). Depression predicts cognitive disorders in older primary care patients. *Journal of Clinical Psychiatry, 71,* 74–79. doi:10.4088/JCP.08m04724gry

Boyle, S. H., Jackson, W. G., & Suarez, E. C. (2007). Hostility, anger, and depression predict increases in C3 over a 10-year period. *Brain, Behavior, and Immunity.*

Braitman, K. A., Kirley, B. B., Chaudhary, N. K., & Ferguson, S. A. (2006). Factors leading to older drivers' intersection crashes. Retrieved from http://www.iihs.org/research/topics/pdf/older_drivers.pdf

Bramlett, M. D., & Mosher, W. D. (2002). Cohabitation, marriage, divorce, and remarriage in the United States. *National Center for Health Statistics. Vital and Health Statistics 23(22).*

Brandt, M., Deindl, C., & Hank, K. (2012). Tracing the origins of successful aging: The role of childhood conditions and social inequality in explaining later life health. *Social Science & Medicine, 74,* 1418–1425. doi:10.1016/j.socscimed.2012.01.004

Brenes, G. A., Ingram, C. W., & Danhauer, S. C. (2012). Telephone-delivered psychotherapy for late-life anxiety. *Psychological Services, 9,* 219–220. doi:10.1037/a0025950

Brenes, G. A., Kritchevsky, S. B., Mehta, K. M., Yaffe, K., Simonsick, E. M., Ayonayon, H. N., ... Penninx, B. W. (2007). Scared to death: Results from the Health, Aging, and Body Composition Study. *American Journal of Geriatric Psychiatry, 15,* 262–265.

Brennan, P. L., Schutte, K. K., & Moos, R. H. (2006). Long-term patterns and predictors of successful stressor resolution in later life. *International Journal of Stress Management, 13*, 253–272.

Brickman, A. M., Zimmerman, M. E., Paul, R. H., Grieve, S. M., Tate, D. F., Cohen, R. A., ... Gordon, E. (2006). Regional white matter and neuropsychological functioning across the adult lifespan. *Biological Psychiatry, 60*, 444–453.

Brill, F. (1967). *Matisse*. London: Paul Hamlyn.

Brim, O. G., Jr., (1976). Theories of the male mid-life crisis. *The Counseling Psychologist, 6*, 2–9.

Briones, T. L. (2006). Environment, physical activity, and neurogenesis: Implications for prevention and treatment of Alzheimer's disease. *Current Alzheimer Research, 3*, 49–54.

Briscoe, J. P., & Finkelstein, L. M. (2009). The "new career" and organizational commitment: Do boundaryless and protean attitudes make a difference? *Career Development International, 14*, 242–260.

Briscoe, J. P., Hall, D. T., & Frautschy DeMuth, R. L. (2006). Protean and boundaryless careers: An empirical exploration. *Journal of Vocational Behavior, 69*, 30–47.

Britto, R. R., Zampa, C. C., de Oliveira, T. A., Prado, L. F., & Parreira, V. F. (2009). Effects of the aging process on respiratory function. *Gerontology, 55*, 505–510. doi:000235853 pii:10.1159/000235853

Broach, K., Joseph, K. M., & Schroeder, D. J. (2003). Pilot age and accident reports 3: An analysis of professional air transport pilot accident rates by age. Retrieved from http://www.faa.gov/library/reports/medical/age60/media/age60_3.pdf

Bronfenbrenner, U., & Ceci, S. J. (1994). Nature-nurture reconceptualized in developmental perspective: A bioecological model. *Psychological Review, 101*, 568–586.

Brooke, L., & Taylor, P. (2005). Older workers and employment: Managing age relations. *Ageing & Society, 25*, 415–429.

Brookmeyer, R., Corrada, M. M., Curriero, F. C., & Kawas, C. (2002). Survival following a diagnosis of Alzheimer disease. *Archives Neurology, 59*, 1764–1767.

Brown, S. L., Bulanda, J. R., & Lee, G. R. (2012). Transitions into and out of cohabitation in later life. *Journal of Marriage and Family, 74*, 774–793.

Brucker, A. J. (2009). Age-related macular degeneration. *Retina, 29*, S2–4. doi:10.1097/IAE.0b013e3181ad255f

Brummett, B. H., Babyak, M. A., Williams, R. B., Barefoot, J. C., Costa, P. T., & Siegler, I. C. (2006). NEO personality domains and gender predict levels and trends in body mass index over 14 years during midlife. *Journal of Research in Personality, 40*, 222–236.

Brydon, L., Strike, P. C., Bhattacharyya, M. R., Whitehead, D. L., McEwan, J., Zachary, I., & Steptoe, A. (2010). Hostility and physiological responses to laboratory stress in acute coronary syndrome patients. *Journal of Psychosomatic Research, 68*, 109–116. doi:S0022-3999(09)00260-8 pii:10.1016/j.jpsychores.2009.06.007

Buckner, R. L., Andrews-Hanna, J. R., & Schacter, D. L. (2008). The brain's default network: anatomy, function, and relevance to disease. *Annals of the New York Academy of Science, 1124*, 1–38. doi:10.1196/annals.1440.011

Buford, T. W., & Willoughby, D. S. (2008). Impact of DHEA(S) and cortisol on immune function in aging: A brief review. *Appl Physiol Nutr Metab, 33*, 429–433. doi: h08-013 pii:10.1139/h08-013

Bugg, J. M., DeLosh, E. L., & Clegg, B. A. (2006). Physical activity moderates time-of-day differences in older adults' working memory performance. *Experimental Aging Research, 32*, 431–446. doi: R15X03172KNU7782 pii:10.1080/03610730600875833

Buja, A., Scafato, E., Sergi, G., Maggi, S., Suhad, M. A., Rausa, G., ... Perissinotto, E. (2009). Alcohol consumption and metabolic syndrome in the elderly: Results from the Italian longitudinal study on aging. *European Journal of Clinical Nutrition.* doi: ejcn2009136 pii:10.1038/ejcn.2009.136

Bureau of Labor Statistics. (2010). Injuries, illnesses, and fatalities. Retrieved from http://www.bls.gov/iif/#News

Bureau of Labor Statistics. (2012). Employment situation of veterans. *News release.* Retrieved from http://www.bls.gov/news.release/pdf/vet.pdf

Bureau of Labor Statistics. (2013a). Education pays. Retrieved from http://www.bls.gov/emp/ep_chart_001.htm

Bureau of Labor Statistics. (2013b). Labor force statistics from the Current Population Survey. Retrieved from http://www.bls.gov/cps/cpsaat07.htm

Bureau of Labor Statistics. (2013c). Usual weekly earnings of wage and salary workers fourth quarter 2012. *News releases.* Retrieved from http://www.bls.gov/news.release/pdf/wkyeng.pdf

Bureau of Labor Statistics. (2013d). Women in the labor force: A databook. Retrieved from http://www.bls.gov/cps/wlf-databook-2012.pdf

Burgio, K. L. (2009). Behavioral treatment of urinary incontinence, voiding dysfunction, and overactive bladder. *Obstetrics and Gynecology Clinics of North America, 36*, 475–491. doi:S0889-8545(09)00062-X pii:10.1016/j.ogc.2009.08.005

Burgio, L. D., Stevens, A., Burgio, K. L., Roth, D. L., Paul, P., & Gerstle, J. (2002). Teaching and maintaining behavior management skills in the nursing home. *Gerontologist, 42*, 487–496.

Burgmans, S., van Boxtel, M. P., Gronenschild, E. H., Vuurman, E. F., Hofman, P., Uylings, H. B., ... Raz, N. (2010). Multiple indicators of age-related differences in cerebral white matter and the modifying effects of hypertension. *Neuroimage, 49*, 2083–2093. doi:S1053-8119(09)01106-9 pii:10.1016/j.neuroimage.2009.10.035

Burke, D. M. (1997). Language, aging, and inhibitory deficits: Evaluation of a theory. *Journal of Gerontology Series B: Psychological Sciences and Social Sciences, 52B*, P254–264.

Burke, K. E., & Wei, H. (2009). Synergistic damage by UVA radiation and pollutants. *Toxicology and Industrial Health, 25*, 219–224. doi:25/4-5/219 pii:10.1177/0748233709106067

Burton, C. L., Strauss, E., Hultsch, D. F., & Hunter, M. A. (2006). Cognitive functioning and everyday problem solving in older adults. *Clinical Neuropsychology, 20,* 432–452.

Burton, C. L., Strauss, E., Hultsch, D. F., & Hunter, M. A. (2009). The relationship between everyday problem solving and inconsistency in reaction time in older adults. *Neuropsychol Dev Cogn B Aging Neuropsychol Cogn, 16,* 607–632. doi:914159307 pii:10.1080/13825580903167283

Burton, C. L., Strauss, E., Hultsch, D. F., Moll, A., & Hunter, M. A. (2006). Intraindividual variability as a marker of neurological dysfunction: A comparison of Alzheimer's disease and Parkinson's disease. *Journal of Clinical and Experimental Neuropsychology, 28,* 67–83.

Burzynska, A. Z., Nagel, I. E., Preuschhof, C., Gluth, S., Bäckman, L., Li, S. C., … Heekeren, H. R. (2012). Cortical thickness is linked to executive functioning in adulthood and aging. *Human Brain Mapping, 33,* 1607–1620. doi:10.1002/hbm.21311

Butler, K. M., & Zacks, R. T. (2006). Age deficits in the control of prepotent responses: Evidence for an inhibitory decline. *Psychology and Aging, 21,* 638–643. doi:2006-11398-019 pii:10.1037/0882-7974.21.3.638

Butler, R. (1974). Successful aging and the role of life review. *Journal of the American Geriatrics Society, 22,* 529–535.

Byberg, L., Melhus, H. K., Gedeborg, R., Sundstrom, J., Ahlbom, A., Zethelius, B., … Michaelsson, K. (2009). Total mortality after changes in leisure time physical activity in 50 year old men: 35-year follow-up of population based cohort. *BMJ: British Medical Journal, 338.*

Byers, A. L., Covinsky, K. E., Barnes, D. E., & Yaffe, K. (2012). Dysthymia and depression increase risk of dementia and mortality among older veterans. *The American Journal of Geriatric Psychiatry, 20,* 664–672. doi:10.1097/JGP.0b013e31822001c1

Byrne, C. M., Solomon, M. J., Young, J. M., Rex, J., & Merlino, C. L. (2007). Biofeedback for fecal incontinence: Short-term outcomes of 513 consecutive patients and predictors of successful treatment. *Diseases of the Colon and Rectum, 50,* 417–427. doi:10.1007/s10350-006-0846-1

Cabrera, E. F. (2009). Protean organizations: Reshaping work and careers to retain female talent. *Career Development International, 14,* 186–201.

Caffrey, C., Sengupta, M., Park-Lee, E., Moss, A., Rosenoff, E., & Harris-Kojetin, L. (2012). Residents living in residential care facilities: United States, 2010. *NCHS Data Brief, No. 91.*

Callahan, C. M., Boustani, M. A., Unverzagt, F. W., Austrom, M. G., Damush, T. M., Perkins, A. J., … Hendrie, H. C. (2006). Effectiveness of collaborative care for older adults with Alzheimer disease in primary care: A randomized controlled trial. *Journal of the American Medical Association, 295,* 2148–2157.

Camp, C. J., Cohen-Mansfield, J., & Capezuti, E. A. (2002). Use of nonpharmacologic interventions among nursing home residents with dementia. *Psychiatric Services, 53,* 1397–1404.

Campayo, A., de Jonge, P., Roy, J. F., Saz, P., de la Camara, C., Quintanilla, M. A., … Lobo, A. (2010). Depressive disorder and incident diabetes mellitus: The effect of characteristics of depression. *American Journal of Psychiatry.* doi: appi.ajp.2009.09010038 pii:10.1176/appi.ajp.2009.09010038

Cao, J. J., Wronski, T. J., Iwaniec, U., Phleger, L., Kurimoto, P., Boudignon, B., & Halloran, B. P. (2005). Aging increases stromal/osteoblastic cell-induced osteoclastogenesis and alters the osteoclast precursor pool in the mouse. *Journal of Bone and Mineral Research, 20,* 1659–1668.

Carnelley, K. B., Wortman, C. B., Bolger, N., & Burke, C. T. (2006). The time course of grief reactions to spousal loss: Evidence from a national probability sample. *Journal of Personality and Social Psychology, 91,* 476–492.

Carr, D. (2012). Death and dying in the contemporary United States: What are the psychological implications of anticipated death? *Social and Personality Psychology Compass, 6,* 184–195. doi:10.1111/j.1751-9004.2011.00416.x

Carroll, C. C., Dickinson, J. M., Haus, J. M., Lee, G. A., Hollon, C. J., Aagaard, P., … Trappe, T. A. (2008). Influence of aging on the in vivo properties of human patellar tendon. *Journal of Applied Physiology, 105,* 1907–1915. doi: 00059.2008 pii:10.1152/japplphysiol.00059.2008

Carroll, J. B. (1993). *Human cognitive abilities: A survey of factor-analytic studies.* New York: Cambridge University Press.

Carstensen, L. L., Isaacowitz, D. M., & Charles, S. T. (1999). Taking time seriously: A theory of socioemotional selectivity. *American Psychologist, 54,* 165–181.

Carstensen, L. L., & Turk-Charles, S. (1994). The salience of emotion across the adult life span. *Psychology and Aging, 9,* 259–264.

Caruso, C., Candore, G., Colonna Romano, G., Lio, D., Bonafe, M., Valensin, S., & Franceschi, C. (2000). HLA, aging, and longevity: A critical reappraisal. *Human Immunology, 61,* 942–949.

Cattell, R. B. (1963). Theory of fluid and crystallized intelligence: A critical experiment. *Journal of Educational Psychology, 54,* 1–22.

Cattell, R. B. (1971). *Abilities: Their structure, growth, and action.* Boston: Houghton Mifflin.

Cauley, J. A., Lui, L. Y., Barnes, D., Ensrud, K. E., Zmuda, J. M., Hillier, T. A., … Newman, A. B. (2009). Successful skeletal aging: A marker of low fracture risk and longevity. The Study of Osteoporotic Fractures (SOF). *Journal of Bone Mineral Research, 24,* 134–143. doi:10.1359/jbmr.080813

Cauley, J. A., Palermo, L., Vogt, M., Ensrud, K. E., Ewing, S., Hochberg, M., … Black, D. M. (2008). Prevalent vertebral fractures in black women and white women. *Journal of Bone Mineral Research, 23,* 1458–1467. doi:10.1359/jbmr.080411

Cavan, R. S., Burgess, E. W., Havighurst, R. J., & Goldhamer, H. (1949). *Personal adjustment in old age.* Chicago: Science Research Associates.

Caycedo, A. M., Miller, B., Kramer, J., & Rascovsky, K. (2009). Early features in frontotemporal dementia. *Current Alzheimer Research, 6,* 337–340.

Center for Medicare and Medicaid Services. (2010a). Medicare enrollment: National trends. Retrieved from http://www.cms.hhs.gov/MedicareEnRpts/Downloads/HISMI08.pdf

Center for Medicare and Medicaid Services. (2010b). Nursing home data compendium, 2010 edition. Retrieved from http://www.cms.gov/Medicare/Provider-Enrollment-and-Certification/CertificationandComplianc/downloads/nursinghomedatacompendium_508.pdf

Center for Medicare and Medicaid Services. (2012). Brief summaries of Medicare and Medicaid: Title XVIII and Title XIX of the Social Security Act. Retrieved from http://www.cms.gov/Research-Statistics-Data-and-Systems/Statistics-Trends-and-Reports/MedicareProgramRatesStats/Downloads/MedicareMedicaidSummaries2012.pdf

Center for Medicare and Medicaid Services. (2013a). 2013 Medicare Part D landscape. Retrieved from http://cms.gov/Medicare/Prescription-Drug-Coverage/PrescriptionDrugCovGenIn/index.html

Center for Medicare and Medicaid Services. (2013b). CMS statistics. Retrieved from http://www.cms.gov/Research-Statistics-Data-and-Systems/Research/ResearchGenInfo/CMSStatistics.html

Center for Medicare and Medicaid Services. (2013c). National health expenditure data. Retrieved from http://www.cms.hhs.gov/nationalhealthexpenddata/

Center for Medicare and Medicaid Services. (2013d). National health expenditures, 2011 highlights. Retrieved from http://www.cms.hhs.gov/NationalHealthExpendData/downloads/highlights.pdf

Centers for Disease Control and Prevention. (2004). National nursing home survey. Retrieved from http://www.cdc.gov/nchs/data/series/sr_13/sr13_167.pdf

Centers for Disease Control and Prevention. (2006). Heat-Related Deaths—United States, 1999–2003. *Morbidity and Mortality Weekly Reports*, 55(29), 796–798.

Centers for Disease Control and Prevention. (2010a). Defining overweight and obesity. Retrieved from http://www.cdc.gov/obesity/defining.html

Centers for Disease Control and Prevention. (2010b). National diabetes fact sheet. Retrieved from http://www.cdc.gov/diabetes/pubs/estimates05.htm

Centers for Disease Control and Prevention. (2012). National Home and Hospice Care Survey fact sheet. Retrieved from http://www.cdc.gov/nchs/data/nhhcs/2007hospicecaresurvey.pdf

Centers for Disease Control and Prevention. (2013). Elder maltreatment prevention. Retrieved from http://www.cdc.gov/features/elderabuse/

Centers for Disease Control and Prevention. (2012). Suicide: Facts at a glance. Retrieved from http://www.cdc.gov/violenceprevention/pdf/Suicide-DataSheet-a.pdf

Centers for Disease Control and Prevention. (2013a). U.S. cancer statistics. Retrieved from http://apps.nccd.cdc.gov/uscs/

Centers for Disease Control and Prevention. (2013b). Web-based Injury Statistics Query and Reporting System (WISQARS). Retrieved from http://webappa.cdc.gov/sasweb/ncipc/mortrate10_us.html

Central Intelligence Agency. (2012). The world factbook. Retrieved from https://www.cia.gov/library/publications/the-world-factbook/rankorder/2066rank.html

Cerella, J., Poon, L. W., & Williams, D. M. (1980). Age and the complexity hypothesis. In L. W. Poon (Ed.), *Aging in the 1980s* (pp. 332–340). Washington DC: American Psychological Association.

Cernin, P. A., Lysack, C., & Lichtenberg, P. A. (2011). A comparison of self-rated and objectively measured successful aging constructs in an urban sample of African American older adults. *Clinical Gerontologist: The Journal of Aging and Mental Health*, 34, 89–102. doi:10.1080/07317115.2011.539525

Chan, D., Cheadle, A. D., Reiber, G., Unutzer, J., & Chaney, E. F. (2009). Health care utilization and its costs for depressed veterans with and without comorbid PTSD symptoms. *Psychiatric Services*, 60, 1612–1617. doi:60/12/1612 pii:10.1176/appi.ps.60.12.1612

Chan, S. W., Chiu, H. F., Chien, W. T., Goggins, W., Thompson, D., & Hong, B. (2009). Predictors of change in health-related quality of life among older people with depression: A longitudinal study. *International Psychogeriatrics*, 21, 1171–1179. doi:S1041610209990950 pii:10.1017/S1041610209990950

Chandola, T., Brunner, E., & Marmot, M. (2006). Chronic stress at work and the metabolic syndrome: Prospective study. *BMJ: British Medical Journal*, 332, 521–525.

Chang, Y. K., & Etnier, J. L. (2009). Exploring the dose-response relationship between resistance exercise intensity and cognitive function. *Journal of Sports Exercise Psychology*, 31, 640–656.

Chapman, B. P., Shah, M., Friedman, B., Drayer, R., Duberstein, P. R., & Lyness, J. M. (2009). Personality traits predict emergency department utilization over 3 years in older patients. *American Journal of Geriatric Psychiatry*, 17, 526–535. doi:10.1097/JGP.0b013e3181a2fbb1pii: 00019442-200906000-00012

Charles, S. T., & Carstensen, L. L. (2010). Social and emotional aging. *Annual Review of Psychology*, 61, 383–409.

Charles, S. T., Reynolds, C. A., & Gatz, M. (2001). Age-related differences and change in positive and negative affect over 23 years. *Journal of Personality & Social Psychology*, 80, 136–151.

Charlton, R. A., Barrick, T. R., Markus, H. S., & Morris, R. G. (2009). The relationship between episodic long-term memory and white matter integrity in normal aging. *Neuropsychologia*. doi:S0028-3932(09)00335-2 pii:10.1016/j.neuropsychologia.2009.08.018

Charney, D. S., Reynolds, C. F., III,, Lewis, L., Lebowitz, B. D., Sunderland, T., Alexopoulos, G. S., ... Young, R. C. (2003). Depression and Bipolar Support Alliance consensus statement on the unmet needs in diagnosis and treatment of mood disorders in late life. *Archives of General Psychiatry*, 60, 664–672.

Chassin, L., Macy, J. T., Seo, D.-C., Presson, C. C., & Sherman, S. J. (2010). The association between membership in the sandwich generation and health behaviors: A longitudinal study. *Journal of Applied Developmental Psychology*, 31, 38–46. doi:10.1016/j.appdev.2009.06.001

Chedraui, P., Perez-Lopez, F. R., Mendoza, M., Leimberg, M. L., Martinez, M. A., Vallarino, V., & Hidalgo, L. (2010). Factors related to increased daytime sleepiness during the menopausal transition as evaluated by the Epworth sleepiness scale. *Maturitas*, 65, 75–80. doi:S0378-5122(09)00402-2 pii:10.1016/j.maturitas.2009.11.003

Chen, J. C., Brunner, R. L., Ren, H., Wassertheil-Smoller, S., Larson, J. C., Levine, D. W., ... Stefanick, M. L. (2008). Sleep duration and risk of ischemic stroke in postmenopausal women. *Stroke*, 39, 3185–3192. doi:STROKEAHA.108.521773 pii:10.1161/STROKEAHA.108.521773

Chen, L. Y., & Hardy, C. L. (2009). Alcohol consumption and health status in older adults: A longitudinal analysis. *Journal of Aging and Health*, 21, 824–847. doi: 0898264309340688 pii:10.1177/0898264309340688

Cheng, S. T., Fung, H. H., & Chan, A. C. (2009). Self-perception and psychological well-being: The benefits of foreseeing a worse future. *Psychol Aging*, 24, 623–633. doi:2009-13203-011 pii:10.1037/a0016410

Cherkas, L. F., Aviv, A., Valdes, A. M., Hunkin, J. L., Gardner, J. P., Surdulescu, G. L., ... Spector, T. D. (2006). The effects of social status on biological aging as measured by white-blood-cell telomere length. *Aging Cell*.

Cherkas, L. F., Hunkin, J. L., Kato, B. S., Richards, J. B., Gardner, J. P., Surdulescu, G. L., ... Aviv, A. (2008). The association between physical activity in leisure time and leukocyte telomere length. *Archives of Internal Medicine*, 168, 154–158. doi:168/2/154 pii:10.1001/archinternmed.2007.39

Cherry, K. E., Silva, J. L., & Galea, S. (2009). Natural disasters and the oldest-old: A psychological perspective on coping and health in late life *Lifespan perspectives on natural disasters: Coping with Katrina, Rita, and other storms.* (pp. 171–193). New York: Springer Science + Business Media.

Chitaley, K., Kupelian, V., Subak, L., & Wessells, H. (2009). Diabetes, obesity and erectile dysfunction: Field overview and research priorities. *Journal of Urology*, 182, S45–S50. doi:S00225347(09)01946-6 pii:10.1016/j.juro.2009.07.089

Chiu, C. J., Milton, R. C., Gensler, G., & Taylor, A. (2006). Dietary carbohydrate intake and glycemic index in relation to cortical and nuclear lens opacities in the Age-Related Eye Disease Study. *American Journal of Clinical Nutrition*, 83, 1177–1184.

Chodzko-Zajko, W. J., Proctor, D. N., Fiatarone Singh, M. A., Minson, C. T., Nigg, C. R., Salem, G. J., & Skinner, J. S. (2009). American College of Sports Medicine position stand. Exercise and physical activity for older adults. *Medicine and Science in Sports and Exercise*, 41, 1510–1530. doi: 10.1249/MSS.0b013e3181a0c95c

Chou, S.-C., Boldy, D. P., & Lee, A. H. (2002). Resident satisfaction and its components in residential aged care. *Gerontologist*, 42, 188–198.

Christiansen, S. L., & Palkovitz, R. (2001). Why the "good provider" role still matters: Providing as a form of paternal involvement. *Journal of Family Issues*, 22, 84–106.

Chu, K. H., Baker, M. A., & Murrmann, S. K. (2012). When we are onstage, we smile: The effects of emotional labor on employee work outcomes. *International Journal of Hospitality Management*, 31, 906–915. doi:10.1016/j.ijhm.2011.10.009

Cicirelli, V. G. (1988). A measure of filial anxiety regarding anticipated care of elderly parents. *Gerontologist*, 28, 478–482.

Cicirelli, V. G. (2010). Attachment relationships in old age. *Journal of Social and Personal Relationships*, 27, 191–199. doi:10.1177/0265407509360984

Clarke, P., Marshall, V. W., & Weir, D. (2012). Unexpected retirement from full time work after age 62: Consequences for life satisfaction in older Americans. *European Journal of Ageing*, 9, 207–219. doi:10.1007/s10433-012-0229-5

Clarke, R., Emberson, J., Fletcher, A., Breeze, E., Marmot, M., & Shipley, M. J. (2009). Life expectancy in relation to cardiovascular risk factors: 38 year follow-up of 19,000 men in the Whitehall study. *BMJ: British Medical Journal*, 339, b3513.

Clerici, F., Vanacore, N., Elia, A., Spila-Alegiani, S., Pomati, S., Da Cas, R., ... Mariani, C. (2009). Memantine in moderately-severe-to-severe Alzheimer's disease: A postmarketing surveillance study. *Drugs and Aging*, 26, 321–332. doi:3

Cluett, C., & Melzer, D. (2009). Human genetic variations: Beacons on the pathways to successful ageing. *Mechanisms of Ageing and Development*, 130, 553–563. doi:S0047-6374(09)00089-X pii:10.1016/j.mad.2009.06.009

Coelho, S. G., Choi, W., Brenner, M., Miyamura, Y., Yamaguchi, Y., Wolber, R., ... Hearing, V. J. (2009). Short- and long-term effects of UV radiation on the pigmentation of human skin. *Journal of Investigative Dermatology Symposium Proceedings*, 14, 32–35. doi: jidsymp200910 pii:10.1038/jidsymp.2009.10

Cohan, C. L., & Kleinbaum, S. (2002). Toward a greater understanding of the cohabitation effect: Premarital cohabitation and marital communication. *Journal of Marriage and Family*, 64, 180–192.

Cohen-Mansfield, J., Shmotkin, D., Malkinson, R., Bartur, L., & Hazan, H. (2013). Parental bereavement increases mortality in older persons. *Psychological Trauma: Theory, Research, Practice, and Policy*, 5, 84–92. doi:10.1037/a0029011

Cohen, A., Houck, P. R., Szanto, K., Dew, M. A., Gilman, S. E., & Reynolds, C. F., III,. (2006). Social inequalities in response to antidepressant treatment in older adults. *Archives of General Psychiatry*, 63, 50–56.

Cohen, C. I., Abdallah, C. G., & Diwan, S. (2010). Suicide attempts and associated factors in older adults with schizophrenia. *Schizophrenia Research*. doi:S0920-9964(10)01180-1 pii:10.1016/j.schres.2010.03.010

Cohn, L. D., & Westenberg, P. M. (2004). Intelligence and maturity: Meta-analytic evidence for the incremental and discriminant validity of Loevinger's measure of ego development. *Journal of Personality and Social Psychology*, 86, 760–772.

Colcombe, S. J., Erickson, K. I., Scalf, P. E., Kim, J. S., Prakash, R., McAuley, E., ... Kramer, A. F. (2006). Aerobic exercise training increases brain volume in aging humans. *Journal of Gerontology Series A: Biological Sciences and Medical Sciences*, 61A, 1166–1170.

Coleman, H. R., Chan, C. C., Ferris, F. L., III,, & Chew, E. Y. (2008). Age-related macular degeneration. *Lancet, 372,* 1835–1845. doi:S0140-6736(08)61759-6 pii:10.1016/S0140-6736(08)61759-6

Coltrane, S. (2000). Research on household labor: Modeling and measuring the social embeddedness of routine family work. *Journal of Marriage and Family, 62,* 1208–1233.

Comijs, H. C., Gerritsen, L., Penninx, B. W., Bremmer, M. A., Deeg, D. J., & Geerlings, M. I. (2010). The association between serum cortisol and cognitive decline in older persons. *American Journal of Geriatric Psychiatry, 18,* 42–50. doi:10.1097/JGP.0b013e3181b970ae

Commons, M., Richards, F., & Armon, C. (Eds.). (1984). *Beyond formal operations: Late adolescent and adult cognitive development.* New York: Praeger.

Comondore, V. R., Devereaux, P. J., Zhou, Q., Stone, S. B., Busse, J. W., Ravindran, N. C., … Guyatt, G. H. (2009). Quality of care in for-profit and not-for-profit nursing homes: systematic review and meta-analysis. *BMJ: British Medical Journal, 4,* b2732.

Congdon, N., Vingerling, J. R., Klein, B. E., West, S., Friedman, D. S., Kempen, J., … Taylor, H. R. (2004). Prevalence of cataract and pseudophakia/aphakia among adults in the United States. *Archives of Ophthalmology, 122,* 487–494. doi:10.1001/archopht.122.4.487122/4/487 pii:

Connidis, I. A. (1992). Life transitions and the adult sibling tie: A qualitative study. *Journal of Marriage and Family, 54,* 972–982.

Connidis, I. A., & McMullin, J. A. (2002). Sociological ambivalence and family ties: A critical perspective. *Journal of Marriage and Family, 64,* 558–567. doi:10.1111/j.1741-3737.2002.00558.x

Connor, S. R., Egan, K. A., Kwilosz, D. M., Larson, D. G., & Reese, D. J. (2002). Interdisciplinary approaches to assisting with end-of-life care and decision making. *American Behavioral Scientist, 46,* 340–356.

Consedine, N. S., & Magai, C. (2003). Attachment and emotion experience in later life: The view from emotions theory. *Attach Hum Dev, 5,* 165–187. doi:10.1080/1461673031000108496 pii:98U1YMG3H66RMMCY

Constantinople, A. (1969). An Eriksonian measure of personality development in college students. *Developmental Psychology, 1,* 357–372.

Conwell, Y., Van Orden, K., & Caine, E. D. (2011). Suicide in older adults. *Psychiatric Clinics of North America, 34,* 451–468. doi:10.1016/j.psc.2011.02.002

Cooney, M. T., Dudina, A., De Bacquer, D., Wilhelmsen, L., Sans, S., Menotti, A., … Graham, I. M. (2009). HDL cholesterol protects against cardiovascular disease in both genders, at all ages and at all levels of risk. *Atherosclerosis, 206,* 611–616. doi:S0021-9150(09)00163-4 pii:10.1016/j.atherosclerosis.2009.02.041

Copen, C. E., Daniels, K., Vespa, J., & Mosher, W. D. (2012). First marriages in the United States: Data from the 2006–2010 National Survey of Family Growth. *National Health Statistics Reports, Number 49* (March 22, 2012). Retrieved from http://www.cdc.gov/nchs/data/nhsr/nhsr049.pdf

Cornelius, S., Gordon, C., & Ackland, A. (2011). Towards flexible learning for adult learners in professional contexts: An activity-focused course design. *Interactive Learning Environments, 19,* 381–393. doi:10.1080/10494820903298258

Cornwell, B. (2012). Spousal network overlap as a basis for spousal support. *Journal of Marriage and Family, 74,* 229–238. doi:10.1111/j.1741-3737.2012.00959.x

Corona, G., & Maggi, M. (2010). The role of testosterone in erectile dysfunction. *Nature Review Urology, 7,* 46–56. doi:nrurol.2009.235 pii:10.1038/nrurol.2009.235

Costa, P. T., Jr.,, & McCrae, R. R. (1992). *NEO-PI-R manual.* Odessa, FL: Psychological Assessment Resources.

Costa, P. T. J., & McCrae, R. R. (1978). Objective personality assessment. In M. Storandt, I. C. Siegler & M. F. Elias (Eds.), *The clinical psychology of aging* (pp. 119–143). New York: Plenum.

Council of Civil Service Unions/Cabinet Office. (2004). *Work, stress, and health: The Whitehall II study.* London, UK: Public and Commercial Services Union.

Covinsky, K. E., Lindquist, K., Dunlop, D. D., & Yelin, E. (2009). Pain, functional limitations, and aging. *Journal of the American Geriatrics Society, 57,* 1556–1561. doi: JGS2388 pii:10.1111/j.1532-5415.2009.02388.x

Cowgill, D. O., & Holmes, L. D. (1972). *Aging and modernization.* New York: Appleton-Century-Crofts.

Coyne, K. S., Margolis, M. K., Jumadilova, Z., Bavendam, T., Mueller, E., & Rogers, R. (2007). Overactive bladder and women's sexual health: What is the impact? *Journal of Sexual Medicine, 4,* 656–666. doi:JSM493 pii:10.1111/j.1743-6109.2007.00493.x

Craik, F. I. M., & Rose, N. S. (2012). Memory encoding and aging: A neurocognitive perspective. *Neuroscience and Biobehavioral Reviews, 36,* 1729–1739. doi:10.1016/j.neubiorev.2011.11.007

Cramer, P. (2003). Personality change in later adulthood is predicted by defense mechanism use in early adulthood. *Journal of Research in Personality, 37,* 76–104.

Cramer, P., & Jones, C. J. (2007). Defense mechanisms predict differential lifespan change in self-control and self-acceptance. *Journal of Research in Personality, 41,* 841–855.

Cramer, P., & Jones, C. J. (2008). Narcissism, identification, and longitudinal change in psychological health: Dynamic predictions. *Journal of Research in Personality, 42,* 1148–1159.

Crawford, S., & Channon, S. (2002). Dissociation between performance on abstract tests of executive function and problem solving in real-life-type situations in normal aging. *Aging and Mental Health, 6,* 12–21.

Crawley, L. M., Marshall, P. A., Lo, B., & Koenig, B. A. (2002). Strategies for culturally effective end-of-life care. *Annals of Internal Medicine, 136,* 673–679.

Crosnoe, R., & Elder, G. H., Jr., (2002). Life course transitions, the generational stake, and grandparent-grandchild relationships. *Journal of Marriage and Family, 64,* 1089–1096.

Crowe, F., Roddam, A., Key, T., Appleby, P., Overvad, K., Jakobsen, M., … Riboli, E. (2011). Fruit and vegetable intake and mortality from ischaemic heart disease: Results from the European Prospective Investigation into Cancer and Nutrition (EPIC)-Heart study. . *European Heart Journal, 32*(10), 1235–1243.

Cuddy, A. J. C., Norton, M. I., & Fiske, S. T. (2005). This old stereotype: The pervasiveness and persistence of the elderly stereotype. *Journal of Social Issues, 61,* 267–285.

Cumming, E., & Henry, W. E. (1961). *Growing old: The process of disengagement.* New York: Basic Books.

Curlin, F. A., Lawrence, R. E., Chin, M. H., & Lantos, J. D. (2007). Religion, conscience, and controversial clinical practices. *New England Journal of Medicine, 356,* 593–600.

Cushman, M., Cantrell, R. A., McClure, L. A., Howard, G., Prineas, R. J., Moy, C. S., … Howard, V. J. (2008). Estimated 10-year stroke risk by region and race in the United States: Geographic and racial differences in stroke risk. *Annals of Neurology, 64,* 507–513. doi:10.1002/ana.21493

da Silva Lara, L. A., Useche, B., Rosa, E. S. J. C., Ferriani, R. A., Reis, R. M., de Sa, M. F., … de Sa Rosa, E. S. A. C. (2009). Sexuality during the climacteric period. *Maturitas, 62,* 127–133. doi:S0378-5122(08)00399-X pii:10.1016/j.maturitas.2008.12.014

Dai, B., Ware, W. B., & Giuliani, C. A. (2012). A structural equation model relating physical function, pain, impaired mobility (IM), and falls in older adults. *Archives of Gerontology and Geriatrics, 55,* 645–652. doi:10.1016/j.archger.2012.06.005

Daly, M. C., & Bound, J. (1996). Worker adaptation and employer accommodation following the onset of a health impairment. *Journal of Gerontology: Social Sciences, 51,* S53–60.

Dangour, A. D., Allen, E., Elbourne, D., Fletcher, A., Richards, M., & Uauy, R. (2009). Fish consumption and cognitive function among older people in the UK: Baseline data from the OPAL study. *Journal of Nutrition, Health, and Aging, 13,* 198–202.

Davidson, D. J., Zacks, R. T., & Williams, C. C. (2003). Stroop interference, practice, and aging. *Neuropsychol Dev Cogn B Aging Neuropsychol Cogn, 10,* 85–98. doi:10.1076/anec.10.2.85.14463

Davidson, P. S. R., Cook, S. P., & Glisky, E. L. (2006). Flashbulb memories for September 11th can be preserved in older adults. *Aging, Neuropsychology and Cognition, 13,* 196–206.

Davis, M. A. (2003). Factors related to bridge employment participation among private sector early retirees. *Journal of Vocational Behavior, 63,* 55–71.

Davis, S. D., Lebow, J. L., & Sprenkle, D. H. (2012). Common factors of change in couple therapy. *Behavior Therapy, 43,* 36–48. doi:10.1016/j.beth.2011.01.009

Davison, E. H., Pless, A. P., Gugliucci, M. R., King, L. A., King, D. W., Salgado, D. M., … Bachrach, P. (2006). Late-life emergence of early-life trauma: The phenomenon of late-onset stress symptomatology among aging combat veterans. *Research on Aging, 28,* 84–114. doi:10.1177/0164027505281560

Dawis, R. (2002). Person–environment–correspondence theory. In S. D. Brown (Ed.), *Career choice and development* (4th ed.) (pp. 427–464). San Francisco, CA: Jossey Bass.

Dawson-Hughes, B., & Bischoff-Ferrari, H. A. (2007). Therapy of osteoporosis with calcium and vitamin D. *Journal of Bone and Mineral Research, 22 Suppl 2,* V59–63. doi:10.1359/jbmr.07s209

De Janasz, S., Sullivan, S., & Whiting, V. (2003). Mentor networks and career success: Lessons for turbulent times. *Academy of Management Executive, 17,* 78–91.

de Jong, F. J., Masaki, K., Chen, H., Remaley, A. T., Breteler, M. M., Petrovitch, H., … Launer, L. J. (2009). Thyroid function, the risk of dementia and neuropathologic changes: The Honolulu-Asia aging study. *Neurobiol Aging, 30,* 600–606. doi:S0197-4580(07)00301-6 pii:10.1016/j.neurobiolaging.2007.07.019

de Jong, P. T. (2006). Age-related macular degeneration. *New England Journal of Medicine, 355,* 1474–1485.

De Raedt, R., & Ponjaert-Kristoffersen, I. (2006). Self-serving appraisal as a cognitive coping strategy to deal with age-related limitations: An empirical study with elderly adults in a real-life stressful situation. *Aging and Mental Health, 10,* 195–203.

De Schutter, B. (2010). Never too old to play: The appeal of digital games to an older audience. *Games and Culture: A Journal of Interactive Media, 6,* 155–170. doi:10.1177/1555412010364978

De Vos, A., & Soens, N. (2008). Protean attitude and career success: The mediating role of self-management. *Journal of Vocational Behavior, 73,* 449–456.

De Vries, B., & Megathlin, D. (2009). The meaning of friendships for gay men and lesbians in the second half of life. *Journal of GLBT Family Studies, 5,* 82–98.

Deacon, A. (2008). Income, health, and well-being from around the world: Evidence from the Gallup World Poll. *Journal of Economic Perspectives, 22.*

Deary, I. J. (2012). Intelligence. *Annual Review of Psychology, 63,* 453–482. doi:10.1146/annurev-psych-120710-100353

Deci, E. L., & Ryan, R. M. (2008). Self-determination theory: A macrotheory of human motivation, development, and health. *Canadian Psychology/Psychologie canadienne, 49,* 182–185.

Degenholtz, H., Arnold, R., Meisel, A., and Lave, J. (2002). Persistence of racial disparities in advance care plan documents among nursing home residents. *Journal of American Geriatrics Society,* 378–381.

Delano-Wood, L., & Abeles, N. (2005). Late-life depression: Detection, risk reduction, and somatic intervention. *Clinical Psychology: Science and Practice, 12,* 207–217.

Delbanco, N. (2011). *Lastingness: The art of old age.* New York: Grand Central Publishing.

Delgoulet, C., & Marquie, J. C. (2002). Age differences in learning maintenance skills: A field study. *Experimental Aging Research, 28,* 25–37.

Dellenbach, M., & Zimprich, D. (2008). Typical intellectual engagement and cognition in old age. *Neuropsychol Dev Cogn B Aging Neuropsychol Cogn, 15,* 208–231. doi: 781708432 pii:10.1080/13825580701338094

Deng, H., Miao, D., Liu, J., Meng, S., & Wu, Y. The regeneration of gingiva: Its potential value for the recession of healthy gingiva. *Medical Hypotheses*, 74, 76–77. doi:S0306-9877(09)00543-X pii:10.1016/j.mehy.2009.07.051

Dennerstein, L., Dudley, E., & Guthrie, J. (2002). Empty nest or revolving door? A prospective study of women's quality of life in midlife during the phase of children leaving and re-entering the home. *Psychological Medicine*, 32, 545–550.

Dennis, N. A., Daselaar, S., & Cabeza, R. (2007). Effects of aging on transient and sustained successful memory encoding activity. *Neurobiology of Aging*, 28, 1749–1758. doi:S0197-4580(06)00239-9 pii:10.1016/j.neurobiolaging.2006.07.006

Dennis, W. (1966). Creative productivity between the ages of 20 and 80 years. *Journal of Gerontology*, 21, 1–8.

Department of Health and Human Services. (1999). *Mental health: A report of the Surgeon General*. Bethesda MD: U.S. Public Health Service.

Depp, C. A., & Jeste, D. V. (2004). Bipolar disorder in older adults: A critical review. *Bipolar Disorders*, 6, 343–367.

Depp, C. A., & Jeste, D. V. (2006). Definitions and predictors of successful aging: A comprehensive review of larger quantitative studies. *American Journal of Geriatric Psychiatry*, 14, 6–20.

Der, G., & Deary, I. J. (2006). Age and sex differences in reaction time in adulthood: Results from the United Kingdom Health and Lifestyle Survey. *Psychol Aging*, 21, 62–73. doi:2006-03906-007 pii:10.1037/0882-7974.21.1.62

Desai, S., Upadhyay, M., & Nanda, R. (2009). Dynamic smile analysis: Changes with age. *American Journal of Orthodontic and Dentofacial Orthopathy*, 136, 310 e311–310; discussion 310–311. doi:S0889-5406(09)00521-6 pii:10.1016/j.ajodo.2009.01.021

Detering, K. M., Hancock, A. D., Reade, M. C., & Silvester, W. (2010). The impact of advance care planning on end of life care in elderly patients: Randomised controlled trial. *BMJ: British Medical Journal*, 340, c1345.

Devine, A., Dick, I. M., Islam, A. F., Dhaliwal, S. S., & Prince, R. L. (2005). Protein consumption is an important predictor of lower limb bone mass in elderly women. *American Journal of Clinical Nutrition*, 81, 1423–1428.

Devore, E. E., Stampfer, M. J., Breteler, M. M., Rosner, B., Hee Kang, J., Okereke, O., ... Grodstein, F. (2009). Dietary fat intake and cognitive decline in women with type 2 diabetes. *Diabetes Care*, 32, 635–640. doi:32/4/635 pii:10.2337/dc08-1741

Di Bonito, P., Di Fraia, L., Di Gennaro, L., Vitale, A., Lapenta, M., Scala, A., ... Capaldo, B. (2007). Impact of impaired fasting glucose and other metabolic factors on cognitive function in elderly people. *Nutrition, Metabolism, and Cardiovascular Diseases*, 17, 203–208.

Diab, T., Condon, K. W., Burr, D. B., & Vashishth, D. (2006). Age-related change in the damage morphology of human cortical bone and its role in bone fragility. *Bone*, 38, 427–431.

Dickin, D. C., Brown, L. A., & Doan, J. B. (2006). Age-dependent differences in the time course of postural control during sensory perturbations. *Aging: Clinical and experimental research*, 18, 94–99.

Dickinson, G. E. (2012). Diversity in death: Body disposition and memorialization. *Illness, Crisis, & Loss*, 20, 141–158. doi:10.2190/IL.20.2.d

Diehl, M., Coyle, N., & Labouvie-Vief, G. (1996). Age and sex differences in coping and defense across the life span. *Psychology and Aging*, 11, 127–139.

Diekelmann, S., Biggel, S., Rasch, B., & Born, J. (2012). Offline consolidation of memory varies with time in slow wave sleep and can be accelerated by cuing memory reactivations. *Neurobiology of Learning and Memory*, 98, 103–111. doi:10.1016/j.nlm.2012.07.002

Diener, E. (1999). Subjective well-being: Three decades of progress. *Psychological Bulletin*, 125, 276–302.

Diener, E., Oishi, S., & Lucas, R. E. (2003). Personality, culture, and subjective well-being: Emotional and cognitive evaluations of life. *Annual Review of Psychology*, 54, 403–425.

Dietrich, A. (2004). The cognitive neuroscience of creativity. *Psychonomic Bulletin & Review*, 11, 1011–1026.

Diez, J. J., & Iglesias, P. (2004). Spontaneous subclinical hypothyroidism in patients older than 55 years: An analysis of natural course and risk factors for the development of overt thyroid failure. *Journal of Clinical Endocrinology and Metabolism*, 89, 4890–4897.

DiGrande, L., Perrin, M. A., Thorpe, L. E., Thalji, L., Murphy, J., Wu, D., ... Brackbill, R. M. (2008). Posttraumatic stress symptoms, PTSD, and risk factors among lower Manhattan residents 2–3 years after the September 11, 2001, terrorist attacks. *Journal of Trauma and Stress*, 21, 264–273. doi:10.1002/jts.20345

Dik, B. J., Eldridge, B. M., Steger, M. F., & Duffy, R. D. (2012). Development and validation of the Calling and Vocation Questionnaire (CVQ) and Brief Calling Scale (BCS). *Journal of Career Assessment*, 20, 242–263. doi:10.1177/1069072711434410

Dillon, C. F., Gu, Q., Hoffman, H. J., & Ko, C. W. (2010). Vision, hearing, balance, and sensory impairment in Americans aged 70 years and over: United States, 1999–2006. *NCHS Data Brief*, 1–8.

DiNardo, P. A., & Barlow, D. H. (1988). *Anxiety Disorders Interview Schedule-Revised (ADIS-R)*. Albany NY: Graywind Publications.

Ding, C., Cicuttini, F., Blizzard, L., Scott, F., & Jones, G. (2007). A longitudinal study of the effect of sex and age on rate of change in knee cartilage volume in adults. *Rheumatology (Oxford)*, 46, 273–290. doi:kel243 pii:10.1093/rheumatology/kel243

Dionne, C. E., Dunn, K. M., & Croft, P. R. (2006). Does back pain prevalence really decrease with increasing age? A systematic review. *Age and Ageing*, 35, 229–234.

Dishman, R. K., Berthoud, H. R., Booth, F. W., Cotman, C. W., Edgerton, V. R., Fleshner, M. R., ... Zigmond, M. J. (2006). Neurobiology of exercise. *Scandinavian Journal of Medicine and Science in Sports*, 16, 379–380.

Dixon, R. A., & Hultsch, D. F. (1999). Intelligence and cognitive potential in late life. In J. C. Cavanaugh & S. K. Whitbourne (Eds.), *Gerontology: Interdisciplinary perspectives* (pp. 213–237). New York: Oxford University Press.

Djousse, L., Lee, I. M., Buring, J. E., & Gaziano, J. M. (2009). Alcohol consumption and risk of cardiovascular disease and death in women: Potential mediating mechanisms. *Circulation, 120*, 237–244. doi:CIRCULATIONAHA.108.832360 pii:10.1161/CIRCULATIONAHA.108.832360

Dobbs, B. M. (2008). Aging baby boomers—a blessing or challenge for driver licensing authorities. *Traffic and Injury Prevention, 9*, 379–386. doi:901525511 pii:10.1080/15389580802045823

Dobrow, S. R., & Tosti-Kharas, J. (2011). Calling: The development of a scale measure. *Personnel Psychology, 64*, 1001–1049. doi:10.1111/j.1744-6570.2011.01234.x

Dodson, C. S., Bawa, S., & Slotnick, S. D. (2007). Aging, source memory, and misrecollections. *Journal of Experimental Psychology: Learning, Memory, and Cognition, 33*, 169–181.

Dolcos, S. M., & Daley, D. (2009). Work pressure, workplace social resources, and work–family conflict: The tale of two sectors. *International Journal of Stress Management, 16*, 291–311.

Dong, X. (2012). Advancing the field of elder abuse: Future directions and policy implications. *Journal of the American Geriatrics Society, 60*, 2151–2156.

Dong, X., Simon, M., Mendes de Leon, C., Fulmer, T., Beck, T., Hebert, L., … Evans, D. (2009). Elder self-neglect and abuse and mortality risk in a community-dwelling population. *Journal of the American Medical Association, 302*, 517–526. doi:302/5/517 pii:10.1001/jama.2009.1109

Donnelly, R. (2009). Career behavior in the knowledge economy: Experiences and perceptions of career mobility among management and IT consultants in the UK and the USA. *Journal of Vocational Behavior, 75*, 319–328.

Donoghue, C. (2006). The percentage of beds designated for Medicaid in American nursing homes and nurse staffing ratios. *Journal of Health and Social Policy, 22*, 19–28.

Donohue, R. (2006). Person–environment congruence in relation to career change and career persistence. *Journal of Vocational Behavior, 68*, 504–515.

Donorfio, L. K. M., D'Ambrosio, L. A., Coughlin, J. F., & Mohyde, M. (2008). Health, safety, self-regulation and the older driver: It's not just a matter of age. *Journal of Safety Research, 39*, 555–561. doi:10.1016/j.jsr.2008.09.003

Donorfio, L. K. M., D'Ambrosio, L. A., Coughlin, J. F., & Mohyde, M. (2009). To drive or not to drive, that isn't the question—The meaning of self-regulation among older drivers. *Journal of Safety Research, 40*, 221–226. doi:10.1016/j.jsr.2009.04.002

Dorshkind, K., Montecino-Rodriguez, E., & Signer, R. A. (2009). The ageing immune system: Is it ever too old to become young again? *Nature Reviews Immunology, 9*, 57–62. doi:nri2471 pii:10.1038/nri2471

Doss, B. D., Rhoades, G. K., Stanley, S. M., Markman, H. J., & Johnson, C. A. (2009). Differential use of premarital education in first and second marriages. *Journal of Family Psychology, 23*, 268–273. doi:2009-04780-015 pii:0.1037/a0014356

Drew, L. M., & Smith, P. K. (2002). Implications for grandparents when they lose contact with their grandchildren: Divorce, family feud, and geographical separation. *Journal of Mental Health & Aging, 8*, 95–119.

Drozdowski, L., & Thomson, A. B. (2006). Aging and the intestine. *World Journal of Gastroenterology, 12*, 7578–7584.

Dubeau, C. E., Simon, S. E., & Morris, J. N. (2006). The effect of urinary incontinence on quality of life in older nursing home residents. *Journal of the American Geriatrics Society, 54*, 1325–1333. doi:JGS861 pii:10.1111/j.1532-5415.2006.00861.x

Duberstein, P. R., & Conwell, Y. (2000). Suicide. In S. K. Whitbourne (Ed.), *Psychopathology in later life* (pp. 245–276). New York: Wiley.

Duffy, R. D., Allan, B. A., Autin, K. L., & Bott, E. M. (2013). Calling and life satisfaction: It's not about having it, it's about living it. *Journal of Counseling Psychology, 60*, 42–52. doi: 10.1037/a0030635

Duffy, R. D., Bott, E. M., Allan, B. A., Torrey, C. L., & Dik, B. J. (2012). Perceiving a calling, living a calling, and job satisfaction: Testing a moderated, multiple mediator model. *Journal of Counseling Psychology, 59*, 50–59. doi:10.1037/a0026129

Dufour, A., & Candas, V. (2007). Ageing and thermal responses during passive heat exposure: Sweating and sensory aspects. *European Journal of Applied Physiology, 100*, 19–26. doi:10.1007/s00421-007-0396-9

Dufour, A. B., Broe, K. E., Nguyen, U. S., Gagnon, D. R., Hillstrom, H. J., Walker, A. H., … Hannan, M. T. (2009). Foot pain: Is current or past shoewear a factor? *Arthritis & Rheumatism, 61*, 1352–1358. doi:10.1002/art.24733

Duner, A., & Nordstrom, M. (2005). Intentions and strategies among elderly people: Coping in everyday life. *Journal of Aging Studies, 19*, 437–451.

Dunifon, R., & Bajracharya, A. (2012). The role of grandparents in the lives of youth. *Journal of Family Issues, 33*, 1168–1194. doi: 10.1177/0192513x12444271

Dustman, R. E., Emmerson, R. Y., Steinhaus, L. A., & Shearer, D. E. (1992). The effects of videogame playing on neuropsychological performance of elderly individuals. *Journals of Gerontology, 47*, P168–P171.

Dy, S., & Lynn, J. (2007). Getting services right for those sick enough to die. *BMJ: British Medical Journal, 334*, 511–513.

Dye, M. W. G., Green, C. S., & Bavelier, D. (2009). Increasing speed of processing with action video games. *Current Directions in Psychological Science, 18*, 321–326. doi:10.1111/j.1467-8721.2009.01660.x

Eby, L. T., Maher, C. P., & Butts, M. M. (2010). The intersection of work and family life: The role of affect. *Annual Review of Psychology, 61*, 599–622.

Economist (2007). Grandparents raising grandchildren: Skipping a generation. *Economist, 383*.

Edelstein, B., Martin, R. R., & McKee, D. R. (2000). Assessment of older adult psychopathology. In S. K. Whitbourne (Ed.), *Psychopathology in later life* (pp. 61–88). New York: Wiley.

Edelstein, B. A., Martin, R. R., & Gerolimatos, L. A. (2013). Assessment in geriatric settings. In J. R. Graham, J. A. Naglieri

& I. B. Weiner (Eds.), *Handbook of psychology, Vol. 10: Assessment psychology* (2nd ed.). (pp. 425–447). Hoboken, NJ: John Wiley & Sons, Inc.

Edwards, C., Rogers, A., Lynch, S., Pylawka, T., Silvis, M., Chinchilli, V., ... Black, K. (2012). The effects of bariatric surgery weight loss on knee pain in patients with osteoarthritis of the knee. *Arthritis.*

Edwards, J. R., & Rothbard, N. P. (2000). Mechanisms linking work and family: Clarifying the relationship between work and family constructs. *The Academy of Management Review, 25,* 178–199. doi:10.2307/259269

Eggermont, L. H., Milberg, W. P., Lipsitz, L. A., Scherder, E. J., & Leveille, S. G. (2009). Physical activity and executive function in aging: The MOBILIZE Boston Study. *Journal of the American Geriatrics Society, 57,* 1750–1756. doi: JGS2441 pii:10.1111/j.1532-5415.2009.02441.x

Eid, M., & Diener, E. (2001). Norms for experiencing emotions in different cultures: Inter- and intranational differences. *Journal of Personality & Social Psychology, 81,* 869–885.

Ekkekakis, P., Lind, E., & Vazou, S. (2009). Affective responses to increasing levels of exercise intensity in normal-weight, overweight, and obese middle-aged women. *Obesity (Silver Spring).* doi:oby2009204 pii:10.1038/oby.2009.204

El Ghissassi, F., Baan, R., Straif, K., Grosse, Y., Secretan, B., Bouvard, V., ... Cogliano, V. (2009). A review of human carcinogens—part D: Radiation. *Lancet Oncology, 10,* 751–752.

Elder, G. H., Jr.,, Shanahan, M., & Clipp, E. C. (1994). When war comes to men's lives: Life course patterns in family, work, and health. *Psychology and Aging, 9,* 5–16.

Elias, M. F., Elias, P. K., D'Agostino, R. B., Silbershatz, H., & Wolf, P. A. (1997). Role of age, education, and gender on cognitive performance in the Framingham Heart Study: Community-based norms. *Experimental Aging Research, 23,* 201–235.

Eliasson, L., Birkhed, D., Osterberg, T., & Carlen, A. (2006). Minor salivary gland secretion rates and immunoglobulin A in adults and the elderly. *European Journal of Oral Sciences, 114,* 494–499.

Elliot, S. J., Karl, M., Berho, M., Xia, X., Pereria-Simon, S., Espinosa-Heidmann, D., & Striker, G. E. (2006). Smoking induces glomerulosclerosis in aging estrogen-deficient mice through cross-talk between TGF-beta1 and IGF-I signaling pathways. *Journal of the Americal Society Nephrology, 17,* 3315–3324. doi:ASN.2006070799 pii:10.1681/ASN.2006070799

Elovainio, M., Kivimaki, M., Ferrie, J. E., Gimeno, D., De Vogli, R., Virtanen, M., ... Singh-Manoux, A. (2009). Physical and cognitive function in midlife: Reciprocal effects? A 5-year follow-up of the Whitehall II study. *Journal of Epidemiology and Community Health, 63,* 468–473. doi: 63/6/468 pii:10.1136/jech.2008.081505

Emaus, N., Berntsen, G. K., Joakimsen, R., & Fonnebo, V. (2006). Longitudinal changes in forearm bone mineral density in women and men aged 45–84 years: The Tromso Study, a population-based study. *American Journal of Epidemiology, 163,* 441–449.

Engels, G. I., Duijsens, I. J., Haringsma, R., & van Putten, C. M. (2003). Personality disorders in the elderly compared to four younger age groups: A cross-sectional study of community residents and mental health patients. *Journal of Personality Disorders, 17,* 447–459.

Engvig, A., Fjell, A. M., Westlye, L. T., Moberget, T., Sundseth, Ø., Larsen, V. A., & Walhovd, K. B. (2012). Memory training impacts short-term changes in aging white matter: A longitudinal diffusion tensor imaging study. *Human Brain Mapping, 33,* 2390–2406. doi:10.1002/hbm.21370

Enserink, M. (1998). First Alzheimer's disease confirmed. *Science, 279,* 2037.

Erickson, K. I., & Kramer, A. F. (2009). Aerobic exercise effects on cognitive and neural plasticity in older adults. *British Journal of Sports Medicine, 43,* 22–24. doi: bjsm.2008.052498 pii:10.1136/bjsm.2008.052498

Erickson, K. I., Prakash, R. S., Voss, M. W., Chaddock, L., Hu, L., Morris, K. S., ... Kramer, A. F. (2009). Aerobic fitness is associated with hippocampal volume in elderly humans. *Hippocampus, 19,* 1030–1039. doi:10.1002/hipo.20547

Erikson, E. H. (1963). *Childhood and society* (2nd ed.). New York: Norton.

Erikson, E. H., Erikson, J. M., & Kivnick, H. Q. (1986). *Vital involvement in old age.* New York: W.W. Norton.

Erqou, S., Kaptoge, S., Perry, P. L., Di Angelantonio, E., Thompson, A., White, I. R., ... Danesh, J. (2009). Lipoprotein(a) concentration and the risk of coronary heart disease, stroke, and nonvascular mortality. *Journal of the American Medical Association, 302,* 412–423. doi:302/4/412 pii:10.1001/jama.2009.1063

Espay, A. J., Mandybur, G. T., & Revilla, F. J. (2006). Surgical treatment of movement disorders. *Clinics in Geriatric Medicine, 22,* 813–825, vi.

Espino, D. V., Lichtenstein, M. J., Palmer, R. F., & Hazuda, H. P. (2004). Evaluation of the mini-mental state examination's internal consistency in a community-based sample of Mexican-American and European-American elders: Results from the San Antonio Longitudinal Study of Aging. *Journal of the American Geriatrics Society, 52,* 822–827.

Espiritu, J. R. (2008). Aging-related sleep changes. *Clin Geriatr Med, 24,* 1–14, v. doi:S0749-0690(07)00072-9 pii:10.1016/j.cger.2007.08.007

European Union. (2010). Progress and key challenges in the delivery of adequate and sustainable pensions in Europe. *Occasional Papers, 71.* Retrieved from http://ec.europa.eu/economy_finance/publications

Evans, S., Patt, I., Giosan, C., Spielman, L., & Difede, J. (2009). Disability and posttraumatic stress disorder in disaster relief workers responding to September 11, 2001, World Trade Center disaster. *Journal of Clinical Psychology, 65,* 684–694. doi:10.1002/jclp.20575

Eyler, L. T., Sherzai, A., Kaup, A. R., & Jeste, D. V. (2011). A review of functional brain imaging correlates of successful cognitive aging. *Biological Psychiatry, 70*, 115–122. doi:10.1016/j.biopsych.2010.12.032

Fallico, F., Siciliano, L., & Yip, F. (2005). Hypothermia-related deaths—United States, 2003–2004. *Morbidity and Mortality Weekly Report, 54*, 173–175.

Farrell, M. P., & Rosenberg, S. D. (1981). *Men at midlife.* Boston: Auburn House.

Farrimond, S., Knight, R. G., & Titov, N. (2006). The effects of aging on remembering intentions: Performance on a simulated shopping task. *Applied Cognitive Psychology, 20*, 533–555.

Féart, C., Samieri, C., Allès, B., & Barberger-Gateau, P. (2013). Potential benefits of adherence to the Mediterranean diet on cognitive health. *Proceedings of the Nutrition Society, 72(1)*, 140–152.

Federal Interagency Forum on Age-Related Statistics. (2010). Older Americans 2010: Key indicators of well-being. Retrieved from http://www.agingstats.gov/agingstatsdotnet/Main_Site/Data/2010_Documents/Docs/OA_2010.pdf

Federmeier, K. D., Kutas, M., & Schul, R. (2010). Age-related and individual differences in the use of prediction during language comprehension. *Brain and Language, 115*, 149–161. doi:10.1016/j.bandl.2010.07.006

Feist, G. J. (2006). How development and personality influence scientific thought, interest, and achievement. *Review of General Psychology, 10*, 163–182.

Feist, G. J., & Barron, F. X. (2003). Predicting creativity from early to late adulthood: Intellect, potential, and personality. *Journal of Research in Personality, 37*, 62–88.

Feldman, H. A., Longcope, C., Derby, C. A., Johannes, C. B., Araujo, A. B., Coviello, A. D., … McKinlay, J. B. (2002). Age trends in the level of serum testosterone and other hormones in middle-aged men: Longitudinal results from the Massachusetts male aging study. *Journal of Clinical Endocrinology and Metabolism, 87*, 589–598.

Felicissimo, M. F., Carneiro, M. M., Saleme, C. S., Pinto, R. Z., da Fonseca, A. M., & da Silva-Filho, A. L. (2010). Intensive supervised versus unsupervised pelvic floor muscle training for the treatment of stress urinary incontinence: A randomized comparative trial. *International Urogynecology: Journal of Pelvic Floor Dysfunction.* doi:10.1007/s00192-010-1125-1

Ferguson, R., & Brohaugh, B. (2010). The aging of Aquarius. *Journal of Consumer Marketing, 27*, 76–81.

Ferrario, S. R., Cardillo, V., Vicario, F., Balzarini, E., & Zotti, A. M. (2004). Advanced cancer at home: Caregiving and bereavement. *Palliative Medicine, 18*, 129–136.

Ferraro, F. R. (2002). *Minority and cross-cultural aspects of neuropsychological assessment.* Bristol, PA: Swets and Zeitlinger.

Ferraro, K. F., & Farmer, M. M. (1996). Double jeopardy, aging as leveler, or persistent health inequality? A longitudinal analysis of white and black Americans. *Journal of Gerontology: Social Sciences, 51*, S319–328.

Ferri, R., Gschliesser, V., Frauscher, B., Poewe, W., & Hogl, B. (2009). Periodic leg movements during sleep and periodic limb movement disorder in patients presenting with unexplained insomnia. *Clinics in Neurophysiology, 120*, 257–263. doi:S1388-2457(08)01257-1 pii:10.1016/j.clinph.2008.11.006

Fetto, J. (2002). Friends forever. Retrieved from http://adage.com/article/american-demographics/friends-forever/44657/

Fetveit, A. (2009). Late-life insomnia: A review. *Geriatrics and Gerontology International, 9*, 220–234. doi:GGI537 pii:10.1111/j.1447-0594.2009.00537.x

Field, A. E., Colditz, G. A., Willett, W. C., Longcope, C., & McKinlay, J. B. (1994). The relation of smoking, age, relative weight, and dietary intake to serum adrenal steroids, sex hormones, and sex hormone-binding globulin in middle-aged men. *Journal of Clinical Endocrinology and Metabolism, 79*, 1310–1316.

Field, M. J., Cassel, C. K., & Committee on Care at the End of Life. (1997). *Approaching death: Improving care at the end of life, Institute of Medicine, Division of Health Care Services.* Washington DC: National Academy Press.

Field, N. P., Gal-Oz, E., & Bonanno, G. A. (2003). Continuing bonds and adjustment at 5 years after the death of a spouse. *Journal of Consulting & Clinical Psychology, 71*, 110–117.

Fiksenbaum, L. M., Greenglass, E. R., & Eaton, J. (2006). Perceived social support, hassles, and coping among the elderly. *Journal of Applied Gerontology, 25*, 17–30.

Fingerman, K. L. (1996). Sources of tension in the aging mother and adult daughter relationship. *Psychology and Aging, 11*, 591–606.

Fingerman, K. L. (2001). *Aging mothers and their adult daughters: A study in mixed emotions.* New York: Springer.

Fingerman, K. L., Cheng, Y. P., Wesselmann, E. D., Zarit, S., Furstenberg, F., & Birditt, K. S. (2012). Helicopter parents and landing pad kids: Intense parental support of grown children. *Journal of Marriage and Family, 74*, 880–896.

Fingerman, K. L., & Griffiths, P. C. (1999). Seasons greetings: Adults' social contacts at the holiday season. *Psychology and Aging, 14*, 192–205.

Fingerman, K. L., Hay, E. L., & Birditt, K. S. (2004). The best of ties, the worst of ties: Close, problematic, and ambivalent social relationships. *Journal of Marriage and Family, 66*, 792–808.

Fingerman, K. L., Pitzer, L. M., Chan, W., Birditt, K. S., Franks, M., & Zarit, S. H. (2010). Who gets what and why? Help middle-aged adults provide to parents and grown children. *Journal of Gerontology: Social Sciences, 66B*, 87–98. doi:10.1093/geronb/gbq009

Fiocco, A. J., & Yaffe, K. (2010). Defining successful aging: The importance of including cognitive function over time. *Archives of Neurology, 67*, 876–880. doi:10.1001/archneurol.2010.130

Fisher, C. D. (2002). Antecedents and consequences of real-time affective reactions at work. *Motivation and Emotion, 26*, 3–30.

Fjell, A. M., Walhovd, K. B., Fennema-Notestine, C., McEvoy, L. K., Hagler, D. J., Holland, D., … Dale, A. M. (2009). One-year brain atrophy evident in healthy aging. *Journal of Neuroscience, 29*, 15223–15231. doi:29/48/15223 pii:10.1523/JNEUROSCI.3252-09.2009

Flint, A. J. (2005). Generalised anxiety disorder in elderly patients: Epidemiology, diagnosis and treatment options. *Drugs and Aging, 22,* 101–114. doi:2222

Flora, C. (2013). *Friendfluence: The surprising ways friends make us who we are.* New York: Random House.

Floyd, K., Boren, J. P., Hannawa, A. F., Hesse, C., McEwan, B., & Veksler, A. E. (2009). Kissing in marital and cohabiting relationships: Effects on blood lipids, stress, and relationship satisfaction. *Western Journal of Communication, 73,* 113–133.

Floyd, K., Pauley, P. M., & Hesse, C. (2012). State and trait affectionate communication buffer adults' stress reactions. *Communication Monographs, 77,* 618–636.

Foley, D. J., Vitiello, M. V., Bliwise, D. L., Ancoli-Israel, S., Monjan, A. A., & Walsh, J. K. (2007). Frequent napping is associated with excessive daytime sleepiness, depression, pain, and nocturia in older adults: Findings from the National Sleep Foundation "2003 Sleep in America" poll. *American Journal of Geriatric Psychiatry, 15,* 344–350.

Folstein, M. F., Folstein, S. E., & McHugh, P. R. (1975). Mini-Mental State: A practical method for grading the cognitive state of patients for the clinician. *Journal of Psychiatric Research, 12,* 189–198.

Ford, D. H., & Lerner, R. M. (Eds.). (1992). *Developmental systems theory: An integrative approach.* Newbury Park CA: Sage.

Fors, S., Lennartsson, C., & Lundberg, O. (2011). Live long and prosper? Childhood living conditions, marital status, social class in adulthood and mortality during mid-life: A cohort study. *Scandinavian Journal of Public Health, 39,* 179–186. doi:10.1177/1403494810395823

Forsmo, S., Langhammer, A., Forsen, L., & Schei, B. (2005). Forearm bone mineral density in an unselected population of 2,779 men and women—the HUNT Study, Norway. *Osteoporos International, 16,* 562–567.

Fossey, J., Ballard, C., Juszczak, E., James, I., Alder, N., Jacoby, R., & Howard, R. (2006). Effect of enhanced psychosocial care on antipsychotic use in nursing home residents with severe dementia: Cluster randomised trial. *BMJ: British Medical Journal, 332,* 756–761. doi:bmj.38782.575868.7C pii:10.1136/bmj.38782.575868.7C

Fraser, J., Maticka-Tyndale, E., & Smylie, L. (2004). Sexuality of Canadian women at midlife. *Canadian Journal of Human Sexuality, 13,* 171–188.

Frazer, K. A., Ballinger, D. G., Cox, D. R., Hinds, D. A., Stuve, L. L., Gibbs, R. A., … Stewart, J. (2007). A second generation human haplotype map of over 3.1 million SNPs. *Nature, 449,* 851–861. doi: nature06258 pii:10.1038/nature06258

Frazier, L., Barreto, M., & Newman, F. (2012). Self-regulation and eudaimonic well-being across adulthood. *Experimental Aging Research, 38,* 394–410. doi:10.1080/0361073x.2012.699367

Frazier, L. D., Johnson, P. M., Gonzalez, G. K., & Kafka, C. L. (2002). Psychosocial influences on possible selves: A comparison of three cohorts of older adults. *International Journal of Behavioral Development, 26,* 308–317.

Friedman, H. S., & Martin, L. R. (2011). *The longevity project: Surprising discoveries for health and long life from the landmark eight-decade study.* New York: Hudson Street Press/Penguin Group USA.

Friedman, H. S., Tucker, J. S., Schwartz, J. E., Martin, L. R., Tomlinson-Keasey, C., Wingard, D. L., & Criqui, M. H. (1995). Childhood conscientiousness and longevity: Health behaviors and cause of death. *Journal of Personality and Social Psychology, 68,* 696–703.

Friedman, M., & Rosenman, R. H. (1974). *Type A behavior and your heart.* New York: Knopf.

Frisby, B. N., Booth-Butterfield, M., Dillow, M. R., Martin, M. M., & Weber, K. D. (2012). Face and resilience in divorce: The impact on emotions, stress, and post-divorce relationships. *Journal of Social and Personal Relationships, 29,* 715–735. doi:10.1177/0265407512443452

Fuiano, G., Sund, S., Mazza, G., Rosa, M., Caglioti, A., Gallo, G., … Conte, G. (2001). Renal hemodynamic response to maximal vasodilating stimulus in healthy older subjects. *Kidney International, 59,* 1052–1058.

Fuller-Thomson, E., & Minkler, M. (2001). American grandparents providing extensive childcare to their grandchildren: Prevalence and profile. *The Gerontologist, 41,* 201–209.

Fung, H. H., Lu, A. Y., Goren, D., Isaacowitz, D. M., Wadlinger, H. A., & Wilson, H. R. (2008). Age-related positivity enhancement is not universal: Older Chinese look away from positive stimuli. *Psychology and Aging, 23,* 440–446.

Funk, L. M. (2004). Who wants to be involved? Decision-making preferences among residents of long-term care facilities. *Canadian Journal on Aging, 23,* 47–58. doi:10.1353/cja.2004.0004

Funk, L. M. (2010). Prioritizing parental autonomy: Adult children's accounts of feeling responsible and supporting aging parents. *Journal of Aging Studies, 24,* 57–64.

Furnham, A., Eracleous, A., & Chamorro-Premuzic, T. (2009). Personality, motivation and job satisfaction: Hertzberg meets the Big Five. *Journal of Managerial Psychology, 24,* 765–779.

Furnham, A., Miller, T., Batey, M., & Johnson, S. (2011). Demographic and individual correlates of self-rated competency. *Imagination, Cognition and Personality, 31,* 247–265. doi:10.2190/IC.31.3.g

Furnham, A., Tang, T. L.-P., Lester, D., O'Connor, R., & Montgomery, R. (2002). Estimates of ten multiple intelligences: Sex and national differences in the perception of oneself and famous people. *European Psychologist, 7,* 245–255. doi:10.1027//1016-9040.7.4.245

Gabelle, A., & Dauvilliers, Y. (2010). Editorial: Sleep and dementia. *Journal of Nutrition Health and Aging, 14,* 201–202.

Gadalla, T. M. (2009). Sense of mastery, social support, and health in elderly Canadians. *Journal of Aging and Health, 21,* 581–595.

Gagne, M., & Deci, E. L. (2005). Self-determination theory and work motivation. *Journal of Organizational Behavior, 26,* 331–362.

Gagnon, M., Hersen, M., Kabacoff, R. L., & Van Hasselt, V. B. (1999). Interpersonal and psychological correlates of marital dissatisfaction in late life: A review. *Clinical Psychology Review, 19,* 359–378.

Galper, D. I., Trivedi, M. H., Barlow, C. E., Dunn, A. L., & Kampert, J. B. (2006). Inverse association between physical inactivity and mental health in men and women. *Medicine and Science in Sports and Exercise, 38,* 173–178.

Galvan, V., Gorostiza, O. F., Banwait, S., Ataie, M., Logvinova, A. V., Sitaraman, S., ... Bredesen, D. E. (2006). Reversal of Alzheimer's-like pathology and behavior in human APP transgenic mice by mutation of Asp664. *Proceedings of the National Academies of Sciences of the United States of America, 103,* 7130–7135.

Garcia-Fabela, L., Melano-Carranza, E., Aguilar-Navarro, S., Garcia-Lara, J. M., Gutierrez-Robledo, L. M., & Avila-Funes, J. A. (2009). Hypertension as a risk factor for developing depressive symptoms among community-dwelling elders. *Revista de Investigación Clínica, 61,* 274–280.

Garden, S. E., Phillips, L. H., & MacPherson, S. E. (2001). Midlife aging, open-ended planning, and laboratory measures of executive function. *Neuropsychology, 15,* 472–482.

Gardner, H. (1983). *Frames of mind: The theory of multiple intelligences.* New York: Basic Books.

Gaunt, R. (2006). Couple similarity and marital satisfaction: Are similar spouses happier? *Journal of Personality, 74,* 1401–1420.

Gauthier, S., & Scheltens, P. (2009). Can we do better in developing new drugs for Alzheimer's disease? *Alzheimers and Dementia, 5,* 489–491. doi:S1552-5260(09)02284-5 pii:10.1016/j.jalz.2009.09.002

Gavrin, J., & Chapman, C. R. (1995). Clinical management of dying patients. *Western Journal of Medicine, 163,* 268–277.

Gazzaley, A., Clapp, W., Kelley, J., McEvoy, K., Knight, R. T., & D'Esposito, M. (2008). Age-related top-down suppression deficit in the early stages of cortical visual memory processing. *Proceedings of the National Academy of Sciences, 105,* 13122–13126. doi:10.1073/pnas.0806074105

Geda, Y. E., Roberts, R. O., Knopman, D. S., Christianson, T. J., Pankratz, V. S., Ivnik, R. J., ... Rocca, W. A. (2010). Physical exercise, aging, and mild cognitive impairment: A population-based study. *Archives of Neurology, 67,* 80–86. doi:67/1/80 pii:10.1001/archneurol.2009.297

Gee, S., & Baillie, J. (1999). Happily ever after? An exploration of retirement expectations. *Educational Gerontology, 25,* 109–128.

Georges, J. J., Onwuteaka-Philipsen, B. D., Muller, M. T., Van Der Wal, G., Van Der Heide, A., & Van Der Maas, P. J. (2007). Relatives' perspective on the terminally ill patients who died after euthanasia or physician-assisted suicide: A retrospective cross-sectional interview study in the Netherlands. *Death Studies, 31,* 1–15.

Gerstorf, D., Ram, N., Hoppmann, C., Willis, S. L., & Schaie, K. W. (2011). Cohort differences in cognitive aging and terminal decline in the Seattle Longitudinal Study. *Developmental Psychology, 47,* 1026–1041. doi:10.1037/a0023426

Gerstorf, D., Ram, N., Lindenberger, U., & Smith, J. (2013). Age and time-to-death trajectories of change in indicators of cognitive, sensory, physical, health, social, and self-related functions. *Developmental Psychology.* doi:10.1037/a0031340

Geurts, T., Poortman, A.-R., van Tilburg, T., & Dykstra, P. A. (2009). Contact between grandchildren and their grandparents in early adulthood. *Journal of Family Issues, 30,* 1698–1713.

Geurts, T., van Tilburg, T. G., & Poortman, A.-R. (2012). The grandparent–grandchild relationship in childhood and adulthood: A matter of continuation? *Personal Relationships, 19,* 267–278.

Ghisletta, P., Rabbitt, P., Lunn, M., & Lindenberger, U. (2012). Two-thirds of the age-based changes in fluid and crystallized intelligence, perceptual speed, and memory in adulthood are shared. *Intelligence, 40,* 260–268. doi:10.1016/j.intell.2012.02.008

Giannoulis, M. G., Sonksen, P. H., Umpleby, M., Breen, L., Pentecost, C., Whyte, M., ... Martin, F. C. (2006). The effects of growth hormone and/or testosterone in healthy elderly men: A randomized controlled trial. *Journal of Clinical Endocrinology and Metabolism, 91,* 477–484.

Gilhooly, M. L., Gilhooly, K. J., Phillips, L. H., Harvey, D., Brady, A., & Hanlon, P. (2007). Real-world problem solving and quality of life in older people. *British Journal of Health Psychology, 12,* 587–600.

Gill, S. C., Butterworth, P., Rodgers, B., Anstey, K. J., Villamil, E., & Melzer, D. (2006). Mental health and the timing of men's retirement. *Social Psychiatry and Psychiatric Epidemiology, 41,* 933–954.

Gilstad, J. R., & Finucane, T. E. (2008). Results, rhetoric, and randomized trials: The case of donepezil. *Journal of the American Geriatrics Society, 56,* 1556–1562. doi:JGS1844 pii:10.1111/j.1532-5415.2008.01844.x

Gimeno, D., Tabak, A. G., Ferrie, J. E., Shipley, M. J., De Vogli, R., Elovainio, M., ... Kivimaki, M. (2010). Justice at work and metabolic syndrome: The Whitehall II study. *Occup Environ Med, 67,* 256–262. doi:oem.2009.047324 pii:10.1136/oem.2009.047324

Gitlin, L. N., Hauck, W. W., Dennis, M. P., Winter, L., Hodgson, N., & Schinfeld, S. (2009). Long-term effect on mortality of a home intervention that reduces functional difficulties in older adults: Results from a randomized trial. *Journal of the American Geriatrics Society, 57,* 476–481. doi:JGS2147 pii:10.1111/j.1532-5415.2008.02147.x

Glaser, B. G., & Strauss, A. L. (1968). *Time for dying.* Chicago: Aldine.

Gleason, M. E. J., Powers, A. D., & Oltmanns, T. F. (2012). The enduring impact of borderline personality pathology: Risk for threatening life events in later middle-age. *Journal of Abnormal Psychology, 121,* 447–457. doi:10.1037/a0025564

Glisky, E. L. (2007). Changes in cognitive function in human aging Brain aging: Models, methods, and mechanisms. (pp. 3–20). Boca Raton, FL: CRC Press.

Global Initiative for Chronic Obstructive Lung Disease. (2009). *Global strategy for the diagnosis, management, and prevention of chronic obstructive pulmonary disease*. Medical Communications Resources, Inc.

Gluck, J., & Bluck, S. (2007). Looking back across the life span: A life story account of the reminiscence bump. *Memory and Cognition, 35*, 1928–1939.

Goh, J. O., & Park, D. C. (2009). Neuroplasticity and cognitive aging: The scaffolding theory of aging and cognition. *Restorative Neurology and Neuroscience, 27*, 391–403. doi:2170W040X0229571 pii:10.3233/RNN-2009-0493

Gold, D. T. (1989). Sibling relationships in old age: A typology. *International Journal of Aging and Human Development, 28*, 37–51.

Goldberg, A. E., & Sayer, A. (2006). Lesbian couples' relationship quality across the transition to parenthood. *Journal of Marriage and Family, 68*, 87–100.

Goldberg, A. E., & Smith, J. Z. (2011). Stigma, social context, and mental health: Lesbian and gay couples across the transition to adoptive parenthood. *Journal of Counseling Psychology, 58*, 139–150. doi:10.1037/a0021684

Goldspink, D. F., George, K. P., Chantler, P. D., Clements, R. E., Sharp, L., Hodges, G., ... Cable, N. T. (2009). A study of presbycardia, with gender differences favoring ageing women. *International Journal of Cardiology, 137*, 236–245. doi:S0167-5273(08)00851-6 pii:10.1016/j.ijcard.2008.06.086

Goldstein, J. H., Cajko, L., Oosterbroek, M., Michielsen, M., van Houten, O., & Salverda, F. (1997). Video games and the elderly. *Social Behavior and Personality, 25*, 345–352. doi:10.2224/sbp.1997.25.4.345

Goodson, I. F. (2013). *Developing narrative theory: Life histories and personal representation*. New York: Routledge/Taylor & Francis Group.

Gottesman, L. E., & Bourestom, N. C. (1974). Why nursing homes do what they do. *Gerontologist, 14*, 501–506.

Gottfredson, G. D. (2002). Interests, aspirations, self-estimates, and the self-directed search. *Journal of Career Assessment, 10*, 200–208.

Gottman, J. M., & Driver, J. L. (2005). Dysfunctional marital conflict and everyday marital interaction. *Journal of Divorce & Remarriage, 43*, 63–78.

Gouin, J. P., Hantsoo, L., & Kiecolt-Glaser, J. K. (2008). Immune dysregulation and chronic stress among older adults: A review. *Neuroimmunomodulation, 15*, 251–259. doi:000156468 pii:10.1159/000156468

Government Accountability Office. (2008). Nursing homes: Federal monitoring surveys demonstrate continued understatement of serious care problems and CMS oversight weaknesses. *GAO*.

Government Accountability Office. (2011). Elder justice: Stronger federal leadership could enhance national response to elder abuse.

Gradinaru, V., Mogri, M., Thompson, K. R., Henderson, J. M., & Deisseroth, K. (2009). Optical deconstruction of parkinsonian neural circuitry. *Science, 324*, 354–359. doi:1167093 pii:10.1126/science.1167093

Green, C. S., & Bavelier, D. (2003). Action video game modifies visual selective attention. *Nature, 423*, 534–537.

Green, C. S., & Bavelier, D. (2006). Effect of action video games on the spatial distribution of visuospatial attention. *Journal of Experimental Psychology: Human Perception and Performance, 32*, 1465–1478. doi:10.1037/0096-1523.32.6.1465

Green, T. L., & Darity, W. A., Jr,. (2010). Under the skin: using theories from biology and the social sciences to explore the mechanisms behind the black-white health gap. *American Journal of Public Health, 100 Suppl 1*, S36–40. doi:AJPH.2009.171140 pii:10.2105/AJPH.2009.171140

Greenhaus, J. H., Collins, K. M., & Shaw, J. D. (2003). The relation between work–family balance and quality of life. *Journal of Vocational Behavior, 63*, 510–531.

Greenhaus, J. H., & Powell, G. N. (2006a). When work and family are allies: A theory of work-family enrichment. *The Academy of Management Review, 31*, 72–92.

Greenhaus, J. H., & Powell, G. N. (2006b). When work and family are allies: A theory of work–family enrichment. *Academy of Management Review, 31*, 72–92.

Greenwald, D. A. (2004). Aging, the gastrointestinal tract, and risk of acid-related disease. *American Journal of Medicine, 117 Suppl 5A*, 8S–13S.

Greenwood, P. M. (2007). Functional plasticity in cognitive aging: Review and hypothesis. *Neuropsychology, 21*, 657–673. doi:10.1037/0894-4105.21.6.657

Gregory, T., Nettelbeck, T., & Wilson, C. (2010). Openness to experience, intelligence, and successful ageing. *Personality and Individual Differences, 48*, 895–899. doi:10.1016/j.paid.2010.02.017

Greif, G. L. (1995). Single fathers with custody following separation and divorce. *Marriage and Family Review, 20*, 213–231.

Greif, G. L., & Deal, K. H. (2012). Platonic couple love: How couples view their close couple friends. In M. A. Paludi (Ed.), *The psychology of love, Vols 1–4* (pp. 19–33). Santa Barbara, CA: Praeger/ABC-CLIO.

Groen, B. E., Smulders, E., de Kam, D., Duysens, J., & Weerdesteyn, V. (2010). Martial arts fall training to prevent hip fractures in the elderly. *Osteoporos International, 21*, 215–221. doi:10.1007/s00198-009-0934-x

Grosse, Y., Baan, R., Straif, K., Secretan, B., El Ghissassi, F., Bouvard, V., ... Cogliano, V. (2009). A review of human carcinogens-Part A: Pharmaceuticals. *Lancet Oncology, 10*, 13–14.

Grossmann, I., Karasawa, M., Izumi, S., Na, J., Varnum, M. E. W., Kitayama, S., & Nisbett, R. E. (2012). Aging and wisdom: Culture matters. *Psychological Science, 23*, 1059–1066. doi:10.1177/0956797612446025

Grossmann, I., Na, J., Varnum, M. E. W., Kitayama, S., & Nisbett, R. E. (2012). A route to well-being: Intelligence versus wise reasoning. *Journal of Experimental Psychology: General, 142*, 944–953. doi:10.1037/a0029560

Grossmann, I., Na, J., Varnum, M. E. W., Park, D. C., Kitayama, S., & Nisbett, R. E. (2010). Reasoning about social conflicts improves into old age. *Proceedings of the National Academy of Sciences, 107,* 7246–7250. doi:10.1073/pnas.1001715107

Grote, N. K., Clark, M. S., & Moore, A. (2004). Perceptions of injustice in family work: The role of psychological distress. *Journal of Family Psychology, 18,* 480–492.

Grubeck-Loebenstein, B. (2010). Fading immune protection in old age: Vaccination in the elderly. *Journal of Comparative Physiology, 142 Suppl 1,* S116–S119. doi: S0021-9975(09)00326-0 pii:10.1016/j.jcpa.2009.10.002

Grundy, E., & Henretta, J. C. (2006). Between elderly parents and adult children: A new look at the intergenerational care provided by the "sandwich generation." *Ageing & Society, 26,* 707–722. doi:10.1017/s0144686x06004934

Gruneir, A., Mor, V., Weitzen, S., Truchil, R., Teno, J., & Roy, J. (2007). Where people die: A multilevel approach to understanding influences on site of death in America. *Medical Care: Research and Review, 64,* 351–378. doi:64/4/351 pii:10.1177/1077558707301810

Guadalupe-Grau, A., Fuentes, T., Guerra, B., & Calbet, J. A. (2009). Exercise and bone mass in adults. *Sports Medicine, 39,* 439–468. doi: 10.2165/00007256-200939060-00002

Gubin, D. G., Gubin, G. D., Waterhouse, J., & Weinert, D. (2006). The circadian body temperature rhythm in the elderly: Effect of single daily melatonin dosing. *Chronobiology International, 23,* 639–658.

Guiney, H., & Machado, L. (2012). Benefits of regular aerobic exercise for executive functioning in healthy populations. *Psychonomic Bulletin & Review.* doi:10.3758/s13423-012-0345-4

Gum, A. M., King-Kallimanis, B., & Kohn, R. (2009). Prevalence of mood, anxiety, and substance-abuse disorders for older Americans in the National Comorbidity Survey-Replication. *American Journal of Geriatric Psychiatry, 17,* 782–792.

Hafkemeijer, A., van der Grond, J., & Rombouts, S. A. (2012). Imaging the default mode network in aging and dementia. *Biochimica et Biophysica Acta, 1822,* 431–441. doi:10.1016/j.bbadis.2011.07.008

Hagestad, G. O., & Neugarten, B. L. (1985). Age and the life course. In R. H. Binstock & E. Shanas (Eds.), *Handbook of aging and the social sciences* (pp. 35–61). New York: Van Nostrand Reinhold.

Haley, W. E., Allen, R. S., Reynolds, S., Chen, H., Burton, A., & Gallagher-Thompson, D. (2002). Family issues in end-of-life decision making and end-of-life care. *American Behavioral Scientist, 46,* 284–298.

Hall, D. T. (1993). The new "career contract": Wrong on both counts. Boston, MA: Boston University Executive Development Roundtable Report.

Hall, D. T., & Briscoe, J. (2004). Becoming protean: Individual and experiential factors in adapting the new career. Boston, MA: Working paper, Boston University Executive Development Roundtable Technical Report.

Hall, D. T., & Chandler, D. E. (2005). Psychological success: When the career is a calling. *Journal of Organizational Behavior, 26,* 155–176. doi:10.1002/job.301

Hall, P. A., Dubin, J. A., Crossley, M., Holmqvist, M. E., & D'Arcy, C. (2009). Does executive function explain the IQ-mortality association? Evidence from the Canadian Study on Health and Aging. *Psychosomatic Medicine, 71,* 196–204.

Hamilton, M. (1959). The assessment of anxiety states by rating. *British Journal of Medical Psychology, 32,* 50–55.

Hamilton, M. (1967). Development of a rating scale for primary depressive illness. *British Journal of Social and Clinical Psychology, 6,* 278–296.

Hank, K., & Buber, I. (2009). Grandparents caring for their grandchildren: Findings from the 2004 Survey of Health, Ageing, and Retirement in Europe. *Journal of Family Issues, 30,* 53–73. doi:10.1177/0192513x08322627

Hanke, T. A., & Tiberio, D. (2006). Lateral rhythmic unipedal stepping in younger, middle-aged, and older adults. *Journal of Geriatric Physical Therapy, 29,* 22–27.

Harber, M. P., Konopka, A. R., Douglass, M. D., Minchev, K., Kaminsky, L. A., Trappe, T. A., & Trappe, S. (2009). Aerobic exercise training improves whole muscle and single myofiber size and function in older women. *American Journal of Physiology: Regulative, Integrative, and Comparative Physiology, 297,* R1452–1459. doi:00354.2009 pii:10.1152/ajpregu.00354.2009

Harding, S., Teyhan, A., Rosato, M., & Santana, P. (2008). All cause and cardiovascular mortality in African migrants living in Portugal: Evidence of large social inequalities. *European Journal of Cardiovascular and Preventive Rehabilitation, 15,* 670–676. doi:10.1097/HJR.0b013e32830fe6ce

Hardy, M. A., & Quadagno, J. (1995). Satisfaction with early retirement: Making choices in the auto industry. *The Journals of Gerontology: Series B: Psychological Sciences and Social Sciences, 50B,* S217–S228. doi:10.1093/geronb/50B.4.S217

Hardy, S. E., Concato, J., & Gill, T. M. (2004). Resilience of community-dwelling older persons. *Journal of the American Geriatrics Society, 52,* 257–262.

Hare, R. D., & Neumann, C. S. (2006). The PCL-R Assessment of Psychopathy: Development, structural properties, and new directions. In C. J. Patrick (Ed.), *Handbook of psychopathy.* (pp. 58–88). New York: Guilford Press.

Harley, T. A., Jessiman, L. J., & MacAndrew, S. B. G. (2011). Decline and fall: A biological, developmental, and psycholinguistic account of deliberative language processes and ageing. *Aphasiology, 25,* 123–153. doi:10.1080/02687031003798262

Harmer, P. A., & Li, F. (2008). Tai Chi and falls prevention in older people. *Medicine and Science in Sports and Exercise, 52,* 124–134. doi:10.1159/000134293 pii:10.1159/000134293

Harmon, L. W., Hansen, J. C., Borgen, F. H., & Hammer, A. L. (1994). *Strong interest inventory: Applications and technical guide.* Palo Alto, CA: Consulting Psychologists Press.

Harms, C. A. (2006). Does gender affect pulmonary function and exercise capacity? *Respiratory Physiology and Neurobiology, 151,* 124–131.

Harold, D., Abraham, R., Hollingworth, P., Sims, R., Gerrish, A., Hamshere, M. L., ... Williams, J. (2009). Genome-wide association study identifies variants at CLU and PICALM associated with Alzheimer's disease. *Nat Genet, 41,* 1088–1093. doi:ng.440 pii:10.1038/ng.440

Harpur, T. J., Hart, S. D., & Hare, R. D. (2002). Personality of the psychopath. In P. T. J. Costa & T. A. Widiger (Eds.), *Personality disorders and the five-factor model of personality* (2nd ed.). (pp. 299–324). Washington DC: American Psychological Association.

Harrington, C., Carrillo, H., Dowdell, M., Tang, P. P., & Blank, B. W. (2011). Nursing facilities, staffing, residents, and facility deficiencies, 2005 through 2010. Retrieved from http://www.theconsumervoice.org/sites/default/files/OSCAR-2011-final.pdf

Harrington, J., & Lee-Chiong, T. (2009). Obesity and aging. *Clinics in Chest Medicine, 30,* 609–614, x. doi:S0272-5231(09)00057-4 pii:10.1016/j.ccm.2009.05.011

Harrison, P. M., & Beck, A. J. (2005). Prisoners in 2004. *Bureau of Justice statistics bulletin, NCJ 210677.*

Harrison, T. M., Weintraub, S., Mesulam, M. M., & Rogalski, E. (2012). Superior memory and higher cortical volumes in unusually successful cognitive aging. *Journal of the International Neuropsychological Society, 18,* 1081–1085. doi:10.1017/s1355617712000847

Hart, C. L., Gruer, L., & Watt, G. C. M. (2011). Cause specific mortality, social position, and obesity among women who had never smoked: 28-year cohort study. *BMJ: British Medical Journal, 343,* 1–14.

Hart, H. M., McAdams, D. P., Hirsch, B. J., & Bauer, J. J. (2001). Generativity and social involvement among African Americans and White adults. *Journal of Research in Personality, 35,* 208–230. doi:10.1006/jrpe.2001.2318

Hartup, W. W., & Stevens, N. (1997). Friendships and adaptation in the life course. *Psychological Bulletin, 121,* 355–370.

Harvey, P. D., & Bowie, C. R. (2013). Schizophrenia spectrum conditions. In G. Stricker, T. A. Widiger & I. B. Weiner (Eds.), *Handbook of psychology, Vol. 8: Clinical psychology* (2nd ed.). (pp. 240–261). Hoboken, NJ: John Wiley & Sons, Inc.

Harwood, D. G., Sultzer, D. L., & Wheatley, M. V. (2000). Impaired insight in Alzheimer disease: Association with cognitive deficits, psychiatric symptoms, and behavioral disturbances. *Neuropsychiatry, Neuropsychology, and Behavioral Neurology, 13,* 83–88.

Haskell, W. L., Lee, I. M., Pate, R. R., Powell, K. E., Blair, S. N., Franklin, B. A., ... Bauman, A. (2007). Physical activity and public health: Updated recommendation for adults from the American College of Sports Medicine and the American Heart Association. *Medicine and Science in Sports and Exercise, 39,* 1423–1434. doi:10.1249/mss.0b013e3180616b27pii:00005768-200708000-00027

Hastings, E. C., & West, R. L. (2009). The relative success of a self-help and a group-based memory training program for older adults. *Psychology and Aging, 24,* 586–594.

Hatfield, E., & Rapson, R. L. (2012). Equity theory in close relationships. In P. A. M. Van Lange, A. W. Kruglanski & E. T. Higgins (Eds.), *Handbook of theories of social psychology,* Vol 2 (pp. 200–217). Thousand Oaks, CA: Sage Publications Ltd.

Hatfield, E., Rapson, R. L., & Aumer-Ryan, K. (2008). Social justice in love relationships: Recent developments. *Social Justice Research, 21,* 413–431.

Hayflick, L. (1994). *How and why we age.* New York: Ballantine Books.

He, W., Sangupta, M., Velkoff, V. A., & DeBarros, K. A. (2005). *65+ in the United States: 2005. Current Population Reports Special Studies. U.S. Census Bureau, Current Population Reports, P23–209.* Washington DC: U.S. Government Printing Office.

Head, D., Kennedy, K. M., Rodrigue, K. M., & Raz, N. (2009). Age differences in perseveration: Cognitive and neuroanatomical mediators of performance on the Wisconsin Card Sorting Test. *Neuropsychologia, 47,* 1200–1203. doi: S0028-3932(09)00006-2 pii:10.1016/j.neuropsychologia.2009.01.003

Hebblethwaite, S., & Norris, J. (2011). Expressions of generativity through family leisure: Experiences of grandparents and adult grandchildren. *Family Relations: An Interdisciplinary Journal of Applied Family Studies, 60,* 121–133. doi:10.1111/j.1741-3729.2010.00637.x

Heckhausen, J. (1997). Developmental regulation across adulthood: Primary and secondary control of age-related challenges. *Developmental Psychology, 33,* 176–187. doi:10.1037/0012-1649.33.1.176

Heckman, G. A., & McKelvie, R. S. (2008). Cardiovascular aging and exercise in healthy older adults. *Clinical Journal of Sports Medicine, 18,* 479–485. doi:10.1097/JSM.0b013e3181865f03pii:00042752-200811000-00002

Hedberg, K., Hopkins, D., & Kohn, M. (2003). Five years of legal physician-assisted suicide in Oregon. *New England Journal of Medicine, 348,* 961–964.

Heilmann, S. G., Holt, D. T., & Rilovick, C. Y. (2008). Effects of career plateauing on turnover: A test of a model. *Journal of Leadership & Organizational Studies, 15,* 59–68.

Heisel, M. J., Duberstein, P. R., Talbot, N. L., King, D. A., & Tu, X. M. (2009). Adapting interpersonal psychotherapy for older adults at risk for suicide: Preliminary findings. *Professional Psychology: Research and Practice, 40,* 156–164. doi:10.1037/a0014731

Helfand, B. T., Evans, R. M., & McVary, K. T. (2009). A comparison of the frequencies of medical therapies for overactive bladder in men and women: Analysis of more than 7.2 million aging patients. *European Urologist.* doi: S0302–2838(09)01272-X pii:10.1016/j.eururo.2009.12.025

Helson, R. (1967). Personality characteristics and developmental history of creative college women. *Genetic Psychology Monographs, 76,* 205–256.

Helson, R., & Soto, C. J. (2005). Up and down in middle age: Monotonic and nonmonotonic changes in roles, status, and personality. *Journal of Personality and Social Psychology, 89*, 194–204.

Helson, R., & Srivastava, S. (2001). Three paths of adult development: Conservers, seekers, and achievers. *Journal of Personality and Social Psychology, 80*, 995–1010.

Henry, J. D., & Phillips, L. H. (2006). Covariates of production and perseveration on tests of phonemic, semantic and alternating fluency in normal aging. *Aging, Neuropsychology and Cognition, 13*, 529–551.

Henz, U. (2010). Parent care as unpaid family labor: How do spouses share? *Journal of Marriage and Family, 72*, 148–164.

Heraclides, A., Chandola, T., Witte, D. R., & Brunner, E. J. (2009). Psychosocial stress at work doubles the risk of type 2 diabetes in middle-aged women: evidence from the Whitehall II study. *Diabetes Care, 32*, 2230–2235. doi:dc09-0132 pii:10.2337/dc09-0132

Heron, M., Hoyert, D. L., Murphy, S. L., Xu, J., Kochanek, K., & Tejeda-Vera, B. (2009). *Deaths: Final data for 2006 Volume 57 Number 14.* Hyattsville MD: National Center for Health Statistics.

Hersch, E. C., & Merriam, G. R. (2008). Growth hormone (GH)-releasing hormone and GH secretagogues in normal aging: Fountain of Youth or Pool of Tantalus? *Clinical Interventions in Aging, 3*, 121–129.

Herzberg, F., Mausner, B., & Bloch Snyderman, B. (2005). *The motivation to work.* New Jersey: Transaction Publishers.

Herzberg, F., Mausner, B., & Snyderman, B. B. (1959). *The motivation to work.* New York: Wiley.

Hess, T. M., Auman, C., Colcombe, S. J., & Rahhal, T. A. (2003). The impact of stereotype threat on age differences in memory performance. *Journals of Gerontology Series B: Psychological Sciences and Social Sciences, 58*, P3–11.

Hess, T. M., & Hinson, J. T. (2006). Age-related variation in the influences of aging stereotypes on memory in adulthood. *Psychology and Aging, 21*, 621–625.

Hetherington, E. M., & Kelly, J. (2002). *For better or for worse: Divorce reconsidered.* New York: W.W. Norton.

Hickman, S. E. (2002). Improving communication near the end of life. *American Behavioral Scientist, 46*, 252–267.

Hill, P. L., Turiano, N. A., Mroczek, D. K., & Roberts, B. W. (2012). Examining concurrent and longitudinal relations between personality traits and social well-being in adulthood. *Social Psychological and Personality Science, 3*, 698–705. doi:10.1177/1948550611433888

Hinrichsen, G. A., & Dick-Siskin, L. P. (2000). Psychotherapy with older adults. In S. K. Whitbourne (Ed.), *Psychopathology in later life.* New York: Wiley.

Hirschi, A. (2012). Callings and work engagement: Moderated mediation model of work meaningfulness, occupational identity, and occupational self-efficacy. *Journal of Counseling Psychology, 59*, 479–485. doi:10.1037/a0028949

Hobfoll, S. E. (2002). Social and psychological resources and adaptation. *Review of General Psychology, 6*, 307–324. doi:10.1037/1089-2680.6.4.307

Hofer, S. M., & Sliwinski, M. J. (2006). Design and analysis of longitudinal studies on aging. In J. E. Birren & K. W. Schaire (Eds.), *Handbook of the psychology of aging* (6th ed.). (pp. 15–37). Amsterdam: Elsevier.

Hoffman, B. J., & Woehr, D. J. (2006). A quantitative review of the relationship between person-organization fit and behavioral outcomes. *Journal of Vocational Behavior, 68*, 389–399.

Hoffman, L., Hofer, S. M., & Sliwinski, M. J. (2011). On the confounds among retest gains and age-cohort differences in the estimation of within-person change in longitudinal studies: A simulation study. *Psychology and Aging, 26*, 778–791. doi:10.1037/a0023910

Hofland, B. F., Willis, S. L., & Baltes, P. B. (1980). Fluid performance in the elderly: Intraindividual variability and conditions of assessment. *Journal of Educational Psychology, 73*, 573–586.

Hogan, M. J., Staff, R. T., Bunting, B. P., Deary, I. J., & Whalley, L. J. (2012). Openness to experience and activity engagement facilitate the maintenance of verbal ability in older adults. *Psychology and Aging, 27*, 849–854. doi:10.1037/a0029066

Hoge, C. W., Castro, C. A., Messer, S. C., McGurk, D., Cotting, D. I., & Koffman, R. L. (2004). Combat duty in Iraq and Afghanistan, mental health problems, and barriers to care. *New England Journal of Medicine, 351*, 13–22. doi:10.1056/NEJMoa040603

Hoge, C. W., Terhakopian, A., Castro, C. A., Messer, S. C., & Engel, C. C. (2007). Association of posttraumatic stress disorder with somatic symptoms, health care visits, and absenteeism among Iraq war veterans. *Americal Journal of Psychiatry, 164*, 150–153. doi:164/1/150 pii:10.1176/appi.ajp.164.1.150

Hogervorst, E., Huppert, F., Matthews, F. E., & Brayne, C. (2008). Thyroid function and cognitive decline in the MRC Cognitive Function and Ageing Study. *Psychoneuroendocrinology, 33*, 1013–1022. doi: S0306-4530(08)00126-1 pii:0.1016/j.psyneuen.2008.05.008

Hogh, A., Hansen, Å. M., Mikkelsen, E. G., & Persson, R. (2012). Exposure to negative acts at work, psychological stress reactions and physiological stress response. *Journal of Psychosomatic Research, 73*, 47–52. doi:10.1016/j.jpsychores.2012.04.004

Holahan, C. J., Moos, R. H., Holahan, C. K., Brennan, P. L., & Schutte, K. K. (2005). Stress generation, avoidance coping, and depressive symptoms: A 10-year model. *Journal of Consulting and Clinical Psychology, 73*, 658–666.

Holder, K. A., & Clark, S. L. (2008). *Working beyond retirement age.* Paper presented at the American Sociological Association Annual Conference, Boston, MA. Retrieved from http://www.census.gov/hhes/www/laborfor/Working-Beyond-Retirement-Age.pdf

Holland, J. L. (1994). *The self-directed search.* Odessa, FL: Psychological Assessment Resources.

Holland, J. L. (1997). *Making vocational choices: A theory of vocational personalities and work environments* (3rd ed.). Odessa, FL: Psychological Assessment Resources.

Holley, C. K., & Mast, B. T. (2007). The effects of widowhood and vascular risk factors on late-life depression. *American Journal of Geriatric Psychiatry, 15*, 690–698. doi:JGP.0b013e3180311209 pii:10.1097/JGP.0b013e3180311209

Hook, J. L., & Chalasani, S. (2008). Gendered expectations? Reconsidering single fathers' child-care time. *Journal of Marriage and Family, 70*, 978–990.

Hooker, K., & Kaus, C. R. (1994). Health-related possible selves in young and middle adulthood. *Psychol Aging, 9*, 126–133.

Horn, J. L., & Cattell, R. B. (1966). Refinement and test of the theory of fluid and crystallized intelligence. *Journal of Educational Psychology, 57*, 253–270.

Hornsby, P. J. (2009). Senescence and life span. *Pflugers Archives.* doi:10.1007/s00424-009-0723-6

House, J. S., Kessler, R. C., Herzog, A. R., & Mero, R. P. (1990). Age, socioeconomic status, and health. *Milbank Quarterly, 68*, 383–411.

Houston, D. K., Nicklas, B. J., & Zizza, C. A. (2009). Weighty concerns: The growing prevalence of obesity among older adults. *Journal of the American Dietetic Association, 109*, 1886–1895. doi:S0002-8223(09)01431-X pii:10.1016/j.jada.2009.08.014

Howard, D., & Adams, E. (2012). Mammography rates after the 2009 US Preventive Services Task Force breast cancer screening recommendation. *Preventive Medicine, 55*(5), 485–487.

Howden, L. M., & Meyer, J. A. (2011). Age and sex composition: 2010. Washington, DC: U.S. Bureau of the Census.

Hoyte, K. J., Brownell, H., & Wingfield, A. (2009). Components of speech prosody and their use in detection of syntactic structure by older adults. *Experimental Aging Research, 35*, 129–151. doi:908222255 pii:10.1080/03610730802565091

Huang, H.-W., Meyer, A. M., & Federmeier, K. D. (2012). A "concrete view" of aging: Event related potentials reveal age-related changes in basic integrative processes in language. *Neuropsychologia, 50*, 26–35. doi:10.1016/j.neuropsychologia.2011.10.018

Hughes, M. E., & Waite, L. J. (2009). Marital biography and health at mid-life. *Journal of Health and Social Behavior, 50*, 344–358.

Hugo, F. N., Hilgert, J. B., de Sousa Mda, L., & Cury, J. A. (2009). Oral status and its association with general quality of life in older independent-living south-Brazilians. *Community Dentistry and Oral Epidemiology, 37*, 231–240. doi:COM459 pii:10.1111/j.1600-0528.2009.00459.x

Huh, J. T., Weaver, C. M., Martin, J. L., Caskey, N. H., O'Riley, A., & Kramer, B. J. (2012). Effects of a late-life suicide risk–assessment training on multidisciplinary healthcare providers. *Journal of the American Geriatrics Society, 60*, 775–780. doi:10.1111/j.1532-5415.2011.03843.x

Humphrey, D. (1991). *Final exit: The practicalities of self-deliverance and assisted suicide for the dying.* Eugene Oregon: Hemlock Society.

Hunter, D. J., & Eckstein, F. (2009). Exercise and osteoarthritis. *Journal of Anatomy, 214*, 197–207. doi:JOA1013 pii:10.1111/j.1469-7580.2008.01013.x

Hurd Clarke, L. (2006). Older women and sexuality: Experiences in marital relationships across the life course. *Canadian Journal of Aging, 25*, 129–140.

Huston, T. L. (2009). What's love got to do with it? Why some marriages succeed and others fail. *Personal Relationships, 16*, 301–327. doi:10.1111/j.1475-6811.2009.01225.x

Hy, L. X., & Keller, D. M. (2000). Prevalence of AD among whites: A summary by levels of severity. *Neurology, 55*, 198–204.

Hy, L. X., & Loevinger, J. (1996). *Measuring ego development* (2nd ed.). Hillsdale, NJ Lawrence Erlbaum Associates, Inc.

Hyer, L., Yeager, C., Hyer, R., & Scott, C. (2010). Psychotherapy with older adults: The importance of assessment. In P. A. Lichtenberg (Ed.), *Handbook of assessment in clinical gerontology* (2nd ed.). (pp. 61–100). San Diego, CA: Elsevier Academic Press.

Iacono, D., Markesbery, W. R., Gross, M., Pletnikova, O., Rudow, G., Zandi, P., & Troncoso, J. C. (2009). The Nun study: Clinically silent AD, neuronal hypertrophy, and linguistic skills in early life. *Neurology, 73*, 665–673. doi:WNL.0b013e3181b01077 pii:10.1212/WNL.0b013e3181b01077

Ice, G. H. (2002). Daily life in a nursing home: Has it changed in 25 years? *Journal of Aging Studies, 16*, 345–359.

Idler, E. L., McLaughlin, J., & Kasl, S. (2009). Religion and the quality of life in the last year of life. *Journals of Gerontology Series B: Psychological Sciences and Social Sciences, 64*, 528–537. doi:gbp028 pii:10.1093/geronb/gbp028

Igwebuike, A., Irving, B. A., Bigelow, M. L., Short, K. R., McConnell, J. P., & Nair, K. S. (2008). Lack of dehydroepiandrosterone effect on a combined endurance and resistance exercise program in postmenopausal women. *Journal of Endocrinological Metabolism, 93*, 534–538. doi:jc.2007-1027 pii:10.1210/jc.2007-1027

Ilies, R., Johnson, M. D., Judge, T. A., & Keeney, J. (2011). A within-individual study of interpersonal conflict as a work stressor: Dispositional and situational moderators. *Journal of Organizational Behavior, 32*, 44–64. doi:10.1002/job.677

Imai, K., Hamaguchi, M., Mori, K., Takeda, N., Fukui, M., Kato, T., … Kojima, T. (2010). Metabolic syndrome as a risk factor for high-ocular tension. *International Journal of Obesity.* doi:ijo201032 pii: 10.1038/ijo.2010.32

Imbimbo, B. P., Solfrizzi, V., & Panza, F. (2012). Are NSAIDs useful to treat Alzheimer's disease or mild cognitive impairment? *Frontiers in Aging Neuroscience, 2.*

IMS Institute for Healthcare Informatics. (2012). The use of medicines in the United States: Review of 2011. Parsippany, NJ: IMS Institute for Healthcare Informatics.

Inkson, K., Gunz, H., Ganesh, S., & Roper, J. (2012). Boundaryless careers: Bringing back boundaries. *Organization Studies, 33*, 323–340. doi:10.1177/0170840611435600

Institute of Medicine. (2008). Retooling for an aging America: Buillding the healthcare workforce. Retrieved from http://www.iom.edu/Reports/2008/Retooling-for-an-Aging-America-Building-the-Health-Care-Workforce.aspx

Isaacowitz, D. M. (2012). Mood regulation in real time: Age differences in the role of looking. *Current Directions in Psychological Science, 21*, 237–242. doi:10.1177/0963721412448651

Isaacowitz, D. M., Toner, K., & Neupert, S. D. (2009). Use of gaze for real-time mood regulation: Effects of age and attentional functioning. *Psychology and Aging, 24*, 989–994.

Isaacowitz, D. M., Wadlinger, H. A., Goren, D., & Wilson, H. R. (2006). Selective preference in visual fixation away from negative images in old age? An eye-tracking study. *Psychology and Aging, 21*, 40–48.

Ishigami, Y., & Klein, R. M. (2009). Is a hands-free phone safer than a handheld phone? *Journal of Safety Research, 40*, 157–164. doi:S0022-4375(09)00029-2 pii:10.1016/j.jsr.2009.02.006

Ivcevic, Z., & Mayer, J. D. (2009). Mapping dimensions of creativity in the life-space. *Creativity Research Journal, 21*, 152–165. doi:10.1080/10400410902855259

Iyer Parameswaran, G., & Murphy, T. F. (2009). Chronic obstructive pulmonary disease: Role of bacteria and updated guide to antibacterial selection in the older patient. *Drugs and Aging, 26*, 985–995. doi:1 pii:10.2165/11315700-000000000-00000

Jackson, R. A., Vittinghoff, E., Kanaya, A. M., Miles, T. P., Resnick, H. E., Kritchevsky, S. B., … Brown, J. S. (2004). Urinary incontinence in elderly women: Findings from the Health, Aging, and Body Composition Study. *Obstetrics and Gynecology, 104*, 301–307. doi:10.1097/01.AOG.0000133482.20685.d1 pii:104/2/301

James, H. S. J. (2005). Why did you do that? An economic examination of the effect of extrinsic compensation on intrinsic motivation and performance. *Journal of Economic Psychology, 26*, 549–566.

James, L. E., & MacKay, D. G. (2007). New age-linked asymmetries: Aging and the processing of familiar versus novel language on the input versus output side. *Psychology and Aging, 22*, 94–103.

Jang, S.-N., Choi, Y.-J., & Kim, D.-H. (2009). Association of socioeconomic status with successful ageing: Differences in the components of successful ageing. *Journal of Biosocial Science, 41*, 207–219.

Janowsky, J. S. (2006). The role of androgens in cognition and brain aging in men. *Neuroscience, 138*, 1015–1020. doi:S0306-4522(05)01036-5 pii:10.1016/j.neuroscience.2005.09.007

Janse, E. (2009). Processing of fast speech by elderly listeners. *Journal of the Acoustical Society of America, 125*, 2361–2373. doi:10.1121/1.3082117

Janson, C., Lindberg, E., Gislason, T., Elmasry, A., & Boman, G. (2001). Insomnia in men—A 10-year prospective population based study. *Sleep, 24*, 425–430.

Jaques, E. (1965). Death and the mid-life crisis. *International Journal of Psychoanalysis, 46*, 502–514.

Jaunin, J., Bochud, M., Marques-Vidal, P., Vollenweider, P., Waeber, G., Mooser, V., & Paccaud, F. (2009). Smoking offsets the metabolic benefits of parental longevity in women:

The CoLaus study. *Preventive Medicine, 48*, 224–231. doi:S0091-7435(08)00665-8 pii:10.1016/j.ypmed.2008.12.007

Jemal, A., Simard, E. P., Dorell, C., Noone, A.-M., Markowitz, L. E., Kohler, B., … Edwards, B. K. (2013). Annual report to the nation on the status of cancer, 1975–2009, featuring the burden and trends in Human Papillomavirus (HPV)–associated cancers and HPV vaccination coverage levels. *Journal of the National Cancer Institute*. doi:10.1093/jnci/djs491

Jeste, D. V., Symonds, L. L., Harris, M. J., Paulsen, J. S., Palmer, B. W., & Heaton, R. K. (1997). Nondementia nonpraecox dementia praecox? Late onset schizophrenia. *American Journal of Geriatric Psychiatry, 5*, 302–317.

Jimenez, D. E., Alegria, M., Chen, C. N., Chan, D., & Laderman, M. (2010). Prevalence of psychiatric illnesses in older ethnic minority adults. *Journal of the American Geriatrics Society, 58*, 256–264. doi:JGS2685 pii:10.1111/j.1532-5415.2009.02685.x

Jobe, T. H., & Harrow, M. (2010). Schizophrenia course, long-term outcome, recovery, and prognosis. *Current Directions in Psychological Science, 19*, 220–225. doi:10.1177/0963721410378034

Johnson, J., Stewart, W., Hall, E., Fredlund, P., & Theorell, T. (1996). Long-term psychosocial work environment and cardiovascular mortality among Swedish men. *American Journal of Public Health, 86*, 324–331.

Jonason, P., & Webster, G. (2010). The dirty dozen: A concise measure of the dark triad. *Psychological Assessment, 22*, 420–432.

Jonassaint, C. R., Boyle, S. H., Williams, R. B., Mark, D. B., Siegler, I. C., & Barefoot, J. C. (2007). Facets of openness predict mortality in patients with cardiac disease. *Psychosomatic Medicine, 69*, 319–322. doi:10.1097/PSY.0b013e318052e27d

Jones, K. M., Whitbourne, S., Whitbourne, S. B., & Skultety, K. M. (2009). Identity processes and memory controllability in middle and later adulthood. *Journal of Applied Gerontology, 28*, 582–599. doi:10.1177/0733464808330823

Jones, T. E., Stephenson, K. W., King, J. G., Knight, K. R., Marshall, T. L., & Scott, W. B. (2009). Sarcopenia—Mechanisms and treatments. *Journal of Geriatric Physical Therapy, 32*, 39–45.

Joo, J. H., Morales, K. H., de Vries, H. F., & Gallo, J. J. (2010). Disparity in use of psychotherapy offered in primary care between older African-American and White adults: Results from a practice-based depression intervention trial. *Journal of the American Geriatrics Society, 58*, 154–160. doi:JGS2623 pii:10.1111/j.1532-5415.2009.02623.x

Jorm, A. F., Windsor, T. D., Dear, K. B., Anstey, K. J., Christensen, H., & Rodgers, B. (2005). Age group differences in psychological distress: The role of psychosocial risk factors that vary with age. *Psychological Medicine, 35*, 1253–1263.

Joseph, J. A., Shukitt-Hale, B., & Willis, L. M. (2009). Grape juice, berries, and walnuts affect brain aging and behavior. *Journal of Nutrition, 139*, 1813S–1817S. doi:jn.109.108266 pii:10.3945/jn.109.108266

Judge, T. A., Heller, D., & Mount, M. K. (2002). Five-factor model of personality and job satisfaction: A meta-analysis. *Journal of Applied Psychology, 87*, 530–541.

Judge, T. A., Locke, E. A., Durham, C. C., & Kluger, A. N. (1998). Dispositional effects on job and life satisfaction: The role of core evaluations. *Journal of Applied Psychology*, 83, 17–34. doi:10.1037/0021-9010.83.1.17

Junco, R. (2012). Too much face and not enough books: The relationship between multiple indices of Facebook use and academic performance. *Computers in Human Behavior*, 28, 187–198. doi:10.1016/j.chb.2011.08.026

Kahlaoui, K., Sante, G. D., Barbeau, J., Maheux, M., Lesage, F., Ska, B., & Joanette, Y. (2012). Contribution of NIRS to the study of prefrontal cortex for verbal fluency in aging. *Brain and Language*, 121, 164–173. doi:10.1016/j.bandl.2011.11.002

Kaiser Family Foundation. (2010a). Prescription drug trends.

Kaiser Family Foundation. (2010b). State Health Facts. Retrieved from http://www.statehealthfacts.org/savemap.jsp?typ=4&ind=180&cat=4&sub=47

Kallio, E. (2011). Integrative thinking is the key: An evaluation of current research into the development of adult thinking. *Theory & Psychology*, 21, 785–801. doi:10.1177/0959354310388344

Kalmijn, M. (2003). Shared friendship networks and the life course: An analysis of survey data on married and cohabiting couples. *Social Networks*, 25, 231–249.

Kalmijn, M., & De Graaf, P. M. (2012). Life course changes of children and well-being of parents. *Journal of Marriage and Family*, 74, 269–280. doi:10.1111/j.1741-3737.2012.00961.x

Kamel, N. S., & Gammack, J. K. (2006). Insomnia in the elderly: Cause, approach, and treatment. *American Journal of Medicine*, 119, 463–469.

Kamimoto, L. A., Easton, A. N., Maurice, E., Husten, C. G., & Macera, C. A. (1999). Surveillance for five health risks among older adults—United States, 1993–1997. *Morbidity and Mortality Weekly Reports*, 48 (SS08), 89–130.

Kane, R. A., Caplan, A. L., Urv-Wong, E. K., Freeman, I. C., Aroskar, M. A., & Finch, M. (1997). Everyday matters in the lives of nursing home residents: Wish for and perception of choice and control. *Journal of the American Geriatrics Society*, 45, 1086–1093.

Kane, R. A., Lum, T. Y., Cutler, L. J., Degenholtz, H. B., & Yu, T. C. (2007). Resident outcomes in small-house nursing homes: A longitudinal evaluation of the initial green house program. *Journal of the American Geriatrics Society*, 55, 832–839. doi:JGS1169 pii:10.1111/j.1532-5415.2007.01169.x

Kanfer, R., & Ackerman, P. L. (2004). Aging, adult development, and work motivation. *Academy of Management Review*, 29, 440–458.

Kannus, P., Uusi-Rasi, K., Palvanen, M., & Parkkari, J. (2005). Nonpharmacological means to prevent fractures among older adults. *Annals of Medicine*, 37, 303–310.

Karakaya, M. G., Bilgin, S. C., Ekici, G., Kose, N., & Otman, A. S. (2009). Functional mobility, depressive symptoms, level of independence, and quality of life of the elderly living at home and in the nursing home. *Journal of the American Medical Directors Association*, 10, 662–666. doi:S1525-8610(09)00221-7 pii:10.1016/j.jamda.2009.06.002

Karavirta, L., Tulppo, M. P., Laaksonen, D. E., Nyman, K., Laukkanen, R. T., Kinnunen, H., … Hakkinen, K. (2009). Heart rate dynamics after combined endurance and strength training in older men. *Medicine and Science in Sports and Exercise*, 41, 1436–1443. doi10.1249/MSS.0b013e3181994a91

Karel, M. J., Holley, C. K., Whitbourne, S. K., Segal, D. L., Tazeau, Y. N., Emery, E. E., … Zweig, R. A. (2012). Preliminary validation of a tool to assess competencies for professional geropsychology practice. *Professional Psychology: Research and Practice*, 43, 110–117. doi:10.1037/a0025788

Karel, M. J., Knight, B. G., Duffy, M., Hinrichsen, G. A., & Zeiss, A. M. (2010). Attitude, knowledge, and skill competencies for practice in professional geropsychology: Implications for training and building a geropsychology workforce. *Training and Education in Professional Psychology*, 4, 75–84. doi:10.1037/a0018372

Karney, B., & Bradbury, T. (1997). Neuroticism, marital interaction, and the trajectory of marital satisfaction. *Journal of Personality and Social Psychology*, 72, 1075–1092.

Karp, J. F., Skidmore, E., Lotz, M., Lenze, E., Dew, M. A., & Reynolds, C. F., III,. (2009). Use of the late-life function and disability instrument to assess disability in major depression. *Journal of the American Geriatrics Society*, 57, 1612–1619. doi:JGS2398 pii:10.1111/j.1532-5415.2009.02398.x

Kastorini, C.-M., Milionis, H. J., Esposito, K., Giugliano, D., Goudevenos, J. A., & Panagiotakos, D. B. (2011). The effect of Mediterranean diet on metabolic syndrome and its components: A meta-analysis of 50 studies and 534,906 individuals. *Journal of the American College of Cardiology (JACC)*, 57, 1299–1313.

Katz, R. (2009). Intergenerational family relations and subjective well-being in old age: A cross-national study. *European Journal of Ageing*, 6, 79–90.

Katzel, L. I., Sorkin, J. D., & Fleg, J. L. (2001). A comparison of longitudinal changes in aerobic fitness in older endurance athletes and sedentary men. *Journal of the American Geriatric Society*, 49, 1657–1664.

Kaufman, A. S., Kaufman, J. L., McLean, J. E., & Reynolds, C. R. (1991). Is the pattern of intellectual growth and decline across the adult life span different for men and women? *Journal of Clinical Psychology*, 47, 801–812.

Kawas, C., Gray, S., Brookmeyer, R., Fozard, J., & Zonderman, A. (2000). Age-specific incidence rates of Alzheimer's disease: The Baltimore Longitudinal Study of Aging. *Neurology*, 54, 2072–2077.

Keefe, S. E., Padilla, A. M., & Carlos, M. L. (1979). The Mexican-American extended family as an emotional support system. *Human Organization*, 38, 144–152.

Keith, S. J., Regier, D. A., & Rae, D. S. (1991). Schizophrenic disorders. In L. N. Robins & D. A. Regier (Eds.), *Psychiatric disorders in America* (pp. 33–52). New York: Free Press.

Kelly, B., Burnett, P., Pelusi, D., Badger, S., Varghese, F., & Robertson, M. (2002). Terminally ill cancer patients' wish to hasten death. *Palliative Medicine*, 16, 339–345.

Kelly, D. L., McMahon, R. P., Liu, F., Love, R. C., Wehring, H. J., Shim, J. C., … Conley, R. R. (2010). Cardiovascular disease mortality in patients with chronic schizophrenia treated with clozapine: A retrospective cohort study. *Journal of Clinical Psychiatry, 71*, 304–311. doi:10.4088/JCP.08m04718yel

Kemper, S., Greiner, L. H., Marquis, J. G., Prenovost, K., & Mitzner, T. L. (2001). Language decline across the life span: Findings from the Nun Study. *Psychology and Aging, 16*, 227–239.

Kemper, S., Marquis, J., & Thompson, M. (2001). Longitudinal change in language production: Effects of aging and dementia on grammatical complexity and propositional content. *Psychology and Aging, 16*, 600–614.

Kemper, S., & McDowd, J. M. (2008). Dimensions of cognitive aging: Executive function and verbal fluency. In S. M. Hofer & D. F. Alwin (Eds.), *Handbook of cognitive aging: Interdisciplinary perspectives.* (pp. 181–192). Thousand Oaks, CA: Sage Publications, Inc.

Kendler, K. S., Myers, J., & Zisook, S. (2008). Does bereavement-related major depression differ from major depression associated with other stressful life events? *American Journal of Psychiatry, 165*, 1449–1455. doi:appi.ajp.2008.07111757 pii:10.1176/appi.ajp.2008.07111757

Kerby, D. S., & Ragan, K. M. (2002). Activity interests and Holland's RIASEC system in older adults. *International Journal of Aging & Human Development, 55*, 117–139.

Kessel, L., Jorgensen, T., Glumer, C., & Larsen, M. (2006). Early lens aging is accelerated in subjects with a high risk of ischemic heart disease: An epidemiologic study. *BMC Ophthalmology, 6*, 16.

Kessler, R. C., Berglund, P., Demler, O., Jin, R., Merikangas, K. R., & Walters, E. E. (2005). Lifetime prevalence and age-of-onset distributions of DSM-IV disorders in the National Comorbidity Survey Replication. *Archives of General Psychiatry, 62*, 593–602.

Kessler, R. C., Chiu, W. T., Demler, O., Merikangas, K. R., & Walters, E. E. (2005). Prevalence, severity, and comorbidity of 12-month DSM-IV disorders in the National Comorbidity Survey Replication. *Archives of General Psychiatry, 62*, 617–627. doi:62/6/617 pii:10.1001/archpsyc.62.6.617

Kessler, R. C., Chiu, W. T., Jin, R., Ruscio, A. M., Shear, K., & Walters, E. E. (2006). The epidemiology of panic attacks, panic disorder, and agoraphobia in the National Comorbidity Survey Replication. *Archives of General Psychiatry, 63*, 415–424. doi:63/4/415 pii:10.1001/archpsyc.63.4.415

Kiecolt-Glaser, J. K., & Glaser, R. (2002). Depression and immune function: Central pathways to morbidity and mortality. *Journal of Psychosomatic Research, 53*, 873–876.

Kieffer, K. M., Schinka, J. A., & Curtiss, G. (2004). Person-environment congruence and personality domains in the prediction of job performance and work quality. *Journal of Counseling Psychology, 51*, 168–177.

Kim, H., Yoshida, H., & Suzuki, T. (2010). The effects of multidimensional exercise on functional decline, urinary incontinence, and fear of falling in community-dwelling elderly women with multiple symptoms of geriatric syndrome: A randomized controlled and 6-month follow-up trial. *Archives of Gerontology and Geriatrics.* doi:S0167-4943(10)00055-5 pii:10.1016/j.archger.2010.02.008

Kim, J. M., Stewart, R., Kim, S. W., Yang, S. J., Shin, I. S., & Yoon, J. S. (2009). Insomnia, depression, and physical disorders in late life: A 2-year longitudinal community study in Koreans. *Sleep, 32*, 1221–1228.

Kim, S., & Hasher, L. (2005). The attraction effect in decision making: Superior performance by older adults. *The Quarterly Journal of Experimental Psychology A: Human Experimental Psychology, 58A*, 120–133. doi:10.1080/02724980443000160

Kimmel, S. B., Gaylor, K. P., Ray Grubbs, M., & Bryan Hayes, J. (2012). Good times to hard times: An examination of adult learners' enrollment from 2004–2010. *Journal of Behavioral & Applied Management, 14*, 18–38.

King, A. C., Atienza, A., Castro, C., & Collins, R. (2002). Physiological and affective responses to family caregiving in the natural setting in wives versus daughters. *International Journal of Behavioral Medicine, 9*, 176–194.

King, L. A., King, D. W., Vickers, K., Davison, E. H., & Spiro, A., III. (2007). Assessing late-onset stress symptomatology among aging male combat veterans. *Aging and Mental Health, 11*, 175–191. doi:773456879 pii:10.1080/13607860600844424

Kinsella, K., & He, W. (2009). An aging world 2008: International Population Reports P95/09-1. Retrieved from http://www.census.gov/prod/2009pubs/p95-09-1.pdf

Kissane, M., & McLaren, S. (2006). Sense of belonging as a predictor of reasons for living in older adults. *Death Studies, 30*, 243–258.

Kite, M. E., & Wagner, L. S. (2002). Attitudes toward older adults. In T. D. Nelson (Ed.), *Ageism: Stereotyping and prejudice against older persons.* (pp. 129–161). Cambridge MA: The MIT Press.

Kiviniemi, M., & Hay, J. (2012). Awareness of the 2009 US Preventive Services Task Force recommended changes in mammography screening guidelines, accuracy of awareness, sources of knowledge about recommendations, and attitudes about updated screening guidelines in women ages 40–49 and 50+. *BMC Public Health, 12*, 899.

Klass, M., Baudry, S., & Duchateau, J. (2006). Voluntary activation during maximal contraction with advancing age: A brief review. *European Journal of Applied Physiology.*

Klemmack, D. L., Roff, L. L., Parker, M. W., Koenig, H. G., Sawyer, P., & Allman, R. M. (2007). A cluster analysis typology of religiousness/spirituality among older adults. *Research on Aging, 29*, 163–183.

Klerman, E. B., Duffy, J. F., Dijk, D. J., & Czeisler, C. A. (2001). Circadian phase resetting in older people by ocular bright light exposure. *Journal of Investigative Medicine, 49*, 30–40.

Klysner, R., Bent-Hansen, J., Hansen, H. L., Lunde, M., Pleidrup, E., Poulsen, D. L., ... Petersen, H. E. (2002). Efficacy of citalopram in the prevention of recurrent depression in elderly patients: Placebo-controlled study of maintenance therapy. *British Journal of Psychiatry, 181*, 29–35.

Knight, B. G., Karel, M. J., Hinrichsen, G. A., Qualls, S. H., & Duffy, M. (2009). Pikes Peak model for training in professional geropsychology. *American Psychologist, 64*, 205–214. doi:2009-04471-004 pii:10.1037/a0015059

Knight, B. G., & Kellough, J. (2013). Psychotherapy with older adults within a family context. In G. Stricker, T. A. Widiger & I. B. Weiner (Eds.), *Handbook of psychology, Vol. 8: Clinical psychology* (2nd ed.). (pp. 474–488). Hoboken, NJ: John Wiley & Sons, Inc.

Knoester, C., & Eggebeen, D. J. (2006). The effects of the transition to parenthood and subsequent children on men's well-being and social participation. *Journal of Family Issues, 27*, 1532–1560.

Knopman, D. S. (2007). Cerebrovascular disease and dementia. *British Journal of Radiology, 80 Spec No 2*, S121–S127. doi:80/Special_Issue_2/S121 pii:10.1259/bjr/75681080

Koropeckyj-Cox, T. (2002). Beyond parental status: Psychological well-being in middle and old age. *Journal of Marriage and Family, 64*, 957–971.

Korte, J., Westerhof, G. J., & Bohlmeijer, E. T. (2012). Mediating processes in an effective life-review intervention. *Psychology and Aging, 27*, 1172–1181. doi:10.1037/a0029273

Kosek, D. J., Kim, J.-s., Petrella, J. K., Cross, J. M., & Bamman, M. M. (2006). Efficacy of 3 days/wk resistance training on myofiber hypertrophy and myogenic mechanisms in young vs. older adults. *Journal of Applied Physiology, 101*, 531–544.

Kostka, T. (2005). Quadriceps maximal power and optimal shortening velocity in 335 men aged 23–88 years. *European Journal of Applied Physiology, 95*, 140–145.

Kousaie, S., & Phillips, N. A. (2012). Ageing and bilingualism: Absence of a "bilingual advantage" in Stroop interference in a nonimmigrant sample. *The Quarterly Journal of Experimental Psychology, 65*, 356–369. doi:10.1080/17470218.2011.604788

Kouvonen, A., Stafford, M., De Vogli, R., Shipley, M. J., Marmot, M. G., Cox, T., ... Kivimäki, M. (2011). Negative aspects of close relationships as a predictor of increased body mass index and waist circumference: The Whitehall II Study. *American Journal of Public Health, 101*, 1474–1480.

Kozbelt, A. (2007). A quantitative analysis of Beethoven as self-critic: Implications for psychological theories of musical creativity. *Psychology of Music, 35*, 144–168.

Kramer, A. F., Boot, W. R., McCarley, J. S., Peterson, M. S., Colcombe, A., & Scialfa, C. T. (2006). Aging, memory and visual search. *Acta Psychologica (Amsterdam), 122*, 288–304.

Kramer, A. F., & Madden, D. J. (2008). Attention. In F. I. M. Craik & T. A. Salthouse (Eds.), *The handbook of aging and cognition* (3rd ed.) (pp. 189–249). New York: Psychology Press.

Kreider, R. M., & Ellis, R. (2011). Number, timing, and duration of marriages and divorces: 2009 *Current Population Reports, 70–125*. Washington DC: U.S. Bureau of the Census.

Krivickas, K. M., & Lofquist, D. (2011). Demographics of same-sex couple households with children. *SEHSD Working Paper, Number 2011-11*.

Kroger, J., & Marcia, J. E. (2011). The identity statuses: Origins, meanings, and interpretations. In S. J. Schwartz, K. Luyckx & V. L. Vignoles (Eds.), *Handbook of identity theory and research,* Vols. *1* and 2 (pp. 31–53). New York: Springer Science + Business Media.

Kryger, A. I., & Andersen, J. L. (2007). Resistance training in the oldest old: Consequences for muscle strength, fiber types, fiber size, and MHC isoforms. *Scandinavian Journal of Medicine and Science in Sports, 17*, 422–430. doi:SMS575 pii:10.1111/j.1600-0838.2006.00575.x

Kübler-Ross, E. (1969). *On death and dying*. New York: MacMillan.

Kubo, N., Kato, A., & Nakamura, K. (2006). Deterioration of planning ability with age in Japanese monkeys (Macaca fuscata). *Journal of Comparative Psychology, 120*, 449–455.

Kubzansky, L. D., Cole, S. R., Kawachi, I., Vokonas, P., & Sparrow, D. (2006). Shared and unique contributions of anger, anxiety, and depression to coronary heart disease: A prospective study in the Normative Aging Study. *Annals of Behavioral Medicine, 31*, 21–29.

Kubzansky, L. D., Koenen, K. C., Spiro, A., III,, Vokonas, P. S., & Sparrow, D. (2007). Prospective study of posttraumatic stress disorder symptoms and coronary heart disease in the Normative Aging Study. *Archives of General Psychiatry, 64*, 109–116.

Kuerbis, A., & Sacco, P. (2012). The impact of retirement on the drinking patterns of older adults: A review. *Addictive Behaviors, 37*, 587–595. doi:10.1016/j.addbeh.2012.01.022

Kujala, U. M. (2009). Evidence on the effects of exercise therapy in the treatment of chronic disease. *British Journal of Sports Medicine, 43*, 550–555. doi:bjsm.2009.059808 pii:10.1136/bjsm.2009.059808

Kukat, A., & Trifunovic, A. (2009). Somatic mtDNA mutations and aging—facts and fancies. *Experimental Gerontology, 44*, 101–105. doi:S0531-5565(08)00154-pii:10.1016/j.exger.2008.05.006

Kumari, M., Badrick, E., Chandola, T., Adler, N. E., Epel, E., Seeman, T., ... Marmot, M. G. (2010). Measures of social position and cortisol secretion in an aging population: Findings from the Whitehall II study. *Psychosomatic Medicine, 72*, 27–34. doi:PSY.0b013e3181c85712 pii:10.1097/PSY.0b013e3181c85712

Kung, H.-C., Hoyert, D. L., Xu, J., & Murphy, S. L. (2008). Deaths: Final data for 2005. *National Vital Statistics Reports, 55*(10).

Kunzmann, U., & Gruhn, D. (2005). Age differences in emotional reactivity: The sample case of sadness. *Psychology and Aging, 20*, 47–59.

Kuzuya, M., Ando, F., Iguchi, A., & Shimokata, H. (2006). Effect of smoking habit on age-related changes in serum lipids: A cross-sectional and longitudinal analysis in a large Japanese cohort. *Atherosclerosis, 185*, 183–190.

Labouvie-Vief, G., & Medler, M. (2002). Affect optimization and affect complexity: Modes and styles of regulation in adulthood. *Psychology and Aging, 17*, 571–588.

Lachman, M. E. (2004). Development in midlife. *Annual Review of Psychology, 55*, 305–331.

Lachman, M. E. (2006). Perceived control over aging-related declines. *Current Directions in Psychological Science, 15*, 282–286.

Lachman, M. E., & Andreoletti, C. (2006). Strategy use mediates the relationship between control beliefs and memory performance for middle-aged and older adults. *Journals of Gerontology Series B: Psychological Sciences and Social Sciences, 61,* P88–94.

Lachman, M. E., Neupert, S. D., Bertrand, R., & Jette, A. M. (2006). The effects of strength training on memory in older adults. *Journal of Aging and Physical Activity, 14,* 59–73.

Lachman, M. E., Rosnick, C. B., Röcke, C., Bosworth, H. B., & Hertzog, C. (2009). The rise and fall of control beliefs and life satisfaction in adulthood: Trajectories of stability and change over ten years. *Aging and cognition: Research methodologies and empirical advances.* (pp. 143–160). Washington, DC: American Psychological Association.

Lafreniere, D., & Mann, N. (2009). Anosmia: Loss of smell in the elderly. *Otolaryngology Clinics of North America, 42,* 123–131, x. doi:S0030-6665(08)00145-X pii:10.1016/j.otc.2008.09.001

Lamina, S., Okoye, C. G., & Dagogo, T. T. (2009). Therapeutic effect of an interval exercise training program in the management of erectile dysfunction in hypertensive patients. *Journal of Clinical Hypertension, 11,* 125–129. doi:JCH086 pii:10.1111/j.1751-7176.2009.00086.x

Lang, F. R., & Carstensen, L. L. (1994). Close emotional relationships in late life: Further support for proactive aging in the social domain. *Psychology and Aging, 9,* 315–324.

Lang, F. R., & Carstensen, L. L. (2002). Time counts: Future time perspective, goals, and social relationships. *Psychology and Aging, 17,* 125–139.

Lang, T., Streeper, T., Cawthon, P., Baldwin, K., Taaffe, D. R., & Harris, T. B. (2009). Sarcopenia: Etiology, clinical consequences, intervention, and assessment. *Osteoporos International.* doi:10.1007/s00198-009-1059-y

Langford, A., & Johnson, B. (2009). Social inequalities in adult female mortality by the National Statistics Socio-economic Classification, England and Wales, 2001–2003. *Health Statistics Quqrterly,* 6–21.

Lapalme, M.-È., Tremblay, M., & Simard, G. (2009). The relationship between career plateauing, employee commitment and psychological distress: The role of organizational and supervisor support. *The International Journal of Human Resource Management, 20,* 1132–1145. doi:10.1080/09585190902850323

Lapointe, J., & Hekimi, S. (2009). When a theory of aging ages badly. *Cellular and Molecular Life Sciences, 67,* 1–8 doi:10.1007/s00018-009-0138-8

Larbi, A., Fulop, T., & Pawelec, G. (2008). Immune receptor signaling, aging and autoimmunity. *Advances in Experimental Medicine and Biology, 640,* 312–324. doi:10.1007/978-0-387-09789-3_21

Larcom, M. J., & Isaacowitz, D. M. (2009). Rapid emotion regulation after mood induction: Age and individual differences. *Journals of Gerontology Series B: Psychological Sciences and Social Sciences, 64,* 733–741. doi:gbp077 pii:10.1093/geronb/gbp077

Lau, A. W., & Gallagher-Thompson, D. (2002). Ethnic minority older adults in clinical and research programs: Issues and recommendations. *Behavior Therapist, 25,* 10–11.

Lau, C. Q. (2012). The stability of same-sex cohabition, different-sex cohabition, and marriage. *Journal of Marriage and Family, 74,* 973–988.

Laub, J. H., & Vaillant, G. E. (2000). Delinquency and mortality: A 50-year follow-up study of 1,000 delinquent and nondelinquent boys. *American Journal of Psychiatry, 157,* 96–102.

Lavender, A. P., & Nosaka, K. (2007). Fluctuations of isometric force after eccentric exercise of the elbow flexors of young, middle-aged, and old men. *European Journal of Applied Physiology, 100,* 161–167.

Lawton, M. P., & Brody, E. M. (1969). Assessment of older people: Self-maintaining and instrumental activities of daily living. *The Gerontologist, 9,* 179–186. doi:10.1093/geront/9.3_Part_1.179

Lawton, M. P., & Nahemow, L. (1973). Ecology and the aging process. In C. Eisdorfer & M. P. Lawton (Eds.), *The psychology of adult development and aging.* Washington, DC: American Psychological Association.

Lease, S. H. (1998). Annual review, 1993–1997: Work attitudes and outcomes. *Journal of Vocational Behavior, 53,* 154–183.

LeBeau, R. T., Glenn, D., Liao, B., Wittchen, H. U., Beesdo-Baum, K., Ollendick, T., & Craske, M. G. (2010). Specific phobia: A review of DSM-IV specific phobia and preliminary recommendations for DSM-V. *Depression and Anxiety, 27,* 148–167. doi:10.1002/da.20655

Leboeuf-Yde, C., Nielsen, J., Kyvik, K. O., Fejer, R., & Hartvigsen, J. (2009). Pain in the lumbar, thoracic or cervical regions: Do age and gender matter? A population-based study of 34,902 Danish twins 20–71 years of age. *BMC Musculoskeletal Disorders, 10,* 39. doi:1471-2474-10-39 pii:10.1186/1471-2474-10-39

Lee, S. Y., Franchetti, M. K., Imanbayev, A., Gallo, J. J., Spira, A. P., & Lee, H. B. (2012). Non-pharmacological prevention of major depression among community-dwelling older adults: A systematic review of the efficacy of psychotherapy interventions. *Archives of Gerontology and Geriatrics, 55,* 522–529. doi:10.1016/j.archger.2012.03.003

Lefevre, M., Redman, L. M., Heilbronn, L. K., Smith, J. V., Martin, C. K., Rood, J. C., … Ravussin, E. (2009). Caloric restriction alone and with exercise improves CVD risk in healthy non-obese individuals. *Atherosclerosis, 203,* 206–213. doi:S0021-9150(08)00378-X pii:101016/j.atherosclerosis.2008.05.036

Lehman, H. C. (1953). *Age and achievement.* Princeton, NJ: Princeton University Press.

Lentz, E., & Allen, T. D. (2009). The role of mentoring others in the career plateauing phenomenon. *Group and Organization Management, 34,* 358–384.

Lenze, E. J., Munin, M. C., Skidmore, E. R., Dew, M. A., Rogers, J. C., Whyte, E. M., … Reynolds, C. F., III,. (2007). Onset of depression in elderly persons after hip fracture: Implications for prevention and early intervention of late-life depression. *Journal of the American Geriatrics Society, 55,* 81–86.

Lenze, E. J., Rollman, B. L., Shear, M. K., Dew, M. A., Pollock, B. G., Ciliberti, C., … Reynolds, C. F., III,. (2009). Escitalopram for older adults with generalized anxiety disorder: A randomized controlled trial. *Journal of the American Medical Association, 301,* 295–303. doi:301/3/295 pii:10.1001/jama.2008.977

Leonardelli, G. J., Hermann, A. D., Lynch, M. E., & Arkin, R. M. (2003). The shape of self-evaluation: Implicit theories of intelligence and judgments of intellectual ability. *Journal of Research in Personality, 37,* 141–168.

Lerma, E. V. (2009). Anatomic and physiologic changes of the aging kidney. *Clinics in Geriatric Medicine, 25,* 325–329. doi:S0749-0690(09)00050-0 pii:10.1016/j.cger.2009.06.007

Lerner, R., M. (1995). Developing individuals within changing contexts: Implications of developmental contextualism for human development, research, policy, and programs. In T. J. Kindermann & J. Valsiner (Eds.), *Development of person-context relations* (pp. 13–37). Hillsdale, NJ: Lawrence Erlbaum.

Lerner, R. M. (1996). Relative plasticity, integration, temporality, and diversity in human development: A developmental contextual perspective about theory, process, and method. *Developmental Psychology, 32,* 781–786.

Letenneur, L., Proust-Lima, C., Le George, A., Dartigues, J. F., & Barberger-Gateau, P. (2007). Flavonoid intake and cognitive decline over a 10-year period. *American Journal of Epidemiology, 165,* 1364–1371.

Leveille, S. G. (2004). Musculoskeletal aging. *Current Opinions in Rheumatology, 16,* 114–118.

Levinson, D. J., Darrow, C. N., Klein, E. B., Levinson, M. H., & McKee, B. (1978). *The seasons of a man's life.* New York: Alfred A. Knopf.

Levinson, D. J., & Levinson, J. D. (1996). *The seasons of a woman's life.* New York: Knopf.

Levy, B. R., Slade, M. D., Kunkel, S. R., & Kasl, S. V. (2002). Longevity increased by positive self-perceptions of aging. *Journal of Personality and Social Psychology, 83,* 261–270.

Licht-Strunk, E., van der Windt, D. A., van Marwijk, H. W., de Haan, M., & Beekman, A. T. (2007). The prognosis of depression in older patients in general practice and the community. A systematic review. *Family Practice, 24,* 168–180

Lichtenberg, P. A., MacNeill, S. E., Lysack, C. L., Bank, A. L., & Neufeld, S. W. (2003). Predicting discharge and long-term outcome patterns for frail elders. *Rehabilitation Psychology, 48,* 37–43. doi:10.1037/0090-5550.48.1.37

Lin, F., Friedman, E., Quinn, J., Chen, D.-G., & Mapstone, M. (2012). Effect of leisure activities on inflammation and cognitive function in an aging sample. *Archives of Gerontology and Geriatrics, 54,* e398–e404. doi:10.1016/j.archger.2012.02.002

Lindau, S. T., & Gavrilova, N. (2010). Sex, health, and years of sexually active life gained due to good health: evidence from two U.S. population based cross sectional surveys of ageing. *BMJ: British Medical Journal, 340.*

Lindauer, M. S. (1998). Artists, art, and arts activities: What do they tell us about aging? In C. Adams-Price (Ed.), *Creativity and successful aging: Theoretical and empirical approaches* (pp. 237–250). New York: Springer.

Lipton, S. A. (2006). Paradigm shift in neuroprotection by NMDA receptor blockade: Memantine and beyond. *Nature Reviews: Drug Discovery, 5,* 160–170.

Lister, J. P., & Barnes, C. A. (2009). Neurobiological changes in the hippocampus during normative aging. *Archives of Neurology, 66,* 829–833. doi:66/7/829 pii:10.1001/archneurol.2009.125

Liu-Ambrose, T., Nagamatsu, L. S., Graf, P., Beattie, B. L., Ashe, M. C., & Handy, T. C. (2010). Resistance training and executive functions: A 12-month randomized controlled trial. *Archives of Internal Medicine, 170,* 170–178. doi: 170/2/170 pii:10.1001/archinternmed.2009.494

Liu, C. Y., Zhou, H. D., Xu, Z. Q., Zhang, W. W., Li, X. Y., & Zhao, J. (2009). Metabolic syndrome and cognitive impairment amongst elderly people in Chinese population: A cross-sectional study. *European Journal of Neurology, 16,* 1022–1027. doi:ENE2640 pii:10.1111/j.1468-1331.2009.02640.x

Liu, H., Bravata, D. M., Olkin, I., Friedlander, A., Liu, V., Roberts, B., ... Hoffman, A. R. (2008). Systematic review: The effects of growth hormone on athletic performance. *Annals of Internal Medicine, 148,* 747–758. doi:0000605-200805200-00215

Liu, I. C., & Chiu, C. H. (2009). Case-control study of suicide attempts in the elderly. *International Psychogeriatrics, 21,* 896–902. doi: S1041610209990056 pii:10.1017/S1041610209990056

Lloyd-Jones, D., Adams, R., Carnethon, M., De Simone, G., Ferguson, T. B., Flegal, K., ... Hong, Y. (2009). Heart disease and stroke statistics—2009 update: A report from the American Heart Association Statistics Committee and Stroke Statistics Subcommittee. *Circulation, 119,* e21–181. doi: CIRCULATIONAHA.108.191261 pii:10.1161/CIRCULATIONAHA.108.191261

Lloyd-Jones, D., Adams, R. J., Brown, T. M., Carnethon, M., Dai, S., De Simone, G., ... Wylie-Rosett, J. (2010). Heart disease and stroke statistics—2010 update: A report from the American Heart Association. *Circulation, 121,* e24–e215. doi:121/7/948 pii:10.1161/CIRCULATIONAHA.109.192666

Lobjois, R., & Cavallo, V. (2009). The effects of aging on street-crossing behavior: From estimation to actual crossing. *Accident Analysis and Prevention, 41,* 259–267. doi:S0001-4575(08)00224-8 pii:10.1016/j.aap.2008.12.001

Lockhart, S. N., Mayda, A. B. V., Roach, A. E., Fletcher, E., Carmichael, O., Maillard, P., ... DeCarli, C. (2012). Episodic memory function is associated with multiple measures of white matter integrity in cognitive aging. *Frontiers in Human Neuroscience, 6.* doi:10.3389/fnhum.2012.00056

Lodi-Smith, J., Jackson, J., Bogg, T., Walton, K., Wood, D., Harms, P., & Roberts, B. W. (2010). Mechanisms of health: Education and health-related behaviours partially mediate the relationship between conscientiousness and self-reported physical health. *Psychology & Health, 25,* 305–319. doi:10.1080/08870440902736964

Loevinger, J. (1976). *Ego development: Conceptions and theories.* San Francisco: Jossey-Bass.

Lofquist, D., Lugaila, T., O'Connell, M., & Feliz, S. (2012). Households and families: 2010.

Lombardi, G., Tauchmanova, L., Di Somma, C., Musella, T., Rota, F., Savanelli, M. C., & Colao, A. (2005). Somatopause: Dismetabolic and bone effects. *Journal of Endocrinological Investigation*, *28*, 36–42.

Lopez-Miranda, J., Perez-Jimenez, F., Ros, E., De Caterina, R., Badimon, L., Covas, M. I., … Yiannakouris, N. (2009). Olive oil and health: Summary of the II international conference on olive oil and health consensus report, Jaén and Córdoba (Spain) 2008. *Nutrition, Metabolism, and Cardiovascular Diseases*. doi:S0939-4753(09)00316-0 pii:10.1016/j.numecd.2009.12.007

Low, K. S. D., Yoon, M., Roberts, B. W., & Rounds, J. (2005). The stability of vocational interests from early adolescence to middle adulthood: A quantitative review of longitudinal studies. *Psychological Bulletin*, *131*, 713–737.

Lu, B., Qian, Z., Cunningham, A., & Li, C.-L. (2012). Estimating the effect of premarital cohabitation on timing of marital disruption: Using propensity score matching in event history analysis. *Sociological Methods & Research*, *41*, 440–466. doi:10.1177/0049124112452395

Lubart, T. I., & Sternberg, R. J. (1998). Life span creativity: An investment theory approach. In C. Adams-Price (Ed.), *Creativity and successful aging: Theoretical and empirical approaches* (pp. 21–41). New York: Springer.

Luber, G. E., & Sanchez, C. A. (2006). Heat-related deaths—United States, 1999–2003. *Morbidity and Mortality Weekly Report*, *55*, 796–798.

Luborsky, M. R., & McMullen, C. K. (1999). Culture and aging. In J. C. Cavanaugh & S. K. Whitbourne (Eds.), *Gerontology: Interdisciplinary perspectives* (pp. 65–90). New York: Oxford University Press.

Lucas, R. E., Clark, A. E., Georgellis, Y., & Diener, E. (2003). Reexamining adaptation and the set point model of happiness: Reactions to changes in marital status. *Journal of Personality and Social Psychology*, *84*, 527–539.

Lüdtke, O., Roberts, B. W., Trautwein, U., & Nagy, G. (2011). A random walk down university avenue: Life paths, life events, and personality trait change at the transition to university life. *Journal of Personality and Social Psychology*, *101*, 620–637. doi:10.1037/a0023743

Luk, G., Bialystok, E., Craik, F. I. M., & Grady, C. L. (2011). Lifelong bilingualism maintains white matter integrity in older adults. *The Journal of Neuroscience*, *31*, 16808–16813. doi:10.1523/jneurosci.4563-11.2011

Lum, T. Y., Kane, R. A., Cutler, L. J., & Yu, T. C. (2008). Effects of Green House nursing homes on residents' families. *Health Care Financing Review*, *30*, 35–51.

Luo, L., Craik, F. I. M., Moreno, S., & Bialystok, E. (2012). Bilingualism interacts with domain in a working memory task: Evidence from Aging. *Psychology and Aging*. doi:10.1037/a0030875

Luo, Y., LaPierre, T. A., Hughes, M. E., & Waite, L. J. (2012). Grandparents providing care to grandchildren: A population-based study of continuity and change. *Journal of Family Issues*, *33*, 1143–1167. doi:10.1177/0192513x12438685

Lupien, S., Lecours, A. R., Schwartz, G., Sharma, S., Hauger, R. L., Meaney, M. J., & Nair, N. P. (1996). Longitudinal study of basal cortisol levels in healthy elderly subjects: Evidence for subgroups. *Neurobiology of Aging*, *17*, 95–105.

Lupien, S. J., McEwen, B. S., Gunnar, M. R., & Heim, C. (2009). Effects of stress throughout the lifespan on the brain, behaviour and cognition. *Nature Reviews Neuroscience*, *10*, 434–445. doi:nrn2639 pii:10.1038/nrn2639

Lüscher, K. (2002). Intergenerational ambivalence: Further steps in theory and research. *Journal of Marriage and Family*, *64*, 585–593. doi:10.1111/j.1741-3737.2002.00585.x

Lynch, N. A., Ryan, A. S., Evans, J., Katzel, L. I., & Goldberg, A. P. (2007). Older elite football players have reduced cardiac and osteoporosis risk factors. *Medicine and Science in Sports and Exercise*, *39*, 1124–1130. doi:10.1249/01.mss.0b013e318055746600005768-200707000-00013 pii:

Lynn, J., Teno, J. M., Phillips, R. S., Wu, A. W., Desbiens, N., Harrold, J., … Connors, A. F., Jr., (1997). Perceptions by family members of the dying experience of older and seriously ill patients. SUPPORT Investigators. Study to Understand Prognoses and Preferences for Outcomes and Risks of Treatments. *Annals of Internal Medicine*, *126*, 97–106.

Lyons, H. Z., & O'Brien, K. M. (2006). The role of person–environment fit in the job satisfaction and tenure intentions of African American employees. *Journal of Counseling Psychology*, *53*, 387–396.

MacDonald, S. W. S., Hultsch, D. F., & Dixon, R. A. (2011). Aging and the shape of cognitive change before death: Terminal decline or terminal drop? *The Journals of Gerontology: Series B: Psychological Sciences and Social Sciences*, *66B*, 292–301. doi:10.1093/geronb/gbr001

Macintyre, S. (1997). The Black report and beyond: What are the issues? *Social Science and Medicine*, *44*, 723–745.

Madden, D. J. (2001). Speed and timing of behavioural processes. In J. E. Birren & K. W. Schaie (Eds.), *Handbook of the psychology of aging* (5th ed.). San Diego CA: Academic Press.

Madden, D. J., Pierce, T. W., & Allen, P. A. (1996). Adult age differences in the use of distractor homogeneity during visual search. [Article]. *Psychology and Aging*, *11*, 454–474.

Magai, C., Consedine, N. S., Krivoshekova, Y. S., Kudadjie-Gyamfi, E., & McPherson, R. (2006). Emotion experience and expression across the adult life span: Insights from a multimodal assessment study. *Psychology and Aging*, *21*, 303–317.

Magnusson, D. (Ed.). (1996). *The lifespan development of individuals: Behavioral, neurobiological, and psychosocial perspectives: A synthesis*. New York: Cambridge University Press.

Magnusson Hanson, L. L., Theorell, T., Oxenstierna, G., Hyde, M., & Westerlund, H. (2008). Demand, control and social climate as predictors of emotional exhaustion symptoms in working Swedish men and women. *Scandinavian Journal of Public Health*, *36*, 737–743. doi:1403494808090164 pii:10.1177/1403494808090164

Mahlberg, R., Tilmann, A., Salewski, L., & Kunz, D. (2006). Normative data on the daily profile of urinary 6-sulfatoxymelatonin in healthy subjects between the ages of 20 and 84. *Psychoneuroendocrinology, 31*, 634–641.

Majer, I. M., Nusselder, W. J., Mackenbach, J. P., & Kunst, A. E. (2011). Socioeconomic inequalities in life and health expectancies around official retirement age in 10 Western-European countries. *Journal of Epidemiology and Community Health, 65*, 972–979. doi:10.1136/jech.2010.111492

Maki, N., & Martikainen, P. (2009). The role of socioeconomic indicators on non-alcohol and alcohol-associated suicide mortality among women in Finland. A register-based follow-up study of 12 million person-years. *Social Science and Medicine, 68*, 2161–2169. doi:S0277-9536(09)00222-6 pii:10.1016/j.socscimed.2009.04.006

Maltais, M. L., Desroches, J., & Dionne, I. J. (2009). Changes in muscle mass and strength after menopause. *Journal of Musculoskeletal and Neuronal Interactions, 9*, 186–197.

Mancini, A. D., & Bonanno, G. A. (2006). Marital closeness, functional disability, and adjustment in late life. *Psychology and Aging, 21*, 600–610.

Mancini, A. D., & Bonanno, G. A. (2009). Predictors and parameters of resilience to loss: Toward an individual differences model. *Journal of Personality, 77*, 1805–1832. doi:JOPY601 pii:10.1111/j.1467-6494.2009.00601.x

Manini, T. M., Everhart, J. E., Anton, S. D., Schoeller, D. A., Cummings, S. R., Mackey, D. C., … Harris, T. B. (2009). Activity energy expenditure and change in body composition in late life. *American Journal of Clinical Nutrition, 90*, 1336–1342. doi:ajcn.2009.27659 pii:10.3945/ajcn.2009.27659

Manzoli, L., Villari, P., Pirone, G. M., & Boccia, A. (2007). Marital status and mortality in the elderly: A systematic review and meta-analysis. *Social Science & Medicine, 64*, 77–94.

Marcia, J. E. (1966). Development and validation of ego-identity status. *Journal of Personality and Social Psychology, 3*, 551–558.

Margrett, J., Martin, P., Woodard, J. L., Miller, L. S., MacDonald, M., Baenziger, J., … Arnold, J. (2010). Depression among centenarians and the oldest old: Contributions of cognition and personality. *Gerontology, 56*, 93–99. doi: 000272018 pii:10.1159/000272018

Markland, A. D., Richter, H. E., Burgio, K. L., Bragg, C., Hernandez, A. L., & Subak, L. L. (2009). Fecal incontinence in obese women with urinary incontinence: Prevalence and role of dietary fiber intake. *American Journal of Obstetrics and Gynecology, 200*, 566 e561–566. doi: S0002-9378(08)02238-2 pii:10.1016/j.ajog.2008.11.019

Marks, B. L., Katz, L. M., & Smith, J. K. (2009). Exercise and the aging mind: Buffing the baby boomer's body and brain. *Physical Sportsmedicine, 37*, 119–125. doi:10.3810/psm.2009.04.1692

Markus, H., & Nurius, P. (1986). Possible selves. *American Psychologist, 41*, 954–969.

Marmot, M. G., Shipley, M. J., Hemingway, H., Head, J., & Brunner, E. J. (2008). Biological and behavioural explanations of social inequalities in coronary heart disease: The Whitehall II study. *Diabetologia, 51*, 1980–1988. doi:10.1007/s00125-008-1144-3

Marshall, V. W. (1980). *Last chapters: A sociology of aging and dying.* Monterey, CA: Brooks-Cole.

Marsiglio, W., Amato, P., Day, R. D., & Lamb, M. E. (2002). Scholarship on fatherhood in the 1990s and beyond. *Journal of Marriage & the Family, 62*, 1173–1191.

Marsiske, M., & Margrett, J. A. (2006). Everyday problem solving and decision making. In J. E. Birren & K. W. Schaire (Eds.), *Handbook of the psychology of aging* (6th ed.). (pp. 315–342) London: Elsevier.

Martens, A., Greenberg, J., Schimel, J., & Landau, M. J. (2004). Ageism and death: Effects of mortality salience and perceived similarity to elders on reactions to elderly people. *Personality and Social Psychology Bulletin, 30*, 1524–1536.

Martin, J. A., Hamilton, B. E., Ventura, S. J., Osterman, M. J. K., Kirmeyer, S., Mathews, T. J., & Wilson, E. C. (2011). Births: Final data for 2009 *National Vital Statistics Reports, 60*(1).

Martin, M. D., Hancock, G. A., Richardson, B., Simmons, P., Katona, C., Mullan, E., & Orrell, M. (2002). An evaluation of needs in elderly continuing-care settings. *International Psychogeriatrics, 14*, 379–388.

Martire, L. M., Schulz, R., Reynolds, C. F., III,, Karp, J. F., Gildengers, A. G., & Whyte, E. M. (2010). Treatment of late-life depression alleviates caregiver burden. *Journal of the American Geriatrics Society, 58*, 23–29. doi:JGS2610 pii:10.1111/j.1532-5415.2009.02610.x

Masayesva, B. G., Mambo, E., Taylor, R. J., Goloubeva, O. G., Zhou, S., Cohen, Y., … Califano, J. (2006). Mitochondrial DNA content increase in response to cigarette smoking. *Cancer Epidemiology Biomarkers and Prevention, 15*, 19–24.

Mast, B. T., Fitzgerald, J., Steinberg, J., MacNeill, S. E., & Lichtenberg, P. A. (2001). Effective screening for Alzheimer's disease among older African Americans. *Clinical Neuropsychologist, 196–202.*

Masuda, A. D., McNall, L. A., Allen, T. D., & Nicklin, J. M. (2012). Examining the constructs of work-to-family enrichment and positive spillover. *Journal of Vocational Behavior, 80*, 197–210. doi:10.1016/j.jvb.2011.06.002

Masunaga, H., & Horn, J. (2001). Expertise and age-related changes in components of intelligence. *Psychol Aging, 16*, 293–311.

Mataix-Cols, D., Rosario-Campos, M. C., & Leckman, J. F. (2005). A multidimensional model of obsessive-compulsive disorder. *American Journal of Psychiatry, 162*, 228–238. doi: 162/2/228 pii:10.1176/appi.ajp.162.2.228

Matsuba, M. K., Pratt, M. W., Norris, J. E., Mohle, E., Alisat, S., & McAdams, D. P. (2012). Environmentalism as a context for expressing identity and generativity: Patterns among activists and uninvolved youth and midlife adults. *Journal of Personality, 80*, 1091–1115. doi:10.1111/j.1467-6494.2012.00765.x

Matthews, R. A., Bulger, C. A., & Barnes-Farrell, J. L. (2010). Work social supports, role stressors, and work–family conflict:

The moderating effect of age. *Journal of Vocational Behavior, 76,* 78–90.

Matthews, S. H. (1986). *Friendships through the life course.* Beverly Hills, CA: Sage.

Maurer, T. J. (2001). Career-relevant learning and development, worker age, and beliefs about self-efficacy for development. *Journal of Management, 27,* 123–140.

Mayhew, P. M., Thomas, C. D., Clement, J. G., Loveridge, N., Beck, T. J., Bonfield, W., ... Reeve, J. (2005). Relation between age, femoral neck cortical stability, and hip fracture risk. *Lancet, 366,* 129–135.

McAdams, D. P. (2008). Generativity, the redemptive self, and the problem of a noisy ego in American life. In H. A. Wayment & J. J. Bauer (Eds.), *Transcending self-interest: Psychological explorations of the quiet ego.* (pp. 235–242). Washington, DC: American Psychological Association.

McAdams, D. P. (2011). Life narratives. In K. L. Fingerman, C. A. Berg, J. Smith & T. C. Antonucci (Eds.), *Handbook of life-span development.* (pp. 589–610). New York: Springer Publishing Co.

McAdams, K. K., Lucas, R. E., & Donnellan, M. B. (2012). The role of domain satisfaction in explaining the paradoxical association between life satisfaction and age. *Social Indicators Research, 109,* 295–303. doi:10.1007/s11205-011-9903-9

McAuley, E., Marquez, D. X., Jerome, G. J., Blissmer, B., & Katula, J. (2002). Physical activity and physique anxiety in older adults: Fitness, and efficacy influences. *Aging and Mental Health, 6,* 222–230.

McCarthy, L. H., Bigal, M. E., Katz, M., Derby, C., & Lipton, R. B. (2009). Chronic pain and obesity in elderly people: Results from the Einstein aging study. *Journal of the American Geriatric Society, 57,* 115–119. doi: JGS2089 pii:10.1111/j.1532-5415.2008.02089.x

McCleane, G. (2007). Pharmacological pain management in the elderly patient. *Clinical Interventions in Aging, 2,* 637–643.

McCrae, R. R., & Costa, P. T. J. (2003). *Personality in adulthood, Personality in adulthood: A five-factor theory perspective,* 2nd ed. New York: Guilford.

McCullough, M. E., Friedman, H. S., Enders, C. K., & Martin, L. R. (2009). Does devoutness delay death? Psychological investment in religion and its association with longevity in the Terman sample. *Journal of Personality and Social Psychology, 97,* 866–882.

McCullough, M. E., Hoyt, W. T., Larson, D. B., Koenig, H. G., & Thoresen, C. (2000). Religious involvement and mortality: A meta-analytic review. *Health Psychology, 19,* 211–222.

McDaniel, M. A., & Einstein, G. O. (2011). The neuropsychology of prospective memory in normal aging: A componential approach. *Neuropsychologia, 49,* 2147–2155. doi:10.1016/j.neuropsychologia.2010.12.029

McDonald-Miszczak, L., Hertzog, C., & Hultsch, D. F. (1995). Stability and accuracy of metamemory in adulthood and aging: A longitudinal analysis. *Psychology and Aging, 10,* 553–564.

McFadden, J. R., & Rawson Swan, K. T. (2012). Women during midlife: Is it transition or crisis? *Family and Consumer Sciences Research Journal, 40,* 313–325. doi:10.1111/j.1552-3934.2011.02113.x

McFadden, S. H., & Basting, A. D. (2010). Healthy aging persons and their brains: Promoting resilience through creative engagement. *Clinics in Geriatric Medicine, 26,* 149–161. doi:S07490690(09)00092-5 pii:10.1016/j.cger.2009.11.004

McGinnis, D. (2012). Susceptibility to distraction during reading in young, young-old, and old-old adults. *Experimental Aging Research, 38,* 370–393.

McGue, M., & Christensen, K. (2002). The heritability of level and rate-of-change in cognitive functioning in Danish twins aged 70 years and older. *Experimental Aging Research, 28,* 435–451.

McKay, S. M., & Maki, B. E. (2010). Attitudes of older adults toward shooter video games: An initial study to select an acceptable game for training visual processing. *Gerontechnology, 9,* 5–17. doi:10.4017/gt.2010.09.01.001.00

McKeith, I. G. (2006). Consensus guidelines for the clinical and pathologic diagnosis of dementia with Lewy bodies (DLB): Report of the Consortium on DLB International Workshop. *Journal of Alzheimers Disease, 9,* 417–423.

McKhann, G., Drachman, D., Folstein, M., Katzman, R., Price, D., & Stadlan, E. M. (1984). Clinical diagnosis of Alzheimer's disease: Report of the NINCDS-ADRDA Work Group under the auspices of Department of Health and Human Services Task Force on Alzheimer's Disease. *Neurology, 34,* 939–944.

McLaughlin, S. J., Connell, C. M., Heeringa, S. G., Li, L. W., & Roberts, J. S. (2010). Successful aging in the United States: Prevalence estimates from a national sample of older adults. *The Journals of Gerontology: Series B: Psychological Sciences and Social Sciences, 65B,* 216–226. doi:10.1093/geronb/gbp101

McLean, K. C. (2008). Stories of the young and the old: Personal continuity and narrative identity. *Developmental Psychology, 44,* 254–264. doi:2007-19851-026 pii:10.1037/0012-1649.44.1.254

McNall, L. A., Masuda, A. D., & Nicklin, J. M. (2010). Flexible work arrangements, job satisfaction, and turnover intentions: The mediating role of work-to-family enrichment. *Journal of Psychology, 144,* 61–81.

McNall, L. A., Nicklin, J. M., & Masuda, A. D. (2010). A meta-analytic review of the consequences associated with work–family enrichment. *Journal of Business and Psychology, 25,* 381–396. doi: 10.1007/s10869-009-9141-1

McNamara, B., & Rosenwax, L. (2010). Which carers of family members at the end of life need more support from health services and why? *Soc Sci Med, 70,* 1035–1041. doi:S0277-9536(09)00845-4 pii:10.1016/j.socscimed.2009.11.029

Medicare Improvements for Patients and Providers Act of 2008, H. R.

Meeks, S. (2000). Schizophrenia and related disorders. In S. K. Whitbourne (Ed.), *Psychopathology in later life* (pp. 189–215). New York: Wiley.

Mehta, K. M., Yaffe, K., Brenes, G. A., Newman, A. B., Shorr, R. I., Simonsick, E. M., ... Covinsky, K. E. (2007). Anxiety symptoms and decline in physical function over 5 years in the health, aging and body composition study. *Journal of the American Geriatrics Society, 55*, 265–270.

Meijer, W. A., van Boxtel, M. P. J., Van Gerven, P. W. M., van Hooren, S. A. H., & Jolles, J. (2009). Interaction effects of education and health status on cognitive change: A 6-year follow-up of the Maastricht Aging Study. *Aging & Mental Health, 13*, 521–529. doi:10.1080/13607860902860821

Mendis, S., Puska, P., & Norrving, B. (2011). Global atlas on cardiovascular disease prevention and control. Geneva, Switzerland: World Health Organization.

Meunier, N., Beattie, J. H., Ciarapica, D., O'Connor, J. M., Andriollo-Sanchez, M., Taras, A., … Polito, A. (2005). Basal metabolic rate and thyroid hormones of late-middle-aged and older human subjects: The ZENITH study. *European Journal of Clinical Nutrition, 59* Suppl 2, S53–57. doi: 1602299 pii:10.1038/sj.ejcn.1602299

Meyer, B. J. F., Talbot, A. P., & Ranalli, C. (2007). Why older adults make more immediate treatment decisions about cancer than younger adults. *Psychology and Aging, 22*, 505–524.

Mhaoláin, A. M. N., Gallagher, D., Connell, H. O., Chin, A. V., Bruce, I., Hamilton, F., … Lawlor, B. A. (2012). Subjective well-being amongst community-dwelling elders: What determines satisfaction with life? Findings from the Dublin Healthy Aging Study. *International Psychogeriatrics, 24*, 316–323. doi:10.1017/s1041610211001360

Miller, M. D., & Reynolds, C. F., III,. (2012). Using interpersonal psychotherapy with older individuals. In J. C. Markowitz & M. M. Weissman (Eds.), *Casebook of interpersonal psychotherapy.* (pp. 243–266). New York: Oxford University Press.

Miller, P. J. E., Niehuis, S., & Huston, T. L. (2006). Positive illusions in marital relationships: A 13-year longitudinal study. *Personality and Social Psychology Bulletin, 32*, 1579–1594.

Miller, S. C., Papandonatos, G., Fennell, M., & Mor, V. (2006). Facility and county effects on racial differences in nursing home quality indicators. *Social Science and Medicine, 63*, 3046–3059. doi:S0277-9536(06)00405-9 pii:10.1016/j.socscimed.2006.08.003

Miner-Rubino, K., Winter, D. G., & Stewart, A. J. (2004). Gender, social class, and the subjective experience of aging: Self-perceived personality change from early adulthood to late midlife. *Personality and Social Psychology Bulletin, 30*, 1599–1610.

Miñino, A. M., & Murphy, S. L. (2010). Deaths in the United States, 2010. *NCHS Data Brief, no 99*.

Minority Staff Special Investigations Division Committee on Government Reform U.S. House of Representatives. (2001, July 30). Abuse of residents is a major problem in U.S. nursing homes. Prepared for Rep. Henry A. Waxman. Retrieved from http://www.cbsnews.com/htdocs/pdf/waxman_nursing.pdf

Mireles, D. E., & Charness, N. (2002). Computational explorations of the influence of structured knowledge on age-related cognitive decline. *Psychology and Aging, 17*, 245–259.

Mitchell, B. A., & Lovegreen, L. D. (2009). The empty nest syndrome in midlife families: A multimethod exploration of parental gender differences and cultural dynamics. *Journal of Family Issues, 30*, 1651–1670. doi:10.1177/0192513x09339020

Mitchell, S. L., Teno, J. M., Kiely, D. K., Shaffer, M. L., Jones, R. N., Prigerson, H. G., … Hamel, M. B. (2009). The clinical course of advanced dementia. *New England Journal of Medicine, 361*, 1529–1538. doi:361/16/1529 pii:10.1056/NEJMoa0902234

Mitnick, D. M., Heyman, R. E., & Smith Slep, A. M. (2009). Changes in relationship satisfaction across the transition to parenthood: A meta-analysis. *Journal of Family Psychology, 23*, 848–852. doi:10.1037/a0017004 pii:10.1037/a0017004.supp (Supplemental)

Mitsumune, T., Senoh, E., Nishikawa, H., Adachi, M., & Kajii, E. (2009). The effect of obesity and smoking status on lung age in Japanese men. *Respirology, 14*, 757–760. doi:RES1541 pii:10.1111/j.1440-1843.2009.01541.x

Mitty, E. (2009). Nursing care of the aging foot. *Geriatric Nursing, 30*, 350–354. doi:S0197-4572(09)00307-3 pii:10.1016/j.gerinurse.2009.08.004

Miyake, A., Friedman, N. P., Emerson, M. J., Witzki, A. H., Howerter, A., & Wager, T. D. (2000). The unity and diversity of executive functions and their contributions to complex "frontal lobe" tasks: A latent variable analysis. *Cognitive Psychology, 41*, 49–100. doi:http://dx.doi.org/10.1006/cogp.1999.0734

Mocchegiani, E., Malavolta, M., Muti, E., Costarelli, L., Cipriano, C., Piacenza, F., … Lattanzio, F. (2008). Zinc, metallothioneins and longevity: Interrelationships with niacin and selenium. *Current Pharmaceutical Design, 14*, 2719–2732.

Moen, P., Kim, J. E., & Hofmeister, H. (2001). Couples' work/retirement transitions, gender, and marital quality. *Social Psychology Quarterly, 64*, 55–71.

Mohammadi, S., Mazhari, M. M., Mehrparvar, A. H., & Attarchi, M. S. (2009). Cigarette smoking and occupational noise-induced hearing loss. *European Journal of Public Health, 20*, 452–455 doi:ckp167 pii:10.1093/eurpub/ckp167

Mohlman, J., & Price, R. (2006). Recognizing and treating late-life generalized anxiety disorder: Distinguishing features and psychosocial treatment. *Expert Reviews in Neurotherapy, 6*, 1439–1445.

Moore, D. E., & Hayward, M. D. (1990). Occupational careers and mortality of elderly men. *Demography, 27*, 31–53.

Moorman, S. M., Booth, A., & Fingerman, K. L. (2006). Women's romantic relationships after widowhood. *Journal of Family Issues, 27*, 1281–1304.

Moos, R. H., Schutte, K., Brennan, P., & Moos, B. S. (2004). Ten-year patterns of alcohol consumption and drinking problems among older women and men. *Addiction, 99*, 829–838.

Morales, A. M., Mirone, V., Dean, J., & Costa, P. (2009). Vardenafil for the treatment of erectile dysfunction: An overview of the clinical evidence. *Clinical Interventions in Aging, 4*, 463–472.

Morone, N. E., Rollman, B. L., Moore, C. G., Li, Q., & Weiner, D. K. (2009). A mind-body program for older adults with chronic low back pain: Results of a pilot study. *Pain*

Medicine, 10, 1395–1407. doi:PME746 pii:10.1111/j.1526-4637.2009.00746.x

Morris, M. C., Evans, D. A., Tangney, C. C., Bienias, J. L., & Wilson, R. S. (2005). Fish consumption and cognitive decline with age in a large community study. *Archives of Neurology, 62,* 1849–1853.

Morrow, D. G., Miller, L. M., Ridolfo, H. E., Magnor, C., Fischer, U. M., Kokayeff, N. K., & Stine-Morrow, E. A. (2009). Expertise and age differences in pilot decision making. *Neuropsychology, Development, and Cognition, B Aging, Neuropsychology and Cognition 16,* 33–55. doi:795235500 pii:10.1080/13825580802195641

Motta, M., Bennati, E., Ferlito, L., Malaguarnera, M., & Motta, L. (2005). Successful aging in centenarians: Myths and reality. *Archives of Gerontology and Geriatrics, 40,* 241–251.

Mottram, P. G., Wilson, K. C., Ashworth, L., & Abou-Saleh, M. (2002). The clinical profile of older patients' response to antidepressants—An open trial of sertraline. *International Journal of Geriatric Psychiatry, 17,* 574–578.

Mount, M. K., Barrick, M. R., Scullen, S. M., & Rounds, J. (2005). Higher-order dimensions of the big five personality traits and the big six vocational interest types. *Personnel Psychology, 58,* 447–478.

Mroczek, D. K., & Kolarz, C. M. (1998). The effect of age on positive and negative affect: A developmental perspective on happiness. *Journal of Personality and Social Psychology, 75,* 1333–1349.

Muchinsky, P. (1999). Application of Holland's theory in industrial and organizational settings. *Journal of Vocational Behavior, 55,* 127–125.

Mueller, M. M., Wilhelm, B., & Elder, G. H., Jr., (2002). Variations in grandparenting. *Research on Aging, 24,* 360–388.

Muntaner, A., Borrell, C., Sola, J., Mari-Dell'olmo, M., Chung, H., Rodriguez-Sanz, M., … Noh, S. (2009). Capitalists, managers, professionals and mortality: Findings from the Barcelona social class and all cause mortality longitudinal study. *Scandinavian Journal of Public Health, 37,* 826–838. doi:1403494809346870 pii:10.1177/1403494809346870

Munzer, T., Harman, S. M., Sorkin, J. D., & Blackman, M. R. (2009). Growth hormone and sex steroid effects on serum glucose, insulin, and lipid concentrations in healthy older women and men. *Journal of Clinical Endocrinology and Metabolism, 94,* 3833–3841. doi:jc.2009-1275 pii:10.1210/jc.2009-1275

Murase, T., Haramizu, S., Ota, N., & Hase, T. (2009). Suppression of the aging-associated decline in physical performance by a combination of resveratrol intake and habitual exercise in senescence-accelerated mice. *Biogerontology, 10,* 423–434. doi:10.1007/s10522-008-9177-z

Murphy, D. R., Daneman, M., & Schneider, B. A. (2006). Why do older adults have difficulty following conversations? *Psychology and Aging, 21,* 49–61.

Murphy, E., Kapur, N., Webb, R., Purandare, N., Hawton, K., Bergen, H., … Cooper, J. (2012). Risk factors for repetition and suicide following self-harm in older adults: Multicentre cohort study. *The British Journal of Psychiatry, 200,* 399–404. doi:10.1192/bjp.bp.111.094177

Murphy, N. A., & Isaacowitz, D. M. (2008). Preferences for emotional information in older and younger adults: A meta-analysis of memory and attention tasks. *Psychology and Aging, 23,* 263–286.

Musil, C., Warner, C., Zauszniewski, J., Wykle, M., & Standing, T. (2009). Grandmother caregiving, family stress and strain, and depressive symptoms. *Western Journal of Nursing Research, 31,* 389–408.

Nadien, M. B. (2006). Factors that influence abusive interactions between aging women and their caregivers. *Annals of the New York Academy of Sciences, 1087,* 158–169.

National Cancer Institute. (2010). Understanding cancer. Retrieved from http://www.cancer.gov/cancertopics/understanding cancer/

National Center for Education Statistics. (2013). Digest of Education statistics: 2011. Retrieved from http://nces.ed.gov/programs/digest/d11/tables/dt11_439.asp?referrer=list

National Center for Elder Abuse. (2013). Retrieved from http://www.ncea.aoa.gov/

National Center for Health Statistics. (2010). Marriage and cohabitation in the United States: A statistical portrait based on Cycle 6 (2002) of the National Survey of Family Growth. Series 23, Number 28. Hyattsville MD: Vital and Health Statistics.

National Center for Health Statistics. (2011). *Health, United States, 2011.* Washington, DC: U.S. Department of Health and Human Services.

National Center for Vital Statistics. (2013). *Deaths: Final data for 2010.* Washington DC: U.S. Department of Health and Human Services.

National Health Interview Survey. (2009). Early release of selected estimates based on data from the January–March 2009 National Health Interview Survey.

National Heart Lung and Blood Institute. (2013). Body Mass Index Table 1. Retrieved from http://www.nhlbi.nih.gov/guidelines/obesity/bmi_tbl.pdf

National Institute of Aging. (2009). Caring for a person with Alzheimer's disease. NIH Publication Number 09-6173. Retrieved from http://www.nia.nih.gov/NR/rdonlyres/6A0E9F3C-E429-4F03-818E-D1B60235D5F8/0/100711_LoRes2.pdf

National Institute of Mental Health. (2013). Suicide in the U.S.: Statistics and prevention. Retrieved from http://www.nimh.nih.gov/health/publications/suicide-in-the-us-statistics-and-prevention/index.shtml

National Institute on Alcohol Abuse and Alcoholism. (2013). Older adults. Retrieved from http://www.niaaa.nih.gov/alcohol-health/special-populations-co-occurring-disorders/older-adults

National Library of Medicine. (2010). Melatonin. Retrieved from http://www.nlm.nih.gov/medlineplus/druginfo/natural/patient-melatonin.html

Negash, S., Smith, G. E., Pankratz, S., Aakre, J., Geda, Y. E., Roberts, R. O., ... Petersen, R. C. (2011). Successful aging: Definitions and prediction of longevity and conversion to mild cognitive impairment. *The American Journal of Geriatric Psychiatry, 19*, 581–588. doi:10.1097/JGP.0b013e3181f17ec9

Nehrke, M. F., Turner, R. R., Cohen, S. H., Whitbourne, S. K., Morganti, J. B., & Hulicka, I. M. (1981). Toward a model of person–environment congruence: Development of the EPPIS. *Experimental Aging Research, 7*, 363–379.

Neider, M. B., Boot, W. R., & Kramer, A. F. (2010). Visual search for real world targets under conditions of high target–background similarity: Exploring training and transfer in younger and older adults. [Article]. *Acta Psychologica, 134*, 29–39. doi: 10.1016/j.actpsy.2009.12.001

Neider, M. B., & Kramer, A. F. (2011). Older adults capitalize on contextual information to guide search. *Experimental Aging Research, 37*, 539–571. doi:10.1080/0361073x.2011.619864

Neikrug, A. B., & Ancoli-Israel, S. (2009). Sleep disorders in the older adult: A mini-review. *Gerontology, 56*, 181–189 doi:000236900 pii:10.1159/000236900

Nelson, E. A., & Dannefer, D. (1992). Aged heterogeneity: Fact or fiction? The fate of diversity in gerontological research. *Gerontologist, 32*, 17–23.

Neugarten, B. L., & Weinstein, K. K. (1964). The changing American grandparent. *Journal of Marriage and the Family, 26*, 199–204.

Neupert, S. D., Almeida, D. M., Mroczek, D. K., & Spiro, A. I. (2006). Daily stressors and memory failures in a naturalistic setting: Findings from the VA Normative Aging Study. *Psychology and Aging, 21*, 424–429.

Neupert, S. D., Lachman, M. E., & Whitbourne, S. B. (2009). Exercise self-efficacy and control beliefs: Effects on exercise behavior after an exercise intervention for older adults. *Journal of Aging and Physical Activity, 17*, 1–16.

Newson, R. S., & Kemps, E. B. (2006). Cardiorespiratory fitness as a predictor of successful cognitive ageing. *Journal of Clinical and Experimental Neuropsychology: Section A, Neuropsychology, Development, and Cognition, 28*, 949–967.

Ng, T. W. H., & Feldman, D. C. (2010). The relationships of age with job attitudes: A meta-analysis. *Personnel Psychology, 63*, 677–718. doi:10.1111/j.1744-6570.2010.01184.x

Ng, T. W. H., & Feldman, D. C. (2012). Evaluating six common stereotypes about older workers with meta-analytical data. *Personnel Psychology, 65*, 821–858. doi:10.1111/peps.12003

Nijs, K. A., de Graaf, C., Kok, F. J., & van Staveren, W. A. (2006). Effect of family style mealtimes on quality of life, physical performance, and body weight of nursing home residents: Cluster randomised controlled trial. *BMJ: British Medical Journal, 332*, 1180–1184. doi:bmj.38825.401181.7C pii:10.1136/bmj.38825.401181.7C

Nikitin, N. P., Loh, P. H., de Silva, R., Witte, K. K., Lukaschuk, E. I., Parker, A., ... Cleland, J. G. (2006). Left ventricular morphology, global and longitudinal function in normal older individuals: A cardiac magnetic resonance study. *International Journal of Cardiology, 108*, 76–83.

Nilsson, L.-G., Sternäng, O., Rönnlund, M., & Nyberg, L. (2009). Challenging the notion of an early-onset of cognitive decline. *Neurobiology of Aging, 30*, 521–524. doi:10.1016/j.neurobiolaging.2008.11.013

Nimrod, G., & Rotem, A. (2012). An exploration of the innovation theory of successful ageing among older tourists. *Ageing & Society, 32*, 379–404. doi:10.1017/s0144686x1100033x

Nissim, R., Gagliese, L., & Rodin, G. (2009). The desire for hastened death in individuals with advanced cancer: A longitudinal qualitative study. *Social Science & Medicine, 69*, 165–171.

Noh, S. R., & Stine-Morrow, E. A. L. (2009). Age differences in tracking characters during narrative comprehension. *Memory & Cognition, 37*, 769–778. doi:10.3758/mc.37.6.769

Noone, J. H., Stephens, C., & Alpass, F. M. (2009). Preretirement planning and well-being in later life: A prospective study. *Research on Aging, 31*, 295–317.

Nordmann, A. J., Suter-Zimmermann, K., Bucher, H. C., Shai, I., Tuttle, K. R., Estruch, R., & Briel, M. (2011). Meta-analysis comparing Mediterranean to low-fat diets for modification of cardiovascular risk factors. *American Journal of Medicine, 124*, 841–851.e842.

Nouchi, R., Taki, Y., Takeuchi, H., Hashizume, H., Akitsuki, Y., Shigemune, Y., ... Kawashima, R. (2012). Brain training game improves executive functions and processing speed in the elderly: A randomized controlled trial. *PLoS ONE, 7*. doi:10.1371/journal.pone.0029676

Nunes, A., & Kramer, A. F. (2009). Experience-based mitigation of age-related performance declines: Evidence from air traffic control. *Journal of Experimental Psychology: Applied, 15*, 12–24. doi:2009-03685-002 pii:10.1037/a0014947

Nygaard, R. W., Echt, K. V., & Schuchard, R. A. (2008). Models of reading performance in older adults with normal age-related vision. *Journal of Rehabilitation Research and Development, 45*, 901–910.

Nyunt, M. S., Fones, C., Niti, M., & Ng, T. P. (2009). Criterion-based validity and reliability of the Geriatric Depression Screening Scale (GDS-15) in a large validation sample of community-living Asian older adults. *Aging and Mental Health, 13*, 376–382. doi:911831778 pii:10.1080/13607860902861027

O'Brien, L. T., & Hummert, M. L. (2006). Memory performance of late middle-aged adults: Contrasting self-stereotyping and stereotype threat accounts of assimilation to age stereotypes. *Social Cognition, 24*, 338–358.

O'Connor, D. W., Gardner, B., Presnell, I., Singh, D., Tsanglis, M., & White, E. (2010). The effectiveness of continuation-maintenance ECT in reducing depressed older patients' hospital re-admissions. *Journal of Affective Disorders, 120*, 62–66. doi:S0165-0327(09)00144-X pii:10.1016/j.jad.2009.04.005

O'Donovan, D., Hausken, T., Lei, Y., Russo, A., Keogh, J., Horowitz, M., & Jones, K. L. (2005). Effect of aging on transpyloric flow, gastric emptying, and intragastric distribution in healthy humans—impact on glycemia. *Digestive Diseases and Sciences, 50,* 671–676.

O'Hanlon, L., Kemper, S., & Wilcox, K. A. (2005). Aging, encoding, and word retrieval: Distinguishing phonological and memory processes. *Experimental Aging Research, 31,* 149–171.

O*NET. (2010). O*NET. Retrieved from http://www.onetcenter.org

Odle-Dusseau, H. N., Britt, T. W., & Greene-Shortridge, T. M. (2012). Organizational work–family resources as predictors of job performance and attitudes: The process of work–family conflict and enrichment. *Journal of Occupational Health Psychology, 17,* 28–40. doi:10.1037/a0026428

Ohtani, N., Mann, D. J., & Hara, E. (2009). Cellular senescence: Its role in tumor suppression and aging. *Cancer Science, 100,* 792–797. doi:CAS1123 pii:10.1111/j.1349-7006.2009.01123.x

Oken, B. S., Zajdel, D., Kishiyama, S., Flegal, K., Dehen, C., Haas, M., ... Leyva, J. (2006). Randomized, controlled, six-month trial of yoga in healthy seniors: Effects on cognition and quality of life. *Alternative Therapies in Health and Medicine, 12,* 40–47.

Okereke, O., Kang, J. H., Ma, J., Hankinson, S. E., Pollak, M. N., & Grodstein, F. (2007). Plasma IGF-I levels and cognitive performance in older women. *Neurobiology of Aging, 28,* 135–142.

Okonkwo, O. C., Crowe, M., Wadley, V. G., & Ball, K. (2008). Visual attention and self-regulation of driving among older adults. *International Psychogeriatrics, 20,* 162–173. doi:S104161020700539X pii:10.1017/S104161020700539X

Okura, T., Plassman, B. L., Steffens, D. C., Llewellyn, D. J., Potter, G. G., & Langa, K. M. (2010). Prevalence of neuropsychiatric symptoms and their association with functional limitations in older adults in the United States: The aging, demographics, and memory study. *Journal of the American Geriatrics Society, 58,* 330–337. doi:JGS2680 pii:10.1111/j.1532-5415.2009.02680.x

Old, S. R., & Naveh-Benjamin, M. (2008a). Differential effects of age on item and associative measures of memory: A meta-analysis. *Psychology and Aging, 23,* 104–118. doi:2008-02853-013 pii:10.1037/0882-7974.23.1.104

Old, S. R., & Naveh-Benjamin, N. (2008b). Age related changes in memory: Experimental approaches. In S. Hofer & D. F. Alwin (Eds.), *Handbook of cognitive aging: Interdisciplinary perspectives* (pp. 151–167). Thousand Oaks, CA: Sage.

Olsson, G., Hemstrom, O., & Fritzell, J. (2009). Identifying factors associated with good health and ill health: Not just opposite sides of the same coin. *International Journal of Behavioral Medicine, 16,* 323–330. doi:10.1007/s12529-009-9033-9

Oltmanns, T. F., & Balsis, S. (2011). Personality disorders in later life: Questions about the measurement, course, and impact of disorders. *Annual Review of Clinical Psychology, 7,* 321–349. doi:10.1146/annurev-clinpsy-090310-120435

ONeill, C., Jamison, J., McCulloch, D., & Smith, D. (2001). Age-related macular degeneration: Cost-of-illness issues. *Drugs and Aging, 18,* 233–241.

Ong, A. D., Bergeman, C. S., Bisconti, T. L., & Wallace, K. A. (2006). Psychological resilience, positive emotions, and successful adaptation to stress in later life. *Journal of Personality and Social Psychology, 91,* 730–749.

Optale, G., Urgesi, C., Busato, V., Marin, S., Piron, L., Priftis, K., ... Bordin, A. (2010). Controlling memory impairment in elderly adults using virtual reality memory training: A randomized controlled pilot study. *Neurorehabilitation and Neural Repair, 24,* 348–357. doi:10.1177/1545968309353328

Organization for Economic Co-operation and Development. (2007). Table 1321. Percentage of the adult population considered to be obese. Retrieved from http://www.oecd.org/document/62/0,2340,en_2649_34489_2345918_1_1_1_1,00.html

Osorio, A., Ballesteros, S., Fay, S., & Pouthas, V. (2009). The effect of age on word-stem cued recall: A behavioral and electrophysiological study. *Brain Research, 1289,* 56–68. doi:S0006-8993(09)01381-X pii:10.1016/j.brainres.2009.07.013

Otsuki, T., Maeda, S., Kesen, Y., Yokoyama, N., Tanabe, T., Sugawara, J., ... Matsuda, M. (2006). Age-related reduction of systemic arterial compliance induces excessive myocardial oxygen consumption during sub-maximal exercise. *Hypertension Research, 29,* 65–73.

Ouwehand, C., de Ridder, D. T. D., & Bensing, J. M. (2007). A review of successful aging models: Proposing proactive coping as an important additional strategy. *Clinical Psychology Review, 27,* 873–884. doi:http://dx.doi.org/10.1016/j.cpr.2006.11.003

Pacheco, J., Hershberger, P. J., Markert, R. J., & Kumar, G. (2003). A longitudinal study of attitudes toward physician-assisted suicide and euthanasia among patients with noncurable malignancy. *American Journal of Hospital Palliative Care, 20,* 99–104.

Packer, D. J., & Chasteen, A. L. (2006). Looking to the future: How possible aged selves influence prejudice toward older adults. *Social Cognition, 24,* 218–247.

Palmer, K. (2009, 28 Jun.). The Nnew parent trap: More boomers help adult kids out financially. *U.S. News & World Report.*

Pamuk, E., Makuc, D., Heck, K., Reuben, C., & Lochner, K. (1998). *Socioeconomic status and health chartbook. Health, United States, 1998.* Hyattsville, MD: National Center for Health Statistics.

Papa, R., & Papa, J. (2011). Leading adult learners: Preparing future leaders and professional development of those they lead. In R. Papa (Ed.), *Technology leadership for school improvement.* (pp. 91–107). Thousand Oaks, CA: Sage Publications, Inc.

Park, D. C., & Reuter-Lorenz, P. (2009). The adaptive brain: Aging and neurocognitive scaffolding. *Annual Review of Psychology, 60,* 173–196. doi:10.1146/annurev.psych.59.103006.093656

Park, S. K., Tedesco, P. M., & Johnson, T. E. (2009). Oxidative stress and longevity in Caenorhabditis elegans as mediated by SKN-1. *Aging Cell, 8,* 258–269. doi:ACE473 pii:10.1111/j.1474-9726.2009.00473.x

Parslow, R. A., Lewis, V. J., & Nay, R. (2011). Successful aging: Development and testing of a multidimensional model using data from a large sample of older Australians. *Journal of the American Geriatrics Society, 59,* 2077–2083. doi:10.1111/j.1532-5415.2011.03665.x

Patterson, T. L., McKibbin, C., Taylor, M., Goldman, S., Davila-Fraga, W., Bucardo, J., & Jeste, D. V. (2003). Functional Adaptation Skills Training (FAST): A pilot psychosocial intervention study in middle-aged and older patients with chronic psychotic disorders. *American Journal of Geriatric Psychiatry, 11*, 17–23.

Paulson, Q. X., Hong, J., Holcomb, V. B., & Nunez, N. P. (2010). Effects of body weight and alcohol consumption on insulin sensitivity. *Nutrition Journal, 9*, 14. doi:1475-2891-9-14 pii:10.1186/1475-2891-9-14

Pavalko, E. K., Elder, G. H., & Clipp, E. C. (1993). Work lives and longevity: Insights from a life course perspective. *Journal of Health and Social Behavior, 34*, 363–380.

Pearson, K. J., Baur, J. A., Lewis, K. N., Peshkin, L., Price, N. L., Labinskyy, N., … de Cabo, R. (2008). Resveratrol delays age-related deterioration and mimics transcriptional aspects of dietary restriction without extending life span. *Cell Metabolism, 8*, 157–168. doi:S1550-4131(08)00182-4 pii:10.1016/j.cmet.2008.06.011

Pedrera-Zamorano, J. D., Lavado-Garcia, J. M., Roncero-Martin, R., Calderon-Garcia, J. F., Rodriguez-Dominguez, T., & Canal-Macias, M. L. (2009). Effect of beer drinking on ultrasound bone mass in women. *Nutrition, 25*, 1057–1063. doi:S0899-9007(09)00136-1 pii:10.1016/j.nut.2009.02.007

Peelle, J. E., Troiani, V., Wingfield, A., & Grossman, M. (2010). Neural processing during older adults' comprehension of spoken sentences: Age differences in resource allocation and connectivity. *Cerebral Cortex, 20*, 773–782. doi:bhp142 pii:10.1093/cercor/bhp142

Pegula, S., Marsh, S. M., & Jackson, L. L. (2007). Fatal occupational injuries—United States, 2005. *Morbidity and Mortality Weekly Report, 56*(13), 297–301.

Pelletier, A. L., Thomas, J., & Shaw, F. R. (2009). Vision loss in older persons. *American Family Physician, 79*, 963–970.

Pellfolk, T., Sandman, P.-O., Gustafson, Y., Karlsson, S., & Lövheim, H. (2012). Physical restraint use in institutional care of old people in Sweden in 2000 and 2007. *International Psychogeriatrics, 24*, 1144–1152. doi:10.1017/s104161021200018x

Pepin, R., Segal, D. L., & Coolidge, F. L. (2009). Intrinsic and extrinsic barriers to mental health care among community-dwelling younger and older adults. *Aging and Mental Health, 13*, 769–777. doi:916358097 pii:10.1080/13607860902918231

Peplau, L. A., & Fingerhut, A. W. (2007). The close relationships of lesbians and gay men. *Annual Review of Psychology, 58*, 405–424.

Peppone, L. J., Hebl, S., Purnell, J. Q., Reid, M. E., Rosier, R. N., Mustian, K. M., … Morrow, G. R. (2009). The efficacy of calcitriol therapy in the management of bone loss and fractures: A qualitative review. *Osteoporosis International.* doi:10.1007/s00198-009-1136-2

Peretz, C., Korczyn, A. D., Shatil, E., Aharonson, V., Birnboim, S., & Giladi, N. (2011). Computer-based, personalized cognitive training versus classical computer games: A randomized double-blind prospective trial of cognitive stimulation. *Neuroepidemiology, 36*, 91–99. doi: 10.1159/000323950

Perez, V. I., Bokov, A., Remmen, H. V., Mele, J., Ran, Q., Ikeno, Y., & Richardson, A. (2009). Is the oxidative stress theory of aging dead? *Biochimica et Biophysica Acta, 1790*, 1005–1014. doi:S0304-4165(09)00169-X pii:10.1016/j.bbagen.2009.06.003

Perlis, R. H., Ostacher, M. J., Patel, J. K., Marangell, L. B., Zhang, H., Wisniewski, S. R., … Thase, M. E. (2006). Predictors of recurrence in bipolar disorder: Primary outcomes from the Systematic Treatment Enhancement Program for Bipolar Disorder (STEP-BD). *American Journal of Psychiatry, 163*, 217–224. doi:163/2/217 pii:10.1176/appi.ajp.163.2.217

Perlman, F., & Bobak, M. (2009). Assessing the contribution of unstable employment to mortality in posttransition Russia: Prospective individual-level analyses from the Russian longitudinal monitoring survey. *American Journal of Public Health, 99*, 1818–1825. doi:AJPH.2008.154815 pii:10.2105/AJPH.2008.154815

Perrig-Chiello, P., & Höpflinger, F. (2005). Aging parents and their middle-aged children: Demographic and psychosocial challenges. *European Journal of Ageing, 2*, 183–191.

Perruccio, A. V., Badley, E. M., & Trope, G. E. (2007). Self-reported glaucoma in Canada: Findings from population-based surveys, 1994–2003. *Canadian Journal of Ophthalmology, 42*, 219–226.

Peters, R., Peters, J., Warner, J., Beckett, N., & Bulpitt, C. (2008). Alcohol, dementia and cognitive decline in the elderly: A systematic review. *Age and Ageing, 37*, 505–512. doi:afn095 pii:10.1093/ageing/afn095

Peterson, B. E. (2006). Generativity and successful parenting: An analysis of young adult outcomes. *Journal of Personality, 74*, 847–869. doi:10.1111/j.1467-6494.2006.00394.x

Petrofsky, J. S., McLellan, K., Bains, G. S., Prowse, M., Ethiraju, G., Lee, S., … Schwab, E. (2009). The influence of ageing on the ability of the skin to dissipate heat. *Medical Science Monitor, 15*, CR261–268. doi:869673

Pew Research Center. (2009). Growing old in America: Expectations vs. reality. Retrieved from http://pewresearch.org/pubs/1269/aging-survey-expectations-versus-reality

Pfaffenberger, A. (2007). Different conceptualizations of optimal development. *Journal of Humanistic Psychology, 47*, 501–523. doi:10.1177/0022167806296858

Pfaffenberger, A. H. (2011). Assessing postconventional personality: How valid and reliable is the Sentence Completion Test? In A. H. Pfaffenberger, P. W. Marko & A. Combs (Eds.), *The postconventional personality: Assessing, researching, and theorizing higher development.* (pp. 9–22). Albany: State University of New York Press.

Pfirrmann, C. W., Metzdorf, A., Elfering, A., Hodler, J., & Boos, N. (2006). Effect of aging and degeneration on disc volume and shape: A quantitative study in asymptomatic volunteers. *Journal of Orthopedics Research, 24*, 1086–1094.

Pfisterer, M. H., Griffiths, D. J., Schaefer, W., & Resnick, N. M. (2006). The effect of age on lower urinary tract function: A study in women. *Journal of the American Geriatrics Society, 54*, 405–412.

Phelps, A. C., Maciejewski, P. K., Nilsson, M., Balboni, T. A., Wright, A. A., Paulk, M. E., ... Prigerson, H. G. (2009). Religious coping and use of intensive life-prolonging care near death in patients with advanced cancer. *Journal of the American Medical Association, 301*, 1140–1147.

Pienta, A. M. (2003). Partners in marriage: An analysis of husbands' and wives' retirement behavior. *Journal of Applied Gerontology, 22*, 340–358. doi:10.1177/0733464803253587

Pietschmann, P., Rauner, M., Sipos, W., & Kerschan-Schindl, K. (2009). Osteoporosis: An age-related and gender-specific disease—a mini-review. *Gerontology, 55*, 3–12. doi: 000166209 pii:10.1159/000166209

Pinilla, F. G. (2006). The impact of diet and exercise on brain plasticity and disease. *Nutrition and Health, 18*, 277–284.

Piolino, P., Desgranges, B., Benali, K., & Eustache, F. (2002). Episodic and semantic remote autobiographical memory in ageing. *Memory, 10*, 239–257.

Plassman, B. L., Langa, K. M., Fisher, G. G., Heeringa, S. G., Weir, D. R., Ofstedal, M. B., ... Wallace, R. B. (2007). Prevalence of dementia in the United States: The aging, demographics, and memory study. *Neuroepidemiology, 29*, 125–132. doi: 000109998 pii:10.1159/000109998

Plaut, V. C., Markus, H. R., & Lachman, M. E. (2003). Place matters: Consensual features and regional variation in American well-being and self. *Journal of Personality & Social Psychology, 83*, 160–184.

Plemons, J. K., Willis, S. L., & Baltes, P. B. (1978). Modifiability of fluid intelligence in aging: A short-term longitudinal training approach. *Journal of Gerontology, 33*, 224–231.

Pollet, T. V., Nelissen, M., & Nettle, D. (2009). Lineage based differences in grandparental investment: Evidence from a large British cohort study. *Journal of Biosocial Science, 41*, 355–379.

Porell, F. W., & Carter, M. W. (2012). Risk of mortality and nursing home institutionalization after injury. *Journal of the American Geriatrics Society, 60*, 1498–1503. doi:10.1111/j.1532-5415.2012.04053.x

Portin, R., Saarijaervi, S., Joukamaa, M., & Salokangas, R. K. R. (1995). Education, gender and cognitive performance in a 62-year-old normal population: Results from the Turva Project. *Psychological Medicine, 25*, 1295–1298.

Powers, A. D., & Oltmanns, T. F. (2012). Personality disorders and physical health: A longitudinal examination of physical functioning, healthcare utilization, and health-related behaviors in middle-aged adults. *Journal of Personality Disorders, 26*, 524–538. doi:10.1521/pedi.2012.26.4.524

Pratt, L. A. (2009). Serious psychological distress, as measured by the K6, and mortality. *Annals of Epidemiology, 19*, 202–209. doi:S1047-2797(08)00364-5 pii:10.1016/j.annepidem.2008.12.005

President's Commission for the Study of Ethical Problems in Medicine and Biomedical and Behavioral Research. (1981). *Defining death*. Washington, DC: U.S. Government Printing Office.

Previti, D., & Amato, P. R. (2004). Is infidelity a cause or a consequence of poor marital quality? *Journal of Social and Personal Relationships, 21*, 217–230.

Price, J. M., & Sanford, A. J. (2012). Reading in healthy ageing: The influence of information structuring in sentences. *Psychology and Aging, 27*, 529–540. doi:10.1037/a0026028

Priem, J. S., Solomon, D. H., & Steuber, K. R. (2009). Accuracy and bias in perceptions of emotionally supportive communication in marriage. *Personal Relationships, 16*, 531–551.

Protopopova, D., Masopust, J., Maly, R., Valis, M., & Bazant, J. (2012). The prevalence of cardiometabolic risk factors and the ten-year risk of fatal cardiovascular events in patients with schizophrenia and related psychotic disorders. *Psychiatria Danubina, 24*, 307–313.

Pruchno, R. A., & McKenney, D. (2002). Psychological well-being of Black and White grandmothers raising grandchildren: Examination of a two-factor model. *Journals of Gerontology Series B: Psychological Sciences and Social Sciences, 57*, P444–452.

Pulkki-Raback, L., Elovainio, M., Kivimaki, M., Raitakari, O. T., & Keltikangas-Jarvinen, L. (2005). Temperament in childhood predicts body mass in adulthood: The Cardiovascular Risk in Young Finns Study. *Health Psychology, 24*, 307–315.

Pynoos, J., & Nishita, C. M. (2007). Aging in place. In S. Carmel, C. Morse & F. Torres-Gil (Eds.), *Lessons on aging from three nations, Volume I: The art of aging well.* (pp. 185–198). Amityville, NY: Baywood Publishing Co.

Qualls, S. H., Segal, D. L., Norman, S. N., George, & Gallagher-Thompson, D. (2002). Psychologists in practice with older adults: Current patterns, sources of training, and need for continuing education. *Professional Psychology: Research & Practice, 33*, 435–442.

Quin, R. C., Clare, L., Ryan, P., & Jackson, M. (2009). "Not of this world": The subjective experience of late-onset psychosis. *Aging and Mental Health, 13*, 779–787. doi:916452340 pii:10.1080/13607860903046453

Raabe, B., Frese, M., & Beehr, T. A. (2007). Action regulation theory and career self-management. *Journal of Vocational Behavior, 70*, 297–311.

Radloff, L. S. (1977). The CES-D Scale: A self-report depression scale for research in the general population. *Applied Psychological Measurement, 1*, 385–401. doi:10.1177/014662167700100306

Radwany, S., Albanese, T., Clough, L., Sims, L., Mason, H., & Jahangiri, S. (2009). End-of-life decision making and emotional burden: Placing family meetings in context. *American Journal of Hospice and Palliative Care, 26*, 376–383. doi:1049909109338515 pii:10.1177/1049909109338515

Rahhal, T. A., Colcombe, S. J., & Hasher, L. (2001). Instructional manipulations and age differences in memory: Now you see them, now you don't. *Psychology and Aging, 16*, 697–706.

Raj, I. S., Bird, S. R., & Shield, A. J. (2010). Aging and the force-velocity relationship of muscles. *Experimental Gerontology, 45*, 81–90. doi:S0531-5565(09)00229-0 pii:10.1016/j.exger.2009.10.013

Ram, N., Rabbitt, P., Stollery, B., & Nesselroade, J. R. (2005). Cognitive performance inconsistency: Intraindividual change and variability. *Psychology and Aging, 20*, 623–633.

Ramírez-Esparza, N., Harris, K., Hellermann, J., Richard, C., Kuhl, P. K., & Reder, S. (2012). Socio-interactive practices and personality in adult learners of English with little formal education. *Language Learning, 62*, 541–570. doi:10.1111/j.1467-9922.2011.00631.x

Raudenbush, S. W., & Bryk, A. S. (2002). *Hierarchical linear models: Applications and data analysis methods*, 2nd ed. Newbury Park, CA: Sage.

Rauthmann, J. F., & Kolar, G. P. (2012). How "dark" are the Dark Triad traits? Examining the perceived darkness of narcissism, Machiavellianism, and psychopathy. *Personality and Individual Differences, 53*, 884–889.

Rawson, N. E. (2006). Olfactory loss in aging. *Science of Aging Knowledge Environment, 2006*, pe6.

Ray, A., Block, S. D., Friedlander, R. J., Zhang, B., Maciejewski, P. K., & Prigerson, H. G. (2006). Peaceful awareness in patients with advanced cancer. *Journal of Palliative Medicine, 9*, 1359–1368.

Reardon, J. Z., Lareau, S. C., & ZuWallack, R. (2006). Functional status and quality of life in chronic obstructive pulmonary disease. *American Journal of Medicine, 119*, 32–37.

Reelick, M. F., van Iersel, M. B., Kessels, R. P., & Rikkert, M. G. (2009). The influence of fear of falling on gait and balance in older people. *Age and Ageing, 38*, 435–440. doi:afp066 pii:10.1093/ageing/afp066

Reeves, N. D., Narici, M. V., & Maganaris, C. N. (2006). Myotendinous plasticity to ageing and resistance exercise in humans. *Experimental Physiology, 91*, 483–498.

Regnier, V., & Denton, A. (2009). Ten new and emerging trends in residential group living environments. *NeuroRehabilitation, 25*, 169–188. doi:A47W1V1R0705P026 pii:10.3233/NRE-2009-0514

Reichstadt, J., Depp, C. A., Palinkas, L. A., Folsom, D. P., & Jeste, D. V. (2007). Building blocks of successful aging: A focus group study of older adults' perceived contributors to successful aging. *American Journal of Geriatric Psychiatry, 15*, 194–201.

Reitz, C., Honig, L., Vonsattel, J. P., Tang, M. X., & Mayeux, R. (2009). Memory performance is related to amyloid and tau pathology in the hippocampus. *Journal of Neurology Neurosurgery and Psychiatry, 80*, 715–721. doi:jnnp.2008.154146 pii:10.1136/jnnp.2008.154146

Reitzes, D. C., & Mutran, E. J. (2004). Grandparent identity, intergenerational family identity, and well-being. *Journals of Gerontology Series B: Psychological Sciences and Social Sciences, 59B*, S213–S219.

Resnick, B., Shaughnessy, M., Galik, E., Scheve, A., Fitten, R., Morrison, T., ... Agness, C. (2009). Pilot testing of the PRAISEDD intervention among African American and low-income older adults. *Journal of Cardiovascular Nursing, 24*, 352–361. doi:10.1097/JCN.0b013e3181ac0301

Reynolds, C. A., Finkel, D., Gatz, M., & Pedersen, N. L. (2002). Sources of influence on rate of cognitive change over time in Swedish twins: An application of latent growth models. *Experimental Aging Research, 28*, 407–433.

Rhoades, G. K., Stanley, S. M., & Markman, H. J. (2009). The pre-engagement cohabitation effect: A replication and extension of previous findings. *Journal of Family Psychology, 23*, 107–111.

Rhone, M., & Basu, A. (2008). Phytochemicals and age-related eye diseases. *Nutrition Reviews, 66*, 465–472. doi:NURE078 pii:10.1111/j.1753-4887.2008.00078.x

Richards, J. B., Kavvoura, F. K., Rivadeneira, F., Styrkarsdottir, U., Estrada, K., Halldorsson, B. V., ... Spector, T. D. (2009). Collaborative meta-analysis: Associations of 150 candidate genes with osteoporosis and osteoporotic fracture. *Annals of Internal Medicine, 151*, 528–537. doi:151/8/528

Richardson, E. D., & Marottoli, R. A. (2003). Visual attention and driving behaviors among community-living older persons. *Journals of Gerontology Series A: Biological Sciences and Medical Sciences, 58*, M832–M836.

Rick, S. I., Small, D. A., & Finkel, E. J. (2011). Fatal (fiscal) attraction: Spendthrifts and tightwads in marriage. *Journal of Marketing Research, 48*, 228–237. doi:10.1509/jmkr.48.2.228

Riesenhuber, M. (2004). An action video game modifies visual processing. *Trends in Neurosciences, 27*, 72–74. doi:10.1016/j.tins.2003.11.004

Riggs, K. M., Lachman, M. E., & Wingfield, A. (1997). Taking charge of remembering: Locus of control and older adults' memory for speech. *Experimental Aging Research, 23*, 237–256.

Rijs, K. J., Cozijnsen, R., & Deeg, D. J. H. (2012). The effect of retirement and age at retirement on self-perceived health after three years of follow-up in Dutch 55–64-year-olds. *Ageing & Society, 32*, 281–306. doi:10.1017/s0144686x11000237

Riordan, C. M., Griffith, R. W., & Weatherly, E. W. (2003). Age and work-related outcomes: The moderating effects of status characteristics. *Journal of Applied Social Psychology, 33*, 37–57.

Rioux, L., & Werner, C. (2011). Residential satisfaction among aging people living in place. *Journal of Environmental Psychology, 31*, 158–169. doi:10.1016/j.jenvp.2010.12.001

Ritchie, R. A., Meca, A., Madrazo, V. L., Schwartz, S. J., Hardy, S. A., Zamboanga, B. L., ... Lee, R. M. (2013). Identity dimensions and related processes in emerging adulthood: Helpful or harmful? *Journal of Clinical Psychology, 69*, 415–432.

Ritchie, R. A., Meca, A., Madrazo, V. L., Schwarz, S. J., Hardy, S. A., Zamboanga, B. L., ... Lee, R. M. (2013). Identity dimensions and related processes in emerging adulthood: Helpful or harmful? *Journal of Clinical Psychology.* doi:10.1002/jclp.21960

Rizzuto, D., Orsini, N., Qiu, C., Wang, H.-X., & Fratiglioni, L. (2012). Lifestyle, social factors, and survival after age 75: Population based study. *BMJ: British Medical Journal, 345*, 1–10.

Roberson, E. D., & Mucke, L. (2006). 100 years and counting: Prospects for defeating Alzheimer's disease. *Science, 314*, 781–784.

Roberto, K. A. (1990). Grandparent and grandchild relationships. In T. H. Brubaker (Ed.), *Family relationships in later life* (2nd ed.). (pp. 100–112). Newbury Park, CA: Sage.

Roberts, B. W., & DelVecchio, W. F. (2000). The rank-order consistency of personality traits from childhood to old age: A quantitative review of longitudinal studies. *Psychological Bulletin*, *126*, 3–25.

Roberts, B. W., Donnellan, M. B., & Hill, P. L. (2013). Personality trait development in adulthood. In H. Tennen, J. Suls & I. B. Weiner (Eds.), *Handbook of psychology, Vol. 5: Personality and social psychology* (2nd. ed.). (pp. 183–196). Hoboken, NJ: John Wiley & Sons, Inc.

Roberts, B. W., Walton, K. E., & Viechtbauer, W. (2006). Patterns of mean-level change in personality traits across the life course: A meta-analysis of longitudinal studies. *Psychological Bulletin*, *132*, 1–25. doi:10.1037/0033-2909.132.1.1

Robins, R. W., & Trzesniewski, K. H. (2005). Self-esteem development across the lifespan. *Current Directions in Psychological Science*, *14*, 158–162.

Rodriguez, L., Schwartz, S. J., & Whitbourne, S. K. (2010). American identity revisited: The relation between national, ethnic, and personal identity in a multiethnic sample of emerging adults. *Journal of Adolescent Research*, *25*, 324–349. doi:10.1177/0743558409359055

Rogers, C. H., Floyd, F. J., Seltzer, M. M., Greenberg, J., & Hong, J. (2008). Long-term effects of the death of a child on parents' adjustment in midlife. *Journal of Family Psychology*, *22*, 203–211. doi:2008-03770-003 pii:10.1037/0893-3200.22.2.203

Roig, M., Macintyre, D. L., Eng, J. J., Narici, M. V., Maganaris, C. N., & Reid, W. D. (2010). Preservation of eccentric strength in older adults: Evidence, mechanisms and implications for training and rehabilitation. *Experimental Gerontology*. doi:S0531-5565(10)00122-1 pii:10.1016/j.exger.2010.03.008

Ronnlund, M., & Nilsson, L.-G. (2006). Adult life-span patterns in WAIS-R Block Design performance: Cross-sectional versus longitudinal age gradients and relations to demographic factors. *Intelligence*, *34*, 63–78.

Rosenberg, D., Depp, C. A., Vahia, I. V., Reichstadt, J., Palmer, B. W., Kerr, J., … Jeste, D. V. (2010). Exergames for subsyndromal depression in older adults: A pilot study of a novel intervention. *The American Journal of Geriatric Psychiatry*, *18*, 221–226. doi:10.1097/JGP.0b013e3181c534b5

Rosenberg, S. D., Rosenberg, H. J., & Farrell, M. P. (1999). The midlife crisis revisited. In J. D. Reid & S. L. Willis (Eds.), *Life in the middle: Psychological and social development in middle age* (pp. 25–45). San Diego: Academic Press.

Ross, L. A., Anstey, K. J., Kiely, K. M., Windsor, T. D., Byles, J. E., Luszcz, M. A., & Mitchell, P. (2009). Older drivers in Australia: Trends in driving status and cognitive and visual impairment. *Journal of the American Geriatrics Society*, *57*, 1868–1873. doi:10.1111/j.1532-5415.2009.02439.x

Rostad, B., Deeg, D. J. H., & Schei, B. (2009). Socioeconomic inequalities in health in older women. *European Journal of Ageing*, *6*, 39–47.

Rostila, M., Saarela, J., & Kawachi, I. (2012). Mortality in parents following the death of a child: A nationwide follow-up study from Sweden. *Journal of Epidemiology and Community Health*, *66*, 927–933. doi:10.1136/jech-2011-200339

Rothbard, N. P., & Wilk, S. L. (2011). Waking up on the right or wrong side of the bed: Start-of-workday mood, work events, employee affect, and performance. *Academy of Management Journal*, *54*, 959–980. doi:10.5465/amj.2007.0056

Rottinghaus, P. J., Coon, K. L., Gaffey, A. R., & Zytowski, D. G. (2007). Thirty-year stability and predictive validity of vocational interests. *Journal of Career Assessment*, *15*, 5–22.

Rowe, G., Hasher, L., & Turcotte, J. (2009). Age and synchrony effects in visuospatial working memory. *Quarterly Journal of Experimental Psychology*, *62*, 1873–1880. doi:911473077 pii:10.1080/17470210902834852

Rowe, J. W., & Kahn, R. L. (1998). *Successful aging*. New York: Pantheon Books.

Rubin, D. C., Rahhal, T. A., & Poon, L. W. (1998). Things learned in early adulthood are remembered best. *Memory and Cognition*, *26*, 3–19.

Rupp, D. E., Vodanovich, S. J., & Crede, M. (2006). Age bias in the workplace: The impact of ageism and causal attributions. *Journal of Applied Social Psychology*, *36*, 1337–1364.

Ryan, E. B., Hummert, M. L., & Boich, L. H. (1995). Communication predicaments of aging: Patronizing behavior toward older adults. *Journal of Language and Social Psychology*, *14*, 144–166.

Ryder, K. M., Shorr, R. I., Bush, A. J., Kritchevsky, S. B., Harris, T., Stone, K., … Tylavsky, F. A. (2005). Magnesium intake from food and supplements is associated with bone mineral density in healthy older white subjects. *Journal of the American Geriatrics Society*, *53*, 1875–1180.

Saarnio, R., & Isola, A. (2010). Nursing staff perceptions of the use of physical restraint in institutional care of older people in Finland. *Journal of Clinical Nursing*, *19*, 3197–3207. doi:10.1111/j.1365-2702.2010.03232.x

Sabia, S., Kivimaki, M., Shipley, M. J., Marmot, M. G., & Singh-Manoux, A. (2009). Body mass index over the adult life course and cognition in late midlife: The Whitehall II Cohort Study. *American Journal of Clinical Nutrition*, *89*, 601–607. doi:ajcn.2008.26482 pii:10.3945/ajcn.2008.26482

Sabia, S., Nabi, H., Kivimaki, M., Shipley, M. J., Marmot, M. G., & Singh-Manoux, A. (2009). Health behaviors from early to late midlife as predictors of cognitive function: The Whitehall II study. *American Journal of Epidemiology*, *170*, 428–437. doi:kwp161 pii:10.1093/aje/kwp161

Sacher, G. A. (1977). Life table modification and life prolongation. In C. E. Finch & L. Hayflick (Eds.), *Handbook of the biology of aging* (pp. 582–638). New York: Van Nostrand Reinhold.

Saczynski, J. S., Sigurdsson, S., Jonsdottir, M. K., Eiriksdottir, G., Jonsson, P. V., Garcia, M. E., … Launer, L. J. (2009). Cerebral infarcts and cognitive performance: Importance of location and number of infarcts. *Stroke*, *40*, 677–682. doi:STROKEAHA.108.530212 pii:10.1161/STROKEAHA.108.530212

Sahni, S., Hannan, M. T., Blumberg, J., Cupples, L. A., Kiel, D. P., & Tucker, K. L. (2009). Inverse association of carotenoid intakes with 4-y change in bone mineral density in elderly men and women: The Framingham Osteoporosis Study. *American Journal of Clinical Nutrition*, 89, 416–424. doi:ajcn.2008.26388 pii:10.3945/ajcn.2008.26388

Sahyoun, N. R., Pratt, L. A., Lentzner, H., Dey, A., & Robinson, K. N. (2001). *The changing profile of nursing home residents: 1985–1997. Aging Trends, 4.* Hyattsville, Maryland: National Center for Health Statistics.

Saito, M., & Marumo, K. (2009). Collagen cross-links as a determinant of bone quality: A possible explanation for bone fragility in aging, osteoporosis, and diabetes mellitus. *Osteoporos International*, 21, 195–214. doi:10.1007/s00198-009-1066-z

Sajatovic, M., Jenkins, J. H., Safavi, R., West, J. A., Cassidy, K. A., Meyer, W. J., & Calabrese, J. R. (2008). Personal and societal construction of illness among individuals with rapid-cycling bipolar disorder: A life-trajectory perspective. *American Journal of Geriatric Psychiatry*, 16, 718–726. doi:JGP.0b013e3180488346 pii:10.1097/JGP.0b013e3180488346

Sala-Llonch, R., Arenaza-Urquijo, E. M., Valls-Pedret, C., Vidal-Piñeiro, D., Bargalló, N., Junqué, C., & Bartrés-Faz, D. (2012). Dynamic functional reorganizations and relationship with working memory performance in healthy aging. *Frontiers in Human Neuroscience*, 6. doi:10.3389/fnhum.2012.00152

Salari, S. M., & Rich, M. (2001). Social and environmental infantilization of aged persons: Observations in two adult day care centers. *International Journal of Aging and Human Development*, 52, 115–134.

Salloway, S. (2008). Taking the next steps in the treatment of Alzheimer's disease: Disease-modifying agents. *CNS Spectrum*, 13, 11–14.

Salthouse, T. (2012). Consequences of age-related cognitive declines. *Annual Review of Psychology*, 63, 201–226. doi:10.1146/annurev-psych-120710-100328

Salthouse, T. A. (1996). The processing-speed theory of adult age differences in cognition. *Psychological Review*, 103, 403–428.

Salthouse, T. A. (2009). When does age-related cognitive decline begin? *Neurobiology of Aging*, 30, 507–514. doi:10.1016/j.neurobiolaging.2008.09.023

Samad, Z., Brealey, S., & Gilbody, S. (2011). The effectiveness of behavioural therapy for the treatment of depression in older adults: A meta-analysis. *International Journal of Geriatric Psychiatry*, 26, 1211–1220. doi:10.1002/gps.2680

Samanez-Larkin, G. R., Robertson, E. R., Mikels, J. A., Carstensen, L. L., & Gotlib, I. H. (2009). Selective attention to emotion in the aging brain. *Psychol Aging*, 24, 519–529. doi:2009-13203-001 pii:10.1037/a0016952

Samuels, J., Eaton, W. W., Bienvenu, O. J. I., Brown, C., Costa, P. T., Jr,, & Nestadt, G. (2002). Prevalence and correlates of personality disorders in a community sample. *British Journal of Psychiatry*, 180, 536–542.

Santos, M., Kovari, E., Hof, P. R., Gold, G., Bouras, C., & Giannakopoulos, P. (2009). The impact of vascular burden on late-life depression. *Brain Res Rev*, 62, 19–32. doi:S0165-0173(09)00082-4 pii:10.1016/j.brainresrev.2009.08.003

Sareen, J., Cox, B. J., Clara, I., & Asmundson, G. J. (2005). The relationship between anxiety disorders and physical disorders in the U.S. National Comorbidity Survey. *Depression and Anxiety*, 21, 193–202. doi 10.1002/da.20072

Sargent-Cox, K. A., Windsor, T., Walker, J., & Anstey, K. J. (2011). Health literacy of older drivers and the importance of health experience for self-regulation of driving behaviour. *Accident Analysis and Prevention*, 43, 898–905. doi:10.1016/j.aap.2010.11.012

Satre, D. D., Knight, B. G., & David, S. (2006). Cognitive-behavioral interventions with older adults: Integrating clinical and gerontological research. *Professional Psychology: Research and Practice*, 37, 489–498.

Sawyer, K. (2011). The cognitive neuroscience of creativity: A critical review. *Creativity Research Journal*, 23, 137–154. doi:10.1080/10400419.2011.571191

Saxer, S., de Bie, R. A., Dassen, T., & Halfens, R. J. (2009). Knowledge, beliefs, attitudes, and self-reported practice concerning urinary incontinence in nursing home care. *Journal of Wound Ostomy and Continence Nursing*, 36, 539–544. doi:10.1097/WON.0b013e3181b35ff1 pii:00152192-200909000-00013 pii:

Sbarra, D. A., & Emery, R. E. (2008). Deeper into divorce: Using actor-partner analyses to explore systemic differences in coparenting conflict following custody dispute resolution. *Journal of Family Psychology*, 22, 144–152. doi:2008-01362-015 pii:10.1037/0893-3200.22.1.144

Scarr, S., & McCartney, K. (1983). How people make their own environments: A theory of genotype–environment effects. *Child Development*, 54, 424–435.

Schaie, K. W. (1965). A general model for the study of developmental change. *Psychological Bulletin*, 64, 92–107.

Schaie, K. W. (1994). The course of adult intellectual development. *American Psychologist*, 49, 304–313.

Schaie, K. W. (1996). Intellectual development in adulthood. In J. E. Birren, K. W. Schaie, R. P. Abeles, M. Gatz & T. A. Salthouse (Eds.), *Handbook of the psychology of aging* (4th ed.). (pp. 266–286). San Diego CA: Academic Press.

Schaie, K. W. (2009). When does age-related cognitive decline begin? Salthouse again reifies the "cross-sectional fallacy." *Neurobiology of Aging*, 30, 528–529. doi:10.1016/j.neurobiolaging.2008.12.012

Schaie, K. W., Nguyen, H. T., Willis, S. L., Dutta, R., & Yue, G. A. (2001). Environmental factors as a conceptual framework for examining cognitive performance in Chinese adults. *International Journal of Behavioral Development*, 25, 193–202.

Schaie, K. W., Willis, S. L., & Caskie, G. I. (2004). The Seattle Longitudinal Study: Relationship between personality and cognition. *Aging, Neuropsychology and Cognition*, 11, 304–324.

Schaie, K. W., & Zanjani, F. A. K. (2006). Intellectual development across adulthood. In C. Hoare (Ed.), *Handbook of adult development and learning.* (pp. 99–122): Oxford University Press.

Schiffman, S. S. (2009). Effects of aging on the human taste system. *Annals of the New York Academy of Science, 1170*, 725–729. doi:NYAS03924 pii:10.1111/j.1749-6632.2009.03924.x

Schlickum, M., Hedman, L., Enochsson, L., Kjellin, A., & Fellander-Tsai, L. (2009). Systematic video game training in surgical novices improves performance in virtual reality endoscopic surgical simulators a prospective randomized study. *World Journal of Surgery, 33*, 2360–2367. doi:10.1007/s00268-009-0151-y

Schneider, C., Jick, S. S., & Meier, C. R. (2009). Risk of gynecological cancers in users of estradiol/dydrogesterone or other HRT preparations. *Climacteric, 12*, 514–524. doi: 10.3109/13697130903075352   pii:10.3109/13697130903075 352

Schnitzspahn, K. M., & Kliegel, M. (2009). Age effects in prospective memory performance within older adults: The paradoxical impact of implementation intentions. *European Journal of Ageing, 6*, 147–155.

Schoenborn, C. A., & Heyman, K. M. (2009). Health characteristics of adults aged 55 years and over: United States, 2004–2007. *National health statistics reports: No. 16.* Hyattsville MD: National Center for Health Statistics.

Schoenfeld, E. A., Bredow, C. A., & Huston, T. L. (2012). Do men and women show love differently in marriage? *Personality and Social Psychology Bulletin, 38*, 1396–1409. doi:10.1177/0146167212450739

Schoenhofen, E. A., Wyszynski, D. F., Andersen, S., Pennington, J., Young, R., Terry, D. F., & Perls, T. T. (2006). Characteristics of 32 supercentenarians. *Journal of the American Geriatrics Society, 54*, 1237–1240.

Schoevers, R. A., Smit, F., Deeg, D. J., Cuijpers, P., Dekker, J., van Tilburg, W., & Beekman, A. T. (2006). Prevention of late-life depression in primary care: do we know where to begin? *American Journal of Psychiatry, 163*, 1611–1621.

Schulte, T., Müller-Oehring, E. M., Chanraud, S., Rosenbloom, M. J., Pfefferbaum, A., & Sullivan, E. V. (2009). Age-related reorganization of functional networks for successful conflict resolution: A combined functional and structural MRI study. *Neurobiology of Aging, 32*, 2075–2090.

Schuurmans, J., Comijs, H., Emmelkamp, P. M., Weijnen, I. J., van den Hout, M., & van Dyck, R. (2009). Long-term effectiveness and prediction of treatment outcome in cognitive behavioral therapy and sertraline for late-life anxiety disorders. *International Psychogeriatrics, 21*, 1148–1159. doi:S1041610209990536 pii:10.1017/S1041610209990536

Schwartz, S. J., Beyers, W., Luyckx, K., Soenens, B., Zamboanga, B. L., Forthun, L. F., ... Waterman, A. S. (2011). Examining the light and dark sides of emerging adults' identity: A study of identity status differences in positive and negative psychosocial functioning. *Journal of Youth and Adolescence, 40*, 839–859. doi:10.1007/s10964-010-9606-6

Schwartz, S. J., Kim, S. Y., Whitbourne, S. K., Zamboanga, B. L., Weisskirch, R. S., Forthun, L. F., ... Luyckx, K. (2012). Converging identities: Dimensions of acculturation and personal identity status among immigrant college students. *Cultural Diversity and Ethnic Minority Psychology, 19*, 155–165 doi:10.1037/a0030753

Scogin, F., Floyd, M., & Forde, J. (2000). Anxiety in older adults. In S. K. Whitbourne (Ed.), *Psychopathology in later life* (pp. 117–140). New York: Wiley.

Scollon, C. N., & Diener, E. (2006). Love, work, and changes in extraversion and neuroticism over time. *Journal of Personality and Social Psychology, 91*, 1152–1165.

Scullin, M. K. (2012). Sleep, memory, and aging: The link between slow-wave sleep and episodic memory changes from younger to older adults. *Psychology and Aging, 28*, 105–114 doi:10.1037/a0028830

Seale, C. (2009). Hastening death in end-of-life care: A survey of doctors. *Social Science & Medicine, 69*, 1659–1666.

Seblega, B. K., Zhang, N. J., Unruh, L. Y., Breen, G. M., Seung Chun, P., & Wan, T. T. (2010). Changes in nursing home staffing levels, 1997 to 2007. *Medical Care: Research and Review, 67*, 232–246. doi:1077558709342253 pii:10.1177/1077558709342253

Secretan, B., Straif, K., Baan, R., Grosse, Y., El Ghissassi, F., Bouvard, V., ... Cogliano, V. (2009). A review of human carcinogens—Part E: Tobacco, areca nut, alcohol, coal smoke, and salted fish. *Lancet Oncology, 10*, 1033–1034.

Segal, D. L., Coolidge, F. L., & Rosowsky, E. (2006). *Personality disorders and older adults: Diagnosis, assessment, and treatment.* Hoboken, NJ: John Wiley & Sons, Inc.

Segal, D. L., Hook, J. N., & Coolidge, F. L. (2001). Personality dysfunction, coping styles, and clinical symptoms in younger and older adults. *Journal of Clinical Geropsychology, 7*, 201–212.

Segal, D. L., Needham, T. N., & Coolidge, F. L. (2009). Age differences in attachment orientations among younger and older adults: Evidence from two self-report measures of attachment. *International Journal of Aging and Human Development, 69*, 119–132.

Seibert, S. E., & Kraimer, M. L. (2001). The Five-Factor Model of personality and career success. *Journal of Vocational Behavior, 58*, 1–21.

Semba, R. D., Bandinelli, S., Sun, K., Guralnik, J. M., & Ferrucci, L. (2010). Relationship of an advanced glycation end product, plasma carboxymethyl-lysine, with slow walking speed in older adults: The InCHIANTI study. *European Journal of Applied Physiology, 108*, 191–195. doi:10.1007/s00421-009-1192-5

Senchina, D. S. (2009). Effects of regular exercise on the aging immune system: A review. *Clinical Journal of Sport Medicine, 19*, 439–440. doi:10.1097/01.jsm.0000358882.07869.20 pii:00042752-200909000-00017

Serfaty, M. A., Haworth, D., Blanchard, M., Buszewicz, M., Murad, S., & King, M. (2009). Clinical effectiveness of individual cognitive behavioral therapy for depressed older people in primary care: A randomized controlled trial. *Archives of General Psychiatry, 66*, 1332–1340. doi: 66/12/1332 pii:10.1001/archgenpsychiatry.2009.165

Serste, T., & Bourgeois, N. (2006). Ageing and the liver. *Acta Gastro-enterologica Belgium, 69*, 296–298.

Settersten, R. A., Jr., (2006). Aging and the life course. In R. H. Binstock & L. K. George (Eds.), *Handbook of aging and the social sciences*, 6th ed (pp. 3–19). Amsterdam: Elsevier.

Shackelford, T. K., Schmitt, D. P., & Buss, D. M. (2005). Mate preferences of married persons in the newlywed year and three years later. *Cognition and Emotion, 19*, 1262–1270.

Shafto, M. A., Burke, D. M., Stamatakis, E. A., Tam, P. P., & Tyler, L. K. (2007). On the tip-of-the-tongue: Neural correlates of increased word-finding failures in normal aging. *Journal of Cognitive Neuroscience, 19*, 2060–2070. doi:10.1162/jocn.2007.19.12.2060

Shafto, M. A., Stamatakis, E. A., Tam, P. P., & Tyler, L. K. (2009). Word retrieval failures in old age: The relationship between structure and function. *Journal of Cognitive Neuroscience, 22*, 1530–1540 doi:10.1162/jocn.2009.21321

Sharma, K. K., & Santhoshkumar, P. (2009). Lens aging: Effects of crystallins. *Biochimica et Biophysica Acta, 1790*, 1095–1108. doi:S0304-4165(09)00143-3 pii:10.1016/j.bbagen.2009.05.008

Sheehy, G. (1974). *Passages: Predictable passages of adult life*. New York: Dutton.

Sheu, Y., Cauley, J. A., Wheeler, V. W., Patrick, A. L., Bunker, C. H., Kammerer, C. M., & Zmuda, J. M. (2009). Natural history and correlates of hip BMD loss with aging in men of African ancestry: The Tobago Bone Health Study. *Journal of Bone Mineral Research, 24*, 1290–1298. doi:10.1359/jbmr.090221

Shih, M., Hootman, J. M., Kruger, J., & Helmick, C. G. (2006). Physical activity in men and women with arthritis National Health Interview Survey, 2002. *American Journal of Preventive Medicine, 30*, 385–393. doi:S0749-3797(06)00010-9 pii:10.1016/j.amepre.2005.12.005

Shin, J. S., Hong, A., Solomon, M. J., & Lee, C. S. (2006). The role of telomeres and telomerase in the pathology of human cancer and aging. *Pathology, 38*, 103–113.

Shu, C. H., Hummel, T., Lee, P. L., Chiu, C. H., Lin, S. H., & Yuan, B. C. (2009). The proportion of self-rated olfactory dysfunction does not change across the life span. *American Journal of Rhinology and Allergy, 23*, 413–416. doi:10.2500/ajra.2009.23.3343

Shumway-Cook, A., Guralnik, J. M., Phillips, C. L., Coppin, A. K., Ciol, M. A., Bandinelli, S., & Ferrucci, L. (2007). Age-associated declines in complex walking task performance: The Walking InCHIANTI toolkit. *Journal of the American Geriatrics Society, 55*, 58–65.

Siebert, D. C., Mutran, E. J., & Reitzes, D. C. (2002). Friendship and social support: The importance of role identity to aging adults. *Social Work, 44*, 522–533.

Siegler, I. C., Costa, P. T., Brummett, B. H., Helms, M. J., Barefoot, J. C., Williams, R. B., … Rimer, B. K. (2003). Patterns of change in hostility from college to midlife in the UNC Alumni Heart Study predict high-risk status. *Psychosomatic Medicine, 65*, 738–745.

Sigurdsson, G., Aspelund, T., Chang, M., Jonsdottir, B., Sigurdsson, S., Eiriksdottir, G., … Lang, T. F. (2006). Increasing sex difference in bone strength in old age: The Age, Gene/Environment Susceptibility-Reykjavik study (AGES-REYKJAVIK). *Bone, 39*, 644–651.

Silveira, M. J., Kim, S. Y., & Langa, K. M. (2010). Advance directives and outcomes of surrogate decision making before death. *New England Journal of Medicine, 362*, 1211–1218. doi:362/13/1211 pii:10.1056/NEJMsa0907901

Silverman, J. M., Schmeidler, J., Beeri, M. S., Rosendorff, C., Sano, M., Grossman, H. T., … Haroutunian, V. (2012). C-reactive protein and familial risk for dementia: A phenotype for successful cognitive aging. *Neurology, 79*, 1116–1123. doi:10.1212/WNL.0b013e3182698c89

Silverstein, M., & Bengtson, V. L. (1997). Intergenerational solidarity and the structure of adult child-parent relationships in American families. *American Journal of Sociology, 103*, 429–460.

Silverstein, M., Gans, D., & Yang, F. M. (2006). Intergenerational support to aging parents: The role of norms and needs. *Journal of Family Issues, 27*, 1068–1084.

Silverstein, M., & Parker, M. G. (2002). Leisure activities and quality of life among the oldest old in Sweden. *Research on Aging, 24*, 528–547.

Simmons, T., & O'Connell, M. (2003). Married-couple and unmarried-partner households: 2000. Retrieved from http://www.census.gov/prod/2003pubs/censr-5.pdf

Simonton, D. K. (1989). The swan-song phenomenon: Last-works effects for 172 classical composers. *Psychology and Aging, 4*, 42–47.

Simonton, D. K. (1997). Creative productivity: A predictive and explanatory model of career trajectories and landmarks. *Psychological Review, 104*, 66–89.

Simonton, D. K. (1998). Achieved eminence in minority and majority cultures: Convergence versus divergence in the assessments of 294 African Americans. *Journal of Personality and Social Psychology, 74*, 804–817.

Simonton, D. K. (2012). Creative productivity and aging: An age decrement—or not? In S. K. Whitbourne & M. J. Sliwinski (Eds.), *Handbook of adult development and aging* (pp. 477–496). Oxford, UK: Wiley-Blackwell.

Singley, S., & Hynes, K. (2005). Transitions to parenthood: Work–family policies, gender, and the couple context. *Gender and Society, 19*, 376–397.

Sinnott, J. D. (1989). A model for solution of ill-structured problems: Implications for everyday and abstract problem solving. In J. D. Sinnott (Ed.), *Everyday problem solving: Theory and applications* (pp. 72–99). New York: Praeger.

Siu, O.-l., Lu, J.-f., Brough, P., Lu, C.-q., Bakker, A. B., Kalliath, T., … Shi, K. (2010). Role resources and work–family enrichment: The role of work engagement. *Journal of Vocational Behavior, 77*, 470–480. doi:10.1016/j.jvb.2010.06.007

Skalicka, V., & Kunst, A. E. (2008). Effects of spouses' socioeconomic characteristics on mortality among men and women in a Norwegian longitudinal study. *Soc Sci Med, 66*, 2035–2047. doi:S0277-9536(08)00047-6 pii:10.1016/j.socscimed.2008.01.020

Skinner, B. F., & Vaughan, M. E. (1983). *Enjoy old age: A practical guide.* New York: W.W. Norton.

Skultety, K. M., & Whitbourne, S. K. (2004). Gender differences in identity processes and self-esteem in middle and later adulthood. *Journal of Women and Aging, 16,* 175–188.

Sliwinski, M. J., Stawski, R. S., Hall, C. B., Katz, M., Verghese, J., & Lipton, R. (2006). Distinguishing preterminal and terminal cognitive decline. *European Psychologist, 11,* 172–181.

Sloane, P. D., Mitchell, C. M., Weisman, G., Zimmerman, S., Foley, K. M., Lynn, M., … Montgomery, R. (2002). The Therapeutic Environment Screening Survey for Nursing Homes (TESS-NH): An observational instrument for assessing the physical environment of institutional settings for persons with dementia. *Journals of Gerontology Series B: Psychological Sciences and Social Sciences, 57,* S69–78.

Sluiter, J. K., & Frings-Dresen, M. H. (2007). What do we know about ageing at work? Evidence-based fitness for duty and health in fire fighters. *Ergonomics, 50,* 1897–1913. doi:783631179 pii:10.1080/00140130701676005

Small, G. W. (2009). Differential diagnoses and assessment of depression in elderly patients. *Journal of Clinical Psychiatry, 70,* e47. doi:10.4088/JCP.8001tx20c

Smith-Ruig, T. (2009). Exploring career plateau as a multi-faceted phenomenon: Understanding the types of career plateaux experienced by accounting professionals. *British Journal of Management, 20,* 610–622. doi:10.1111/j.1467-8551.2008.00608.x

Smith, A. D., & Refsum, H. (2009). Vitamin B-12 and cognition in the elderly. *American Journal of Clinical Nutrition, 89,* 707S–711S. doi:ajcn.2008.26947D pii:10.3945/ajcn.2008.26947D

Smith, C. D., Walton, A., Loveland, A. D., Umberger, G. H., Kryscio, R. J., & Gash, D. M. (2005). Memories that last in old age: Motor skill learning and memory preservation. *Neurobiology of Aging, 26,* 883–890.

Smith, D. B., Hanges, P. J., & Dickson, M. W. (2001). Personnel selection and the five-factor model: Reexamining the effects of appplicant's frame of reference. *Journal of Applied Physiology, 86,* 304–315.

Smith, J., & Freund, A. M. (2002). The dynamics of possible selves in old age. *Journals of Gerontology Series B: Psychological Sciences and Social Sciences, 57,* P492–500.

Smith, T. J., & Campbell, C. (2006). The Structure of ONET Occupational Values. *Journal of Career Assessment, 14,* 437–448. doi:10.1177/1069072706286511

Sneed, J. R., Kasen, S., & Cohen, P. (2007). Early-life risk factors for late-onset depression. *International Journal of Geriatric Psychiatry, 22,* 663–667.

Sneed, J. R., & Whitbourne, S. K. (2003). Identity processing and self-consciousness in middle and later adulthood. *Journals of Gerontology Series B: Psychological Sciences and Social Sciences, 58,* P313–P319.

Sneed, J. R., Whitbourne, S. K., Schwartz, S. J., & Huang, S. (2012). The relationship between identity, intimacy, and midlife well-being: Findings from the Rochester Adult Longitudinal Study. *Psychology and Aging, 27,* 318–323. doi:10.1037/a0026378

Snitz, B. E., O'Meara, E. S., Carlson, M. C., Arnold, A. M., Ives, D. G., Rapp, S. R., … DeKosky, S. T. (2009). Ginkgo biloba for preventing cognitive decline in older adults: A randomized trial. *Journal of the American Medical Association, 302,* 2663–2670. doi:302/24/2663 pii:10.1001/jama.2009.1913

Social Security Administration. (2012). Fast facts and figures about Social Security, 2012. Retrieved from http://www.ssa.gov/policy/docs/chartbooks/fast_facts/2012/fast_facts12.pdf

Social Security Administration. (2013). Monthly statistical snapshot, January 2013. Retrieved from http://www.ssa.gov/policy/docs/quickfacts/stat_snapshot/

Sohal, R. S. (2002). Role of oxidative stress and protein oxidation in the aging process. *Free Radical Biology and Medicine, 33,* 37–44.

Solano, N. H., & Whitbourne, S. K. (2001). Coping with schizophrenia: Patterns in later adulthood. *International Journal of Aging and Human Development, 53,* 1–10.

Soldz, S., & Vaillant, G. E. (1998). A 50-year longitudinal study of defense use among inner city men: A validation of the DSM-IV defense axis. *Journal of Nervous and Mental Disease, 186,* 104–111.

Solfrizzi, V., Scafato, E., Capurso, C., D'Introno, A., Colacicco, A. M., Frisardi, V., … Panza, F. (2009). Metabolic syndrome and the risk of vascular dementia. The Italian Longitudinal Study on Aging. *Journal of Neurological and Neurosurgical Psychiatry, 81,* 433–440. doi:jnnp.2009.181743 pii:10.1136/jnnp.2009.181743

Solomon, S., Greenberg, J. & Pyszczynski, T. (1991). A terror management theory of social behavior: The psychological functions of self-esteem and cultural worldviews. In M. P. Zanna (Ed.), *Advances in experimental social psychology* (Vol. 24, pp. 93–159). Orlando, FL: Academic Press.

Spearman, C. (1904). "General intelligence": Objectively determined and measured. *American Journal of Psychology, 15,* 201–292.

Spearman, C. (1927). *The abilities of man.* New York: Macmillan.

Spindler, H., & Pedersen, S. S. (2005). Posttraumatic stress disorder in the wake of heart disease: Prevalence, risk factors, and future research directions. *Psychosomatic Medicine, 67,* 715–723.

Spira, A. P., Stone, K., Beaudreau, S. A., Ancoli-Israel, S., & Yaffe, K. (2009). Anxiety symptoms and objectively measured sleep quality in older women. *American Journal of Geriatric Psychiatry, 17,* 136–143. doi:10.1097/JGP.0b013e3181871345 pii:00019442-200902000-00006

Squire, L. R. (1989). On the course of forgetting in very long term memory. *Journal of Experimental Psychology: Learning, Memory, and Cognition, 15,* 241–245.

St John, P. D., & Montgomery, P. R. (2009). Do depressive symptoms predict mortality in older people? *Aging and Mental Health, 13,* 674–681. doi:916352953 pii:10.1080/13607860902774493

Stanley, S. M., Amato, P. R., Johnson, C. A., & Markman, H. J. (2006). Premarital education, marital quality, and marital stability: Findings from a large, random household survey. *Journal of Family Psychology, 20,* 117–126.

Starr, J. M., Deary, I. J., Fox, H. C., & Whalley, L. J. (2007). Smoking and cognitive change from age 11 to 66 years: A confirmatory investigation. *Addictive Behaviors, 32*, 63–68.

Staudinger, U. M., & Kunzmann, U. (2005). Positive adult personality development: Adjustment and/or growth? *European Psychologist, 10*, 320–329.

Staudinger, U. M., Marsiske, M., & Baltes, P. B. (1995). Resilience and reserve capacity in later adulthood: Potentials and limits of development across the life span. In D. Cicchetti & D. J. Cohen (Eds.), *Developmental psychopathology, Vol. 2: Risk, disorder, and adaptation* (pp. 801–847). New York: Wiley.

Steele, C. M., Spencer, S. J., Aronson, J., & Zanna, M. P. (2002). Contending with group image: The psychology of stereotype and social identity threat. *Advances in experimental social psychology, Vol. 34.* (pp. 379–440). San Diego, CA: Academic Press.

Stengel, B., Couchoud, C., Cenee, S., & Hemon, D. (2000). Age, blood pressure and smoking effects on chronic renal failure in primary glomerular nephropathies. *Kidney International, 57*, 2519–2526.

Sterns, H. L., & Gray, J. H. (1999). Work, leisure, and retirement. In J. C. Cavanaugh & S. K. Whitbourne (Eds.), *Gerontology: Interdisciplinary perspectives* (pp. 355–390). New York: Oxford University Press.

Steunenberg, B., Beekman, A. T., Deeg, D. J., Bremmer, M. A., & Kerkhof, A. J. (2007). Mastery and neuroticism predict recovery of depression in later life. *American Journal of Geriatric Psychiatry, 15*, 234–242.

Stevens, J. A., Ryan, G., & Kresnow, M. (2006). Fatalities and injuries from falls among older adults—United States, 1993–2003 and 2001–2005. *Morbidity and Mortality Weekly Report, 55*(45), 1221–1224.

Stewart, K. A., Grabowski, D. C., & Lakdawalla, D. N. (2009). Annual expenditures for nursing home care: Private and public payer price growth, 1977 to 2004. *Medical Care: Research and Review, 47*, 295–301. doi:10.1097/MLR.0b013e3181893f8e

Stewart, R., & Wingfield, A. (2009). Hearing loss and cognitive effort in older adults' report accuracy for verbal materials. *Journal of the American Academy of Audiology, 20*, 147–154.

Stine-Morrow, E. A., Milinder, L., Pullara, O., & Herman, B. (2001). Patterns of resource allocation are reliable among younger and older readers. *Psychology and Aging, 16*, 69–84.

Stine-Morrow, E. A., Soederberg Miller, L. M., Gagne, D. D., & Hertzog, C. (2008). Self-regulated reading in adulthood. *Psychol Aging, 23*, 131–153. doi:2008-02853-015 pii:10.1037/0882-7974.23.1.131

Stine-Morrow, E. A. L., & Miller, L. M. S. (1999). Basic cognitive processes. In J. C. Cavanaugh & S. K. Whitbourne (Eds.), *Gerontology: Interdisciplinary perspectives* (pp. 186–212). New York: Oxford University Press.

Story, T. N., Berg, C. A., Smith, T. W., Beveridge, R., Henry, N. J., & Pearce, G. (2007). Age, marital satisfaction, and optimism as predictors of positive sentiment override in middle-aged and older married couples. *Psychology and Aging, 22*, 719–727. doi:2007-18670-007 pii:10.1037/0882-7974.22.4.719

Straif, K., Benbrahim-Tallaa, L., Baan, R., Grosse, Y., Secretan, B., El Ghissassi, F., … Cogliano, V. (2009). A review of human carcinogens—Part C: Metals, arsenic, dusts, and fibres. *Lancet Oncology, 10*, 453–454.

Strenger, C. (2009). Paring down life to the essentials: An epicurean psychodynamics of midlife changes. *Psychoanalytic Psychology, 26*, 246–258.

Strobach, T., Frensch, P. A., & Schubert, T. (2012). Video game practice optimizes executive control skills in dual-task and task switching situations. *Acta Psychologica, 140*, 13–24. doi:10.1016/j.actpsy.2012.02.001

Stroebe, M., Schut, H., & Boerner, K. (2010). Continuing bonds in adaptation to bereavement: Toward theoretical integration. *Clinical Psychology Review, 30*, 259–268.

Stroebe, M., Schut, H., & Stroebe, W. (2007). Health outcomes of bereavement. *Lancet, 370*, 1960–1973.

Stroebe, W., Schut, H., & Stroebe, M. S. (2005). Grief work, disclosure and counseling: Do they help the bereaved? *Clinical Psychology Review, 25*, 395–414.

Styczynska, M., Strosznajder, J. B., Religa, D., Chodakowska-Zebrowska, M., Pfeffer, A., Gabryelewicz, T., … Barcikowska, M. (2008). Association between genetic and environmental factors and the risk of Alzheimer's disease. *Folia Neuropathologica, 46*, 249–254. doi:11573

Suarez, E. C., Williams, R. B., Kuhn, C. M., & Zimmerman, E. A. (1991). Biobehavioral basis of coronary-prone behavior in middle-aged men: II. Serum cholesterol, the Type A behavior pattern, and hostility as interactive modulators of physiological reactivity. *Psychosomatic Medicine, 53*, 528–537.

Subramaniam, H., Dennis, M. S., & Byrne, E. J. (2006). The role of vascular risk factors in late onset bipolar disorder. *International Journal of Geriatric Psychiatry, 22*, 733–737

Substance Abuse and Mental Health Services Administration. (2009). Illicit drug use among older adults. *Findings from the SAMHSA 2006 to 2008 National Surveys on Drug Use and Health* (NSDUHs).

Substance Abuse and Mental Health Services Administration. (2012). Results from the 2011 National Survey on Drug Use and Health: Summary of national findings. NSDUH Series H-44, HHS Publication No. (SMA) 12-4713. Rockville, MD: Substance Abuse and Mental Health Services Administration.

Suitor, J. J., Sechrist, J., Plikuhn, M., Pardo, S. T., Gilligan, M., & Pillemer, K. (2009). The role of perceived maternal favoritism in sibling relations in midlife. *Journal of Marriage and Family, 71*, 1026–1038.

Sullivan, S. E., Martin, D. F., Carden, W. A., & Mainiero, L. A. (2003). The road less traveled: How to manage the recycling career stage. *Journal of Leadership & Organizational Studies, 10*, 34–42. doi:10.1177/107179190301000204

Sun, M. K., Hongpaisan, J., & Alkon, D. L. (2009). Postischemic PKC activation rescues retrograde and anterograde long-term memory. *Proceedings of the National Academies of Sciences of the United States of America, 106,* 14676–14680. doi:0907842106 pii:10.1073/pnas.0907842106

Sun, X., Chen, Y., Chen, X., Wang, J., Xi, C., Lin, S., & Liu, X. (2009). Change of glomerular filtration rate in healthy adults with aging. *Nephrology (Carlton), 14,* 506–513. doi:NEP1098 pii:10.1111/j.1440-1797.2009.01098.x

Super, D. E. (1957). *The psychology of careers.* New York: Harper.

Super, D. E. (1990). A life span, life-space approach to career development. In D. Brown & L.Brooks (Eds.), *Career choice and development* (2nd ed.). San Francisco: Jossey-Bass.

Sutin, A. R., Beason-Held, L. L., Resnick, S. M., & Costa, P. T. (2009). Sex differences in resting-state neural correlates of openness to experience among older adults. *Cerebral Cortex, 19,* 2797–2802.

Sutin, A. R., Terracciano, A., Deiana, B., Naitza, S., Ferrucci, L., Uda, M., … Costa, P. T. (2009). High neuroticism and low conscientiousness are associated with interleukin-6. *Psychological Medicine,* 1–9. doi:S0033291709992029 pii:10.1017/S0033291709992029

Sutin, A. R., Terracciano, A., Deiana, B., Uda, M., Schlessinger, D., Lakatta, E. G., & Costa, P. T., Jr,. (2010). Cholesterol, triglycerides, and the Five-Factor Model of personality. *Biological Psychology, 84,* 186–191 doi:S0301-0511(10)00017-7 pii:10.1016/j.biopsycho.2010.01.012

Sweeney, M. M., & Cancian, M. (2004). The changing importance of White women's economic prospects for assortative mating. *Journal of Marriage and Family, 66,* 1015–1028.

Sweeper, S., & Halford, K. (2006). Assessing adult adjustment to relationship separation: The Psychological Adjustment to Separation Test (PAST). *Journal of Family Psychology, 20,* 632–640.

Sweet, M. G., Sweet, J. M., Jeremiah, M. P., & Galazka, S. S. (2009). Diagnosis and treatment of osteoporosis. *American Family Physician, 79,* 193–200.

Swick, K. J., & Williams, R. D. (2006). An analysis of Bronfenbrenner's bio-ecological perspective for early childhood educators: Implications for working with families experiencing stress. *Early Childhood Education Journal, 33,* 371–378. doi:10.1007/s10643-006-0078-y

Swift, D., Lavie, C., Johannsen, N., Arena, R., Earnest, C., O'Keefe, J., … Church, T. (2013). Physical activity, cardiorespiratory fitness, and exercise training in primary and secondary coronary prevention. *Circulation, 77,* 281–292.

Szanton, S. L., Thorpe, R. J., Boyd, C., Tanner, E. K., Leff, B., Agree, E., … Gitlin, L. N. (2011). Community aging in place, advancing better living for elders: A bio-behavioral-environmental intervention to improve function and health-related quality of life in disabled older adults. *Journal of the American Geriatrics Society, 59,* 2314–2320. doi:10.1111/j.1532-5415.2011.03698.x

Tadic, S. D., Zdaniuk, B., Griffiths, D., Rosenberg, L., Schafer, W., & Resnick, N. M. (2007). Effect of biofeedback on psychological burden and symptoms in older women with urge urinary incontinence. *Journal of the American Geriatrics Society, 55,* 2010–2015. doi:JGS1461 pii:10.1111/j.1532-5415.2007.01461.x

Takahashi, K., Takahashi, H. E., Nakadaira, H., & Yamamoto, M. (2006). Different changes of quantity due to aging in the psoas major and quadriceps femoris muscles in women. *Journal of Musculoskeletal and Neuronal Interactions, 6,* 201–205.

Tanaka, H., & Seals, D. R. (2003). Invited review: Dynamic exercise performance in masters athletes: Insight into the effects of primary human aging on physiological functional capacity. *Journal of Applied Physiology, 95,* 2152–2162.

Tang, H. Y., Harms, V., Speck, S. M., Vezeau, T., & Jesurum, J. T. (2009). Effects of audio relaxation programs for blood pressure reduction in older adults. *European Journal of Cardiovascular Nursing, 8,* 329–336. doi:S1474-5151(09)00061-9 pii:10.1016/j.ejcnurse.2009.06.001

Tanzi, R. E., & Bertram, L. (2008). Alzheimer's disease: The latest suspect. *Nature, 454,* 706–708. doi:454706a pii:10.1038/454706a

Taylor, J. L., Kennedy, Q., Noda, A., & Yesavage, J. A. (2007). Pilot age and expertise predict flight simulator performance: A 3-year longitudinal study. *Neurology, 68,* 648–654.

Teichtahl, A. J., Wluka, A. E., Wang, Y., Hanna, F., English, D. R., Giles, G. G., & Cicuttini, F. M. (2009). Obesity and adiposity are associated with the rate of patella cartilage volume loss over 2 years in adults without knee osteoarthritis. *Annals of the Rheumatic Diseases, 68,* 909–913. doi:ard.2008.093310 pii:10.1136/ard.2008.093310

Teixeira, C. V. L., Gobbi, L. T. B., Corazza, D. I., Stella, F., Costa, J. L. R., & Gobbi, S. (2012). Non-pharmacological interventions on cognitive functions in older people with mild cognitive impairment (MCI). *Archives of Gerontology and Geriatrics, 54,* 175–180.

Teno, J. M., Gruneir, A., Schwartz, Z., Nanda, A., & Wetle, T. (2007). Association between advance directives and quality of end-of-life care: A national study. *Journal of the American Geriatrics Society, 55,* 189–194.

Teno, J. M., Weitzen, S., Fennell, M. L., & Mor, V. (2001). Dying trajectory in the last year of life: Does cancer trajectory fit other diseases? *Journal of Palliative Medicine, 4,* 457–464.

Tentori, K., Osherson, D., Hasher, L., & May, C. (2001). Wisdom and aging: Irrational preferences in college students but not older adults. *Cognition, 81,* B87–96.

Teri, L. (1994). Behavioral treatment of depression in patients with dementia. *Alzheimer's Disease and Associated Disorders, 8,* 66–74.

Terracciano, A., & Costa, P. T. J. (2004). Smoking and the five-factor model of personality. *Addiction, 99,* 472–481.

Terracciano, A., Löckenhoff, C. E., Crum, R. M., Bienvenu, O. J., & Costa, P. T., Jr., (2008). Five-Factor Model personality profiles of drug users. *BMC Psychiatry, 8,* 22. doi:10.1186/1471-244X-8-22

Terracciano, A., Löckenhoff, C. E., Zonderman, A. B., Ferrucci, L., & Costa, P. T., Jr., (2008). Personality predictors of longevity:

Activity, emotional stability, and conscientiousness. *Psychosomatic Medicine, 70,* 621–627.

Thanvi, B., & Treadwell, S. (2009). Drug induced parkinsonism: A common cause of parkinsonism in older people. *Postgrad Med J, 85,* 322–326. doi:85/1004/322 pii:10.1136/pgmj.2008.073312

The President's Council on Bioethics. (2005). Taking care: Ethical caregiving in our aging society. Washington, DC.

Theodoraki, A., & Bouloux, P. M. (2009). Testosterone therapy in men. *Menopause Int, 15,* 87–92. doi: 15/2/87 pii:10.1258/mi.2009.009025

Thomas, A. K., & Bulevich, J. B. (2006). Effective cue utilization reduces memory errors in older adults. *Psychology and Aging, 21,* 379–389.

Thompson-Torgerson, C. S., Holowatz, L. A., & Kenney, W. L. (2008). Altered mechanisms of thermoregulatory vasoconstriction in aged human skin. *Exercise and Sport Sciences Review, 36,* 122–127. doi:10.1097/JES.0b013e31817bfd47 pii:00003677-200807000-00004

Thompson, O., Barrett, S., Patterson, C., & Craig, D. (2012). Examining the neurocognitive validity of commercially available, smartphone-based puzzle games. *Psychology, 3,* 525–526. doi:10.4236/psych.2012.37076

Thorne, A. (1993). On contextualizing Loevinger's stages of ego development. *Psychological Inquiry, 4,* 53–55. doi:10.1207/s15327965pli0401_11

Thornton, W. J. L., & Dumke, H. A. (2005). Age differences in everyday problem-solving and decision-making effectiveness: A meta-analytic review. *Psychology and Aging, 20,* 85–99.

Thornton, W. L., Paterson, T. S. E., & Yeung, S. E. (2013). Age differences in everyday problem solving: The role of problem context. *International Journal of Behavioral Development, 37,* 13–20. doi:10.1177/0165025412454028

Tiikkaja, S., Hemstrom, O., & Vagero, D. (2009). Intergenerational class mobility and cardiovascular mortality among Swedish women: A population-based register study. *Soc Sci Med, 68,* 733–739. doi:S0277-9536(08)00605-9 pii:10.1016/j.socscimed.2008.11.017

Tinetti, M. E., Baker, D., Gallo, W. T., Nanda, A., Charpentier, P., & O'Leary, J. (2002). Evaluation of restorative care vs usual care for older adults receiving an acute episode of home care. *Journal of the American Medical Association, 287,* 2098–2105.

Tinetti, M. E., & Kumar, C. (2010). The patient who falls: "It's always a trade-off." *Journal of the American Medical Association, 303,* 258–266. doi:303/3/258 pii:10.1001/jama.2009.2024

Titone, D. A., Koh, C. K., Kjelgaard, M. M., Bruce, S., Speer, S. R., & Wingfield, A. (2006). Age-related impairments in the revision of syntactic misanalyses: Effects of prosody. *Language and Speech, 49,* 75–99.

Tolomio, S., Ermolao, A., Travain, G., & Zaccaria, M. (2008). Short-term adapted physical activity program improves bone quality in osteopenic/osteoporotic postmenopausal women. *Journal of Physical Activity and Health, 5,* 844–853.

Toossi, M. (2009). Labor force projections to 2018: Older workers stay active despite their age. *Monthly Labor Review,* 30–51. Retrieved from http://www.bls.gov/opub/mlr/2009/11/art3full.pdf

Toossi, M. (2012). Projections of the labor force to 2050: A visual essay. *Monthly Labor Review.* Retrieved from http://www.bls.gov/opub/mlr/2012/10/art1full.pdf

Tostain, J. L., & Blanc, F. (2008). Testosterone deficiency: A common, unrecognized syndrome. *Nat Clin Pract Urol, 5,* 388–396. doi:ncpuro1167 pii:10.1038/ncpuro1167

Tran, K., Levin, R. M., & Mousa, S. A. (2009). Behavioral intervention versus pharmacotherapy or their combinations in the management of overactive bladder dysfunction. *Advances in Urology, 345324.* doi:10.1155/2009/345324

Travis, S. S., Bernard, M., Dixon, S., McAuley, W. J., Loving, G., & McClanahan, L. (2002). Obstacles to palliation and end-of-life care in a long-term care facility. *Gerontologist, 42,* 342–349.

Travison, T. G., Araujo, A. B., Beck, T. J., Williams, R. E., Clark, R. V., Leder, B. Z., & McKinlay, J. B. (2009). Relation between serum testosterone, serum estradiol, sex hormone-binding globulin, and geometrical measures of adult male proximal femur strength. *Journal of Clinical Endocrinology and Metabolism, 94,* 853–860. doi:jc.2008-0668 pii:10.1210/jc.2008-0668

Travison, T. G., O'Donnell, A. B., Araujo, A. B., Matsumoto, A. M., & McKinlay, J. B. (2007). Cortisol levels and measures of body composition in middle-aged and older men. *Clinical Endocrinology, 67,* 71–77. doi:CEN2837 pii:10.1111/j.1365-2265.2007.02837.x

Tremblay, S., & Pierce, T. (2011). Perceptions of fatherhood: Longitudinal reciprocal associations within the couple. *Canadian Journal of Behavioural Science/Revue canadienne des sciences du comportement, 43,* 99–110. doi:10.1037/a0022635

Troll, L. E. (1985). The contingencies of grandparenting. In V. L. Bengston & J. F. Robertson (Eds.), *Grandparenthood* (pp. 135–149). Beverly Hills, CA: Sage.

Trouillet, R. l., Gana, K., Lourel, M., & Fort, I. (2009). Predictive value of age for coping: The role of self-efficacy, social support satisfaction and perceived stress. *Aging and Mental Health, 13,* 357–366.

Trunk, D. L., & Abrams, L. (2009). Do younger and older adults' communicative goals influence off-topic speech in autobiographical narratives? *Psychology and Aging, 24,* 324–337. doi:10.1037/a0015259

Tu, J. V., Nardi, L., Fang, J., Liu, J., Khalid, L., & Johansen, H. (2009). National trends in rates of death and hospital admissions related to acute myocardial infarction, heart failure and stroke, 1994–2004. *Canadian Medical Association Journal, 180,* E118–125. doi:180/13/E118 pii:10.1503/cmaj.081197

Tucker-Drob, E. M. (2011). Neurocognitive functions and everyday functions change together in old age. *Neuropsychology, 25,* 368–377. doi:10.1037/a0022348

Tucker-Samaras, S., Zedayko, T., Cole, C., Miller, D., Wallo, W., & Leyden, J. J. (2009). A stabilized 0.1% retinol facial moisturizer improves the appearance of photodamaged skin in an eight-week, double-blind, vehicle-controlled study. *Journal of Drugs and Dermatology, 8,* 932–936.

Tucker, K. L. (2009). Osteoporosis prevention and nutrition. *Current Osteoporosis Reports, 7,* 111–117.

Turcotte, M. (2006). Parents with adult children living at home. *Canadian Social Trends, March 2006,* 11–14.

Turiano, N. A., Mroczek, D. K., Moynihan, J., & Chapman, B. P. (2013). Big 5 personality traits and interleukin-6: Evidence for "healthy neuroticism" in a U.S. population sample. *Brain, Behavior, and Immunity, 28,* 83–89. doi:10.1016/j.bbi.2012.10.020

Turiano, N. A., Spiro, A., III,, & Mroczek, D. K. (2012). Openness to experience and mortality in men: Analysis of trait and facets. *Journal of Aging and Health, 24,* 654–672. doi:10.1177/0898264311431303

Tyler, L. K., Shafto, M. A., Randall, B., Wright, P., Marslen-Wilson, W. D., & Stamatakis, E. A. (2010). Preserving syntactic processing across the adult life span: The modulation of the frontotemporal language system in the context of age-related atrophy. *Cerebral Cortex, 20,* 352–364. doi:bhp105 pii:10.1093/cercor/bhp105

U.S. Bureau of the Census. (2010a). America's families and living arrangements: 2009.

U.S. Bureau of the Census. (2010b). International data base. Retrieved from http://sasweb.ssd.census.gov/idb/worldpopinfo.html

U.S. Bureau of the Census. (2010c). Statistical abstract of the United States. Retrieved from http://www.census.gov/compendia/statab/cats/education.html

U.S. Bureau of the Census. (2010d). U.S. Interim projections by age, sex, race, and hispanic origin: 2000–2050. Retrieved from http://www.census.gov/population/www/projections/usinterimproj/

U.S. Bureau of the Census. (2012a). 2012 national population projections: Summary tables. Retrieved from http://www.census.gov/population/projections/data/national/2012/summarytables.html

U.S. Bureau of the Census. (2012b). America's families and living arrangements: 2011. Table FG6.

U.S. Bureau of the Census. (2012c). Statistical abstract of the United States. Retrieved from http://www.census.gov/compendia/statab/cats/education.html

U.S. Bureau of the Census. (2013a). America's families and living arrangements: 2012.

U.S. Bureau of the Census. (2013b). American Community Survey.

U.S. Department of Labor. (2013). Labor force characteristics by race and ethnicity, 2011. Retrieved from http://www.bls.gov/cps/cpsrace2011.pdf

U.S. National Highway Traffic Safety Administration. (2012). Traffic safety facts. Retrieved from http://www.census.gov/compendia/statab/2012/tables/12s1113.pdf

U.S. News and World Reports, H. (2012). Best nursing homes 2012: Behind the rankings. Retrieved from http://health.usnews.com/health-news/best-nursing-homes/articles/2012/02/07/best-nursing-homes-2012-behind-the-rankings

Uchino, B. N., Berg, C. A., Smith, T. W., Pearce, G., & Skinner, M. (2006). Age-related differences in ambulatory blood pressure during daily stress: Evidence for greater blood pressure reactivity with age. *Psychology and Aging, 21,* 231–239.

Urien, B., & Kilbourne, W. (2011). Generativity and self-enhancement values in eco-friendly behavioral intentions and environmentally responsible consumption behavior. *Psychology & Marketing, 28,* 69–90. doi:10.1002/mar.20381

Vahia, I. V., Thompson, W. K., Depp, C. A., Allison, M., & Jeste, D. V. (2012). Developing a dimensional model for successful cognitive and emotional aging. *International Psychogeriatrics, 24,* 515–523. doi:10.1017/s1041610211002055

Vail, K. E., III,, Juhl, J., Arndt, J., Vess, M., Routledge, C., & Rutjens, B. T. (2012). When death is good for life: Considering the positive trajectories of terror management. *Personality and Social Psychology Review, 16,* 303–329. doi:10.1177/1088868312440046

Vaillant, G. E. (1993). *The wisdom of the ego.* Cambridge MA: Harvard University Press.

Vaillant, G. E. (2000). Adaptive mental mechanisms: Their role in a positive psychology. *American Psychologist, 55,* 89–98.

Vaillant, G. E. (2003). A 60-year follow-up of alcoholic men. *Addiction, 98,* 1043–10451.

Valentijn, S. A. M., Hill, R. D., Van Hooren, S. A. H., Bosma, H., Van Boxtel, M. P. J., Jolles, J., & Ponds, R. W. H. M. (2006). Memory self-efficacy predicts memory performance: Results from a 6-year follow-up study. *Psychology and Aging, 21,* 165–172.

Van Assche, L., Luyten, P., Bruffaerts, R., Persoons, P., van de Ven, L., & Vandenbulcke, M. (2013). Attachment in old age: Theoretical assumptions, empirical findings and implications for clinical practice. *Clinical Psychology Review, 33,* 67–81. doi:10.1016/j.cpr.2012.10.003

van den Berg, E., Dekker, J. M., Nijpels, G., Kessels, R. P., Kappelle, L. J., de Haan, E. H., … Biessels, G. J. (2008). Cognitive functioning in elderly persons with type 2 diabetes and metabolic syndrome: The Hoorn study. *Dement Geriatr Cogn Disord, 26,* 261–290. doi:000160959 pii:10.1159/000160959

Van den Block, L., Deschepper, R., Bilsen, J., Bossuyt, N., Van Casteren, V., & Deliens, L. (2009). *Euthanasia and other end of life decisions and care provided in final three months of life: Nationwide retrospective study in Belgium.* BMJ: British Medical Journal, 339, b2772. doi: 10.1136/bmj.b2772.

van den Kommer, T. N., Dik, M. G., Comijs, H. C., Jonker, C., & Deeg, D. J. (2008). Homocysteine and inflammation: Predictors of cognitive decline in older persons? *Neurobiology of Aging, 31,* 1700–1709. doi:S0197-4580(08)00349-7 pii:10.1016/j.neurobiolaging.2008.09.009

Van der Elst, W., Van Boxtel, M. P. J., & Jolles, J. (2012). Occupational activity and cognitive aging: A case-control study based on the Maastricht Aging Study. *Experimental Aging Research, 38,* 315–329. doi:10.1080/0361073x.2012.672137 van Hooff, M. L., Geurts, S. A., Taris, T. W., Kompier, M. A., Dikkers, J. S., Houtman, I. L., & van den Heuvel, F. M. (2005). Disentangling the causal relationships between work–home interference and employee health. *Scandinavian Journal of Work and Environmental Health*, *31*, 15–29.

Van Manen, K. J., & Whitbourne, S. K. (1997). Psychosocial development and life experiences in adulthood: A 22-year sequential study. *Psychology and Aging*, *12*, 239–246.

van Muijden, J., Band, G. P. H., & Hommel, B. (2012). Online games training aging brains: Limited transfer to cognitive control functions. *Frontiers in Human Neuroscience*, *6*. doi: 10.3389/fnhum.2012.00221

Van Ness, P. H., & Larson, D. B. (2002). Religion, senescence, and mental health: The end of life is not the end of hope. *American Journal of Geriatric Psychiatry*, *10*, 386–397.

Van Volkom, M. (2006). Sibling relationships in middle and older adulthood: A review of the literature. *Marriage and Family Review*, *40*, 151–170.

Vandewater, E. A., Ostrove, J. M., & Stewart, A. J. (1997). Predicting women's well-being in midlife: The importance of personality development and social role involvements. *Journal of Personality and Social Psychology*, *72*, 1147–1160.

Vannorsdall, T. D., Waldstein, S. R., Kraut, M., Pearlson, G. D., & Schretlen, D. J. (2009). White matter abnormalities and cognition in a community sample. *Archives of Clinical Neuropsychology*, *24*, 209–217. doi:acp037 pii:10.1093/arclin/acp037

Vartanian, O. (2012). Dissociable neural systems for analogy and metaphor: Implications for the neuroscience of creativity. *British Journal of Psychology*, *103*, 302–316. doi:10.1111/j.2044-8295.2011.02073.x

Vaughan, L., & Giovanello, K. (2010). Executive function in daily life: Age-related influences of executive processes on instrumental activities of daily living. *Psychology and Aging*, *25*, 343–355. doi:10.1037/a0017729

Vazey, E. M., & Aston-Jones, G. (2013). New tricks for old dogmas: Optogenetic and designer receptor insights for Parkinson's disease. *Brain Research*, *1511*, 153–163. doi: 10.1016/j.brainres.2013.01.021.

Velagaleti, R. S., & O'Donnell, C. J. (2010). Genomics of heart failure. *Heart Failure Clinics*, *6*, 115–124.

Velkoff, V. A., & Lawson, V. A. (1998). Gender and aging: Caregiving. Washington, DC: U.S. Department of Commerce.

Verghese, J., Wang, C., Katz, M. J., Sanders, A., & Lipton, R. B. (2009). Leisure activities and risk of vascular cognitive impairment in older adults. *Journal of Geriatric Psychiatry and Neurology*, *22*, 110–118.

Verweij, L. M., van Schoor, N. M., Deeg, D. J., Dekker, J., & Visser, M. (2009). Physical activity and incident clinical knee osteoarthritis in older adults. *Arthritis Rheumatology*, *61*, 152–157. doi:10.1002/art.24233

Vespa, J. (2009). Gender ideology construction: A life course and intersectional approach. *Gender & Society*, *23*, 363–387. doi:10.1177/0891243209337507

Vig, E. K., Davenport, N. A., & Pearlman, R. A. (2002). Good deaths, bad deaths, and preferences for the end of life: A qualitative study of geriatric outpatients. *Journal of the American Geriatrics Society*, *50*, 1541–1548.

Vincent, G. K., & Velkoff, V. A. (2010). The next four decades. The older population in the United States: 2010 to 2050. *Current Population Reports*. Retrieved from http://www.census.gov/prod/2010pubs/p25-1138.pdf

Vita, A. J., Terry, R. B., Hubert, H. B., & Fries, J. F. (1998). Aging, health risks, and cumulative disability. *New England Journal of Medicine*, *338*, 1035–1041. doi:10.1056/nejm199804093381506

Vitale, S., Cotch, M. F., & Sperduto, R. D. (2006). Prevalence of visual impairment in the United States. *Journal of the American Medical Association*, *295*, 2158–2163.

Vitiello, M. V., Rybarczyk, B., Von Korff, M., & Stepanski, E. J. (2009). Cognitive behavioral therapy for insomnia improves sleep and decreases pain in older adults with co-morbid insomnia and osteoarthritis. *Journal of Clinical Sleep Medicine*, *5*, 355–362.

von Arnim, C. A. F., Herbolsheimer, F., Nikolaus, T., Peter, R., Biesalski, H. K., Ludolph, A. C., ... Nagel, G. (2012). Dietary antioxidants and dementia in a population-based case-control study among older people in South Germany. *Journal of Alzheimer's Disease*, *31*, 717–724.

von Muhlen, D., Laughlin, G. A., Kritz-Silverstein, D., & Barrett-Connor, E. (2007). The Dehydroepiandrosterone and WellNess (DAWN) study: Research design and methods. *Contemporary Clinical Trials*, *28*, 153–168.

Voorpostel, M., & Blieszner, R. (2008). Intergenerational solidarity and support between adult siblings. *Journal of Marriage and Family*, *70*, 157–167.

Wagg, A., Wyndaele, J. J., & Sieber, P. (2006). Efficacy and tolerability of solifenacin in elderly subjects with overactive bladder syndrome: A pooled analysis. *American Journal of Geriatric Pharmacotherapy*, *4*, 14–24.

Waite, L. J., Laumann, E. O., Das, A., & Schumm, L. P. (2009a). Sexuality: Measures of partnerships, practices, attitudes, and problems in National Social Life, Health, and Aging Study. *The Journals of Gerontology: Series B: Psychological Sciences and Social Sciences*, *64B*, I56–I66.

Waiter, G. D., Deary, I. J., Staff, R. T., Murray, A. D., Fox, H. C., Starr, J. M., & Whalley, L. J. (2010). Exploring possible neural mechanisms of intelligence differences using processing speed and working memory tasks: An fMRI study. *Intelligence*, *37*, 199–206.

Walford, R. L., Mock, D., Verdery, R., & MacCallum, T. (2002). Calorie restriction in biosphere 2: Alterations in physiologic, hematologic, hormonal, and biochemical parameters in humans restricted for a 2-year period. *Journal of Gerontology Series A: Biological Sciences and Medical Sciences*, *57*, B211–224.

Walker, A. E., Eskurza, I., Pierce, G. L., Gates, P. E., & Seals, D. R. (2009). Modulation of vascular endothelial function by low-density lipoprotein cholesterol with aging: Influence of habitual exercise. *American Journal of Hypertension*, *22*, 250–256. doi:ajh2008353 pii:10.1038/ajh.2008.353

Walster, E., Walster, G. W., & Berscheid, E. (1978). *Equity: Theory and research*. Boston: Allyn & Bacon.

Walton, A., Scheib, J. L., McLean, S., Zhang, Z., & Grondin, R. (2008). Motor memory preservation in aged monkeys mirrors that of aged humans on a similar task. *Neurobiol Aging, 29*, 1556–1562. doi:S0197-4580(07)00125-X pii:10.1016/j.neurobiolaging.2007.03.016

Wang, H., Dwyer-Lindgren, L., Lofgren, K. T., Rajaratnam, J. K., Marcus, J. R., Levin-Rector, A., … Murray, C. J. L. (2012). Age-specific and sex-specific mortality in 187 countries, 1970–2010: A systematic analysis for the Global Burden of Disease Study 2010. *The Lancet, 380*, 2071–2094.

Wang, M. (2007). Profiling retirees in the retirement transition and adjustment process: Examining the longitudinal change patterns of retirees' psychological well-being. *Journal of Applied Psychology, 92*, 455–474. doi:10.1037/0021-9010.92.2.455

Wang, M., Henkens, K., & van Solinge, H. (2011). Retirement adjustment: A review of theoretical and empirical advancements. *American Psychologist, 66*, 204–213. doi:10.1037/a0022414

Wang, M., & Shultz, K. S. (2010). Employee retirement: A review and recommendations for future investigation. *Journal of Management, 36*, 172–206.

Wang, S. Q., & Dusza, S. W. (2009). Assessment of sunscreen knowledge: A pilot survey. *British Journal of Dermatology, 161* Suppl 3, 28–32. doi:BJD9446 pii:10.1111/j.1365-2133.2009.09446.x

Ward, R. A., Spitze, G., & Deane, G. (2009). The more the merrier? Multiple parent–adult child relations. *Journal of Marriage and Family, 71*, 161–173.

Warr, P. (1994). Age and employment. In H. C. Triandis, M. D. Dunnette & L. M. Hough (Eds.), *Handbook of industrial and organizational psychology* (pp. 485–550). Palo Alto, CA: Consulting Psychologists Press.

Wayne, J. H., Randel, A. E., & Stevens, J. (2006). The role of identity and work–family support in work–family enrichment and its work-related consequences. *Journal of Vocational Behavior, 69*, 445–461.

Weatherbee, S. R., & Allaire, J. C. (2008). Everyday cognition and mortality: Performance differences and predictive utility of the Everyday Cognition Battery. *Psychology and Aging, 23*, 216–221.

Webster, G. D., & Jonason, P. K. (2013). Putting the "irt" in "dirty": Item response theory analyses of the Dark Triad dirty dozen—an efficient measure of narcissism, psychopathy, and Machiavellianism. *Personality and Individual Differences, 54*, 302–306.

Wechsler, D. (2008). Wechsler Adult Intelligence Scales–IV, from http://www.pearsonassessments.com/HAIWEB/Cultures/en-us/Productdetail.htm?Pid=015-8980-808

Wedisinghe, L., & Perera, M. (2009). Diabetes and the menopause. *Maturitas, 63*, 200–203. doi:S0378-5122(09)00130-3 pii:10.1016/j.maturitas.2009.04.005

Wegge, J., von Dick, R., Fisher, G. K., West, M. A., & Dawson, J. F. (2006). A test of basic assumptions of Affective Events Theory (AET) in call centre work. *British Journal of Management, 17*, 237–254.

Weige, C. C., Allred, K. F., & Allred, C. D. (2009). Estradiol alters cell growth in nonmalignant colonocytes and reduces the formation of preneoplastic lesions in the colon. *Cancer Res, 69*, 9118–9124. doi:0008-5472.CAN-09-2348 pii:10.1158/0008-5472.CAN-09-2348

Weinberger, M. I., Hofstein, Y., & Whitbourne, S. K. (2008). Intimacy in young adulthood as a predictor of divorce in midlife. *Personal Relationships, 15*, 551–557. doi:10.1111/j.1475-6811.2008.00215.x

Weinberger, M. I., & Whitbourne, S. K. (2010). Depressive symptoms, self-reported physical functioning, and identity in community-dwelling older adults. *Ageing International, 35*, 276–285. doi: 10.1007/s12126-010-9053-4

Weiner, D. K., Rudy, T. E., Morrow, L., Slaboda, J., & Lieber, S. (2006). The relationship between pain, neuropsychological performance, and physical function in community-dwelling older adults with chronic low back pain. *Pain Medicine, 7*, 60–70.

Weiss, A., & Costa, P. T., Jr,. (2005). Domain and facet personality predictors of all-cause mortality among Medicare patients aged 65 to 100. *Psychosomatic Medicine, 67*, 724–733. doi:67/5/724 pii:10.1097/01.psy.0000181272.58103.18

Weiss, H. M., & Cropanzano, R. (1996). Affective events theory: A theoretical discussion of the structure, causes and consequences of affective experiences at work. In B. M. Staw & L. L. Cummings (Eds.), *Research in organizational behavior: An annual series of analytical essays and critical reviews*, Vol. *18* (pp. 1–74). Middlesed UK: Elsevier Science/JAI Press.

Welge-Lussen, A. (2009). Ageing, neurodegeneration, and olfactory and gustatory loss. *B-ENT, 5* Supplement 13, 129–132.

Weltman, A., Weltman, J. Y., Roy, C. P., Wideman, L., Patrie, J., Evans, W. S., & Veldhuis, J. D. (2006). Growth hormone response to graded exercise intensities is attenuated and the gender difference abolished in older adults. *Journal of Applied Physiology, 100*, 1623–1629.

Werner, P., Buchbinder, E., Lowenstein, A., & Livni, T. (2005). Mediation across generations: A tri-generational perspective. *Journal of Aging Studies, 19*, 489–502.

West, G. L., Al-Aidroos, N., & Pratt, J. (2013). Action video game experience affects oculomotor performance. *Acta Psychologica, 142*, 38–42. doi: http://dx.doi.org/10.1016/j.actpsy.2011.08.005

West, R., & Schwarb, H. (2006). The influence of aging and frontal function on the neural correlates of regulative and evaluative aspects of cognitive control. *Neuropsychology, 20*, 468–481.

West, R. L., Bagwell, D. K., & Dark-Freudeman, A. (2008). Self-efficacy and memory aging: The impact of a memory intervention based on self-efficacy. *Neuropsychol Dev Cogn B Aging Neuropsychol Cogn, 15*, 302–329.

West, R. L., Thorn, R. M., & Bagwell, D. K. (2003). Memory performance and beliefs as a function of goal setting and aging. *Psychol Aging, 18*, 111–125.

Westen, D. (1998). Loevinger's theory of ego development in the context of contemporary psychoanalytic theory. In P. M. Westenberg, A. Blasi & L. D. Cohn (Eds.), *Personality development: Theoretical, empirical, and clinical investigations of Loevinger's conception of ego development.* (pp. 59–69). Mahwah, NJ: Lawrence Erlbaum Associates Publishers.

Westerhof, G. J., Whitbourne, S. K., & Freeman, G. P. (2012). The aging self in a cultural context: The relation of conceptions of aging to identity processes and self-esteem in the United States and the Netherlands. *The Journals of Gerontology: Series B: Psychological Sciences and Social Sciences, 67B,* 52–60. doi:10.1093/geronb/gbr075

Westoby, C. J., Mallen, C. D., & Thomas, E. (2009). Cognitive complaints in a general population of older adults: Prevalence, association with pain and the influence of concurrent affective disorders. *European Journal of Pain, 13,* 970–976. doi:S1090-3801(08)00230-9 pii:10.1016/j.ejpain.2008.11.011

Wetherell, J. L., Reynolds, C. A., & Gatz, M. P., Nancy L. (2002). Anxiety, cognitive performance, and cognitive decline in normal aging. *Journals of Gerontology Series B: Psychological Sciences and Social Sciences, 57B,* P246–P255.

Wethington, E., Kessler, R. C., Pixley, J. E., Brim, O. G., & Ryff, C. D. (2004). Turning points in adulthood. In O. G. Brim, C. D. Ryff & R. C. Kessler (Eds.), *How healthy are we?: A national study of well-being at midlife.* (pp. 586–613). Chicago, IL: University of Chicago Press.

Wheeler, I. (2001). Parental bereavement: The crisis of meaning. *Death Studies, 25,* 51–66.

Whisman, M. A., Uebelacker, L. A., Tolejko, N., Chatav, Y., & McKelvie, M. (2006). Marital discord and well-being in older adults: Is the association confounded by personality? *Psychology and Aging, 21,* 626–631.

Whitbourne, S. K. (1985). The life-span construct as a model of adaptation in adulthood. In J. E. Birren & K.W. Schaie (Eds.), *Handbook of the psychology of aging* (2nd ed.). (pp. 594–618). New York: Van Nostrand Reinhold.

Whitbourne, S. K. (1986). *The me I know: A study of adult identity.* New York: Springer-Verlag.

Whitbourne, S. K. (2010). *The search for fulfillment.* New York: Ballantine.

Whitbourne, S. K., & Collins, K. C. (1998). Identity and physical changes in later adulthood: Theoretical and clinical implications. *Psychotherapy, 35,* 519–530.

Whitbourne, S. K., & Connolly, L. A. (1999). The developing self in midlife. In J. D. Reid & S. L. Willis (Eds.), *Life in the middle: Psychological and social development in middle age* (pp. 25–45). San Diego: Academic Press.

Whitbourne, S. K., Culgin, S., & Cassidy, E. (1995). Evaluation of infantilizing intonation and content of speech directed at the aged. *International Journal of Aging and Human Development, 41,* 107–114.

Whitbourne, S. K., & Halgin, R. P. (2013). *Abnormal psychology: Clinical perspectives on psychological disorders,* 7th ed. New York: McGraw-Hill.

Whitbourne, S. K., & Meeks, S. (2010). Psychopathology, bereavement, and aging. In K. W. Schaie & S. L. Willis (Eds.), *Handbook of the psychology of aging.* New York: Cambridge University Press.

Whitbourne, S. K., & Sneed, J. R. (2002). The paradox of well-being, identity processes, and stereotype threat: Ageism and its potential relationships to the self in later life. In T. D. Nelson (Ed.), *Ageism: Stereotyping and prejudice against older persons.* (pp. 247–273): Cambridge, MA: The MIT Press.

Whitbourne, S. K., Sneed, J. R., & Sayer, A. (2009). Psychosocial development from college through midlife: A 34-year sequential study. *Developmental Psychology, 45,* 1328–1340. doi:2009-12605-011 pii:10.1037/a0016550

Whitbourne, S. K., Sneed, J. R., & Skultety, K. M. (2002). Identity processes in adulthood: Theoretical and methodological challenges. *Identity, 2,* 29–45.

Whitbourne, S. K., & Waterman, A. S. (1979). Psychosocial development during the adult years: Age and cohort comparisons. *Developmental Psychology, 15,* 373–378.

Whitbourne, S. K., & Willis, S. L. (Eds.). (2006). *The baby boomers grow up: Contemporary perspectives on midlife.* Mahwah, NJ: Lawrence Erlbaum.

Whitbourne, S. K., & Wills, K.-J. (1993). Psychological issues in institutional care of the aged. In S. B. Goldsmith (Ed.), *Long-term care administration handbook* (pp. 19–32). Gaithersburg, MD: Aspen.

Whitbourne, S. K., Zuschlag, M. K., Elliot, L. B., & Waterman, A. S. (1992). Psychosocial development in adulthood: A 22-year sequential study. *Journal of Personality & Social Psychology, 63,* 260–271.

Whitfield, K. E., Allaire, J. C., & Wiggins, S. A. (2004). Relationships among health factors and everyday problem solving in African Americans. *Health Psychology, 23,* 641–644.

Whiting, W. L., Madden, D. J., Pierce, T. W., & Allen, P. A. (2005). Searching from the top down: Ageing and attentional guidance during singleton detection. *Quarterly Journal of Experimental Psychology: Section A, 58,* 72–97. doi:10.1080/02724980443000205

Whitlock, G., Lewington, S., Sherliker, P., Clarke, R., Emberson, J., Halsey, J., … Peto, R. (2009). Body-mass index and cause-specific mortality in 900,000 adults: Collaborative analyses of 57 prospective studies. *Lancet, 373,* 1083–1096. doi:S0140-6736(09)60318-4 pii:10.1016/S0140-6736(09)60318-4

Whitmer, R. A., Gustafson, D. R., Barrett-Connor, E., Haan, M. N., Gunderson, E. P., & Yaffe, K. (2008). Central obesity and increased risk of dementia more than three decades later. *Neurology, 71,* 1057–1064. doi:01.wnl.0000306313.89165.ef pii:10.1212/01.wnl.0000306313.89165.ef

Whitton, S. W., Rhoades, G. K., Stanley, S. M., & Markman, H. J. (2008). Effects of parental divorce on marital commitment and confidence. *Journal of Family Psychology, 22,* 789–793. doi:2008-14158-014 pii:10.1037/a0012800

Wickremaratchi, M. M., & Llewelyn, J. G. (2006). Effects of ageing on touch. *Postgraduate Medical Journal, 82,* 301–304.

Wieser, M. J., Muhlberger, A., Kenntner-Mabiala, R., & Pauli, P. (2006). Is emotion processing affected by advancing age? An event-related brain potential study. *Brain Research*, *1096*, 138–147.

Wiggs, C. L., Weisberg, J., & Martin, A. (2006). Repetition priming across the adult lifespan—The long and short of it. *Aging, Neuropsychology and Cognition*, *13*, 308–325.

Wijngaards-de Meij, L., Stroebe, M., Schut, H., Stroebe, W., van den Bout, J., van der Heijden, P. G. M., & Dijkstra, I. (2008). Parents grieving the loss of their child: Interdependence in coping. *British Journal of Clinical Psychology*, *47*, 31–42.

Wilcox, S., Evenson, K. R., Aragaki, A., Wassertheil-Smoller, S., Mouton, C. P., & Loevinger, B. L. (2003). The effects of widowhood on physical and mental health, health behaviors, and health outcomes: The Women's Health Initiative. *Health Psychology*, *22*, 513–522.

Wilkins, C. H., Mathews, J., & Sheline, Y. I. (2009). Late life depression with cognitive impairment: Evaluation and treatment. *Clinical Interventions and Aging*, *4*, 51–57.

Wilkins, C. H., Sheline, Y. I., Roe, C. M., Birge, S. J., & Morris, J. C. (2006). Vitamin D deficiency is associated with low mood and worse cognitive performance in older adults. *American Journal of Geriatric Psychiatry*, *14*, 1032–1040.

Williams, B. R., Zhang, Y., Sawyer, P., Mujib, M., Jones, L. G., Feller, M. A., … Ahmed, A. (2011). Intrinsic association of widowhood with mortality in community-dwelling older women and men: Findings from a prospective propensity-matched population study. *The Journals of Gerontology: Series A: Biological Sciences and Medical Sciences*, *66A*, 1360–1368. doi:10.1093/gerona/glr144

Williams, K., & Dunne-Bryant, A. (2006). Divorce and adult psychological well-being: Clarifying the role of gender and child age. *Journal of Marriage and Family*, *68*, 1178–1196.

Williams, K. N., & Warren, C. A. (2009). Communication in assisted living. *Journal of Aging Studies*, *23*, 24–36. doi:10.1016/j.jaging.2007.09.003

Williams, P. G., Rau, H. K., Cribbet, M. R., & Gunn, H. E. (2009). Openness to experience and stress regulation. *Journal of Research in Personality*, *43*, 777–784.

Willis, S. L., Blieszner, R., & Baltes, P. B. (1981). Intellectual training research in aging: Modification of performance on the fluid ability of figural relations. *Journal of Educational Psychology*, *73*, 41–50.

Willis, S. L., & Schaie, K. W. (2009). Cognitive training and plasticity: Theoretical perspective and methodological consequences. *Restorative Neurology and Neuroscience*, *27*, 375–389.

Willis, S. L., Schaie, K. W., Martin, M., Bengston, V. L., Gans, D., Pulney, N. M., & Silverstein, M. (2009). Cognitive plasticity *Handbook of theories of aging* (2nd ed.). (pp. 295–322). New York: Springer Publishing Co.

Willis, S. L., Tennstedt, S. L., Marsiske, M., Ball, K., Elias, J., Koepke, K. M., … Wright, E. (2006). Long-term effects of cognitive training on everyday functional outcomes in older adults. *Journal of the American Medical Association*, *296*, 2805–2814.

Wilsgaard, T., Emaus, N., Ahmed, L. A., Grimnes, G., Joakimsen, R. M., Omsland, T. K., & Berntsen, G. R. (2009). Lifestyle impact on lifetime bone loss in women and men: The Tromso Study. *American Journal of Epidemiology*, *169*, 877–886. doi:kwn407 pii:10.1093/aje/kwn407

Wilson, M. N. (1986). The black extended family: An analytical consideration. *Developmental Psychology*, *22*, 246–258.

Wilson, R. S., Arnold, S. E., Tang, Y., & Bennett, D. A. (2006). Odor identification and decline in different cognitive domains in old age. *Neuroepidemiology*, *26*, 61–67.

Wilson, R. S., Schneider, J. A., Arnold, S. E., Bienias, J. L., & Bennett, D. A. (2007). Conscientiousness and the incidence of Alzheimer disease and mild cognitive impairment. *Archives of General Psychiatry*, *64*, 1204–1212. doi:64/10/1204 pii:10.1001/archpsyc.64.10.1204

Winch, R. F. (1958). *Mate selection: A study of complementary needs*. New York: Harper & Row.

Wittchen, H. U. (2002). Generalized anxiety disorder: Prevalence, burden, and cost to society. *Depression and Anxiety*, *16*, 162–171. doi:10.1002/da.10065

Wittchen, H. U., Gloster, A. T., Beesdo-Baum, K., Fava, G. A., & Craske, M. G. (2010). Agoraphobia: A review of the diagnostic classificatory position and criteria. *Depression and Anxiety*, *27*, 113–133. doi:10.1002/da.20646

Wlotko, E. W., Federmeier, K. D., & Kutas, M. (2012). To predict or not to predict: Age-related differences in the use of sentential context. *Psychology and Aging*, *27*, 975–988. doi:10.1037/a0029206

Wojtkowiak, J., & Rutjens, B. T. (2011). The postself and terror management theory: Reflecting on after death identity buffers existential threat. *International Journal for the Psychology of Religion*, *21*, 137–144. doi:10.1080/10508619.2011.557008

Wolkove, N., Elkholy, O., Baltzan, M., & Palayew, M. (2007). Sleep and aging: 2. Management of sleep disorders in older people. *Canadian Medical Association Journal*, *176*, 1449–1454. doi:176/10/1449 pii:10.1503/cmaj.070335

Womack, C. J., Harris, D. L., Katzel, L. I., Hagberg, J. M., Bleecker, E. R., & Goldberg, A. P. (2000). Weight loss, not aerobic exercise, improves pulmonary function in older obese men. *Journal of Gerontology Series A: Biological Sciences and Medical Sciences*, *55*, M453–457.

Wong, P. C. M., Jin, J. X., Gunasekera, G. M., Abel, R., Lee, E. R., & Dhar, S. (2009). Aging and cortical mechanisms of speech perception in noise. *Neuropsychologia*, *47*, 693–703.

Wood, R. G., Goesling, B., & Avellar, S. (2007). The effects of marriage on health *ASPE Research Brief*.

Woods, J., Woods, C. A., & Fonn, D. (2009). Early symptomatic presbyopes—what correction modality works best? *Eye and Contact Lens*, *35*, 221–226. doi:10.1097/ICL.0b013e3181b5003b

Woolcott, J. C., Richardson, K. J., Wiens, M. O., Patel, B., Marin, J., Khan, K. M., & Marra, C. A. (2009). Meta-analysis of the impact of 9 medication classes on falls in elderly persons.

Archives of Internal Medicine, 169, 1952–1960. doi:169/21/1952 pii:10.1001/archinternmed.2009.357

Woolf, S. H. (2010). The 2009 breast cancer screening recommendations of the U.S. Preventive Services Task Force. *Journal of the American Medical Association, 303,* 162–163. doi:303/2/162 pii:10.1001/jama.2009.1989

World Health Organization. (1948). Preamble to the Constitution of the World Health Organization as adopted by the International Health Conference, New York, 19–22 June 1946; signed on 22 July 1946 by the representatives of 61 States (Official Records of the World Health Organization, no. 2, p. 100) and entered into force on 7 April 1948.

World Health Organization. (2001). The World Health Report 2001. Mental health: New understanding, new hope. Retrieved from http://www.who.int/whr2001/2001/main/en/index.htm

World Health Organization. (2002a). Active ageing: A policy framework. Geneva, Switzerland: World Health Organization.

World Health Organization. (2002b). *National cancer control programmes: Policies and managerial guidelines.* Geneva: World Health Organization.

World Health Organization. (2009). Disease and injury country estimates. Retrieved from http://www.who.int/healthinfo/global_burden_disease/estimates_country/en/index.html

World Health Organization. (2010a). Diabetes. Retrieved from http://www.who.int/dietphysicalactivity/publications/facts/diabetes/en/

World Health Organization. (2010b). Globocan 2008.

World Health Organization. (2013). Epidemiology. Retrieved from http://www.who.int/topics/epidemiology/en/

Worthy, D. A., Gorlick, M. A., Pacheco, J. L., Schnyer, D. M., & Maddox, W. T. (2011). With age comes wisdom: Decision making in younger and older adults. *Psychological Science, 22,* 1375–1380. doi:10.1177/0956797611420301

Wu, E. Q., Shi, L., Birnbaum, H., Hudson, T., & Kessler, R. (2006). Annual prevalence of diagnosed schizophrenia in the USA: A claims data analysis approach. *Psychological Medicine, 36,* 1535–1540. doi:S0033291706008191 pii:10.1017/S0033291706008191

Wu, J., Bie, B., Yang, H., Xu, J. J., Brown, D. L., & Naguib, M. (2013). Activation of the CB_2 receptor system reverses amyloid-induced memory deficiency. *Neurobiology of Aging, 34,* 791–804.

Wunderlich, G. S., Kohler, P. O., & Committee on Improving Quality in Long-Term Care, D. o. H. C. S., Institute of Medicine (Eds.). (2001). *Improving the quality of long-term care.* Washington, DC: National Academies Press.

Wyatt, C. M., Kim, M. C., & Winston, J. A. (2006). Therapy insight: How changes in renal function with increasing age affect cardiovascular drug prescribing. *Nature Clinical Practice: Cardiovascular Medicine, 3,* 102–109.

Xiong, K. L., Yang, Q. W., Gong, S. G., & Zhang, W. G. (2010). The role of positron emission tomography imaging of beta-amyloid in patients with Alzheimer's disease. *Nuclear Medicine Communications, 31,* 4–11.

Yabiku, S. T., & Gager, C. T. (2009). Sexual frequency and the stability of marital and cohabiting unions. *Journal of Marriage and Family, 71,* 983–1000.

Yamamoto, Y., Uede, K., Yonei, N., Kishioka, A., Ohtani, T., & Furukawa, F. (2006). Effects of alpha-hydroxy acids on the human skin of Japanese subjects: The rationale for chemical peeling. *Journal of Dermatology, 33,* 16–22.

Yan, E., & Tang, C.S.-K. (2001). Prevalence and psychological impact of Chinese elder abuse. *Journal of Interpersonal Violence, 16,* 1158–1174.

Yeung, S. E., Fischer, A. L., & Dixon, R. A. (2009). Exploring effects of type 2 diabetes on cognitive functioning in older adults. *Neuropsychology, 23,* 1–9. doi:2008-19137-001 pii:10.1037/a0013849

Yin, H., Lin, S.-J., Kong, S. X., Benzeroual, K., Crawford, S. Y., Hedeker, D., … Muramatsu, N. (2011). The association between physical functioning and self-rated general health in later life: The implications of social comparison. *Applied Research in Quality of Life, 6,* 1–19. doi:10.1007/s11482-010-9109-3

Yong, H. H. (2006). Can attitudes of stoicism and cautiousness explain observed age-related variation in levels of self-rated pain, mood disturbance and functional interference in chronic pain patients? *European Journal of Pain, 10,* 399–407.

Yoshida, M., Takashima, Y., Inoue, M., Iwasaki, M., Otani, T., Sasaki, S., & Tsugane, S. (2007). Prospective study showing that dietary vitamin C reduced the risk of age-related cataracts in a middle-aged Japanese population. *European Journal of Nutrition, 46,* 118–124. doi:10.1007/s00394-006-0641-8

Yung, L. M., Laher, I., Yao, X., Chen, Z. Y., Huang, Y., & Leung, F. P. (2009). Exercise, vascular wall and cardiovascular diseases: An update (part 2). *Sports Medicine, 39,* 45–63. doi:10.2165/00007256-200939010-00004

Zamboni, M., Mazzali, G., Fantin, F., Rossi, A., & Di Francesco, V. (2008). Sarcopenic obesity: A new category of obesity in the elderly. *Nutrition, Metabolism, and Cardiovascular Diseases, 18,* 388–395. doi:S0939-4753(07)00185-8 pii:10.1016/j.numecd.2007.10.002

Zanetti, M. V., Cordeiro, Q., & Busatto, G. F. (2007). Late onset bipolar disorder associated with white matter hyperintensities: A pathophysiological hypothesis. *Progress in Neuropsychopharmacology and Biological Psychiatry, 31,* 551–556.

Zanon-Moreno, V., Garcia-Medina, J. J., Zanon-Viguer, V., Moreno-Nadal, M. A., & Pinazo-Duran, M. D. (2009). Smoking, an additional risk factor in elder women with primary open-angle glaucoma. *Molecular Vision, 15,* 2953–2959.

Zarit, S. H., & Zarit, J. M. (2007). *Mental disorders in older adults: Fundamentals of assessment and treatment* (2nd ed.). New York: Guilford Press.

Zeleznik, J. (2003). Normative aging of the respiratory system. *Clinics in Geriatric Medicine, 19,* 1–18.

Zhang, C., Wu, B., Beglopoulos, V., Wines-Samuelson, M., Zhang, D., Dragatsis, I., … Shen, J. (2009). Presenilins are essential for regulating neurotransmitter release. *Nature, 460,* 632–636. doi:nature08177 pii:10.1038/nature08177

Zhang, F., & Labouvie-Vief, G. (2004). Stability and fluctuation in adult attachment style over a 6-year period. *Attachment and Human Development, 6,* 419–437.

Zhang, Y., Qiu, C., Lindberg, O., Bronge, L., Aspelin, P., Backman, L., ... Wahlund, L. O. (2010). Acceleration of hippocampal atrophy in a non-demented elderly population: The SNAC-K study. *International Psychogeriatrics, 22,* 14–25. doi:S1041610209991396 pii:10.1017/S1041610209991396

Zijlstra, G. A., van Haastregt, J. C., Ambergen, T., van Rossum, E., van Eijk, J. T., Tennstedt, S. L., & Kempen, G. I. (2009a). Effects of a multicomponent cognitive behavioral group intervention on fear of falling and activity avoidance in community-dwelling older adults: Results of a randomized controlled trial. *Journal of the American Geriatrics Society, 57,* 2020–2028. doi:JGS2489 pii:10.1111/j.1532-5415.2009.02489.x

Zijlstra, G. A., van Haastregt, J. C., Ambergen, T., van Rossum, E., van Eijk, J. T., Tennstedt, S. L., & Kempen, G. I. (2009b). Effects of a multicomponent cognitive behavioral group intervention on fear of falling and activity avoidance in community-dwelling older adults: Results of a randomized controlled trial. *Journal of the American Geriatrics Society, 57,* 2020–2028. doi:JGS2489 pii:10.1111/j.1532-5415.2009.02489.x

Zisook, S., Corruble, E., Duan, N., Iglewicz, A., Karam, E. G., Lanuoette, N., ... Young, I. T. (2012). The bereavement exclusion and DSM-5. *Depression and Anxietyy 29,* 425–443. doi:10.1002/da.21927

AUTHOR INDEX

SUBJECT INDEX